Cisco® Switching
Black Book

Sean Odom

Hanson Nottingham

D1341106

President and CEO
Keith Weiskamp

Publisher
Steve Sayre

Acquisitions Editor
Charlotte Carpentier

Product Marketing Manager
Tracy Rooney

Project Editor
Toni Zuccarini Ackley

Technical Reviewer
Deniss Suhanovs

Production Coordinator
Carla J. Schuder

Cover Designer
Jody Winkler

Layout Designer
April Nielsen

Cisco® Switching Black Book

Limits of Liability and Disclaimer of Warranty

The author and publisher of this book have used their best efforts in preparing the book and the programs contained in it. These efforts include the development, research, and testing of the theories and programs to determine their effectiveness. The author and publisher make no warranty of any kind, expressed or implied, with regard to these programs or the documentation contained in this book.

The author and publisher shall not be liable in the event of incidental or consequential damages in connection with, or arising out of, the furnishing, performance, or use of the programs, associated instructions, and/or claims of productivity gains.

Trademarks

Trademarked names appear throughout this book. Rather than list the names and entities that own the trademarks or insert a trademark symbol with each mention of the trademarked name, the publisher states that it is using the names for editorial purposes only and to the benefit of the trademark owner, with no intention of infringing upon that trademark.

The Coriolis Group, LLC
14455 N. Hayden Road
Suite 220
Scottsdale, Arizona 85260

(480) 483-0192
FAX (480) 483-0193
www.coriolis.com

Library of Congress Cataloging-in-Publication Data
Odom, Sean
 Cisco switching black book / by Sean Odom.
  p. cm.
 Includes index.
 ISBN 1-57610-706-X
 1. Packet switching (Data transmission) I. Title.
TK5105.3 .O36 2000
004.6'6--dc21   00-064415

Printed in the United States of America
10 9 8 7 6 5 4 3 2 1

⑥ CORIOLIS™

The Coriolis Group, LLC • 14455 North Hayden Road, Suite 220 • Scottsdale, Arizona 85260

Dear Reader:

Coriolis Technology Press was founded to create a very elite group of books: the ones you keep closest to your machine. Sure, everyone would like to have the Library of Congress at arm's reach, but in the real world, you have to choose the books you rely on every day *very* carefully.

To win a place for our books on that coveted shelf beside your PC, we guarantee several important qualities in every book we publish. These qualities are:

- *Technical accuracy*—It's no good if it doesn't work. Every Coriolis Technology Press book is reviewed by technical experts in the topic field, and is sent through several editing and proofreading passes in order to create the piece of work you now hold in your hands.

- *Innovative editorial design*—We've put years of research and refinement into the ways we present information in our books. Our books' editorial approach is uniquely designed to reflect the way people learn new technologies and search for solutions to technology problems.

- *Practical focus*—We put only pertinent information into our books and avoid any fluff. Every fact included between these two covers must serve the mission of the book as a whole.

- *Accessibility*—The information in a book is worthless unless you can find it quickly when you need it. We put a lot of effort into our indexes, and heavily cross-reference our chapters, to make it easy for you to move right to the information you need.

Here at The Coriolis Group we have been publishing and packaging books, technical journals, and training materials since 1989. We're programmers and authors ourselves, and we take an ongoing active role in defining what we publish and how we publish it. We have put a lot of thought into our books; please write to us at **ctp@coriolis.com** and let us know what you think. We hope that you're happy with the book in your hands, and that in the future, when you reach for software development and networking information, you'll turn to one of our books first.

Keith Weiskamp
President and CEO

Jeff Duntemann
VP and Editorial Director

This book is dedicated to all those who endeavor to turn dreams into realities.
—Sean Odom

❧

To my wife, Sonia, and my daughter, Sabrina.
—Hanson Nottingham

❧

About the Authors

Sean Odom is a CCNP, MCSE, and CNX-Ethernet. He has been in the computer networking field for over 12 years and can be found instructing a number of Cisco courses, including the Switching and Remote Access courses for Globalnet Training Solutions, Inc. (**www.globalnettraining.com**). Sean is a former president and currently on the board of the Sacramento Placer County Cisco Users Group (SPCCUG). In addition, Sean has been a consultant for many companies including Advanced Computer Systems, American Licorice, CH2M Hill, The Money Store, NCR, Wells Fargo Bank, and Intel. Sean has authored and co-authored many industry books, labs, and white papers. You can reach Sean by email at (**sodom@rcsis.com**) or see his Web site at **www.thequestforcertification.com**.

Hanson Nottingham is a CCNA, MCSE, and MCP+I. He is an experienced Windows NT Systems Engineer with over eight years experience in the Information Systems industry. Hanson is currently working as a systems manager on the E:Services NT Team at Hewlett-Packard Company. Prior to HP, Hanson helped manage Vision Service Plan's Web farm as an Internet systems engineer. He specializes in Web farm management and integration, SOHO network designs, and e-commerce solutions. Hanson is currently working to further his Cisco Certified Networking Professional certification.

Acknowledgments

It's always exciting when you get to the acknowledgments because that means the book is almost done. First off, I must thank Erin for putting up with me during the writing of this book. She is a wonderful person who is as smart as she is good looking and puts up with a lot of extra responsibility while I am working on books. I also need to thank Albert Ip and Hanson Nottingham for their defined knowledge of the Cisco switches. Thanks to my favorite English teacher, Mr. Strange, for being the one who originally thought I would be a great writer some day, and I guess it shows here in my third book. Coriolis deserves many thanks. A few people in particular at Coriolis need to be thanked: Steve Sayre, for believing in my idea of a *Cisco Switching Black Book*; my project editor for the second time, Toni Zuccarini Ackley; Tiffany Taylor for finding all my mistakes; Charlotte Carpentier and Shari Jo Hehr for handling the many contract issues for this book; Jody Winkler for making the cover; Carla Schuder for making the inside of the book look good; and Paul LoPresto for all his help in acquisitions.

—Sean Odom

Sean, thank you for giving me the opportunity and the privilege to become a co-author on this book—I appreciate all your help, assistance, and encouragement! To my wonderful wife, Sonia, and my beautiful daughter, Sabrina, thank you for giving me the time—dealing with my complicated and difficult schedules I know has not been easy and your support does not go unnoticed! To Toni and the rest of the Coriolis team, thank you for this opportunity and your undying patience throughout my process development learning curve—I owe you guys mochas!

—Hanson Nottingham

Contents at a Glance

Table of Contents

Chapter 3
WAN Switching 75

In Depth

Chapter 8
WAN Cell Switching 241

In Depth

Immediate Solutions

Chapter 11
Multilayer Switching 345

In Depth

Immediate Solutions

Immediate Solutions

Introduction

For many years I have been a consultant for different companies and have written books on switch and router configurations and troubleshooting. During my years as a consultant I have had to either install, administer, or troubleshoot switching problems and configurations for switches without a good handbook. I have constantly gone through bookstores looking for a book on Cisco switch troubleshooting and configurations that didn't deal with a Cisco curriculum. Guess what? I couldn't find one!

I have written books related to the CCDP and CCNP curricula and always thought about writing a book that concentrated on Cisco switches. One day I was walking through a bookstore and noticed a book from The Coriolis Group called *Cisco Routers for IP Routing Little Black Book*. I immediately thought to myself that a *Cisco Switching Little Black Book* would be a great configuration handbook for many people. After contacting Coriolis and pitching them the idea for the book, I received a call from Steve Sayre, the publisher at Coriolis, who was excited about publishing a book of this nature. As I pondered and started putting my idea into an outline, I realized that I could not place everything that an administrator needed in a *Little Black Book*.

To make a long story short, a few months later, with a great big outline and help from Albert Ip and Hanson Nottingham, the book became this *Black Book*—the most feature-packed handbook for Cisco switching an administrator can buy. Not only do we cover the Cisco Catalyst switching line but we also cover the LightStream ATM switch series, Gigabit Switch Router Series (GSR), and the IGX and MGX WAN switch series.

Thanks for buying the *Cisco Switching Black Book*.

Is This Book for You?

The Cisco Switching Black Book was written with the intermediate or advanced user in mind. Among the topics that are covered, are:

- Cisco Catalyst switch configuration and troubleshooting
- Cisco IGX and MGX switch configuration
- Cisco GSR switch configuration

- Cisco switch troubleshooting

- Cisco switch features

- ATM LightStream switch configuration and troubleshooting

- Switched network design issues

How to Use This Book

The examples in the Immediate Solutions are intended to teach you the basic steps in configuring Cisco Catalyst switches and their interfaces. Primarily, the Immediate Solutions will cover the information discussed in the In Depth section of each chapter. When we explain each scenario we will use the following notations:

- *<Italics in angle brackets>* will be used to denote command elements that have a specific value that needs to be input, such as characters or numbers. Occasionally some other entry will be needed, which will be explained in each individual instance.

- [Text in square brackets] is used to denote optional commands that can be configured.

- Words in brackets that are separated by bars are used when indicating that there are multiple choices of commands. For example, when configuring VTP you can enable the trunk port to choose one mode: on, off, desirable, or auto mode. This will be shown like this: [on|off|desirable|auto].

Knowledge of what configuration mode you are in and how to enter each configuration mode on the Cisco Command Line Interface is important. Knowing what each mode configures will aid you in using the proper configuration mode. The Set/Clear command-based IOS CLI uses similar command modes as the Cisco CLI used on Cisco routers and switches, but uses mainly the **enable**, **set**, **show**, and **clear** commands. Chapter 1 will cover the different CLI command modes.

The *Black Book* Philosophy

Written by experienced professionals, Coriolis *Black Books* provide immediate solutions to global programming and administrative challenges, helping you complete specific tasks, especially critical ones that are not well documented in other books. The *Black Book*'s unique two-part chapter format—thorough technical overviews followed by practical immediate solutions—is structured to help you use your knowledge, solve problems, and quickly master complex technical issues to become an expert. By breaking down complex topics into easily manageable components, this format helps you quickly find what you're looking for, with commands, jump tables, and step-by-step configurations located in the Immediate Solutions section.

I welcome your feedback on this book. You can either email The Coriolis Group at **ctp@coriolis.com** or email me directly at **sodom@rcsis.com**. Errata, updates, information on classes I teach, and more are available at my Web site: **www.thequestforcertification.com**.

Chapter 1

Network Switching Fundamentals

In Depth

Although writing the first paragraph of a book is probably the least important part, it's invariably the most difficult section to write. To get a good picture of the different parts of networking, readers need to know where networking began and the history behind the networks of today. You may have seen a lot of what is in the first section of this chapter in any basic networking course, such as Networking Essentials; or you may have covered most of it in a CCNA class; but a refresher never hurt.

In this chapter, you will become acquainted with the history of networks and how networks evolved into those you see in today's corporate environments. I will also discuss the inventors of the different types of networking equipment found at each layer of the network.

As we progress through the chapter I will also cover the different network architectures, from legacy networks to the fast high-speed media types found in today's networks. A clear understanding of the networking technologies and challenges found at each layer of the network will aid you in assessing problems with the switches you'll deal with later.

I have a favorite quote that helps me to remember why I continuously study, so that I can better support my customers' equipment. It is a quote by Albert Einstein, and I remember it from one of my mentors: "The significant [technical] problems we face cannot be solved by the same level of thinking that created them."

This chapter will contain some of the following information:

- The history of networking
- The different pieces of networking equipment
- How to identify problems in a flat network topology
- The how to's and the when to's of upgrading to a switched network
- When to upgrade your flat topology network
- Network upgrade planning and basic strategies

Two terms to keep in mind when reading this chapter are *resource nodes* and *demand nodes*. A resource node is a node on an interface attached to a device that provides resources to the network. These nodes can be everything from printers, servers, and mainframes, to wide area network (WAN) routers. A demand node is an interface on the network that makes requests or queries to the resource nodes. The interfaces can be devices such as workstations, terminals, or even client applications. Network conversations occur when resource nodes and demand nodes send a series of requests and responses through the network.

Physical Media and Switching Types

The following are the most popular types of physical media in use today:

- *Ethernet*—Based on the Institute of Electrical and Electronics Engineers (IEEE) 802.3 standard. However, it doesn't rely on the Carrier Sense Multiple Access Collision Detection (CSMA/CD) technology. It includes 10Mbps LANs, as well as Fast Ethernet and Gigabit Ethernet.

- *Token-Ring*—Not as popular as Ethernet switching. Token-Ring switching can also be used to improve LAN performance.

- *FDDI*—Rarely used, chiefly due to the high expense of Fiber Distributed Data Interface (FDDI) equipment and cabling.

The following are some of the protocol and physical interface switching types in use today:

- *Port switching*—Takes place in the backplane of a shared hub. For instance, ports 1, 2, and 3 could be connected to backplane 1, whereas ports 4, 5, and 6 could be connected to backplane 2. This method is typically used to form a collapsed backbone and to provide some improvements in the network.

- *Cell switching*—Uses Asynchronous Transfer Mode (ATM) as the underlying technology. Switch paths can be either permanent virtual circuits (PVCs) that never go away, or switched virtual circuits (SVCs) that are built up, used, and torn down when you're finished.

A Bit of History

The first local area networks (LANs) began as a result of the introduction of personal computers into the workplace environment. As computers became more common, the need arose to share resources, such as printers or files. These early networks were pretty simple, with a handful of computers sharing a few printers and not much more. As more items such as servers, applications, and peripherals came along, the increasing numbers of interfaces—along with application designs that could take advantage of the network—created a weakness in the current network design.

The limitations of traditional Ethernet technology brought forth a number of innovations that soon became standard in the Ethernet protocol. Innovations such as full duplexing, Fast Ethernet, and Gigabit Ethernet began to appear—innovations that have also made possible a transition to switches from shared hubs.

Other limitations to the way networks operated in a shared environment created a need for alternative methods to permit the use of bandwidth-intensive applications such as video and voice. Switches are one of these alternative methods. In many respects, switches are relatively simple devices. A switch's design and self-learning features require very little manual configuration to get it up and running. To properly use these devices in your network, you must have an in-depth knowledge of the issues involved in implementing switching.

Knowing the basics of Ethernet technology can help you effectively troubleshoot and install switches in the network. You also need a good grasp of the different technologies and how switches work, as well as the constraints of each type of device you may use in the network. As you read the following sections, make sure you get a clear understanding of the fundamentals and basics of Ethernet technology.

The types of devices you use in the network have important implications for network performance. For example, bridges and routers are both devices that network administrators use to extend the capabilities of their networks. Both of them have advantages and disadvantages.

Bridges, for example, can easily solve distance limitations and increase the number of stations you can have on a network, but they can have real problems with broadcast traffic. Routers can be used to prevent this problem, but they increase the time it takes to forward the traffic.

This has been the pattern throughout the history of networking. When a new product is introduced, problems or bottlenecks are soon found that limit the product's usefulness. Then, innovations are invented or implemented to aid the product and allow it to perform better. To see this occurrence in action, let's take a look at some of the traditional network architectures. As you will see in upcoming sections, the pattern of new innovation after new innovation started in the earliest days of networking and continues in today's networks.

Networking Architectures

Network designers from the beginnings of networking were faced with the limitations of the LAN topologies. In modern corporate networks, LAN topologies such as Ethernet, Token Ring, and FDDI are used to provide network connectivity. Network designers often try to deploy a design that uses the fastest functionality that can be applied to the physical cabling.

Many different types of physical cable media have been introduced over the years, such as Token Ring, FDDI, and Ethernet. At one time, Token Ring was seen as a technically superior product and a viable alternative to Ethernet. Many networks still contain Token Ring, but very few new Token Ring installations are being implemented. One reason is that Token Ring is an IBM product with very little support from other vendors. Also, the prices of Token Ring networks are substantially higher than those of Ethernet networks.

FDDI networks share some of the limitations of Token Ring. Like Token Ring, FDDI offers excellent benefits in the area of high-speed performance and redundancy. Unfortunately, however, it has the same high equipment and installation costs. More vendors are beginning to recognize FDDI and are offering support, services, and installation for it—especially for network backbones.

Network backbones are generally high-speed links running between segments of the network. Normally, backbone cable links run between two routers; but they can also be found between two switches or a switch and a router.

Ethernet has by far overwhelmed the market and obtained the highest market share. Ethernet networks are open-standards based, more cost-effective than other types of physical media, and have a large base of vendors that supply the different Ethernet products. The biggest benefit that makes Ethernet so popular is the large number of technical professionals who understand how to implement and support it.

Early networks were modeled on the peer-to-peer networking model. These worked well for the small number of nodes, but as networks grew they evolved into the client/server network model of today. Let's take a look at these two models in more depth.

Peer-to-Peer Networking Model

A small, flat network or LAN often contains multiple segments connected with hubs, bridges, and repeaters. This is an Open Systems Interconnection (OSI) Reference Model Layer 2 network that can actually be connected to a router for access to a WAN connection. In this topology, every network node sees the conversations of every other network node.

In terms of scalability, the peer-to-peer networking model has some major limitations—especially with the technologies that companies must utilize to stay ahead in their particular fields. No quality of service, prioritizing of data, redundant links, or data security can be implemented here, other than encryption. Every node sees every packet on the network. The hub merely forwards the data it receives out of every port, as shown in Figure 1.1.

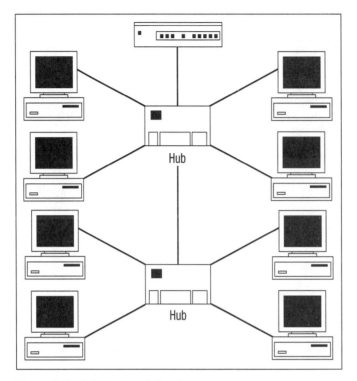

Figure 1.1   A flat network topology.

Early networks consisted of a single LAN with a number of workstations running peer-to-peer networks and sharing files, printers, and other resources. Peer-to-peer networks share data with one another in a non-centralized fashion and can span only a very limited area, such as a room or building.

Client/Server Network Model

Peer-to-peer model networks evolved into the client/server model, in which the server shares applications and data storage with the clients in a somewhat more centralized network. This setup includes a little more security, provided by the operating system, and ease of administration for the multiple users trying to access data.

A LAN in this environment consists of a physical wire connecting the devices. In this model, LANs enable multiple users in a relatively small geographical area to exchange files and messages, as well as to access shared resources such as file servers and printers. The isolation of these LANs makes communication between different offices or departments difficult, if not impossible. Duplication of resources means that the same hardware and software have to be supplied to each office or department, along with separate support staff for each individual LAN.

WANs soon developed to overcome the limitations of LANs. WANs can connect LANs across normal telephone lines or other digital media (including satellites), thereby ignoring geographical limitations in dispersing resources to network clients.

In a traditional LAN, many limitations directly impact network users. Almost anyone who has ever used a shared network has had to contend with the other users of that network and experienced the impacts. These effects include such things as slow network response times, making for poor network performance. They are due to the nature of shared environments.

When collision rates increase, the usefulness of the bandwidth decreases. As applications begin having to resend data due to excessive collisions, the amount of bandwidth used increases and the response time for users increases. As the number of users increases, the number of requests for network resources rises, as well. This increase boosts the amount of traffic on the physical network media and raises the number of data collisions in the network. This is when you begin to receive more complaints from the network's users regarding response times and timeouts. These are all telltale signs that you need a switched Ethernet network. Later in this chapter, we will talk more about monitoring networks and solutions to these problems. But before we cover how to monitor, design, and upgrade your network, let's look at the devices you will find in the network.

The Pieces of Technology

In 1980, a group of vendors consisting of Digital Equipment Corporation (DEC), Intel, and Xerox created what was known as the *DIX standard*. Ultimately, after a few modifications, it became the IEEE 802.3 standard. It is the 802.3 standard that most people associate with the term *Ethernet*.

The Ethernet networking technology was invented by Robert M. Metcalfe while he was working at the Xerox Palo Alto Research Center in the early 1970s. It was originally designed to help support research on the "office of the future." At first, the network's speed was limited to 3Mbps.

Ethernet is a multiaccess, packet-switched system with very democratic principles. The stations themselves provide access to the network, and all devices on an Ethernet LAN can access the LAN at any time. Ethernet signals are transmitted serially, one bit at a time, over a shared channel available to every attached station.

To reduce the likelihood of multiple stations transmitting at the same time, Ethernet LANs use a mechanism known as Carrier Sense Multiple Access Collision Detection (CSMA/CD) to listen to the network and see if it is in use. If a station has data to transmit, and the network is not in use, the station sends the data. If two stations transmit at the same time, a collision occurs. The stations are notified of this event, and they instantly reschedule their transmissions using a specially designed back-off algorithm. As part of this algorithm, each station involved chooses a random time interval to schedule the retransmission of the frame. In effect, this process keeps the stations from making transmission attempts at the same time and prevents a collision.

After each frame transmission, all stations on the network contend equally for the next frame transmission. This competition allows access to the network channel in a fair manner. It also ensures that no single station can lock out the other stations from accessing the network. Access to the shared channel is determined by the Media Access Control (MAC) mechanism on each Network Interface Card (NIC) located in each network node. The MAC address uses a physical address which, in terms of the OSI Reference Model, contains the lowest level address. This is the address used by a switch. The router at Layer 3 uses a protocol address, which is referred as a *logical address*.

CSMA/CD is the tool that allows collisions to be detected. Each collision of frames on the network reduces the amount of network bandwidth that can be used to send information across the physical wire. CSMA/CD also forces every device on the network to analyze each individual frame and determine if the device was the intended recipient of the packet. The process of decoding and analyzing each individual packet generates additional CPU usage on each machine, which degrades each machine's performance.

As networks grew in popularity, they also began to grow in size and complexity. For the most part, networks began as small isolated islands of computers. In many of the early environments, the network was installed over a weekend—when you came in on Monday, a fat orange cable was threaded throughout the organization, connecting all the devices. A method of connecting these segments had to be derived. In the next few sections, we will look at a number of approaches by which networks can be connected. We will look at repeaters, hubs, bridges, and routers, and demonstrate the benefits and drawbacks to each approach.

Repeaters

The first LANs were designed using thick coaxial cables, with each station physically tapping into the cable. In order to extend the distance and overcome other limitations on this type of installation, a device known as a *repeater* is used. Essentially, a repeater consists of a pair of back-to-back transceivers. The transmit wire on one transceiver is hooked to the receive wire on the other, so that bits received by one transceiver are immediately retransmitted by the other.

Repeaters work by regenerating the signals from one segment to another, and they allow networks to overcome distance limitations and other factors. Repeaters amplify the signal to further transmit it on the segment because there is a loss in signal energy caused by the length of the cabling. When data travels through the physical cable it loses strength the further it travels. This loss of the signal strength is referred to as *attenuation*.

These devices do not create separate networks; instead, they simply extend an existing one. A standard rule of thumb is that no more than three repeaters may be located between any two stations. This is often referred to as the *5-4-3 rule*, which states that no more than 5 segments may be attached by no more than 4 repeaters, with no more than 3 segments populated with workstations. This limitation prevents *propagation delay*, which is the time it takes for the packet to go from the beginning of the link to the opposite end.

As you can imagine, in the early LANs this method resulted in a host of performance and fault-isolation problems. As LANs multiplied, a more structured approach called *10BaseT* was introduced. This method consists of attaching all the devices to a hub in the wiring closet. All stations are connected in a point-to-point configuration between the interface and the hub.

Hubs

A *hub*, also known as a *concentrator*, is a device containing a grouping of repeaters. Similar to repeaters, hubs are found at the Physical layer of the OSI Model. These devices simply collect and retransmit bits. Hubs are used to connect multiple cable runs in a star-wired network topology into a single network. This design is similar to the spokes of a wheel converging on the center of the wheel.

Many benefits derive from this type of setup, such as allowing interdepartmental connections between hubs, extending the maximum distance between any pair of nodes on the network, and improving the ability to isolate problems from the rest of the network.

Six types of hubs are found in the network:

- *Active hubs*—Act as repeaters and eliminate attenuation by amplifying the signals they replicate to all the attached ports.

- *Backbone hubs*—Collect other hubs into a single collection point. This type of design is also known as a *multitiered* design. In a typical setup, servers and other critical devices are on high-speed Fast Ethernet or Gigabit uplinks. This setup creates a very fast connection to the servers that the lower-speed networks can use to prevent the server or the path to the server from being a bottleneck in the network.

- *Intelligent hubs*—Contain logic circuits that shut down a port if the traffic indicates that malformed frames are the rule rather than the exception.

- *Managed hubs*—Have Application layer software installed so that they can be remotely managed. Network management software is very popular in organizations that have staff responsible for a network spread over multiple buildings.

- *Passive hubs*—Aid in producing attenuation. They do not amplify the signals they replicate to all the attached ports. These are the opposite of active hubs.

- *Stackable hubs*—Have a cable to connect hubs that are in the same location without requiring the data to pass through multiple hubs. This setup is commonly referred to as *daisy chaining*.

In all of these types of hub configurations, one crucial problem exists: All stations share the bandwidth, and they all remain in the same collision domain. As a result, whenever two or more stations transmit simultaneously on any hub, there is a strong likelihood that a collision will occur. These collisions lead to congestion during high-traffic loads. As the number of stations increases, each station gets a smaller portion of the LAN bandwidth. Hubs do not provide microsegmentation and leave only one collision domain.

Bridges

A *bridge* is a relatively simple device consisting of a pair of interfaces with some packet buffering and simple logic. The bridge receives a packet on one interface, stores it in a buffer, and immediately queues it for transmission by the other interface. The two cables each experience collisions, but collisions on one cable do not cause collisions on the other. The cables are in separate *collision domains*.

NOTE: *Some bridges are capable of connecting dissimilar topologies.*

The term *bridging* refers to a technology in which a device known as a *bridge* connects two or more LAN segments. Bridges are OSI Data Link layer, or Layer 2, devices that were originally designed to connect two network segments. *Multiport bridges* were introduced later to connect more than two network segments, and they are still in use in many networks today. These devices analyze the frames as they come in and make forwarding decisions based on information in the frames themselves.

To do its job effectively, a bridge provides three separate functions:

- Filtering the frames that the bridge receives to determine if the frame should be forwarded

- Forwarding the frames that need to be forwarded to the proper interface
- Eliminating attenuation by amplifying received data signals

Bridges learn the location of the network stations without any intervention from a network administrator or any manual configuration of the bridge software. This process is commonly referred to as *self-learning*. When a bridge is turned on and begins to operate, it examines the MAC addresses located in the headers of frames passed through the network. As the traffic passes through the bridge, the bridge builds a table of known source addresses, assuming the port from which the bridge received the frame is the port to which the device is a sending device is attached.

In this table, an entry exists that contains the MAC address of each node along with the bridge interface and port on which it resides. If the bridge knows that the destination is on the same segment as the source, it drops the packet because there is no need to transmit it. If the bridge knows that the destination is on another segment, it transmits the packet on that segment or port to that segment only. If the bridge does not know the destination segment, the bridge transmits a copy of the frame to all the interface ports in the source segment using a technique known as *flooding*. For each packet an interface receives, the bridge stores in its table the following information:

- The frame's source address
- The interface the frame arrived on
- The time at which the switch port received the source address and entered it into the switching table

---

NOTE: *Bridges and switches are logically equivalent.*

There are four kinds of bridges:

- *Transparent bridge*—Primarily used in Ethernet environments. They are called transparent bridges because their presence and operation are transparent to network hosts. Transparent bridges learn and forward packets in the manner described earlier.
- *Source-route bridge*—Primarily used in Token Ring environments. They are called source-route bridges because they assume that the complete source-to-destination route is placed in frames sent by the source.
- *Translational bridge*—Translators between different media types, such as Token Ring and Ethernet.
- *Source-route transparent bridge*—A combination of transparent bridging and source-route bridging that enables communication in mixed Ethernet and Token Ring environments.

Broadcasts are the biggest problem with bridges. Some bridges help reduce network traffic by filtering packets and allowing them to be forwarded only if needed. Bridges also forward broadcasts to devices on all segments of the network. As networks grow, so does broadcast traffic. Instead of frames being broadcast through a limited number of devices, bridges often allow hundreds of devices on multiple segments to broadcast data to all the devices. As a result, all devices on all segments of the network are now processing data intended for one device. Excessive broadcasts reduce the amount of bandwidth available to end users. This situation causes bandwidth problems called *network broadcast storms*. Broadcast storms occur when broadcasts throughout the LAN use up all available bandwidth, thus grinding the network to a halt.

Network performance is most often affected by three types of broadcast traffic: inquiries about the availability of a device, advertisements for a component's status on the network, and inquiries from one device trying to locate another device. The following are the typical types of network broadcasts:

- Address Resolution Protocol (ARP)
- Internetwork Packet Exchange (IPX) Get Nearest Server (GNS) requests
- IPX Service Advertising Protocol (SAP)
- Multicast traffic broadcasts
- NetBIOS name requests

These broadcasts are built into the network protocols and are essential to the operation of the network devices using these protocols.

Due to the overhead involved in forwarding packets, bridges also introduce a delay in forwarding traffic. This delay is known as *latency*. Latency delay is measured from the moment a packet enters the input port on the switch until the time the bridge forwards the packet out the exit port. Bridges can introduce 20 to 30 percent loss of throughput for some applications. Latency is a big problem with some timing-dependent technologies, such as mainframe connectivity, video, or voice.

High levels of latency can result in loss of connections and noticeable video and voice degradation. The inherent problems of bridging over multiple segments including those of different LAN types with Layer 2 devices became a problem to network administrators. To overcome these issues, a device called a *router*, operating at OSI Layer 3, was introduced.

Routers

Routers are devices that operate at Layer 3 of the OSI Model. Routers can be used to connect more than one Ethernet segment with or without bridging. Routers perform the same basic functions as bridges and also forward information and

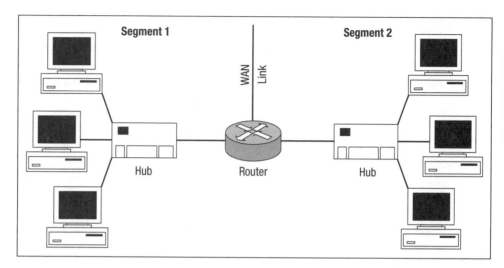

Figure 1.2 Routers connecting multiple segments.

filter broadcasts between multiple segments. Figure 1.2 shows routers segmenting multiple network segments. Using an OSI network Layer 3 solution, routers logically segment traffic into subnets.

Routers were originally introduced to connect dissimilar network media types as well as to provide a means to route traffic, filter broadcasts across multiple segments, and improve overall performance. This approach eliminated broadcasts over multiple segments by filtering broadcasts. However, routers became a bottleneck in some networks and also resulted in a loss of throughput for some types of traffic.

When you are connecting large networks, or when you are connecting networks to a WAN, routers are very important. Routers will perform media conversion, adjusting the data link protocol as necessary. With a router, as well as with some bridges, you can connect an Ethernet network and a Token Ring network.

Routers do have some disadvantages. The cost of routers is very high, so they are an expensive way to segment networks. If protocol routing is necessary, you must pay this cost. Routers are also difficult to configure and maintain, meaning that you will have a difficult time keeping the network up and running. Knowledgeable workers who understand routing can be expensive.

Routers are also somewhat limited in their performance, especially in the areas of latency and forwarding rates. Routers add about 40 percent additional latency from the time packets arrive at the router to the time they exit the router. Higher latency is primarily due to the fact that routing requires more packet assembly and disassembly. These disadvantages force network administrators to look elsewhere when designing many large network installations.

Switches

A new option had to be developed to overcome the problems associated with bridges and routers. These new devices were called *switches*. The term *switching* was originally applied to packet-switch technologies, such as Link Access Procedure, Balanced (LAPB); Frame Relay; Switched Multimegabit Data Service (SMDS); and X.25. Today, switching is more commonly associated with LAN switching and refers to a technology that is similar to a bridge in many ways.

Switches allow fast data transfers without introducing the latency typically associated with bridging. They create a one-to-one dedicated network segment for each device on the network and interconnect these segments by using an extremely fast, high-capacity infrastructure that provides optimal transport of data on a LAN; this structure is commonly referred to as a *backplane*. This setup reduces competition for bandwidth on the network, allows maximum utilization of the network, and increases flexibility for network designers and implementers.

Ethernet switches provide a number of enhancements over shared networks. Among the most important is *microsegmentation*, which is the ability to divide networks into smaller and faster segments that can operate at the maximum possible speed of the wire (also known as *wire-speed*).

To improving network performance, switches must address three issues:

• They must stop unneeded traffic from crossing network segments.

• They must allow multiple communication paths between segments.

• They cannot introduce performance degradation.

Routers are also used to improve performance. Routers are typically attached to switches to connect multiple LAN segments. A switch forwards the traffic to the port on the switch to which the destination device is connected, which in turn reduces the traffic to the other devices on the network. Information from the sending device is routed directly to the receiving device. No device other than the router, switch, and end nodes sees or processes the information.

The network now becomes less saturated, more secure, and more efficient at processing information, and precious processor time is freed on the local devices. Routers today are typically placed at the edge of the network and are used to connect WANs, filter traffic, and provide security. See Figure 1.3.

Like bridges, switches perform at OSI Layer 2 by examining the packets and building a forwarding table based on what they hear. Switches differ from bridges by helping to meet the following needs for network designers and administrators:

• Provide deterministic paths

• Relieve network bottlenecks

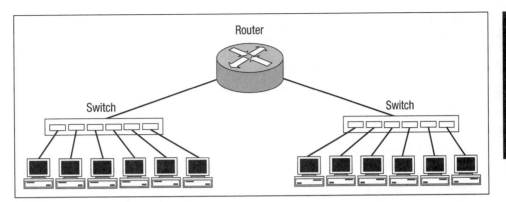

Figure 1.3   Routers and switches.

- Provide deterministic failover for redundancy
- Allow scalable network growth
- Provide fast convergence
- Act as a means to centralize applications and servers
- Have the capacity to reduce latency

Network Design

When designing or upgrading your network, you need to keep some basic rules of segmenting in mind. You segment your network primarily to relieve network congestion and route data as quickly and efficiently as possible. Segmentation is often necessary to satisfy the bandwidth requirements of a new application or type of information that the network needs to support. Other times, it may be needed due to the increased traffic on the segment or subnet. You should also plan for increased levels of network usage or unplanned increases in network population.

Some areas you need to consider are the types of nodes, user groups, security needs, population of the network, applications used, and the network needs for all the interfaces on the network. When designing your network, you should create it in a hierarchical manner. Doing so provides you with the ability to easily make additions to your network. Another important consideration should be how your data flows through the network.

For example, let's say your users are intermingled with your servers in the same geographical location. If you create a switched network in which the users' data must be switched through a number of links to another geographical area and then back again to create a connection between the users and file servers, you have not designed the most efficient path to the destination.

Single points of failure need to be analyzed, as well. As we stated earlier, every large-network user has suffered through his or her share of network outages and downtime. By analyzing all the possible points of failure, you can implement redundancy in the network and avoid many network outages. *Redundancy* is the addition of an alternate path through the network. In the event of a network failure, the alternate paths can be used to continue forwarding data throughout the network.

The last principle that you should consider when designing your network is the behavior of the different protocols. The actual switching point for data does not have to be the physical wire level. Your data can be rerouted at the Data Link and Network layers, as well. Some protocols introduce more network traffic than others. Those operating at Layer 2 can be encapsulated or tagged to create a Layer-3–like environment. This environment allows the implementation of switching, and thereby provides security, protocol priority, and Quality of Service (QoS) features through the use of Application-Specific Integrated Circuits (ASICs) instead of the CPU on the switch. ASICs are much faster than CPUs. ASICs are silicon chips that provide only one or two specific tasks faster than a CPU. Because they process data in silicon and are assigned to a certain task, less processing time is needed, and data is forwarded with less latency and more efficiency to the end destinations.

In order to understand how switches work, we need to understand how collision domains and broadcast domains differ.

Collision Domains

A switch can be considered a high-speed multiport bridge that allows almost maximum wire-speed transfers. Dividing the local geographical network into smaller segments reduces the number of interfaces in each segment. Doing so will increase the amount of bandwidth available to all the interfaces. Each smaller segment is considered a collision domain.

In the case of switching, each port on the switch is its own collision domain. The most optimal switching configuration places only one interface on each port of a switch, making the collision domain two nodes: the switch port interface and the interface of the end machine.

Let's look at a small collision domain consisting of two PCs and a server, shown in Figure 1.4. Notice that if both PCs in the network transmit data at the same time, the data will collide in the network because all three computers are in their own collision domain. If each PC and server was on its own port on the switch, each would be in its own collision domain.

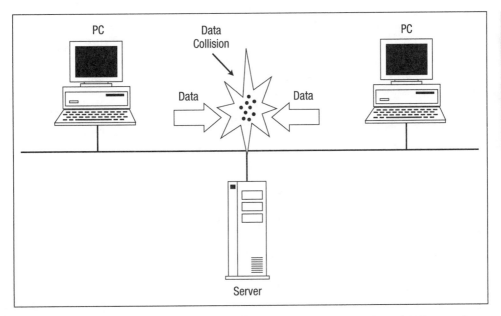

Figure 1.4 **A small collision domain consisting of two PCs sending data simultaneously to a server.**

Switch ports are assigned to virtual LANs (VLANs) to segment the network into smaller broadcast domains. If you are using a node attached to a switch port assigned to a VLAN, broadcasts will only be received from members of your assigned VLAN. When the switch is set up and each port is assigned to a VLAN, a broadcast sent in VLAN 1 is seen by those ports assigned to VLAN 1 even if they are on other switches attached by trunk links. A switch port can be a member of only one VLAN and requires a Layer 3 device such as an internal route processor or router to route data from one VLAN to another.

Although the nodes on each port are in their own collision domain, the broadcast domain consists of all of the ports assigned to a particular VLAN. Therefore, when a broadcast is sent from a node in VLAN 1, all the devices attached to ports assigned to VLAN 1 will receive that broadcast. The switch segments the users connected to other ports, thereby preventing data collisions. For this reason, when traffic remains local to each segment or workgroup, each user has more bandwidth available than if all the nodes are in one segment.

On a physical link between the port on the switch and a workstation in a VLAN with very few nodes, data can be sent at almost 100 percent of the physical wire speed. The reason? Virtually no data collisions. If the VLAN contains many nodes, the broadcast domain is larger and more broadcasts must be processed by all ports on the switch belonging to each VLAN. The number of ports assigned to a VLAN make up the broadcast domain, which is discussed in the following section.

Broadcast Domains

In switched environments, broadcast domains consist of all the ports or collision domains belonging to a VLAN. In a flat network topology, your collision domain and your broadcast domain are all the interfaces in your segment or subnet. If no devices (such as a switch or a router) divide your network, you have only one broadcast domain. On some switches, the number of broadcast domains or VLANs that can be configured is almost limitless. VLANs allow a switch to divide the network segment into multiple broadcast domains. Each port becomes its own collision domain. Figure 1.5 shows an example of a properly switched network.

NOTE: *Switching technology complements routing technology, and each has its place in the network. The value of routing technology is most noticeable when you get to larger networks that utilize WAN solutions in the network environment.*

Why Upgrade to Switches?

As an administrator, you may not realize when it is time to convert your company to a switched network and implement VLANs. You may also not be aware of the benefits that can occur from replacing your Layer 2 hubs and bridges with switches, or how the addition of some modules in your switches to implement routing and filtering ability can help improve your network's performance.

When your flat topology network starts to slow down due to traffic, collisions, and other bottlenecks, you may want to investigate the problems. Your first

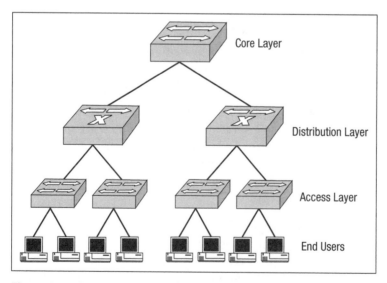

Figure 1.5   An example of a properly switched network.

reaction is to find out what types of data are flowing through your network. If you are in command of the network sniffer or other such device, you may begin to find over-utilization errors on the sniffer occurring when the Ethernet network utilization reaches above only 40 percent.

Why would this happen at such a low utilization percentage on the network? Peak efficiency on a flat topology Ethernet network is about 40 percent utilization. Sustained utilization above this level is a strong indicator that you may want to upgrade the physical network into a switched environment.

When you start to notice that your state-of-the-art Pentiums are performing poorly, many network administrators don't realize the situation may be due to the hundreds of other computers on their flat hub and bridged networks. To resolve the issue, your network administrator may even upgrade your PC to a faster CPU or more RAM. This allows your PC to generate more input/output (I/O), increasing the saturation on the network. In this type of environment, every data packet is sent to every machine, and each station has to process every frame on the network.

The processors in the PCs handle this task, taking away from the processing power needed for other tasks. Every day, I visit users and networks with this problem. When I upgrade them to a switched network, it is typically a weekend job. The users leave on Friday with their high-powered Pentiums stacked with RAM acting like 486s. When they come back Monday morning, we hear that their computers boot up quickly and run faster, and that Internet pages come up instantly.

In many cases, slow Internet access times were blamed on the users' WAN connections. The whole time, the problem wasn't their WAN connections—it was their LAN saturated to a grinding halt with frames from every interface on the network.

When network performance gets this bad, it's time to call in a Cisco consultant or learn how to implement switching. Either way, you are reading this book because you are very interested in switching or in becoming Cisco certified. Consider yourself a network hero of this generation in training.

To fix the immediate problems on your 10BaseT network with Category 3 or Category 4 cabling, you might need to upgrade to Category 5 cabling and implement a Fast Ethernet network. Then you need to ask yourself, is this only a temporary solution for my network? What types of new technologies are we considering? Are we going to upgrade to Windows 2000? Will we be using Web services or implementing Voice Over IP? Do we have any requirements for using multicast, unicast, video conferencing, or CAD applications? The list of questions goes on. Primarily, you need to ask yourself if this is a temporary solution or one that will stand the test of time.

Unshielded Twisted-Pair Cable

Category 3 unshielded twisted-pair (UTP) is cable certified for bandwidths of up to 10Mbps with signaling rates of up to 16MHz. Category 4 UTP cable is cable certified for bandwidths of up to 16Mbps with signaling rates up to 20MHz. Category 4 cable is classified as voice and data grade cabling. Category 5 cabling is cable certified for bandwidths of up to 100Mbps and signaling rates of up to 100MHz. New cabling standards for Category 5e and Category 6 cable support bandwidths of up to 1Gbps.

In many cases, network administrators don't realize that implementing a switched network will allow your network to run at almost wire speed. Upgrading the backbone (not the wiring), eliminating the data collisions, making the network segments smaller, and getting those users off hubs and bridges is the answer. In terms of per-port costs, this is usually a much cheaper solution. It's also a solution you can grow with. Of course, a 100Mbps network never hurts; but even a switched 10BaseT network that has been correctly implemented can have almost the same effect of providing your network with increased performance.

Network performance is usually measured by throughput. *Throughput* is the overall amount of data traffic that can be carried by the physical lines through the network. It is measured by the maximum amount of data that can pass through any point in your network without suffering packet loss or collisions.

Packet loss is the total number of packets transmitted at the speed of the physical wire minus the number that arrive correctly at their destination. When you have a large percentage of packet losses, your network is functioning less efficiently than it would if the multiple collisions of the transmitted data were eliminated.

The *forwarding rate* is another consideration in network throughput. The forwarding rate is the number of packets per second that can be transmitted on the physical wire. For example, if you are sending 64-byte packets on a 10BaseT Ethernet network, you can transmit a maximum of about 14,880 packets per second.

Poorly designed and implemented switched networks can have awful effects. Let's take a look at the effects of a flat area topology and how we can design, modify, and upgrade Ethernet networks to perform as efficiently as possible.

Properly Switched Networks

Properly switched networks use the Cisco hierarchical switching model to place switches in the proper location in the network and apply the most efficient functions to each. In the model you will find switches in three layers:

- Access layer
- Distribution layer
- Core layer

NOTE: *Chapter 2 will introduce the layers at which each switch can be found and the basic configuration steps for both of the command line interfaces.*

The Access layer's primary function is to connect to the end-user's interface. It routes traffic between ports and broadcasts collision domain traffic to its membership broadcast domain. It is the access point into the network for the end users. It can utilize lower-end switches such as the Catalyst 1900, 2800, 2900, 3500, 4000, and 5000 series switches.

The Access layer switch blocks meet at the Distribution layer. It uses medium-end switches with a little more processing power and stronger ASICs. The function of this layer is to apply filters, queuing, security, and routing in some networks. It is the main processor of frames and packets flowing through the network. Switches found at this layer belong to the 5500, 6000, and 6500 series.

The Core layer's only function is to route data between segments and switch blocks as quickly as possible. No filtering or queuing functions should be applied at this layer. The highest-end Cisco Catalyst switches are typically found at this layer, such as the 5500, 6500, 8500, 8600 GSR, and 12000 GSR series switches.

How you configure your broadcast and collision domains—whether in a switched network or a flat network topology—can have quite an impact on the efficiency of your network. Let's take a look at how utilization is measured and the different effects bandwidth can have on different media types and networks.

Network Utilization

Network administrators vary on the utilization percentage values for normal usage of the network. Table 1.1 shows the average utilization that should be seen on the physical wire. Going above these averages of network utilization on the physical wire is a sign that a problem exists in the network, that you need to make changes to the network configuration, or that you need to upgrade the network.

Table 1.1   The average limits in terms of physical wire utilization. Exceeding these values indicates a network problem.

Utilization (%)	Medium Type
100	Full duplex
90 to 100	FDDI
90 to 100	Switched LAN segments
60 to 65	WAN links
35 to 45	Non-switched Ethernet segments or subnets
5 to 7	Collisions

You can use a network monitor such as a sniffer to monitor your utilization and the type of traffic flowing through your network. Devices such as WAN probes let you monitor the traffic on the WAN.

Switched Forwarding

Switches route data based on the destination MAC address contained in the frame's header. This approach allows switches to replace Layer 2 devices such as hubs and bridges.

After a frame is received and the MAC address is read, the switch forwards data based on the switching mode the switch is using. This strategy tends to create very low latency times and very high forwarding rates. Switches use three switching modes to forward information through the switching fabric:

- Store-and-forward
- Cut-through
- FragmentFree

TIP: Switching fabric *is the route data takes to get from the input port on the switch to the output port on the switch. The data may pass through wires, processors, buffers, ASICs, and many other components.*

Store-and-Forward Switching

Pulls the entire packet received into its onboard buffers, reads the entire packet, and calculates its cyclic redundancy check (CRC). It then determines if the packet is good or bad. If the CRC calculated on the packet matches the CRC calculated by the switch, the destination address is read and the packet is forwarded out the correct port on the switch. If the CRC does not match the packet, the packet is discarded. Because this type of switching waits for the entire packet before forwarding, latency times can become quite high, which can result in some delay of network traffic.

Cut-Through Switching

Sometimes referred to as *realtime switching* or *FastForward switching*, cut-through switching was developed to reduce the latency involved in processing frames as they arrive at the switch and are forwarded on to the destination port. The switch begins by pulling the frame header into its network interface card buffer. As soon as the destination MAC address is known (usually within the first 13 bytes), the switch forwards the frame out the correct port.

This type of switching reduces latency inside the switch; however, if the frame is corrupt because of a late collision or wire interference, the switch will still forward the bad frame. The destination receives the bad frame, checks its CRC, and discards it, forcing the source to resend the frame. This process will certainly waste bandwidth; and if it occurs too often, major impacts can occur on the network.

In addition, cut-through switching is limited by its inability to bridge different media speeds. In particular, some network protocols (including NetWare 4.1 and some Internet Protocol [IP] networks) use windowing technology, in which multiple frames may be sent without a response. In this situation, the latency across a switch is much less noticeable, so the on-the-fly switch loses its main competitive edge. In addition, the lack of error checking poses a problem for large networks. That said, there is still a place for the fast cut-through switch for smaller parts of large networks.

FragmentFree Switching

Also known as *runtless switching*, FragmentFree switching was developed to solve the late-collision problem. These switches perform a modified version of cut-through switching. Because most corruption in a packet occurs within the first 64 bytes, the switch looks at the entire first 64 bytes to get the destination MAC address, instead of just reading the first 13 bytes. The minimum valid size for an Ethernet frame is 64 bytes. By verifying the first 64 bytes of the frame, the switch then determines if the frame is good or if a collision occurred during transit.

Combining Switching Methods

To resolve the problems associated with the switching methods discussed so far, a new method was developed. Some switches, such as the Cisco Catalyst 1900, 2820, and 3000 series, begin with either cut-through or FragmentFree switching. Then, as frames are received and forwarded, the switch also checks the frame's CRC. Although the CRC may not match the frame itself, the frame is still forwarded before the CRC check and after the MAC address is reached. The switch performs this task so that if too many bad frames are forwarded, the switch can take a proactive role, changing from cut-through mode to store-and-forward mode. This method, in addition to the development of high-speed processors, has reduced many of the problems associated with switching.

Only the Catalyst 1900, 2820, and 3000 series switches support cut-through and FragmentFree switching. You might ponder the reasoning behind the faster Catalyst series switches not supporting this seemingly faster method of switching. Well, store-and-forward switching is not necessarily slower than cut-through switching—when switches were first introduced, the two modes were quite different. With better processors and integrated-circuit technology, store-and-forward switching can perform at the physical wire limitations. This method allows the end user to see no difference in the switching methods.

Switched Network Bottlenecks

This section will take you step by step through how bottlenecks affect performance, some of the causes of bottlenecks, and things to watch out for when designing your network. A *bottleneck* is a point in the network at which data slows due to collisions and too much traffic directed to one resource node (such as a server). In these examples, I will use fairly small, simple networks so that you will get the basic strategies that you can apply to larger, more complex networks.

Let's start small and slowly increase the network size. We'll take a look at a simple way of understanding how switching technology increases the speed and efficiency of your network. Bear in mind, however, that increasing the speed of your physical network increases the throughput to your resource nodes and doesn't always increase the speed of your network. This increase in traffic to your resource nodes may create a bottleneck.

Figure 1.6 shows a network that has been upgraded to 100Mbps links to and from the switch for all the nodes. Because all the devices can send data at 100Mbps or wire-speed to and from the switch, a link that receives data from multiple nodes will need to be upgraded to a faster link than all the other nodes in order to process and fulfill the data requests without creating a bottleneck.

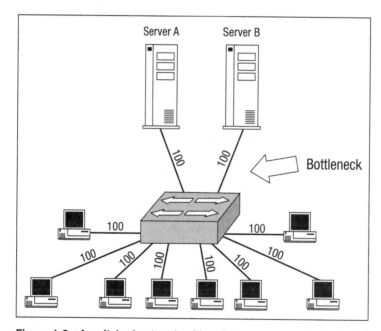

Figure 1.6   A switched network with only two servers. Notice that the sheer number of clients sending data to the servers can overwhelm the cable and slow the data traffic.

However, because all the nodes—including the file servers—are sending data at 100Mbps, the link between the file servers that is the target for the data transfers for all the devices becomes a bottleneck in the network.

Many types of physical media topologies can be applied to this concept. In this demonstration, we will utilize Ethernet 100BaseT. Ethernet 10BaseT and 100BaseT are most commonly found in the networks of today.

We'll make an upgrade to the network and alleviate our bottleneck on the physical link from the switch to each resource node or server. By upgrading this particular link to a Gigabit Ethernet link, as shown in Figure 1.7, you can successfully eliminate this bottleneck.

It would be nice if all network bottleneck problems were so easy to solve. Let's take a look at a more complex model. In this situation, the demand nodes are connected to one switch and the resource nodes are connected to another switch. As you add additional users to switch A, you'll find out where our bottleneck is. As you can see from Figure 1.8, the bottleneck is now on the trunk link between the two switches. Even if all the switches have a VLAN assigned to each port, a trunk link without VTP pruning enabled will send all the VLANs to the next switch.

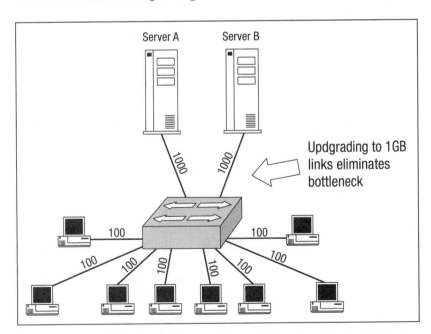

Figure 1.7   The addition of a Gigabit Ethernet link on the physical link between the switch and the server.

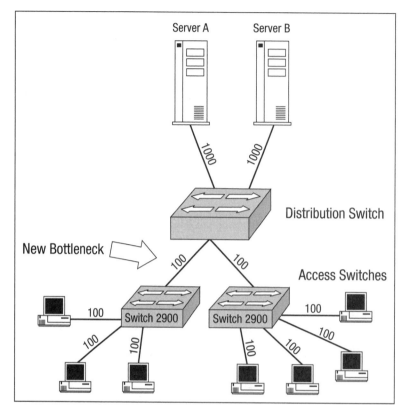

Figure 1.8   A new bottleneck on the trunk link between the two switches.

To resolve this issue, you could implement the same solution as the previous example and upgrade the trunk between the two switches to a Gigabit Ethernet. Doing so would eliminate the bottleneck. You want to put switches in place whose throughput is never blocked by the number of ports. This solution is referred to as using *non-blocking switches.*

Non-Blocking Switch vs. Blocking Switch

We call a switch a *blocking switch* when the switch bus or components cannot handle the theoretical maximum throughput of all the input ports combined. There is a lot of debate over whether every switch should be designed as a non-blocking switch; but for now this situation is only a dream, considering the current pricing of non-blocking switches.

Let's get even more complicated and introduce another solution by implementing two physical links between the two switches and using full-duplexing technology. *Full duplex* essentially means that you have two physical wires from each port—data is sent on one link and received on another. This setup not only virtually guarantees a collision-free connection, but also can increase your network traffic to almost 100 percent on each link.

You now have 200 percent throughput by utilizing both links. If you had 10Mbps on the wire at half duplex, by implementing full duplex you now have 20Mbps flowing through the wires. The same thing goes with a 100BaseT network: Instead of 100Mbps, you now have a 200Mbps link.

TIP: *If the interfaces on your resource nodes can implement full duplex, it can also be a secondary solution for your servers.*

Almost every Cisco switch has an acceptable throughput level and will work well in its own layer of the Cisco hierarchical switching model or its designed specification. Implementing VLANs has become a popular solution for breaking down a segment into smaller collision domains.

Internal Route Processor vs. External Route Processor

Routing between VLANs has been a challenging problem to overcome. In order to route between VLANs, you must use a Layer 3 route processor or router. There are two different types of route processors: an external route processor and an internal route processor. An external route processor uses an external router to route data from one VLAN to another VLAN. An internal route processor uses internal modules and cards located on the same device to implement the routing between VLANs.

Now that you have a pretty good idea how a network should be designed and how to monitor and control bottlenecks, let's take a look at the general traffic rule and how it has changed over time.

The Rule of the Network Road

Network administrators and designers have traditionally strived to design networks using the *80/20 rule*. Using this rule, a network designer would try to design a network in which 80 percent of the traffic stayed on local segments and 20 percent of the traffic went on the network backbone.

This was an effective design during the early days of networking, when the majority of LANs were departmental and most traffic was destined for data that resided on the local servers. However, it is not a good design in today's environment, where the majority of traffic is destined for enterprise servers or the Internet.

A switch's ability to create multiple data paths and provide swift, low-latency connections allows network administrators to permit up to 80 percent of the traffic on the backbone without causing a massive overload of the network. This ability allows for the introduction of many bandwidth-intensive uses, such as network video, video conferencing, and voice communications.

Multimedia and video applications can demand as much as 1.5Mbps or more of continuous bandwidth. In a typical environment, users can rarely obtain this bandwidth if they share an average 10Mbps network with dozens of other people. The video will also look jerky if the data rate is not sustained. In order to support this application, a means of providing greater throughput is needed. The ability of switches to provide dedicated bandwidth at wire-speed meets this need.

Switched Ethernet Innovations

Around 1990, many vendors offered popular devices known as *intelligent multiport bridges*; the first known usage of the term *switch* was the Etherswitch, which Kalpana brought to the market in 1990. At the time, these devices were used mainly to connect multiple segments—they usually did very little to improve performance other than the inherent benefits bridges provide, such as filtering and broadcast suppression.

Kalpana changed that by positioning its devices as performance enhancers. A number of important features made the Kalpana switches popular, such as using multiple transmission paths for network stations and cut-through switching.

Cut-through switching reduced the delay problems associated with standard bridges by providing the means to have multiple transmissions paths to network devices. Each device could have its own data path to the switch and did not need to be in a shared environment.

Kalpana was able to do this by dedicating one pair of the station wiring to transmitting data and one pair to receiving data. This improvement allowed the Kalpana designers to ignore the constraints of collision detection and carrier sense, because the cables were dedicated to one station. Kalpana continued its history of innovation with the introduction in 1993 of full-duplex Ethernet.

Full-Duplex Ethernet

Prior to the introduction of full-duplex (FDX) Ethernet, Ethernet stations could either transmit or receive data; they could not do both at the same time, because there was no way to ensure a collision-free environment. This was known as half-duplex (HDX) operation.

FDX has been a feature of WANs for years, but only the advent of advances in LAN switching technology made it practical to now consider FDX on the LAN. In FDX operation, both the transmission and reception paths can be used simultaneously. Because FDX operation uses a dedicated link, there are no collisions, which greatly simplifies the MAC protocol. Some slight modifications in the way the packet header is formatted enable FDX to maintain compatibility with HDX Ethernet.

You don't need to replace the wiring in a 10BaseT network, because FDX operation runs on the same two-pair wiring used by 10BaseT. It simultaneously uses one pair for transmission and another pair for reception. A switched connection has only two stations: the station itself and the switch port. This setup makes simultaneous transmission possible and has the net effect of doubling a 10Mbps LAN.

This last point is an important one. In theory, FDX operation can provide double the bandwidth of HDX operation, giving 10Mbps speeds in each direction. However, achieving this speed would require that the two stations have a constant flow of data and that the applications themselves would benefit from a two-way data flow. FDX links are extremely beneficial in connecting switches to each other. If there were servers on both sides of the link between switches, the traffic between switches would tend to be more symmetrical.

Fast Ethernet

Another early innovation in the switching industry was the development of Fast Ethernet. Ethernet as a technology has been around since the early 1970s, but by the early 1990s its popularity began to wane. Competing technologies such as FDDI running at 100Mbps showed signs of overtaking Ethernet as a de facto standard, especially for high-speed backbones.

Grand Junction, a company founded by many of the early Ethernet pioneers, proposed a new Ethernet technology that would run at 10 times the 10Mbps speed of Ethernet. They were joined by most of the top networking companies—with the exception of Hewlett-Packard (HP), which had a competing product. HP's product, known as 100Mbps VG/AnyLAN, was in most respects far superior to the product proposed by Grand Junction. It had a fatal flaw, though: It was incompatible with existing Ethernet standards and was not backward compatible to most of the equipment in use at the time. Although the standards bodies debated the merits of each of the camps, the marketplace decided for them. Fast Ethernet is the overwhelming winner, so much so that even HP sells Fast Ethernet on almost all its products.

NOTE: *In 1995, Cisco purchased both Kalpana and Grand Junction and incorporated their innovations into its hardware. These devices became the Catalyst line of Cisco products.*

Gigabit Ethernet

In order to implement Gigabit Ethernet (GE), the CSMA/CD method was changed slightly to maintain a 200-meter collision diameter at gigabit-per-second data rates. This slight modification prevented Ethernet packets from completing transmission before the transmitting station sensed a collision, which would violate the CSMA/CD rule.

GE maintains a packet length of 64 bytes, but provides additional modifications to the Ethernet specification. The minimum CSMA/CD carrier time and the Ethernet slot time have been extended from 64 bytes to 512 bytes. Also, packets smaller than 512 bytes have an extra carrier extension added to them. These changes, which can impact the performance of small packets, have been offset by implementing a feature called *packet bursting*, which allows servers, switches, and other devices to deliver bursts of small packets in order to utilize the available bandwidth.

Because it follows the same form, fit, and function as its 10- and 100Mbps predecessors, GE can be integrated seamlessly into existing Ethernet and Fast Ethernet networks using LAN switches or routers to adapt between the different physical line speeds. Because GE is Ethernet, only faster, network managers will find the migration from Fast Ethernet to Gigabit Ethernet to be as smooth as the migration from Ethernet to Fast Ethernet.

Avoiding Fork-Lift Upgrades

Although dedicated switch connections provide the maximum benefits for network users, you don't want to get stuck with *fork-lift upgrades.* In a fork-lift upgrade, you pay more to upgrade your computer or networking equipment than it would cost to buy the equipment already installed. The vendor knows that you are not going to buy all new equipment, so the vendor sells you the upgrade at an enormous price. In order to exchange it for the bigger, better, faster equipment It may sometimes be necessary to support legacy equipment.

Fortunately for Ethernet switches you can provide connectivity in a number of ways. You can attach shared hubs to any port on the switch in the same manner that you connect end stations. Doing so makes for a larger collision domain, but you avoid paying the high costs of upgrades.

Typically, your goal would be to migrate toward single-station segments as bandwidth demands increase. This migration will provide you with the increased bandwidth you need without wholesale replacement of existing equipment or cabling.

In this lower cost setup, a backbone switch is created in which each port is attached to the now-larger collision domain or segment. This switch replaces existing connections to routers or bridges and provides communication between each of the shared segments.

The Cisco IOS

The Cisco Internetwork Operating System (IOS) is the kernel of Cisco routers and switches. Not all Cisco devices run the same IOS. Some use a graphical interface, some use a Set/Clear command-line interface, and some use a Cisco Command Line Interface (CLI). Cisco has acquired more devices than they have designed and built themselves. Therefore, Cisco has adapted the operating systems designed for each device they have acquired to use the protocols and standards of the company. Almost all Cisco routers run the same IOS, but only about half of the switches currently run the Cisco CLI IOS.

Knowing what configuration mode you are in and how to enter each configuration mode on the Cisco CLI is important. Recognizing what each mode configures will aid you in using the proper configuration mode. The Set/Clear command-based IOS is similar in modes, but uses the **enable**, **set**, **show**, and **clear** commands (covered in the next chapter).

Connecting to the Switch

You can connect to a Cisco switch to configure the switch, verify the configuration, or check statistics. Although there are different ways of connecting to a Cisco switch, typically you would connect to its console port.

In lower-end Cisco switches, the console port is usually an RJ-45 connection on the back of the switch. On a higher-end switch, you may find console ports on the line cards such as a Supervisor Engine. By default there is no password set on the console port.

Another way to connect to a Cisco switch or router is through an auxiliary port. This is basically the same as connecting through a console port, but it allows you to connect remotely by using a modem. This means you can dial up a remote switch and perform configuration changes, verify the configuration, or check statistics.

A third way to connect to a Cisco switch is through the program Telnet. Telnet is a program that emulates a dumb terminal. You can use Telnet to connect to any active port on the switch, such as an Ethernet or serial port.

Cisco also allows you to configure the switch by using Switch Manager, which is a way of configuring your switch through a Web browser using HTTP. This method creates a graphical interface for configuring your switch. The Switch Manager allows you to perform most of the same configurations as you can with the CLI.

Powering Up the Switch

When you first power up a Cisco switch, it runs the power on self test (POST), which runs diagnostics on the internal workings of the switch. If the switch passes this test, it will look for and load the Cisco IOS from Flash memory if a file is present. *Flash memory* is read-only memory kept on an EEPROM (a silicon chip inside of the switch). The IOS then loads the configuration contained in nonvolatile RAM (NVRAM). NVRAM is similar to random access memory (RAM) but is not lost when the power is cycled on the switch. This loads the configuration of the Cisco IOS and the Cisco user interface becomes available.

The Cisco IOS user interface is divided into several different modes. The commands available to you in each mode determine the mode you are in. When you start a session on the switch, you begin in User EXEC mode, often called EXEC mode. Only a limited subset of the commands is available in EXEC mode. In order to have access to all commands, you must enter Privileged EXEC mode. From Privileged EXEC mode, you can enter any EXEC command or enter Global Configuration mode, which offers even more command options. From global configuration mode you can also enter into any interface configuration mode to configure an interface (port) or a subinterface.

Subinterfaces

Subinterfaces allow you to create virtual interfaces within an interface or port on a switch. When entering an interface number with a decimal subinterface number, the prompt changes to **(config-subif)#**. Let's look at an example:

```
Router(config)#interface e0/0.?
  <0-4294967295>  Ethernet interface number
Router(config)#interface e0/0.1
Router(config-subif)#
```

Let's take a look at the commands available in the User EXEC mode of a Cisco Catalyst 1912 EN switch:

```
SeansSwitch>?
Exec commands:
  enable    Turn on privileged commands
  exit      Exit from the EXEC
  help      Description of the interactive help system
  ping      Send echo messages
  session   Tunnel to module
  show      Show running system information
  terminal  Set terminal line parameters
SeansSwitch>
```

The following commands are available in Privileged EXEC mode:

```
SeansSwitch#?
Exec commands:
  clear             Reset functions
  configure         Enter configuration mode
  copy              Copy configuration or firmware
  delete            Reset configuration
  disable           Turn off privileged commands
  enable            Turn on privileged commands
  exit              Exit from the EXEC
  help              Description of the interactive help system
  menu              Enter menu interface
  ping              Send echo messages
  reload            Halt and perform warm start
  session           Tunnel to module
  show              Show running system information
  terminal          Set terminal line parameters
  vlan-membership   VLAN membership configuration
SeansSwitch#
```

Finally, the following commands are available in Global Configuration mode:

```
SeansSwitch(config)#?
Configure commands:
  address-violation          Set address violation action
  back-pressure              Enable back pressure
  bridge-group               Configure port grouping using bridge groups
  cdp                        Global CDP configuration subcommands
  cgmp                       Enable CGMP
  ecc                        Enable enhanced congestion control
  enable                     Modify enable password parameters
  end                        Exit from configure mode
  exit                       Exit from configure mode
  help                       Description of the interactive help system
  hostname                   Set the system's network name
  interface                  Select an interface to configure
  ip                         Global IP configuration subcommands
  line                       Configure a terminal line
  login                      Configure options for logging in
  mac-address-table          Configure the mac address table
  monitor-port               Set port monitoring
  multicast-store-and-forward  Enables multicast store and forward
  network-port               Set the network port
  no                         Negate a command or set its defaults
```

```
    port-channel                    Configure Fast EtherChannel
    rip                             Routing information protocol configuration
    service                         Configuration Command
    snmp-server                     Modify SNMP parameters
    spantree                        Spanning tree subsystem
    spantree-template               Set bridge template parameter
    storm-control                   Configure broadcast storm control parameters
    switching-mode                  Sets the switching mode
    tacacs-server                   Modify TACACS query parameters
    tftp                            Configure TFTP
    uplink-fast                     Enable Uplink fast
    vlan                            VLAN configuration
    vlan-membership                 VLAN membership server configuration
    vtp                             Global VTP configuration commands
SeansSwitch(config)#
```

Notice that as you progress through the modes on the Cisco IOS, more and more commands become available.

TIP: *If your switch does not boot correctly, it may mean that you are in ROM Configuration mode, which is covered in Chapter 2.*

The Challenges

Sending data effectively through the network is a challenge for network designers and administrators regardless of the LAN topology. The first data-processing environments consisted mostly of time-sharing networks that used mainframes and attached terminals. Communications between devices were proprietary and dependent on your equipment vendor. Both IBM's System Network Architecture (SNA) and Digital's network architecture implemented such environments.

In today's networks, high-speed LANs and switched internetworks are universally used, owing largely to the fact that they operate at very high speeds and support such high-bandwidth applications as voice and video conferencing. Internetworking evolved as a solution to three key problems: isolated LANs, duplication of resources, and a lack of network management.

Implementing a functional internetwork is no simple task. You will face many challenges, especially in the areas of connectivity, reliability, network management, and flexibility. Each area is important in establishing an efficient and effective internetwork. The challenge when connecting various systems is to support communication between disparate technologies. Different sites, for example, may use different types of media, or they may operate at varying speeds.

Reliable service is an essential consideration and must be maintained in any internetwork. The entire organization sometimes depends on consistent, reliable access to network resources to function and to prosper. Network management must provide centralized support and troubleshooting capabilities. Configuration, security, performance, and other issues must be adequately addressed for the internetwork to function smoothly. Flexibility, the final concern, is necessary for network expansion and new applications and services, among other factors.

Today's Trend

In today's networks, the trend is to replace hubs and bridges with switches. This approach reduces the number of routers connecting the LAN segments while speeding the flow of data in the network. A smart network administrator uses switches to inexpensively increase network bandwidth and ease network administration.

A switch is a low-cost solution to provide more bandwidth, reduce collisions, filter traffic, and contain broadcasts. But, switches don't solve all network routing problems. Routers provide a means of connecting multiple physical topologies, restricting broadcasts, and providing network security. Using switches and routers together, you can integrate large networks and provide a high level of performance without sacrificing the benefits of either technology.

Immediate Solutions

Entering and Exiting Privileged EXEC Mode

After the switch has gone through the power on self test (POST), it will come to a User EXEC mode prompt with the hostname and an angle bracket as shown here, assuming no password has been configured:

```
Switch>
```

To enter Privileged EXEC mode, use the following command. You will notice that the prompt changes to indicate that you are in Privileged EXEC mode:

```
Switch>enable
Switch>(enable)
```

To exit Privileged Exec mode and return to User EXEC mode, use the **disable** command.

Entering and Exiting Global Configuration Mode

From Privileged EXEC mode, you can enter Global Configuration mode by using the following command. Notice again that the prompt changes for each successive mode:

```
Switch>(enable)configure terminal
Switch(config)#
```

To exit Global Configuration mode and return to Privileged Exec mode, you can use the **end** or **exit** command, or press Ctrl+Z.

Entering and Exiting Interface Configuration Mode

To configure an interface, you must enter Interface Configuration mode. From the Global Configuration mode command prompt, use the following command.

You must specify the interface and number; this example configures the Ethernet 0 port:

```
Switch(config)#interface e0
Switch(config-if)#
```

To exit to Global Configuration mode, use the **exit** command or press Ctrl+Z.

Entering and Exiting Subinterface Configuration Mode

To configure a subinterface on an interface, use the following command. You must specify the interface and the subinterface, separated by a decimal; the second number identifies the subinterface:

```
Switch(config-if)#interface e0.1
Switch(config-subif)#
```

TIP: *You can abbreviate any command as much as you want, as long as it remains unique (no other command exists that matches your abbreviation). For instance, the command **interface e0.1** can be abbreviated as **int e0.1**.*

To exit to Global Configuration mode, use the **exit** command or press Ctrl+Z.

TIP: *Entering a question mark (**?**) in any mode will display the list of commands available for that particular mode. Typing any command followed by a question mark—such as **clock ?**—will list the arguments associated with that command. You can also type the first few letters of a command immediately followed by a question mark. This will list all the commands starting with the entered letters.*

Saving Configuration Changes

When you're saving the configuration, the Set/Clear IOS-based switches are identical to the IOS-based CLI. The configuration modes allow you to make changes to the running configuration. In order to save these changes, you must save the configuration.

There are two types of configuration files: Startup configuration files are used during system startup to configure the software, and running configuration files contain the current configuration of the software. The two configuration files do not always agree.

To make a change to the running configuration file:

1. Issue the command **configure terminal**.

2. Make any necessary changes.

3. When you are done, copy the running configuration to the startup configuration.

In the following example, the hostname is being changed and then saved to the start-up configuration:

```
Switch> enable
Switch# configure terminal
Enter configuration commands, one per line. End with CNTL/Z.
Switch(config)# hostname BBSwitch
BBSwitch (config) end
BBSwitch# copy running-config startup-config
```

Chapter 2
Basic Switch Configuration

(continued)

In Depth

Throughout the last decade, Cisco has acquired some major switching vendors such as Kalpana and Crescendo. As a result, Cisco switches have a variety of command-line interfaces you need to be familiar with in order to set up and maintain the devices.

Command-Line Interfaces

The most common interface found on the Cisco Catalyst line of switches is the original Crescendo interface (named for the vendor Cisco purchased). This interface is often termed the *Set/Clear command-based switch*, because these switches are limited to **set**, **clear**, and **show** commands. The Crescendo interface can be found in the following switches:

- Catalyst 2900G series
- Catalyst 2926
- Catalyst 4000 series
- Catalyst 5000 series
- Catalyst 5500 series
- Catalyst 6000 series
- Catalyst 6500 series

A second type of interface is found on more recent models. It is called the *Command-Line Interface (CLI)*. The Enterprise Edition Software of these switches uses the standard Cisco Internetwork Operating System (IOS), which is virtually identical to the IOS found on Cisco's line of routers. The CLI can be found on the following switches:

- Catalyst 1900 series
- Catalyst 2820 series
- Catalyst 2900 XL series
- Catalyst 8500 GSR series
- Catalyst 12000 GSR series

A third type of interface is found on Cisco's legacy switches. These devices have a menu-driven interface that you use to enter commands. The menu selections are fairly intuitive, so you don't have to memorize a lot of commands to get around the switches. The interface is found on these switches:

- Catalyst 1900 series
- Catalyst 2820 series
- Catalyst 3000 series

On each of the three different interfaces of Cisco Catalyst switch IOSs, you will need to perform certain common configuration tasks in order to configure the switch initially. Unless your switch was preconfigured, in most cases you will need to connect to the console port to begin the initial configuration of the device.

After the switch has been powered on and has completed its power on self test (POST) sequence, it's a good idea to assign the switch a hostname to help to identify the switch. Doing so is particularly useful if you have multiple switches at multiple layers of the network. You should choose a name that identifies the switch type and its placement in the network. For example, if two Cisco Catalyst 5000 switches are on the third floor of your building, you might want to name the second switch 50002FL3. So long as you use the same naming convention on all the switches in your network, they will be easy to identify when you're configuring them remotely.

For security reasons, you should change the default password and add an enable password on the Crescendo and IOS CLI-based interface switches. In the next stage of the configuration, you should assign an IP address, subnet mask, and default route to the route processor for routing and management purposes.

Once you have finished the preceding basic steps, you can connect the switch to the rest of the local network. You can use many different types of physical media, such as Ethernet, Fast Ethernet, and Gigabit Ethernet.

Switches have two types of connections: the connection to the switch console where you can initially configure the switch or monitor the network, and the connection to an Ethernet port on the switch.

Different classifications of switches permit the switches to be placed in different layers of the network architecture. Cisco prefers to use a hierarchal campus model for switches, to break down the complexity of the network.

Campus Hierarchical Switching Model

Cisco defines a *campus* as a group of buildings connected into an enterprise network of multiple LANs. A campus has a fixed geographic location and is owned and controlled by the same organization.

The *campus hierarchical switching model*, sometimes referred to as Cisco's hierarchical internetworking model, has been widely deployed in switching environments. However, telephone companies have been adopting this system in their own switching environments—particularly recently, as they branch out as providers of Internet, Digital Subscriber Line (DSL), and other digital technologies. This model provides the maximum bandwidth to the users of the network while also providing Quality of Service (QoS) features, such as queuing.

Queuing

Queuing is a way of withholding bandwidth from one data process to provide a guarantee of bandwidth for another. You can define queuing priorities for different traffic types; these priorities can be used in many networking environments that require multiple high-priority queues, including Internet Protocol (IP), Internetwork Packet Exchange (IPX), and System Network Architecture (SNA) environments. Queues are provided dynamically, which means that traffic can filter through the switch or router without congestion—bandwidth is not withheld from use by queues.

Queuing offers a number of different types of configurations and ways to base traffic to be queued: Cisco comes out with new solutions frequently. Here are a few of the most frequently used and recommended ways to control traffic:

- *First in, first out (FIFO)*—The queuing method most network administrators are familiar with. It allows for buffering control, storing data traffic in buffers and then releasing it slowly when congestion occurs on the network. This type of queuing works well on LANs where a switch or router is the demarcation point for a high-speed link and a slower link.

- *Priority queuing (PQ)*—Provides absolute preferential treatment, giving an identified type of data traffic higher priority than other traffic. This method ensures that critical data traffic traversing various links gets priority treatment over other types of data traffic. PQ also provides a faster response time than other methods of queuing. Although you can enable priority output queuing for any interface, it is best used for low-bandwidth, congested serial interfaces. Remember that PQ introduces extra overhead, which is acceptable for slow interfaces but may not be acceptable for high-speed interfaces.

- *Custom queuing (CQ)*—Based on a packet or application identifier. This type of queuing is different from PQ in that it assigns a varying window of bandwidth to each source of incoming bandwidth, assigning each window to a queue. The switch then services each queue in a round-robin fashion.

- *Weighted fair queuing (WFQ)*—Allows for multiple queues so that no one queue can starve another of all its bandwidth. WFQ is enabled by default on all serial interfaces that run at or below 2Mbps, except for those interfaces with Link Access Procedure, Balanced (LAPB), X.25, or Synchronous Data Link Control (SDLC) encapsulations. Most networks fail when their design creates unstable network links, hardware failures, or routing loops. When a failure occurs in such a network, and then the network does not converge in time to prevent a major problem for network processes or users, redundancy must be built in.

When designing a network using the Cisco campus hierarchical switching model, you create redundancy; doing so aids in the case of a network failure by providing logical points to aggregate and summarize network traffic. This setup prevents a failure in one part of the network from affecting the entire enterprise network. This model divides the network into three distinct layers:

- *Access layer*—The first layer, which is the first point of access for the end user interface. This layer passes traffic from the end user interface to the rest of the network. Security at this layer is port-based and provides verification of an authentic MAC address, local device security, and access lists.

- *Distribution layer*—The second layer, which serves to combine the traffic of the Access layer, summarize traffic, and combine routes. This layer also processes data traffic and applies security and queuing policies, allowing data traffic to be filtered and providing a guarantee of bandwidth availability for certain traffic.

- *Core layer*—Reads headers and forwards traffic as quickly as possible through the network. This is its only function. This layer needs to have high reliability and availability because any losses at this layer can greatly affect the rest of the network.

The Cisco campus hierarchical switching model is depicted in Figure 2.1.

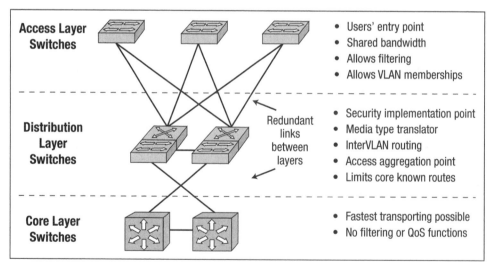

Figure 2.1   The Cisco campus hierarchical switching model.

Access Layer

The Access layer provides some important functionality, such as shared bandwidth, switched bandwidth, Media Access Control (MAC) layer filtering, and microsegmentation. Two goals of this layer are to pass traffic to the network for valid network users and to filter traffic that is passed along.

The Access layer switch connects the physical wire from the end user interface, thereby providing the means to connect to the devices located on the Distribution layer. It provides connections to both the local LAN and remote devices. The Access layer is the entry point to the network. This layer makes security and policy decisions and becomes the logical termination point for virtual private networks (VPNs).

Distribution Layer

The Distribution layer is the demarcation point between the Access and Core layers. This layer terminates network traffic that originates in the Access layer and then summarizes the traffic before passing it along to the highest Core layer. The Distribution layer also provides policy-based network connectivity, such as queuing and data termination.

The Distribution layer defines the boundaries for the network and provides packet manipulation of the network traffic. It aids in providing isolation from topology changes such as media translations, defining broadcast domains, QoS, security, managing the size of the routing table, aggregating network addresses, static route distribution, dynamic route redistribution, remote site connectivity, and inter-domain traffic redistribution.

Core Layer

The Core layer is designed to do one thing and one thing only: It switches packets at the fastest possible speed, providing the final aggregation point for the entire network. The devices at this layer must be fast and reliable. They should contain the fastest processors in the network. Connections at the Core layer must be of the highest possible bandwidth.

The Core layer makes no decisions about packet filtering or policy routing for two basic reasons. First, any filtering or policy decisions at this layer will add to the processing requirements of the system, thereby introducing latency in forwarding packets. Second, any forwarding mistakes at this level will severely impact the rest of the network.

Devices placed in the Core layer should be able to reach any device in the network. This doesn't mean that they have to have a physical link directly to each device, but all devices must be reachable in the routing table. To prevent Core layer devices from having a path to every device in their routing tables, you should use *network route summarization*, which means defining the available routes for data traffic. If the Core layer is poorly designed, network instability can easily develop due to the demands placed on the network at this layer. A good tool in your toolbox to determine some of the problems in your network is Remote Monitoring.

Remote Network Monitoring

Remote Monitoring (RMON) is an industry-standard method used to monitor statistics on a network using Simple Network Management Protocol (SNMP). RMON allows a network administrator to obtain information about a switch's Layer 1 or Layer 2 statistics. This type of information cannot be obtained by using the console port of the switch.

RMON collects information regarding connections, performance, configuration, and other pertinent statistics. Once RMON is configured on the switch, it runs continuously even when no clients are checking statistics. In fact, communication with an SNMP management station is not necessary. RMON can be configured to send trap messages to notify a management station when an error condition occurs that exceeds a currently configured maximum threshold.

With IP, nine different groups can provide RMON information. Four can be configured to provide information on a switch without an external device, such as a Switched Port Analyzer (SPAN). Cisco Catalyst switches support RMON information for IP traffic for the following four groups:

- *Statistics Group*—Maintains utilization and error statistics. This group monitors collisions, oversized packets, undersized packets, network jabber, packet fragmentation, multicast, and unicast bandwidth utilization.

- *History Group*—Provides periodical statistical information such as bandwidth utilization, frame counts, and error counts. The data can be stored for later use.

- *Alarm Group*—Allows you to configure thresholds for alarms and the intervals at which to check statistics. Any monitored event can be set to send the management station a trap message regarding an absolute or relative value or threshold.

- *Event Group*—Monitors log events on the switches. This group also sends trap messages to the management station with the time and date of the logged event, allowing the management station to create customized reports based on the Alarm Group's thresholds. Reports can be printed or logged for future use.

RMON provides support for the following groups of Token Ring extensions:

- *MAC-Layer Statistics Group*—A collection of statistics from the MAC sublayer of the Data Link layer, kept for each Token Ring interface. This group collects information such as the total number of MAC layer packets received and the number of times the port entered a beaconing error state.

- *Promiscuous Statistics Group*—A collection of promiscuous statistics kept for non-MAC packets on each Token Ring interface. This group collects information such as the total number of good non-MAC frames received that were directed to a Logical Link Control (LLC) broadcast address.

- *Ring Station Group*—A collection of statistics and status information associated with each Token Ring station on the local ring. This group also provides status information for each ring being monitored.

- *Ring Station Order Group*—A list of the order of stations on the monitored Token Ring network's rings.

To see a list of available commands, use the **?** command. Table 2.1 provides a list of the ROM command-line interface commands and a brief description of each.

Table 2.1   ROM command-line interface commands.

Command	Description
alias	Configures and displays aliases
boot	Boots up an external process
confreg	Configures the configuration register utility
dev	Shows device IDs available on a platform
dir	Shows files of the named device
history	Shows the last 16 commands
meminfo	Shows switch memory information
repeat	Repeats a specified command
reset	Performs a switch reboot/reset
set	Shows monitor variable names with their values
sync	Saves the ROM monitor configuration
unalias	Deletes the alias name and associated value from the alias list
unset=*varname*	Deletes a variable name from the variable list
varname=*value*	Assigns a value to a variable

Connecting to the Console Port

To initially configure a switch, you must make a connection to the console port and enter instructions to the switch from this port. The console comes preconfigured on a Cisco device and ready to use. You can access the console port in a number of ways, as shown in Figure 2.2.

The console port must be accessed through a PC or another device (such as a dumb terminal) to view the initial configuration. From the console port, you can configure other points of entry—such as the VTY line ports—to allow you to use Telnet to configure the switch from other points in your network.

On switches where the console port is an RJ-45 port, you must plug a rolled RJ-45 cable straight into the port. If it is a DB-25 port, you must use an RJ-45-to-DB-25 connector to connect. If the switch uses a DB-9 port, you will need a DB-9-to-RJ-45 connector. Fortunately, these connectors come with every switch—you only need to know which connector and cables to use.

Whatever the type of console port in use on the switch, you will need to connect an RJ-45 cable from the console port or connector to the dumb terminal or PC. On a PC, you can use a third-party program to gain access, such as HyperTerminal (included with most Microsoft Windows operating systems).

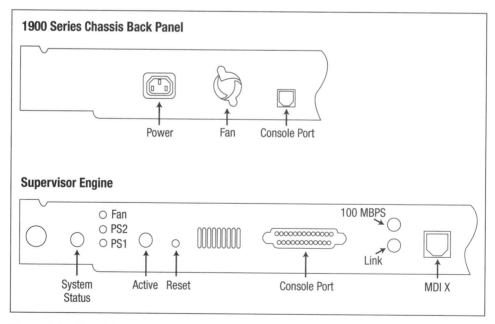

Figure 2.2   The different types of console ports on the switches.

NOTE: *The HyperTerminal version included with Microsoft Windows is very limited. One of its most notable limitations is its failure to perform the **break** command, which does not allow you to obtain a lost password from some switches and routers. You can download an upgrade to HyperTerminal from the Hilgraeve Web site, **www.hilgraeve.com**; the upgrade will allow you to use this feature.*

Console Cable Pinouts

Two types of RJ-45 cables are used with Cisco switches: a straight-through cable and a rolled cable. To figure out what type of cable you have, hold the two RJ-45 ends side by side. You will see eight colored wires, known as *pins*, at each end. If the order of the colored pins matches at both ends, then you are holding a straight-through cable. If the colors are reversed, then you are holding a rolled cable.

When a problem occurs, having access to all the accessories to build your own cable is a big advantage. Finding the correct cable or connector on a moment's notice is not always convenient. I have always wanted a quick reference that lists the pinouts of each cable and connector, so that I could easily make my own cable or connectors. Because I've never found such a reference, I've created it myself; the lists appear in Tables 2.2 and 2.3.

Table 2.2   Straight-through cable RJ-45-to-RJ-45 pinouts.

RJ-45	RJ-45
1	1
2	2
3	3
4	4
5	5
6	6
7	7
8	8

Table 2.3   Rollover cable RJ-45-to-RJ-45 pinouts.

RJ-45	RJ-45
1	8
2	7
3	6
4	5
5	4
6	3
7	2
8	1

Console Connectors

Different console adapters connect different interfaces in order to connect to the console port. The following are the types of console connectors for each switch:

- Catalyst 1900, 2820, and 2900 XL series switches each have an RJ-45 console port. You can connect to the console port using a straight-through Category 5 cable.

- The Catalyst 3000 uses a DB-9 connector to access the console port.

- The Catalyst 5000 line uses a Supervisor Engine. To connect a console to a Supervisor Engine I or II, use a DB-25 connection. If the switch uses a Supervisor Engine III, use the RJ-45-to-RJ-45 rollover cable.

- The Catalyst 6000 family also uses a Supervisor Engine with an RJ-45 style connector and an RJ-45-to-RJ-45 straight-through cable.

- The Catalyst 6500 uses a rolled cable from the console port.

You can use a number of connectors when connecting different devices using your rolled or straight-through cable:

- To connect a PC to any console cable, attach the RJ-45-to-DB-9 female Data Terminal Equipment (DTE) adapter to one of the nine-pin serial ports on the PC.

- To attach to a Unix workstation, use the RJ-45-to-DB-25 Data Communications Equipment (DCE) adapter (female).

- To connect a modem to the console port, use the RJ-45-to-DB-25 (male) adapter.

NOTE: Console port settings by default are 9600 baud, 8 data bits, 1 stop bit, and no parity.

Normally, all three connectors will come with your switch. You will need to use the appropriate adapter for the device with which you are configuring your switch.

Cisco uses two types of RJ-45-to-DB-25 connectors: the DCE style (used for modem connections) and the DTE style (used to connect to terminals or PCs).

The RJ-45-to-AUX Port Console Connector Pinouts

Most often, you will use a connection to a PC or a laptop. The connector signal appointments for each pin on the auxiliary (AUX) port DB-9 connector are shown in Table 2.4. Table 2.5 shows the connector pinouts for an RJ-45-to-DB-9 AUX port connector by color.

Table 2.4   The RJ-45-to-AUX port DB-9 connector signal appointments for each pin.

Pin	Signal	Input/Output
1	RTS	Out
2	DTR	Out
3	TXD	Out
4	GND	N/A
5	GND	N/A
6	RXD	In
7	DSR	In
8	CTS	In

Table 2.5   The RJ-45-to-DB-9 AUX port pinouts by color.

Color	RJ-45	DB-9
Brown	1	6
Blue	2	7
Yellow	3	2
Green	4	5
Red	5	5
Black	6	3
Orange	7	4
White	8	8

Table 2.6   DCE connector pinouts for an RJ-45 to a DB-25 male.

RJ-45	DCE
1	5
2	8
3	3
4	7
5	7
6	2
7	20
8	4

Table 2.6 shows the connectors most often used for modem connections. Table 2.7 shows the connectors most often used with Unix workstation connections to the console port.

In the event that you need a DB-25-to-DB-9 connector, Table 2.8 shows the pinouts.

Table 2.7   DTE connectors for an RJ-45 to a DB-25 female.

RJ-45	DTE
1	4
2	20
3	2
4	7
5	7
6	3
7	6
8	5

Table 2.8   DB-25-to-DB-9 connector pinouts.

DB-25	Signal	DB-9
2	TXD	3
3	RXD	2
4	RTS	7
5	CTS	8
6	DSR	6
7	GND	5
8	DCD	1
20	DTR	4

Switch IOSs

Three types of Cisco operating systems are in use:

- *Set/Clear command interface*—Found on models of the Catalyst 2926, 2926G, 2948G, 2980G, 4000, 5000, 5500, 6000, and 6500 series of switches. They are called Set/Clear because most commands on the switches start with **set**, **clear**, or **show**.

- *Cisco IOS-based Command Line Interface*—Most closely resembles a Cisco router's IOS Command Line Interface. This interface is found on Catalyst 1900EN, 2820, 2900 XL, 8500, and 12000 series models.

- *Menu-driven*—Found exclusively on the Catalyst 1900SE, 2820SE, 3000, 3100, and 3200 series switches.

You have to do very little in order to get a Cisco switch to work. By default, the Set/Clear command set switches and the Cisco CLI IOS interface switches have the following default attributes:

- The prompt name is set to **Console>**.
- No hostname is configured.
- No passwords are set.
- All ports default to VLAN1.
- The console port has no IP information.
- No contact name or location information is defined.
- RMON is disabled.
- SNMP traps are disabled.
- SNMP community strings are set Public for read-only, Private for read-write, and Secret for read-write-all access.
- VLAN Trunking Protocol (VTP) mode is set to Server.
- No VTP domain or password is configured.
- All VLANs are eligible for trunking.
- Inter-Switch Link (ISL) defaults to Auto.

The IOS Configuration Modes

The CLI of IOS-based switches is similar to that of IOS-based routers. Commands can be recalled by using the up or down arrows or by using a combination of Ctrl or Esc sequences to perform certain editing functions in the command-line history buffers.

On an IOS-based switch, you can access many command modes to enter commands. Here are some of the more important modes:

- *EXEC mode*—When you log in to a switch, you are automatically in User EXEC command mode. The EXEC commands are a subset of those available at the Privileged level. In general, EXEC commands allow you to test connectivity, perform basic tests, and list system information.

- *Privileged EXEC mode*—The Privileged command set includes those commands contained in User EXEC mode, as well as the **configure** command, through which you can access the remaining command modes. Privileged EXEC mode also includes high-level testing commands, such as **debug**.

- *Global Configuration mode*—Global Configuration mode commands apply to features that affect the system as a whole. Use the **configure privileged EXEC** command to enter Global Configuration mode.

- *Interface Configuration mode*—Many features are enabled on a per-interface basis. Interface Configuration commands modify the operation of an interface such as an Ethernet port or a VLAN.

Configuring Passwords

Passwords can be configured on every access method to a Cisco Catalyst switch. Passwords can be applied to the console port, auxiliary (AUX) port, and VTY lines.

Limiting Telnet Access

VTY access can be secured with a password. However, when a careless administrator walks away from a logged-in Telnet session, the door is open with full access to the entire network. This situation allows anyone with access to the terminal the administrator was using to make changes and attack the network.

A solution is to add another layer of security. You can do this by applying a time-out condition to unused VTY sessions. The Cisco IOSs calculate unused sessions in seconds or minutes, depending on the IOS version. Should the session not receive a character input from the administrator's session for the configured amount of time, the session is closed, and the administrator using the session is logged out.

Implementing Privilege Levels

Privilege levels can be assigned to limit switch users' ability to perform certain commands or types of commands. You can configure two types of levels in the IOS: user levels and privilege levels. A *user level* allows a user to perform a subset of commands that does not allow for configuration changes or debug functions. A *privilege level*, on the other hand, allows the user to use all the available commands, including configuration change commands.

You can assign a user 16 different levels, from level 0 to level 15. Level 1 is set to User EXEC Mode by default. This level gives the user very limited access, primarily to **show** commands. Level 15 defaults to Privileged EXEC mode, which gives the user full access to all configuration commands in the IOS (including the **debug** command).

Privilege level 0 is a special level that allows the user to use a more specific defined set of commands. As an example, you could allow a certain user to use only the **show arp** command. This command is useful when a third party is using a sniffer on your network and needs to match a MAC address to an IP address and vice versa.

Immediate Solutions

Configuring an IOS-Based CLI Switch

In this section, we will walk through the basic configuration of the IOS-based CLI switches. Although these tasks are not all mandatory, knowing them will help you to better manage your switches.

Setting the Login Passwords

By default, Cisco switches have no passwords configured when they are shipped. On the Cisco IOS-based switches, different priority levels of authority are available for console access. You can define two levels on IOS-based switches: privilege level 1, which is equivalent to User EXEC mode; and privilege level 15, which is equivalent to Privileged EXEC mode. Use the following commands to set the two levels' passwords (the password for level 1 will be *noaccess*, and the password for level 15 will be *noone*):

```
Switch> enable
Switch# Configure terminal
Switch (config) enable password level 1 noaccess
Switch (config) enable password level 15 noone
```

Related solutions:	*Found on page:*
Creating a Standard Access List	402
Creating an Extended Access List	403
Enabling Port Security	411

Setting Privilege Levels

Using the **privilege level** command allows you to assign a better-defined set of commands for a selected user. Let's walk through how to do this:

1. Select a user and associate that user with a privilege level. In this example I will use myself and the login name SeanO. I'll assign myself a privilege level of 3. To do this, use the following command in Global Configuration Mode:

```
5000RSM(config)# privilege configure level 3 seano
5000RSM(config)#
```

2. You should assign an enable password for each configured privilege level. To assign the password a privilege level of 3, use the following command:

```
5000RSM(config)# enable secret level 3 sean1
```

3. To get into the switch, I will now use the following command:

```
5000RSM(config)# username seano password sean1
```

Assigning Allowable Commands

To allow a user to use only certain **show** commands, but give him no access to **debug** or configuration commands, use the following command:

```
5000RSM(config)#  privilege exec level 3 show
5000RSM(config)#
```

To allow users with privilege level 3 a specific command syntax for **debug**, such as **debug ip**, use the following command:

```
5000RSM1(config)#  privilege exec level 3 debug ip
5000RSM1(config)#
```

NOTE: *Privilege level 0 includes five commands:* ***disable***, ***enable***, ***exit***, ***help***, *and* ***logout***.

Setting the Console Port Time-out Value

To configure a time-out value for IOS-based Cisco switches, use the following command:

```
CAT2924XL(config)# line console
CAT2924XL(config)# time-out 300
```

The time-out value is now set to five minutes, using seconds.

TIP: *You can use the **lock** command to lock an unused Telnet session. After you issue the **lock** command, the system will ask you to enter and verify an unlocking password.*

To configure a Set/Clear command-based switch to five minutes, use the following command:

```
CAT5009(enable) set logout 5
```

To configure the time-out value to five minutes on the console port of an IOS-based route processor or router, use the following command:

```
5000RSM(config)# line console 0
5000RSM(config-line)# exec-timeout 5
```

Configuring the Telnet Time-out Value

To configure the time-out value to five minutes on the VTY port of an IOS-based route processor or router, use the following command:

```
5000RSM(config)# line vty 0 4
5000RSM(config-line)# exec-timeout 5
```

TIP: *To configure seconds beyond a minute, you can add an additional value to the command. For example, if you want the **exec-timeout** to be 5 minutes and 10 seconds, the command is **exec-timeout 5 10**.*

Configuring the Hostname

On a Cisco IOS-based switch, configure the hostname using the following command in Global Configuration mode:

```
Switch (config)  hostname CORIOLIS8500
CORIOLIS8500>
```

Configuring the Date and Time

To set the system clock on an IOS-based switch and to put it in the PST time zone, use the following command:

```
CORIOLIS8500(config)  clock set 22:09:00 08 Oct 00
CORIOLIS8500(config)  clock timezone PST -8
```

Configuring an IP Address and Netmask

To configure an IP address on a Cisco IOS-based switch, enter the following commands in Global Configuration mode (the IP address being used is 68.187.127.254 and the subnet mask is 255.255.0.0):

```
CORIOLIS8500(config) interface vlan 1
CORIOLIS8500(config-int) ip address 68.187.127.254 255.255.0.0
CORIOLIS8500(config-int) exit
```

Configuring a Default Route and Gateway

To configure the default route for data routing out of the subnet or VLAN, enter the following commands (the address of the local router is 68.187.127.1):

```
CORIOLIS8500(config) ip default-gateway 68.187.127.1
CORIOLIS8500(config) end
```

Configuring Port Speed and Duplex

To configure the port speed—whether 10Mbps or 100Mbps—use the following commands:

```
CORIOLIS5500(config) interface fastethernet 2/3
CORIOLIS5500(config-int) speed 100
CORIOLIS5500(config-int) duplex full
```

The **auto** command can be used when the port on the other side is manually set. Links should not be configured with the **auto** setting on both devices connecting the links because both sides will try to determine the speed on the other side of the link and neither will agree.

You can change the port duplex from full duplex to half duplex, as shown in the following commands:

```
CORIOLIS8500(config) interface fastethernet 0/1
CORIOLIS8500(config-int) speed auto
CORIOLIS8500(config-int) duplex half
```

Enabling SNMP Contact

To set the SNMP contact for RMON support, configure your switch with a contact name, location, and chassis identification to make the device easily identifiable by an SNMP management station. You can set the SNMP system contact, location, serial number, and, most importantly, the community that is the same as the community configured on your SNMP management station. You can configure these items as shown here in the same order as discussed, from the Global Configuration mode prompt:

```
CORIOLIS8500(config) snmp-server contact Joe Snow
CORIOLIS8500(config) snmp-server location Coriolis Wiring Closet
CORIOLIS8500(config) snmp-server chassis-id 987654321
CORIOLIS8500(config) snmp-server community coriolis
```

Configuring a Set/Clear-Based CLI Switch

In this section, you'll walk through the basic configuration of the Set/Clear command-based CLI switches. Although these tasks are not all mandatory, completing them will help you to better manage your switches.

Logging On to a Switch

To begin configuring your switch, do the following:

1. Connect the console cable and connector to a terminal or PC and power on the switch. The switch will then go through its initial POST, which runs diagnostics and checks for the reliability of the switch components.

2. Once the POST has completed successfully, the initial prompt should show a User EXEC mode prompt:

```
Enter Password:
```

3. No password has been configured at this point, so just press the Enter key to continue.

4. Cisco switches have two levels of access by default: User EXEC mode and Privileged EXEC mode. User EXEC mode will allow you to do some basic tasks, such as show the port or VLAN information. To get more advanced configuration options, you will need to enter Privileged EXEC mode. Use the following command to enter Privileged EXEC mode:

```
Console> enable
Enter password:
```

5. Because you have not yet set a Privileged EXEC mode password, pressing Enter will put you into Privileged EXEC mode. The console will show the following prompt:

```
Console> (enable)
```

You are now in Privileged EXEC mode.

WARNING! *Starting here, all configuration changes are executed and saved to memory immediately.*

Setting the Login and Enable Passwords

Because you don't want the janitor coming in and trying to configure your networks, you need to configure a password. You should close your security hole to prevent unauthorized access to your switch.

1. To set a password for user access, enter the following command in Privileged EXEC mode (the new password is *noaccess*):

```
Console> (enable)  set password
Enter old password: <press enter>
Enter new password: noaccess
Retype new password: noaccess
Password changed.
```

2. Now add an additional layer of security by changing the password to enter Privileged EXEC mode on your switch. It looks similar to the User EXEC mode change. For security purposes, the password will be masked. To change the Privileged EXEC mode password, enter the following (set the password as *noone*):

```
Console> (enable)    set enablepass
Enter old password: <press enter>
Enter new password: noone
Retype new password: noone
Password changed.
```

TIP: *At any time, you can type "?" or "help" to access the CLI help facility. For help on specific commands, you can enter the command followed by a question mark; for example,* **set ?** *or* **set help**.

Related solutions:	Found on page:
Creating a Standard Access List	402
Creating an Extended Access List	403
Enabling Port Security	411

Changing the Console Prompt

The switch prompt is set by default to **Console>**. To help you to identify the switch you are configuring—especially when you Telnet into your switch—you should name the switch prompt something that identifies it. If you fail to identify the switch correctly, it can be pretty embarrassing to work on the wrong switch. To change your hostname to CORIOLIS5000, use the following command:

```
Console(enable) set prompt CORIOLIS5000
CORIOLIS5000(enable)
```

Remember, you are still in Privileged EXEC mode, and the change will take place immediately.

Entering a Contact Name and Location Information

Next, let's set the contact name for the person or organization that is administering this switch. Use the following commands to set the switch contact and location:

```
CORIOLIS5500(enable) set system contact Joe Snow
CORIOLIS5500(enable) set system location Coriolis Wiring Closet
```

Configuring System and Time Information

For troubleshooting with SNMP and Cisco Discovery Protocol (CDP), you need to configure system information to identify the switch. By setting the correct date and time, you can be assured that error or log messages will be accurate. To make changes to the system information, use the following commands:

```
CORIOLIS5500(enable) set system name CORIOLIS-5500
CORIOLIS5500(enable) set time Sun 10/08/00 23:59:00
```

Configuring an IP Address and Netmask

Before you can Telnet, ping, or manage the switch remotely, you need to define an IP address and netmask for the console port and assign it to a VLAN. By default, the switch console is in VLAN1. The syntax for setting up a console interface is:

```
set interface sc0 [vlan] [ip address] [subnet mask] [broadcast address]
```

For example, to set up a console with the IP address 68.187.127.1 and a netmask of 255.255.255.0 in VLAN2, you would enter the following command:

```
Console (enable) set interface sc0 2 68.187.127.1 255.255.255.0
Interface sc0 vlan set, IP address and netmask set.
```

NOTE: *It is only necessary to enter the broadcast address if the address entered is something other than a Class A, B, or C address.*

Serial Line Internet Protocol (SLIP) access can also be set up for the console port. SLIP is an older method of connecting to network devices. When you configure the SLIP (sl0) interface, you can open a point-to-point connection to the switch through the console port from a workstation. The command syntax for configuring a SLIP interface is:

```
set interface sl0 slip_addr dest_addr
```

To configure a SLIP interface, enter the following:

```
Console> (enable) set interface s10 68.187.127.1 68.187.127.2
Interface s10 slip and destination address set.
Console> (enable) slip attach
Console Port now running SLIP.
```

The console port must be used for the SLIP connections. If you use the console port to access the switch when you enter the **slip attach** command, you will lose the console port connection. When the SLIP connection is enabled and SLIP is attached on the console port, an Electronic Industries Association/Telecommunications Industry Association-232 (EIA/TIA-232) or dumb terminal cannot connect through the console port.

To see the interface IP information that has been configured, use the following command:

```
Console> (enable) show interface
s10: flags=51<UP,POINTOPOINT,RUNNING>
        slip 68.187.127.1 dest 68.187.127.2
sc0: flags=63<UP,BROADCAST,RUNNING>
        vlan 1 inet 68.187.127.1 netmask 255.255.255.0 broadcast
          68.187.127.1
Console> (enable)
```

Configuring a Default Route and Gateway

Data traffic not addressed to the local subnet or VLAN must be sent to a default route or destination. For redundancy purposes, a secondary default gateway can be configured if the primary gateway link is lost. The switch attempts to use the secondary gateways in the order they were configured, unless the syntax **primary** is used. The switch will send periodic pings to determine if each gateway has lost connectivity. If the primary gateway loses its link, it begins forwarding to the secondary default gateway. When connectivity to the primary gateway link is restored, the switch resumes sending traffic to the primary gateway.

You can define up to three default IP gateways. The first gateway configured becomes the primary default gateway. If multiple gateways are defined, the last primary gateway configured is the primary default gateway. You can also use the **primary** subcommand to make a certain IP address the defined primary default gateway. The rest become secondary in the event of a network problem, as shown here:

```
Console> (enable) set ip route default 68.187.127.1
Route added.
```

```
Console> (enable) set ip route default 68.187.127.2 primary
Route added.
```

Viewing the Default Routes

The following command allows you to see the default routes on both the Cisco IOS-based command-line interfaces:

```
Console> (enable) show ip route

Fragmentation    Redirect    Unreachable
-------------    --------    -----------
enabled          enabled     enabled

The primary gateway: 68.187.127.1
Destination      Gateway         RouteMask    Flags   Use       Interface
-------------    -------------   ----------   -----   --------  ---------
default          68.187.127.1    0x0          UG      100             sc0
default          68.187.127.2    0x0          G       0               sc0
```

Configuring Port Speed and Duplex

You can manually set 10Mbps and 100Mbps ports. Occasionally, you will find an interface that cannot autonegotiate the speed correctly. You can choose from three syntaxes:

- **10**—10Mbps traffic only

- **100**—100Mbps traffic only

- **auto**—Autonegotiates the speed of the traffic on the port

Let's take a look at some examples. To configure port 3 on module 2 to auto-negotiate, use the following command:

```
Console? (enable) set port speed 2/3 auto
Port 2/3 set to auto-sensing mode.
```

You can also enter multiple ports' consecutive port numbers. The following example configures ports 1 through 8 on the same line card used in the previous example to 100Mbps:

```
SeansSwitch (enable) set port speed ?
  <mod/port>                 Module number and Port number(s)
SeansSwitch (enable) set port speed 2/1 ?
  auto                       Set speed to auto
  <port_speed>               Port speed (4, 10, 16, 100 or 1000)
```

```
SeansSwitch (enable) set port speed 2/1-8 100
Ports 2/1-8 transmission speed set to 100Mbps.
SeansSwitch (enable)
```

To manually configure a line card port to full duplex, use the following command:

```
SeansSwitch (enable) set port duplex ?
  <mod/port>                    Module number and Port number(s)
SeansSwitch (enable) set port duplex 2/1 ?
  full                          Full duplex
  half                          Half duplex
SeansSwitch (enable) set port duplex 2/1 full
Port(s)  2/1 set to full-duplex.
SeansSwitch (enable)
```

NOTE: *The possible syntaxes are **full** or **half**, representing full duplex or half duplex.*

Enabling SNMP

SNMP is used by SNMP management stations to monitor network devices such as switches. By configuring operating thresholds, you can configure SNMP to generate trap messages when changes or problems occur on a switch.

There are three levels of access for configuring SNMP. The levels of access are defined by the information configured on the switch; the accessing management station must abide by those given sets of rights. The levels can be defined with community string configuration or by trap receivers, as follows:

- *Read-only*—Allows management stations to read the SNMP information but make no configuration changes.

- *Read-write*—Allows management stations to set SNMP parameters on the switch with the exception of community strings.

- *Read-write-all*—Allows complete access to the switch. The SNMP management stations can alter all information and community strings.

The following commands are examples of how to configure all three types of access and set the functions of the SNMP management stations:

```
Console> (enable) set snmp community read-only public
SNMP read-only community string set to 'public'.
Console> (enable) set snmp community read-write public2
SNMP read-write community string set to 'public2'.
Console> (enable) set snmp community read-write-all public3
SNMP read-write-all community string set to 'public3'.
```

Configuring Trap Message Targets

You can configure trap message receivers by specifying the IP address of each receiver and the access type allowed. You must then enable SNMP traps, as shown here:

```
Console> (enable) set snmp trap 68.187.127.6 read-write-all
SNMP trap receiver added.
Console> (enable) set snmp trap 68.187.127.4 read-write
SNMP trap receiver added.
Console> (enable) set snmp trap enable all
All SNMP traps enabled.
```

Configuring a Menu-Driven IOS

The Catalyst 3000 series has a menu-driven switch interface, which allows you to use the arrow keys on your keyboard to select the different options used to configure the switch. As with the other two types of interfaces, you need to connect the switch to a dumb terminal or PC. This switch, however, supports a process known as *autobaud*, which allows you to press the Enter key several times to get the switch's attention. The switch will then automatically configure the console port to the correct baud rate. Here's how to do it:

1. The first screen you come to shows the MAC address assigned to the switch and the system contact, and asks you to type in the password. If this is the initial configuration, press the Enter key to continue. This will bring you to the Main menu, shown in Figure 2.3. No password is configured when the switch has just been loaded with a new IOS or straight out of the box.

2. Because you are going to configure the switch, choose the Configuration option. You are presented with two options. You can choose either Serial Link Configuration to configure the console port, or Telnet Configuration to configure Telnet.

   When you enter the Configuration menu, you will notice that you are given the option to configure your switch for options that are not available without certain add-on or module cards for your switch. This is more evident if you have the Enhanced Feature Set, which is now the standard for the Cisco 3000 series. Without the Enhanced Feature Set, you will not have VLAN and EtherChannel menu options. In this example you'll be configuring a Cisco 3000 series switch with the Enhanced Feature Set, as depicted in Figure 2.4.

Figure 2.3 The main menu of the menu-driven IOS.

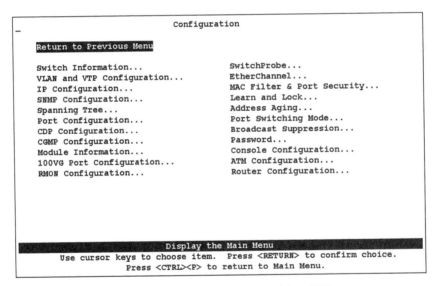

Figure 2.4 The Configuration menu of the menu-driven IOS.

TIP: *If you make a mistake in your configuration, you can use Ctrl+P to exit the switch without saving changes. Use the Exit Console or Return To Previous Menu option to save your changes and exit the switch configuration mode.*

---

3. You have the option of choosing a time-out value for the console session. If you would like to disable time-outs, enter a zero. Otherwise, enter a time in minutes from 1 to 1,440.

Configuring the Console Port

To configure the Console port, do the following:

1. Choose Configuration|Serial Configuration.

2. As shown in Figure 2.5, you can configure four options: the Hardware Flow Control, the Software Flow Control, the Autobaud Upon Break feature, and the Console Baud Rate. Under normal circumstances, you will never change these defaults. However, the option you probably won't be familiar with—and which Cisco recommends not changing—is the Autobaud Upon Break feature. By enabling this feature, you force the switch to automatically sense the baud rate of the switch by pressing the Break key on the PC or dumb terminal. You can set the baud rate on the switch from 2,400 to 57,600 baud.

Configuring Telnet

To configure Telnet, do the following:

1. Using a Telnet emulator supporting VT100 or VT200, use Telnet to access your switch configuration.

2. Choose Configuration|Console Configuration. The Telnet Configuration screen appears. This screen allows you to configure three options:

   • The number of Telnet sessions allowed simultaneously, from 0 to 5

   • The switch to disallow new Telnet sessions

   • The ability to terminate all Telnet sessions

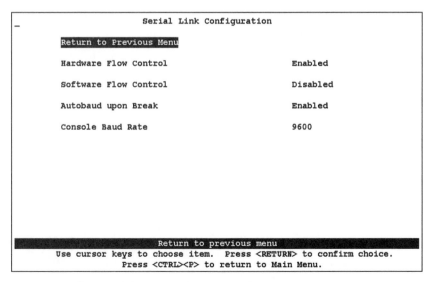

Figure 2.5   The Console Port Serial Link configuration screen.

TIP: *Disallowing new Telnet sessions is a great feature to invoke when you are configuring or upgrading the switch. That way, another administrator can't come in and try to change the configuration while you are working on the switch.*

Configuring the Password

The Password menu is available from the Configuration menu. It has just two options, and only one password needs to be configured for the whole switch. You can set or delete the password.

When changing the password, you will need to supply the current password. If no password is configured, just press Enter. You will then be asked for the new password. The new password can be up to 15 characters long.

Configuring an IP Address and Default Gateway

Configuring the default gateway and the IP address on the menu-driven IOS is pretty straightforward, as well. As you can see from Figure 2.6, the MAC address comes preconfigured; you need only enter the IP address, subnet mask, and default gateway of your router or route processor for individual VLANs you have configured.

Related solutions:	Found on page:
Creating a Standard Access List	402
Creating an Extended Access List	403
Enabling Port Security	411

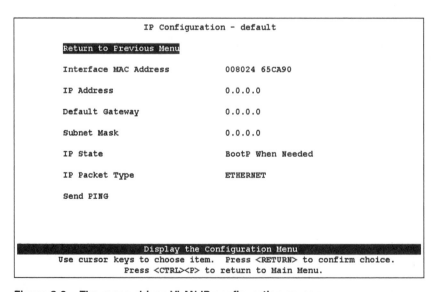

```
                    IP Configuration - default

        Return to Previous Menu

        Interface MAC Address          008024 65CA90

        IP Address                     0.0.0.0

        Default Gateway                0.0.0.0

        Subnet Mask                    0.0.0.0

        IP State                       BootP When Needed

        IP Packet Type                 ETHERNET

        Send PING




                   Display the Configuration Menu
         Use cursor keys to choose item.   Press <RETURN> to confirm choice.
                   Press <CTRL><P> to return to Main Menu.
```

Figure 2.6   The menu-driven VLAN IP configuration screen.

Configuring SNMP

You can configure up to 10 community strings on the menu-driven switch IOS by following these steps:

1. Enter the appropriate IP configurations as shown in Configuring an IP Address and Default Gateway.

2. Select Configuration|SNMP Configuration. You are then presented with three configuration options: Send Authentication Traps, Community Strings, or Trap Receivers. As with the SNMP configurations on the other two IOS configurations, we will concern ourselves with the configuration necessary to receive information to our SNMP management station.

3. Choose the option Community Strings. The screen shown in Figure 2.7 will appear.

You have five options at the bottom of the screen:

- *Return*—Automatically saves the configuration and returns to the Main menu.

- *Add Entry*—Allows you to add an SNMP entry and the mode.

NOTE: *The Mode option allows you to configure two modes. R (for read access) allows a management station to receive messages but make no configuration changes. W (for write access) allows the SNMP management station to receive messages and make configuration changes.*

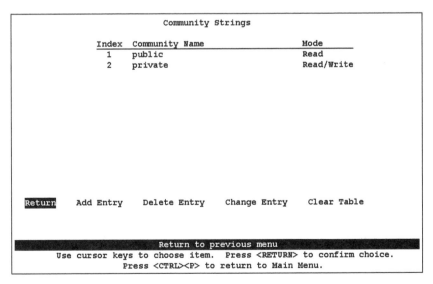

Figure 2.7   The Community Strings configuration screen.

- *Delete Entry*—Deletes the highlighted community string.
- *Change Entry*—Allows you to modify a community string entry.
- *Clear Table*—Deletes all community string entries.

Configuring ROM

ROM monitor is a ROM-based program that can be configured to execute upon the following conditions:

- Upon boot-up
- Upon recycling the switch power
- When a fatal exception error occurs
- When the switch fails to find a valid system image
- If the nonvolatile RAM (NVRAM) configuration is corrupt
- If the configuration register is set to enter ROM monitor mode

The ROM monitor CLI is present only on the Supervisor Engine III, Catalyst 4000, and the 2948G series switch Supervisor Engine modules. When the switch is in the ROM monitor mode, the switch will allow you to load a system image manually from Flash memory, from a Trivial File Transfer Protocol (TFTP) file, or from the bootflash.

Entering ROM Configuration Mode

You can enter ROM configuration mode by using one of these two methods:

- Cycle the power on the switch and press the Break key during the first 60 seconds of startup. (The Break key is enabled for the first 60 seconds after cycling the power on the switch.)
- Enter ROM mode through a terminal server, using Telnet or another terminal emulation program. Enter the **break** command as soon as the power is cycled on the switch.

ROM monitor has its own unique prompt that informs you when you have entered ROM monitor mode. The prompt you will see when you have entered ROM configuration mode is **rommon>**.

Booting ROM Mode from a Flash Device

To boot from a flash device, you can use the following syntax, which is shown in Table 2.9:

```
boot [-xv] [device][imagename]
```

Table 2.9   The boot command syntaxes.

Syntax	Meaning
-x	Identifies the image to load but not execute
-v	Identifies a need to use verbose mode
device	Identifies the device
imagename	Identifies the image to use

The image name is optional. If no image name is presented, the system defaults to the first valid file in the device. Remember that file names are case sensitive. Let's look at an example of using this command:

```
rommon> boot -x bootflash:cat5000-sup2.2-2.bin
CCCCCCCCCCCCCCCCCCCCCCCCCCCCCCCCCCCCCCCCCCCCCCCCCCCCCCCCCCCCCC
Uncompressing file:
##########################################################################
##########################################################################
##########################################################################
```

Configuring SNMP

RMON works in conjunction with SNMP and requires a protocol analyzer or probe to use its full features. To use SNMP-based monitoring, you need to verify that SNMP is running on your IOS-based switch.

1. Verify that SNMP is running, using the following command in User or EXEC mode:

   ```
   show snmp
   ```

2. Enable SNMP and allow read-only access to hosts using the public SNMP string by using this command in Configuration mode:

   ```
   snmp-server community public
   ```

3. After enabling SNMP, you need to define a host IP address to send SNMP trap messages. Here is an example:

   ```
   snmp server host 130.77.40.05 public
   ```

Configuring RMON

To configure RMON, use the following steps:

1. To show RMON statistics on a certain interface, use the following command:

   ```
   show rmon statistics
   ```

This command shows statistics for the number of packets, octets, broadcast packets, and multicast packets received, as well as errors detected and packet lengths received.

2. Configure the SNMP community using this command:

```
set snmp community <read-only|read-write|read-write-all>
   <community string>
```

3. Assign the SNMP log server responsible for receiving traps with this command:

```
set snmp trap <hostaddress> <community-string>
```

Configuring RMON on a Set/Clear-Based Interface

To configure RMON on a Set/Clear-based interface, perform the following steps:

1. On a Set/Clear command-based interface, configure the SNMP community using this command:

```
set snmp community <read-only|read-write|read-write-all>
 <community string>
```

2. Assign the SNMP log server responsible for receiving traps with the following command:

```
set snmp trap <hostaddress> <community-string>
Enable snmp with "set snmp enable"
Console> (enable) set snmp rmon enable
SNMP RMON support enabled.
Console> (enable) show snmp
RMON:                        Enabled
Extended RMON:               Extended RMON module is not present
Traps Enabled:
Port,Module,Chassis,Bridge,Repeater,Vtp,Auth,ippermit,Vmps,config,
    entity,stpx
Port Traps Enabled: 1/1-2,3/1-8
Community-Access    Community-String
----------------    --------------------
read-only           Everyone
read-write          Administrators
read-write-all      Root
```

```
Trap-Rec-Address                              Trap-Rec-Community
-----------------------------------------     --------------------
168.187.127.4                                 read-write
168.187.127.6                                 read-write-all
Console> (enable)
```

3. To verify that RMON is running, use the following command in EXEC mode:

```
show rmon
```

Using Set/Clear Command Set Recall Key Sequences

The CLI of a Set/Clear interface is based on Unix, so certain c-shell commands can be issued to recall commands previously issued. The switch by default stores the previous 20 commands in its buffer. Unlike the Cisco IOS routers or switches, the up arrows do not work. You can, however, use the key sequences shown in Table 2.10 to recall or modify commands:

Table 2.10   Command recall key sequences.

Command	Action
!!	Repeats the last command
!-*nn*	Repeats the *nn*th number of commands
!*n*	Repeats command *n* in the list
!*zzz*	Repeats the command that starts with the *zzz* string
!?*zzz*	Repeats the command containing the *zzz* string
^*yyy*^*zzz*	Replaces the string *yyy* with *zzz* in the previous command
!!*zzz*	Adds the string *zzz* to the previous command
!*n zzz*	Adds the string *zzz* to command *n*
!*yyy zzz*	Adds the string *zzz* to the end of the command that begins with *yyy*
!?*yyy zzz*	Adds the string *zzz* to the end of the command containing *yyy*

Using IOS-Based Command Editing Keys and Functions

In the Cisco IOS, certain keys allow you to edit or change the configuration. The keys and their functions are listed in Table 2.11.

Table 2.11   Cisco IOS basic command editing keys and functions.

Key	Function
Tab	Completes a partial command name
Delete	Erases the character to the left of the cursor
Return	Performs a command
Space	Scrolls down a page
Left arrow	Moves a character to the left
Right arrow	Moves a character to the right
Up arrow	Recalls commands in the history buffer
Down arrow	Returns to more recent commands
Ctrl+A	Moves to the beginning of a line
Ctrl+B	Moves back one character
Ctrl+D	Deletes a character
Ctrl+E	Moves to the end of the command line
Ctrl+F	Moves forward one character
Ctrl+K	Deletes all characters to the end of the line
Ctrl+L	Redisplays the system prompt and command line
Ctrl+T	Transposes the character to the left of the cursor with the character at the cursor
Ctrl+U	Deletes all characters to the beginning
Ctrl+V	Indicates that the next keystroke is a command
Ctrl+W	Deletes to the left of the cursor
Ctrl+Y	Recalls the most recently deleted command
Ctrl+Z	Ends the configuration mode and returns you to EXEC mode

Chapter 3

WAN Switching

(continued)

In Depth

Switches are not only used in LAN networks; they are also used extensively in wide area networks (WANs). Chapters 1 and 2 gave you an overview of LAN switching. Well, WAN switching is the same in some ways and completely different in others.

In an Ethernet switching environment, the switch utilizes Carrier Sense Multiple Access with Collision Detection (CSMA/CD). The switch or host sends out a packet and detects if a collision occurs. If there is a collision, the sender waits a random amount of time and then retransmits the packet. If the host does not detect a collision, it sends out the next packet. You may think that if the switch or host is set to full-duplex, there will be no collision—that is correct, but the host still waits between sending packets.

In a Token Ring switching environment, a token is passed from one port to the next. The host must have possession of the token to transmit. If the token is already in use, the host passes the token on and waits for it to come around again. All stations on the network must wait for an available token. An *active monitor*, which could be any station on the segment, performs a ring maintenance function and generates a new token if the existing token is lost or corrupted.

As you can see, both Token Ring and Ethernet switching require the node to wait. The node must wait either for the token or for the frame to reach the other nodes. This is not the most efficient utilization of bandwidth. In a LAN environment, this inefficiency is not a major concern; in a WAN, it becomes unacceptable. Can you imagine if your very expensive T1 link could be used only half the time? To overcome this problem, WAN links utilize *serial transmission.*

Serial transmission sends the electric signal (bits) down the wire one after another. It does not wait for one frame to reach the other end before transmitting the next frame. To identify the beginning and the end of the frame, a timing mechanism is used. The timing can be either synchronous or asynchronous. *Synchronous* signals utilize an identical clock rate, and the clocks are set to a reference clock. *Asynchronous* signals do not require a common clock; the timing signals come from special characters in the transmission stream.

Asynchronous serial transmissions put a start bit and a stop bit between each character (usually 1 byte). This is an eight-to-two ratio of data to overhead, which is very expensive in a WAN link.

Synchronous serial transmissions do not have such high overhead, because they do not require the special characters; they also have a larger payload. Are synchronous serial transmissions the perfect WAN transmission method? No; the problem lies in how to synchronize equipment miles apart. Synchronous serial transmission is only suitable for distances where the time required for data to travel the link does not distort the synchronization.

So, first we said that serial is the way to go, and now we've said that serial has either high overhead or cannot travel a long distance. What do we use? Well, we use both, and cheat a little bit. We use synchronous serial transmission for a short distance and then use asynchronous for the remaining, long distance. We cheat by putting multiple characters in each frame and limiting the overhead.

When a frame leaves a host and reaches a router, the router uses synchronous serial transmission to pass the frame on to a WAN transmission device. The WAN device puts multiple characters into each WAN frame and sends it out. To minimize the variation of time between when the frames leave the host and when they reach the end of the link, each frame is divided and put into a slot in the WAN frame. This way, the frame does not have to wait for the transmission of other frames before it is sent. (Remember, this process is designed to minimize wait time.) If there is no traffic to be carried in a slot, that slot is wasted. Figure 3.1 shows a diagram of a packet moving from LAN nodes to the router and the WAN device.

Let's take a look at how this process would work in a T1 line. T1 has 24 slots in each frame; each slot is 8 bits, and there is 1 framing bit:

24 slots × 8 bits + 1 framing bit = 193 bits

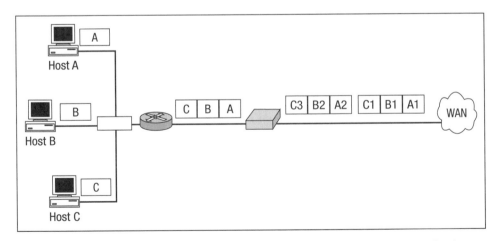

Figure 3.1   A packet's journey from a host to a WAN device. The WAN transmission is continuous and does not have to wait for acknowledgement or permission.

T1 frames are transmitted 8,000 frames per second, or one frame every 125 micro-seconds:

193 bits × 8,000 = 1,544,000 bits per second (bps)

When you have a higher bandwidth, the frame is bigger and contains more slots (for example, E1 has 32 slots). As you can see, this is a great increase in the effective use of the bandwidth.

Another asynchronous serial transmission method is Asynchronous Transfer Mode (ATM). ATM is a cell-based switching technology. It has a fixed size of 53 octets: 5 octets of overhead and 48 octets of payload. Bandwidth in ATM is available on demand. It is even more efficient relative to the serial transmission method be-cause it does not have to wait for assigned slots in the frame. One Ethernet frame can consist of multiple consecutive cells. ATM also enables Quality of Service (QoS). Cells can be assigned different levels of priority. If there is any point of congestion, cells with higher priority will have preference to the bandwidth. ATM is the most widely used WAN serial transmission method.

NOTE: *ATM is covered in more detail in Chapter 8.*

WAN Transmission Media

The physical transmission media that carry the signals in WAN are divided into two kinds: narrowband and broadband. A *narrowband* transmission consists of a single channel carried by a single medium. A *broadband* transmission consists of multiple channels in different frequencies carried on a single medium.

The most common narrowband transmission types are T1, E1, and J1. See Table 3.1 for the differences among the transmission types and where each is used. The time slots specify how much bandwidth (bit rate) the narrowband transmissions have.

Narrowband is most commonly used by businesses as their WAN medium be-cause of its low cost. If more bandwidth is needed than narrowband can provide, most businesses use multiple narrowband connections.

Table 3.1   Narrowband transmission types.

Transmission Type	Number of Slots	Bit Rate	Region
T1	24	1.544Mbps	North America
E1	32	2.048Mbps	Africa, Asia (not including Japan), Europe, Australia, South America
J1	32	2.048Mbps	Japan

The capability of broadband to carry multiple signals enables it to have a higher transmission speed. Table 3.2 displays the various broadband transmissions, which require more expensive and specialized transmitters and receivers.

Digital signal 2 (DS2), E2, E3, and DS3 describe digital transmission across copper or fiber cables. OC/STS resides almost exclusively on fiber-optic cables. The OC designator specifies an optical transmission, whereas the STS designator specifies the characteristics of the transmission (except the optical interface). There are two types of fiber-optic media:

- *Single-mode fiber*—Has a core of 8.3 microns and a cladding of 125 microns. A single light wave powered by a laser is used to generate the transmission. Single-mode can be used for distances up to 45 kilometers; it has no known speed limitation. Figure 3.2 shows an example of a single-mode fiber.

- *Multimode fiber*—Has a core of 62.5 microns and a cladding of 125 microns. Multiple light waves powered by a light-emitting diode (LED) are used to power the transmission. Multimode has a distance limit of two kilometers; it has a maximum data transfer rate of 155Mbps in WAN applications. (It has recently been approved for use for Gigabit Ethernet.) Figure 3.3 shows an example of a multimode fiber. The core and cladding boundary work as a mirror to reflect the light waves down the fiber.

Table 3.2   The different broadband transmission types and their bandwidth.

Transmission Type	Bit Rate
DS2	6.312Mbps
E2	8.448Mbps
E3	34.368Mbps
DS3	44.736Mbps
OC/STS-1	51.840Mbps
OC/STS-3	155.520Mbps
OC/STS-9	466.560Mbps
OC/STS-12	622.080Mbps
OC/STS-18	922.120Mbps
OC/STS-24	1.244Gbps
OC/STS-36	1.866Gbps
...	...
OC/STS-768	39.820Gbps

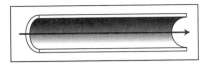

Figure 3.2   Single mode fiber.

Figure 3.3   Multimode fiber.

Synchronous Transport Signal (STS)

Synchronous transport signal (STS) is the basic building block of the Synchronous Optical Network (SONET). It defines the framing structure of the signal. It consist of two parts: STS overhead and STS payload. In STS-1, the frame is 9 rows of 90 octets. Each row has 3 octets of overhead and 87 octets of payload, resulting in 6,489 bits per frame. A frame occurs every 125 microseconds, yielding 51.84Mbps. STS-n is an interleaving of multiple (n) STS-1s. The size of the payload and the overhead are multiplied by n. Figure 3.4 displays an STS diagram.

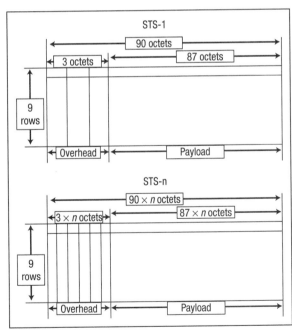

Figure 3.4   The STS-1 framing and STS-n framing. The overhead and payload are proportionate to the n value, with the STS-1 frame as the base.

You may wonder why we're talking about synchronous transmission when we said it is only used over short distances. Where did the asynchronous transmission go? Well, the asynchronous traffic is encapsulated in the STS payload. The asynchronous serial transmission eliminates the need for the synchronization of the end transmitting equipment. In SONET, most WAN links are a point-to-point connection utilizing light as the signaling source. The time required for the signal to travel the link does not distort the synchronization. The OC-n signal itself is used for the synchronization between equipment. This combination of asynchronous and synchronous serial transmission enables signals to reach across long distances with minimal overhead.

Cisco WAN Switches

The current Cisco WAN product line consists of the following switches:

- MGX 8200 series
- IGX 8400 series
- BPX 8600 series wide-area switches
- MGX 8800 series wide-area edge switches

MGX 8200 Series

The Cisco MGX 8200 series is designed to function as a WAN edge device. It combines multiple narrowband transmissions into a single broadband trunk. It functions as a standalone unit to connect to the ATM network or it can be used as a feeder device to other WAN switches. The series consists of the MGX 8220 Edge Concentrator, the MGX 8240 Private Line Service Gateway, and the MGX 8260 Media Gateway.

The MGX 8220 Edge Concentrator has 16 slots with the capability for full redundancy. It accepts two classes of modules: common control cards and function modules. Six slots are reserved for common control cards, and 10 slots are reserved for function modules. The common control card consists of an AXIS Shelf Controller (ASC) card, a Service Resource Module (SRM) card, and a service trunk card. Each card can use either of two specific slots. When both slots are occupied, one of them acts as a hot standby. The ASC card provides a user interface for the overall control, configuration, and management of the unit. The SRM controls the flow of traffic from the trunk card to various function modules. The service trunk module is the only broadband interface (OC-3 or T3) that transports the aggregated traffic to the ATM network. The function modules are narrowband interface cards. The narrowband transmission can be T1, high-speed Frame Relay, ATM frame user-network interface (UNI), or System Network Architecture (SNA).

The MGX 8240 Private Line Service Gateway is designed to terminate private lease lines (T1, T3, or DS0). It has 16 slots with 1 reserved for a redundant control card. It can support up to 1,260 channelized T1s. It is designed for large Internet service providers (ISPs) to aggregate dial-in traffic, which is delivered by the local central office's Class 4 or Class 5 switch in a T1 or T3 interface. The combined traffic is delivered to the broadband network via OC-3 trunk ports.

The MGX 8260 Media Gateway is a high-density, carrier-class gateway for voice and data traffic. It is designed to move data traffic from voice line to packet network. It can also function as a Voice over IP (VoIP) gateway. The chassis has 14 slots for interface modules and 2 slots for switch control cards. A fully configured system has over 16,000 VoIP ports. The gateway has advanced voice features: echo cancellation, dynamic de-jitter, Voice Activity Detection (VAD), Comfort Noise Generation (CNG), and announcement play-outs (AU or WAV files). It can connect to the broadband network via six broadband service cards (BSCs). Each BSC has six channelized DS3 interfaces.

IGX 8400 Series

The IGX is the successor to the IPX switch. It was the first commercial implementation of Cisco's fastpacket cell technology. It employs fixed-length cells for switching all types of traffic (voice, data, and Frame Relay). The IGX adds a higher bus capacity, a higher access rate, and ATM. The series has three models:

- *IGX 8410*—Has 8 slots with 2 reserved for redundant processor modules.
- *IGX 8420*—Has 16 slots with 2 reserved for redundant processor modules.
- *IGX 8430*—Has 32 slots with 2 reserved for redundant processor modules.

One of the major differences between the MGX and IGX series is the trunk ports. The IGX can use any of the module interfaces as the trunk connection to an edge device. The speed ranges from 256Kbps to OC-3. The IGX also has advanced switching and routing capabilities: It uses a distributed intelligence algorithm to route new connections and react to failures in transmission media. It provides full control of network resources with multiple classes of service, and it can provide different QoS to individual applications.

Each of the service modules has a large buffer. The ATM module can buffer 128,000 cells, and the Frame Relay can buffer 100,000 frames. The buffer can be allocated by QoS to each virtual circuit based on the amount of traffic and service-level agreements.

The IGX is marketed to the enterprise as its core WAN switch. The ability of the IGX to switch and route between multiple trunks enables it to connect a large number of sites. The capability to handle voice, data, fax, and video traffic in a single network minimizes the overall expense for the enterprise.

IGX is also marketed to carriers in situations where there is not enough traffic to justify purchasing a high-end WAN switch (such as a BPX). It enables the carrier to gradually increase the capacity of the network.

NOTE: *Another Cisco product that belongs with the IGX (but that is not considered a WAN device) is the MC3810 Multiservice Concentrator. It has the same switch technology as the IGX series. It utilizes the Cisco Internetwork Operating System (IOS) for configuration commands. The MC3810 can combine data, voice, and video traffic into a channelized ATM T1/E1.*

BPX 8600 Series Wide-Area Switches

The BPX 8600 series, first introduced in 1993, is the flagship of the Cisco WAN switch line. It is designed to function as the core of the WAN ATM network. The series has three models: BPX 8620, BPX 8650, and BPX 8680. All three models have the same chassis type with 15 slots; 2 slots are reserved for redundant control and switch modules, 1 slot is reserved for an alarm status monitor module, and 12 slots are reserved for interface modules.

The BPX 8620 is a pure ATM broadband switch. It has a nonblocking 9.6Gbps architecture. The interface modules range from T3 to OC-12. Each trunk port can buffer up to 32,000 cells. The OC-12 interface module has two OC-12 ports. The OC-3 interface module has eight OC-3 ports. The BPX is commonly used in conjunction with multiple MGX switches. The MGX concentrator terminates narrowband traffic to an OC-3 trunk to the BPX 8620, which aggregates it to multiple OC-12s to the WAN ATM network.

With the popularity and the increase of TCP/IP traffic on the WAN, Cisco introduced the BPX 8650 to enhance the functionality of the BPX series. The BPX 8650 adds a Label Switch Controller (LSC) to the BPX 8620. The LSC provides Layer 3 functionality to the ATM traffic. It enables the use of Multiprotocol Label Switching (MPLS) and virtual private networks (VPNs). Currently, the LSC is a Cisco 7200 series router with an ATM interface. The plan is to have native LSC modules for the BPX series (similar to a Route Switch Module [RSM] for the Catalyst LAN switches). The BPX 8650 also introduced a new control and switch module to increase the throughput to 19.2Gbps.

The BPX 8680 is the newest member of the series. This addition is a combination of the BPX 8650 and the MGX 8850 edge switch. It incorporates a modular design. Up to 16 MGX 8850s can be added to the BPX 8680 as feeders to a BPX 8620, creating a port density of up to 16,000 DS1s (T1). The 16 MGX 8850s and the BPX 8680 are managed as a single node; this design enables the use of MPLS for all the ports on every connected MGX. A service provider can install a BPX 8680 with a single MGX 8850 connected at a new location. Then, when the traffic warrants, the service provider can simply add MGX 8850s to the cabinet.

MGX 8800 Series Wide-Area Edge Switches

The MGX 8800 series is the newest line of WAN switches. It is designed as an edge device to connect narrowband traffic to broadband. The capability of the switch enables you to move it closer to the core. It has the greatest flexibility of all the WAN switches. It has 32 single-height (16 double-height) module slots. Two of the double-height slots are reserved for redundant processor switch modules, 4 single-height slots are reserved for optional value-added service resource modules, and 24 single-height slots are reserved for interface modules.

The throughput can scale from 1.2Gbps to 45Gbps. A route processor module can be added for Layer 3 functionality (a Cisco 7200 series router in a single double-height module). The network interfaces range from Ethernet, Fiber Distributed Data Interface (FDDI), and channelized T1 to OC-48c. A Voice Interworking Service Module (VISM) can be added to terminate T1/E1 circuits. Each module has 8 T1/E1 interfaces, and up to 24 modules can be added to the chassis (a total of 4,608 voice calls for T1 and 6,144 voice calls for E1). The VISM provides toll-quality voice services. All the packetization and processing are handled by the module. It supports echo canceling, voice compression, silence suppression, VoIP/VoATM, auto fax/modem tone detection, and more.

WAN Switch Hardware Overview

Cisco WAN switches have a wide range of capabilities and features. Physically, they share many common characteristics. All the WAN switches are designed to have a minimum 99.999 percent service availability when configured properly—that is, 5.256 minutes of downtime in 1 year of continuous operation. Each component can have a hot standby to act as a failsafe. All the components are hot swappable, and all the chassis have redundant power feeds.

For ease of replacement and upgrades, all the modules consist of a front card and a back card. The front card contains the intelligent part of the card set: the processor, memory, storage, control button, and other components. The back card contains the Physical layer component. If there is no backplane for the set, a blank faceplate is used. This system enables the quick replacement/upgrade of the front card without distributing the physical connections. The front card and back card are connected to a system bus backplane when inserted.

The system bus backplane contains multiple buses for connecting the modules. It has no active component. Different buses provide power to the modules, transfer of data, timing control, system commands, and other functionality.

Cisco WAN Switch Network Topologies

We've talked about the transmission media, the signal, and the equipment. Let's put it all together. Cisco classifies WAN topologies into three designs: flat, tiered, and structured.

In a flat design, the WAN switches are connected in a fully meshed network. All the nodes are aware of one another. Each node can send traffic to another node with a direct connection. This design is only suitable in a small WAN network (private enterprise network). Figure 3.5 displays a typical flat WAN network.

In a tiered network, the core WAN switches have to route traffic for other nodes. This design utilizes edge switches as feeders to the network. The feeders aggregate multiple narrowband transmissions into broadband trunk connections to the core switches. The edge switches can be right next to the core switch, or they can be miles apart. The IGX series and the MGX 8800 series can be configured as core switches or feeders. The BPX can only be configured as a core switch, whereas the MGX 8200 series can only be a feeder node. Figure 3.6 displays how a tiered network combines different equipment.

The structured network design is a combination of flat networks and tiered networks. Each of these networks is considered a domain. All domains have a unique number. Each domain is attached to others through switches called *junction nodes* that are responsible for routing across domains. Switches other than junction nodes in the domain have limited contact with switches outside the domain. You will rarely see this design today, because the current switching software no longer supports it.

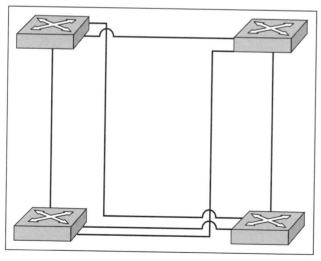

Figure 3.5   A flat WAN network.

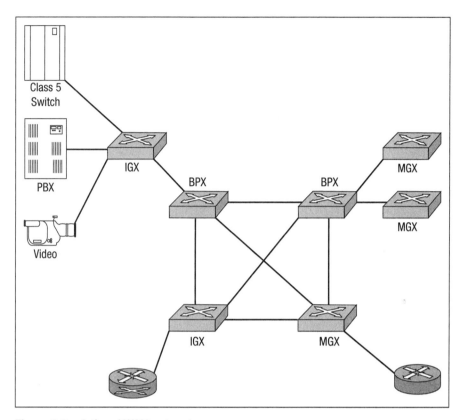

Figure 3.6   A tiered WAN network.

Network Management

In managing a wide area network, you have to understand the basic network management technology common to both LANs and WANs. You must understand IP addressing, Simple Network Management Protocol (SNMP), out-of-band management/in-band management, Management Information Bases (MIBs), network management tools, configuration of systems, and so on. Let's look at some WAN specifics.

The CLI

Everyone who has worked with Cisco equipment is familiar with the Command Line Interface (CLI). The WAN interface is very different from the interfaces in other Cisco equipment. To gain access to the CLI, you will have to use the serial port on the control module, the Ethernet connection, or a virtual terminal. Figure 3.7 displays an initial login screen. You are provided with this display when you first Telnet into the equipment.

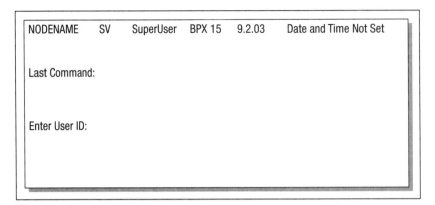

```
NODENAME    SV    SuperUser    BPX 15    9.2.03    Date and Time Not Set


Last Command:



Enter User ID:
```

Figure 3.7   An initial login screen.

The login screen is divided into three parts: system information, display, and input. The system information appears at the top of the screen. It contains the name of the unit, method of accessing the CLI, current user ID and privilege level, chassis model, system software version, and date/time/time zone. The display portion shows the result and the last command given. The input portion has a prompt for your next command.

You can enter commands on the CLI in three ways:

- *Via a menu*—Pressing the Esc key opens a menu; you highlight a command using the arrow keys and press Enter to issue the command.

- *In response to prompts*—A prompt will request the required parameters. Using the prompt method, you enter the desired command, and the switch asks you for all the required parameters.

- *Using direct entry*—Direct entry is the only way to issue optional parameters in the CLI; all the parameters must follow the command in exact order, separated by spaces.

Every command falls into a privilege level. The levels are superuser, service, StrataCom, and 1 to 6. A level is assigned when the user account is created. The user can issue commands only at his or her level or lower. The superuser, service, and StrataCom levels rank above level 1 (the highest numerical level).

WAN Manager

The Cisco WAN Manager software manages an entire WAN infrastructure. It operates on Sun Solaris and IBM AIX systems. The software's components are as follows:

- *Topology Management*—Provides an automatically generated topology map. The map can be formatted as a standalone or for HP Open View, CiscoWorks, or IBM NetView. A multicolor map can be generated that's updated in real time. It can provide the network manager with a global view of the network while highlighting any local problems.

- *Connection Management*—Provides a graphic interface to configure WAN switches. It provides templates to minimize the work in setting up many connections. All interface modules are supported, including VoIP/VoATM setups.

- *Performance and Accounting Data Management*—Controls the collection of SNMP information from the network. The statistics collected are stored in an Informix database. Reports can be generated by the built-in report generator or by SQL.

- *Element Management*—Provides a reactive response to events on the network. It can forward information to HP Open View and IBM NetView (CiscoWorks is an integrated part of Cisco WAN Manager). External action is also supported; a page or an email can be sent when a specific event happens on the network.

3. WAN Switching

Immediate Solutions

Accessing and Setting Up IGX and BPX Switches

The setup and the interface of IGX and BPX switches are very similar. During initial setup, you will have to attach a terminal or computer with a terminal program to the DB25 control port or DB25 auxiliary port with a straight-through EIA/TIA-232 cable. The terminal must be set at 9600bps, with no parity, eight data bits, one stop bit, and no flow control (hardware or software).

Adding New Users

Anyone can add a user account. The new user must have a lower privilege level than the user account's creator. User accounts and passwords are global in the network—when you create a user account on one node, that user account can access any other node in the network.

To add a user, use the **adduser** command. This command has a privilege level of 5. Figure 3.8 displays a login screen.

Displaying a User's Password

You can display the password of a current user and any user with a lower privilege level than the current user by using the **dsppwd** command, which has a privilege level of 6. The passwords will be displayed for 10 seconds.

```
NODENAME       SV      SuperUser   BPX 15   9.2.03    Date and Time Not Set


Super User
Newuser        1




Last Command:   adduser Newuser 1

Next Command:
                                                                  MAJOR ALARM
```

Figure 3.8   The **adduser** command.

Changing a User's Password

To change your password, use the **cnfpwd** command; it has a privilege level of 6. When you enter "cnfpwd" on the command line, the system will prompt you for your current password. You must enter the new password twice for the system to save it. The password must be between 6 and 15 characters long, and it is case sensitive.

You cannot change the password of any other user. To change another user's password, you must log in as that user. You can use the **dsppwd** command to view another user's password and log in as that user.

Using the History Command

You can display a list of the previous 12 commands by pressing the period (.) key; this command has a privilege level of 6. You can select which command to repeat by entering a number from 1 through 12. (Entering "1" repeats the most current command, "5" repeats the command five back in the list, and so on.) After you enter the number, the previous command is copied to the command line. You can edit the command or parameters before issuing the command. Use the arrow keys to move along the command line, and use the backspace key to erase the character to the left of the cursor.

Displaying a Summary of All Card Modules

The **dspcds** command displays a summary of all the modules. The privilege level for this command is 6. The information is generated by the switch and does not need to be configured. The command displays the front card's name and revision code, the back card's name and revision code, and the status of the card. The revision code indicates the model, hardware revision, and firmware revision.

Displaying Detailed Information for a Card Module

To display more detailed information about the card module, use the **dspcd** command followed by a space and the module number. This is a privilege level 6 command. The command provides the card serial numbers, card features, features supported, number of connections supported, buffer size, memory size, and software version.

Displaying the Power and Temperature of a Switch

The **dsppwr** command provides the status of the power supply and the cabinet temperature. The privilege level for this command is 6. This command's display is different on the IGX than on the BPX. The IGX displays the power supply type and status, actual cabinet temperature, temperature alarm threshold, and monitor status; the BPX displays the ASM status, AC power supply and status, and fan speed.

Displaying the ASM Statistics for BPX

To have the BPX's ASM provide environment information and statistics, use the **dspasm** command; it has a privilege level of 6. The statistics count displays the successful polling of the environmental conditions. The statistics timeout displays the unsuccessful attempts.

Configuring the ASM Setting for BPX

The command **cofasm** is used to change the Alarm Service Monitor alarm thresholds and to configure alarm notification. It has a privilege level of 1. When you enter "cofasm" on the command line, a list of current settings is displayed. The command line will prompt you for the selection and setting. You can set the alarm level for the temperature threshold, power deviation from –48, polling interval, fan threshold, power voltage, and power failure.

Logging Out

To log out of the CLI session, use the **bye** command; it has a privilege level of 6. If you are using Telnet, your session will be disconnected. On the control port or auxiliary port, you will see the logon screen.

Resetting the Switch

The clear configuration command, **clrcnf**, will erase the connections, trunks, circuit lines, and other network settings. This is a fast way to clear settings if you're moving the switch to another location. The switch name, IP address, user, and other function settings are maintained. To change all the settings back to their factory defaults, use the **clrallcnf** command; this is a service-level command. You must be logged in at the superuser, service, or StrataCom level.

Displaying Other Switches

To display a list of known switches, use the **dspnds** command. This command is privilege level 6. You should see only the one switch on the display until connectivity is established with other switches. You can add the optional parameter **+n** to display the switch number.

Setting the Switch Name

You can configure a name by which the switch will be known in the network using the command **cnfname** followed by the hostname. The switch name will be distributed automatically on the network. The name is case sensitive and must be unique on the network. This is a level 1 command.

Setting the Time Zone

The command **cnftmzn** will set the local time zone for the switch. This command ensures that the switch has the correct local time. The time zone is identified by an abbreviation after the command (PST, EST, or GMT). You can also set the time zone to an offset from GMT (for example, **g-8**). This is a privilege level 1 command.

Configuring the Time and Date

The **cnfdate** command has network-wide effects; the new time and date are automatically distributed to other switches on the network. It has a privilege level of 1. To set the time and date, use **cnfdate** followed by the year, month, day, hour, minute, and second. The format of the time must use a 24-hour clock. The switch will prompt you for confirmation before executing the command.

Configuring the Control and Auxiliary Ports

The command **cnfterm** sets the transmission characteristics of the control port and auxiliary port. You can set the baud rate, parity, data bits, stop bits, and flow control. You cannot change just one parameter—you must enter all the parameters after the command separated by spaces. This is a privilege level 6 command.

Modifying the Functions of the Control and Auxiliary Ports

The command **cnftermfunc** is used to modify the control port and auxiliary port. You can modify the control port's terminal emulation or disable switch-initiated transmission. On the auxiliary port, you can set the printer type, autodial of the modem, and terminal emulation. This is a privilege level 0 command, equivalent to the superuser and service account.

Configuring the Printing Function

You can print log messages and error messages on a printer. The printer can be directly connected on the auxiliary port or connected to another switch's auxiliary port on the network. To change the setting, use the command **cnfprt**. The parameter can specify no printing, local printing, or remote printing. For remote printing, the remote hostname must be set up on the network. This is a privilege level 6 command.

Configuring the LAN Interface

The **cnflan** command is used to set up the 10Mbps Ethernet port. You can set the IP address, subnet mask, default gateway, and service port (the port used by WAN Manager). The maximum LAN transmit units and MAC addresses will be displayed but cannot be changed. This is a privilege level 0 command, equivalent to the superuser and service account.

Accessing the MGX 8850 and 8220

The MGX 8850 has a control port, maintenance port, and LAN port. The control port is an EIA/TIA-232 Data Communications Equipment (DCE) interface. To access the control, you must use a terminal or a PC with a terminal emulation program. The maintenance port is an EIA/TIA-232 DCE interface that utilizes Serial Line Internet Protocol (SLIP). You must configure an IP address to the interface before it can be used. The LAN port is a DB15 attachment unit interface (AUI). You must have the appropriate media converter.

The MGX 8220 also has the control port and maintenance port. The ports are the reverse of those on the MGX 8850—you use SLIP to connect to the control port and you use a terminal to connect to the maintenance port.

The MGX series' CLI is different from that on the IGX and BPX. The inputs are entered one line at a time, and the results scroll up the screen. MGX commands are case sensitive; most of the commands are lowercase, except for **Help**.

Adding New Users

The **adduser** command will create a new user who can access the switch:

```
MGX.1.3.ASC.a > adduser user 2
MGX.1.3.ASC.a >
```

The user must have a lower privilege level than the user creating the account. The privilege level for this command is 6.

Changing Passwords

The MGX 8220 and MGX 8850 use different commands for changing user passwords. You can change the password of the user account you are logged in to. The password must be 6 to 15 characters. The privilege level for this command is 6.

To change the password on an MGX 8220, use **cnfpwd** followed by the old password and the new password twice:

```
MGX.1.3.ASC.a > cnfpwd oldpassword newpassword newpassword
The password for user is newpassword

This screen will self-destruct in ten seconds
```

To change the password on an MGX 8850, use the command **passwd**. The new password follows the command twice:

```
MGX.1.3.ASC.a > passwd newpassword newpassword
```

Assigning a Switch Hostname

Use the command **cnfname** to assign a hostname for the switch:

```
MGX.1.3.ASC.a > cnfname MGX2
MGX2.1.3.ASC.a >
```

The name is case sensitive and must be unique on the network. The command has a privilege level of 1.

Displaying a Summary of All Modules

The command **dspcds** will display the summary information of all the modules. This is a level 6 command. The card number, card status, card type, switch name, date, time, time zone, and IP address are all displayed. The information is displayed one screen at a time. Press the Enter key to display a second screen, and press Q to stop the display.

Displaying Detailed Information for the Current Card

The command **dspcd** will display detailed information for the current card. The information displayed includes the slot number, active state, type, serial number, hardware revision, firmware revision, line module type, line module state, and fabrication number. The privilege level for this command is 6.

NOTE: *To switch between cards, use the command **cc** followed by the card number.*

Changing the Time and Date

In the MGX series, changing the time and date requires two different commands. Both commands have a privilege level of 0, equivalent to the superuser and service account. The time and date are not distributed out to the network.

To change the switch's time, use **cnftime**. The format must use a 24-hour clock:

```
MGX2.1.3.ASC.a > cnftime
cnftime "hh:mm:ss"
  Time = hh:mm:ss

MGX2.1.3.ASC.a > cnftime 15:23:00
```

To change the date on the switch, use the command **cnfdate** followed by the date in month-first format:

```
MGX2.1.3.ASC.a > cnfdate
cnfdate "mm/dd/yyyy"
  Date = mm/dd/yyyy

MGX2.1.3.ASC.a > cnfdate 09/24/2000
```

Displaying the Configuration of the Maintenance and Control Ports

The command **xdsplns** with the parameter **-rs232** displays the port, type, status, and baud rate for both the maintenance port and the control port.

To display the information on a specific port, use the command **xdspln**. One of the following parameters must be used with this command:

- **-rs232**—Information on the control or maintenance port
- **-ds3**—Information on the Broadband Network Module (BNM) DS3 line characteristics
- **-plcp**—Information on the BNM Physical layer convergence procedure line characteristics
- **-srmds3**—Information on the Single Route Explorer (SRE) DS3 line characteristics

The parameter is followed by a number identifying the control port (1) or maintenance port (2). Both the **xdsplns** and **xdspln** commands have a privilege level of 6.

Displaying the IP Address

The command **dspifip** displays the IP address, interface, netmask, and broadcast address. It will only display the interface that is configured. This command has a privilege level of 6.

Configuring the IP Interface

The command **cnfifip** is used to set the IP address, netmask, and broadcast address. Each parameter must be entered one at a time. The parameters are as follows:

- **-if**—The interface (26 for Ethernet, 28 for SLIP, or 37 for ATM)
- **-ip**—The IP address
- **-msk**—The network mask
- **-bc**—The broadcast address

This command has a privilege level of 1.

Displaying the Alarm Level of the Switch

The command **dspshelfalm** is used to display the alarm level and current status of the temperature, power supply, fans, and voltage. This is a level 6 command.

This command provides the following information for each alarm type: the threshold, severity, measurable (temperature-related or not), current value, and status.

Chapter 4

LAN Switch Architectures

In Depth

Knowing the internal architectures of networking devices can be a great asset when you're working with Cisco switches. Knowing how the internal components work together, as well as how Application-Specific Integrated Circuits (ASICs) and CPUs are used, can give you an advantage in determining what Cisco device will work best at every point in the network.

The Catalyst Crescendo Architecture

When you're looking at the architecture of the switch, ASICs are among the most important components. ASICs are very fast and relatively inexpensive silicon chips that do one or two specific tasks faster than a processor can perform those same functions. These chips have some advantages over a processor but lack functions such as filtering and advanced management functions, and they have limited support for bridging modes. ASICs make today's switches less expensive than processor-based switches. Processor-based switches are still available, but they are expensive and limited in the number of tasks they can take on and still maintain reliable and acceptable limits of throughput.

The Set/Clear command-based Command Line Interface (CLI) switches (also known as Crescendo Interface switches) found in the Cisco Catalyst 2900G, 5000, 5500, 6000, and 6500 series of switches, give the best example of how the Broadcast and Unknown Server (BUS), ASICs, Arbiters, and logic units work inside the switch. Let's look at Figure 4.1, which shows a diagram of the ASICs and processors found inside a Cisco 5000 series switch. We'll examine these components and then look at several other ASICs that are for more specialized or earlier model Cisco Catalyst switches.

First, we need to look at the components involved: the ASICs, Catalyst processors, bus, and other units of logic. Let's begin by examining each of the BUSs; then we will define the ASICs shown in Figure 4.1.

BUS

Every switch must have at least two interfaces. But what fun would just two be? Today's switches can have hundreds of ports. The BUS connects all these interfaces—it moves frames from one interface to the other. All these frames require an arbitration process using processors, ASICs, and logic units to make sure data doesn't slip out the wrong port or ports.

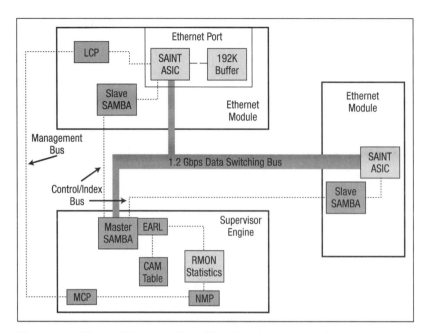

Figure 4.1   The architecture of the Cisco Catalyst 5000 series switch.

Single BUS vs. Crossbar Matrix

A single-BUS architecture is pretty simple: One BUS connects all the ports together. This setup creates a bandwidth problem called a *blocking architecture*, or what the networking industry likes to call *over-subscription*. Over-subscription is characterized as a condition in which the total bandwidth of all the ports on the switch is greater than the capacity of the switching fabric or backplane. As a result, data is held up at the port because the tunnel-through switch is too small. Examples of Cisco switches with a single-BUS architecture are the Cisco Catalyst 1900, 2820, 3000, and 5000 series.

A cross-bar matrix is used to solve the problems of a single BUS architecture by creating a multiple BUS architecture in which more than one BUS services the switch ports. In this architecture, the BUS can handle all the data the ports can possibly send—and more. It is sometimes referred to as a *non-blocking architecture*, and it requires a very sophisticated arbitration scheme.

TIP: *The switching fabric is the "highway" the data takes from the point of entry to the port or ports from which the data exits.*

Each switch employs some kind of queuing method in order to solve blocking problems. An Ethernet interface may receive data when the port does not have access to the BUS. In this situation, the port has a buffer in which it stores the frame it receives until the BUS can process it. The frame uses queuing to determine which frame will be processed next. Let's look at the three queuing components: input queuing, output queuing, and shared buffering.

Input Queuing

Input queuing is the simpler of the two forms of queuing. The frame is buffered into the port's buffer until it becomes its turn to enter the bus. When the frame enters the bus, the exit port must be free to allow the frame to exit. If another frame is exiting the port, a condition called *head-of-line blocking* occurs: The frame is dropped because it was blocked by other data.

Output Queuing

Output queuing can be used with input queuing; it allows the frame to be buffered on the outbound port if other data is in the way. This is a way to resolve head-of-line blocking, but if a large burst of frames occurs, head-of-line blocking still can occur. The problem of large bursts can be resolved by using shared buffering. All the Cisco Catalyst switches (with the exception of the 1900 and 2820 series) use both input and output queuing.

Shared Buffering

Although there is no sure way to stop head-of-line blocking, shared buffering can be used in a switch as a safeguard. Shared buffering is a derivative of output queuing and provides each port with access to one large buffer instead of smaller, individual buffering spaces. If a frame is placed in this buffer, the frame is extracted from the shared memory buffer and forwarded. This method is used on the 1900 and 2820 series of Cisco Catalyst switches.

ASICs

The ASICs shown in Figure 4.1 are used in the Catalyst 5000 series Supervisor Engine and an Ethernet Module. Let's take a look at each:

- Encoded Address Recognition Logic (EARL) ASIC
- Encoded Address Recognition Logic Plus (EARL+) ASIC
- Synergy Advanced Interface and Network Termination (SAINT) ASIC
- Synergy Advanced Multipurpose Bus Arbiter (SAMBA) ASIC

EARL ASIC

The Encoded Address Recognition Logic (EARL) ASIC performs functions that are very similar to those of the Content Addressable Memory (CAM) table. Switches use this CAM to make filtering and forwarding decisions. The EARL ASIC connects directly to the data switching bus, allowing the ASIC access to all the frames that cross the switching fabric. The switch makes forwarding decisions based on the destination Media Access Control (MAC) address.

NOTE: *The CAM table contains the MAC address of the interfaces connected to the port and the time the switch last read a frame from that source port and address. The CAM table receives updated information by examining frames it receives from a segment; it then updates the table with the source MAC address from the frame.*

The EARL ASIC aids in building a table containing all the information the switch has extracted from incoming frames. This information includes the source MAC address, the port of arrival, the virtual LAN (VLAN) membership of the port of arrival, and the time the frame was received. This table can contain up to 128,000 entries. Entries in the table are removed after the time to live (TTL) has expired. The default TTL at which entries are removed is 300 seconds; this time can be set from 1 to 20 minutes.

The EARL ASIC tags each frame as it arrives at the switch before the frame is buffered. This tagging includes the source port's identity, the VLAN, and a checksum. This tagging should not be confused with the tagging used in trunking for Inter-Switch Link (ISL) or 802.1Q, discussed in Chapter 5. The tagging the EARL places in the frame is removed before the frame exits the switch. The EARL ASIC's placement is shown in Figure 4.2.

EARL+ ASIC

The Encoded Address Recognition Logic Plus (EARL+) ASIC allows the EARL to support Token Ring line modules. The EARL+ ASIC is an enhancement to the EARL ASIC and is used on the Supervisor Engine III Module.

SAINT ASIC

The Synergy Advanced Interface and Network Termination (SAINT) ASIC allows a switch interface to support both half-duplex and full-duplex Ethernet. This ASIC has a second responsibility to handle frame encapsulation and de-encapsulation, and gathering statistics for trunked ports.

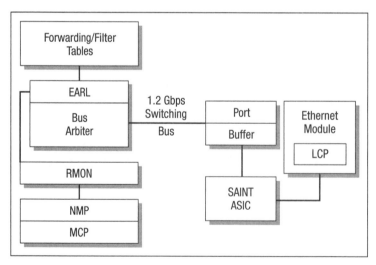

Figure 4.2   EARL ASIC placement on the Crescendo architecture.

SAMBA ASIC

The Synergy Advanced Multipurpose Bus Arbiter (SAMBA) ASIC and the EARL ASIC work in tandem to let ports access the bus, thus allowing frames to be forwarded correctly. Both the Supervisor Engine and the installed line modules utilize this ASIC; it can support up to 13 separate line modules.

This ASIC operates in either master or slave mode. In master mode, the ASIC allows ports access to the bus based on a priority level of normal, high, or critical. In slave mode, each port must post a request to each SAMBA ASIC, negotiate local port decisions, and arbitrate requests with the Supervisor Engine's SAMBA ASIC.

The Crescendo Processors

Although we have ASICs to do some of the hard work of the processors, processors still must be involved to handle the more dynamic administrative items. They carry the intelligence behind the frame-switching process. Inside the Crescendo Interface Internetwork Operating System (IOS) switches, the processors connect to a bus; the bus in turn connects to other ASICs and processors inside the switch. In the following sections, I will examine the processors listed here and their assigned functions. You will find these processors in the Crescendo Interface Catalyst switches:

• Line Module Communication Processor (LCP)

• Master Communication Processor (MCP)

• Network Management Processor (NMP)

LCP

The Line Module Communication Processor (LCP) can be found on each line module in the switch. This ASIC's responsibility is to provide communications for access to the Master Communication Processor (MCP) located on the Supervisor Engine.

The LCP automatically boots from read-only memory (ROM) and is an 8051 processor. Immediately upon boot up, the ASIC forwards an information package called a *Resetack* to the MCP. Resetack includes information regarding the switch's boot diagnostics and module information. This information is then forwarded from the MCP to the Network Management Processor (NMP).

MCP

The Master Communication Processor (MCP), which is sometimes called the Management Control Processor, uses a serial management bus to communicate between the NMP on the Supervisor Engine module and the LCP on the individual line cards located in the switch. The MCP also has a secondary job: to test and check the configuration of the local ports, control of local ports, downloading of runtime code, and performing continuous port diagnostics. This ASIC handles the diagnostics and obtains the usage statistics of the on-board memory, ASICs, Local Target Logic (LTL), and Color Blocking Logic (CBL).

NMP

The Network Management Processor (NMP) is used to control the system hardware, configuration, switch management, the Spanning-Tree Protocol (STP) (discussed in Chapter 10), and diagnostic functions.

Crescendo Logic Units

Logic units provide logic-based forwarding by VLAN, MAC address, or port assignment. The Catalyst Crescendo Interface switches contain the following logic units:

- Arbiter (ARB)
- Local Target Logic (LTL)
- Color Blocking Logic (CBL)
- Remote Network Monitoring (RMN)

ARB

The Arbiter (ARB) is located on each line module. It uses a two-tiered method of arbitration to assign queuing priorities and control data traffic through the switch. The arbiter controls the traffic coming to and from the line modules. In addition, a Central Bus Arbiter located on the Supervisor Engine module obtains permission to transmit frames to the switching engine.

The Central Bus Arbiter provides special handling of high-priority frames by using a round-robin approach. Frames with other priority levels can be set to handle support of time-sensitive traffic, such as multimedia.

LTL

The Local Target Logic (LTL) works in conjunction with the EARL ASIC to determine if a frame is switched to one individual port or sent to multiple ports. The LTL also helps identify the port or ports on the switch to which the frame needs to be forwarded, and it can look at the frame to determine if the frame is a unicast or a multicast frame for broadcast forwarding. This process is handled using index values provided by the EARL ASIC table. The LTL then uses this information to select the port or ports to forward the frame to.

CBL

The Color Block Logic (CBL) blocks data frames from entering a port that does not belong to the same VLAN as the port of arrival. This ASIC aids STP in deciding which ports to block and which ports to place in the learning, listening, or forwarding modes.

Other Cisco Switch Processors, Buses, ASICs, and Logic Units

In addition to the items we just discussed, other ASICs and significant components are used in the Cisco 5000 architecture as well as that of other Cisco Catalyst and Gigabit Switch Routers (GSRs).

NOTE: *ASIC is not a Cisco term. ASICs are vendor specific, and differently named ASICs can be found on other vendor networking products.*

Let's take a closer look at the functions of these switch components:

- Content Addressable Memory (CAM)
- AXIS bus
- Cisco Express Forwarding (CEF) ASIC
- Phoenix ASIC
- Line Module Communication Processor (LCP)
- Synergy Advanced Gate-Array Engine (SAGE) ASIC
- Quad Token Ring Port (QTP) ASIC
- Quad Media Access Controller (QMAC)

CAM

The CAM table is used by a bridge to make forwarding and filtering decisions. The CAM table contains MAC addresses with port addresses leading to the physical interfaces. It uses a specialized interface that is faster than RAM to make forwarding and filtering decisions. The CAM table updates information by examining frames it receives from a segment and then updating the table with the source MAC address from the frame.

AXIS Bus

The architecture of the Catalyst 3900 centers around the AXIS bus, which uses a 520Mbps switching fabric through which all switched ports communicate.

The AXIS bus is a partially asynchronous time division multiplexed bus used for switching packets between heterogeneous LAN modules.

CEF ASIC

The Cisco Express Forwarding (CEF) ASIC and Distributed Cisco Express Forwarding (dCEF) ASIC are Cisco's newest ASICs, found in Cisco's lines of routers and switches. In Cisco's switching line, you will find this ASIC available in the 8500 GSR and 12000 GSR series.

dCEF

The dCEF ASIC is a mode that can be enabled on line cards; this mode uses interprocess communication (IPC) to synchronize a copy of the Forwarding Information Base (FIB). This synchronization enables identical copies of the FIB and adjacency tables to be stored on the Versatile Interface Processor (VIP), GSR, or other line card. The line cards can then express forward between port adapters. This process relieves the Route Switch Processor (RSP) of its involvement. The Cisco 12000 series routers have dCEF enabled by default. This is valuable troubleshooting information, because when you view the router configuration, it does not indicate that dCEF is enabled.

The CEF ASIC (CEFA) is a small CPU-type silicon chip that makes sure Layer 3 packets have fair access to the switch's internal memory. An internal CEFA search engine performs fast lookups using arbitration to make sure lookups have metered access to the ASIC. CEF's features include optimized scalability and exceptional performance. Cisco has made an excellent component that fits well into large networks, particularly those using Web-based applications that like to eat up the available bandwidth in slower processed networks. Such applications include Voice over IP, multimedia, large graphics, and other critical applications.

The CEFA microcontroller is local to four ports on the Catalyst 8500 GSR series line module; it uses a round-robin approach for equal access to data traffic on each port. The CEF microprocessor also has the responsibility to forward system messages back to the centralized CPU. These messages can include such data as Bridge Protocol Data Units (BPDUs), routing protocol advertisements, Internet Protocol (IP) Address Resolution Protocol (ARP) frames, Cisco Discovery Protocol (CDP) packets, and control-type messages.

CEF is a very complex ASIC that is less CPU-intensive than fast-switching route caching (discussed later in this chapter). It allows more processing ability for other Layer 3 services such as Quality of Service (QoS) queuing, policy networking (including access lists), and higher data encryption and decryption. As a result, CEF offers a higher level of consistency and stability in very large networks.

The FIB, which contains all the known routes to a destination, allows the switch to eliminate the route cache maintenance and fast switching or process switching that doesn't scale well to large network routing changes.

The Routing Information Base (RIB) table is created first, and information from the routing table is forwarded to the FIB. The FIB is a highly optimized routing lookup algorithm. Through the use of prefix matching of the destination address, the FIB makes the process of looking up the destination in a large routing table occur much more quickly than the line-by-line lookup of the RIB.

The FIB maintains a copy of the forwarding information contained in the IP routing table based on the next-hop address. An adjacency table is then used to determine the next hop. The IP table is updated if routing or topology changes occur. Those changes are then recorded in the FIB, and the next hop is then recomputed by the adjacency table based on those changes. This process eliminates the need for fast or optimum switching (discussed later in this chapter) in previous versions of the IOS.

CEF allows you to optimize the resources on your switch by using multiple paths to load-balance traffic. You can configure per-destination or per-packet load balancing on the outbound interface of the switch:

- *Per-destination load balancing*—Enabled by default when you enable CEF. It allows multiple paths to be used for load sharing. Packets destined for a given destination or source host are guaranteed to take the same path, although multiple destinations are available.

- *Per-packet load balancing*—Uses a round-robin approach to determine what path individual packets will take over the network. Per-packet load balancing ensures balancing when multiple paths are available to a given destination. This method allows packets for a given destination to take different paths. However, per-packet load balancing does not work well with data such as Voice over IP and video; these types of data packets need a guarantee that they will arrive at the destination in the same sequence they were sent.

The Adjacency Table
The adjacency table maintains a one-to-one correspondence to the FIB. All entries in the FIB are maintained in the adjacency table. A node is said to be *adjacent* if the node can be reached in one hop. CEF uses the adjacency table to apply Layer 2 address information determined by such protocols as Address Resolution Protocol (ARP) when the next hop must use the physical hardware address of the interface. The adjacency table provides the Layer 2 information necessary to switch the packet to its next point destination; the table is updated as adjacencies are discovered.

The adjacency table contains the MAC address for routers that map to Layer 2 to Layer 3 addresses. It uses the IP ARP to populate neighbors gleaned from IP and Internetwork Packet Exchange (IPX) updates, indexed by interface and address. For each computed path, a pointer is added for the adjacency corresponding to the next hop. This mechanism is used for load balancing where more than one path exists to a destination.

Using host-to-route adjacencies, a few other types of adjacencies are used to expedite switching in certain instances. Let's look at these instances and the conditions in which other adjacencies are used:

- *Null adjacency*—Packets destined for a Null0. The Null0 address is referred to as the *bit bucket*. Packets sent to the bit bucket are discarded. This is an effective form of access filtering.

- *Glean adjacency*—A node connected directly to more than one host, such as a multihomed PC. In this situation, the router or switch maintains a prefix for the subnet instead of the individual host. If a packet needs to reach a specific host, the adjacency table is gleaned for the information specific to that node.

- *Punt adjacency*—Packets that need to be sent to another switching layer for handling. This is done when a packet needs special handling, or when the packets need to be forwarded to a higher switching layer.

- *Discard adjacency*—Packets that are sent to the bit bucket and whose prefix is checked. The Cisco 12000 GSR is the only Cisco device using this type of adjacency.

CEF Search Engine

The CEF search engine can make either Layer 2-based or Layer 3-based switching decisions. The FIB places incoming packets into the internal memory. From there, the first 64 bytes of the frame are read. If a Layer 2 adjacency resolution needs to be made, the microcode sends the search engine the relevant source MAC address, destination MAC address, or the Layer 3 network destination. The search engine then conducts a lookup of the CAM table for the corresponding information. CEF uses the search engine to find the MAC address or the longest match on the destination network address. It does this very quickly and responds with the corresponding rewrite information; it then stores this information in the CAM table.

The CEFA now knows the port-of-exit for the packet, based either on its MAC address or on the Layer 3 IP or IPX network numbers. The packet is now transferred across the switching fabric to its point of destination to be sent to its next hop. The destination interface prepares the packet prior to exiting the switch. Figure 4.3 shows the CEFA components.

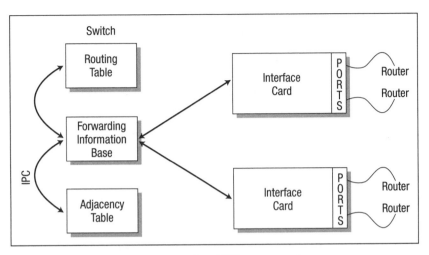

Figure 4.3   Cisco Express Forwarding ASIC components.

NOTE: *CEF supports Ethernet, Fiber Distributed Data Interface (FDDI), Point-to-Point Protocol (PPP), High-Level Data Link Control (HDLC), Asynchronous Transfer Mode (ATM)/AAL5snap, ATM/AAL5mux, ATM/AAL5nlpid, and tunnels.*

Phoenix ASIC

The Phoenix ASIC is another ASIC used to handle high-speed data traffic on the Supervisor Engine III. This ASIC provides a gigabit bridge between each of the buses located on the module. The Phoenix ASIC has a 384K buffer used to handle traffic between buses located on the module. From the perspective of the EARL and the SAMBA, the Phoenix ASIC appears as another port on the box. Figure 4.4 depicts the Phoenix ASIC.

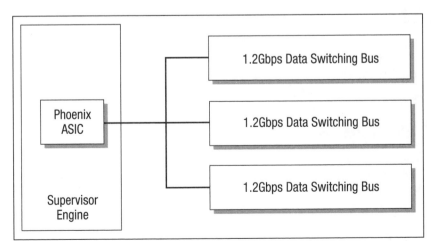

Figure 4.4   The Phoenix ASIC used on the Supervisor Engine III.

It is important to note that some line modules do not have access to all three buses. In the case of the Catalyst 5500 13-slot chassis, slots 1 through 5 are connected to bus A, slots 1 through 9 are connected to bus B, and slots 1 through 5 and 10 through 12 are connected to bus C. The placement of line modules in the chassis becomes important. You will learn more about this topic in Chapter 6.

LCP

The LCP is located on each line module. It is the responsibility of the LCP to provide communications for the MCP located on the Supervisor Engine.

SAGE ASIC

The Synergy Advanced Gate-Array Engine (SAGE) ASIC performs the same functions as the SAINT. This ASIC also has some additional functions, such as gaining access to the token in FDDI or Token Ring networks. Processing performed by SAGE takes place in the hardware ASICs, requires no CPU cycles, and adds no additional latency to the switching process.

QTP ASIC

The architecture of the Catalyst 3900 is centered around the AXIS bus (discussed earlier), using the Quad Token Ring Port (QTP) ASIC. Cisco uses the 3900 series line of switches as its primary switch dedicated to Token Ring topology networks. This line of switches uses a 520Mbps switching fabric through which all switched interfaces communicate. The ASIC interfaces directly with the Quad Media Access Controller (QMAC) ASIC and provides the necessary functions for switching directly between the four Token Ring ports connected to the QMAC ASIC.

QMAC

The QMAC uses four protocol handlers to support four Token Ring physical interfaces directly connected to the QTP ASIC. Together, these two ASICs provide support for early token release (ETR) and Token Ring Full Duplex (FDX) concentrator and adapter modes for dedicated Token Ring.

Bridging Types

In the early 1980s, IBM developed a non-routable protocol called NetBIOS as part of its implementation strategy. NetBIOS joined other non-routable protocols that came into wide use, such as System Network Architecture (SNA) and Local Area Transport (LAT). IBM also developed a physical network topology called Token Ring. With Token Ring came a bridging technology called Source Route Bridging (SRB).

The SRB algorithm for Token-Ring LAN bridging became the IEEE 802.5 Token Ring LAN specification. SRB has various combinations, which will be discussed in more detail in the next chapter:

- Source Route Bridging (SRB)
- Source Route Transparent Bridging (SRT)
- Source Route Translational Bridging (SR/TLB)

Transparent Bridging (TB) is another bridging technology that was developed later by DEC, and which is now used in Ethernet networks. Although it was developed for DEC, it is the primary bridging algorithm for today's switches and routers. It maintains a routing table, building tables composed of destination addresses. It has the ability to switch network packets based upon a match of the destination address, such as those used with IP, IPX, and AppleTalk.

TB tables are built differently than routing tables. Whereas routing tables rely heavily on routing protocols to learn about foreign networks, TB tables learn the location of each MAC address by logging the port from which the frame arrived. Thus, assuming that the network the frame arrived from is attached to the port of entry, TB logs the information along with a maximum age or TTL. When this maximum is reached, TB removes the entry from the table.

Let's take a look at each bridging type.

Source Route Bridging

SRB is a method of bridging used to connect Token Ring segments. It makes all forwarding decisions based upon data in the RIF. It cannot acquire or look up MAC addresses. Therefore, SRB frames without a corresponding RIF are not forwarded.

With SRB, every port on the switch is assigned a ring number. The switch itself is assigned one or more bridge numbers. SRB uses this information to build the RIF; it then searches the RIF to determine where to forward incoming frames.

SRB frames are modified when they arrive using explorer frames. Explorer frames are typically one of two types: All Routes Explorer (ARE) or Spanning-Tree Explorer (STE). SRB bridges copy ARE and STE frames and modify the RIF with their own routing information.

Source Route Transparent Bridging

Source Route Transparent Bridging (SRT) is a combination of SRB and TB. SRT bridges make forwarding decisions based on either the Routing Information Field (RIF) for the destination or the MAC address in the frame.

4. LAN Switch Architectures

Some protocols attempt to establish a connection using a frame without using a RIF. These applications send a test frame to see if the destination is on the same ring as the source. If no response is received from this test frame, then an All Routes Explorer (ARE) test frame with a RIF is sent. If the destination receives the ARE, it responds, and the spanning-tree path through the bridge is used.

If the network is configured with parallel full-duplex backbones, this detected path may be very undesirable. If the spanning-tree path is used, then only one of the backbones will carry the traffic.

Source Route Translational Bridging

Source Route Translational Bridging (SR/TLB) has a Token Ring attached to at least one port of the bridge and another media-type topology (such as FDDI or Ethernet) attached to another port. SR/TLB's main function is to make the two media types transparent to one another. The bridge receives the token, converts the data to a readable format for the Ethernet segment, and then forwards the data out the Ethernet to the receiving host address. All this takes place transparently to both hosts on the network—the Ethernet host believes that the Token Ring host is on Ethernet, and vice versa.

Transparent Bridging

Transparent bridges get their name because they are invisible to all the network nodes for which they provide services. Transparent bridges and switches acquire knowledge of the network by looking at the source address of all frames coming into their interfaces. The bridge then creates a table based on the information from the frames it received.

If a host sends a frame to a single host on another port, then if the bridge or switch has learned the port the destination resides on and it is on the local switch, the switch forwards the frame out the destination interface. If the bridge or switch does not know the port the destination host resides on, it will flood the frame received out all the ports except for the port the frame was received on. Broadcasts and multicasts are also flooded in the same way out all the ports.

Source Route Switching

Source Route Switching (SRS) was created to overcome the disadvantages of standard TB. TB does not support source-routing information. SRS forwards frames that do not contain routing information based on the MAC address the same way that TB does. All the rings that are source-route switched have the same ring number, and the switch learns the MAC addresses of adapters on these rings.

SRS also learns the route descriptors. A *route descriptor* is a portion of a RIF that indicates a single hop. It defines a ring number, a bridge number, and the hop closest to the switch. Future frames received from other ports with the same next-hop route descriptor are forwarded to that port.

If you have a Token Ring switch that has reached the limitation of ring stations on the current ring, SRS is your best choice for bridging. Unlike SRB, SRS looks at the RIF; it never makes the changes to the RIF. Using SRS, the switch does not need to obtain the MAC addresses of the devices. This method reduces the number of MAC addresses that the switch must learn and maintain.

Switching Paths

The switch is commonly referred to in marketing terms as a Layer 2 device. If you keep thinking that way, this section will confuse you. By definition, switching paths are logical paths that Layer 3 packets follow when they are switched through a Layer 3 device such as a router or internal route processor. These switching types allow the device to push packets from the incoming interface to the interface where the packet must exit using switching paths or table lookups. By using switching paths, unnecessary table lookups can be avoided, and the processor can be freed to do other processing.

You're probably wondering, "Sean, this is a switching book. Why am I learning about switching paths in Layer 3 devices?" Well, inside switches are Layer 3 devices such as the Route Switch Module (RSM), Multilayer Switching Module (MSM), Multilayer Switch Feature Card (MSFC), and NetFlow Feature Card (NFFC). Later in this book, I will cover trunk links, which are links that carry more than one VLAN. Doesn't it seem logical that if you need to have a "router on a stick," which is an external router used for interVLAN routing, it might help to know if the router you are using can handle the traffic for all of your VLANs? Better yet, you should learn the internal working paths and types of switching paths through the route processor. Let's take a look at all the switching paths used on Layer 3 devices.

In this section, we will focus on the following switching path types and the functions of each:

- Process switching
- Fast switching
- Autonomous switching
- Silicon switching
- Optimum switching

4. LAN Switch Architectures

- Distributed switching
- NetFlow switching

Process Switching

Process switching uses the processor to determine the exit port for every packet. As a packet that needs to be forwarded arrives on an interface, it is copied to the router's process buffer, where the router performs a lookup based on the Layer 3 destination address and calculates the Cyclic Redundancy Check (CRC). Subsequent packets bound for the same destination interfaces follow the same path as the first packet.

This type of switching can overload the processor. Making Layer 3 lookups the responsibility of the processor used to determine which interface the packet should exit takes away from more essential tasks the processor needs to handle. It is recommended that you use other types of switching whenever possible.

Fast Switching

Consider fast switching an enhancement to process switching. This switching type uses a fast switching cache found on the route processor board. The first received packet of a data flow or session is copied to the interface's processor buffer. The packet is copied to the Cisco Extended Bus (CxBus) and then sent to the switch processor. If a silicon or autonomous switching cache does not contain an entry for the destination address, fast switching is used because no entries for the destination address are in any other more efficient caches.

Fast switching copies the header and then sends the packet to the route processor that contains the fast switching cache. If an entry exists in the cache, the packet is encapsulated for fast switching, sent back to the switch processor, and then buffered on the outgoing interface processor.

NOTE: *Fast switching is used on the 2500 and the 4000 series of Cisco routers by default.*

Autonomous Switching

With autonomous switching, when a packet arrives on an interface, it is forwarded to the interface processor. The interface processor checks the silicon-switching cache; if the destination address is not contained in that cache, the autonomous cache is checked. The packet is encapsulated for autonomous switching and sent back to the interface processor. The header is not sent to the route processor with this type of switching.

NOTE: *Autonomous switching is available only on AGS+ and Cisco 7000 series routers that have high-speed controller interface cards.*

Silicon Switching

Silicon-switched packets use a silicon-switching cache on the Silicon Switching Engine (SSE) found on the Silicon Switch Processor (SSP). This is a dedicated switch processor used to offload the switching process from the route processor. Packets must use the router's backplane to get to and from the SSP.

NOTE: *Silicon switching is used only on the Cisco 7000 series router with an SSP.*

Optimum Switching

Optimum switching is similar to all the other switching methods in many ways. As the first packet for a flow arrives on an interface, it is compared to the optimum switching cache, appended, and sent to the destination exit interface. Other packets associated with the same session then follow the same path. Just as with process switching, all the processing is carried out on the interface processor.

Unlike process switching, optimum switching is faster than both fast switching or NetFlow switching when the route processor is not using policy networking such as access lists. Optimum switching is used on higher-end route processors as a replacement for fast switching.

Distributed Switching

Distributed switching is used on the VIP cards, which use a very efficient switching processor. Processing is done right on the VIP card's processor, which maintains a copy of the router's own route cache. This is another switching type in which the route processor is never copied with the packet header. All the processing is offloaded to the VIP card's processor. The router or internal route processor's efficiency is dramatically increased with a VIP card added.

NetFlow Switching

NetFlow switching is usually thought of as utilizing the NetFlow Feature Card (NFFC) or NFFC II inside the Catalyst 5000 or 6000 family of switches. These switches use the NFFCs to let a router or internal route processor make a routing decision based on the first packet of a flow. The NFFCs then determine the forwarding interface decision made by the router or internal route processor and send all subsequent packets in the same data flow to that same interface. This method offloads work that the router used to do on to the switch's NFFC card.

However, NetFlow switching is not just a switching type; it can be used as an administrative tool to gather statistics in an ATM-, LAN-, and VLAN-implemented network. This type of switching actually creates some added processing for the router or an internal route processor by collecting data for use with circuit accounting and application-utilization information. NetFlow switching packets are processed using either the fast or optimum switching methods, and all the information obtained by this switching type is stored in the NetFlow switching cache; this cache includes the destination address, source address, protocol, source port, destination port, and router's active interfaces. This data can be sent to a network management station for analysis.

The first packet that's copied to the NetFlow cache contains all security and routing information. If policy networking (such as an access list) is applied to an interface, the first packet is matched to the list criteria. If there is a match, the cache is flagged so that any other packets arriving with the flow can be switched without being compared to the list.

NOTE: *NetFlow switching can be configured on most 7000 series router interfaces and can be used in a switched environment. NetFlow switching can also be configured on VIP interfaces.*

System Message Logging

The system message logging software can save messages to a log file or direct the messages to other devices. By default, the switch logs normal but significant system messages to its internal buffer and sends these messages to the system console. You can access logged system messages using the switch CLI or by saving them to a properly configured syslog server.

NOTE: *When the switch first boots, the network is not connected until the initialization and power on self test (POST) are completed. Therefore, messages that are sent to a syslog server are delayed up to 90 seconds.*

System logging messages are sent to console and Telnet sessions based on the default logging facility and severity values. You can disable logging to the console or logging to a given Telnet session. When you disable or enable logging to console sessions, the enable state is applied to all future console sessions. In contrast, when you disable or enable logging to a Telnet session, the enable state is applied only to that session.

Most enterprise network configurations include a Unix-based or Windows-based system log server to log all messages from the devices in the network. This server provides a central location from which you can extract information about all the devices in the event of a network failure or other issue. You can use several **set**

logging commands. Let's take a look at those that will not be covered in the Immediate Solutions section and what each will do:

- **set logging server**—Specifies the IP address of one or more syslog servers. You can identify up to three servers.

- **set logging server facility**—Sets the facility levels for syslog server messages.

- **set logging server severity**—Sets the severity levels for syslog server messages.

- **set logging server enable**—Enables system message logging to configured syslog servers.

Immediate Solutions

Loading an Image on the Supervisor Engine III

Trivial File Transfer Protocol (TFTP) boot is not supported on the Supervisor Engine III or on either the Catalyst 4000 series and the 2948G switch Supervisor Engine modules. You can use one of two commands to load a saved image. To load copies to a TFTP server, use the following:

```
copy file-ld tftp
```

To load copies to Flash memory, use the following:

```
copy file-ld flash
```

Booting the Supervisor Engine III from Flash

To boot from a Flash device, use the following command:

```
boot [device][image name]
```

NOTE: *If you do not specify an image file name, the system defaults to the first valid file in the device. Remember that file names are case sensitive. Use the* **show flash** *command to view the Flash files. The device can be the local Supervisor Engine's Flash memory or a TFTP server.*

Related solution:	Found on page:
Using the **show flash** Command on a Set/Clear Command-Based IOS	493

Setting the Boot Configuration Register

You can set the boot method for the switch manually using the boot field in the configuration register. This command affects the configuration register bits that control the boot field, similar to the way a router does. There are three syntaxes for the **set boot config-register boot** command:

- **rommon**—This syntax forces the switch to remain in ROM Monitor mode at startup.
- **bootflash**—This syntax causes the switch to boot from the first image stored in Flash memory.
- **system**—This syntax allows the switch to boot from the image specified in the BOOT environment variable.

To set the configuration register boot field, use the following command in Privileged EXEC mode:

```
set boot config-register boot {rommon|bootflash|system} [module number]
```

Here's an example of using the command:

```
Seans5002> (enable) set boot config-register boot rommon 1
Configuration register is 0x140
ignore-config: enabled
console baud: 9600
boot: the ROM monitor
Seans5002> (enable)
```

Configuring Cisco Express Forwarding

You configure CEF in the Global Configuration mode. The following commands for configuring CEF and dCEF are available on the Cisco 8500 and 12000 GSR series.

Enabling CEF

To enable standard CEF, use the following command:

```
ip cef
```

Disabling CEF

To disable standard CEF, use the following command:

```
no ip cef
```

Enabling dCEF

To enable dCEF operation, use the following command:

```
ip cef distributed
```

Disabling dCEF

To disable dCEF operation, use the following command:

```
no ip cef distributed
```

WARNING! Never disable dCEF on a Cisco 12000 series.

Disabling CEF on an Individual Interface

When you enable or disable CEF or dCEF in Global Configuration mode, all supported interfaces that support CEF or dCEF are affected. Some features on interfaces do not support CEF, such as policy routing. In that case, you will need to disable CEF on that interface.

To disable CEF on an interface, use the following command:

```
no ip route-cache cef
```

Configuring CEF Load Balancing

To enable per-packet load balancing, use the following command:

```
ip load-sharing per-packet
```

Disabling CEF Load Balancing

To disable per-packet sharing, use the following command:

```
no ip load-sharing per-packet
```

Enabling Network Accounting for CEF

To enable network accounting for CEF on the 8500 GSR to collect the numbers of packets and bytes forwarded to a destination, use the following command:

```
ip cef accounting per-prefix
```

Setting Network Accounting for CEF to Collect Packet Numbers

To set network accounting for CEF to collect the numbers of packets express-forwarded through a destination, use this command:

```
ip cef accounting non-recursive
```

Viewing Network Accounting for CEF Statistics

The information collected by network accounting for CEF is collected at the route processor. Distributed CEF information is collected by the line cards, not the route processor.

To view the statistics collected, use the following command:

```
show ip cef
```

Viewing CEF Packet-Dropped Statistics

To view the number of packets dropped from each line card, use the following command:

```
show cef drop
```

Viewing Non-CEF Path Packets

To view what packets went to a path other than CEF, use the following command:

```
show cef not-cef-switched
```

Disabling Per-Destination Load Sharing

If you want to use per-packet load balancing, you need to disable per-destination load balancing. To disable per-destination load balancing, use this command:

```
no ip load-sharing per-destination
```

Viewing the Adjacency Table on the 8500 GSR

The following command allows you to display the adjacency table on the Cisco 8500 GSR:

```
show adjacency
```

The following command will allow you to get a more detailed look at the Layer 2 information adjacencies learned by the CEF ASIC:

```
show adjacency detail
```

Clearing the Adjacency Table on the 8500 GSR

To clear the adjacency table on a Cisco 8500 GSR, use the following command:

```
clear adjacency
```

Enabling Console Session Logging on a Set/Clear Command-Based IOS

Different variations of the **set logging** command affect session logging differently. To enable session logging for a console session, use the following command:

```
set logging console enable
```

Enabling Telnet Session Logging on a Set/Clear Command-Based IOS

To enable session logging for a Telnet session, use the following command:

```
set logging session enable
```

Disabling Console Session Logging on a Set/Clear Command-Based IOS

To disable session logging for a console session, use the following command:

```
Catalyst5000> (enable) set logging console disable
System logging messages will not be sent to the console.

Catalyst5000> (enable)
```

Disabling Telnet Session Logging on a Set/Clear Command-Based IOS

To disable logging for the current Telnet session, use the following command:

```
Catalyst5000> (enable) set logging session disable
System logging messages will not be sent to the current login session.

Catalyst5000> (enable)
```

Setting the System Message Severity Levels on a Set/Clear Command-Based IOS

The severity level for each logging facility can be set using the **set logging level** command. Use the **default** keyword to make the specified severity level the default for the specified facilities. If you do not use the **default** keyword, the specified severity level applies only to the current session. The command syntax is:

```
set logging level [all|facility] severity [default|value]
```

Here's an example of the command's use:

```
Catalyst5000> (enable) set logging level all 5
All system logging facilities for this session set to
    severity 5(notifications)

Catalyst5000> (enable)
```

Enabling the Logging Time Stamp on a Set/Clear Command-Based Switch

You can use the logging timestamps in your system logging to help you keep track of when events happen. To enable the logging time stamp, use the following command in Privileged mode:

```
Catalyst5000> (enable) set logging timestamp enable
System logging messages timestamp will be enabled.

Catalyst5000> (enable)
```

Disabling the Logging Time Stamp on a Set/Clear Command-Based Switch

To disable the logging time stamp, use the following command in Privileged mode:

```
Catalyst5000> (enable) set logging timestamp disable
System logging messages timestamp will be disabled.

Catalyst5000> (enable)
```

Configuring the Logging Buffer Size on a Set/Clear Command-Based Switch

By default, the logging buffer will hold 1,024 messages in memory. If you do not want to keep this many in memory, either to conserve memory or because they are not needed, use the **set logging buffer** command followed by the net buffer size:

```
set logging buffer 2048
```

Clearing the Server Logging Table

To clear a syslog server table, use the **clear logging server** command followed by the server IP address:

```
Catalyst5000> (enable) clear logging server 63.78.39.164
System logging server 63.78.39.164 removed from system logging server table.

Catalyst5000> (enable)
```

Disabling Server Logging

The **set logging server disable** command disables system logging to all config- ured system logging servers:

```
Catalyst5000> (enable) set logging server disable
System logging messages will not be sent to the configured syslog servers.

Catalyst5000> (enable)
```

Displaying the Logging Configuration

Use the **show logging** command to display the current system message logging configuration. Use the **no alias** keyword to display the IP addresses instead of the host names of the configured syslog servers.

This output shows how to display the current system message logging configuration:

```
Catalyst5000> (enable) show logging

Logging buffered size:       500
        timestamp option:    enabled
Logging history size:        1
Logging console:             enabled
Logging server:              disabled
        server facility:     LOCAL7
        server severity:     warnings(4)
```

Facility	Default Severity	Current Session Severity
acl	2	2
cdp	4	4
cops	2	2
dtp	5	5
dvlan	2	2
earl	2	2
filesys	2	2
gvrp	2	2
ip	2	2
kernel	2	2
ld	2	2
mcast	2	2
mgmt	5	5
mls	5	5
pagp	5	5
protfilt	2	2
pruning	2	2
privatevlan	2	2
qos	2	2
radius	2	2
rsvp	2	2
security	2	2
snmp	2	2
spantree	2	2
sys	5	5
tac	2	2
tcp	2	2
telnet	2	2
tftp	2	2
udld	4	4
vtp	2	2

4. LAN Switch Architectures

```
0(emergencies)        1(alerts)           2(critical)
3(errors)             4(warnings)         5(notifications)
6(information)        7(debugging)

Catalyst5000> (enable)
```

Displaying System Logging Messages

You can use the **show logging buffer** command to display the messages in the switch logging buffer. If you do not specify the number of messages, the default is to display the last 20 messages in the buffer (**-20**).

To display the first five messages in the buffer, use the following code:

```
Catalyst5000> (enable) show logging buffer 5
2000 Aug 21 09:41:12 %SYS-5-MOD_OK:Module 1 is online
2000 Aug 21 09:41:14 %SYS-5-MOD_OK:Module 3 is online
2000 Aug 21 09:41:14 %SYS-5-MOD_OK:Module 2 is online
2000 Aug 21 09:42:16 %PAGP-5-PORTTOSTP:Port 2/1 joined bridge port 2/1
2000 Aug 21 09:42:16 %PAGP-5-PORTTOSTP:Port 2/2 joined bridge port 2/2
Catalyst5000> (enable)
```

To display the last five messages in the buffer, use this code:

```
Catalyst5000> (enable) show logging buffer -5
%PAGP-5-PORTFROMSTP:Port 3/1 left bridge port 3/1
%SPANTREE-5-PORTDEL_SUCCESS:3/2 deleted from vlan 1 (PAgP_Group_Rx)
%PAGP-5-PORTFROMSTP:Port 3/2 left bridge port 3/2
%PAGP-5-PORTTOSTP:Port 3/1 joined bridge port 3/1-2
%PAGP-5-PORTTOSTP:Port 3/2 joined bridge port 3/1-2
Catalyst5000> (enable)
```

Chapter 5

Virtual Local Area Networks

(continued)

In Depth

Faced with the problems of a slow network, many network administrators make expensive mistakes. Several times, I have come across companies that have a fiber link to every desktop. In fact, an architectural firm I consulted for comes to mind. The company used hubs to deliver data to each desktop. When the company reached about 150 workstations in its LAN, the users began to complain about how slow their network and PCs were becoming.

To deal with this problem, the two Microsoft NT administrators decided to upgrade their existing Category 4 cabling—which could adequately handle 10Mbps links to the desktops—to a fiber link. This was an expensive mistake, to the tune of about $150,000. Both the administrators now know it was a mistake; but because of their lack of knowledge of networking products, at the time they thought it was the best solution.

If the administrators had decided to implement a switched solution, they would have saved nearly $50,000 in labor costs and $60,000 in cabling costs. Upgrading the cabling and line speed is a solution—not the best, in most situations, but it resolves the issue. A much cheaper solution is available; it will segment your network into smaller broadcast domains, eliminate most collisions, and resolve your network and PC performance problems.

In this chapter, you will learn not only about switched networks, but how virtual LANs (VLANs) can be used in place of a router to segment your LANs. Most Ethernet and network problems are caused by too many nodes trying to send data at one time, thereby causing collisions and overutilization of the network wire. As an administrator, you may not even realize when it is time to convert your company to a switched network and implement VLANs. You also may not be aware of the benefits that can occur from replacing your Layer 2 hubs and bridges with switches, or how adding some modules in your switches to implement routing and filtering can improve your network's performance. Let's begin with a quick review of a flat topology network.

The Flat Network of Yesterday

The flat topology network was discussed in Chapter 1. As you will remember, a flat topology is a LAN connected by bridges and hubs. Every node in the network sees the data being passed by every other node on the network. This arrangement

5. Virtual Local Area Networks

eats up an incredible amount of processing power and bandwidth, even without collisions forcing data to be re-sent on the physical wire. A flat topology network begins to slow down due to traffic, collisions, and other bottlenecks. When problems of this nature occur, you must investigate them.

As a network administrator, you should have the resources to adequately determine the types of data that are flowing throughout your network. You should have a good network Sniffer, or other such device, to find over-utilization problems as well as faulty equipment and unnecessary protocols running on the network.

Of the Layer 3 protocols, TCP/IP is the most popular because it is less chatty than the other common Layer 3 protocols, IPX and Appletalk. Most network administrators agree that if you have bandwidth to kill, you can add Internetwork Packet Exchange (IPX) and Appletalk, which like to scream "I'm here on the network" quite frequently—thereby eating up bandwidth. A few devices on the network won't use too much bandwidth; but as the number of network nodes increases, so does the number of broadcasts required to identify the nodes running those protocols on the network.

Users are usually the first to notice the problems of an over-utilized network. For example, the users' state-of-the-art Pentiums begin to perform poorly. Because many network administrators are fluent in operating systems and not the network, most don't realize that the problem may be due to the hundreds of computers on a flat topology that uses hub and bridges. In this type of environment, every data packet is sent to every node on the network; and every node on that segment of the network has to process every frame on the network.

The processors in each node handle this task, which takes away from the processing power needed for other tasks and application—thus causing a slowdown that the users discover and complain about. Most network administrators pass off this slowness as a problem with the PCs, and the most vital PCs are rebuilt or replaced. When the companies finally decide to upgrade to a switched network, they can typically do so over a weekend. When the network users leave on Friday, their high-powered Pentiums stacked with RAM have the speed of 386s. When they return Monday morning, nothing is more exciting than hearing comments all over the office about how their computers boot up more quickly and run so much faster, and how they like the faster network. But did the users get a faster network? In one sense, the network did get an upgrade; but this upgrade merely eliminated the problems of a flat topology network by segmenting the network into smaller collision and broadcast domains.

How did they do this? By replacing the hubs (which send data they receive out every single port, forcing every node attached to them to process the data whether the node is meant to receive the data or not) with switches. In terms of per-port costs, replacing your hubs with switches is a solution at a quarter of the cost of upgrading the network cabling. So, what segments the network? VLANs.

NOTE: *Sometimes, if you have a 10BaseT network with Category 3 or 4 cabling, the best solution is to fix the immediate problems by upgrading to Category 5 cabling and implementing a Fast Ethernet network in conjunction with installing switches. However, most network users do not need more than true 10Mbps from the Access layer switches to their desktops even if they are using high-bandwidth applications. After all, before they had switches, the users were getting along with only 3Mbps or 4Mbps on their 10Mbps link, due to broadcasts, collisions, and network utilization.*

Why Use VLANs?

VLANs are used to segment the network into smaller broadcast domains or segments. The primary reason to segment your network is to relieve network congestion and increase bandwidth. Segmentation is often necessary to satisfy the bandwidth requirements of a new application or a type of information the network needs to be able to support, such as multimedia or graphical design applications. Other times, you may need to segment the network due to the increased traffic on the segment or subnet.

Be careful not to oversegment. Placing each port in an individual VLAN is like placing a router to stop broadcasts between each individual VLAN. Routers are like bug poison—they kill broadcasts *dead*. Broadcasts can't escape through routers and they can't escape a VLAN, either. Each VLAN becomes its own individual broadcast domain. When a network node or workstation sends out an advertisement or broadcast to the other nodes on a segment, only the nodes assigned to the VLAN to which the node sending the broadcast is assigned will receive that broadcast.

Another definition of a VLAN is a logical grouping of network users and resources connected administratively to defined ports on a switch. By creating VLANs, you are able to create smaller broadcast domains within a switch by assigning different ports on the switch to different subnetworks. Ports assigned to a VLAN are treated like their own subnet or broadcast domain. As a result, frames broadcast are only switched between ports in the same VLAN at Layer 2.

Using virtual LANs, you're no longer confined to physical locations. VLANs can be organized by location, function, department, or even the application or protocol used, regardless of where the resources or users are located. In a flat network topology, your broadcast domain consists of all the interfaces in your segment or subnet. If no devices—such as switches or routers—divide your network, you have only one broadcast domain. On some switches, an almost limitless number of broadcast domains or VLANs can be configured.

VLAN Basics

Inter-Switch Link (ISL) protocol was designed to allow VLAN traffic to flow from one Cisco device to another. The protocol adds a header that uniquely identifies the source and destinations of the data as well as the VLAN the data is a member of. If data from one VLAN needs to be forwarded to another VLAN, it requires some type of Layer 3 routing.

Layer 3 routing can be provided by any number of modules known as *internal route processors*. The internal route processors available from Cisco for Cisco switches are the Route Switch Feature Card (RSFC), NetFlow Feature Card (NFFC), Multilayer Switch Feature Card (MSFC), Multilayer Switching Module (MSM), and Route Switch Module (RSM). Layer 3 routing for VLANs can also be provided by some Cisco routers that support ISL, such as the Cisco 4000 series and the Cisco 7000 series.

Spanning Tree Protocol (STP), which can be applied to each individual VLAN, keeps the network from forming bridging loops when a packet can reach a given destination multiple ways. This means you can provide multiple ways to get data from point A in your network to point B, thereby providing redundancy in case one link fails. STP blocks the redundant ports so only one path exists for data in the network.

VLANs allow you to use these links to load balance data. By assigning different VLANs to each link, data from one VLAN can use one link and another VLAN can use the second, redundant link. A VLAN would use the other link only during a link failure in the network; in this case the VLANs assigned to the lost link would converge and use the link that was still available.

A Properly Switched Network

Let's take a look at how a properly switched network should look. This network implements the switches using a hierarchical model, as shown in Figure 5.1. Notice that you don't need a high-speed link to every workstation in order to create an efficient network, even when using high-end applications such as graphical CAD applications. In the figure, you see 10Mbps links to each workstation, a Fast Ethernet trunk to the switch containing the servers, and 100Mbps links to each server. This way, the amount of bandwidth entering from the 10Mbps switch will not overwhelm all the server links, and you create an efficiently switched network without bottlenecks.

NOTE: Switching technology complements routing technology, and both have their place in the networks of today.

Using Layer 2 switches to create individual collision domain segments for each node residing on a switch port increases the number of nodes that can reside on an Ethernet segment. This increase means that larger networks can be built, and the number of

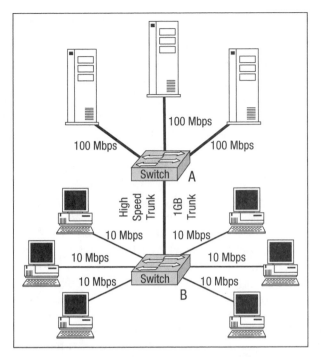

Figure 5.1   An example of a properly switched network.

users and devices will not overload the network with more broadcasts and packets than each device on the network can handle (and still maintain a consistent level of processing).

Broadcasts are used in each and every networking protocol. How often they occur depends upon the protocol, the applications running on the network, and how these network services are used.

To avoid the older, chatty protocols, older applications have been rewritten to reduce their bandwidth needs even though bandwidth availability to desktops has increased since the applications were written. New-generation applications utilizing multimedia—such as video conferencing, Voice Over IP, Web applications, multicast, and unicast—are bandwidth-greedy and like to consume all the bandwidth they can find.

When your company or organization tries to keep up with technology, you'll find that faulty equipment, inadequate segmentation, non-switched networks, and poorly designed networks each contribute to the problems of broadcast-intensive applications. To add insult to injury, protocol designers have found ways to propagate application data through the switched internetwork. Not only that, but by using applications from the Web that utilize unicast and multicast, you continue to receive constant broadcasts even between routers. The old rule—that a router stops broadcasts dead—doesn't work.

As an administrator, you must make sure the network is properly segmented, to keep problems on one segment from propagating through the internetwork; you must also create ways of killing the unwanted traffic. You can do so most effectively through a combination of switching and routing. Switches have become more cost effective, allowing many companies to replace their flat network hubs and bridges with a pure switched network utilizing VLANs. As mentioned earlier, all devices in a VLAN are members of the same broadcast domain and receive all broadcasts from members of the same VLAN. The broadcasts, by default, are filtered from all ports on a switch that are not members of the same VLAN.

Routers and switches that utilize internal route processors (such as RSMs) are used in conjunction with Access layer switches and provide connections between network segments or VLANs. If one VLAN wants to talk to another, the process must be routed at Layer 3. This arrangement effectively stops broadcasts from propagating through the entire internetwork.

Security is also a benefit of VLANs and switches. A flat Layer 2 network has almost no security. Users on every network device can see the conversations that take place between all users and devices on the network. Using certain software, not only can they see the network conversations, the users can alter the data and send it on to its destination; this action is referred to as a *man in the middle attack*. In a flat area network, you cannot stop devices from broadcasting and other devices from trying to respond to broadcasts. Your only security lies in the passwords assigned to your workstation or other devices on the network. Unfortunately, the passwords can only be used on the local machine, not on data traversing the network. Let's take a better look at how switches improve security in the network.

Switched Internetwork Security

In the previous paragraph, I described the network security issues in a flat internetwork that is implemented by connecting hubs and switches with routers. In this type of network, security is maintained by the router to disallow unwanted access—but anyone connecting to the physical network can easily gain access to the network resources on that physical LAN or network segment. An intrusion in your local network could easily happen when a person (even a somewhat educated employee) runs certain software (like that available in Windows NT) to analyze the network packets and obtain passwords and user information without the knowledge of the network administrators. To make matters worse, in a flat network, the intrusion can be done from any port—even at a user's desk. The user does not need access to the wiring closet to see all the traffic in that network.

By using switches and implementing VLANs, the switch takes care of making sure that data is sent directly from the port on the switch containing the source node, and that the data only exits out the port on which the destination node resides. The switch also makes sure that when a broadcast is received, only the ports assigned to the VLAN that the source port is a member of receive that broadcast.

This setup allows for a more secure network. In addition, network administrators now have more control over each port as well as the ability to deny the user based on the Layer 2 or Layer 3 address the user is using to access the port. Users no longer have the ability to just plug their workstation into any network port in the office and access network resources. The administrator controls each port and the resources the user may access.

The best way to design a switched network and implement VLANs is to either assign VLANs to ports based on the network resources a user requires or group them according to departments such as Engineering and Accounting. Switches can also be configured to inform a network management station of any unauthorized access to the network resources. If interVLAN communication needs to take place, a Layer 3 device such as a router is required, but it allows for restrictions to be placed on ports based on the hardware addresses, protocols, or applications.

Scaling with VLANs

A *switch block* consists of all the equipment found in the hierarchical network model. By taking multiple blocks and connecting them, you can create larger and larger networks. By connecting more blocks, you can create networks that are virtually unrestricted in how large they can become. The Access layer is the point in the network that connects servers, workstations, and other nodes to the network and then connects to the Distribution layer switches, which handle routing and security issues for VLAN distribution.

You need to understand many issues when configuring VLANs within a switch block. Let's look at the concerns you need to address in determining how you should design and scale your VLAN infrastructure. We've already discussed access to resources and group commonality; now let's take a look at the following:

- VLAN boundaries
- VLAN membership types
- Traffic patterns flowing through the network
- IP addressing used in the network
- Cisco's VLAN recommendations

VLAN Boundaries

VLANs can be broken into two different types of boundaries: local and end-to-end. A *local* VLAN is configured in one local geographical location. This type of VLAN is the most common and the least difficult to maintain in corporations with centralized server and mainframe blocks.

Local VLANs are designed around the fact that the business or corporation is using centralized resources, like a server farm. Users will spend most of their time utilizing these centralized resources, which are local to the users and not located on the other side of the router that connects their network to the outside world or other parts of the company.

Networks are becoming faster. Because this is the case, the Layer 3 devices in your network must be able to keep up with the number of packets being switched through the local network and out to the rest of the world. As the administrator, you must take into account the number of packets your network's Layer 3 devices must handle or implement multiple Layer 3 devices to handle load balancing.

An *end-to-end* VLAN spans the entire switch fabric from one end of the network to the other. With this type of VLAN boundary, all the switches in the network know about all the configured VLANs in the network. End-to-end VLANs are configured to allow membership based on a project, a department, or many other groupings.

One of the best features of end-to-end VLANs is that users can be placed in a VLAN regardless of their physical location. The VLAN the port becomes a member of is defined by an administrator and assigned by a VLAN Membership Policy Server (VMPS, discussed in the next section).

In this situation, the administrator must have very defined goals, and network planning must be more detailed so as to not create bottlenecks in the WAN. Your goal in defining an end-to-end VLAN solution must be centered around the 20/80 Rule: Maintain 20 percent of the network traffic as local, or within the VLAN, and design the WAN network to support speeds that will accommodate this use. (Just a few years ago, this rule was reversed—the administrators' goal was to keep all the servers local and to allow only 20 percent or less of the network traffic to extend outside the local network.)

NOTE: *The ISL protocol, IEEE 802.10, IEEE 802.1, and LAN Emulation (LANE) all provide ways of sending multiple VLAN data traffic over certain physical media types, adding tagging information to frames to send data through the network, and creating trunk ports that carry VLAN data. ATM and LANE are covered in Chapter 8. Virtual Trunking Protocol (VTP) is used to let switches know about the VLANs that have been configured in the network. We will cover all of these topics in the rest of this chapter.*

VLAN Membership Types

You can create two types of VLANs: static and dynamic. An administrator can configure the Access layer switches with a VLAN for each individual workgroup, and then assign each switch port to a particular VLAN. These are *static* VLANs; the port is assigned a VLAN number, and any device connecting to that port becomes a member of that VLAN by default.

A static VLAN is the most common and easiest in terms of administration. The switch port that you assign a VLAN association always remains in the VLAN you assign until you change the port assignment. Static VLAN configurations are easy to configure and monitor, and they work well in a network where the movement of users remains controlled. You can also use network management software such as CiscoWorks for Switched Internetworks (CWSI) to configure the ports on the switch.

A dynamic VLAN determines a node's VLAN assignment automatically using a VLAN Membership Policy Server (VMPS) service to set up a database of Media Access Control (MAC) addresses. This database can be used for dynamic addressing of VLANs. VMPS is a MAC-address-to-VLAN mapping database that contains allowable MAC or physical addresses that are mapped to a particular VLAN. When the user boots up, the switch learns the MAC address and checks the database for the appropriate VLAN assigned to that MAC address. This process allows a switch port to remain in the same VLAN throughout the network regardless of the location at which the node resides.

It takes a lot of network management to maintain the databases of MAC addresses. Therefore, these types of VLANs are not very effective in larger networks. You can use intelligent network management software to allow you to match a VLAN number to a hardware (MAC) address, protocol, or even application address to create dynamic VLANs.

Traffic Patterns Flowing through the Network

VLANs need to be configured for optimal use through the network. If your servers do not support trunk links, you don't want everyone outside the VLAN that the server resides in to have to route all the packets to and from a router or internal route processor. Therefore, you should place servers in the most optimal VLAN, to route the data traffic of as few VLANs as possible to and from the server. It doesn't make sense to place your server in one VLAN and the rest of your workstations in another.

Cisco's VLAN Recommendations

Cisco makes certain recommendations to ensure that the switch block performs as it should. The first recommendation is that the Core layer not contain any routing and filtering policies. VLANs should not be a part of the Core layer, with the exception of those being routed along the backbone through trunk links. So, VLANs should not extend past the Distribution layer switches for interVLAN routing.

Cisco also recommends a one-to-one ratio between VLANs and subnets. This means that you must understand how users are broken up by subnets. If you have 1,000 users in a building and 100 users are in each subnet, then you should have 10 VLANs.

VLAN Trunking

There are two types of VLAN links: a trunk link and an access link. An *access link* is part of only one VLAN, referred to as the *native* VLAN of the port. All the devices are attached to an access link, which connects your physical workstation to the network. Access link devices are totally unaware of a VLAN membership, or that a switched network exists at all. The devices only know that they are part of a broadcast domain. They have no understanding of the network they are attached to and don't need to know this information.

TIP: Remember, an access link device cannot communicate with devices outside of its VLAN or subnet without the use of a router or internal route processor.

Trunk links, on the other hand, can carry multiple VLANs. A *trunk link* is a link that carries all the VLANs in a network and tags each frame as it enters the trunk link and spans the network. You probably have heard this term used in telephone systems. The trunk link of a telephone system carries multiple telephone conversation and lines on a single cable. Trunk links that connect switches and carry VLANs to other switches, routers, or servers use the same theory.

When an administrator assigns a port to a VLAN, that port can be a member of only one VLAN. In order for VLANs to span multiple connected switches, a trunk link must be used. This link cannot be used to connect to the average Network Interface Card (NIC) found on the back of the PC.

Frame tagging is used when a frame travels between two devices that support a trunked link. Each switch that the frame reaches must be able to identify the VLAN the frame is a member of based on the tagging information, in order to determine what to do with the frame and how to apply it to the filtering table.

Because the trunk link uses frame tagging to identify which VLAN a frame belongs to, each device connecting to the trunk link must be able to interpret and read this VLAN tag. Intel has created some NICs for servers that understand the frame tagging involved with a trunk link. However, in most situations, this trunk link tagging is removed at the Access layer switch, and the destination address never knows that the frame it received was tagged with information to allow it to span the switch fabric.

What happens if the frame reaches a switch or router that has another trunk link? The device will simply forward the frame out of the proper trunk link port. Once the frame reaches a switch at the Access layer, the switch will remove the frame tagging. It does this because the end device needs to receive the frames without having to understand the VLAN tagging. Remember, the end device (such as a workstation) does not understand this frame tagging identification.

If you are using NetFlow switching hardware (discussed in Chapter 6) on your Cisco switches, it will allow devices on different VLANs to communicate after taking just the first packet through the router. The router will then send the correct routing information back to the NetFlow device. This process allows the router to be contacted only once to let VLAN frames be routed from port to port on a switch, rather than from port to router and back to the port for each frame.

Trunk Types

Trunk links are point-to-point, high-speed links from 100 to 1000Mbps. These trunked links between two switches, a switch and a router, or a switch and a server carry the traffic of up to 1,005 VLANs at any given time.

Four different methods or protocols allow you to track VLAN frames as they traverse the switch fabric:

- IEEE 802.10
- IEEE 802.1Q
- Inter-Switch Link (ISL)
- LAN Emulation (LANE)

IEEE 802.10

The IEEE 802.10 standard is used to send VLAN information over a Fiber Distributed Data Interface (FDDI) physical link. In this situation, ISL is disabled and IEEE 802.10 is used to forward the VLAN frames. The Clear Header on a FDDI frame contains a Security Association Identifier (SAID), a Link Service Access Point (LSAP), and the Management Defined Field (MDF). The SAID field in the frame header is used to identify the VLAN.

The 802.10 protocol is used primarily to transport VLAN information over FDDI, and you will only find it used on this type of physical media, primarily in FDDI backbones to transport VLAN information and data.

Cisco Standards

A *standard* is a basis that participating vendors use to maintain functionality and compatibility between different vendors' products on a network. For example, when you get a 100BaseT NIC from one vendor and you purchase a second card from another vendor, standards ensure that they will work with each other in your network.

With so many ideas for the implementation of virtual LANs, Cisco found it essential to set certain standards. Cisco chose to submit its standardization to the IEEE Internetworking Subcommittee.

Other standards have been created for VLANs by the Internet Engineering Task Force (IETF). Standards related to the use of Asynchronous Transfer Mode (ATM) and LANE have been designated by the ATM forum. This section will concentrate on the standards created by the IEEE, IETF, and ATM forum. The main focus will be on those standards created and submitted for standardization by Cisco to enhance VLANs in their route processors and other switching products.

Organizations install high-speed switched networks in order to create a network that can efficiently handle the growing demands of software and hardware applications. These installations can cause some unexpected problems in the network. Some of the standards discussed in this section relate to monitoring and managing VLAN networks and resources. This management enables organizations to reduce problems in their networks and to increase functionality and compatibility of different vendor products on the networks.

IEEE 802.1Q

IEEE 802.1Q is called the "Standard for Virtual Bridged Local Area Networks"; it was created by the IEEE as a standard method of frame tagging. It actually inserts a field into the frame to identify the VLAN, and it creates a method used for identifying VLANs over a trunk link. The IEEE 802.1Q standard calls for a frame tag identifier to identify VLANs in the frame header. This protocol calls for no encapsulation of the data, and is used in only Ethernet physical media.

As a frame enters the switch fabric, it is tagged with additional information regarding the VLAN properties. Just as in ISL (discussed next), the tag remains in the frame while it is forwarded from switch to switch; the tag is removed prior to exiting the access link to the destination interface. Unlike ISL, which uses an external tagging process, 802.1Q uses an internal tagging process by modifying the existing Ethernet frame itself. To both access links and trunk links, the frame looks like a standard Ethernet frame. This process remains completely transparent to the source interface and the destination interface.

Unlike ISL, IEEE 802.1Q is not a Cisco proprietary protocol. It can be used to carry the traffic of more than one subnet down a single cable, and it is compatible with devices that are not running the Cisco IOS. 802.1Q changes the frame header with a standard VLAN format, which allows multiple-vendor VLAN implementations. For example, a Bay Networks switch or a 3COM switch can work with a Cisco switch to pass VLAN information on a trunk link.

Inter-Switch Link (ISL) Protocol

Cisco created the ISL protocol, and therefore ISL is proprietary to Cisco devices. Several NIC cards from Intel and other companies support ISL trunking. If you need a non-proprietary VLAN protocol over Ethernet, you will need to use the 802.1Q protocol.

Along with being proprietary to Cisco switches, ISL is used for Fast Ethernet and Gigabit Ethernet trunk links only. ISL is a way of explicitly tagging VLAN information onto an Ethernet frame traversing the network through trunk links. This tagging information allows VLANs to be multiplexed over a trunk link through an external encapsulation method. By running ISL, you can interconnect multiple switches and still maintain VLAN information as traffic travels between switches on trunk links. Along with switches, you can also use ISL to create trunk links between two Cisco routers that support ISL, a switch and a router, and a switch and a server that has a NIC that supports ISL.

On a trunk port, each frame is tagged as it enters the switch. Once the frame is tagged with the appropriate VLAN information, it can go though multiple routers or switches without retagging the frame, which reduces latency. It is important to understand that ISL VLAN information is added to a frame only if the frame is forwarded out a port configured as a trunk link. The ISL encapsulation is removed from the frame if the frame is forwarded out an access link.

ISL is an external tagging process. The original frame is not altered; it is encapsulated within a new 26-byte ISL header. This tagging adds a new 4-byte frame check sequence (FCS) at the end of the frame, as shown in Figure 5.2.

Remember, only a Cisco device or an ISL-aware NIC is capable of interpreting frames with an ISL frame tag. By using ISL, the frame encapsulation means that the frame can violate the normal Ethernet maximum transmission unit size of 1,518 bytes.

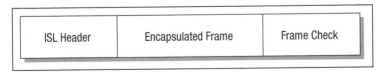

| ISL Header | Encapsulated Frame | Frame Check |

Figure 5.2   A typical ISL frame.

The ISL header, shown in Figure 5.3, is entered into the frame. The ISL header contains the following:

- *Destination address (DA)*—A 40-bit multicast address set to 01-00-0c-00-00. This address signals the receiver that this packet is in ISL format.

- *Frame type field*—Indicates the media type the frame is supporting. The possible options are 0000 for Ethernet, 0001 for Token Ring, 0010 for FDDI, and 0011 for ATM.

- *4-bit User field*—Identifies one of four possible priorities of the frame: XX00 for normal, XX01 for priority 1, XX02 for priority 2, and XX11 for the highest priority.

- *Source MAC address (SA)*—Set to the sending switch port's IEEE 802.3 MAC address. Some receiving devices ignore the SA field.

- *16-bit LEN field*—Shows the length of the packet in bytes minus the excluded fields. The excluded fields are the CRC, DA, Type, User, Source Address, and LEN field itself. The total of the excluded fields is 18 bytes. Therefore, the LEN field contains the total packet size minus 18 bytes from the excluded fields.

- *802.2 LLC header*—For ISL frames, this field is always set to AAAA03.

- *High bit of source address (HSA)*—The 3-byte manufacturer's portion of the SA field or vendor field of the source port's MAC address.

- *15-bit descriptor*—Used to distinguish the frame from other VLANs or colors. 10 bits are used to indicate the source port.

- *Bridge Protocol Data Units (BPDU) bit*—Used to indicate Spanning Tree Protocol (STP) or Cisco Discovery Protocol (CDP) topology information.

- *16-bit index value*—Used to indicate the port address. This index can be set to any value and may be used for diagnostic purposes only.

- *Reserved field*—Used only by FDDI and Token Ring. In Token Ring, the Frame Control (FC) and Token Ring AC bits (AC) fields are placed in the header. For FDDI, the FC is placed in the field. For Ethernet, the field includes all zeros.

DA	Media Type	Frame Priority	SA	Frame Length	AAAA03	HSA	VLAN	BPDU	Index	Reserve

Figure 5.3   The ISL header inserted into an ISL encapsulated packet.

LAN Emulation (LANE)

LANE is an IEEE standard for transporting VLANs over networks utilizing ATM. It uses no encapsulation or tagging. This process will be covered in detail in Chapter 8.

VLAN Trunking Protocol (VTP)

From the name of this protocol, you might think it is used to create trunk links. Sorry—the closest it gets to trunk links is sending its VTP information between switches by using a trunk port between the switches and routers. VTP was created by Cisco to manage and distribute VLAN configuration information across a switched internetwork. When you configure VTP on all of your switches and assign them to the same VTP domain name, you can merely configure one switch to make changes on all the switches—the changes will be propagated to all the other switches in the network. Not only can you add VLANs, but you can delete and rename VLANs as well; the new configuration will be propagated to all the switches.

VTP maintains consistent VLAN configurations throughout the network by propagating the VLAN mapping scheme of the VTP domain across the network using many different physical media types. VTP provides for plug-and-play–type connections when you add additional VLANs. It also provides tracking, monitoring, and reporting of VLANs in the network.

In order to allow VTP to manage your VLANs across the switched internetwork, you must first designate one or more of your Cisco switches as a VTP server. All the VTP servers that need to share VLAN information must use the same domain name, and a switch can only be a member of one VTP domain. A switch configured as a server can only share VTP configuration information with switches configured as members of the same VTP domain.

VTP is used to avoid situations in which security violations occur when VLANs cross-connect and thus produce duplicate names on the network. This duplication results in a disconnection, particularly when VLANs are connected from one physical media type to another.

On Cisco Catalyst switches, the default configuration places VTP in non-secure mode. This allows other switches in the network to join the VTP domain at will and either use the domain's configuration information or make changes to the configuration. To ensure that other switches do not join your domain without your knowledge, and to avoid security violations that can occur when inconsistent VLAN configurations reside on the network (caused when VLANs cross-connect using duplicate names on the network), you need to configure a secure mode password for your VTP management domain. The management domain name can be up to 32 characters long. You must also provide a password to place the switches in secure mode; the password can be from 8 to 64 characters long.

NOTE: *A switch can be a member of only one VTP management domain. All the switches in the domain must share the same VTP domain name.*

VTP Versions

VTP comes in two versions: version 1 and version 2. The primary differences between the two version are few, but they are significant enough to render the two versions incompatible. The two versions will not work together in the same network. Version 1 is the default on Cisco Catalyst switches and supports Ethernet media. Version 2 provides the following additional features beyond support for Ethernet:

- Consistency checks
- Token Ring support
- Transparent mode change support
- Unrecognized Type Length Value support

If all the switches in the network support VTP version 2, then only one switch needs to have version 2 enabled to enable version 2 on all other switches.

Consistency Checks

Consistency checks are performed when new information is entered by an administrator through the command line interface (CLI) or through Simple Network Management Protocol (SNMP). Normally, no consistency checks are performed when information for each switch is obtained through a VTP advertising message or read from nonvolatile RAM (NVRAM). If information is received by an advertisement or read from NVRAM, a switch will check the MD5 digest on a VTP message; only if it is incorrect will a consistency check be made.

Token Ring Support

Token-Ring support is provided only in VTP version 2. This support includes Token Ring LAN switching and VLANs.

Transparent Mode Change Support

In transparent mode, switches will only forward messages and advertisements; the switches will not add any new information received to its own database. Version 1 allows switches to check the domain name and version before forwarding. Version 2 allows switches to forward VTP messages and advertisements without checking the version number.

Unrecognized Type Length Value

If a VTP advertisement is received and has an unrecognized type length value (TLV), the version 2 VTP switches will still propagate the changes through their trunk links. A VTP server or client propagates its configuration changes to the configured trunk links, even for TLVs it is not able to parse. The unrecognized TLV is then saved in NVRAM.

VTP Advertisements

Switches in a VTP management domain share VLAN information through VTP advertisement messages. There are three types of advertisement messages:

- *Advertisement request*—Occurs when clients request VLAN information for the current network. A VTP sends these types of advertisements in response to requests with the appropriate summary and subset advertisements. The advertisement frame includes a version field, code field, reserved field, management domain name field (up to 32 bytes), and start value field.

- *Summary advertisement*—Sent automatically every 5 minutes (300 seconds) to all the switches on the network. A summary advertisement can also be sent when a topology change occurs on the network, such as a switch drop or addition. The summary advertisement frame contains the version field, the code field, a followers field, a management domain name field, a configuration revision number field, the updater's identity, the updater's timestamp, and the MD5 digest field.

- *Subset advertisement*—Contains very detailed information about the network, including the version, code, sequence number, management domain name, configuration revision number, and VLAN information fields.

VTP advertisements can contain the following information:

- *802.10 SAID values*—For FDDI physical media.

- *Configuration revision number*—The higher the number, the more updated the information.

- *Emulated LAN names*—Used for ATM LANE.

- *Frame format*—Information about the format and content of the frame.

- *Management domain name*—The name of the VTP management domain. If the switch is configured for one name and receives a frame with another name, the information is ignored.

- *MD5 digest*—Used when a password is used throughout the domain. The key must match the key on the given destination or the update information is ignored.

- *Updater identity*—The identity of the switch that forwarded the summary advertisement to the switch.

- *VLAN configuration*—Includes known VLAN information, specific parameters, and a maximum transmission unit (MTU) size for each VLAN in the VTP management domain.

- *VLAN identification*—The ISL or 802.1Q information.

The advertisement frames are sent to a multicast address so all the VTP devices in the same management domain can receive the frames. The frames are not forwarded using normal bridging controls. All VTP management domain clients and servers update their databases on all deletions and additions on the network. Therefore, only the VTP client operating in server mode needs to be updated with the deleted or additional VLAN to allow all the members of the VTP management domain to update their databases.

There are two types of VTP management domain advertisements:

- Server originating advertisements

- Request advertisements from clients needing VLAN information upon power cycling or bootup

Each advertisement has a revision number. The revision number is one of the most important parts of the VTP advertisement. As a VTP database is modified, the VTP server increments the revision number by one. The VTP server then advertises this information from its own database to other switches with the newly updated revision number.

When VTP switches receive an advertisement that has a higher revision number, the switches will overwrite the current database information stored in NVRAM with the new database information being advertised. If it receives a lower revision number, the switch believes it has newer information and disregards the received advertisement.

Can the VTP Revision Number on a New VTP Server Be a Problem?

When a new VTP revision number is sent throughout the VTP domain, the switches believe the highest revision number has the most up-to-date information about all the VLANs. So, when switches detect the additional VLANs within a VTP advertisement, they process the information received as authentic information.

What happens when a new switch is configured as a server and the revision number is higher than the current revision number used in the domain? Oops! If the rest of the domain gets that information, it reconfigures every single member with the configuration on that new switch. This event could create a disaster on your network. Unfortunately, any time a switch sees a higher revision number, it takes the information it just received, considers it more current, and overwrites the existing database with the new configuration information, even if this clears the VLAN information.

Many network administrators make the mistake of using the **clear config all** command, believing that it will erase the current revision number. Doing so is a bad mistake on the network administrator's part. This command doesn't do what it says it does—it doesn't really "clear all." VTP has its own NVRAM, so the VTP information as well as the revision number will still be present if you perform the clear config all command. You can take care of this problem two ways. The easiest way is to cycle the power on the switch after placing the switch in client mode. The switch must be in client mode because the switch will store VTP information in special NVRAM when the server is in server mode. As a result, merely powering down the switch will not reset the revision number or cause the switch to lose its VTP database.

The other way is to make the switch a client, connect it to the network to get new revisions, and then configure the switch as a VTP server.

Each time a server sends out an updated advertisement, it increases the revision number by one. If a client switch receives two advertisements simultaneously, it knows which one to use by selecting the advertisement with the highest revision number.

VTP Switch Modes

Three switch modes can be configured on a switch that will be used to participate in a VTP domain. The three switching modes are as follows:

- Client mode
- Server mode
- Transparent mode

Client Mode

Client mode allows the switch to have the same functions as server mode, with the exception that it cannot change any VLAN information. A switch in client mode cannot create, modify, or delete VLANs on any VTP client or switch except when it receives an advertisement from a switch operating in server mode. It can, however, advertise its own VLAN configuration, synchronize the VLAN information with other switches on the network, specify VTP configuration information such as VTP version, and participate in VTP pruning. Client mode switches receive their information from other VTP servers in the VTP management domain. In this mode, the global VLAN information is lost when the switch power is cycled.

VTP Pruning

VLAN Trunk Protocol pruning is used to increase network bandwidth by reducing VLAN traffic across switch trunk links. VTP pruning filters network traffic such as broadcasts, multicasts, and unicasts on trunk links that connect switches that contain no VLAN ports in the particular VLAN the data is destined for.

When VTP pruning is enabled on a VTP server, the information is propagated to all other client and server mode switches in the VTP management domain. This step automatically enables VTP pruning on these switches. By default, VLANs 2 through 1,000 are eligible for VTP pruning, and VLAN 1 is always ineligible. VTP pruning usually takes several seconds to propagate to the other VTP management domain clients after it is enabled or the switch power is cycled.

Server Mode

Server mode, which is configured by default, allows you to create, modify, and delete VLANs for the management domain. Configuration changes are then sent to all other participating members of the VTP domain. At least one VTP server should exist in the VTP management domain. Two or more switches can be configured as servers for redundancy. When a server's power is cycled, the switch configured as a server maintains its global VLAN information.

Transparent Mode

Transparent mode allows VTP switches to be configured to not accept VTP information and to merely forward advertisements the switch receives to other switches participating in the VTP domain. Even though switches configured for transparent mode will still send VTP information and advertisements, they will not update their databases or send out information on VLAN or topology changes. In this mode, switches do not participate in any VTP functions, such as sending VTP advertisements or synchronizing VLAN information. VTP version 2 does allow a switch operating in transparent mode to forward the advertisements it receives out any configured trunk ports, thus allowing other switches participating in VTP to obtain the advertisements.

Methods for VLAN Identification

To logically identify which packets belong to which VLAN or VLAN group, Cisco Catalyst switches support many trunking protocols to put a header on frames. The headers identify the VLAN associated with the frame; each switch in the switch block removes the header before the frame exits the access link port or ports belonging to the identified VLAN.

Dynamic Trunking Protocol

The Dynamic Trunking Protocol (DTP) is another way of allowing trunk links to carry VLAN tagged frames across multiple switches or routers. DTP manages trunk negotiation in the Catalyst Supervisor Engine software releases 4.2 and later.

With previous versions of the Catalyst Supervisor Engine software, trunk negotiation was managed by the Dynamic Inter-Switch Link (DISL) protocol. Version 4.1 of the Catalyst Supervisor Engine software allows DISL auto-negotiation of ISL trunks only. In this version, you can manually configure DISL to auto-negotiate IEEE 802.1Q trunks.

In versions 4.2 and later, DTP supports and manages IEEE 802.1Q and ISL trunk links.

WARNING! If you have non-DTP–compatible networking devices on the network, you might want to disable this feature because non-DTP internetworking devices forward DTP frames improperly. When you disable DTP, the link still can become a trunk, but DTP frames will no longer be generated.

InterVLAN Routing

Access layer switches occupy the same place in the network as hubs. However, unlike hubs operating at Layer 1, switches examine the frames at Layer 2 and try to process the frames. A hub simply repeats the data to every single port, whereas a switch filters the data and forwards it directly to the destination port if the destination does not require routing. If data arrives on a port assigned to a VLAN and the destination is unknown, the switch repeats the signal only to the port or ports assigned to the VLAN, except for the port of arrival.

The switch also has the ability to regenerate packets, enabling the data to be forwarded even greater distances than a simple hub can achieve. This ability enables a switch to take the place of another device, called a repeater. A *repeater* is a device dedicated only to data regeneration. Repeaters allow data to be forwarded over greater distances, allowing the data to overcome regular data distance limitations for the type of physical media being used.

By filtering frames and regenerating forwarded frames and packets, the switch can split the network into many separate collision domains. This splitting allows for greater distances, dramatically lower collision rates, and higher numbers of nodes on the network. Each VLAN in the network is its own broadcast domain, and each port is its own collision domain. In a shared or flat network, every node is part of the same collision and broadcast domain.

Switches do not have the ability to forward frames based on Layer 3 addresses or the ability to forward data from one VLAN to another. A switch must forward these frames to a Layer 3 device for a routing decision. This device can be an external or internal route processor. An external route processor is your typical router. An internal router processor is considered a "router on a stick"; it is a module inside of the switch, but the switch must access it remotely to make forwarding decisions. Let's take a look at an internal route processor.

Internal Route Processors

When a switch receives a packet from a port on one VLAN destined for the port of another VLAN, the switch must find a path on which to send the frame. Switches work at Layer 2 and are designed to isolate traffic to collision domains or subnets; they cannot by default forward data from one VLAN to another VLAN or network without some other Layer 3 devices. The Layer 2 device known as a "router on a stick" is used to route the data and create routing tables of other networks and devices.

Route processors can be used to route data between foreign VLANs and other logically segmented parts of the network, such as subnets. They also route data to remote WAN segments, networks, or the Internet.

Quite a few types of route processors are available for Catalyst switches. They include:

- Route Switch Module (RSM)
- Route Switch Feature Card (RSFC)
- Multilayer Switch Module (MSM)
- Multilayer Switch Feature Card (MSFC)

NOTE: *InterVLAN routing using RSM, RSFC, MSM, and MSFC will be covered in Chapter 6.*

How InterVLAN Routing Works

Layer 3 routing takes place between VLANs. This can become a challenging problem for an administrator to overcome. As you already learned, there are two types of route processors: external and internal. An external route processor uses an external router (such as the Cisco devices you are familiar with) to route data from one VLAN to another VLAN. An internal route processor uses internal modules and cards located inside the switch route data between VLANs.

Each type of Layer 3 routable protocol that does not have to be IP can have its own mapping for a VLAN. In an IP network, each subnetwork is mapped to an individual VLAN. In an IPX network, each VLAN is mapped to the IPX network number. With AppleTalk, a cable range and AppleTalk zone name are associated with each VLAN.

By configuring VLANs, you control the size of your broadcast domains and keep local traffic local. However, when an end station in one VLAN needs to communicate with an end station in another VLAN, this communication is supported by interVLAN routing. You configure one or more routers to route traffic to the appropriate destination VLAN.

Figure 5.4 shows Switch 1 handling traffic for a PC in VLAN 1 and Switch 2 handing traffic for VLAN 2. The router has an ISL-configured interface connecting both switches.

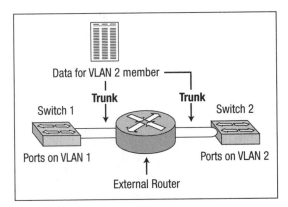

Figure 5.4   An example of an external router routing interVLAN traffic.

Immediate Solutions

Configuring a Static VLAN on a Catalyst 5000 Series Switch

The Cisco Catalyst 2900G series, 5000 family, and 6000 family of switches use the Cisco Set/Clear-based CLI. It is important to understand the difference between the Catalyst 5000 series VLAN configuration and the Enterprise IOS edition that runs on the other series of Cisco switches, which use an IOS-based VLAN configuration.

The command used to configure a VLAN on a Catalyst 5000 switch is as follows:

```
set vlan [vlan number] [slot/port(s)]
```

By default, all VLANs are in VLAN 1. Let's place the module in slot 2 with a port number of 3 in VLAN 2:

```
Catalyst5002> (enable) set vlan 2 2/3
VLAN 3 modified.
VLAN 1 modified.
VLAN  Mod/Ports
----  ---------------------
2     2/3
```

You should notice that although only one port was placed in VLAN 3, the port was in VLAN 1 to begin with, so both VLANs are updated.

Configuring Multiple VLANs on a Catalyst 5000 Series Switch

You can configure multiple consecutive ports on a module at one time. You do this by using the same command as in the previous section (**set vlan**) but identifying the beginning and ending port numbers, separated by a hyphen:

```
Catalyst5002> (enable) set vlan 2 2/1-3
VLAN 3 modified.
```

```
VLAN 2 modified.
VLAN 1 modified.
VLAN  Mod/Ports
----  ---------------------
2     2/1-3
```

TIP: *The **set vlan** command allows you create both the VLAN and the ports assigned to the VLAN at the same time.*

Creating VLANs on a Catalyst 1900EN Series

When you first turn on the Cisco 1912 or 1924EN series switch, you will see a screen asking you to choose an interface. Choose K from the initial user interface menu to get into IOS configuration:

```
1 user(s) now active on Management Console.

        User Interface Menu

    [M] Menus
    [K] Command Line
    [I] IP Configuration

Enter Selection:   K
```

Once a CLI session on the switch is open, you must create a VLAN number and name. The command used to do this is as follows:

```
vlan [vlan#] name [vlan name] command
```

To use this command, you must be in Global Configuration mode on the switch. To enter Global Configuration mode and create VLANs, take a look at the following example:

```
>enable
#config terminal
Enter configuration commands, one per line.   End with CNTL/Z
1912EN(config)#vlan 2 name sales
1912EN(config)#vlan 3 name marketing
1912EN(config)#exit
```

WARNING! *A created VLAN is unused until it is assigned to a switch port or ports. By default, all ports remain in VLAN 1 until the port is assigned to another VLAN.*

Assigning a Static VLAN to an Interface on a 1900EN Series

You can assign each port on an interface to a VLAN by using the **vlan-membership** command. Unlike the Set/Clear interface, which allows you to assign and configure a VLAN to multiple ports with one command, you must configure VLANs port by port on the 1900EN series. To configure VLANs on the 1900EN series, follow these steps:

1. First you need to enter Interface Configuration mode, as shown here:

```
1912EN#config terminal
Enter configuration commands, one per line.  End with CNTL/Z
1912EN(config)#interface e0/2
```

2. Next, you need to issue the **vlan-membership** command. There are two options for this command:

   - **dynamic**—Allows the port to be set to a specific MAC address based on the MAC address of the end user.

   - **static**—The port number you as the administrator selects will remain the same regardless of the MAC address used by the end user of that port.

3. In the following examples we will be using static VLANs. To see how many VLANs are available to assign to an interface, use the following command:

```
1912EN(config-if)#vlan-membership static ?
  <1-1005>  ISL VLAN index
```

4. Next, take the VLANs created in the previous two steps and assign them to Ethernet ports 4 and 5. You can only assign one VLAN per port, as shown here:

```
1912EN(config-if)#vlan-membership static 2
1912EN(config-if)#interface e0/4
1912EN(config-if)#vlan-membership static 3
1912EN(config-if)#interface e0/5
```

Viewing the VLAN Configuration on a 1900 Series

Now that we have created the VLANs we want, we can use the **show vlan** command to see the configured VLANs. Notice that all unconfigured ports on the switch are in VLAN 1. The command is used from the Privileged mode prompt, as follows:

```
1912#show vlan
```

The results are shown here:

```
VLAN Name               Status    Ports
----------------------------------------
1    default            Enabled   1, 3, 6-12, AUI, A, B
2    sales              Enabled   2
3    marketing          Enabled   4
1002 fddi-default       Suspended
1003 token-ring-defau   Suspended
1004 fddinet-default    Suspended
1005 trnet-default      Suspended
----------------------------------------


VLAN Type           SAID    MTU  Parent RingNo BridgeNo Stp  Trans1 Trans2
--------------------------------------------------------------------------
1    Ethernet       100001 1500  0      0      0        Unkn 1002   1003
2    Ethernet       100002 1500  0      1      1        Unkn 0      0
3    Ethernet       100003 1500  0      1      1        Unkn 0      0
1002 FDDI           101002 1500  0      0      0        Unkn 1      1003
1003 Token-Ring     101003 1500  1005   1      0        Unkn 1      1002
1004 FDDI-Net       101004 1500  0      0      1        IEEE 0      0
1005 Token-Ring-Net 101005 1500  0      0      1        IEEE 0      0
--------------------------------------------------------------------------
```

Viewing an Individual VLAN Configuration on a 1900 Series

To view an individual VLAN on a 1900EN series switch, you use the **show vlan** command followed by the VLAN number, as shown here:

```
1912#show vlan 2

VLAN Name              Status     Ports
-------------------------------------
3    sales             Enabled    4
-------------------------------------


VLAN Type            SAID   MTU   Parent RingNo BridgeNo Stp  Trans1
Trans2
-------------------------------------------------------------------
3    Ethernet        100002 1500  0      1      1        Unkn 0      0
-------------------------------------------------------------------

1912#
```

Configuring a Trunk Port on a Cisco 5000 Series

To configure a trunk on a 5000 series switch, you use the **set trunk** command. You can see the command and its syntaxes by typing "set trunk ?":

```
5000> (enable) set trunk ?
Usage: set trunk <mod_num/port_num> [on|off|desirable|auto|nonegotiate]
       [vlans] [trunk_type]
(vlans = 1..1005 An example of vlans is 2-10,1005)
(trunk_type = isl,dot1q,dot10,lane,negotiate)
```

The different port negotiation types are described in Table 5.1, and the different trunk encapsulation types are described in Table 5.2.

Let's set port 2/1 as a trunk link using ISL with the following command:

```
5000> (enable) set trunk 2/1 on isl
Port(s) 2/1 trunk mode set to on.
Port(s) 2/1 trunk type set to isl.
5000> (enable) 2000 Dec 21 05:12:01 %DTP-5-TRUNKPORTON:Port 2/1 has
    become trunked.
```

Table 5.1   Port negotiation syntaxes for configuring VLAN trunks.

Variable	Description
auto	This trunking mode is used if the port uses DISL to initiate trunking. This is the default mode for Fast Ethernet and mimics plug-and-play. You cannot configure a trunk when both ends' switch ports are configured for **auto** mode. One switch must be set to **on** or **desirable** mode.
desirable	This trunking mode, if using DISL, actively tries to configure itself as a trunk link. The other end of the trunk link must be configured to **on** or **desirable** to complete the trunk initiation.
off	This option disables the port from becoming a trunk. It is typically used when the device on the other end does not support ISL or IEEE 802.1Q. The port on the other end might be a 10Mbps Ether port or FDDI interface.
on	This option basically makes the port a trunk port, whether the other end is configured to be or cannot become a trunk. Use this option when the port on the other end does not understand DTP, such as a third-party adapter.
nonegotiate	Use this option when DISL negotiation that takes place on ISL trunks is not supported. When using **dot1q** as the final parameter, this option tells the switch that ISL will not be used for trunking the ports.

Table 5.2   Encapsulation type syntaxes that can be used when configuring VLAN trunk links.

Variable	Description
isl	Applies the ISL protocol encapsulation to an Ethernet trunk.
dot1q	Used for Ethernet trunks using the IEEE 802.1Q standard.
dot10	Used when assigning a FDDI trunk link to the port.
lane	Used when applying ATM to a trunk link port.
negotiate	Puts the port into permanent trunking mode. This option disallows the port from generating DTP frames. Typically, this command is used with switch-to-router trunks.

Mapping VLANs to a Trunk Port

In the last example, we assigned port 2/1 as a trunk port using ISL encapsulation. Notice that we did not specify the VLANs to trunk. By default, all VLANs would be trunked. You can assign only VLANs 1 through 200 to be trunked across this configured trunk link, as shown here:

```
Console> (enable) set trunk 2/1 on 1-200 isl
Adding vlans 1-1005 to allowed list.
Please use the 'clear trunk' command to remove vlans from allowed list.
Port(s) 2/1 allowed vlans modified to 1-1005.
Port(s) 2/1 trunk mode set to on.
Port(s) 2/1 trunk type set to isl.
```

Configuring a Trunk Port on a Cisco 1900EN Series

To configure a trunk on a 1900EN series switch, you use the **trunk** command. The 1900 switch has the same port negotiation options as the 5000 series, but only runs the DISL encapsulation method. You can see the syntaxes available for configuring a 1900EN series switch by using the **trunk** option from Interface Configuration mode:

```
1912(config)#int f0/26
1912(config-if)#trunk ?
   auto         Set DISL state to AUTO
   desirable    Set DISL state to DESIRABLE
   nonegotiate  Set DISL state to NONEGOTIATE
   off          Set DISL state to OFF
   on           Set DISL state to ON
```

trunk is the only command needed to trunk a port once you are in Interface Configuration mode for the port that needs to be trunked. You can set the trunked port to always be a trunk link, using the following command:

```
1900EN(config-if)#trunk on
```

Clearing VLANs from Trunk Links on a Cisco 5000 Series

All VLANs are configured on a trunk by default. They remain configured unless cleared by an administrator. If you want a trunk link not to carry certain VLAN information—perhaps because you want to stop broadcasts on a certain VLAN from traversing the trunk link, or you want to stop topology change information from being sent across a link where a VLAN is not supported—use the **clear trunk** command:

```
5000> (enable) clear trunk 2/1 4-1005
Removing Vlan(s) 4-1005 from allowed list.
```

Clearing VLANs from Trunk Links on a Cisco 1900EN Series

To remove VLANs from a trunk port on a 1900, use the **no trunk-vlan** command in Interface Configuration mode. First, to view the possible options for the command, use the following:

```
1912(config-if)#no trunk-vlan ?
  <1-1005>  ISL VLAN index
```

To remove VLAN 2 from a trunked port use the following command:

```
1912(config-if)#no trunk-vlan 2
1912(config-if)#
```

NOTE: *No command is available to clear more then one VLAN at a time on the 1900.*

Verifying a Trunk Link Configuration on a 5000 Series

To verify your trunk ports on a Catalyst 5000 series, use the **show trunk** command as follows:

```
Console> (enable) show trunk 2/1
```

The following shows the results:

```
Port     Mode        Encapsulation Status        Native vlan
-------- ----------- ------------- ------------  ----------
2/1      on          isl           trunking      1

Port     Vlans allowed on trunk
-------- -------------------------------------------------------------
2/1      1-3
```

```
Port      Vlans allowed and active in management domain
--------  ------------------------------------------------------------
 2/1      1

Port      Vlans in spanning tree forwarding state and not pruned
--------  ------------------------------------------------------------
 2/1      1
Console> (enable)
```

Verifying a Trunk Link Configuration on a 1900EN Series

The 1900EN series uses the **show trunk** command just as the 5000 series does, but can view only the two Fast Ethernet ports 26 and 27. The IOS on the 1900EN identifies these ports as Port A and Port B. To verify the trunk link configuration, do the following:

1. First, look at the syntaxes available for the **show trunk** command:

```
1912#show trunk ?
  A   Trunk A
  B   Trunk B
```

2. Now, look at the syntaxes available for the Fast Ethernet port 26, which is identified by an "a":

```
1912#sh trunk a ?
  allowed-vlans   Display allowed vlans
  joined-vlans    Display joined vlans
  joining-vlans   Display joining vlans
  prune-eligible  Display pruning eligible vlans
```

Configuring the VTP Version on a Catalyst 5000 Switch

To configure VTP version 2, use the **set vtp v2 enable** command. Let's look at an example:

```
5000> (enable) set vtp v2 enable
This command will enable the version 2 function in the entire
 management domain.
```

```
All devices in the management domain should be version2-capable
 before enabling.
Do you want to continue (y/n) [n]? y
VTP domain  modified
5000> (enable)
```

Configuring a VTP Domain on a Catalyst 1900 Switch

The 1900EN series switches only use VTP version 1. The switch can be a member of only one VTP domain. To set the switch to the Coriolis domain, use the following command:

```
1912(config)# vtp domain coriolis
```

Setting a VTP Domain Password on a Catalyst Switch

To set the VTP domain password to 1234 on a Catalyst 1900, use the following command:

```
1912(config)# vtp password 1234
```

Configuring a Catalyst 1900 Switch as a VTP Server

The 1900EN series switches only use VTP version 1. No configuration options exist for VTP versions. To set the switch as a VTP server for the domain use the following command:

```
1912(config)# vtp server
```

Configuring a Catalyst 1900 Switch as a VTP Client

To configure the switch as a VTP client use the following command:

```
1912(config)# vtp client
```

Configuring a Catalyst 1900 Switch for Transparent Mode

To configure the switch to operate in transparent mode, use the following command:

```
1912(config)# vtp transparent
```

Configuring VTP Pruning on a Catalyst 1900 Switch

To configure the switch for VTP pruning, use the following command:

```
1912(config)# vtp pruning
```

Configuring VTP on a Set/Clear CLI Switch

Before you can configure a router or internal route processor for interVLAN routing, you must enable VTP, assign a mode, and configure a domain.

1. You enable and configure VTP and VLANs on the switch in Privileged mode. To enable VTP and specify a VTP mode, use the **set vtp mode {client | server | transparent}** command, as follows:

```
5002> (enable) set vtp mode server
VTP domain modified
```

2. If you set the mode to **client** or **server**, then you need to set the VTP domain name and password on the first switch. The VTP name can be up to 32 characters long. The password is a minimum of 8 characters with a maximum of 64. For our example, we set the mode to **server**. The following shows the available syntaxes for the **set vtp domain** option:

```
5002> (enable) set vtp domain ?
Usage: set vtp [domain <name>] [mode <mode>] [passwd <passwd>]
               [pruning <enable|disable>] [v2 <enable|disable>
          (mode = client|server|transparent)
           Use passwd '0' to clear vtp password)
```

```
Usage: set vtp pruneeligible <vlans>
       (vlans = 2..1000
         An example of vlans is 2-10,1000)
```

You must configure a VTP domain name if you choose to configure the switch as a VTP client or server. To do so, use the **set vtp domain *name*** command, as follows:

```
5002> (enable) set vtp domain Coriolis
VTP domain Coriolis modified
```

3. Set the password to "pass1" for the VTP domain with the following command:

```
5002> (Enable) set vtp passwd pass1
```

Configuring VTP on a 1900 Cisco IOS CLI Switch

The 1900 switch does not require you to set the VTP password, just the domain name. The following shows the options available for the **vtp domain** command:

```
1900EN(config)#vtp domain ?
  WORD  Name of the VTP management domain
1900EN(config)#vtp domain Coriolis ?
  client       VTP client
  pruning      VTP pruning
  server       VTP server
  transparent  VTP transparent
  trap         VTP trap
```

Here is an example of setting the domain to "Coriolis" on the 1912EN:

```
1900EN(config)#vtp domain Coriolis
1900EN(config)#
```

To set a VTP domain password on a 1900EN to "pass1" use the following command:

```
1900EN(config)# vtp password pass1
1900EN(config)#
```

Verifying the VTP Configuration on a Set/Clear CLI

To verify the VTP domain information, use the command **show vtp domain**. This command will show you the domain name, mode, and pruning information:

```
5002> (enable) show vtp domain
Domain Name            Domain Index VTP Version  Local Mode  Password
------------------     ----------   ----------   ----------  ----------
Coriolis               1            2            server      -
Vlan-count Max-vlan-storage Config Revision Notifications
---------- ---------------- -------------- ------------
2          1023             1              disabled


Last Updater     V2 Mode  Pruning   PruneEligible on Vlans
--------------   -------- --------   ----------------------
130.10.10.14     enabled  disabled  2-1000
Console> (enable)
```

WARNING! *You cannot use the show vtp domain command on a 1900. You should use the show vtp statistics command instead.*

Displaying VTP Statistics

The **show vtp statistics** command shows a summary of the VTP advertisement messages that have been sent and received, as well as errors. The command is the same on the Set/Clear and Cisco CLI switches.

```
5002> (enable) show vtp statistics
VTP statistics:
summary advts received         0
subset  advts received         0
request advts received         0
summary advts transmitted      5
subset  advts transmitted      2
request advts transmitted      0
No of config revision errors   0
No of config digest errors     0
```

```
VTP pruning statistics:
Trunk      Join Transmitted  Join Received  Summary advts received from
                                            non-pruning-capable device
--------   ----------------  -------------  --------------------------
 2/12      0                 0              0
5000> (enable)


1912EN#sh vtp stat
            Receive Statistics                    Transmit Statistics
-----------------------------------    -------------------------------
Summary Adverts                    0    Summary Adverts               0
Subset Adverts                     0    Subset Adverts                0
Advert Requests                    0    Advert Requests              56
Configuration Errors:
  Revision Errors                  0
  Digest Errors                    0
VTP Pruning Statistics:
Port    Join Received   Join Transmitted   Summary Adverts received
                                           with no pruning support
----    -------------   ----------------   ------------------------
A       0               0                  0
B       0               0                  0
1912#
```

Configuring VTP Pruning on a Set/Clear CLI Switch

Enabling pruning on a VTP server enables pruning for the entire domain, which is by default VLANs 2 through 1005. VLAN 1 can never prune.

Before you can set a VLAN to be eligible for VTP pruning, you should go to the switch to see what the available syntaxes are for the command:

```
5002> (enable) set vtp pruneeligible ?
Usage: set vtp [domain <name>] [mode <mode>] [passwd <passwd>]
   [pruning <enable|disable>] [v2 <enable|disable>
         (mode = client|server|transparent
         Use passwd '0' to clear vtp password)
         Usage: set vtp pruneeligible <vlans>
         (vlans = 2..1000 An example of vlans is 2-10,1000)
```

Now, let's set VLAN 2 to become eligible for VTP pruning so switches that do not use VLAN 2 will not receive VLAN 2's broadcast traffic on their trunk links:

```
5002> (enable) set vtp pruneeligible 2
Vlans 2-1000 eligible for pruning on this device.
VTP domain Coriolis modified.
```

Disabling Pruning for Unwanted VLANs

To disable pruning for VLANs that are not used or that you do not wish to prune, use the following command:

```
5002> (enable) clear vtp pruneeligible 3-1005
Vlans 1,3-1005 will not be pruned on this device.
VTP domain Globalnet modified.
5002> (enable)
```

Configuring IP InterVLAN Routing on an External Cisco Router

In order to understand this section, you should be familiar with Cisco IOS software running on Cisco routers. In this demonstration, we will configure a Cisco 7505:

1. To enable IP routing on the router, enter Global Configuration mode and use the **ip routing** command:

```
7505#configure terminal
Enter configuration commands, one per line.  End with CNTL/Z.
7505 (config)#ip routing
```

2. Specify an IP routing protocol such as Open Shortest Path First (OSPF), Routing Information Protocol (RIP), Internet Gateway Routing Protocol (IGRP), or Enhanced IGRP (EIGRP) and identify the network:

```
Cisco7505(config)#router rip
Cisco7505(config-router)#network 192.1.0.0
```

3. Create a subinterface on a physical interface in Interface Configuration mode for the port connected to the switch:

```
7505(config-router)#interface fastethernet2/0.100
```

4. Specify the encapsulation type and VLAN number to use on the subinterface:

```
7505(config-subif)#encapsulation isl 100
```

5. Assign an IP address and subnet mask to the subinterface:

```
7505(config-subif)#ip address 192.1.1.1 255.255.255.0
```

6. To configure any other interfaces, repeat Steps 3 through 5 for each VLAN between the switches that you want to route traffic:

```
7505(config-router)#interface fastethernet2/0.200
7505(config-subif)#encapsulation isl 200
7505(config-subif)#ip address 192.1.2.3 255.255.255.0
```

Configuring IPX InterVLAN Routing on an External Router

In order to understand this section, you should be familiar with Cisco IOS software running on Cisco routers. In this demonstration, we will configure a Cisco 7505:

1. To enable IP routing on the router, enter Global Configuration mode and use the **ipx routing** command:

```
7505#configure terminal
Enter configuration commands, one per line.  End with CNTL/Z.
7505(config)#ipx routing
```

2. Specify an IPX routing protocol, such as RIP, and identify all the networks:

```
Cisco7505(config)#ipx router rip
Cisco7505(config-router)#network all
```

3. Create a subinterface on a physical interface in Interface Configuration mode for the port connected to the switch:

```
7505(config-router)#interface fastethernet2/0.1
```

4. You must specify the encapsulation type and VLAN number to use on the subinterface:

```
7505 (config-subif)#ipx encapsulation isl 1
```

5. Assign a network number to the subinterface and identify an encapsulation type for IPX, such as **snap**, **novell-ether**, **arpa** or **sap**:

```
7505(config-subif)# ipx network 1 encapsulation sap
```

6. To configure any other interfaces, repeat Steps 3 through 5 for each VLAN between the switches you want to route traffic:

```
7505(config-subif)#interface fastethernet2/0.2
7505(config-subif)#encapsulation isl 2
7505(config-subif)#ipx network 2 encapsulation sap
```

Chapter 6

InterVLAN and Basic Module Configuration

In Depth

One of the first things you will discover in this chapter is that *switch* is merely a marketing term. When we think of a switch, we think of a device that operates at Layer 2. Well, in this chapter we'll walk through the process of configuring Cisco switch-swappable cards and modules, and you'll find that today's switches have modules and cards that allow them to operate not just at Layer 2 but at Layers 3 and 4, as well. Although this chapter does not include the new Cisco 11000 series Web switches, they operate at Layer 5. This makes the term *switch* very blurry, doesn't it?

Normally, regardless of the vendor, routing is not considered a switch function. As you will learn, today's Cisco switches have plenty of features that involve routing. Today's switches can also run routing protocols that can be used for path determination and building routing tables; more to the point, they use Routing Information Bases (RIBs). (A RIB is what you see when you use the **show ip route** command on a router.)

You can add many modules to a Cisco switch. In fact, we'd need this book and three others like it to completely cover every module that can be placed in the switches. This chapter will focus on configuring three internal route processors: the Route Switch Feature Card (RSFC), the Route Switch Module (RSM), and the Multilayer Switch Module (MSM). It will also supplement what you have already learned in the book about configuring the Supervisor Engine and Ethernet module interfaces.

Internal Route Processors

An internal route processor can be thought of as a router on a card. In a typical situation, the first packet to a destination must go through the RIB to see if a route has been discovered by matching the destination address field of the packet header. Routing protocols are used to learn the topology of the network and place the information the protocols learn in a topology table called the *Forwarding Information Base (FIB)*. Based on information contained in the FIB, routes are calculated based on metrics used by the routing protocol and the best route (and sometimes a feasible successor) is placed in the RIB. The RIB examines an incoming packet to select the outgoing interface to which the packet is to be sent. The forwarding decision can be based on a minimal amount of information, such as the destination address.

Cisco defines the FIB as a forwarding table that has an entry for every entry in the RIB. When Cisco speaks of a *forwarding cache*, it means the forwarding table that contains the most recently used subset of the routes in the RIB.

In a device using the Cisco Express Forwarding (CEF) Application-Specific Integrated Circuit (ASIC), each forwarding element has its own copy of the FIB, which contains every route contained in the RIB. One of the advantages of having the CEF ASIC, in comparison with other switching ASICs, is a one-to-one correspondence between the RIB and FIB entries, thus making it unnecessary for the switch to maintain a cache. When a destination address is received and is not present in the cache, the cache is invalidated and a new FIB is generated. Depending on the platform, routing may slow or come to a stop during the cache reconstruction.

The switch creates a routing table first and then forwards the information from the routing table to the FIB. The FIB uses a highly optimized routing lookup algorithm. By prefix-matching the destination address, the FIB can look up the destination in a large routing table much more quickly than it could using the line-by-line lookup of a traditional routing table.

The FIB maintains a copy of the forwarding information contained in the IP routing table based on the next-hop address. The routing table is updated if routing or topology changes are detected in the network. Those changes are then forwarded to the FIB, and the next-hop information is recomputed based on those changes.

Cisco Express Forwarding ASIC

The CEF ASIC and Distributed Cisco Express Forwarding (dCEF) ASIC are Cisco's newest ASICs; the company uses them in high-end devices. These are the most functional and efficient ASICs in Cisco's product line, including the internal route processors.

The CEF ASIC is used to ensure that all packets have equal access to the switch's internal memory. It performs lookups via the CEF ASIC (CEFA) search engine. CEFA uses a round-robin approach, giving fair access to data traffic on each port as well as cycling data between ports and processing requests as needed.

The CEFA search engine is used to make IP prefix-based switching decisions using an adjacency table. The CEFA operates at Layer 2 and Layer 3 and uses Address Resolution Protocol (ARP) to resolve next-hop adjacencies at Layer 2. (A network interface is said to be *adjacent* if it can be reached in a single hop.) CEFA looks at the first 64 bytes of an incoming frame, obtains information such as the destination for the frame, and then uses information contained in the switch's Content Addressable Memory (CAM) table to rewrite the relevant source Media Access Control (MAC) address, destination MAC address, or destination network address to the frame's or packet's header.

Because of the efficiency and speed of the CEF ASIC, this ASIC makes more processing available for other Layer 3 services performed within the main processor, such as queuing, higher encryption levels, and higher-level decryption.

When using process switching, the RIB and FIB have almost identical data structures. In fast switching, however, the FIB remains in the Random Access Memory (RAM), and the forwarding is done by the CPU rather than an ASIC. This process is slower than having ASICs handle the task.

NOTE: *Autonomous switching and silicon switching are used on the AGS, AGS+, and 7000 routers. The FIB has its own separate memory, and the bus controller on an AGS(+) or a Silicon Switch Processor on the Cisco 7000 series handles the forwarding process. The FIB is on the same board as the forwarding engine. FIB memory is quite small, so if a particular route or destination address has not been learned or recently used, cache misses can occur. Cache misses take place when the FIB is invalidated and must be rebuilt from the knowledge gained by the RIB.*

Optimum switching uses both an FIB and RIB. The Route Switch Processor (RSP) card uses them but also has its own separate physical memory allotted for these processes. With this type of switching, one processor and one memory set handle the path determination and forwarding.

Distributed switching (either in the CEF ASIC or NetFlow routing) uses only one RIB but copies the FIB to multiple Versatile Interface Processor (VIP) cards. Each VIP card runs a separate instance of the forwarding process. The VIP cards have large memories; as a result, in a CEF ASIC the FIB and RIB have a one-to-one correspondence with each other, so there are no cache misses. Only the first packet to a destination goes through the RIB to be resolved to a destination. Subsequent packets relating to the same data flow are forwarded the same as the first packet.

Cisco switches such as the Catalyst 5000 family use distributed Layer 3 switching. This type of switching uses only one route-determination engine. Although this is a Layer 2 switch, the physical chassis can contain a separate module such as an RSM, RSFC, or (in the 6000 series) an MSM. Routing can also be handled with one of the processes described earlier in an external route processor known as an *external router*. A Cisco proprietary protocol transfers the FIB information to a NetFlow Feature Card (NFFC or NFFC II) on a Cisco Catalyst 5000 series, or to another forwarding board or module on the higher-speed Cisco distributed switches.

There is little difference between using an external router and an internal route processor as your source of the FIB to route Layer 3 protocol data traffic or to perform inter-VLAN routing; it is basically a design choice. If you need to route using an external router, keep cost and speed in mind as you decide which router is best. In the Immediate Solutions sections, we will walk through configuring a Cisco 2600 for trunking, which allows for inter-VLAN routing. Let's look at how to decide whether to use an internal or external route processor:

- *Cisco 2600 series*—A good choice if you just need to do inter-VLAN routing.
- *Cisco 3600 series*—A good choice if you need to do inter-VLAN routing a little more quickly. You can use the 3600 as a path determination engine and use an NFFC or equivalent on the switch.

- *Route Switch Module*—If you need to handle routing very quickly, use an RSM with an NFFC or equivalent, such as the RSFC, MSM, or Multilayer Switch Feature Card (MSFC).

- *Cisco 10000 or 12000*—A good choice if you need to route huge amounts of data very quickly, especially if you have multiple WAN interfaces. If you need to use an external route processor because of a lack of open slots on your switch, a Cisco 7200 or 7500 might be a good alternative.

You can configure one or more Hot Standby Routing Protocol (HSRP) groups on an external route processor or on internal route processor interfaces such as the RSM or the RSFC VLAN interfaces. This protocol (discussed in more detail in Chapter 12) provides a way to transparently create redundant Layer 3 routing devices in the network. Interfaces in an HSRP group share the same virtual IP and MAC addresses. You configure all the devices' default gateway addresses to the virtual IP address assigned to the HSRP-enabled router's interface. In the event of a failure of a link to one device or a failure of one router interface, the other takes over so service is not interrupted.

Multimodule vs. Fixed Configuration Switches

So far, we have talked about the internal route processors and their features. Several Cisco switches, such as the Catalyst 4000, 5000, 6000, 8500, and 12000 families of switches, are considered *multimodule* switches. Many Layer 3 switches, such as the Cisco Catalyst 2926G-L3, 2948G-L3, and 4912G, do not have internal cards. Instead, these switches have built-in modules and are considered *logically modular switches* or *fixed configuration switches*. The Catalyst 2926G has 24 ports of 10/100 Fast Ethernet and 2 ports of Gigabit Ethernet built in. The ports are considered to be located on module 2 logically, although the module cannot be removed from the switch like an add-on card.

On an internal or external route processor, each interface can be divided into many subinterfaces. Doing so creates a flexible solution for routing streams of multiple data types through one interface. On each switch interface connected to a route processor's interface, you need to identify the VLAN encapsulation method and assign an IP address and subnet mask to the interface.

Now, let's look at the features of the internal route processors.

Available Route Processors

When a switch receives a packet from a port on one VLAN destined for the port of another VLAN, the switch must find a path on which to send the frame. Because switches are designed to isolate traffic to collision domains or subnets, they cannot by default forward data to another VLAN or network without some other device's intervention to route the data and create routing tables of networks and devices.

As you learned in the previous section, route processors can be used to route data between foreign VLANs and other logically segmented parts of the network, such as subnets. They also route data to remote WAN segments, networks, or the Internet. A few types of route processors are available for Catalyst switches. They include:

- NetFlow Feature Card and NetFlow Feature Card II
- Route Switch Module
- Route Switch Feature Card
- Multilayer Switch Module

NetFlow Feature Card and NetFlow Feature Card II

The NFFC and NFFC II are feature cards that work primarily with an RSM or other high-end router. Both are daughter cards of the Supervisor Engine III Module on the Catalyst 5000 family of switches running version 11.3.4 or higher of the Cisco IOS. This Cisco solution provides frame and packet filtering at wire speeds, utilizing ASICs instead of processors and allowing the switch to scale forwarding rates from millions of packets per second to gigabit wire speeds.

Both cards provide protocol-filtering support for Ethernet VLANs and on non-trunked Ethernet, Fast Ethernet, and Gigabit Ethernet ports. By default, the protocol filtering feature is disabled on all Ethernet VLANs. In addition to assigning a VLAN to a port, you can configure the port to be a member of one or more groups based on a common protocol.

TIP: *Trunk ports and links are members of all VLANs; no filtering can be done on trunk links. Dynamic ports and ports that have port security enabled are members of all protocol groups.*

The NFFC's primary functions are to enable multilayer switching, NetFlow accounting, NetFlow data exporting, filtering by protocol, enhanced multicast packet replication, filtering by application, and Internet Group Management Protocol (IGMP) snooping. It is also a Quality of Service (QoS) enhancement for Cisco's CiscoAssure end-to-end solutions.

NFFCs can filter based not only on Layer 3 IPs or VLANs but by Transport layer (Layer 4) application port addresses, as well. This ability adds a layer of security by preventing unauthorized applications on the network. This feature is critical in today's networks, especially those needing the ability to forward Voice Over IP traffic or video conferencing.

The RSM or another switch running Multilayer Switch Protocol (MLSP) must still provide the routing functionality for the NFFC. Routers that can run MLSP and utilize the features of the NFFCs are the 4500, 4700, 7200, and 7500 series routers.

MLSP is also used to flush cache entries when a topology change occurs and to make modifications to the access lists used for filtering.

NFFCs populate their Layer 3 and 4 switching cache dynamically by observing and learning from the flow of data. They parse data using NetFlow Data Export to collect and export detailed information about data flows. This parsing is accomplished without introducing any additional latency into the switching or routing process.

NetFlow Data Export provides a look into all Layer 2 port traffic, as well as Layer 3 statistics. It records the statistics into User Datagram Protocol (UDP) and exports them to any Remote Monitoring 2 (RMON2)-compliant network analysis package, such as CWSI TrafficDirector. Some of the information that NetFlow Data Export provides is as follows:

- Source address
- Destination address
- Traffic type
- Byte count
- Packet count
- Timestamp

NFFC also provides protocol filtering to allow segmentation by VLANs. It can provide per-port filtering of data in four different groups:

- Internet Protocol (IP)
- Internetwork Packet Exchange (IPX)
- AppleTalk, DECnet, and Banyan Vines
- Other group

TIP: *By default, the IP group is on, but it can be turned off for the other groups listed. Remember, the NFFC and NFFC II do not process Token Ring packets. A port where a server resides and that is configured for IP can be turned off for other protocols such as IPX and AppleTalk. No broadcasts from these protocols will reach the server or end-user interface, because the NFFC will filter them.*

IGMP snooping is another feature of the NFFC II. Spawned by multicast applications such as video conferencing, it provides advanced features that help keep multicast traffic from flooding all the ports and degrading network performance. Using this feature, Catalyst 5500 switches are able to intelligently forward multicast to the correct destination. IGMP snooping reads IGMP messages from the end-user's interface and learns their port location. This process allows the NFFC II card to forward multicast data streams out the port attached to the destination interface.

Both cards also provide broadcast and unicast traffic filtering based on the port's membership in the different protocol groups in addition to the port's assigned VLAN. The NFFC II also has the ability to become a multicast forwarder. The ASICs on the NFFC II replicate multicast packets to allow wire-speed multicast forwarding.

Route Switch Module

The RSM enhances the Catalyst 5000 switch family by letting the switch provide some of the same Layer 3 switching capabilities as a router. As a result, a switch that normally forwards only Layer 2 command broadcasts and VLAN traffic and that relies on a router to forward traffic to other segments or VLANs can now route the traffic itself without relying on a router.

The RSM contains a MultiChannel Interface Processor (MIPS) R47000, 32MB Dynamic RAM (DRAM) expandable to 128MB, a 16MB Flash card expandable to 40MB, 1.5MB high-speed RAM for the backplane interface, and 8MB of Flash memory. It connects directly into the backplane of the switch. The RSM adds to the Cisco IOS such features as multiprotocol routing for the Ethernet interfaces, security control, multicast control, interVLAN routing, and some basic QoS features. The routing protocols supported by the RSM are as follows:

- AppleTalk
- Enhanced Interior Gateway Routing Protocol (EIGRP)
- Hot Standby Routing Protocol (HSRP)
- Interior Gateway Routing Protocol (IGRP)
- Internet Protocol (IP)
- Internetwork Packet Exchange (IPX)
- NetWare Link Services Protocol (NLSP)
- Open Shortest Path First (OSPF)
- Routing Information Protocol (RIP)
- Routing Table Maintenance Protocol (RTMP) for AppleTalk

A Catalyst 5500 has 13 slots available for additional modules. Slots 1 and 2 are reserved for the Supervisor Engine and a redundant Supervisor Engine. If there is no redundant Supervisor Engine card, up to seven RSMs can be installed in the switch in slots 2 through 12.

The RSM interface to the Catalyst 5000 series backplane is through VLAN 0 mapped to channel 0 and VLAN 1 mapped to channel 1. The switch uses VLAN 0 to communicate with the RSM; the user cannot access VLAN 0. VLAN 1 is the switch default, but this default can be changed and mapped to a specific channel to load-balance the channels.

VLAN 0's MAC address is the address assigned to the programmable ROM (PROM) on the line communication processor (LCP) located on the RSM. This MAC address can be used for diagnostic purposes and to identify the RSM's slot number. All the other VLANs are assigned the base MAC address from the RSM PROM, which is preprogrammed with 512 MAC addresses. The RSM can route up to 256 VLANs.

Route Switch Feature Card

The RSFC is another daughter card of the Supervisor Engine IIG or the Supervisor Engine IIIG. This card basically transforms your switch into a Level 3 router with lots of ports. Two great features of this card are Web browser support, which provides a graphical navigation tool through the Command Line Interface (CLI), and the integration of NetFlow switching services, which include those services built into the NetFlow Feature Card. Included in these features are security services, QoS, Cisco Group Management Protocol (CGMP), Protocol-Independent Multicast (PIM), and queuing.

This card builds on the RSP found in the Cisco 7200 series router and provides exceptional performance in the routing process for the Catalyst 5000 family of switches. It uses a R4700 150MHz processor, 128MB of DRAM memory, 32MB of flash memory, 2MB of high-speed packet memory, and 6MB of high-speed RAM for the Catalyst switching bus interface.

This feature card, like the others, uses a Cisco IOS that supports a wide array of routed protocols and services. The following protocols are supported by the RSFC's IOS:

- AppleTalk
- Banyan Vines
- DECnet
- IP
- IPX
- Xerox Network Systems (XNS)

Multilayer Switch Module

The MSM is for the internal route processor used on the Catalyst 6000 family using the Supervisor Engine software version 5.2(1)CSX or later. This module uses the Cisco IOS which plugs directly into an interface's switch backplane to provide Layer 3 switching. This module connects directly to the switch with four full-duplex Gigabit Ethernet interfaces. The Catalyst switch sees the MSM as an external route processor not connected to the switch itself. You can group the four Gigabit interfaces into a single Gigabit EtherChannel or configure them as independent interface links. The MSM supports channeling trunks for use with 802.1Q or Inter-Switch Link (ISL).

The port-channel interface on the MSM must be configured with one subinterface for every VLAN on the switch, providing interVLAN routing with EtherChannel and trunk ports. Each of the four Gigabit interfaces must be independently configured as a separate VLAN trunk port or non-trunked routed interface. The MSM supports the following routing protocols:

- *Interior Gateway Routing Protocol*—IGRP is a Cisco-developed distance vector routing protocol. A distance vector routing protocol sends all or a portion of its routing table in the form of routing update messages at regular intervals to each neighboring router. As routing information proliferates through the network, routers can calculate the distance to all the nodes in the network. IGRP uses a combination of metrics such as internetwork delay, bandwidth, reliability, and load factors to make routing decisions.

- *Enhanced Interior Gateway Routing Protocol*—EIGRP is an enhanced version of IGRP that combines the advantages of the link-state routing protocols with distance vector protocols. EIGRP uses the Diffusing Update Algorithm (DUAL) and includes features such as variable-length subnet masks, fast convergence, and multiple network layer support. When a network topology change occurs, EIGRP checks its topology table for a suitable new route to the destination. If a route exists in the table, EIGRP updates the routing table with the new route and purges the old route from the table. Unlike other routing protocols, EIGRP saves WAN-link bandwidth by sending routing updates only when routing information changes. It also takes into account the available bandwidth between the paths to determine the rate at which it transmits updates.

- *Open Shortest Path First*—OSPF is an IP-based link-state routing protocol designed to overcome the limitations of RIP. It sends link-state advertisements (LSAs) to all other routers within the network. Information is included in the LSAs about the interfaces on which OSPF is running and the metrics used. As routers collect the link-state information, they use the Shortest Path First (SPF) algorithm to calculate the shortest path to each node.

- *Routing Information Protocol*—RIP is another distance-vector routing protocol that works well in small networks. However, in larger, more complex internetworks, RIP has many limitations, such as a maximum hop count of 15, lack of support for variable-length subnet masks (VLSMs), slow convergence, and inefficient use of bandwidth.

Routing Protocol Assignment

All devices communicate with each other through a path or route. If the destination interface does not reside in the same network segments as the sender, a route to the destination must be found using a dynamic routing protocol or a static route. If you have stacks of cash to spend on IOSs for your internal route processors, you can support any number of the following routing protocols:

- Enhanced Interior Gateway Routing Protocol (EIGRP)
- Hot Standby Routing Protocol (HSRP)
- Interior Gateway Routing Protocol (IGRP)
- NetWare Link Services Protocol (NLSP)
- Open Shortest Path First (OSPF)
- Routing Information Protocol (RIP)
- Routing Table Maintenance Protocol (RTMP) for AppleTalk

To use a dynamic protocol, you must first assign a routing protocol to the route prcessor being configured just as you would an external router. Then, you identify the network and, in some cases, an area ID and an autonomous system number.

Supervisor Engine Modules

The Supervisor Engine (SE) is basically the brains of the Cisco 4000, 5000, and 6000 families of switches. There are three series of Supervisor Engines; each has its own individual features and the newer ones add features that go beyond those of their predecessors. Let's take a look at the features of each Supervisor Engine.

Supervisor Engines I and II

As shown in Figure 6.1, the SE I and SE II provide a switching engine using a 25MHz Motorola MC68EC040 Network Management Processor (NMP). The processor's ability to switch more than one million packets per second (pps) provides data path and data control for all the switch's network interfaces, including two on-board integrated Fast Ethernet interfaces that can support redundancy using the Spanning-Tree Algorithm or load sharing. Other features supported by these SEs are:

- *Media Access Control Addressing and VLANs*—Support for 16,000 active MAC addresses for up to 1,024 VLANs allocated dynamically between active ports.

- *Management*—Support for Simple Network Management Protocol (SNMP) for statistical management. The SE also supports access and management through the console and Telnet interface.

The SE II includes a few upgraded features, such as:

- Support for redundant supervisor engines
- Support for redundant clock modules
- Support for core-switching logic

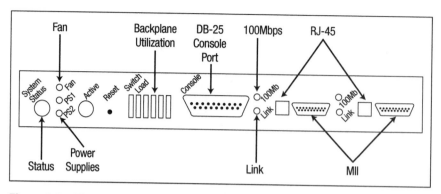

Figure 6.1   The Catalyst Supervisor Engine I and II.

The Supervisor Engine II G supports additional features, such as:

• An optional NetFlow Feature Card II (NFFC II) chipset built in

• Route Switch Feature Card (RSFC)

• Modular uplink ports

Supervisor Engine III

The Supervisor Engine III is available in three models:

• Supervisor Engine III with Enhanced Address Recognition Logic (EARL) ASIC

• Supervisor Engine III with the NFFC

• Supervisor Engine III with the NFFC II

The Supervisor Engine III shown in Figure 6.2 has a few more features than SEs I and II:

• 150MHz RISC 4700 processor

• Three switching buses that can simultaneously provide 1.2GB of throughput, resulting in a 3.6Gbps throughput engine

• Two Flash PC card slots that can be used for memory upgrades or to serve as additional I/O devices

The Supervisor Engine III G shown in Figure 6.3 provides the following additional features:

• Gigabit Interface Converter (GBIC) for use with multimode fiber (MMF) or single-mode fiber (SMF) interfaces using SC connectors

• An MCF5102 processor

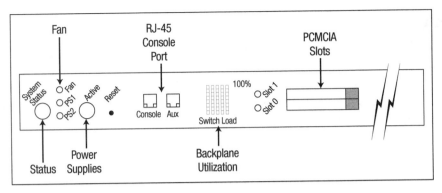

Figure 6.2   The Supervisor Engine III.

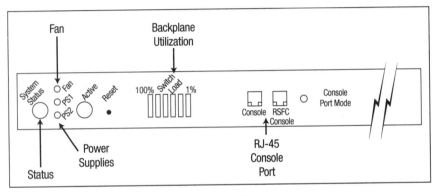

Figure 6.3   The Catalyst Supervisor Engine III G.

Using the Supervisor Engine

If you installed the Supervisor Engine from another switch, it probably has been configured for other interfaces; as a result, the configuration needs to be cleared. To do this, use the **clear config** command to return the Supervisor Engine to its factory defaults.

You can determine the boot process the switch will use when you recycle the power by setting the boot field in the configuration register. There are three different settings for the boot field. These are as follows:

- *ROM monitor*—Use the **rommon** syntax, which will instruct the switch to remain in ROM-monitor mode.

- *Bootflash*—Use the **bootflash** syntax, which instructs the switch to boot from the first image stored in Flash memory.

- *System*—Use the **system** syntax to instruct the switch to boot from the image specified in the boot environment, which is the default on the switch.

Etherport Modules

One of the most common interfaces found on switches is the Ethernet port. Leaving an Ethernet interface to autonegotiate the speed and duplex of a port should allow any device to connect to it. Many times, however, you must adjust the speed and duplex configuration so the device can talk on the network. A good example of a switch using Ethernet ports is shown in Figure 6.4.

There are three types of Ethernet interfaces: Ethernet, Fast Ethernet, and Gigabit Ethernet. The same port speed and duplex must be used on both interfaces participating in the point-to-point link. Ethernet and Fast Ethernet ports can autonegotiate the duplex mode, using either half or full duplex. Fast Ethernet interfaces can be set to autonegotiate the port speed. Gigabit Ethernet ports are always full duplex.

To set the port speed on a Fast Ethernet port on a Set/Clear command-based switch, use the following command:

```
set port speed mod_num/port_num {10|100|auto}
```

The **auto** syntax allows the port to autonegotiate the port speed. On an Ethernet or Fast Ethernet interface, use the command

```
set port duplex mod_num/port_num {full|half|auto}
```

to set the port duplex mode. Again, the **auto** syntax can be used to allow the port to autonegotiate the duplex mode.

Port Security

You can use port security to block a NIC on an Ethernet, Fast Ethernet, or Gigabit Ethernet port when the MAC address of the station attempting to access the port is different than the MAC addresses specified to access that port. There must be

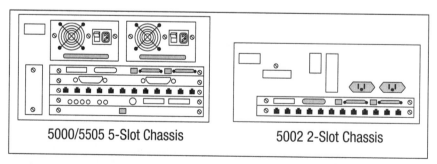

5000/5505 5-Slot Chassis   5002 2-Slot Chassis

Figure 6.4   The 5000/5500 and the 5002 chassis with installed Ethernet modules.

at least one default MAC address per port for the port to be secured. The total number of MAC addresses on any port cannot exceed 1,025. You must also follow other guidelines when configuring port security:

- You cannot configure port security on a trunk port.
- Port security is not supported on the three-port Gigabit Ethernet module.
- You cannot enable port security on a Switched Port Analyzer (SPAN) destination or source port.
- You cannot configure dynamic, static, or permanent CAM entries for a secure port.

When port security on a port is enabled, any static or dynamic CAM entries associated with the port are cleared. Any currently configured permanent CAM entries are treated as secure.

Manually Configured MAC Addresses

Different IP addresses can be assigned to the virtual VLAN interfaces on the device; all of them utilize the same global MAC address. However, specifying an individual MAC address to each interface does have benefits in some situations. Assigning an individual MAC address to each interface offers these two main benefits:

- Allows the best use of Fast EtherChannel for load distribution
- Enhanced management with the use of the Multilayer Switching (MLS) cache

Immediate Solutions

Determining the Slot Number in Which a Module Resides

To determine the slot number in which a module or card resides, use the following steps:

1. On the switch console, enter the **enable** command and the password to enter Privileged mode:

```
Coriolis5000# enable
Password: ********

Coriolis5000>(enable)
```

2. Enter the **show module** command to determine what cards are present:

```
Coriolis5000>(enable) show module

Mod  Module-Name Ports Module-Type          Model      Serial-Num Status
---  ----------- ----- -------------------- -------    --------   ----
1                0     Supervisor III       WS-X5530   010854649  ok
2                24    10/100baseTX Ethernet WS-X5225R 012453433  ok
3                1     Route Switch         M-X5302    007673460  ok


Mod MAC-Address(es)                            Hw     Fw     Sw
--  -----------------------------------------  ------ ------ --------
1   00-40-0b-80-54-00 to 00-40-0b-80-57-fi 2.0        3.1.2  4.3(1a)
2   00-40-0b-03-5d-58 to 00-40-0b-03-5d-6f 3.1        4.3(1) 4.3(1a)
3   00-43-0d-91-45-66 to 00-43-0d-91-dc-67 5.0        20.14  11.3(6)WAA4(9)


Mod Sub-Type Sub-Model Sub-Serial Sub-Hw
--- -------- --------- ---------- ------
1   NFFC II  WS-F5531  0036457641
```

Accessing the Internal Route Processor from the Switch

The session command, followed by the slot number on the switch in which the internal routing processor module resides, allows you to access the module from the switch's CLI. You can then end the session by using the **exit** command. Let's take a look at an example of accessing the internal route processor:

```
Seans5002> (enable) session 15
Trying Router-15...
Connected to Router-15.
Escape character is '^]'.

User Access Verification

Password:
RSFC1>exit
Seans5002> (enable)
```

Let's take a look at this process from the initial User EXEC mode prompt:

1. On the switch console, enter the **enable** command and the password to enter Privileged mode:

```
Coriolis5000# enable
Password: ********
Coriolis5000>(enable)
```

2. To open a session from the console port for the RSM, use the following command:

```
Coriolis5000> session 3
```

The prompt will look like this if it is the initial configuration:

```
Router>
```

Configuring a Hostname on the RSM

To configure the hostname on an RSM, follow these steps:

1. On the switch console, enter the **enable** command and the password to enter Privileged mode:

```
Coriolis5000# enable
Password: ********
Coriolis5000>(enable)
```

2. To open a session from the console port for the RSM, use the following command:

```
Coriolis5000> session 3
```

The prompt will look like this if it is the initial configuration:

```
Router>
```

3. Enter Global Configuration mode with the following commands:

```
Router> enable
Router# configure terminal
```

WARNING! When you make changes in this mode, they must be saved to NVRAM. Otherwise, the next time you recycle the switch, the changes will be lost. The command to save changes is copy running-config startup-config.

4. Assign the RSM a unique hostname with the following command. Call it RSM1:

```
Router>(config)# hostname RSM1
RSM1>(config)#
```

TIP: *The hostname can be up to 255 characters, using alphanumeric characters only. Although in this example we use uppercase to identify the hostname, in some instances when you connect to the switch with different software, the hostname may appear in lowercase.*

Assigning an IP Address and Encapsulation Type to an Ethernet Interface

To assign an IP address and a trunking encapsulation type to an Ethernet interface so interVLAN routing can take place, follow these steps:

1. To enter Interface Configuration mode for Ethernet on the subinterface that needs to be configured, enter the following command in Global Configuration mode:

```
Catalyst5000(config)#interface ethernet 3/1.2
```

In this example, **3** indicates the module number/slot number, **1** indicates the port number, and **2** indicates the number of the subinterface to be configured.

NOTE: No changes take effect until the **no shutdown** command is issued.

---

2. Once in Interface Configuration mode, you can configure the port for the encapsulation type and identify the VLAN number that will be carried by the port. The most common encapsulation type is ISL; this will be the encapsulation type configured in our example. Configure the interface for VLAN 2. Each VLAN packet destined for a non-local network is tagged with a VLAN ID within the packet header, to help identify the VLAN to the subinterface:

```
Coriolis5000(config-if)#encapsulation isl 2
```

3. Assign the subinterface its own unique IP address and subnet mask. To do this, use the following commands followed by a **no shutdown** command to apply the changes and exit:

```
Coriolis5000(config-if)#ip address 130.77.20.18 255.255.254.0
Coriolis5000(config-if)#no shutdown
Coriolis5000(config-if)#exit
```

Setting the Port Speed and Port Name on an Ethernet Interface

Here is an example of setting the port speed and port name:

```
Coriolis5000> (enable) set port speed 2/3 auto
Port 2/3 speed set to auto detect.
Coriolis5000> (enable) set port name 2/3 VLAN 1 FileServer1
Port 2/3 name set.
Coriolis5000> (enable) show port 2/3
```

```
Port  Name               Status     Vlan Level  Duplex Speed Type
----  ------------------ ---------- ---- ------  ------ ----  ------------
 2/3 FileServer1         connect    1    normal  a-half a-100 10/100BaseTX
```

Configuring a Default Gateway on a Catalyst 5000

Before IP management from another subnet or network can take place through Telnet, the sending device must know the routers that are connected to the local network to forward data for destinations outside the local network. Just as an end-user interface needs to have a defined default gateway, a switch needs to know the address of the interface of the route processor connected to the local subnet.

To define the gateway, in Global Configuration mode use the following command combined with the route processor or router IP address that is acting as the default gateway for the network:

```
Coriolis5000(config)# ip default-gateway 130.77.20.1
```

Verifying the IP Configuration on a Catalyst 5000

You can verify the IP configuration of the switch by using the **show ip** command:

```
Coriolis5000#show ip
IP Address: 130.77.20.15
Subnet Mask: 255.255.254.0
Default Gateway: 130.77.20.1
Management VLAN: 1
Domain name: coriolis.com
Name server 1: 130.77.17.190
Name server 2: 130.77.16.191
HM server : Enabled
HTTP port : 80
RIP : enabled
```

Enabling RIP on an RSM

To assign an IP routing protocol and network number, perform the following steps:

1. Assign a routing protocol (RIP) to the RSM. To do this, use the following commands in Global Configuration mode:

```
RSM1(config)#ip routing
RSM1(config)#router rip
```

2. Assign a network number to the route processor on the RSM by using the **network** command followed by the network number just as you would use with an external Cisco router's interface:

```
RSM1(config-router)#network 172.16.0.0
```

3. Assign a VLAN to an IP address:

```
RSM1(config-router)#interface vlan 100
RSM1(config-if)#ip address 172.16.1.1 255.255.255.0
RSM1(config-if)#^Z
RSM1#
```

NOTE: *The commands for configuring the RSM, RSFC, and MSM are the same.*

Viewing the RSM's Running Configuration

To view the RSM's running configuration, use the **show running-config** command as shown here:

```
Coriolis5000RSM# show running-config
Building configuration...

Current configuration:
!
version 11.2
no service udp-small-servers
no service tcp-small-servers
!
hostname Coriolis5000RSM
!
enable book1234
!
!
interface Vlan1
 ip address 130.77.20.15 255.255.254.0
!
interface Vlan2
 ip address 130.77.20.15 255.255.254.0
```

```
!
interface Vlan3
ip address 130.77.20.16 255.255.254.0
 shutdown
!
router eigrp 100
network 130.77.0.0
no auto-summary
!
ip default-gateway 130.77.20.254
no ip classless
snmp-server community public RO
snmp-server community private RW
!
line con 0
line aux 0
line vty 0 4
password book1234
login
!
end

Coriolis5000RSM#
```

WARNING! In order to keep new changes when the switch is cycled, don't forget to save the configuration to the NVRAM.

Configuring InterVLAN Routing on an RSM

Before you configure the RSM, you must configure the switch as a VTP server and assign a VTP domain name. You must also configure the ISL trunk links and assign the switch ports on each switch to the appropriate VLAN. To configure the RSM for interVLAN routing, use the following steps:

1. Start a session on the RSM for module 5:

```
Coriolis5002> (enable) session 5
Trying Router-5...
Connected to Router-5.
Escape character is '^]'.
```

2. Create one VLAN interface for each VLAN configured on the switch:

```
RSM1>enable
RSM1#configure terminal
Enter configuration commands, one per line. End with CNTL/Z.
RSM1(config)#interface vlan 2
RSM1(config-if)#
%LINEPROTO-5-UPDOWN: Line protocol on Interface Vlan2, changed state to
down
```

3. Assign IP addresses to the VLAN interfaces:

```
RSM1(config-if)#ip address 172.20.52.33 255.255.255.224
RSM1(config-if)#no shutdown
%LINEPROTO-5-UPDOWN: Line protocol on Interface Vlan2, changed state to
up
RSM1(config-if)#interface vlan 3
RSM1(config-if)#
```

Repeat these steps for each VLAN. After you successfully configure the network, all end stations should be able to communicate with one another. Communication between hosts in the same VLAN is handled only by the switches. All interVLAN traffic must be routed by the RSM.

Configuring IPX InterVLAN Routing on the RSM

To configure interVLAN routing for IPX, perform these steps in Global Configuration mode:

1. Enable IPX routing on the router:

```
RSM1(config)#ipx routing
```

2. Specify an IPX routing protocol, in this example IPX RIP:

```
RSM1(config)#ipx router rip
RSM1(config-ipx-router)#network all
```

3. Specify a VLAN interface on the RSM:

```
RSM1(config-ipx-router)#interface vlan50
```

4. Assign a network number to the VLAN and an encapsulation method; then exit:

```
RSM1(config-if)#ipx network 50 encapsulation snap
RSM1(config-if)#^Z
RSM1#
```

Configuring AppleTalk InterVLAN Routing on an RSM

To configure interVLAN routing for AppleTalk, perform these tasks beginning in Global Configuration mode:

1. Enable AppleTalk routing on the router:

```
RSM1#configure terminal
Enter configuration commands, one per line. End with CNTL/Z.
RSM1(config)#appletalk routing
```

2. Specify a VLAN interface number on the RSM and assign a cable range to the VLAN:

```
RSM1(config)#interface vlan100
RSM1(config-if)#appletalk cable-range 200-200
```

3. Assign a zone name to the VLAN; then exit:

```
Router(config-if)#appletalk zone artdept
Router(config-if)#^Z
Router#
```

Viewing the RSM Configuration

Just as on a router, you use the **show running-config** to view the running configuration:

```
Coriolis5000RSM# show running-config
Building configuration...

Current configuration:
!
version 11.2
no service udp-small-servers
no service tcp-small-servers
!
```

```
hostname Coriolis5000RSM
!
enable book1234
!
!
interface Vlan1
 ip address 130.77.20.15 255.255.254.0
!
interface Vlan2
 ip address 130.77.20.15 255.255.254.0
!
interface Vlan3
 ip address 130.77.20.16 255.255.254.0
```

Assigning a MAC Address to a VLAN

In Interface Configuration mode, you can assign a MAC address to the interface by using the **mac-address** command. Use the 48-bit IEEE MAC address written as a dotted triplet of four-digit hexadecimal numbers, as shown here:

```
Coriolis5000RSM(config-if)#mac-address 0040.0b03.5d6f
Coriolis5000RSM(config-if)#exit
```

Viewing the MAC Addresses

To see the MAC addresses assigned to each VLAN, use the following command:

```
CoriolisRSM5000> (enable) show cam dynamic
* = Static Entry. + = Permanent Entry. # = System Entry.
R = Router Entry. X = Port Security Entry

VLAN   Dest MAC/Route Des [CoS]   Destination Ports or VCs
----   ----------------------     --------------------------
1      00-60-29-43-a2-29          1/1
1      00-60-94-c5-2e-a1          1/1
1      00-60-2c-03-f4-43          1/1
1      00-60-94-d8-a1-92          1/1
1      00-60-38-a4-28-0e          2/1
1      00-60-67-6b-12-3b          2/1
1      00-60-15-be-55-80          2/1

Total Matching CAM Entries Displayed = 7
```

Configuring Filtering on an Ethernet Interface

To configure protocol filtering for IP only, follow these steps:

1. To configure protocol filtering on the Ethernet, Fast Ethernet, or Gigabit Ethernet ports, you must first enable protocol filtering on the switch. To enable protocol filtering, use this command in Privileged mode:

```
Coriolis5002 (enable) set protocolfilter enable
```

2. Configure port 2 on module 2 to filter all traffic unless it is IP based:

```
Coriolis5002(enable) set port protocol 2/2 ip on
IP protocol set to on mode on module 2/2.
Coriolis5002>(enable)
```

3. Do the same for port 3 on module 2:

```
Coriolis5002>(enable) set port protocol 2/3 ip on
IP protocol set to on mode on module 2/3.
Coriolis5002>(enable)
```

Configuring Port Security on an Ethernet Module

To enable port security on a switch interface, use the following steps:

1. Enable port security on the desired ports. Optionally, you can specify the secure MAC address:

```
set port security mod_num/port_num {enable|disable} [mac_address]
```

2. Add MAC addresses to the list of secure addresses:

```
set port security module number/port number mac_address
```

Here's an example of using this command:

```
Catalyst5000> (enable) set port security 2/3 enable
Port 2/3 port security enabled with the learned mac address.
Trunking disabled for Port 2/1 due to Security Mode
```

```
Catalyst5000> (enable) show port 2/1
Port  Name                 Status      Vlan        Level  Duplex Speed Type
----  -------------------- ----------- ----------- ------ ------ ----- --------
 2/3                       connected   522         normal half    100 100BaseTX


Port  Security Secure-Src-Addr   Last-Src-Addr     Shutdown Trap     IfIndex
----  -------- ----------------- ----------------- -------- -------- ------
 2/3  enabled  00-60-1a-30-a1-d2 00-60-1a-30-a1-d2 No       disabled 1081


Port     Broadcast-Limit Broadcast-Drop
-------- --------------- --------------
 2/3                   -              0


Port  Align-Err  FCS-Err    Xmit-Err   Rcv-Err    UnderSize
----  ---------- ---------- ---------- ---------- --------
 2/3           0          0          0          0         0


Port  Single-Col Multi-Coll Late-Coll  Excess-Col Carri-Sen Runts     Giants
----  ---------- ---------- ---------- ---------- -------- -------- ------
 2/3           0          0          0          0        0        0        0


Last-Time-Cleared
-------------------------
Fri Nov 24 2000, 21:53:38
```

Clearing MAC Addresses

The **clear port security** command is used to clear the MAC address from a list of secure addresses on a port. If the **clear** command is executed on a MAC address that is in use by an interface, the MAC address may be relearned by the switch and made secure again if dynamic port security is being used. Dynamic port security is when a switch is configured to allow only the first MAC address used on an interface to use the switch port. If another interface using another MAC address tries to use the switch port, the switch will automatically place the port in the disabled state. The light color on the switch will change from green to amber indicating the port is disabled. Cisco recommends that you disable port security before you clear any MAC addresses. Here is the command and its possible syntaxes, and an example of using the command:

```
clear port security mod_num/port_num {mac_addr|all}
```

```
Coriolis5000> (enable) clear port security 3/10-20 all
All addresses cleared from secure address list for ports 3/10-20

Coriolis5000> (enable)
```

Configuring the Catalyst 5000 Supervisor Engine Module

To configure the basic configuration on a Catalyst 5000 Supervisor Engine Module, follow these steps:

1. Access the Cisco Catalyst 5000 through the console port located on the Supervisor Engine 3. The initial password is just pressing the Enter key, as shown here:

```
Cisco Systems Console

Enter password:

Console> enable

Enter password:

Console>(enable)
```

2. Configure the hostname:

```
Console>(enable) set prompt Catalyst5000>
Catalyst5000> (enable)
```

3. Configure a password for the switch. Press Enter for the old password if none has ever been configured:

```
Catalyst5000> (enable) set password
Enter old password:
Enter new password: coriolis1
Retype new password: coriolis1
Password changed.
```

4. Configure the password for Enable mode. Press Enter for the old password if none has ever been configured:

```
Catalyst5000> (enable) set enablepass
Enter old password:
Enter new password: coriolis2
Retype new password: coriolis2
Password changed.
Catalyst5000(enable)
```

5. Enter the IP address and the default gateway (router) for the switch on the Supervisor Engine module SC0:

```
Catalyst5000> (enable) set interface sc0 63.78.39.174 255.255.255.0
Interface sc0 IP address and netmask set.
Catalyst5000>(enable) set ip route default 38.68.127.254
Route added.
```

6. Enable trunking on interface 2/2 to complete your trunk link to the 1912EN switch and on interface 2/24 to the router for interVLAN routing:

```
Catalyst5000> (enable) set trunk 2/2 mode on isl
Port(s) 2/2 trunk mode set to on.
Port(s) 2/2 trunk type set to isl.
2000 Nov 19 12:31:54 %DTP-5-TRUNKPORTON:Port 2/2

Catalyst5000> (enable) set trunk 2/24 mode on isl
Port(s) 2/24 trunk mode set to on.
Port(s) 2/24 trunk type set to isl.
2000 Nov 19 12:32:46 %DTP-5-TRUNKPORTON:Port 2/24
```

7. Enable the switch to be a VTP client for the Coriolis VTP domain. Doing so will propagate the VLAN information from the 1912EN switch:

```
Catalyst5000> (enable) set vtp domain ?
Usage: set vtp [domain <name>] [mode <mode>] [passwd <passwd>]
           [pruning <enable|disable>] [v2 <enable|disable>
(mode = client|server|transparent Use passwd '0' to clear vtp password)
Usage: set vtp pruneeligible <vlans>
(vlans = 2..1000 An example of vlans is 2-10,1000)

Catalyst5000> (enable) set vtp domain Coriolis mode client
VTP domain Coriolis modified.
```

Related solution:	**Found on page:**
Testing the Supervisor Engine Hardware on a Set/Clear Command-Based Switch	494

6. InterVLAN and Basic Module Configuration

Setting the **boot config-register** on the Supervisor Engine Module

Here is an example of setting the **boot config-register** on the Supervisor Engine module. Let's look at the command and the available syntaxes and then an example of using the command:

```
set boot config-register boot {rommon|bootflash|system} [module number]

Catalyst5000> (enable) set boot config-register boot rommon
Configuration register is 0x0
ignore-config: disabled
auto-config: non-recurring
console baud: 9600
boot: the ROM monitor
Catalyst5000> (enable)
```

Several other commands can be used to configure the Supervisor Engine. The following list shows some of them:

- **set boot config-register ignore-config enable**—Sets the switch to ignore the contents of the configuration on NVRAM at startup

- **set boot config-register 0xvalue [*module number*]**—Sets the configuration register value

- **set boot system flash device:[*filename*] [*prepend*] [*module number*]**—Sets the system image to add to the **BOOT** environment variable

- **clear boot system flash device:[*filename*] [*module number*]**—Clears a specific image from the **BOOT** environment variable

- **clear boot system all [*module number*]**—Clears the entire **BOOT** environment variable

- **show boot [*module number*]**—Shows the current configuration register, **BOOT** environment variable, and configuration file (**CONFIG_FILE**) environment variable settings

Changing the Management VLAN on a Supervisor Engine

By default, the switch places all of its ports into what Cisco refers to as a native management VLAN. The native management VLAN is always configured for VLAN 1 on a Cisco switch. Cisco recommends adding another layer of security by changing the default management VLAN from VLAN 1, which is the default of all the ports on the module. To change the default VLAN from VLAN 1 to VLAN 3 on a Set/Clear command-based IOS, you use the **set interface sc0 <VLAN number>** command. Let's look at the command and then examine the interface to see the changes:

```
Catalyst5002> (enable) set interface sc0 3
Interface sc0 vlan set.

Catalyst5002> (enable) show interfaces
sc0: flags=63<UP,BROADCAST,RUNNING>
 vlan 3 inet 38.187.127.11 netmask 255.255.255.0 broadcast 38.187.127.255


Catalyst5002> (enable)
```

Viewing the Supervisor Engine Configuration

Using the **show version** command, you can see the software version installed on the Supervisor Engine:

```
Catalyst5000> (enable) show version

WS-C5000 Software, Version McpSW: 5.5(2) NmpSW: 5.5(2)
Copyright (c) 1995-2000 by Cisco Systems
NMP S/W compiled on Jul 28 2000, 16:43:52
MCP S/W compiled on Jul 28 2000, 16:38:40


System Bootstrap Version: 3.1.2


Hardware Version: 2.0  Model: WS-C5000  Serial #: 011454261


Mod Port Model      Serial #  Versions
--  ---- ---------- --------  ----------------------------------------
1   0    WS-X5530   011454261 Hw : 2.0
                              Fw : 3.1.2
                              Fw1: 4.2(1)
                              Sw : 5.5(2)
         WS-F5521   011455134 Hw : 1.1
2   24   WS-X5225R  013405523 Hw : 3.1
                              Fw : 4.3(1)
                              Sw : 5.5(2)
        DRAM                    FLASH                  NVRAM
Module Total   Used    Free    Total   Used    Free   Total Used Free
------ ------  ------  ------  ------  ------  ------  ----- ---- ----
1       32640K 20331K 12309K   8192K  5548K   2644K   512K  185K 327K
```

```
Uptime is 2 days, 19 hours, 3 minutes

Catalyst5000> (enable)
```

You can also use the **show module** command, as shown in the following output:

```
Catalyst5000> (enable) show module

Mod Slot Ports Module-Type              Model               Sub Status
--  ---- ----  ------------------------ ------------------- --  --------
1   1    0     Supervisor III           WS-X5530            yes ok
2   2    24    10/100BaseTX Ethernet     WS-X5225R           no  ok

Mod Module-Name        Serial-Num
--  -----------------  --------------------
1                      00011454261
2                      00013405523


Mod MAC-Address(es)                           Hw      Fw          Sw
--  ----------------------------------------- ------  ----------  --------
1   00-50-bd-a0-b0-00 to 00-50-bd-a0-b3-ff 2.0      3.1.2       5.5(2)
2   00-50-0f-b7-ff-50 to 00-50-0f-b7-ff-67 3.1      4.3(1)      5.5(2)

Mod Sub-Type Sub-Model Sub-Serial Sub-Hw
--  -------- --------- ---------- ------
1   NFFC     WS-F5521  0011455134 1.1

Catalyst5000> (enable)
```

Configuring the Cisco 2621 External Router for ISL Trunking

If you are going to use an external router for interVLAN routing, it helps to know how to configure it. Follow these steps to configure a 2621 for interVLAN routing:

1. Enter Interface Configuration mode for the Fast Ethernet 0/2 interface and force the port to use full duplex. Disable any IPs and use the **no shutdown** command:

```
Cisco2621(conf)# interface fastethernet 0/2
Cisco2621(conf-if)# no ip address
Cisco2621(conf-if)# no shutdown
Cisco2621(conf-if)# full-duplex
```

2. Create a subinterface for each VLAN and assign a description (optional), an IP address for the VLAN, an encapsulation type, and the VLAN number:

```
Cisco2621(conf-if)# interface fastethernet 0/2.2
Cisco2621(conf-if)# description vlan2
Cisco2621(conf-if)# ip address 63.78.39.2 255.255.255.0
Cisco2621(conf-if)# encapsulation isl 2
Cisco2621(conf-if)# interface fastethernet 0/2.3
Cisco2621(conf-if)# description vlan3
Cisco2621(conf-if)# ip address 63.78.39.3 255.255.255.0
Cisco2621(conf-if)# encapsulation isl 3
```

TIP: *Don't forget to save your configuration. Use the **show config** command on each device to verify the configuration.*

Configuring Redundancy Using HSRP

To configure HSRP on router interfaces, perform the following steps:

1. Enter Interface Configuration mode and identify a standby group and an IP address:

```
standby [group-number] ip [ip-address]
```

2. Identify the priority for the HSRP interface. The interface with the highest priority becomes active for that HSRP group; the default is 100:

```
standby [group-number] priority priority
```

3. You can optionally configure the interface to preempt the current active HSRP interface and become active if the interface priority is higher than the priority of the current active interface:

```
standby [group-number] preempt [delay delay]
```

4. You can also optionally set the HSRP **Hello** timer and **holdtime** timer for the interface. The default values are 3 (**Hello**) and 10 (**holdtime**). All the interfaces in the HSRP group should use the same timer values:

```
standby [group-number] timers hellotime holdtime
```

5. You can optionally identify a clear-text HSRP authentication string for the interface. Again, all HSRP member interfaces in the HSRP group should use the same authentication string:

```
standby [group-number] authentication string
```

Now that you have seen the steps to configure HSRP on an interface, let's take a look at an example of configuring HSRP on two different interfaces connected to the same network segment:

```
RSM1#configure terminal
Enter configuration commands, one per line. End with CNTL/Z.
RSM1(config)#ip routing
RSM1(config)#router rip
RSM1(config-router)#network 172.16.0.0
RSM1(config-router)#interface vlan10
RSM1(config-if)#ip address 172.16.10.1 255.255.255.0
RSM1(config-if)#no shutdown
RSM1(config-if)#standby 10 ip 172.16.10.10
RSM1(config-if)#standby 10 priority 110
RSM1(config-if)#standby 10 preempt
RSM1(config-if)#standby 10 timers 5 15
RSM1(config-if)#standby 10 authentication Secret
RSM1(config-if)#interface vlan200
RSM1(config-if)#ip address 172.16.20.1 255.255.255.0
RSM1(config-if)#no shutdown
RSM1(config-if)#standby 20 ip 172.16.20.10
RSM1(config-if)#standby 20 priority 110
RSM1(config-if)#standby 20 preempt
RSM1(config-if)#standby 20 timers 5 15
RSM1(config-if)#standby 20 authentication Covert
RSM1(config-if)#^Z
RSM1#

RSM2#configure terminal
Enter configuration commands, one per line. End with CNTL/Z.
RSM2(config)#ip routing
RSM2(config)#router rip
RSM2(config-router)#network 172.16.0.0
RSM2(config-router)#interface vlan10
RSM2(config-if)#ip address 172.16.10.2 255.255.255.0
RSM2(config-if)#no shutdown
RSM2(config-if)#standby 10 ip 172.16.10.10
RSM2(config-if)#standby 10 preempt
```

```
RSM2(config-if)#standby 10 timers 5 15
RSM2(config-if)#standby 10 authentication Secret
RSM2(config-if)#interface vlan20
RSM2(config-if)#ip address 172.16.20.2 255.255.255.0
RSM2(config-if)#no shutdown
RSM2(config-if)#standby 20 ip 172.16.20.10
RSM2(config-if)#standby 20 preempt
RSM2(config-if)#standby 20 timers 5 15
RSM2(config-if)#standby 20 authentication Covert
RSM2(config-if)#^Z
RSM2#
```

Chapter 7

IP Multicast

In Depth

Over time, our use of computers has moved from the local desktop to the local network. Most of this network traffic consists of using local network sources, such as printing and file transfers. As our personal computers become more powerful, the applications that we use now contain more audio and video components. We've now started to move this traffic onto the network.

Today, it is still the norm for network traffic to be between one sender and one recipient. That is slowly changing. As different network resources become available, new resources such as messaging, multimedia, distance learning, and Internet access are causing a large increase in data traffic. This type of traffic usually involves one server sending a data stream to multiple users; a good example of this would be video conferencing and software updates in the intranet.

This type of traffic can be very demanding in terms of data usage. For example, if 100 people want a 1.5MB file, the result is a demand for more than 150MB of data-link usage. Even on a T3, that's a lot of simultaneous use. What's more, this calculation doesn't take into account the rest of the users' applications and data requirements.

One way to provide users with this high-bandwidth information and at the same time minimize the traffic on the network is to utilize *IP multicast*. IP multicast enables data to be sent once and received by all the recipients that requested it.

The concept behind IP multicasting is that end recipients join a multicast group. The information that is requested is then delivered to all members of that group by the network infrastructure. The sender of the data doesn't need to know anything about the recipients. In this manner, only one copy of a multicast message will pass over any link in the network, and copies of the message will be made only where the paths diverge. This is a much more effective method of delivering traffic destined for multiple locations, and it provides significant performance improvements for the network.

In this chapter, we will explain the concepts behind IP multicasting. We will cover the types of multicast traffic and introduce you to the way multimedia traffic types are routed on the network. Finally, we will look at the methods to configure IP routing on your Catalyst switches and how to manage the resulting multicast traffic. We will begin with a discussion of the different types of multicast traffic.

IP Multicasting Overview

IP multicasting is an extension of the standard IP protocol and is described in RFC 1112, "Host Extensions for IP Multicasting." IP multicasting is the transmission of an IP datagram to a group identified by a single IP destination address. A multicast datagram is delivered to all members of its destination host group using User Datagram Protocol (UDP). Membership in these groups is unrestricted—hosts can be members of multiple groups, and they may join or leave at any time.

IP multicast datagrams are handled by multicast routers. A host transmits an IP multicast datagram as a local network multicast that reaches a multicast router. The router examines the packet and begins to provide the host with the requested multicast traffic. If the router is not receiving the requested multicast traffic, it will pass the request to other multicast routers.

IP traffic can travel the network in one of three ways:

- Broadcast
- Unicast
- Multicast

Broadcast

In its simplest form, broadcast traffic consists of packets that reach every point of the network. In a typical network, broadcasts are stopped at the router. You can set the router to forward broadcasts, but doing so is not very efficient—it creates a lot of traffic on the network and slows the end users' machines. Every host on the network must process the packet to see if it is destined for that host. Data broadcasts are typically small frames used in the local network—so, the performance effect is negligible, unless there is a broadcast storm.

NOTE: *In a broadcast storm, an incorrect packet is broadcast on the network. This causes most hosts to respond with incorrect answers, which in turn causes even more hosts to respond again. This process continues until the network can no longer carry any other traffic. A broadcast storm can also occur when there is more than one path through the network, allowing broadcasts to circle the network until there are so many that the network comes to a stop.*

Multimedia broadcasts, in contrast, can be huge packets. Processing these types of broadcasts can quickly use up all the available bandwidth on the network and bring the end station to a crawl—particularly if you are in a shared 10BaseT environment.

Figure 7.1 illustrates broadcast traffic in the network.

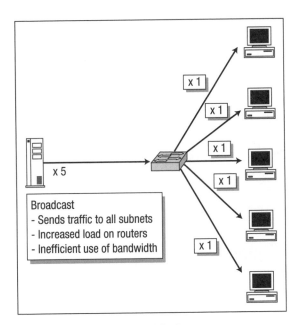

Figure 7.1   Broadcast traffic flow.

Unicast

In unicast, a single packet is sent from the source to the destination. It is a one-to-one relationship: For every packet that reaches the destination, one packet was sent by the source. This process is fine if the source is having different conversations with only a few hosts. Now, imagine that same source talking to hundreds of hosts on the same conversation—each identical packet must be generated by the source and must travel on the network.

Audio and video transmissions are so large that a high-bandwidth link is consumed very quickly. A 100Mbps link can support about 60 to 70 full-screen, full-motion video streams if each stream uses approximately 1.5Mbps of server-to-client bandwidth. You will need gigabit-per-second (Gbps) links between the server and the network in order to provide one audio/video broadcast to a couple hundred hosts. Unicast multimedia applications do not scale very well.

Figure 7.2 illustrates unicast traffic flow.

Multicast

Multicast is a combination of broadcast and unicast. It sends one copy of the packet to many hosts that requested it, thereby using less bandwidth. It also saves bandwidth by not sending the packet to the portion of the network whose hosts

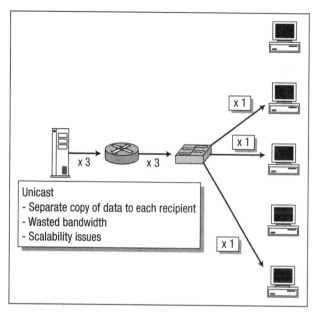

Figure 7.2   Unicast traffic flow.

didn't request the transmission. Multicast accomplishes this task by transmitting to an identified group, called a *multicast group*, rather than to an individual host. Each interface/host can be a member of multiple multicast groups. The membership is dynamic; a host can leave and join any time it wants. The traffic is also not limited by any boundary; it can reach the farthest point of the Internet.

Figure 7.3 illustrates multicast traffic flow.

The characteristics of multicast enable it to take three different forms:

- *One-to-many*—One-to-many is the most common form of multicast traffic. Examples include database updates, live concerts, news, music/audio broadcasts, announcements, lectures, and many more.

- *Many-to-one*—Many-to-one multicasts are less common; they include data collection, auctions, and polling.

- *Many-to-many*—Many-to-many multicasts are rare, but they are gaining popularity as programmers begin to utilize multicast in some imaginative ways. Chat groups, multimedia conferencing, concurrent processing, interactive music sessions, and collaboration are examples of many-to-many multicasts. But don't forget the rising star (and my favorite): interactive multiplayer games.

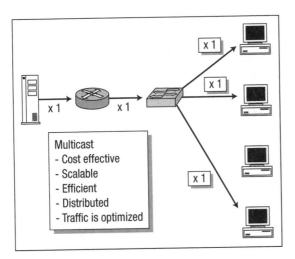

Figure 7.3   Multicast traffic flow.

Want to Join the Military?

The U.S. military has one of the largest interactive multicast-based war-game simulations I've heard of. The battlefield is divided into map grids, and each grid square is a multicast group. Individuals communicate with each other and with the server by multicast. When an individual driving a tank or a fighter enters a grid square, it joins the multicast group to receive that square's simulation traffic. As the individual moves from square to square, the individual's multicast group membership changes.

IP multicasting uses Class D network addresses to route data to different groups and hosts. Most basic networking classes cover Classes A, B, and C, but usually don't go into depth about Classes D and E. Maybe you were told that they are used for experimental purposes and not to worry about them. Well, as you will see in the next few sections, things have changed.

IP Multicasting Addresses

IP multicasting uses a variation of a Class D network address space assigned by the Internet Assigned Number Authority (IANA). A Class D address is denoted with a binary 1110 prefix in the first octet. The range spans from 224.0.0.0 to 239.255.255.255. Applications use one of the addresses in this range as the multicast group address on the Internet.

NOTE: *A permanent IP multicast address is rarely assigned to an application. Instead, the address is assigned to a specific network protocol or network application. Applications on the Internet must dynamically request a multicast address when needed and release the address when it is no longer being used.*

Due to the nature of multicast addresses, they are frequently referred to as *multicast groups*. In addition, certain well-known groups have been identified by the IANA. These are detailed in RFC 2365 and are known as *administrative scopes*. We will discuss this topic later in this section.

The Multicast IP Structure

An IP multicast frame contains a single IP address. The host group is also identified by a single IP address. This process operates at Layer 3. However, switches do not understand IP addresses; they operate with Media Access Control (MAC) addresses. Let's look at how the Layer 3 address is mapped to a Layer 2 address.

IP MAC addresses are 48 bits long. If the first 24 bits are set to 01-00-5e, with the next bit set to 0, that leaves 23 bits for the IP address to be mapped to the MAC address. The multicast IP address is 32 bits long with 28 unique bits. So, only the last 23 bits of the IP address are mapped to the MAC address.

Figure 7.4 shows the MAC address and IP address mapping.

Let's take a quick look at how this process works. Consider the multicast address 224.138.8.5:

```
1110 0000 1000 1010 0000 1000 0000 0101
XXXX XXXX X000 1010 0000 1000 0000 0101
```

The X bits are not used. The remaining bits

```
000 1010 0000 1000 0000 0101
```

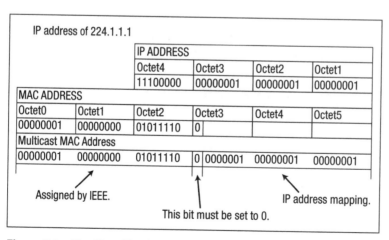

Figure 7.4   The IP multicast address structure.

give you 0a:08:05. Put that result together with 01:00:5e: and you get 01:00:5e:0a:08:05.

Here is another example, using the multicast address 224.127.15.10:

```
1110 0000 0111 1111 0000 1111 0000 1010
XXXX XXXX X111 1111 0000 1111 0000 1010
```

After removing the X portion, the section

```
111 1111 0000 1111 0000 1010
```

yields 7f:0f:0a. Again, you put this result together with 01:00:5e to get 01:00:5e:7f:0f:0a.

This process creates an ambiguity when a Layer 3 IP address is mapped to the Layer 2 MAC address. A 32-to-1 relationship (2^5) exists, meaning that for every multicast MAC address, there are 32 corresponding IP addresses. Figure 7.5 shows the MAC address ambiguities.

A host that is set up to receive multicast group 224.127.15.10 will have the network interface card interrupt the CPU when a frame with the destination MAC address 01:00:5e:7f:0f:0a arrives. This MAC address is also used by 31 other multicast groups. If any of these groups are active on the LAN, the CPU will have to examine the frames for both multicast groups to decide if the frame that interrupted the CPU belongs to the desired multicast group. This process could degrade the performance of the host PC if many multicast groups are on the network. You must consider this fact when assigning multicast groups to applications.

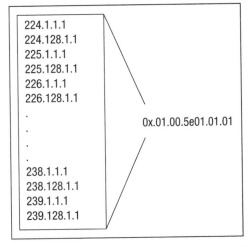

Figure 7.5   The 32-to-1 relationship of IP addresses to MAC address.

Special Multicast Addresses

The range from 224.0.0.0 to 224.0.0.255 is reserved for use on the network by network protocols. Cisco routers by default do not forward IP multicast frames that arrive for this range. Routers that forward these packets are known as *broken routers*. Routing protocols use this range to communicate with each other (see Table 7.1).

The range from 224.0.1.0 to 224.1.255.255 is assigned by IANA to network protocols and network applications on a permanent basis. To obtain one of these addresses, you must have a really good technical justification.

The range from 239.0.0.0 to 239.255.255.255 contains administratively scoped addresses for use in private networks, similar to the use of 10.x.x.x for IP addresses. The network administrator must ensure that this kind of multicast traffic does not leave the private network.

The range from 224.2.0.0 to 233.255.255.255 is dynamically assigned to applications that require a multicast address. This process is similar to the way Dynamic Host Configuration Protocol (DHCP) assigns IP addresses to hosts. The multicast address is allocated or leased when it's needed and released to be used by others when it's not needed. The Session Directory (SDR) program currently is the most widely used method of dynamically allocating IP multicast addresses. The Internet Engineering Task Force (IETF) is considering modifying SDR to enable it to scale well or to define and develop a new form of dynamic multicast address allocation.

NOTE: *IANA has started to assign blocks of multicast addresses from this range. To review a current list of multicast addresses, visit **www.isi.edu/in-notes/iana/assignments/multicast-addresses**.*

Table 7.1   Partial list of non-routed local multicast addresses.

Address	Destination
.1	All systems in this subnet
224.0.0.2	All routers in this subnet
.4	Distance Vector Multicast Routing Protocol
.5	Open Shortest Path First (OSPF) routers
.6	Open Shortest Path First (OSPF) designated routers
.7	Routing Information Protocol 2 (RIP2) routers
.8	Internet Gateway Routing Protocol (IGRP) routers
.9	Dynamic Host Configuration Protocol (DHCP) server/relay agent
.10	All Protocol-Independent Multicast (PIM) routers

Delivery of Multicast Datagrams

When the sender and recipients are members of the same subnet, delivery of multicast frames is a simple matter. The source station addresses the IP packet to the multicast group, the Network Interface Card (NIC) maps the IP address to the multicast MAC address, and the frame is sent. Recipients that want to capture the frame notify their IP layer that they want to receive datagrams addressed to the group.

When the sender is on one subnet and the recipients are on different subnets, the routers need to use a multicast routing protocol that permits the construction of multicast delivery trees and supports multicast data packet forwarding.

Multicast Distribution Tree

The multicast model uses one source and many destinations. The packet travels from one router to many routers on different paths. This route forms a *multicast distribution tree*, with the first router as the root. Multicast distribution tree is a dynamic visualization of how the multicast packet travels the network. The packet travels from one router to the next until it reaches the destination—it follows a line from end to end.

NOTE: *In unicast, there is no such tree.*

There are two types of distribution trees: *source trees* and *shared trees*.

The source tree is the simplest type of tree. The source of the multicast traffic forms the root of the tree and the branches are the paths through the network to the destination. This form is commonly referred to as the *shortest path tree (SPT)* because it uses the shortest path to reach the destination. This design functions very well in a one-to-many model, but it has drawbacks when used in a many-to-many model. For example, a live concert has only one source, so there will be only one distribution tree in the router for the multicast group. But in a video conference with 20 participants, you will have 20 different trees for the same multicast group.

In a shared tree design, the entire multicast group utilizes the same distribution path. The root is placed at a selected point in the network. Protocol Independent Multicast (PIM) refers to this router/point as the *rendezvous point*; Core-Based Tree (CBT) multicast routing protocol refers to this router as the *core*. All multicast traffic for that group is first sent to the root/rendezvous point. It then flows out the branches to the destination. Only one distribution tree exists for the multicast group, which in turn means each router only has to keep track of one path for that multicast group.

> **NOTE:** CBT is a rarely implemented multicast routing protocol. It is in a constant state of development. The newest version (version 3) is already in draft form, even though the current version 2 is not yet widely used. Unfortunately, there is no backward compatibility from version 3 to version 2. It will be a while before you see mainstream hardware support for this protocol. PIM, which is more commonly used, will be discussed later in this chapter.

The only difference between the source tree and the shared tree in a one-to-many multicast is that the root moves from the first router to some other point in the network. In a many-to-many multicast, the differences and advantages become more significant. The shared tree is subdivided into unidirectional and bidirectional trees. In the unidirectional shared tree, the multicast traffic can first be unicast to the root for distribution to the rest of the multicast group; it can also be sent as a multicast using the source tree model with the source as the root and the shared tree root as the branch. A bidirectional shared tree takes advantage of the existing routing table to distribute multicast traffic to the multicast group. Multicast traffic can go back the same path by which it came to the rendezvous point and be distributed from the root. Before the traffic reaches the root, it follows the multicast routing table to the other destinations. This way, the multicast traffic flows only one time on any path on the network.

Multicast Forwarding

Let's look at how the routers make the distribution tree. In unicast traffic, the router makes a forwarding decision based on the destination address. It looks up the address in the routing table and forwards the packet to the next hop via the associated interface. In multicast traffic, rather than a single IP address, a multicast address is associated with multiple hosts; this addressing makes the forwarding decision more complex.

The router utilizes Reverse Path Forwarding (RPF) to make the forwarding decision. Instead of using the destination address, the router uses the source address. It checks the source address and determines whether the packet comes from an interface that leads back to the source address. If the packet did not arrive on an interface that leads back to the source, the RPF check fails and the packet is discarded. If the packet comes from the interface that leads back to the source, the packet is forwarded out the other interfaces on the router.

The router determines which interface is on the reverse path back to the source using either the unicast routing table or a separate multicast routing table. This routing decision is based on the multicast routing protocol.

IGMP Protocols

In order to build multicast routes for each multicast group, routers communicate with each other via one of the following protocols:

- *DVMRP*—Distance Vector Multicast Routing Protocol
- *PIM*—Protocol Independent Multicast
- *MOSPF*—Multicast Open Shortest Path First

Distance Vector Multicast Routing Protocol

DVMRP is based on RIP and is widely used. Just like RIP, it uses a distance vector (hops) and sends out periodic route updates. It's different from RIP in that it is classless and has a hop limit of 32 rather than 16. When DVMRP is first implemented on a router, it sends a probe packet with its IP address out all the interfaces. Another DVMRP router receives the probe and adds the IP address to its list of DVMRP neighbors on that interface. It then sends back a probe with its IP address and the first router's IP address. When the first router receives a probe with its own IP address, it knows that it has a two-way adjacency between itself and the other router. The two routers will then begin to exchange routing information.

As stated earlier, the router uses RPF to ensure that a packet arrives on the correct interface. If the packet fails the RPF check, it is discarded. When it passes the RPF check, the packet is forward out all other interfaces. As the multicast traffic is sent out, it reaches every point in the network. That's great if every host on the network wants the multicast—but if part of the network does not need the multicast, the traffic is just taking up bandwidth. To overcome this problem, the multicast routers use a process called *pruning*. If the router is not connected to a recipient (multicast destination), it sends a prune message to the upstream router to stop the flow of unnecessary multicast traffic. The upstream router responds by pruning the connection to the router. If the interface on the upstream router is connected to another router, it also must send a prune message before the upstream router will prune traffic from that interface. As the prune message traffic flows from one router to another, the multicast traffic is only sent to the portion of the network that wants it. If the router wants to receive multicast traffic after being pruned, it must send a graft message to the upstream router. When the upstream router receives the graft message, it sends out a graft-ack message. If that router is not receiving the multicast traffic, it will also send a graft message to its upstream router. The graft message will be sent until it reaches a router that is receiving the multicast traffic.

DVMRP sends out periodic updates. It cannot be used in a network with a diameter greater than 31 hops, and it does not consider the bandwidth of the link. It was the first multicast routing protocol, so, despite its limitations, it is deployed in the Internet Multicast Backbone (MBONE). The MBONE is used primarily to transmit desktop video conferencing and—due to the use of DVMRP as its protocol—it has been responsible for several Internet meltdowns when the volume of traffic has become overwhelming.

7. IP Multicast

Protocol Independent Multicast

Protocol Independent Multicast (PIM) is an IP multicast routing protocol that is independent of the unicast routing protocol on the router. It does not maintain a multicast routing table, but instead uses the unicast routing table. The routing table can be populated in many ways: OSPF, static routes, Enhanced IGRP (EIGRP), Border Gateway Protocol (BGP), and so on. By using the existing routing table to perform reverse path forwarding checks, PIM sends out no updates and the overhead on the router is significantly reduced.

PIM operates in two modes:

- *Dense mode (DM)*—Utilizes the source tree distribution model. It is designed to operate in an environment where bandwidth is plentiful and the multicast traffic is destined for all LANs. DM is suitable for environments with a small number of senders and many recipients. DM is also a good choice in high-traffic networks with a constant stream of multicast traffic. PIM-DM enabled routers that have no local members of a multicast group will prune themselves from that group with prune messages sent to neighboring IP multicast routers. The neighbors that receive the prune messages stop sending multicast messages and start a timer. When this timer expires, they begin sending multicast messages to the pruned group again. This process is known as the *broadcast and prune cycle*.

- *Sparse mode (SM)*—Uses the unidirectional shared tree design. It is designed to operate in environments where group members are distributed across many regions of the Internet and bandwidth may not be widely available. SM does not imply that the group has few members, just that they are widely dispersed across the Internet. The objective of SM is to prevent situations in which a relatively small number of devices want to participate in a multicast environment and cause the multicast traffic to overwhelm the network. SM is designed to limit multicast traffic so that only those routers interested in receiving traffic for a particular group participate in it. Each router that wishes to receive the multicast traffic sends a PIM join message toward the root node (rendezvous point). As this join message travels up the tree, the multicast routers along the way forward the requested traffic back down the tree to the destination.

To put it in a simple form, PIM-DM will send the multicast traffic everywhere until it is told not to. PIM-SM will not send any multicast traffic until it is asked to.

NOTE: *Cisco routers use PIM-SM. They can receive and forward messages to DVMRP neighbors, but they do not actually implement DVMRP in their networks.*

Multicast Open Shortest Path First

Multicast Open Shortest Path First (MOSPF) is an extension of the Open Shortest Path First (OSPFv2) unicast routing protocol. OSPF must be running on the network for MOSPF to work. OSPF is a link-state routing protocol that allows a network to be split into multiple areas. The OSPF link-state database provides the complete map of an area at each router. MOSPF's extension is a new link-state advertisement (LSA) to distribute multicast group membership throughout the OSPF area. The group membership LSA includes the multicast group address, the router ID, and the interfaces on the router that have members in the multicast group. This information reaches all the MOSPF routers in the area, so each router will have a complete database of all the multicast group members. Each router will then construct a source tree from the link-state information.

MOSPF is a very bandwidth-efficient multicast routing protocol, but it does have a downside: It is very CPU intensive. If the network topology is not stable, the router will have to recalculate the routing tabling. Multicast increases the problem, because each membership change will cause a new computation. In a many-to-many multicast environment, by utilizing the source tree model, a new SPT is created for each source. Because of this, MOSPF is most suitable in a stable environment where the location of sources, number of sources, number of groups, and group membership are under tight control.

Internet Group Management Protocol (IGMP)

Internet Group Management Protocol (IGMP) is used by hosts to request multicast traffic. An individual host sends out an IGMP member report to inform the multicast router that it wants to receive data transmissions. The router maintains a list of multicast group memberships learned from IGMP. The multicast group membership list is built on a per-interface basis and is considered active if one host maintains its membership.

There are currently two versions of IGMP: version 1 (IGMPv1), which is defined in RFC 1112; and version 2 (IGMPv2), which is defined in RFC 2236. Let's look at the two versions of IGMP and how they differ.

IGMPv1

You may wonder why we're explaining version 1, when version 2 is the standard. Well, there are PCs that still use IGMPv1. Windows 95 (the OS that never goes away) supports IP multicast utilizing IGMPv1, unless you download an upgrade version of Microsoft's Winsock dynamic link library (DLL). (Windows 98 and Windows 2000 have native support for IGMPv2.) The same situation applies to the different versions of Unix. Unless all of the computers on your network are running the latest version of an OS or you've installed a patch, you're going to have computers using IGMPv1.

IGMP uses a query and response format. The router sends a *host membership query* message to the all-hosts multicast address, 244.0.0.1. (If multiple routers are on the network, one will be designated to send the message.) When a host receives the query message, it responds with a *membership report* to the multicast group of which the host is a member. If more than one host on the subnet belongs to the same multicast group, it will see the membership report and not respond to the membership query. As the router receives the responses, it will build a list of all the multicast groups for that interface. Any other router on the same subnet will also receive the responses and will have the same information.

NOTE: *A host does not have to wait for a host membership query to send out a membership report. It could send an unsolicited membership report, a process sometimes mistakenly referred to as sending out an IGMP join to the router.*

To minimize the traffic, IGMP utilizes a report suppression mechanism. The host starts a countdown with a random value between zero and the maximum response interval for each multicast group to which it belongs. When the value reaches zero, the host sends a membership report. All members of the same multicast group receive this message and reset their own countdown values. As long as the router receives a membership response, it will not send out a host membership query.

To leave a multicast group, a host simply stops sending membership responses. If no group members send member responses, the router begins its own timer (usually one minute). It will then send a membership query and reset its timer. If the router sends a membership query three times and does not get a reply, it will stop sending the multicast group's traffic out that interface.

The time interval from when the last host leaves the multicast group until the router stops transmitting traffic can create network problems. Assume that a user is trying to find a channel (multicast group) on a multimedia application. As the user surfs the different channels to locate the one he wants, he will join multiple multicast groups. If he goes through six channels before finding the one he wants, the router will transmit all six multicast groups' traffic until the timer runs out. This process may not affect the user much, but if the traffic is coming across a WAN link, the unnecessary high-bandwidth multimedia traffic will bog down the link. IGMPv2 was developed with this situation in mind.

IGMPv2

IGMPv2 functions the same as version 1, with the following enhancements:

- *Querier election process*—Allows the routers on the local subnet to elect the designated IGMP querier utilizing IGMP rather than using an upper-layer protocol, as in version 1. The router with the lowest IP address is elected and is responsible for sending out the multicast query for that subnet.

- *Maximum response time*—Allows the router to set an upper limit for the value the host will use to determine when to send a membership report. This limit enables you to fine-tune your IGMP traffic.

- *Multicast group-specific query message*—An enhancement to the original all-host membership query. Rather that being sent to everyone, a multicast query will be sent only to the specific multicast group.

- *Leave group message*—The biggest improvement in IGMPv2. In version 2, a host joins a multicast group the same way as in version 1. However, the process of leaving is completely different. Instead of just keeping quiet, the host sends a leave group message to the all-routers (224.0.0.2) multicast group. When a router receives this message, it sends out a multicast group-specific query. (The router must send this query because it only keeps a list of multicast groups associated with each interface. It doesn't know if any other multicast group members exist.) When another host on the same subnet receives the query, it responds with a membership report. The router will then maintain that multicast group's association to that interface. Just as in version 1, other members of the same multicast group will see the reply and not respond to the query. If the host is the last member of the multicast group and no other host responds to the query, the router will wait a last member query interval (default value one second) and send out another group-specific query. If it doesn't receive any reply to this second query, the router will stop transmitting multicast traffic out that interface. This process results in a much faster response time than in version 1 when a host leaves the multicast group.

TIP: *By default, Cisco routers utilize version 2. If any host on the subnet does not support version 2, you must change the router to version 1.*

Time to Live

Using the IP time to live (TTL) field is an important IGMP topic. The TTL field is a value in an IP packet that tells a network router whether the packet has been in the network too long and should be discarded. A multicast datagram with a TTL of 0 is allowed only on the same host. A TTL of 1 (the default value) is allowed only on the local subnet. If a higher TTL is set, the router is allowed to forward the packet.

By increasing the TTL value, a multicast application can look further from its origin for a server. This process works in the following manner: The host first sends a multicast message with a TTL of 1. If it doesn't receive a response, it sends a multicast message with a TTL of 2, then 3, and so on, until it reaches its limit. In this manner, the application can locate the nearest server that can be reached.

You can also change the multicast TTL value on a router's interface to prevent multicast traffic from leaving your network. If you set the TTL value higher than the multicast application's TTL value, the traffic will never leave the network.

Multicast at Layer 2

You must be wondering by now why we keep talking about routers when this book's title is *Cisco Switching Black Book*. Let's get down to how multicast behaves in a switch environment. As you are well aware, the difference between a hub and a switch is how the device forwards the frames out the ports: A hub will forward a frame out every port except the receiving port, whereas a switch will forward the frame to the ports based on the destination MAC address.

A switch accomplishes this task by comparing the destination MAC address with a forwarding table. This forwarding table is populated by looking at the source MAC addresses of frames sent between every port and keeping track of the port from which the frame arrived. This information creates a forwarding table that is usually kept in Content Addressable Memory (the table is commonly referred to as a *CAM table*). When the switch receives a frame with a destination MAC address that is not in the forwarding table, it has no choice but to send it out every port in hopes that it will reach its destination. This usually happens in two situations: when the destination MAC address has not been seen before, or when the destination MAC address is a broadcast/multicast address.

If the MAC address has never been seen before, the switch will eventually receive a frame with that MAC address as the source; the address will then be put into the forwarding table. This process takes a little time. If the MAC address is a broadcast/multicast address, the switch will never see a frame with that MAC address as the source address. If you have multicast traffic, this situation will turn your Catalyst 5000 into a very expensive hub. To overcome this problem, Cisco has the following solutions:

- IGMP snooping
- Cisco Group Management Protocol (CGMP)
- Router Group Management Protocol (RGMP)
- GARP Multicast Registration Protocol (GMRP)

IGMP Snooping

IGMP snooping works as its name implies: The switch snoops on the traffic between the host and the multicast router. When the switch sees an IGMP report from a host for a multicast group, it associates that port with the multicast MAC address in the CAM table. When the switch sees an IGMP leave group message, it removes the port from the association.

NOTE: *The source port must also be added to the association for that multicast group in the CAM table.*

This process looks simple. As a host joins the multicast group, its port number is added to the CAM table; as the host leaves, its port is removed from the CAM table. However, this entire process forgets about the switch's processor. The switch must also receive the multicasts in order to receive the join and leave messages. If a steady stream of multicast traffic is received by the switch, the processor will be so busy checking the multicast traffic that it will have no time to process any other traffic. To overcome this problem, Cisco redesigned its switch to enable the ports to examine frames for Layer 3 information. When the port sees an IGMP frame, the frame will only be forwarded to the processor. This way, the processor will see all the IGMP traffic but will not receive any non-IGMP multicast traffic.

Let's look at the entire process. When a host broadcasts an IGMP report, the report is processed by the switch and sent out to every port. The router will begin to send multicast traffic to the switch. The switch will add the source port to the CAM table along with the first port. As more hosts send IGMP reports, their ports are added to the forwarding table. When the router sends a general query to the switch, the switch will send the multicast to every port. All the multicast group members will send a reply to the router (all IGMP replies are sent to the processor). The processor will send one IGMP report to the router so that it will continue to receive the multicast traffic. When a host sends a leave group message, the switch sends a general query out the same port to ensure that no other host wishes to receive the multicast (if the port is connected to another switch/hub). It will remove the port from the CAM table if it does not get a reply.

IGMP snooping is very efficient and is vendor independent. Unfortunately, it is only available for the enterprise class Catalyst switches.

Cisco Group Management Protocol

Cisco Group Management Protocol (CGMP) is a lightweight Layer 2 protocol that will only work between a Cisco router and a Cisco switch. CGMP is supported by almost the full line of routers and switches. A router and a switch utilize CGMP to communicate the multicast member states in the CAM table entries. The router communicates with the host using IGMP, but these IGMP messages are ignored by the switch.

When a host sends a membership report to the multicast router, the router sends a CGMP message to the switch with the host's MAC address and the multicast

MAC address. The CGMP switch uses the host's MAC address to look up the port. Depending on the CGMP message, the switch will either remove the port from or add it to the CAM table of the specific multicast MAC address.

This entire process moves the administration of the multicast from the switch to the router. The switch only has to follow the instructions and add/remove MAC addresses from the CAM table (which is what it is designed to do).

TIP: *When you enable the router's interface with CGMP, ensure that the CGMP-enabled switch is already connected to that interface. When CGMP is enabled on the router, the router will send an assign router port message to the switch.*

Router Group Management Protocol

Router Group Management Protocol (RGMP) is used by the switch to manage the multicast router. It is supported by Catalyst enterprise LAN switches. It lets a switch reduce multicast traffic by sending multicasts to the routers that are configured to receive them.

All the routers on the network must support RGMP and have PIM-SM running. IGMP snooping must also be enabled on the switch. The router sends a hello packet to the switch. The hello packet tells the switch when it will receive multicast traffic. This message is called an *RGMP join*. When the router wants to stop receiving multicast traffic, it sends an RGMP leave message to the switch. These messages greatly reduce the multicast traffic on the network.

GARP Multicast Registration Protocol

Generic Attribute Registration Protocol (GARP) Multicast Registration Protocol (GMRP) prevents multicast flooding on the switch. This protocol provides a way for the host to communicate with the switch at the MAC level. It runs independently of the Layer 3 protocol.

GMRP software must be running on both the host and the Cisco switch. GMRP is generally used with IGMP on the host. The GMRP application sends a message when the host sends an IGMP message. The switch uses the GMRP information to manage the multicast traffic. The switch periodically sends GMRP queries. If it does not receive a response, the port will be removed from the multicast group.

GMRP requires the installation of special software on the host; for this reason, it is not widely used. This protocol is most suitable in a situation where the switch cannot run IGMP snooping or CMGP.

Immediate Solutions

Configuring IP Multicast Routing

To enable IP multicast routing, use the following command in Global mode:

```
Router(config)# ip multicast-routing
```

NOTE: *The hostname "Router" indicates that this must be configured on an external router or an internal route processor, such as the RSM, RSFC, MSM, or MSFC. The hostname "Coriolis" indicates that the configuration is taking place on a Set/Clear-based IOS switch, such as the 2900G, 5000, or 6000 family of switches.*

Disabling IP Multicast Routing

To disable IP multicast routing, use the following command in Global mode:

```
Router(config)# no ip multicast-routing
```

Enabling PIM on an Interface

When you enable PIM on an interface, IGMP is enabled at the same time on that interface. PIM operates in either Dense mode or Sparse mode on each interface. The different modes dictate how the router populates the multicast routing table, as well as how the router will forward multicast packets.

Use the following commands to configure each interface:

```
Router(config-if)# ip pim dense-mode
Router(config-if)# ip pim sparse-mode
```

You can also let the multicast group decide which mode the interface will be in:

```
Router(config-if)# ip pim sparse-dense-mode
```

Disabling PIM on an Interface

Use the following commands to disable PIM on the interface:

```
Router(config-if) no ip pim sparse-mode
Router(config-if) no ip pim dense-mode
Router(config-if) no ip pim sparse-dense-mode
```

7. IP Multicast

Configuring the Rendezvous Point

You can configure the rendezvous point (RP) manually or let it be auto-discovered. To configure the RP manually, you have to configure the routers that have either the sender of the multicast traffic or the receiver of the multicast traffic connected to its segment. The RP router can be any router on the network and does not need to know that it is the rendezvous point:

```
Router(config-if) ip pim rp-address [ip address]
```

To configure Auto-RP, you set up the RP router to send an rp-announce message:

```
Router(config)# ip pim send-rp-announce [interface] scope 11 group-list 1
Router(config)# access-list 1 permit 239.0.0.0 0.255.255.255
```

You can use any interface on the router, including the loop-back interface, as the IP address of the administrative group (just make sure all the routers know the route to that IP address).

Adding a Router to a Multicast Group

This feature lets the router accept and forward multicast traffic. You can use this command if the host on the segment cannot report its group memberships:

```
Router(config-if)# ip igmp join-group 225.01.02.112
```

NOTE: *One of the side effects to this is that the router will no longer use fast switching.*

Configuring a Router to Be a Static Multicast Group Member

This command will forward the desired multicast group to the specified segment of the network. Perform it on the interface connected to that segment:

```
Router(config-if)# ip igmp static-group 225.01.02.112
```

Restricting Access to a Multicast Group

Use this command when you want to restrict certain portions of the network from accessing multicast traffic:

```
Router(config-if)# ip igmp access-group [access-list-number]
```

Changing the IGMP Version

Cisco routers use IGMP version 2 by default. You must change the version of IGMP if you have version 1 equipment on the subnet, because all systems on the subnet must use the same version of IGMP. The router will not automatically change to version 1 if it detects version 1 equipment. Use the following command to change to version 1:

```
Router(config-if)# ip igmp version 1
```

Changing the IGMP Host-Query Message Interval

As mentioned earlier, the router sends IGMP host-query messages to the network to discover which multicast group is still active. You can modify the message interval setting to accommodate your network's bandwidth/utilization (the default is 60 seconds):

```
Router(config-if)# ip igmp query-interval 90
```

Configuring Multicast Groups

To manually add a multicast group to the switch, enter the following command:

```
Coriolis> (enable) set cam static 01-00-5e-0c-8-5 2/1-12
Static multicast entry added to CAM table.
```

This multicast group exists only until you reset the switch. To store the entry in the NVRAM, replace **static** with **permanent**:

```
Coriolis> (enable) set cam permanent 01-00-5e-0c-8-5 2/1-12
Permanent multicast entry added to CAM table.
```

Removing Multicast Groups

Use the following command to remove a multicast group manually:

```
Coriolis> (enable) clear cam 01-00-5e-0c-8-5
CAM entry cleared.
```

This command will remove the entire multicast group from the switch. When you want to remove only one port from the multicast group, you will have to remove the entire group and re-enter the desired port back into the switch.

Configuring Multicast Router Ports

To configure which port the multicast router is connected to, use the following command:

```
Coriolis> (enable) set multicast router 2/14
Port 2/14 added to multicast router port list.
```

You can use this command even if you are using IGMP snooping, CGMP, or GMRP.

Displaying Multicast Routers

To verify or display all the multicast router's ports, use the **show multicast router** command as shown here:

```
Coriolis> (enable) show multicast router
CGMP enable
IGMP disable
Port        Vlan
--------    ----------------
2/14   *    3
3/1         1

Total Number of Entries = 2
'*' - Configured
```

The asterisk between the port and the VLAN number means the multicast router port was manually configured.

Removing the Multicast Router

Use the following command to remove the multicast router port:

```
Coriolis> (enable) clear multicast router 2/14
Port 2/14 cleared from multicast router port list.
```

Configuring IGMP Snooping

IGMP snooping is disabled by default. To enable IGMP snooping, use the following command:

```
Coriolis> (enable) set igmp enable
IGMP Snooping is enabled.
CGMP is disabled.
```

NOTE: The switch will not let you enable IGMP snooping if CGMP or GMRP is enabled.

Disabling IGMP Snooping

To disable IGMP snooping, use the following command:

```
Coriolis> (enable) set igmp disable
IGMP feature for IP multicast disabled.
```

Configuring IGMP Fast-Leave Processing

To enable IGMP fast-leave processing, enter the following command:

```
Coriolis> (enable) set igmp fastleave enable
IGMP fastleave set to enabled.
CGMP is disabled.
```

Disabling IGMP Fast-Leave Processing

To disable IGMP fast-leaving processing, use the following command:

```
Coriolis> (enable) set igmp fastleave disable
IGMP fastleave set to disable.
```

Displaying IGMP Statistics

To display IGMP statistics for all VLANs, use the **show igmp multicast statistics** command as shown here:

```
Coriolis> (enable) show igmp statistics
IGMP enabled
IGMP fastleave disabled
```

7. IP Multicast

```
IGMP statistics for vlan1:
Total valid pkts rcvd:           17564
Total invalid pkts recvd         0
General Queries recvd            235
Group Specific Queries recvd     0
MAC-Based General Queries recvd  0
Leaves recvd                     4
Reports recvd                    14584
Other Pkts recvd                 0
Queries Xmitted                  0
GS Queries Xmitted               18
Reports Xmitted                  0
Leaves Xmitted                   0
Failures to add GDA to EARL      0
Topology Notifications rcvd      6
```

This is a good way to verify that IGMP is set up correctly. If you have more than one VLAN on the switch and want to display only the specific VLAN, use the command **show igmp multicast statistics [*vlan*]**.

Displaying Multicast Routers Learned from IGMP

To display multicast router ports that were learned from IGMP, use the following command:

```
Coriolis> (enable) show multicast router igmp
CGMP disable
IGMP enable
Port      Vlan
--------  ----------------
3/1       1

Total Number of Entries = 1
'*' - Configured
```

Displaying IGMP Multicast Groups

To display the total number of multicast groups, use the following command:

```
Coriolis> (enable) show multicast group count [vlan]
CGMP disable
IGMP enable
```

```
Total Number of Entries = 2
```

If you only want to display the number of multicast groups that were learned from IGMP, use the following command:

```
Coriolis> (enable) show multicast group count igmp [vlan]
CGMP disable
IGMP enable


Total Number of Entries = 1
```

To get more detail about the multicast groups, use this command:

```
Coriolis> (enable) show multicast group [vlan]
CGMP disable
IGMP enable

VLAN  Dest MAC/Route Des  Destination Ports or VCs / [Protocol Type]
----  ------------------  ------------------------------------------
1     01-88-75-88-08-57*  2/1-12
1     11-87-96-54-22-11*  2/1-12

Total Number of Entries = 2
```

Again, if you only want to see the entries that were learned from IGMP, you can use the command **show multicast group igmp [vlan]**.

Configuring CGMP

CGMP is disabled by default. Use the following command to enable CGMP:

```
Coriolis> (enable) set cgmp enable
CGMP support for IP multicast enabled.
```

Disabling CGMP

To disable CGMP, use the following command:

```
Coriolis> (enable) set cgmp disable
CGMP support for IP multicast disabled.
```

Enabling CGMP Fast-Leave Processing

To enable CGMP fast-leave processing, enter the following command:

```
Coriolis> (enable) set cgmp leave enable
CGMP leave processing enabled.
```

Disabling CGMP Fast-Leave Processing

To disable CGMP fast-leave processing, enter the following command:

```
Coriolis> (enable) set cgmp leave disable
CGMP leave processing disabled.
```

Displaying CGMP Statistics

To display CGMP statistics, use the following command:

```
Coriolis> (enable) show cgmp stat
CGMP enabled.

CGMP statistics for vlan 1:
valid rx pkts received          12548
invalid rx pkts received        0
valid cgmp joins received       12865
valid cgmp leaves received      147
valid igmp leaves received      0
valid igmp queries received     568
igmp gs queries transmitted     0
igmp leaves transmitted         0
failures to add GDA to EARL     0
topology notifications received 10
number of CGMP packets dropped  2456875
```

Configuring RGMP on the Switch

RGMP is disabled by default. Use the following command to enable RGMP globally:

```
Coriolis> (enable) set rgmp enable
RGMP enabled.
```

Disabling RGMP on the Switch

To disable RGMP, use the following command:

```
Coriolis> (enable) set rgmp disable
RGMP disabled.
```

Configuring RGMP on the Router

RGMP must be enabled on each interface that has the appropriate topology. Use this command:

```
Router(config)# vlan-interface 3
Router(config-if)# ip rgmp
```

Disabling RGMP on the Router

To disable RGMP, use the following command:

```
Router(config)# vlan-interface 3
Router(config-if)# no ip rgmp
```

NOTE: *Here are some related commands that you can try on the router:*

```
debug ip rgmp [group_name | group_address]
show ip rgmp interface [interface_unit_name]
show ip rgmp groups [group_name | group_address]
```

Displaying RGMP Groups

To display all the multicast groups that were joined by RGMP-capable routers, use the following command:

```
Coriolis> (enable) show rgmp group
VlanDest MAC/Route DesRGMP Joined Router Ports
-----------------------------------------------------------------------
201-00-5e-46-85-111/1,2/14
101-00-5e-14-11-285/1
Total Number of Entries = 2
'*' - Configured
```

To display the total number of RGMP groups, use the following command:

```
Coriolis> (enable) show rgmp group count [vlan]
Total Number of Entries = 2
```

Displaying RGMP-Capable Router Ports

To display the ports to which RGMP routers are connected, use the following command:

```
Coriolis> (enable) show multicast router rgmp
PortVlan
------------------
2/1 +1
2/16 +2

Total Number of Entries = 2
'*' - Configured
```

Displaying RGMP VLAN Statistics

To display RGMP statistics, use the following command:

```
Coriolis> (enable) show rgmp statistics 1
RGMP enabled
RGMP statistics for vlan <1>:
Receive:
Valid pkts:10
Hellos:5
Joins:3
Leaves:2
Byes:0
Discarded:0
Transmit:
Total Pkts:10
Failures:0
Hellos:10
Joins:
Leaves:0
Byes:0
```

You can reset the statistics with the command **clear rgmp statistics**.

Configuring GMRP

To enable GMRP globally, use the following command:

```
Coriolis> (enable) set gmrp enable
GMRP enabled.
```

Disabling GMRP

To disable GMRP globally, use the following command:

```
Coriolis> (enable) set gmrp disable
GMRP disabled.
```

Enabling GMRP on Individual Ports

You can enable GMRP on a per-port basis using this command:

```
Coriolis> (enable) set port gmrp enable 2/1-12
GMRP enabled on ports 2/1-12.
```

But don't be fooled—the switch will let you configure GMRP on a per-port basis, but it will not work unless you enable it globally.

Disabling GMRP on Individual Ports

To disable GMRP on each port, use the following command:

```
Coriolis> (enable) set port gmrp disable 2/1-12
GMRP disabled on ports 2/1-12.
```

Enabling GMRP Forward-All

When GMRP forward-all is enabled, a copy of all multicast traffic is forwarded to that port. You may want to use this feature when a probe or network analyzer is connected to a port. Cisco's documentation recommends that you enable forward-all on any port that is connected to a router. Use this command to enable forward-all:

```
Coriolis> (enable) set gmrp fwdall enable 2/1
GMRP Forward All groups option enabled on port 2/1.
```

Disabling GMRP Forward-All

To disable GMRP forward-all on a port, use the following command:

```
Coriolis> (enable) set gmrp fwdall disable 2/1
GMRP Forward All groups option disabled on port 2/1.
```

7. IP Multicast

Configuring GMRP Registration

GMRP registration has three modes:

- *Normal mode*—Allows dynamic GMRP multicast registration and de-registration on the port.

- *Fixed mode*—Registers all multicast group on all ports to this single port and ignores any subsequent registration and de-registration on other ports. To de-register any multicast group, you must first return the port to Normal mode.

- *Forbidden mode*—Un-registers all GMRP multicasts and will not accept any GMRP multicast registration on that port.

To configure Normal mode, use the following command:

```
Coriolis> (enable) set gmrp registration normal 2/1
GMRP Registration is set normal on port 2/1.
```

To configure Fixed mode, use the following command:

```
Coriolis> (enable) set gmrp registration fixed 2/1
GMRP Registration is set fixed on port 2/1.
```

To configure Forbidden mode, use the following command:

```
Coriolis> (enable) set gmrp registration forbidden 2/1
GMRP Registration is set forbidden on port 2/1.
```

Displaying the GMRP Configuration

To display the GMRP configuration setting on the switch, use the following command:

```
Coriolis> (enable) show gmrp configuration
Global GMRP Configuration:
GMRP Feature is currently enabled on this switch.
GMRP Timers (milliseconds):
Join = 200
Leave = 600
LeaveAll = 10000
GMRP-Status Registration ForwallAll Port(s)
---------- ------------ ---------- --------------------------------
Enabled    Normal       Disabled   1/1-12
                                   2/1-11,2/13-48
Enabled    Forbidden    Disabled   2/12
```

Setting GMRP Timers

If you have many multicast groups, you can change the GMRP timer value to improve performance. The **leave** timer value must be equal to or greater than three times the **join** timer value. The **leaveall** timer value must be greater than the **leave** timer value.

You must change the timer values in this order: **leaveall** timer value, **leave** timer value, and then **join** timer value. If you try to set the **join** timer value before you change the **leave** timer value, an error message will result.

Let's look at the commands to change the timer values:

```
Coriolis> (enable) set gmrp timer leaveall 8000
GMRP/GARP leaveAll timer value is set to 8000 milliseconds.

Coriolis> (enable) set gmrp timer leave 900
GMRP/GARP leave timer value is set to 900 milliseconds.

Coriolis> (enable) set gmrp timer join 300
GMRP/GARP join timer value is set to 300 milliseconds.
```

Displaying GMRP Timers

To display the GMRP timers, use the following command:

```
Coriolis> (enable) show gmrp timer

Timer     Timer Value (milliseconds)
--------  --------------------------
Join      300
Leave     900
LeaveAll  8000
```

TIP: *GMRP and GARP are interchangeable for the set and show commands. GMRP is considered an alias of GARP.*

Configuring Bandwidth-Based Suppression

Bandwidth-based suppression is a hardware-based suppression method. The threshold is set as a percentage of the port's bandwidth. When the multicast/broadcast traffic exceeds the threshold within a one second period, the switch stops forwarding multicast/broadcast traffic. Unicast traffic will still be forwarded. Use the following command to configure bandwidth-based suppression:

```
Coriolis> (enable) set port broadcast 2/12 75%
Port(s) 2/12 broadcast traffic limited to 75%.
```

Configuring Packet-Based Suppression

Packet-based suppression is a software-based suppression method. The threshold is set as a number of packets travelling through the port. When the multicast/broadcast traffic exceeds the threshold within a one-second period, the switch stops all incoming traffic for the remainder of the period. Use the following command to configure packet-based suppression:

```
Coriolis> (enable) set port broadcast 2/12 500
Port(s) 2/12 broadcast traffic limited to 500 packets/second.
```

Disabling Multicast Suppression

Use the following command to disable both bandwidth-based and packet-based suppression:

```
Coriolis> (enable) clear port broadcast 2/12
Port 2/12 broadcast traffic unlimited.
```

TIP: *Bandwidth-based suppression is preferable to packet-based suppression. Packet sizes vary, and it is difficult to determine the right number of packets to specify for packet-based suppression. For example, you could have 500 small broadcast packets that used only 10 percent of the bandwidth—but a packet-based suppression value of 500 would still shut down the port.*

Chapter 8

WAN Cell Switching

In Depth

WAN switching is defined as the process of forwarding data traffic across a wide area network. WAN switching uses *cell relay technology* to multiplex all network traffic across WAN trunk links without a predefined timeslot for each type of connection. Cell relay networks use small, fixed-length packets called *cells* to send control information in a header attached to the user's data. Using a common cell format for the encapsulation and transport of all network traffic, voice, video, and data over the WAN results in simplified, efficient, and quick routing and multiplexing of data.

These cell relay networks provide for very high throughput, short delays, and very low error rates. The industry standard for cell switching at Layer 2 is Asynchronous Transfer Mode (ATM) and LAN Emulation (LANE).

ATM was developed by the ATM Forum, which is part of the International Telecommunications Union Telecommunication Standardization Sector (ITU-T). Cisco—which is a leading member and one of the original founding members of the ATM Forum LAN Emulation Sub-Working group—has implemented LANE in most of its Core layer products.

The following Cisco WAN switches support ATM:

- BPX 8600 series wide area switches (8620, 8650, 8680)
- IGX 8400 series wide area switches (8410, 8420, 8430)
- MGX 8220 edge concentrator
- MGX 8800 wide area edge switch

These switches, which are also called *nodes*, fall into three Cisco WAN switched architectures:

- *Feeder nodes*—The MGX 8220 concentrator shelves, which are used to aggregate narrowband UNI connections and multiplex traffic onto a single trunk link to a BPX switch or routing node.
- *Hybrid nodes*—The IGX 8400 and the MGX 8800 switches, which are used to aggregate UNI connections. These switches are also used to route and switch packets to the trunks that lead to the final destination.
- *Routing nodes*—The BPX switches that actually render the switching decisions and forward packets to appropriate trunk links.

In the Cisco LAN and Catalyst switching line, you can use the Cisco Catalyst 5000 ATM module or the LightStream series of switches for ATM cell switching. The LightStream series of switches is covered in Chapter 9.

ATM Overview

ATM is a cell-based networking technology designed to be a high-speed, efficient method of supporting multiple types of traffic, including voice, data, and video. ATM's characteristics allow it to effectively support today's networking requirements.

Some of the major benefits of ATM are:

• *Efficient bandwidth*—ATM efficiently supports most transmission requirements of the network and allocates bandwidth as necessary. One of the primary reasons ATM is such a great protocol is its ability to accomplish this task without any manual intervention.

• *Scalability*—ATM is highly flexible, accommodating a wide range of traffic types, traffic rates, and communications applications.

An ATM network includes two types of devices: ATM switches and ATM endpoints. One type of ATM interface, called a user-network interface (UNI), connects an ATM device to a switch; a second type, called a network-to-network interface (NNI), connects an ATM switch to another ATM switch.

ATM has built-in support for Quality of Service (QoS), which is used to guarantee a level of service for networks that use ATM. This guarantee includes bandwidth utilization and data throughput. This type of service is critical when dealing with newer multimedia technologies.

LANE

LANE is a method used to provide backward compatibility to legacy Ethernet and Token Ring networks. LANE makes an ATM interface look like an Ethernet or Token Ring network interface, so no modifications to existing network drivers or applications need to be made to support ATM environments. LANE allows ATM networks to emulate Media Access Control (MAC) broadcast networks. Before the implementation of LANE, a proprietary emulation device was needed to connect ATM to a LAN topology.

ATM LANE works with a client/server architecture to create an emulated LAN (ELAN). An ELAN is very similar to a VLAN, in that it limits local broadcasts and multicast traffic to the ELAN. LANE devices can be either clients or servers. The LANE Emulation service (LE service) consists of several different components:

- *LAN Emulation Client (LEC)*—Resides in every ATM device and provides a LAN interface to higher layer protocols.

- *LAN Emulation Server (LES)*—The centerpiece of the LANE architecture. A single LES is responsible for address registry and resolution for an ELAN.

- *Broadcast and Unknown Server (BUS)*—The means by which ATM provides broadcasting support for an ELAN.

- *LAN Emulation Configuration Server (LECS)*—Contains the database of LES/BUS pairs for all the configured ELANs.

LANE is discussed in much more detail later in this chapter.

ATM—Easy to Learn?

Nothing in ATM makes it easy to comprehend and learn. It defies a lot of what today's network administrators have learned. Telling you that ATM is used as a backbone protocol in the network makes you think that you do not need to worry about packet-based broadcast LANs trying to communicate with cell-based ATM networks (which will be discussed in the following sections). In this chapter, I discuss how to connect ATM—which is a connection-oriented, point-to-point protocol—to the Layer 2 addresses of the broadcast domains in the LAN.

ATM is a difficult subject for most people, because they rarely are exposed to it on a day-to-day basis like Ethernet or Token Ring. In today's networking environment, however, increased emphasis is being put on integrating data, voice, and video in networks, and ATM is a driving force. No other protocol today has ATM's ability to ensure timely delivery of packets based on their type. In addition, ATM can be used on both LANs and WANs on almost any types of media, with speeds that can scale up to gigabits per second.

ATM Protocols

The protocols used in ATM have been specifically designed to support high-speed networks at speeds ranging up to gigabits per second (Gbps). Other physical LAN topologies, such as Gigabit Ethernet, provide high-speed networking and work very well in LANs. ATM, on the other hand, can handle network Gbps traffic in both LAN and WAN environments and could care less about the type of physical media being used.

ATM works on the theory that it is possible to expect upper-layer protocols to use a connectionless service to communicate with the lower layers. LANE is used to allow an upper-layer protocol to make connections to lower-layer ATM connection-oriented services. Thus, LANE provides a switching service that is transparent to the 802.x networks.

Traditional methods of transporting data use one of two ways to send data: character-based or frame-based. ATM is a cell-based switching technology that uses both circuit switching and frame switching to move packets through the network. Let's take a closer look at ATM's method of cell-based circuit switching.

ATM Circuit Switching

ATM is an efficient, high-bandwidth switching and multiplexing technology that also utilizes the benefits of circuit switching. *Circuit switching* is the process of using straight-through circuits between two points to ensure minimal transmission latency and guarantee equal bandwidth availability. Let's take a look at the ATM technology components used in ATM circuit switching services:

- *Circuit emulation (CE)*—A connection-oriented, constant bit rate ATM transport service. This service handles the heavy-duty, end-to-end timing requirements for the user's chosen bandwidth and QoS requirements for establishing a connection. This is typically a dedicated line for applications such as video conferencing and multimedia.

- *Frame Relay*—A widely used industry standard for WAN traffic that works by switching Data Link layer data. It uses multiple virtual circuits by implementing High-Level Data Link Control (HDLC) encapsulation between connected devices.

- *Switched Multimegabit Data Services (SMDS)*—A high-speed, packet-switched, datagram-based WAN technology typically offered by telephone companies.

- *Cell relay services (CRS)*—The basis for networking protocols, including ATM, SMDS, and IEEE 802.6. This networking technology uses small, fixed-length cells that can be switched in hardware at very high speeds.

Frame Relay, SMDS, and CRS are *fastpacket* transmission technologies used in today's network. Most standard ATM platforms can support all three of these fastpacket technologies. Typically, these transmission technologies support two types of network connections:

- *Permanent virtual circuit (PVC)*—A logical physical connection between two communicating ATM peers. This type of connection remains active (static) between two endpoints regardless of whether data is being transmitted over the connection. PVCs are typically used for interconnectivity between two fixed locations, such as a data center or company locations. This type of connection allows the network bandwidth to be predictable and constant.

- *Switched virtual circuit (SVC)*—A switched connection that is established by means of a defined and standardized ATM signaling protocol. Such connections are set up dynamically and are activated only when data must be

8. WAN Cell Switching

sent to the other end of the logical link. The connection is made *on demand* and is then terminated.

ATM Cells

ATM transports network data in fixed-sized units commonly called *cells*. Each cell is 53 bytes in length and is divided into a 5-byte header and 48 bytes of data. The 53-byte size of the cell, illustrated in Figure 8.1, is a compromise between the voice, data, and video advocates—one side wanted small cells (32 bytes) and another wanted larger packets (64 bytes). The final decision was to add the defaults (32 + 64 = 96) and divide the result by 2—and thus the data portion of the ATM cell contains 48 bytes.

The fixed size of the ATM cells provides some the following benefits:

- Efficient bandwidth use of the physical medium
- Ability of applications to share the network more fairly
- Accommodation for bursty applications
- Effective recovery of data loss on the physical wire

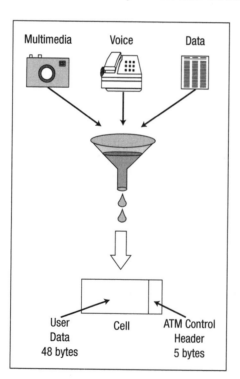

Figure 8.1   The ATM cell.

NOTE: *ATM is based on the switching and multiplexing techniques proposed by the ITU for Broadband Integrated Services Digital Network (BISDN) access.*

Time Division Multiplexing

ATM uses a switching and multiplexing method called *Time Division Multiplexing (TDM)*. This method places voice, multimedia, and data into fixed-length cells. These cells are then routed to their destination without regard to content.

TDM combines the information from different resources onto a single serial trunk link that dedicates a predefined timeslot on the multiplexed line for a piece of each resource's data, as shown in Figure 8.2. If a source has nothing to send, then the timeslot goes unused, and the bandwidth is considered wasted.

The ATM Cell Header

The ATM cells can be found in one of two formats, depending on whether the endpoints are a UNI or an NNI connection. The two differ in one way: The NNI header does not contain a Generic Flow Control (GFC) field. The NNI header has a Virtual Path Identifier (VPI) that occupies the entire first 12 bits. A cell header for a UNI cell is shown in Figure 8.3.

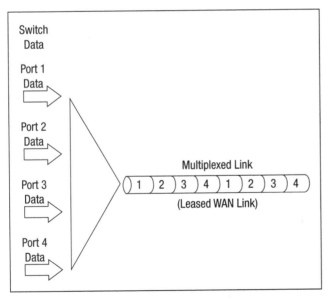

Figure 8.2   Data from multiple switch ports (resources) is sent down a single multiplexed serial link.

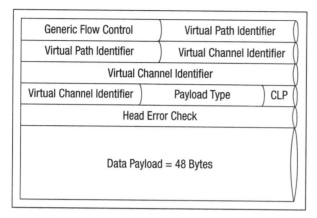

Generic Flow Control	Virtual Path Identifier	
Virtual Path Identifier	Virtual Channel Identifier	
Virtual Channel Identifier		
Virtual Channel Identifier	Payload Type	CLP
Head Error Check		
Data Payload = 48 Bytes		

Figure 8.3   An ATM UNI cell header.

Let's take a look at the fields in a cell header:

- *Generic Flow Control (GFC)*—An 8-bit field that is used to provide information to identify multiple stations that share a single ATM interface. The GFC is typically not used.

- *Virtual Path Identifier (VPI)*—An 8-bit field used with the VCI to identify the next destination of a cell as it passes through a series of ATM switches on its way to its destination.

- *Virtual Channel Identifier (VCI)*—An 8-bit field used in conjunction with the VPI to identify a cell's next destination.

- *Payload Type (PT)*—A 3-bit field that indicates whether the cell contains user data or control data. If the cell contains user data, the second bit in the user data indicates congestion, and the third bit indicates whether the cell is the last in a series of cells that represent a single AAL5 frame.

- *Congestion Loss Priority (CLP)*—A 1-bit field that indicates whether the cell should be discarded if it encounters extreme congestion as it moves through the network.

- *Header Error Check (HEC)*—An 8-bit field that indicates a checksum calculated only on the header itself.

The ATM Switch and ATM Endpoints

ATM networks use one of two types of devices for each end of the network: ATM switches and ATM endpoints. An *ATM endpoint* is a device that has an ATM network interface adapter, such as a workstation, router, Data Service Unit (DSU), or LAN switch. These devices in turn transmit data to an ATM switch, which is responsible for receiving this data, updating the header information, and then sending the data out the proper interface port to its intended destination.

As mentioned earlier in the chapter, in a UNI, the ATM interface connects an endpoint to a switch. In an NNI, the interface connects two ATM switches together. The UNI and NNI connections can be used to further divide the network into private and public networks. As the name implies, a *private network* connects the ATM endpoint to a private network, whereas a *public network* connects an ATM endpoint to a public switch (possibly owned by a telephone company or other WAN service provider).

The ATM Reference Model

The ATM standard uses a reference model to describe the functions of the protocol. The ATM Reference Model has three layers (which roughly correspond to those in the OSI model) and three management planes. The ATM Physical layer is similar to the Physical layer of the OSI model. The Physical layer controls the transmission and receipt of bits on the physical medium.

The ATM layer and the ATM Adaptation layer (AAL) are similar to the Data Link layer of the OSI chart. The ATM layer is responsible for establishing connections and passing cells through the ATM network. The ATM Adaptation layer translates the different types of network traffic. Four AALs are defined, but only three are actively in use:

- *AAL1*—Used to transport timing-dependent traffic such as voice

- *AAL3/4*—Used by network service providers in Switched Multimegabit Data Service (SMDS) networks

- *AA5*—The primary AAL used for non-SMDS traffic that doesn't require the pacing AAL1 would provide

Figure 8.4 shows the mapping of the ATM Reference Model compared to the OSI Reference Model.

The Physical Layer

The ATM Physical layer controls transmission and receipt of bits on the physical media. This layer also tracks the ATM cell boundaries and packages cells into the appropriate frame type. This layer is divided into two sublayers: the physical medium dependent (PMD) sublayer and the transmission convergence (TC) sublayer.

The PMD sublayer is responsible for sending and receiving a continuous flow of bits with the timing information to synchronize the transmission and reception of data. ATM does not care about the physical media being used, and all widely used physical topologies are capable of supporting ATM cells. Existing high-speed topologies capable of supporting ATM cells include Synchronous Optical Network (SONET), DS3/E3, Fiber Distributed Data Interface (FDDI), and unshielded twisted pair (UTP).

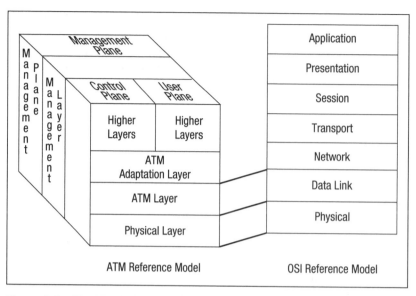

Figure 8.4   The ATM Reference Model layers compared to OSI Reference Model layers.

The TC sublayer is used to maintain the ATM cell boundaries, verify the validity of data, maintain data synchronization, create and check header error control to ensure valid data, and put the cells into a format that the physical media can use. This sublayer also extracts and inserts ATM cells within either a Plesiochronous Digital Hierarchy (PDH) or a Synchronous Digital Hierarchy (SDH) Time Division Multiplexed (TDM) frame and passes this frame to and from the ATM layer.

The ATM Layer

The ATM layer is responsible for establishing connections, passing cells to and from the AAL, inserting the ATM header, and extracting the ATM header. This layer is also responsible for multiplexing and demultiplexing data through the ATM network. To do this, ATM uses information contained in the header of each ATM cell. ATM switches use a VPI and a VCI field inside the ATM cell header to identify the next network segment a cell needs to transit on its way to its final destination.

A VCI is also known as a *virtual channel.* It is an identifier for the physical connection between the two ends that form a logical connection. A VPI is the identifier for a group of VCIs that allows an ATM switch to perform operations on a group of virtual connections (VCs).

The ATM Adaptation Layer

The ATM Adaptation Layer (AAL) provides the translation between the larger service data units of the upper layers of the OSI Reference Model and ATM cells. It works by receiving packets from the upper-level protocols and breaking them into 48-byte segments to be dumped into the payload of an ATM cell. The AAL has two sublayers: segmentation and reassembly (SAR) and the convergence sublayer (CS). The CS has further sublayers: the common part (CP) and the service specific (SS). Like protocols specified in the OSI Reference Model, Protocol Data Units (PDUs) are used to pass information between these layers.

The AAL translates between the different types of network traffic—such as video streams, data packets, and voice packets—of upper-layer processes and ATM cells. In other words, the AAL receives packets from upper-level protocols and breaks them into the 48-byte segments that form the payload field of an ATM cell. Several types of AAL standards are defined for this layer. Which AAL you use will largely depend on the type of traffic and what you are trying to do with the traffic. The characteristics of each AAL are as follows:

- *AAL1 (Class A)*—This layer is a connection-oriented service that provides end-to-end timing provisions. It maintains a constant data transfer rate, which is used for transporting telephone traffic and uncompressed video traffic. This is known as a constant bit rate (CBR) service. It is appropriate to use AAL1 to transport voice and video traffic or another type of timing-sensitive data.

- *AAL2 (Class B)*—This layer is reserved for data traffic that requires variable bit rates (VBR) and timing sensitivity, such as multimedia. It multiplexes short packets from multiple sources into a single cell with end-to-end timing and connection orientation.

- *AAL3/4 (Class C)*—This layer was designed for network service providers; it closely aligns with SMDS. This layer uses no VBR and has no timing requirements. It supports both connection-oriented and connectionless data for WAN links using Frame Relay or X.25. This layer is perfectly suited for use in environments that need to send or receive large files. AAL3 is identical to AAL4, with the exception that the AAL3 layer is connection-oriented only, whereas AAL4 is both connection-oriented and connectionless.

- *AAL5 (Class D)*—This layer is the primary AAL used to transfer non-SMDS data. It supports both connection-oriented and connectionless data. This layer is used for such applications as classical IP (CLIP) over ATM and LANE. Catalyst switches use this layer to provide LANE services for ATM.

ATM networks provide the transport method for several different independent emulated LANs. When a device is attached to one of these emulated LANs, its physical location no longer matters to the administrator or implementation. This process allows you to connect several LANs in different locations with switches to create one large emulated LAN. This arrangement can make a big difference, because attached devices can now be moved easily between emulated LANs. Thus, an engineering group can belong to one ELAN and a design group can belong to another ELAN, without the groups ever residing in the same location.

LANE also provides translation between multiple-media environments, allowing data sharing. Thus, Token Ring or FDDI networks can share data with Ethernet networks as if they were part of the same network.

Specifying ATM Connections

ATM networks manage traffic by establishing and configuring each connection. When establishing the connection, the connection type and the resources required to support the connection are specified as a class of service. This class is used to provide users with a guaranteed QoS.

The classes of service for QoS are defined by the ATM Forum and are as follows:

- *Available bit rate (ABR)*—Supports variable-rate data transmissions without preserving any timing relationships between the source and destination nodes. This connection type provides for a best effort service above a specified minimum cell rate (MCR).

- *Constant bit rate (CBR)*—Typically used to carry constant rate traffic and represented by fixed timing. CBR is typically used for circuit emulation, uncompressed voice, and multimedia data traffic.

- *Variable bit rate-real time (VBR-RT)*—Typically used for connections that carry VBR traffic in which a fixed timing relationship exists between either VBR video or voice compression.

- *Variable bit rate-non real time (VBR-NRT)*—Used to carry VBR traffic in which no timing relationship exists for data traffic where a guarantee of bandwidth or latency is needed. This type of connection is used in Frame Relay where the committed information rate (CIR) of the Frame Relay connection is mapped into a bandwidth guarantee within the ATM network.

- *Unspecified bit rate-real time (UBR-RT)*—Does not offer any service guarantees whatsoever. This type of connection is typically for the bursty or unpredictable traffic patterns from LAN protocols served by ATM routers.

ATM Addressing

ATM devices must have unique ATM addresses in order to connect to other ATM devices. The device at the other end of your circuit must know your address. ATM uses both private and public types of addresses. Because the ATM standard has adopted the subnetwork model of addressing, the ATM layer is responsible for mapping Network layer addresses to the ATM addresses.

Currently, two types of ATM addressing plans are used. The ATM UNI address format defined by ITU-T uses telephone-type E.164 addresses. This format is used to connect an endpoint to a telephone carrier's network. One drawback to this type of address is that E.164 addresses are available only from large telephone carriers, which prevents the addresses from being assigned to competitors and private businesses.

The ISO has defined a second address type that uses a Network Service Access Point (NSAP) format. This format is used to connect an ATM endpoint to a private network. The ATM Forum has now used this method to incorporate the E.164 address of the public networks into the address of customers using NSAP addresses. The ATM Forum is also working on a method for the phone carriers to use NSAP-based addressing on their networks. Let's take a look at the components of an NSAP address, as shown in Figure 8.5:

- *Authority and format identifier (AFI)*—Used to indicate which standard is being used for the ATM address. An AFI of 47 indicates a British Standards Institute address (used by Cisco on all its ATM devices); an AFI of 39 indicates an ISO address and an E.164 address.

- *Initial domain identifier (IDI)*—Indicates the address allocation and administrative authority.

- *Domain specific part (DSP)*—Contains the actual routing information.

- *End-system identifier (ESI)*—Places the end system's MAC address in the frame.

- *NSAP selector field (SEL)*—Identifies the LANE components.

Local Area Network Emulation (LANE)

In a LAN environment, broadcast support is an inherent part of the networking technology. Legacy networks have native broadcast support to perform address mapping resolution. In contrast, ATM networks are Non-Broadcast Multiple Access (NBMA) networks with no such support. The LANE standard was created by the ATM Forum in 1994 to provide connectivity for ATM networks to legacy Ethernet and Token-Ring networks.

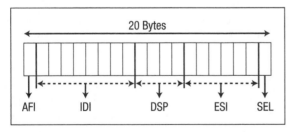

Figure 8.5   The format of an ATM NSAP address.

LANE provides these broadcast services by making an ATM interface look like an Ethernet or Token Ring interface. LANE gives ATM devices MAC addresses, just like Ethernet or Token Ring devices. Because the ATM interfaces can use the same frame format as legacy devices, LAN-based applications can run without changing the application itself or Layer 3 drivers.

This approach allows backward compatibility with existing LANs, broadcast support, and connectionless delivery. LANE has some drawbacks, however: It prevents the use of ATM-specific benefits such as QoS and doesn't have the ability to provide flexible bandwidth allocations.

LANE is the primary component that provides connectivity between ATM devices and the devices residing on the Layer 2 LAN. This connectivity extends to devices attached to ATM stations and devices attached to LAN devices spanning the ATM network. This connectivity between ATM devices and other LAN devices is done through ELANs.

What Are ELANs?

ELANs are just like VLANs—one of their functions is to create independent broadcast domains in ATM, the same way that VLANs do in Ethernet and Token Ring networks. ELAN workstations are independent of the physical location, and like VLANs, ELANs must be connected to a Layer 3 device in order to communicate with members of another ELAN.

The Data Link layer's MAC sublayer allows ELANs to use the Microsoft or Novell upper-level NDIS/ODI driver interfaces. This method allows ELANs to transmit Layer 3 protocols such as TCP/IP, IPX, and AppleTalk.

LANE is a standardized conversion process that allows a connectionless environment in a LAN to connect to a connection-oriented ATM environment. LANE fragments an incoming Layer 3 into a 48-byte payload and places a 5-byte ATM-specific identification header on the front of the packet, yielding a 53-byte cell. It then removes the checksum from the cell and forwards the cell through the ATM network. When the cell has traveled the ATM network, the ATM information is removed and the cell fragments are reassembled and returned to the LAN environment as a packet.

The LANE 1.0 standard can be summed up as a software interface for the Layer 3 protocol environment that encapsulates user data for either Ethernet or Token Ring packets. LANE isn't actually the media access method for this conversion process—LANE uses three servers, which clients access over the ATM connections. The LANE servers provide address registration and resolution functions, including collecting address and route descriptor types based on the LANE standard. Let's take a look at the LANE components.

NOTE: *FDDI can be used with LANE 1.0; however, it is not accurately defined like Ethernet and Token Ring protocols. ATM uses translational bridging techniques to map FDDI packets into either Ethernet or Token Ring.*

LANE Components

LANE uses several components to provide LAN-based network connectivity. The interaction of these components allows address registration, address caching, and searchable databases. LANE uses the following components:

- *LAN Emulation Client (LEC)*—Emulates a LAN interface to higher-layer protocols and applications of the OSI Reference Model.

- *LAN Emulation Server (LES)*—Provides a database of LANE services, resolves addresses, manages stations that make up an ELAN, and provides registration services to LANE clients for the emulated LAN.

- *LAN Emulation Configuration Server (LECS)*—Uses a database to track device memberships in each ELAN.

- *Broadcast and Unknown Server (BUS)*—Sends broadcasts, sequences cells, controls unicast flooding, and distributes multicast packets.

WARNING! Notice that although LEC and LECS sound the same, they are completely different terms and components in LANE.

LAN Emulation Client (LEC)

The LEC resides in every ATM end system. It provides services to emulate the Data Link layer interface that allows communication of all higher-level protocols and applications to occur. It provides both ATM-attached devices and ATM-capable Token Ring, Ethernet, and legacy LAN topologies the ability to coexist within an ATM emulated LAN and WAN environment.

The LEC is the component responsible for passing traffic between separate VLANs on the Catalyst switches and between ELANs on the ATM switch. You can configure multiple LECs for one or more ELANs on the ATM modules. Prior to configuring a LEC on an ATM module, a VLAN must be configured on the switch, and the LES/BUS or an ELAN must be configured on one or more ATM module subinterfaces.

The LEC forwards data to other LANE components in the ELAN and performs control functions. Each LEC is a member of only one ELAN. In many instances, an Ethernet switch may have multiple LECs for each ELAN. Examples of LEC implementations include servers, routers, switches, or other network hosts. The LEC has the following functions:

- Resolves MAC addresses
- Transfers data

8. WAN Cell Switching

- Performs address caching
- Interfaces with other LANE components
- Provides interface driver support

LAN Emulation Server (LES)

The LES for an ELAN is the central piece of LANE. It gives the LECs the information they need to establish ATM connections to other LECs in their ELAN. A single LES is responsible for address registry and resolution for an ELAN. When a LEC joins an ELAN, it forms a connection with the LES. The LEC registers its MAC and ATM addresses with the LES. The LES has the following functions:

- Supports LECs
- Registers addresses from LECs
- Resolves addresses from LECs
- Interfaces to the LEC, LECS, and BUS

The LES performs traffic control for all LECs connecting to an ELAN. This component provides the address resolution, registration, broadcast, and unknown server information that guides communication among LECs. When configuring each LEC, the LEC must request a connection from the LES. The request information contains the ATM address of the LEC, a LAN identifier, and an optional MAC address. This component also performs verification of each LEC during the initial connection with the server, checking to make sure that each LEC has permission to join the requested ELAN.

Address registration is also a function of the LES. It must maintain a database to aid in resolving addresses. This registration occurs after the LEC joins an ELAN. Each LEC provides the LES with one registered address with a join request, and no separate registrations are required.

The LES with the ATM address database responds to all address resolution queries and attempts to locate partnering LECs. The LES responds with the ATM addresses for the targeted ELANs. If no address can be found, the LES attempts to forward the request to other LECs on other ELANs.

The ultimate goal of the LES is to arrange and control connections with a LEC. This connection is commonly known as a *control direct ATM virtual channel connection (VCC)*. After this connection is established, it will handle address resolution and registration responses.

NOTE: *The LES establishes communication with the LECS and provides verification information for LECs attempting to join. The LES does not maintain a constant connection with the BUS. The LES only provides each LEC with the ATM address of the BUS for forwarding.*

The LANE servers provide the address registration and resolution functions. These functions include collecting address and route descriptor types based on the LANE standard. Let's take a look at the address resolution process, which is shown in Figure 8.6 and outlined as follows:

1. A workstation connects to a router or ATM switch and performs a physical outbound packet transmission. This example uses the Address Resolution Protocol (ARP) query to try to locate a device on a remote segment.

NOTE: *The local router is typically the ATM LEC and provides the circuit for the initial ATM address mapping.*

2. The LEC takes an Ethernet frame and assigns an immediate LEC link, which is used to obtain the ATM address identifier needed to establish an ATM connection. If this process is not successful, the LEC must locate a LES.

3. The LES circuit holds the main ATM network address table and returns with the VCI assignment.

LAN Emulation Configuration Server (LECS)

The LECS provides key services such as registration for Integrated Local Management Interface (ILMI) and configuration support for the LES addresses for the corresponding emulated LAN identifiers.

The LECS contains a database of ATM addresses for the LES and BUS pairs for known ELANs. The LEC consults the LECS to determine the LES's ATM address when it first joins an ELAN.

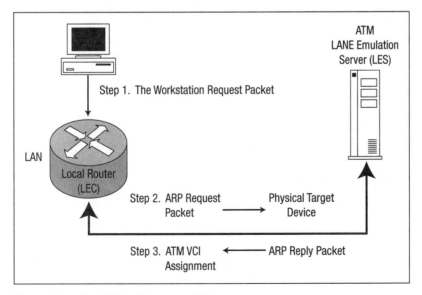

Figure 8.6   The LES address resolution process.

NOTE: *At least one LECS is required per ATM LANE switch cloud.*

The LECS has the following functions:

- Registers the LECS ATM addresses for known ELANs
- Supplies LECs with LESs' ATM addresses
- Provides interfaces to the LEC and the LES

The registration process of the LECS ATM address uses the ILMI functions to connect to the ATM network; this situation usually includes an ATM switch. Support for configurations from the LECS ensures that the correct LES address is supplied to the LEC.

Broadcast and Unknown Server (BUS)

The BUS provides broadcasting support for an ELAN. The BUS distributes multicast data, sends or distributes unicast data, and connects the other LANE components. When the destination address of an Ethernet or Token Ring frame contains a local broadcast or a multicast address, the LEC forwards the traffic to the BUS, which forwards it to all the other LECs in the ELAN. At least one combined LES and BUS is required per ELAN. The BUS has the following functions:

- Distributes multicast data
- Sends or distributes unicast data
- Interfaces to LEC and LES

The LES is the component responsible for resolving MAC addresses to ATM addresses, and the BUS is the component responsible for servicing multicast, Ethernet, and Token Ring broadcasts. The Cisco LANE implementation calls for the LES and the BUS to be configured in the same end-station.

ATM Module Subinterfaces

In order to configure ATM components on an ATM LANE module for the Catalyst 5000 or 6000 family of switches, you need to use subinterfaces. Depending on the level of traffic you expect on your network, you may want to place different LES/BUS components throughout the framework of your network. To configure a LES or BUS on the ATM module, you need to complete the following tasks:

1. Enter Interface Configuration mode.
2. Specify the subinterface for the ELAN.
3. Specify the type of link: Ethernet or Token Ring.
4. Enable the LES and BUS on the ELAN.
5. Repeat this process for each LES/BUS.

The BUS must be used to sequence and distribute broadcast data to all the LECs. However, sending a large volume of broadcast data to all the LECs can severely impact the overall performance of the network. For this reason, it may be necessary for the BUS to place restrictions on the LANE components to control the maximum throughput rate for each device. The BUS's primary function is to provide broadcast management support for LANs. The BUS must supply the following services:

- Distribute unicast and multicast data to all the LECs in the network

- Connect interfaces to the ELAN

Distribution of unicast and multicast data includes the transmission of data to the LECs in the network. Whenever possible, the LEC will establish a direct connection to another LEC. If this isn't possible, then data the BUS receives is broadcast to each LEC on the ELAN. This option can be enabled and disabled, and you should carefully consider whether you need this option, because it can eat up costly bandwidth.

NOTE: *When interfacing to ELANs, the BUS establishes a bi-directional connection that allows forwarding of multicast and unicast frames with unknown destinations.*

LEC Queries

LECs send queries for configuration information to receive the LES address. The LECS then assigns the correct LES address for each LEC. The LES also has the ability to establish a connection with the LECS.

A reply to a query can be as simple as providing a single LES address or it can provide more information, such as:

- The default ELAN name

- The LEC address and corresponding LES

- The ELAN name and corresponding LES

- The ATM address prefix and corresponding LES

- The ELAN type and corresponding LES

- The ELAN name

- The corresponding ATM address of a LANE server

- A LANE client MAC address

- A client MAC address with the corresponding ELAN name

- The LANE client ATM template

8. WAN Cell Switching

ATM Addresses

ATM addresses are 40-digit addresses that use the ILMI protocol to provide the ATM prefix address of the switch for the LECs. This process configures the initial 26 (hexadecimal) digits of the ATM address, which are identical for each LEC. The next 12 (hexadecimal) digits of the ATM address are known as the ESI. There is also a two-digit SEL field. To provide this part of the ATM address, Cisco provides a pool of 16 MAC addresses for each ATM module, although only 4 are used. The following assignments pertain to the LANE components:

- The prefix fields are the same for all LANE components and indicate the identity of the ATM switch.
- All LECSs are assigned an ESI field value from the first pool of MAC addresses assigned to the interface.
- All LESs are assigned an ESI field value from the second pool of MAC addresses.
- The BUS is assigned an ESI value from the third pool of MAC addresses.
- The LECS is assigned an ESI value from the fourth pool of MAC addresses.

Integrated Local Management Interface (ILMI)

The ILMI protocol was defined by the ATM Forum. It aids in initialization and configuration of ATM LECs. ILMI uses the Simple Network Management Protocol (SNMP) to share information between an ATM client and an ATM switch. It uses a well-known permanent connection to the LECS that has a VPI of 0 and a VCI of 17.

The basic functions of ILMI are to enable the LEC to discover the ATM address of the LECS and to allow the LEC to tear down virtual circuits when they are no longer in use. ILMI allows the ATM switch to share its ATM prefix with the LECs, which lets the LECs share the same initial 13 bytes of their own 20-byte ATM address. This scheme makes it easier to route traffic between switches, because the switch only needs to look at the first 13 bytes to determine which ATM switch has the end-station. ILMI is an extremely popular way to resolve addressing in ATM networks.

LANE Communication

Now that we have looked at the individual components that make up the LANE model, let's examine the communication process. Like X.25 and Frame Relay, LANE components communicate by using SVCs. Several different types of SVCs exist in the ATM LANE implementation; they are called *virtual channel connections* or *virtual circuit connections (VCCs)*, depending on the standards documents you refer to. These VCCs are as follows:

- Unidirectional VCCs
- Bidirectional VCCs

- Point-to-multipoint control distribute VCCs

- Point-to-point configure direct VCCs

In the ATM LANE communications process, when a client wants to join an ELAN, the client must build a table that links ATM addresses to Ethernet MAC addresses. Let's take a close look at this process:

1. The LEC first sends a LAN Emulation ARP (LE_ARP) message to the LES that is using a point-to-point configure direct VCC. This query is made to the ATM switch containing the LECS, using ILMI. The query is a request for the ATM address of the LES for its emulated LAN. The switch contains a Management Information Base (MIB) variable containing the requested ATM address. The LEC will attempt to locate the LES using these steps:

   a. Uses ILMI to connect to the LECS

   b. Checks to see if any locally configured ATM addresses exist

   c. Checks to see if it has received a fixed address defined by the MIB variable using UNI

   d. Checks to see if this is a well-known permanent virtual circuit

2. The LES forwards the LE_ARP to all clients on the ELAN using a point-to-multipoint control distribute VCC.

3. The LECS responds across the established connection with the ATM address and name of the LES for the LEC's ELAN. The LEC can establish a connection with the LES based on the configuration data received. This connection is a bidirectional point-to-point control direct VCC; it remains open throughout the remainder of the communications process.

4. The LES forwards the response using a point-to-multipoint control distribute VCC to the LEC. While the connection is established with the LEC requesting entry to the ELAN, the LES attempts to make a bidirectional connection to the LECS to request verification that the requesting LEC may enter the ELAN. After this verification is completed, the server configuration that was received in the first connection is verified against the LECS database; if authentication is approved, the client gains membership in the ELAN.

5. The LEC creates another packet with the correct ATM address for the LES and establishes a control direct VCC to make the connection. The LEC sends out a LE_JOIN_REQUEST to the LES containing the LEC ATM address as well as the MAC address, in order to register with the ELAN.

6. The LES checks with the LECS to verify the LEC. The LES receives the data, creates a new entry in the cache for the LEC, and sends a LE_JOIN_RESPONSE back to the LEC.

7. The LES replies to the LEC using the existing configure direct VCC. This process is completed by either allowing or denying membership in the ELAN. If the LES rejects the LEC's request, the session is terminated.

8. If the LES connection is allowed, the LEC is added to the point-to-multipoint control distribute VCC connection. The LEC is granted a connection using the point-to-point control VCC to the corresponding LEC, and the higher-level protocols take over.

9. If permission is granted by the LES, the LEC must determine the ATM address for the BUS in order to become a member of the broadcast group.

10. The LEC must locate the BUS, so it sends an LE_ARP_REQUEST packet containing the MAC address 0xFFFFFFFF. This packet is sent down the control direct VCC to the LES, which understands the request for the BUS. The LES responds with the ATM address for the BUS.

11. When the BUS is located, the LEC can become a member of the ELAN.

LE Messages

An LE_ARP message is used to allow a LEC to indicate that a particular MAC address resides on a local node on the local network. This message can then be redistributed to all other LECs in the ELAN to allow those LECs to update their address cache.

Once a client has joined an ELAN and built an address cache based on the LE_ARP messages received, the client can establish a VCC to the desired destination and transmit packets to the ATM address mapped to the physical MAC address using a bidirectional point-to-point data direct VCC. Let's take a look at four types of packets:

- *LE_ARP_REQUEST*—Contains the broadcast MAC address 0xFFFFFFFF. This packet is sent on a control direct VCC to the LES to query for the ATM address of the BUS.

- *LE_ARP_RESPONSE*—Sent in response to an LE_ARP_REQUEST; it contains the ATM address of the BUS.

- *LE_JOIN_RESPONSE*—Contains the LANE client identifier (LECID) that is a unique identifier for each client. This ID is used to filter return broadcasts from the BUS.

- *LE_JOIN_REQUEST*—Allows the LEC to register its own MAC and ATM addresses with the LES as well as any other MAC addresses for which it is proxying. This information is maintained to make sure that no two LECs will register the same MAC or ATM address.

Joining and Registering with the LES

After a LEC joins the LES, the LEC uses its own ATM and MAC addresses. The following process shows how this is done:

1. After the LEC obtains the LES address, the LEC clears the connection to the LECS to set up a control-direct VCC to the LES. It then sends an LE_JOIN_REQUEST on that VCC.

2. When the LES receives the LE_JOIN_REQUEST, the LES checks with the LECS with its open connection, verifies the request, and confirms the client's membership.

3. If this verification is successful, the LES adds the LEC as a branch in its ATM point-to-multipoint control-distribute VCC.

4. The LES issues the LEC a successful LE_JOIN_RESPONSE that contains a unique LECID.

NOTE: *The LECID is used by the LEC to filter its own broadcasts from the BUS.*

When this process is complete, LANE will have created an ATM forwarding path for unicast traffic between the LECs. This forwarding path will enable you to move data across the ATM network.

LANE Configuration Guidelines

When setting up LANE components, you should consider the following list:

- The LANE subsystem supports as many as 16 LECS addresses.

- The LECS must always be assigned to the major interface.

- Two separate ELANs cannot be configured on the same subinterface.

- LES/BUSs for different ELANs cannot be configured on the same subinterface.

- Each ELAN can define an unlimited number of LES/BUSs.

- LECSs come up as masters automatically until a higher-level LECS takes priority.

- If multiple LES/BUS pairs are configured for an ELAN, the priority of a pair is determined by the order in which it was entered in the LECS database. When a higher-priority LES/BUS pair comes online, it takes over the functions of the current LES/BUS on the ELAN.

- It may take up to one minute for changes made to the list of LECS addresses to propagate through the network. However, changes made to the configuration database for LES/BUS addresses take place almost immediately.

- The ATM Forum-defined well-known LECS address is used if no LECS is operational on an ELAN.

8. WAN Cell Switching

NOTE: *The operating LECSs must use the same configuration database. An identical database can be created by configuring a LECS database on one device and then copying the database to other devices by using the* **config net** *command.*

How LANE Works

Earlier, I discussed how the different LANE components interact with each other to support the LAN emulation services. A LEC goes through three stages to join an ELAN:

- Initialization and configuration
- Joining and registering with the LES
- Finding and joining the BUS

Let's step through the process. Suppose that you were working on an ELAN and you wanted to access a file stored on a server that was located on a physically separate LAN:

1. You send the file request. Your LEC determines if it knows the ATM address of its LES.

2. If your LEC does not know this address, the client queries the LECS and asks for the ATM address of the LES.

3. After your LEC receives the correct address, it queries the LES for the ATM address of the LES where the file is located. If the LES knows this address, it sends the address to your LEC.

4. If the LES does not know this address, it queries the LANE BUS. The LANE BUS, in turn, asks all the LECs on the ELAN for their ATM addresses. The LANE BUS returns the correct address to the LES, which returns the address to your LEC.

5. Your LEC establishes a virtual circuit to the server on which the file is stored. The LEC converts its Ethernet or Token Ring frames into cells and sends these cells over the virtual circuit to the server.

Implementing LANE

LANE is supported on many of the products offered by Cisco, including all Cisco switches from the Catalyst 1900 series through the 12000 series, the Cisco LightStream switches, and the 8000 series of WAN switches. Routers such as the Cisco 4000, 4500, 7000, and 7500 can support LANE, as well.

If you're designing an ATM LANE network, you need to examine each switch's level of performance and functionality. Doing so allows you to determine which switching product is needed at each point in the network. Cisco has created four product lines for specific network types. Each product provides a certain level of performance and functionality. Cisco provides ATM devices that fit well in all sizes of ATM implementations, from the smallest to the largest. These four product lines are as follows:

- *Workgroup switches*—The smallest switches, typically found in the Access layer of the network. Workgroup switches begin with the 1900 series switches and includes the Cisco Catalyst 5000. Most workgroup switches are located in the wiring closet closest to the end user. These switches are usually Ethernet based for the local LAN environment and provide an ATM uplink to a campus switch.

- *Campus switches*—Typically implemented to relieve the congested nature of the network and to eliminate bandwidth problems across the existing backbone. These switches include the LightStream family of ATM switches. Campus switches support a wide variety of interfaces, including those that have connections to backbone and to the WAN.

- *Enterprise switches*—The next level of ATM switches. These switches allow multilevel campus ATM switches to be connected for enterprise installations. They also provide the internetworking processes necessary to route multiprotocol traffic in the network. These switches are not used in the Core layer or backbone; they are used in the enterprise or WAN to meet the needs of high-traffic enterprises or even public service providers. These are Cisco's BPX and AXIS switches.

- *Multiservice access switches*—Provide a multitude of services for the growing needs of networks. They can provide services to support MANs, WANs, and the campus network.

Configuring ATM on the 5000 Switch

The LANE module for the Catalyst 5000 and 5500 series is available with three different types of interfaces: multimode fiber (MMF), single-mode fiber (SMF), and unshielded twisted pair (UTP). On each module, two interfaces of each type are available—but only one may be used at any time. This arrangement provides redundancy in the event of a hardware failure or the loss of ILMI signaling.

NOTE: *When ILMI was first introduced, it was referred to as Interim Local Management Interface because the protocol was anticipated to have a short life span.*

ILMI provides sufficient information for the ATM end-station to find a LECS. The ILMI also provides the ATM NSAP prefix information to the end-station. This prefix is configured on a local ATM switch. The prefix is 13 bytes long; it is then combined with the MAC address (6 bytes) of the end-node (end system identifier), and a 1-byte selector, to create a 20-byte ATM address.

LANE Modules

The following ATM LANE modules are available for the 5000 family of switches; the list also indicates the cable types that can connect to each. Tables 8.1 and 8.2 show the LED lights and functions on the LANE modules. These modules provide a connection between multiple ATM networks connecting through the ATM switch:

- *ATM LANE Single PHY Module (UTP)*—Provides a connection between the 155Mbps ATM network, Category 5 UTP cables, and one RJ-45 connector

- *ATM LANE Single PHY Module (MMF)*—Provides a connection between a 155Mbps ATM network and one multimode SC fiber-optic connector

- *ATM LANE Single PHY Module (SMF)*—Provides a connection between a 155Mbps ATM network and one single-mode, SC fiber-optic connector

- *ATM LANE Dual PHY Module (UTP)*—Provides two connections between the ATM network, Category 5 UTP cables, and two RJ-45 connectors

- *ATM LANE Dual PHY Module (MMF)*—Provides two connections between an ATM network, multimode fiber-optic cable, and two multimode, SC fiber-optic connectors

- *ATM LANE Dual PHY Module (SMF)*—Provides two connections between an ATM network, a single-mode fiber-optic cable, and two single-mode, SC fiber-optic connectors

- *ATM Dual PHY OC-12 Module (MMF)*—Provides two connections between the OC-12 (622Mbps) ATM network, a single-mode fiber-optic cable, and two single-mode, SC fiber-optic connectors

- *ATM Dual PHY DS3 Module*—Provides two interfaces for two DS3 (45Mbps) connections between an ATM network, 75-ohm RG-59 coaxial cable, and two Bayonet-Neill-Concelman (BNC) twist-lock connectors

Table 8.1   LANE module status LEDs.

Port Color	Meaning
Red	Diagnostics failure
Orange	Module disabled
Green	Functioning normally

Table 8.2   ATM LANE module indicator LEDs.

LED	Meaning
TX (Transmit)	Port is transmitting a cell
RX (Receive)	Port is receiving a cell
Link	Active link

- *ATM Dual PHY OC-3 Module (MMF)*—Provides two direct connections between an OC-3 (155Mbps) ATM network, multimode fiber-optic cable, and two multimode, SC fiber-optic connectors

- *ATM Dual PHY OC-3 Module (SMF)*—Provides two direct connections between an OC-3 (155Mbps) ATM network, a single-mode fiber-optic cable, and two single-mode, SC fiber-optic connectors

The single-mode LANE module is better equipped for longer distances. It uses a laser optical source and has a maximum distance of 10 kilometers. The multi-mode module uses an LED optical source and has a maximum distance of two kilometers. Both modules have a SAR of 512, meaning that the module can segment and reassemble up to 512 packets simultaneously.

Network Management on the LANE Module

The LANE modules in the Catalyst 5000 and 5500 series switches are configured by using the standard Cisco command-line interface (CLI), which is similar to that of a router. This interface can be accessed through the Supervisor Engine's console port.

TIP: *Even though the LANE module is configured through the Supervisor Engine, the Supervisor Engine maintains no configuration information regarding the LANE module. This information is stored on the LANE module itself.*

Segmentation and Reassembly

In a frame-based network such as Ethernet, packets sent on the physical wire require a minimum frame size. Ethernet requires a minimum frame size of 64 bytes; this size is larger than an ATM cell, which is only 53 bytes with the header information included.

A process must occur to segment or reassemble the data into the needed minimum size for the physical media. This is the job of segmentation and reassembly (SAR), which is a task performed by the Adaptation layer of the ATM Reference Model. SAR is responsible for breaking frames into cells and padding cells to result in a larger payload than the 48 bytes from the cells. This process allows the data in cells to traverse the local LAN and meet the minimum frame size requirements.

Unfortunately, SAR is one area in which ATM switches fail to perform up to the standard of the physical wire's available bandwidth. As a result, SAR alone on the LANE module may have a problem processing packets fast enough to keep up with frames or cells arriving and being sent on a 155Mbps OC-3. To resolve this issue, Cisco installed two LSI ATMizers to provide low-latency and wire-speed performance on the LANE module. Each ATMizer operates by itself—one is used for receiving, and the other transmits cells and frames.

TIP: *The LANE module is capable of addressing 4,096 virtual circuits; however, the default is 1,024, which provides sufficient capability for most installations. To provide for data bursts (associated with LANs and not WANs), the LANE module SAR is capable of traffic shaping using a single-rate queue.*

Connecting in an ATM Network

To provide a basis for troubleshooting, it helps to evaluate proper placement of the LES/BUS and LECS components in your network. Most ATM LANE environments use LECS to provide configuration information to the end-node. This connection uses a configuration direct VCC to query for a LECS. This query uses three processes to try to locate the LECS, in the following order:

1. Checks the local LECS for a preconfigured address on the local LEC.

2. Checks the ILMI to locate the LECS.

3. Uses 47:00:79:00:00:00:00:00:00:00:00:00:00:00:00:A0:3E:00:01:00, which is the LECS's well-known address. This address is specified by the ATM Forum.

After the end-node has contacted the LECS, the LES sends the end-node the information it needs to continue contact with the LES. This information includes the operating information for the ELAN. The LES will register the LEC and permit it to join the ELAN. The communication between the LEC and the LES is established with the use of a **join** command on a bidirectional control direct VCC.

At this point, the LEC is responsible for locating the BUS. This is done through the use of an LE_ARP request message. The LES responds to this request with the address of the BUS. The LEC then registers and joins the BUS.

Now, when a client needs to send data to an unknown resource, the LES and BUS establish direct communication to provide the address information and answer address queries. The LEC sends an LE_ARP request to the LES for the destination station and also sends the initial data cells to the BUS, which will forward the data cells to the destination and all the other stations.

After the destination node receives the LE_ARP response from the LES, the destination client responds to the source with its address information. The source sends a "flush" message to the BUS, which instructs the BUS to stop sending any unsent cells—the source will now establish a direct connection with the destination and send the remaining data.

Immediate Solutions

Monitoring and Maintaining LANE

The following commands can be used to monitor and maintain your LANE network:

- **show lane**—Displays the complete LANE configuration and status information for the LES/BUSs, LECs, and LECSs

- **show lane server**—Displays the global and per-VCC LANE information for all the LANE components

- **show lane bus**—Displays the global and virtual circuit LANE information for the BUS configured on any subinterface or ELAN

- **show lane client**—Displays the global and virtual circuit LANE information for all LECs configured on any subinterface or ELAN

- **show lane config**—Displays the global and virtual circuit LANE information for the LECS configured on any interface

- **show lane database**—Displays the LECS database

- **show lane le-arp**—Displays the LAN Emulation ARP table contained on the LECs

- **show atm vc**—Displays the ATM virtual circuit information

Related solutions:	Found on page:
Configuring Virtual Private Tunnels	288
Configuring LANE on a LightStream 1010	295

Accessing the ATM LANE Module

The process of accessing and configuring the ATM LANE module on the Cisco Catalyst 5000 and 6000 family of switches is identical. The 5000 and 6000 switches both use the Set/Clear CLI, and the LANE module uses a CLI similar to a router.

Use the **session** command followed by the slot number in which the LANE module resides to access the CLI of the LANE module:

```
Console> (enable) session 5
Trying ATM-5...
Connected to ATM-5.
Escape character is '^]'.
```

Displaying the Selector Field

The last two digits of an ATM address are known as the *selector field*. This value is assigned on the subinterface on which a LANE component resides. The LECS must reside on the primary interface, making the selector value a static **00**. To determine the default ATM addresses the ATM LANE module has assigned, use the **show lane default-atm-addresses** command. An example of this command and the related output is as follows:

```
ATM#show lane default-atm-addresses
interface ATM1/0/0:
LANE Client:        47.00817200000000E04BAAA006.00E04BAAA060.**
LANE Server:        47.00817200000000E04BAAA006.00E04BAAA061.**
LANE Bus:           47.00817200000000E04BAAA006.00E04BAAA062.**
LANE Config Server: 47.00817200000000E04BAAA006.00E04BAAA063.00
note: ** is the subinterface number byte in hex
```

NOTE: *The asterisks in this example indicate that the addresses are in hexadecimal. The ATM LANE module does not list these addresses with this command.*

Configuring the LES/BUS

Follow these steps to configure a LES/BUS for two ELANS—the default ELAN and ELAN2:

1. Enter Global Configuration mode on the LANE module:

   ```
   ATM#configure terminal
   Enter configuration commands, one per line. End with CNTL/Z.
   ```

2. Enter Interface Configuration mode for the ATM0 interface, subinterface 1, and indicate whether the link is point-to-point or multipoint:

   ```
   ATM(config)#interface atm0.1 point-to-point
   ```

3. Make this subinterface the Ethernet default LES/BUS and identify the ELAN:

```
ATM(config-subif)#lane server-bus ethernet ELAN2
```

NOTE: *You cannot configure more than one LES/BUS per subinterface.*

---

4. Repeat Steps 2 and 3 for each LES/BUS you want to configure on this LANE module.

5. Enter Interface Configuration mode for the ATM0 subinterface 2:

```
ATM(config-subif)#interface atm0.2
```

6. Map the LES bus to the Ethernet ELAN named ELAN2:

```
ATM(config-subif)#lane server-bus ethernet ELAN2
ATM(config-subif)#end
```

Verifying the LES/BUS Configuration

To verify the configuration, issue the following command:

```
ATM#show lane server
LE Server ATM0.1  ELAN name: default  Admin: up  State: operational
type: ethernet        Max Frame Size: 1516
ATM address: 47.00918100000000E04FACB401.00100DAACC41.01
LECS used: 47.00790000000000000000000.00A03E000001.00 NOT yet connected

LE Server ATM0.2  ELAN name: TEST_ELAN  Admin: up  State: operational
type: ethernet        Max Frame Size: 1516
ATM address: 47.00918100000000E04FACB401.00100DAACC41.02
LECS used: 47.00790000000000000000000.00A03E000001.00 NOT yet connected
```

Configuring a LEC for an ELAN

Follow these steps to configure two LECs for two ELANS—the default ELAN and ELAN2:

1. Enter Global Configuration mode on the LANE module:

```
ATM#configure terminal
Enter configuration commands, one per line. End with CNTL/Z.
```

2. Enter Interface Configuration mode for the ATM0 interface, subinterface 1:

```
ATM(config)#interface atm0.1
```

3. Map the LEC bus to the Ethernet ELAN named "default":

```
ATM(config-subif)#lane client ethernet default
```

4. Repeat Steps 2 and 3 for each LEC you want to configure on this LANE module.

5. Enter Interface Configuration mode for the ATM0 subinterface 2:

```
ATM(config-subif)#interface atm0.2
```

6. Map the LEC bus to the Ethernet ELAN named ELAN2:

```
ATM(config-subif)#lane client ethernet ELAN2
ATM(config-subif)#end
```

Verifying a LEC Configuration on an ELAN

To verify the previous operation, issue the following command:

```
ATM#show lane client
LE Client ATM0.1  ELAN name: default  Admin: up  State: initialState
Client ID: unassigned          Next join attempt in 0 seconds
Join Attempt: 4
Last Fail Reason: Config VC being released
HW Address: 0010.0daa.cc40   Type: ethernet          Max Frame Size: 1516
        VLANID: 1
ATM Address: 47.00918100000000E04FACB401.00100DAACC40.01

  VCD  rxFrames  txFrames  Type      ATM Address
    0         0         0  configure
47.007900000000000000000000.00A03E000001.00
    0         0         0  direct
00.000000000000000000000000.000000000000.00
    0         0         0  distribute
00.000000000000000000000000.000000000000.00
    0         0         0  send
00.000000000000000000000000.000000000000.00
    0         0         0  forward
00.000000000000000000000000.000000000000.00
```

```
LE Client ATM0.2  ELAN name: TEST_ELAN  Admin: up  State: initialState
Client ID: unassigned          Next join attempt in 1 seconds
Join Attempt: 2
Last Fail Reason: Config VC being released
HW Address: 0010.0daa.cc40   Type: ethernet          Max Frame Size: 1516
        VLANID: 2
ATM Address: 47.00918100000000E04FACB401.00100DAACC40.02


 VCD  rxFrames  txFrames  Type      ATM Address
  0         0         0  configure
47.00790000000000000000000000.00A03E000001.00
 VCD  rxFrames  txFrames  Type      ATM Address
  0         0         0  direct
00.00000000000000000000000000.000000000000.00
  0         0         0  distribute
00.00000000000000000000000000.000000000000.00
  0         0         0  send
00.00000000000000000000000000.000000000000.00
  0         0         0  forward
00.00000000000000000000000000.000000000000.00
```

In the previous example, the state is **initialState**. This state indicates that the LEC is not yet a member of the ELAN. The zeroes in the ATM address columns are an indication that the LECS database has not yet been configured. This is normal—LECS will not come up until the LES/BUS is configured and the LECS database has been configured.

Configuring the LECS

Prior to configuring the LECS, you will need to go to each LES and get its ATM address. This address can be gathered with the following command:

```
ATM#show lane server
LE Server ATM0.1  ELAN name: default  Admin: up  State: operational
type: ethernet        Max Frame Size: 1516
ATM address:47.00918100000000E04FACB401.00100DAACC41.01
LECS used:47.00790000000000000000000000.00A03E000001.00 NOT yet connected
```

Make a note of the address following the **ATM address:** label. To set up this LEC in a default unrestricted ELAN, perform the following commands:

1. Enter Global Configuration mode on the LANE module:

```
LANEMODULE#configure terminal
Enter configuration commands, one per line. End with CNTL/Z.
```

8. WAN Cell Switching

2. Configure a LANE database and specify the LANE database name with the following command:

```
LANEMODULE(config)#lane database LANE_DB
```

3. To bind the ELAN name to the ATM address of the LES/BUS for each ELAN, use the ATM address displayed when using the **show lane server** command:

```
LANEMODULE(lane-config-database)#name ELAN2 server-atm-address
   47.00918100000000E04FCCB100.00100DAACC51.01
```

4. Repeat this step for each ELAN in the LANE network.

5. You can optionally specify an ELAN as the default ELAN. Doing so will allow the LECs not to be bound to an ELAN:

```
ATM(lane-config-database)#default-name default
ATM(lane-config-database)#end
```

Viewing the LANE Database

To see the results of the previous operation, issue the following command:

```
ATM#show lane database

LANE Config Server database table 'LANE_Backbone'
default elan: default
elan 'default': un-restricted
   server 47.00918100000000E04FACB401.00100DAACC41.01 (prio 0)
```

Binding the LECS Address to an Interface

After you have finished configuring the LECS database, use the following steps to configure the LECS address and bind it to the interface:

1. Enter Interface Configuration mode for ATM0 interface:

```
ATM(config)#interface atm0
```

2. Use the **lane config auto-config-atm-address** command to allow the ATM address to be computed automatically for the LECS:

```
ATM(config-if)#lane config auto-config-atm-address
```

3. Use the **lane config database** command to associate a database with the configuration server on the selected ATM interface:

```
ATM(config-if)#lane config database ELAN2
ATM(config-if)#end
```

Verifying the LECS Configuration

Verify the proper setup with the following command:

```
ATM#show lane config
LE Config Server ATM0 config table: ELAN2
Admin: up  State: operational
LECS Mastership State: active master
list of global LECS addresses (58 seconds to update):
47.00918100000000E04FACB401.00100DAACC43.00
ATM Address of this LECS: 47.00918100000000E04FACB401.
   00100DAACC43.00 (auto)
 vcd  rxCnt  txCnt  callingParty
  11    1      1    47.00918100000000E04FACB401.00100DAACC41.01
     LES default 0
active
cumulative total number of unrecognized packets received so far: 0
cumulative total number of config requests received so far: 3
cumulative total number of config failures so far: 1
    cause of last failure: no configuration
    culprit for the last failure: 47.00918100000000E04FACB401.
       00E04FACB070.04
```

Chapter 9

LightStream Switches

In Depth

The demand for high-speed network communications has skyrocketed in the past 20 to 30 years. In the early 1970s, 9.6Kbps was considered a high-speed network. Now that we have entered the next century, network speeds have surpassed 1Gbps with the introduction of 10Gbps technologies. This advancement has led to the introduction of many applications that require massive quantities of data to be transferred over LAN and WAN physical connections.

As we learned in Chapter 8, Asynchronous Transfer Mode (ATM) has become an industry standard for transporting large quantities of data through the network. However, ATM is not supported on all Cisco Catalyst switches. To meet the need for ATM support, Cisco introduced the LightStream series; this line of switches is used primarily for ATM cell switching.

The LightStream series of Cisco switches are ATM switches meant primarily to run multiservice applications. The LightStream series works well for campus back-bones, service provider backbones, ATM workgroups, metropolitan area networks (MANs), and multiple service applications. The LightStream can be found in three primary versions: LightStream 100 (LS100), LightStream 1010 (LS1010), and LightStream 2020 (LS2020).

In Chapter 8, we looked at ATM and how ATM is configured on Catalyst switches. This chapter will supplement Chapter 8 by discussing the features and benefits of the LightStream series of Cisco switches. The configuration steps for each switch feature discussed in this chapter will be explained in the Immediate Solutions section.

LightStream 100

As with all the LightStream switches, the LS100 switch shown in Figure 9.1 is a desktop ATM switch used in the LAN, WAN, or campus backbone. This switch supports a maximum of 16 ATM lines; it supports a maximum of 155Mbps per line, for an aggregate throughput of 2.5Gbps.

This switch carries a unique core called the expandable ATM output-buffer modular switch (XATOMSW). The XATOMSW component supports the buffering that takes place in order to allow the switch to provide a guaranteed Quality of Service (QoS), making this switch a great asset in a multimedia environment. The switch also supports mixed-media interfaces. Interface types can be mixed on an LS100

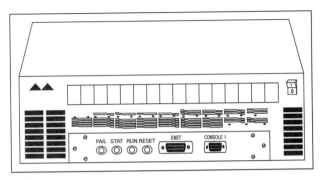

Figure 9.1   The LS100 switch.

Table 9.1   LS100 supported interface types and media speeds.

Interface	Media Speed
DS3/T3	45Mbps
E3	34Mbps
FDDI	100Mbps
STS-3c/STM-1	155Mbps
TAXI 4B/5B	100Mbps

ATM switch used as a backbone, workgroup, or WAN access switch. Table 9.1 shows the supported media types and the supported line speeds.

LightStream 1010

The LS1010, shown in Figure 9.2, is the most recent addition to the LightStream series of ATM switches used for multiservice applications. The switch has a five-slot, modular chassis with two fault-tolerant, load-sharing power supplies. The switch contains a central slot that is dedicated to a single, field-replaceable switch processor module. The switch processor module supports 5Gbps of shared memory that is fully non-blocking. *Non-blocking* means the switch fabric can process and switch just as much or more data than all the ports on the switch combined can possibly bring in. This is possible because the switch uses a feature card and a high-performance reduced instruction set computer (RISC) processor that provides the speed and routing intelligence for the architecture.

The RISC processor provides traffic management mechanisms that allow for bursty data traffic and QoS for such data as voice, video, multimedia, and other applications that require guaranteed bandwidth. The LS1010 can buffer up to 65,536 cells in its on-board shared buffers; this buffering minimizes the possibility of cell loss. Policies and scheduling with user-definable thresholds permit flexible support of multiple service classes.

9. LightStream Switches

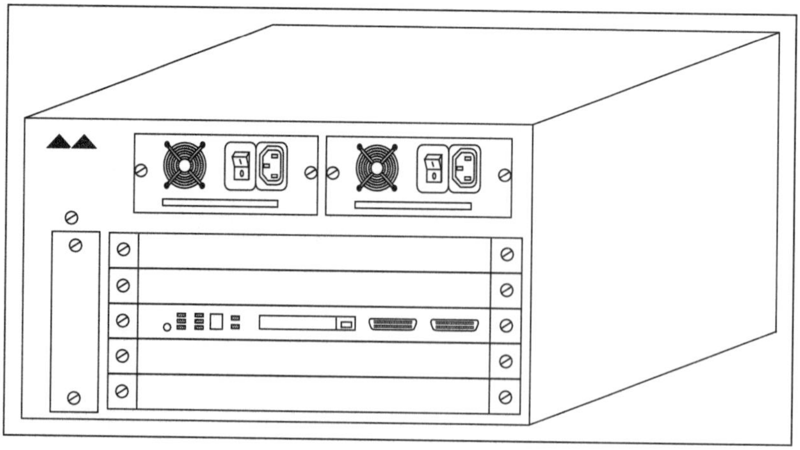

Figure 9.2   The LS1010 switch.

The LS1010 family's architecture is flexible. The switch architecture is scalable and can support WAN interfaces with speeds ranging from a T1 to an OC-12. The LS1010 supports many traffic classes, such as those listed in Table 9.2.

One of the great features of the LightStream 1010 switch is its ability to use the same interface modules as the Cisco Catalyst 5500 series of switches. This feature allows the LS1010 to be controlled in the same way as the Catalyst 5500 series, with the AtmDirector, CiscoView, and CiscoWorks for Switched Internetworks (CWSI) software available from Cisco.

Table 9.2   Traffic classes supported on the LightStream 1010.

Traffic Class	Designation
Constant bit rate (CBR)	Used for telephony, legacy, and site-to-site videoconferencing applications.
Real-time variable	Used for time-delay or jitter-sensitive applications such as those used for videoconferencing at the desktop level.
Variable bit rate (VBR)	Comes in two forms: real time (VBR-RT) and non real time (VBR-NRT). These forms are used in high-delay, high-jitter-tolerant, and high-bandwidth applications, including many video broadcasts.
Available bit rate (ABR) + minimum cell rate (MCR)	Used in the WAN. This class provides best-effort delivery with congestion feedback notification. Optionally, you can define a minimum bandwidth requirement.
Unspecified bit rate (UBR)	Used by many legacy data applications. This class provides best-effort delivery.
UBR + MCR	A unique Cisco class for best-effort data traffic delivery with a specified minimum bandwidth. This class is used in a LAN for high-end resource applications or in a WAN with an ATM for a guarantee of a certain amount of bandwidth (also called a committed information rate [CIR]).

LightStream 2020

The LS2020 is one of Cisco's most powerful LAN, WAN, backbone, campus, and multiservice-type ATM switches. This switch offers cost-effective bandwidth coupled with superior QoS handling in the network. Several other features make this switch a perfect solution for ATM: This switch works well with existing devices and will scale well with future technologies and applications. The switch supports not only ATM but also fastpacket switching applications, which means that it can support Frame Relay, circuit emulation, and LAN technologies such as Fiber Distributed Data Interface (FDDI) and Ethernet.

Switching and communications on the LS2020 are performed at wire speed, so no noticeable latency is caused by the switch processor or the Application-Specific Integrated Circuits (ASICs) used to switch data traffic from one interface to another. Processing tasks are handled by three components based solely on the speed required for each task. Let's take a look at these three components:

- *Line card*—Used when a particular function must be completed in a tenth of a millisecond or less. Such functions include implementing traffic policies and cell forwarding.

- *Line card control processor*—Performs complex tasks that must be completed in a tenth of a millisecond or less. These functions include interface management, error handling, and line-up and line-down protocol processing.

- *Network processor software*—Performs less critical processing that can be handled in more than a tenth of a millisecond, such as cell processing and network management request processing.

The LightStream 2020 processor card is shown in Figure 9.3.

The LS2020 switch can use a software package called ControlStream, which is a traffic management application used to control data traffic. This software allows very high line utilization while at the same time maintaining users' QoS guarantees. ControlStream software employs congestion avoidance and traffic control techniques that allow network links to operate at high levels of utilization by scaling back data that has a much lower priority, including data traffic that is tolerant to traffic delays in the network. As a result, traffic selection can occur at congestion points in the network.

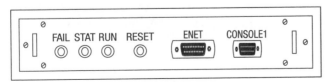

Figure 9.3   The LightStream 2020 processor card.

9. LightStream Switches

The LightStream 2020 uses an internal routing mechanism to provide a path through an ATM virtual channel connection (VCC). These routing mechanisms allow the LS2020 network to provide paths through permanent virtual connections (PVCs) and switched virtual connections (SVCs). Through these virtual connections, the LS2020 supports synchronous connections over ATM user-network interface (UNI) PVCs, Frame Relay PVCs, and circuit emulation PVCs. The switch also provides connections over physical LAN medias such as Ethernet and FDDI.

Neighborhood Discovery Function

The neighborhood discovery function (NDF) can be used to provide a means for locating all the other nodes in the network and to simplify the network configuration process. This tool helps to eliminate the need to manually configure some of the attributes of interface modules inside the LS2020 switch.

CDF enables the switch to find nodes in the network; the found nodes are placed in a database to make internal routing decisions. This neighborhood discovery process runs on the network processor (NP) inside the LS2020's attached network. The neighborhood discovery function provides two functions:

* Discovering the local network topology

* Determining the network processor processes

Discovering the Local Network Topology

This function keeps track of the interface modules added to or removed from service manually or by a hardware fault. When another module is installed into the switch, the NDF automatically locates and distributes functions to each network processor. If an interface module is removed from the switch, NDF must be used to move processes running on that network processor to another or to terminate the processes if they are no longer necessary.

Determining Network Processor Processes

When a resource is added to or removed from an LS2020, the NDF process notifies the global information distribution (GID) system. The GID then floods information about the change from the local network processor module to all the network processors in the network. A function called the connection admission control (CAC) is used by the network processors to generate new routes through the network. Using this process, the internal routing module provides a directed set of links from one source node to a destination node, providing link state and bandwidth information that can be advertised throughout the network.

Virtual Path Connections

Virtual path (VP) is a generic term used to define more than one virtual channel directed to the same ATM endpoint. A virtual path essentially makes for a much larger pipe by combining the redundant paths and creating a logical grouping of virtual connections between multiple ATM sites. The advantage of using VPs in an ATM network is that they enable cell streams from multiple users to be bundled together, resulting in transit over multiple links that is much faster than transit over one link. This process is referred to as *load-sharing*. In an ATM cell (discussed in Chapter 8), the Virtual Path Identifier (VPI) field in the cell header identifies the VP. If a virtual circuit (VC) cell is traversing the network, the network pays attention to the Virtual Channel Identifier (VCI) field.

There is another reason to use a VP between LightStream switches. This path can be used if an end user needs to define the route of certain ATM cells in a manually defined manner that must remain entirely transparent to the network service provider.

Before you can enable a PVC and an SVC between any two endpoints in the network, an internal routing database must first be established. The internal database is established during the network configuration process by downloading the necessary configuration information to each of the LS2020 switches installed in your network. An internal routing module keeps the database information up to date with the required information that confirms the state of every link in the network.

This routing database is replicated from the NP used in each of the LS2020 switches in the network. The database is synchronized with the other ATM switches in the network; the ATM switches then use a routing algorithm to determine the path for any data that arrives and needs to be switched through the network. The routing algorithm calculates the minimum distance path through the network, verifies the availability of bandwidth, and then sets up a connection between the two ATM endpoints in the network. The routing algorithm can use metrics to determine the least-cost route for setting up a virtual connection.

A route that is selected through the route generation function is based on the smallest number of hops to the destination. If two equal paths exist, the routing algorithm uses the bandwidth of the links as the tie-breaker: It uses the fastest link with the most available bandwidth.

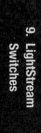

9. LightStream
Switches

When a route needs to be generated, the routing algorithm creates the most efficient route based on the following information:

- Source and destination addresses (the internal addresses used to designate the VCC endpoints in the network)

- Bandwidth type (indicates the pool to be used for allocation, data, or control purposes)

- Service specification of the desired bandwidth or a minimum acceptable bandwidth

Scaling factors allow for a partial allocation of bandwidth for certain types of data traffic. The primary scaling factor is not definable and is always set to 1. A secondary scaling factor can be defined by an administrator; it's typically set to a range of 1 to 2 percent.

When identifying a minimum acceptable bandwidth, you must set a parameter that will be an enforced rate for the VCC. This parameter will make the routing algorithm choose a link that has bandwidth equal to or greater than the assigned minimum acceptable bandwidth value. Doing so prevents the possibility of an output port sending data at a greater rate than an intermediate link can handle and guarantees a certain amount of bandwidth for those applications that require it.

LightStream Troubleshooting Tools

The LightStream series of Cisco switches has many troubleshooting and monitoring tools. The boot process can be used to find hardware or software problems, certain protocols can be used for troubleshooting, and a unique tool called a *snooping* mechanism allows all or some of the connections to be transparently mirrored to a port. Let's take a better look at these troubleshooting tools in the following sections.

LightStream Boot Process

When you power-on a LightStream for the first time, you should be able to access the console port. Within the first few seconds of turning on the power, you should see the following three lines:

```
System Bootstrp, Version 201 (1025), SOFTWARE
Copyright (c) 1986-1996 by Cisco Systems
ASP processor with 16384 Kbytes of main memory
```

These lines indicate how much memory is installed in the switch. Checking the amount of memory installed in the switch against the amount displayed here can identify a hardware problem. If the bootstrap fails to load, the boot ROM could have a problem. If the switch has no configuration, it will default to setup mode.

If you see the following notice during the boot process and you're prompted to set up the switch, then the installed nonvolatile RAM (NVRAM) may have a problem—particularly if a saved configuration existed when the power was recycled. Let's take a look:

```
Notice: NVRAM invalid, possibly due to a write erase.
   -- System Configuration Dialog --
At any point you may enter a question mark '?' for help.
Use ctrl-c to abort configuration dialog at any prompt.
Default settings are in square brackets '[]'
Would you like to enter the initial configuration dialog? [yes]
```

From this prompt, you can enter the initial configuration dialog or decline and manually enter the configuration. This choice allows an administrator to use the Command Line Interface (CLI) on the LightStream switch. If you are not familiar with configuring a LightStream switch, you may want to continue using the System Configuration Dialog screen.

Supported Troubleshooting Protocols

LightStream switches support many protocols, such as Bootstrap Protocol (BOOTP) and Telnet, for remote access to the switch and autoconfiguration. In-band management access is possible through the ATM interfaces or the Ethernet port. Out-of-band management can be handled by the console port or either of the two serial ports. One serial port allows a dedicated port to attach a local terminal, and one can be used to attach an external modem for dial-in access through an analog telephone line.

Trivial File Transfer Protocol (TFTP) can be used for remote access to upload new firmware upgrades, save configurations, or upload configurations.

NOTE: *Security for LightStream switches can be provided by the Cisco IOS software or a Terminal Access Controller Access Control System Plus (TACACS+)/authentication, authorization, and accounting (AAA). The Cisco IOS can be configured with multiple password levels. A TACACS+/AAA server can be used for remote access validation.*

Snooping Mechanisms

Snooping mechanisms used by the LightStream 1010's ports allow a mirrored connection from one or more ports to be mirrored to another port. As a result, any data on a selected mirrored port will be copied and sent to the mirror port. This process is completely transparent to the end devices connected to the port or ports being monitored, and the data can be analyzed by an external ATM analyzer attached to the mirrored port.

9. LightStream Switches

Snooping mechanisms are one of the most important monitoring and trouble-shooting tools used in ATM switches. ATM analyzers can be used to monitor the traffic flows in and out of the selected ports. No external devices can be connected to monitored ports to easily identify problems associated with ATM.

Multiprotocol Over ATM

Multiprotocol Over ATM (MPOA) enables the fast routing of internetwork-layer packets across a nonbroadcast, multiaccess (NBMA) network. MPOA replaces multihop routing with point-to-point routing using a direct VCC between ingress and egress edge devices or hosts.

Two components will be discussed here:

- MPOA Server (MPS)
- MPOA Client (MPC)

The MPS

The MPS supplies the forwarding information used by MPCs. Once the MPS receives a query from a client, it responds with forwarding information. MPOA uses Next Hop Resolution Protocol (NHRP) to support the query and response. The MPS on the router can also terminate shortcuts.

Although, a router is usually designated as an MPS, it can also be designated as an MPC.

The MPC

Configuring an MPC on a router provides router-initiated and router-terminated shortcuts for non-NBMA networks. The MPC functionality involves the following:

- Data-plane and control-plane VCC management
- Ingress/egress cache management
- MPOA frame processing
- MPOA protocol and flow detection

An MPC identifies packets sent to an MPOA-capable router over the NBMA network and establishes a shortcut VCC to the egress MPC, if possible.

Immediate Solutions

Configuring the Hostname

You can change the default prompt of **Switch>** and distinguish a switch from other devices in your network by naming it. The following code lists the command to change the prompt name to **CoriolisLS1010>** (this setting has only local significance on the switch):

```
Switch> enable

Switch# configure terminal
Enter configuration commands, one per line. End with CNTL/Z.

Switch(config)# hostname CoriolisLS1010
CoriolisLS1010(config)#
```

Configuring an Enable Password

In order to keep unauthorized people from making configuration changes on your switch, you should use the **enable password** command followed by the new password. Let's take a look at an example:

1. Use the **enable** command to enter Privileged EXEC mode:

   ```
   CoriolisLS1010> enable
   ```

2. Use the **config terminal** command to enter Global Configuration mode:

   ```
   CoriolisLS1010# config terminal
   ```

3. Use the **enable password** command followed by a password to configure the enable password:

   ```
   CoriolisLS1010(config)# enable password book1
   ```

9. LightStream Switches

287

Configuring the Processor Card Ethernet Interface

You must configure the Ethernet port on the processor card in order to allow Telnet access to the switch CLI. To configure the Ethernet interface, you must have local administrative access. Connect a PC or workstation to the console port on the processor card and follow these steps:

1. Use the **enable** command to enter Privileged EXEC mode:

```
CoriolisLS1010> enable
```

2. Use the **config terminal** command to enter Global Configuration mode:

```
CoriolisLS1010# config terminal
```

3. You must identify the route for traffic to take to the internal network (referred to as a *static route*) using the **ip route** command, as shown here:

```
CoriolisLS1010(config)# ip route 63.78.127.0 255.255.255.0 ethernet 0
```

4. Enter Interface Configuration mode for the Ethernet interface:

```
CoriolisLS1010(config)# interface ethernet 0
```

5. Assign the IP address and subnet mask to the interface just as you would a switch or router Ethernet interface, and then exit:

```
CoriolisLS1010(config-if)# ip address 63.78.127.2 255.255.255.0
CoriolisLS1010(config-if)# ^C
CoriolisLS1010#
```

Configuring Virtual Private Tunnels

A *virtual private tunnel* provides a way to link two private ATM networks across a public network. This type of network only supports PVCs. Connecting this way provides a permanent path through the public network. The public network trunks all the virtual channels in the VP between the two networks. The following example shows how to configure the VP tunnel when the VPI equals 2:

1. Use the **enable** command to enter Privileged EXEC mode:

```
CoriolisLS1010> enable
```

2. Use the **config terminal** command to enter Global Configuration mode:

```
CoriolisLS1010# config terminal
```

3. Enter the interface on the module:

```
CoriolisLS1010(config)# interface atm 3/0/2
```

4. Identify the private virtual path (PVP) number:

```
CoriolisLS1010(config-if)# atm pvp 2
```

5. Create an ATM subinterface. This example uses the PVP number as the sub-interface number:

```
CoriolisLS1010(config-if)# interface atm 3/0/2.2
CoriolisLS1010(config-subif)# end
CoriolisLS1010#
```

Verifying an ATM Interface Connection Status

When the VP tunnel is configured correctly, the connection status displayed in the AutoCfgState shows the word *completed*. You display this information by using the **show atm interface** command followed by the ATM interface. Let's take a look at an example of the command:

```
CoriolisLS1010# show atm interface atm 3/0/2.2

Interface:      ATM3/0/2.2      Port-type:      vp tunnel
IF Status:      UP              Admin Status:   up

Auto-config:    enabled         AutoCfgState:   completed
IF-Side:        Network         IF-type:        NNI
Uni-type:       not applicable  Uni-version:    not applicable

CoriolisLS1010#
```

9. LightStream Switches

Viewing the Configured Virtual Connections

To view the configured virtual connections, use the **show atm vp** command as shown here:

```
CoriolisLS1010# show atm vp

Interface   VPI  Type   X-Interface   X-VPI      Status
ATM3/0/2    2    PVP    TUNNEL

CoriolisLS1010#
```

Configuring the LECS ATM Address on a LightStream 1010 Switch

To configure the LAN Emulation Configuration Server (LECS) ATM address on a LightStream 1010 switch, follow these steps:

1. Use the **enable** command to enter Privileged EXEC mode.

2. Use the **config terminal** command to enter Global Configuration mode.

3. Enter Interface Configuration mode for the correct ATM interface.

4. Use the **atm** command followed by the address of the LECS:

   ```
   atm lecs-address atm-address
   ```

TIP: To verify the address configuration, use the show atm ilmi-configuration command.

Configuring the Advertised LECS Address

To configure the LECS address advertised by the switch to the end system, use the **atm lecs-address-default** Global Configuration command. The syntax is as follows:

```
atm lecs-address-default lecsaddress [sequence #]
```

Viewing the LANE Configuration

To view the LANE configuration on a LightStream series switch, use the **show lane** command as follows:

```
CoriolisLS1010# show lane

LE Server ATM2/0.2  ELAN name: elan1  Admin: up  State: operational

type: ethernet        Max Frame Size: 1516
ATM address: 47.009181000000060707B8A01.1122334455AA.02
LECS used: 47.009181000000060707B8A01.0060705A8F05.00 connected, vcd 1450
control distribute: vcd 1452, 3 members, 196 packets

proxy/ (ST: Init, Conn, Waiting, Adding, Joined, Operational, Reject,
Term)
lecid ST vcd pkts Hardware Addr  ATM Address
   1  0 1451     6 0060.705a.8f02 47.009181000000060707B8A01.0060705A8B12.01
   2  0 1455    10 00e0.d7b1.ba12 47.009181000000060707B8A01.112233461176.02
  3P  0 1466    59 0090.a2fb.b430 47.009181000000060707B8A01.009086FB1021.01

LE BUS ATM2/0.2  ELAN name: elan1  Admin: up  State: operational
type: ethernet        Max Frame Size: 1516
ATM address: 47.009181000000006007B8A01.1B2133CC51BA.02
data forward: vcd 1454, 3 members, 244 packets, 5 unicasts

lecid  vcd pkts    ATM Address
   1 1453    32 47.009181000000060707B8A01.0060705A8B12.01
   2 1458    28 47.009181000000060707B8A01.112233461176.02
   3 1467    58 47.009181000000060707B8A01.0060705A8B12.01

LE Client ATM2/0.2  ELAN name: elan1  Admin: up  State: operational

Client ID: 2                LEC up for 22 minutes 53 seconds
Join Attempt: 605
HW Address: 00e0.f9b1.b410   Type: ethernet  Max Frame Size: 1516
ATM Address: 47.009181000000060707B8A01.112233461176.02
```

9. LightStream Switches

```
VCD   rxFrames  txFrames  Type        ATM Address
  0          0         0  configure
00.000000000000000000000000.000000000000.00
1456         1        10  direct
47.009181000000000060707B8A01.112233461176.02
1457       196         0  distribute
47.009181000000000060707B8A01.112233461176.02
1459         0        28  send
47.009181000000000060707B8A01.112233461176.02
1460       245         0  forward
47.009181000000000060707B8A01.112233461176.02
```

Related solution:	Found on page:
Verifying a LEC Configuration on an ELAN	272

Viewing the Installed Modules

Just as you can on a Catalyst switch, you can use the **show module** command to look at the installed modules on the LightStream switch. Remember, the LS1010 can use the same modules as the 5500 series switch. Here's an example of the command's results:

```
CoriolisLS1010> show module

Mod Module-Name       Ports Module-Type           Model     Serial-Num Status
-- ---------------    ----  --------------------  --------  ---------- ------
2                     2     100BaseTX Supervisor  WS-X5509  002261212  ok
3                     24    3 Segment 100BaseTX E ws-x5223  000000021  ok
4                     1     MM OC-3 ATM           WS-X5155  003125674  ok
5                     2     MM MIC FDDI           WS-X5101  002774545  ok
6                           Route Switch Ext Port
7                     1     Route Switch          WS-X5302  002274941  ok

Mod MAC-Address(es)                             Hw     Fw     Sw
--- ----------------------------------------    ------ ------ ----------
2   00-e0-a3-a5-00-00 thru 00-e0-a3-a5-03-ff    1.2    2.2(1) 3.1(1)
3   00-60-83-42-e4-4b thru 00-60-83-42-e4-4d    0.1    2.2(4) 3.1(1)
4   00-40-0b-43-02-64                           1.0    1.3    2.2
5   00-60-3e-cd-42-95                           1.0    1.1    2.1(2)
7   00-40-0b-91-42-16 thru 00-40-0b-91-42-17    1.0    20.2   11.2
```

```
Mod Sub-Type Sub-Model Sub-Serial Sub-Hw
--- -------- --------- ---------- ------
2   EARL 1+  WS-F5511  0002278010 1.0

Mod SMT User-Data            T-Notify CF-St    ECM-St   Bypass
--- ------------------------ -------- -------- -------- ------
5   WorkGroup Stack          30       isolated in       absent

CoriolisLS1010>
```

Configuring the MPC

This example configures the MPC and binds an LEC to the MPC:

1. Define the MPC with the name THEMPC, as follows:

   ```
   mpoa client config name THEMPC
   ```

2. Specify the ATM interface to which the MPC is attached. In this example, the interface is 1/2:

   ```
   interface ATM 1/2
   ```

3. Associate the interface to the MPC named MYMPC as follows:

   ```
   mpoa client name MYMPC
   ```

4. Enter Subinterface Configuration mode for the ATM interface that contains the LEC to which you will bind the MPC:

   ```
   interface atm 1/2.1
   ```

5. To bind a LANE client to the specified MPC, use this command:

   ```
   lane client mpoa client name MYMPC
   ```

Configuring the MPS

The following example shows the proper configuration of the MPS and attaches the MPS to a hardware interface:

9. LightStream Switches

1. Define the MPS named THEMPS:

    ```
    mpoa server config name THEMPS
    ```

2. Enter Interface Configuration mode for the ATM interface:

    ```
    interface ATM 1/1
    ```

3. Attach the MPS called THEMPS to a hardware interface:

    ```
    mpoa server name THEMPS
    ```

Changing the MPS Variables

MPS variables affect only a particular MPS. Perform the following tasks starting in MPS Configuration mode:

1. To identify an MPS with a specific name, use the following command:

    ```
    mpoa server config name mps-name
    ```

2. The ATM address that specifies the control ATM can be optionally identified using this command:

    ```
    atm-address atm-address
    ```

3. To specify the network ID, use the following command:

    ```
    network-id id
    ```

4. To identify a keepalive time value, use the following command:

    ```
    keepalive-time time
    ```

5. To change the holding-time value, use the following command:

    ```
    holding-time time
    ```

Monitoring the MPS

To monitor the MPS, use the following command in Privileged EXEC mode:

```
show mpoa server
```

Enabling ILMI Autoconfiguration

The following example shows how to enable Integrated Local Management Interface (ILMI) autoconfiguration on interface ATM 3/1/2:

```
CoriolisLS1010(config)# interface atm 3/1/2
CoriolisLS1010(config-if)# atm auto-configuration
CoriolisLS1010(config-if)#

%ATM-5-ATMSOFTSTART:Restarting ATM signaling and ILMI on ATM3/1/2
```

Configuring LANE on a LightStream 1010

To configure a LANE client connection from a remote ATM switch router to the processor card (CPU) of a local switch, follow these configuration steps:

1. Use the **enable** command to enter Privileged EXEC mode:

```
CoriolisLS1010> enable
```

2. Use the **config terminal** command to enter Global Configuration mode:

```
CoriolisLS1010# config terminal
```

3. Enter Subinterface mode for the processor card using the following command:

```
CoriolisLS1010(config)# interface atm 0[.subinterface]
```

4. You must specify an ATM address to override the automatic ATM address assigned to a LANE client:

```
CoriolisLS1010(config-if)# lane client-atm-address atm-address-template
```

5. Use the **lane client ethernet** command followed by the name of the ELAN to configure a LANE client:

```
CoriolisLS1010(config-if)# lane client ethernet elan-name
```

Powering on the LightStream 100 ATM Switch

To power on the LightStream 100 ATM switch, use the following steps:

1. Turn the power switch to the on position, which is depicted by a symbol that looks like this: (I).

2. The switch will execute the diagnostic power on self test (POST). The results can be viewed by connecting to the console port. If there is a problem with the POST, you can see the error on screen and you will be notified with a lit alarm LED. A red alarm LED indicates a failure that must be resolved before the boot process can continue. The screen displays NG (for "no good") when a POST item doesn't pass; you will see a Not Installed error if the switch has an empty slot.

Configuring the LS100 Switch

To perform the basic configuration on the LS100 switch, follow these steps:

1. Use the **show interface** or **show module** command to display the interfaces installed. Make sure there is a line number for each module installed.

2. If a card or module does not appear, turn off the power, reseat the module or card, and turn the power back on. If the card or module still does not appear, contact Cisco's Technical Assistance Center (TAC).

3. Use the **enable** command to enter Privileged EXEC command mode. The system requests a password; if one has not been assigned, just hit the Enter key.

4. Type in a lowercase *c* to allow changes. The prompt changes from > to #.

5. You must set the time and date on the LS100 switch. The following command shows how to set the time to 7:37 P.M. in military time and the date to November 30, 2000:

```
CoriolisLS100# set time 00-11-30 19:37:00
System Timer is set.
00-11-30 19:37:00
```

6. Use the **set clock** command to set the clock to synchronize the time with the other connected LightStream switches. This step will also determine if the switch is a master or slave time synchronizer unit.

7. Use the **set interface** command to register a line. This command sets the interface type to user-network interface (UNI) or network-to-network interface (NNI), the standard body conformance to either ATM or ITU, the length of the VPI valid bits, and the length of VCI valid bits.

8. Use the **pvc establish** command to configure a point-to-point PVC.

WARNING! This command becomes active immediately.

9. To optionally set PVC multicast, use the **pvc add** command to add the endpoint. The **pvc add** command can also be used to add a PVC endpoint for point-to-multipoint connection. If you are using an SVC, use the **route add** command instead of the **pvc add** command. The **pvc establish** command allows you to enter the line number, VPI, and VCI.

---

*NOTE: To delete an endpoint, use the **pvc remove** command.*

---

10. Use the **save** command to save the configuration data.

11. Use the **exit** command to exit Privileged EXEC command mode.

Recovering a Lost Password

To recover a password, such as that used for the root account, look at the following example (the output is quite long, so unnecessary information has been omitted):

```
Type '. to get a Test and Control System (TCS) hub prompt.
user name:'.
TCS HUB<>
At the TCS hub prompt, use reset and connect to reset the NP card.

Note: Be prepared to press Enter at the prompt, as shown below.
TCS HUB<>  reset 1
TCS HUB<>  connect 1

Memory Autosizing...(32Meg)...Done
Clearing 32Meg Memory...Done
NP1 POST Version 0.220 Nov 23 1994

NP1 POST SUMMARY:
----------------
0 Tests Failed
```

9. LightStream
Switches

```
System will boot in 5 seconds: hit  to interrupt.
Press Enter now.
Choose option 5 to boot the system for a single-user:
Network Processor bootstrap(version 1.3: Sep 13 1993)
1 - Boot ATM switch application
2 - Begin full installation with boot from floppy disk
3 - List contents of hard disk root directory
4 - List contents of floppy disk root directory
5 - Boot system single-user
6 - Escape to full set of bootstrap options
7 - Extended help
Option> 5

booting: drive:0, partition:0, kernel:"lynx.os", flags:0x4100
Resetting SCSI bus
Kernel linked for 0xea010000
LOAD AT 0x10000
483328+49152+262564[+62796+51901]
TOTAL SIZE: 909744 at 0x1001c
START AT 0x10020
NP memory size: 32 MB
ILACC: EEPROM enet addr:8:0:8:0:ae:61, Silicon Rev:0x5, IB:0xea1dfce0
virtual console: IB: 0xea1dfe68
NCR 53C710: Chip Revision: 0x2, IB: 0xec18e000

Memory Autosizing...(32Meg)...Done
Clearing 32Meg Memory...Done
NP1 POST Version 0.220 Nov 23 1994

NP1 POST SUMMARY:
----------------
0 Tests Failed

booting: drive:0, partition:0, kernel:"lynx.os", flags:0x5104
Resetting SCSI bus
Kernel linked for 0xea010000
LOAD AT 0x10000
483328+49152+262564[+62796+51901]
TOTAL SIZE: 909744 at 0x1001c
START AT 0x10020
NP memory size: 32 MB
ILACC: EEPROM enet addr:8:0:8:0:ae:61, Silicon Rev:0x5, IB:0xea1dfce0
virtual console: IB: 0xea1dfe68
NCR 53C710: Chip Revision: 0x2, IB: 0xec18e000
```

```
LynxOS/68040-MVME167 Version 2.1.0
Copyright 1992 Lynx Real-Time Systems Inc.
All rights reserved.

LynxOS release 2.1.0, level 1: NP-LynxOS #112: compiled Nov 08 1994 19:49:33
Single-user boot
single-user$
Type '. to get a TCS hub prompt:
single-user$ '.
TCS HUB<>
Reset the NP card:
TCS HUB<>    reset 1
TCS HUB<>    connect 1

Memory Autosizing...(32Meg)...Done
Clearing 32Meg Memory...Done
NP1 POST Version 0.220 Nov 23 1994

NP1 POST SUMMARY:
----------------
0 Tests Failed

The following accounts do not have passwords:
root fldsup npadmin oper

Install a password on the root account? (y/n) [y] y
Changing password for root
Enter new password:
Retype new password:

Install a password on the fldsup account? (y/n) [y] y
Changing password for fldsup
Enter new password:
Retype new password:

Install a password on the npadmin account? (y/n) [y] y
Changing password for npadmin
Enter new password:
Retype new password:

Install a password on the oper account? (y/n) [y] y
Changing password for oper
Enter new password:
Retype new password:
```

```
Starting VM system ... Virtual Memory Engaged!
inetd started
Starting crond ...
Initializing the switch hardware interface ...
Using switch A, cards are NOT synchronized, fast cutover is supported
PCP version: 0x410, CMP version: 0x12, FSU version 0x109
Starting the switch software
LightStream 2020 Version 2.0.6
Copyright 1993 LightStream Corp. All rights reserved.
Portions copyright 1992 by Lynx Real-Time Systems Inc., 1983 by the Regents
of the University of California, 1988 and 1990 by Paul Vixie, and 1991 by
SNMP Research Inc.

This software contains unpublished proprietary and trade secret information
of LightStream Corp.

LightStream 2020 Software provided to the U.S. Government is subject to the
notices on the software and on the LightStream user documentation copyright
page.
PROGRAM: cbuf: (ls2_0) compiled Nov 08 1994 @ 23:33:35 [pid:50]
Login as root and check the new password:
user name: coriolisuser
password:
```

This process changes the password and recovers any lost passwords.

Chapter 10

Layer 2 Redundant Links

(continued)

In Depth

If your company has ever experienced a critical work stoppage due to a downed server or a network outage, you understand how critical it is to implement redundancy in your network. No matter what happens with an individual link in your network, the other links should take over using redundant links.

The Spanning-Tree Protocol (STP) provides the components needed to ensure consistent network availability when a problem occurs with a link in the network. Not only can you use these redundant links in the case of a network failure, but—because your company is paying to implement the redundant links—it makes sense to load balance over those links and use them to handle twice the traffic load when they are operating correctly.

This chapter will concentrate on using Layer 2 redundant links as well as using STP to block redundant links to prevent data loops from forming in the network. Layer 3 devices, which are typically routers, give the routing protocols the responsibility for making sure routing loops do not occur in the network.

Layer 2 Switching Overview

Here's a quick reminder of how Layer 2 switching works. The Open System Interconnection (OSI) Layer 2 uses the Network Interface Card's (NIC) physical address, called the Media Access Control (MAC) address, which is assigned to the card by the vendor of the card. In Chapter 2, I covered how Application Specific Integrated Circuits (ASICs) are used to build the switches' Content Addressable Memory (CAM) table—similar to a router's routing table—which is used to calculate and maintain loop-free paths through the network.

At Layer 3, you use software to create filtering tables and make filtering decisions. Switches use hardware ASIC chips to help make filtering decisions—filtering with hardware is much faster.

Both switches and bridges track the source hardware address of each frame received on each port and enter this information in their filtering table. This table allows the bridge or switch to make a forwarding or filtering decision for data it receives based on the information learned.

Bridges have up to 16 ports but only one instance of STP for all the ports. Cisco switches can have hundreds of ports and an instance of STP running for each virtual LAN (VLAN). On some Cisco Catalyst switches, thousands of instances of STP can be running on the network.

When a frame is received on a switch port, the switch looks at the destination address in the frame header and compares the address with known source addresses the switch has learned to see if it knows the port the destination resides on. If the address is known, the switch forwards the frame to the destination port. If the address is unknown, the switch forwards the frame to all its ports, which are members of the same broadcast domain as the arriving switch port. This broadcast domain consists of all the members of the same VLAN as the port of arrival. This domain does not necessarily include just VLAN members on the switch of arrival—it can include all the switches in the network that share the same VLAN number.

Frames

A switch will typically receive three types of frames without a specific destination. These frames in turn become a broadcast and are flooded out all the ports except for the port of arrival. These frame types are:

- Broadcast frames
- Multicast frames
- Unknown unicasts

Broadcast and Multicast Frames

Broadcast and multicast frames are unique in that neither has a specified destination hardware address. The source address is also the hardware address of the device that sent the frame. In the case of broadcasts, the destination address shown in the header is all 1s, indicating that the broadcast goes to all nodes in a network. A multicast specifies a network but changes all the host address bits to all 1s. For example, a broadcast and multicast in binary would appear as shown in Table 10.1.

Table 10.1   Broadcast and multicast destination addresses.

Frame Type	Binary Value	Broadcast Address
Broadcast	11111111.11111111.11111111.11111111	255.255.255.255
Multicast	00001010.00000001.11111111.11111111	10.1.255.255

When a switch receives a broadcast or a multicast, the frame is sent out all the ports of the switch by default, with the exception of the port on which the frame arrived. VLANs can be used to break down the broadcasts into smaller broadcast domains. In the case of a VLAN, if a broadcast arrives on a port assigned to VLAN 5, only ports assigned to VLAN 5 will receive the broadcast.

Unknown Unicasts

An *unknown unicast* is similar to a broadcast. This type of unicast is sent when a destination address is unknown by the switch. In this case, the bridge forwards the frame just like a broadcast; the frame is sent out all ports except the port on which it arrived.

Layer 2 Network Loops

To sum up STP in one sentence, Spanning Tree Protocol is used to allow the Layer 2 network to have more than one path to a destination by blocking ports that can cause a packet to make a complete circle through the network. This circle, shown in Figure 10.1, is known as a *data loop*. The data will move in a continuous circle unless some protocol or algorithm is used to stop the data or a maximum time to live is assigned to the data packet. STP reliably monitors the network topology to find all the links and make sure that data loops do not occur.

Manufacturers needed a consistent standard that they all could use to block redundant paths through a network. Digital Equipment Corporation (DEC) answered

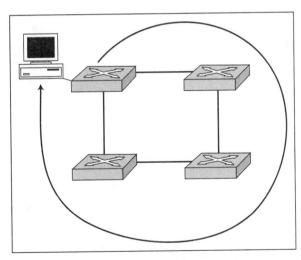

Figure 10.1   A network with more than one path in the network. Data can return to the source node on a second link, causing a data loop.

the call and submitted to the Institute of Electrical and Electronics Engineers (IEEE) a protocol similar to STP to become a networking standard. However, after the IEEE 802 committee revised it into what is now known as the IEEE 802.1D standard (Spanning Tree Protocol), the protocol differed just enough from DEC's version that they were incompatible.

Danger! Data Loops!

Data loops can easily become a network disaster. A transparent bridge always likes to retransmit a broadcast it receives and never mark the frame with a time to live (TTL) or an identifier that says "Hey I started here!" or "I've been around here a few times already." The result? Your transparent bridge keeps re-creating broadcasts in an expanding fashion. The bridge actually begins rebroadcasting broadcasts. Think this situation will last forever? Not likely—the bridges will eventually cause a broadcast storm and bring down the entire network.

STP fixes this problem and forces all the redundant data paths into a blocked state. By blocking the paths to destinations other than the given root path, STP creates only one path through the network. If any of the forwarding paths through one of the network segments in the spanning tree become unreachable, STP will reconfigure the spanning-tree topology and use the once blocked links in the network. STP calculates the network topology using the Spanning-Tree Algorithm (STA).

To avoid confusion, let me clarify that the Spanning-Tree Protocol and the Spanning-Tree Algorithm are two separate entities. STA chooses a reference point in the network and calculates the redundant paths to that reference point. If the STA finds a redundant path, it will choose one path to forward and the redundant paths to block. Using this process, STP and the STA effectively sever all the redundant links within the network.

STA is based on the graph theory developed by Edsger Dijkstra to construct a loop-free subset of the network topology. Let's take a look at this theory.

Edsger Dijkstra's Graph Theory

The STA uses solutions obtained by a graph theory also known as the Shortest Path Algorithm. As I mentioned earlier, this algorithm is used to construct a loop-free subset of the network's topology. The same theory is also used in other link state protocols, such as Open Shortest Path First (OSPF), to calculate routing solutions. The theory states that for a connected graph consisting of interfaces and edges connecting pairs of interfaces, a spanning tree of the edges maintains the connectivity of the graph while containing no loops.

The algorithm provides a directed graph where each link is represented by vertices and weighted edges, as shown in Figure 10.2. Each link represents a cost. The weighted edges, which usually have more hops in the link than do the straight-through points, are assigned higher values. Each link in the path has a value, and the total of the values to a given point or destination is the total weighted value of the path. The lowest total weighted value represents the most efficient path from one point to another point.

STA assigns each switch in the network a unique identifier. This identifier is one of the switch's MAC addresses, as well as an assigned priority (explained in more detail later in this chapter in "The Selection Process"). After STA assigns each switch this unique identifier, it then assigns each port in every switch a unique identifier. This port identifier is typically the port's own individual interface MAC address. Each bridge port is then associated with a path cost, which represents the cost of transmitting a frame onto the network through the port. Path costs are assigned by default, but can be assigned manually by a network administrator.

As I stated in the last section, the graph theory chooses a reference point in the network and calculates the redundant paths to that particular point in the network

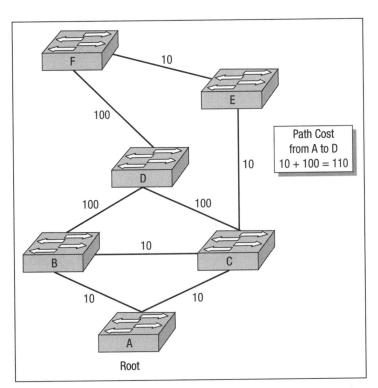

Figure 10.2 An example of a directed graph.

topology. After STP discovers all the links in the network, the STA chooses a single path through the network and blocks the redundant links. It does so by electing a root bridge. Let's take a look at root bridges in the next section.

STP Root Bridges

When STP initially comes online in a network, one of its first actions is to use the STA to select a root bridge and a root port. The *root bridge* is the bridge with the lowest-value bridge identifier. Switches or bridges using STP exchange multicast frames called Bridge Protocol Data Units (BPDUs) (discussed in the next section). All the switches on the network use these BPDUs to broadcast their bridge IDs to the other switches in the network. After the root bridge is selected, the root ports on all other bridges are determined.

Switch A in Figure 10.3 is acting as the root bridge, calculating the least-cost path to switch D. Notice the numbers associated with the root bridge's path to each individual destination; the path with the lowest number has the highest priority. The higher the number between individual segments, the higher the cost of transmitting a frame between those two segments. The port through which the root bridge can be reached with the least amount of hops or cost determines a bridge's root port; this is referred to as the *least path cost*.

The lowest calculated path is not always the most ideal path. For example, if multiple high-speed links to a destination exist, the links may total more than the cost of a very slow link, such as a modem. Even though the straight path has the

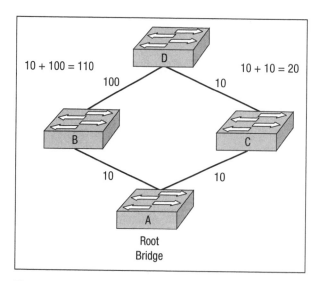

Figure 10.3   The root bridge calculating the path cost to switch D.

fewest hops, it is much slower than using a high-speed, longer path. To overcome this problem, you as the administrator can manually change a slower-speed link to have a higher port cost, which STP will use to calculate a higher path cost. The goal is to make changes to the network so that the fastest, most efficient route to the root port is designated for the switch to use. The fastest links should always have the lowest port costs.

A *designated bridge* is the bridge or switch on each LAN that provides the shortest route with the least path cost. The designated bridge is the only bridge that is allowed to forward frames to and from the other bridges. A *designated port* on the switch is the port that connects the switch to the physical interface of the designated bridge.

Bridge Protocol Data Units

BPDUs are messages passed between bridges and switches to help STP calculate and learn the topology of the network. The multicast messages contain information that identifies the network link, the bridge presumed to be the root bridge, the calculated root path cost, other STP bridges, port identifiers, and the age of the information contained in the message.

STP member bridges and switches exchange BPDU messages at configurable intervals—typically, every one to four seconds. By default, BPDUs are sent out every two seconds on every port to ensure a stable network without accidental data loops. Should one or more bridges fail or another STP member join the network, BPDU messages will help the other STP member bridges and switches to notice this change in the network topology. The neighboring bridges will detect the lack of configuration messages and initiate an immediate STA recalculation.

NOTE: *BPDU messages are never forwarded by any member. Instead, each STP bridge or switch makes a decision locally based on BPDU messages received. The switch or bridge then creates a new BPDU message based on the new information and sends that message out its ports.*

Let's take a look at the fields of a BPDU, as shown in Figure 10.4:

- *Protocol Identifier*—Contains 2 bytes and the value of zero.
- *Version*—Contains 1 byte and the value of zero.
- *Message Type*—Contains 1 byte and the value of zero.
- *Flag*—Contains 1 byte; only the first 2 bits are used. The topology change (TC) bit signals that there has been a topology change. The topology change acknowledgment (TCA) bit is then set to acknowledge receipt of a configuration message with the TC signal bit set.

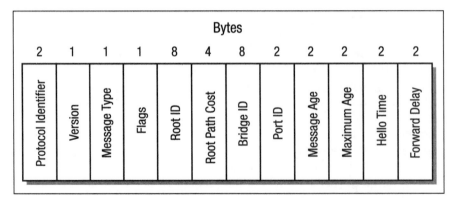

Figure 10.4   The 12 fields of a BPDU message.

- *Root ID*—Contains 8 bytes that identify the root bridge by listing a 2-byte priority followed by a 6-byte ID.

- *Root Path Cost*—Contains 4 bytes containing the cost of the path from the bridge sending the configuration message to the root bridge.

- *Bridge ID*—Contains 8 bytes identifying the priority and ID of the bridge sending the message.

- *Port ID*—Contains 2 bytes identifying the port from which the configuration message was sent. This field allows loops created by multiple attached bridges to be detected immediately by STP.

- *Message Age*—Contains 2 bytes specifying the amount of time since the root sent the configuration message on which the current configuration message is based.

- *MaxAge*—Contains 2 bytes indicating when the current configuration message should be discarded.

- *Hello Time*—Contains 2 bytes indicating the time period between root bridge configuration messages.

- *FwdDelay*—Contains 2 bytes indicating the length of time that the bridge should wait before transitioning to a new state following a topology change in the network.

Timer's affect the way BPDUs operate in a network and converge in the event of a data loop or network topology change. Let's take a look at these timers.

BPDU Timers

STP uses timers to prevent data loops and to determine how long it will take STP to converge after a link failure or change in the network topology. As frames and packets travel through the switched network, this data faces propagation delays. Propagation delays occur due to such things as bandwidth utilization, packet length, switch processing, or any other port-to-port delay encountered as data traverses the network.

As a result of propagation delays, BPDUs can be late to their destinations, making the switch think that a network topology change has occurred. Because propagation delays can occur at any time in the network, when a switch port converts from a blocked state to a forwarding state, the port can inadvertently create temporary data loops because it has not received a complete picture of the network topology.

To overcome network propagation delays, STP members use timers to force the ports to wait for the correct topology information. The timers are set by default on the switch. Table 10.2 shows the three different STP timers and the default timer settings based on a default setting of 2 for the Hello Time and 7 for the switch diameter. Based on these assumptions, the network should always form a stable topology.

Selecting the root bridge is important in calculating the port cost in the network. The port cost from each child switch in the network is calculated from the network's root bridge. In the next section, we'll take a look at how the BPDUs are used in the process of selecting a root bridge.

Parent and Child Switches

A switch's *diameter* is a unit of measurement between the root switch and child switches. The root bridge counts as the first switch. Each subsequent child switch out from the root bridge is counted to yield the diameter number. A parent switch brings you one switch closer to the root bridge, and a child switch takes you one switch farther away from the root bridge.

Each root bridge can be configured with a diameter from a minimum of two switches to a maximum of seven switches. By modifying the diameter, you will subsequently change the timer values that are advertised by the root to reflect a more accurate network diameter. For example, a diameter of 2 yields a MaxAge of 10 seconds and a FwdDelay of 7 seconds. Cisco recommends that you change the diameter to correctly reflect your network rather than manually changing the timers.

Table 10.2   The default STP timers and their default settings.

STP Timer Variable	Description	Default
Hello Time	Determines how often the switch will broadcast hello messages to other switches	2 seconds
Maximum Time/MaxAge	Determines how long protocol information received on a port is stored by the switch	20 seconds
FwdDelay	Determines how long listening and learning will last before the port begins forwarding	15 seconds

Root Bridge Selection

One of the most important decisions that you make when configuring the STP protocol on your network is the placement of the root bridge. In the spanning tree, the root bridge should be located as close as possible to the center of the network. Certain commands can help the administrator determine which device will become the root bridge. The proper placement of the root bridge(s) optimizes the paths that are chosen by the STP to allow data traffic to flow through the network. It also provides deterministic paths for data to take.

In order to get the most optimal paths through the network, you must sometimes ignore the default root bridge used by STP. This means you must manually configure the bridge that should be the root bridge, as well as the secondary root bridge. The function of the secondary root bridge is to become the root bridge, should the original root bridge fail.

TIP: *Typically, root bridges are Distribution layer switches, not Access layer switches. The root bridge should never be a Core layer switch, because the Core layer's responsibility is to move traffic as quickly as possible.*

The Selection Process

The root bridge selection process begins as soon as the switch powers up. The root bridge is the reference point in the network from which graph theory is used to calculate the cost of each link for each instance of a spanning tree. Using these calculations, the switches must determine if loops exist in the network and the path costs associated with each path through the network. The switch immediately assumes at startup that it gets to be the root bridge, and it configures its bridge ID equal to the root ID in the BPDU. The bridge ID field of a BPDU message is actually made up of two parts, as follows:

- *Bridge priority*—A 2-byte value set by the switch. By default, the priority is set to 0x8000 or 32,768.

- *Media Access Control (MAC) address*—The 6-byte MAC address of the switch or bridge.

These two fields of the bridge ID help an STP switch yield a value that can be compared with other switches' bridge IDs to determine which switch will become the root bridge. The lower the bridge ID value, the higher the chance of a root-bridge assignment. If more than one switch has the same low bridge priority value, the bridge with the lowest MAC address then becomes the root bridge. Table 10.3 shows the bridge priority values assigned by STP.

The switches participating in STP (other than the root bridge) must form an association with the root bridge shortly after the root bridge has been elected. Each switch examines each BPDU as it arrives on each port. When a switch receives

Table 10.3   The bridge priority values assigned by Spanning Tree Protocol.

Priority Assignment	Value
Default bridge priority	32,768
Secondary root bridge priority	16,384
Root bridge priority	8,192

the same information on more than one port, it is an indication that the switch has a redundant path to the root bridge. The switch then determines which port will forward data and which ports will be blocked from sending data. This decision is made by analyzing the path cost and port ID fields of the BPDUs.

Bridges look at the path cost first to determine if the port has the lowest-cost path to the root switch. If the port has the lowest port cost, the port is placed in forwarding mode. All the other ports that are receiving the same BPDU information are placed in blocking mode.

In blocking mode, the port will still forward BPDU and system information to the switch processor. If the path cost is equal, as in the case of identical links, the bridge looks at the port ID as a tie breaker. The port with the lowest port ID forwards, and all other ports are blocked.

Port Costs, Path Costs, and Port Priorities

After the root bridge has been elected, all the switches determine the best loop-free path to the root switch. STP uses several different costs, with the port priority as the tiebreaker. The sum of all the port costs to a destination through all the ports the frames must travel makes up the path cost. Table 10.4 shows the default port cost and port priority assigned to each port.

When the BPDU is sent to the other bridges, it carries the path cost. The spanning tree looks first at the path cost and decides which ports should forward and which ports should be blocked. If the path costs are equal for more than one port, then the spanning tree looks at the port ID. The port with the lower port ID has priority, making that port the forwarding port. If the path cost and the port ID are the same, then the STP will use the port priority as the tiebreaker. We'll look more at equal cost paths in the next section.

Table 10.4   The default port settings for STP.

Variable	Default
Port priority	32 (Except 1900 and 2820 series—128)
Port cost	62

TIP: *On both the Command Line Interface (CLI) based IOS and the Set/Clear command-based IOS, you should assign lower numbers to ports attached to faster media and higher numbers to ports attached to slower media. The defaults differ for media, as shown in Table 10.5.*

The port priority on each port can be modified to influence the links that will be forwarding. The port with the lowest priority value forwards frames for all VLANs. In the event that all ports have the same priority value, the port with the lowest port number will forward the frames. The possible port priority value range is from 0 to 63.

Equal Cost Paths

If two or more links have the same root path cost, such as two identical links running between two switches, STA has a problem choosing the designated port or a root path through the network using the lowest path cost. The bridge ID is used to determine the root bridge in the network and also the root port. By default, the priority on all devices running STP is 32,768.

If two switches or bridges have the same priority value, then the MAC address is used to break the tie. The bridge or port with the lowest ID wins. For example, let's look at the two switches depicted in Figure 10.5. One switch uses the MAC

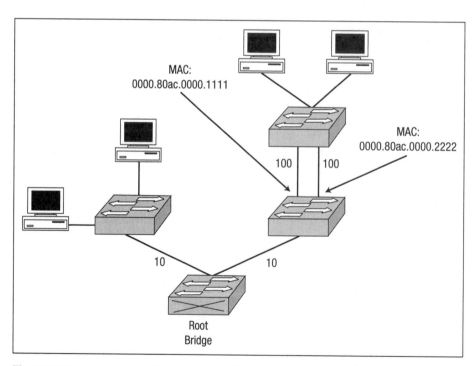

Figure 10.5   Two ports on two switches with equal cost paths through the network.

Table 10.5   Examples of path cost calculations.

Physical Wire Speed	Path Cost
10Mbps	100
100Mbps	10
155Mbps	6
1000Mbps (1Gbps)	1
10000Mbps (10Gbps)	1

address 0000.80ac.0000.1111, and the other switch uses the MAC address 0000.80ac.0000.2222. The switch using 0000.80ac.0000.1111 would become the root bridge or the root port, depending on which decision the switch is making.

We didn't consider another option: As the administrator, you can assign a lower path cost to faster physical media, or you can assign slower media a higher path cost. You can also decide which link to give a higher cost path when multiple links are equal. The range of numbers that can be assigned to the port costs are 1 through 65,535. Typically, the path cost is determined by dividing 1,000 by the physical wire speed in megabits per second (Mbps), as shown in Table 10.5.

NOTE: *The path cost can never be lower than one.*

STA recalculates the cost of using each link whenever a bridge joins the network or when a topology change is detected in the network. This calculation requires communication between the spanning tree bridges, which is accomplished through the passing of BPDU messages between switches.

Spanning Tree Convergence Time

The *convergence time* is the time it takes STP members to begin transmitting data on a redundant link after a link in forwarding mode has failed. It is also the initial period between the time an STP member powers up and when all the active links are placed in forwarding mode. In both cases, during the convergence time, no data is forwarded.

NOTE: *Convergence is necessary to make sure that all devices have the same topology information.*

Earlier in this chapter we discussed the STP default timers. The MaxAge default is set to 20 seconds and the FwdDelay is set to 30 seconds, because FwdDelay is used by both the listening and learning states (discussed in the next section). The values have meaning only at a root bridge. You can adjust FwdDelay and MaxAge; however, doing so may cause a data loop temporarily in more complex networks. The downtime could be as high as 50 seconds using the following formula:

```
2 * FwdDelay + MaxAge = Down Time
```

For example, the downtime caused by using the defaults would be the following:

```
2 * 15 + 20 = 50 seconds
```

Now that you have learned about the timers and how BPDUs operate in the network, let's take a closer look at how ports transition through different states before forwarding data.

STP Port States

Each port participating in STP transitions through four port states, or modes, in a designated order before the port can forward frames it receives. These states are blocking, listening, learning, and forwarding. A fifth state—the disabled state—can be manually configured by the switch.

Let's look at the different port states and when each is used (see Figure 10.6):

- *Blocking*—The port will not forward frames. It merely accepts BPDUs the port receives and processes them. All ports are in the blocking state by default when the switch is powered up. The port stays in a blocked state if STP determines that a lower-cost path exists to the root bridge. The port does not put any of the information it hears into the address table.

- *Listening*—The port continues to process BPDUs to make sure no loops occur on the network before it passes data frames. In this state the port is not forwarding frames or learning new addresses.

- *Learning*—The port is not forwarding frames but is learning addresses and putting them in the address table. The learning state is similar to the listening

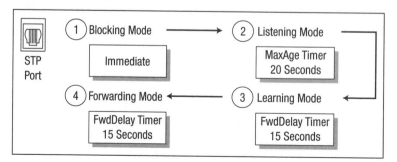

Figure 10.6   The convergence process of the port states in Spanning Tree Protocol.

state, except the port can now add information it has learned to the address table. The port is still not allowed to send or receive frames.

- *Forwarding*—The port now begins to learn from the BPDUs and starts to build a filter table. A port is not placed in a forwarding state until there are no redundant links or the port determines the lowest cost path to the root bridge or switch.

- *Disabled*—The port has been manually shut down by the network administrator or by the system due to a hardware problem.

Let's take a step-by-step look at what happens to a port when the switch is powered up:

1. After the switch's initialization or startup, all the ports immediately go to a blocking state.

2. After the configured MaxAge has been reached, the switch transitions from the blocking state to the learning state.

3. After the configured FwdDelay time has been reached, the port enters the learning state.

4. After the configured FwdDelay has been reached in the learning state, the port either transitions into forwarding mode or back to blocking mode. If STP has decided the port will be a forwarding port, the port is placed in forwarding mode; but if the port is a higher-cost redundant link, the port is placed in blocking mode again.

Each port state can be manually modified using the Cisco IOS. If properly configured, the ports should create a stable network, and the ports of each switch should transition to either a forwarding or blocking state.

Per-VLAN Spanning Tree

You can have many instances of STP running in your network. By running a different instance of STP on a per-VLAN basis, you can run some VLANs on ports that are blocked by another instance of STP running on another VLAN. In this way, you can set the priority of each port on a per-VLAN basis, allowing you to use the redundant links in your network to run an equal amount of traffic on each link. The VLANs individually determine which links to forward and which links to block.

Just as with the port priority setting, the port with the lowest priority value for each VLAN gets to forward the frames. If more than one or all the ports have the same priority value for a particular VLAN, the port with the lowest port number gets to forward the frames for that VLAN.

PVST and PVST+

Per-VLAN Spanning Tree (PVST) is a Cisco proprietary solution to the scaling and stability problems associated with Common Spanning Tree (CST) in large-scale spanning tree networks. PVST creates a separate instance of STP on each VLAN in the switch block. This setup gives each VLAN a unique STP topology containing its own port cost, path cost, priority, and root switch.

By using separate instances of PVST on each VLAN, you reduce the convergence time for STP recalculation and increase reliability of the network. By implementing PVST, the overall size of the spanning tree topology is reduced significantly. PVST improves scalability and decreases convergence time, providing faster recovery in the event of network faults. It also allows control of forwarding paths on a per-subnet basis while providing a simple technique for Layer 2 redundancy.

PVST does have some disadvantages in the spanning tree. PVST uses more processing power and consumes more bandwidth to support spanning tree maintenance and BPDUs for each VLAN. Inter-Switch Link (ISL) uses one spanning tree per VLAN, using PVST over ISL trunks. PVST implementation requires the use of Cisco ISL encapsulation in order to function.

Per-VLAN Spanning Tree Plus (PVST+) is not well documented by Cisco. IEEE 802.1Q can use PVST+ to map multiple spanning trees to the spanning tree of authentic IEEE 802.1Q switches.

PVST+ is available in Catalyst software versions 4.1 or newer. Cisco Catalyst switches configured with version 4.1 or later are considered Cisco PVST+ switches. PVST+ is compatible and interoperable with legacy type Mono Spanning Tree (MST) and PVST switches without any user intervention—thus PVST+ has a type of plug-and-play functionality.

Configuring the port priority by VLAN is useful for distributing data across parallel paths. If a parallel connection exists between two devices, STP will block one of the links. If the port priority is not changed on one of the ports for each VLAN, the traffic from all VLANs will travel on one link, and one link will be used only as a backup.

When you need to have multiple links to a destination be able to transmit data as though they were one link, you can use EtherChannel. Let's take a look at EtherChannel in the next section.

EtherChannel

Fast EtherChannel can provide scaled bandwidth within the campus using full-duplex bandwidth at wire speed for up to eight bundled links. A *bundle* is a series of links acting like a single link between two points in the network. Thus, eight wires can be used to simulate one link able to handle up to 800Mbps and load balance data across those links, as shown in Figure 10.7.

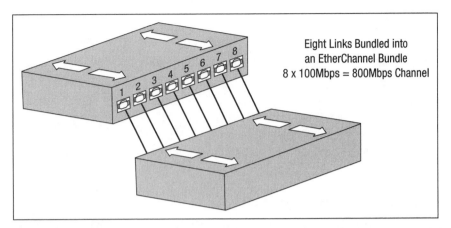

Figure 10.7   Eight equal-cost links between two switches, creating a bundle of eight channels acting as a single link.

Let's take a look at what occurs during a link failure in an EtherChannel bundle. We'll also examine the Port Aggregation Protocol (PAgP).

Link Failure

Fast EtherChannel provides redundancy in the event of a link failure. The EtherChannel bundle is managed by the Fast EtherChannel process and the Ethernet Bundle Controller (EBC). Should one link in the bundle fail, the EBC informs the Enhanced Address Recognition Logic (EARL) ASIC of the failure. The EARL ASIC immediately ages out all addresses learned on that link. The EBC and the EARL then recalculate in the hardware, sending queries to the other switches and learning the destination link based on the responses. The data traffic is rerouted on one of the other links in just a few milliseconds, making the convergence transparent to the user.

EtherChannel Administrative Groups

You can define an EtherChannel administrative group to identify groups of ports that are allowed to form an EtherChannel bundle together. When you create an EtherChannel port bundle, an administrative group is defined automatically. Administrative group membership is limited by hardware restrictions.

The administrative group can be any value between 1 and 1,024, inclusive. It is defined using the

```
set port channel <port list> <administrative group number>
```

command. To view the configured administrative groups, use this command:

```
show channel group <administrative group number>
```

Modifying a member port of an EtherChannel administrative group will cause the port to be removed from the group when STP realizes that a change has occurred in the network topology. The modified port that was a member of the EtherChannel administrative group must go through listening and learning mode again before it can return to forwarding mode and rejoin the EtherChannel bundle.

Port Aggregation Protocol

The Port Aggregation Protocol (PAgP) is used to manage the Fast EtherChannel bundles and aids in the automatic creation of Fast EtherChannel links. PAgP packets are sent between Fast EtherChannel-capable ports. PAgP learns of the neighbors and their group capabilities dynamically and then informs its neighbors of the local group capabilities. After the protocol determines all the paired, point-to-point, or bi-directional links, it groups into a single channel those ports that have the same neighbor device ID and neighbor group capability. The channel is then added to the spanning tree as a bridge port.

WARNING! Dynamic VLAN ports can force a VLAN change; as a result, PAgP cannot be used to form a bundle on ports that are configured for dynamic VLANs. The VLANs must be static VLANs, meaning that the port on the switch must be assigned to a VLAN. PAgP also requires that all ports in the channel belong to the same VLAN or be configured as trunk ports.

If you have a pre-existing EtherChannel bundle, and a VLAN of a port contained in the bundle is modified, all ports in the bundle are modified to match the VLAN configuration. PAgP will not group ports running at different speeds or duplex. PAgP will change the port speed and duplex for all ports in the bundle.

All ports in a Fast EtherChannel bundle should be assigned to the same VLAN or be configured as trunked ports. You must also configure both ends of the link with the same trunking mode.

TIP: You can configure the broadcast limits by percentage limit or by packets-per-second. Packets-per-second allows unicast packets to be dropped when the broadcast limit is exceeded.

Fast Convergence Components of STP

There are a number of protocols for STP that allow for fast convergence, including PortFast, UplinkFast, and BackboneFast. In the following sections I'll discuss the functions of these protocols and components.

PortFast

PortFast is a switch function that can be used on ports where a single server or workstation is connected, to allow a port to enter the forwarding mode almost immediately. Doing so prevents the port from entering the listening and learning states.

As we've discussed, when a switch using STP is powered up, the ports running STP go through four states before forwarding frames through each port. In order to get to the forwarding state, the STA makes each port wait up to 50 seconds before data is allowed to be forwarded. This delay may cause problems with certain protocols and applications. By implementing PortFast, you can avoid these delays.

UplinkFast

One of the most important factors in a network is the convergence time when a link fails. By implementing the UplinkFast function, you can reduce the time it takes for the network to converge by optimizing convergence times. Because of the convergence time of STP, some end stations become inaccessible, depending on the current state of each switch port.

By decreasing convergence time, you reduce the length of the disruption. UplinkFast allows a port in a blocked state on a switch to almost immediately begin forwarding when the switch detects a link failure or a topology change. However, UplinkFast must have direct knowledge of the link failure in order to move a blocked port into a forwarding state.

NOTE: *An Uplink Group is a root port that is in a forwarding state and a set of blocked ports that does not include self-looping ports. The Uplink Group is the alternate path when the currently forwarding link fails.*

The UplinkFast feature should be placed only on Access layer switches that are connected to the end-user nodes. In order to utilize UplinkFast, several criteria must be met:

- UplinkFast must be enabled on the switch.
- The switch must have at least one blocked port.
- The failure must be on the root port.

If a link fault occurs on the primary root link, UplinkFast transitions the blocked port to a forwarding state. UplinkFast changes the port so that it bypasses the listening and learning phases. This change occurs in three to four seconds, allowing convergence to begin immediately without waiting for the MaxAge timer to expire.

NOTE: *UplinkFast becomes a global setting on the switch. It affects all the VLANs on the switch and cannot be applied on just one VLAN. When you enable UplinkFast, it automatically increases the path cost, making it unlikely that the switch will become the root switch. If UplinkFast is not being used, you should use the Catalyst default settings.*

BackboneFast

BackboneFast is a function that allows the switch to converge more quickly in the event that a redundant link fails. An inferior BPDU is sent when a link from the designated switch has been lost to the root bridge. When the root port or a blocked port on a switch receives an inferior BPDU from its designated bridge, if BackboneFast is enabled, this event in turn triggers a root Link Query.

The designated switch transmits these BPDUs with the new information that it is now the root bridge as well as the designated bridge, and the BPDUs begin arriving on a port that is blocked on the switch. The switch receiving inferior BPDUs will ignore the message until the configured MaxAge timer expires, to give the network time to overcome the network problem.

If inferior BPDU messages continue to arrive after the MaxAge timer has been used, the root port and other blocked ports on the switch become alternate paths to the root bridge. The switch will send another kind of BPDU called the root Link Query PDU if more than one link exists to the root bridge. The switch will send a root Link Query PDU out all the available alternate paths to the root bridge to determine which one will forward.

If there are no other blocked ports, the switch automatically assumes that it has lost connectivity to the root bridge, causes the maximum aging time on the root to expire, and becomes the root switch. BackboneFast must be enabled on all switches in the network in order to function properly.

TIP: *BackboneFast cannot be used in a Token Ring network.*

Immediate Solutions

Enabling STP on a Set/Clear Command-Based Switch

The Set/Clear command-based switch allows you to enable and disable STP on a per-port basis. Every port on the switch is enabled for STP by default. If STP has been disabled on the switch, you can re-enable STP from the Privileged mode prompt.

NOTE: *Cisco recommends that STP remain enabled on the switch. It is important that it remain enabled on any trunk port where the possibility exists of a bridging loop in the network.*

To enable STP on a Set/Clear command-based switch, use the following Privileged mode command:

```
catalyst5000> (enable) set spantree enable
```

After using this command you must use the **set spantree enable all** command to enable STP on all the VLANs. An example is shown in the next section.

Enabling STP on a Set/Clear Command-Based Switch for All VLANs

To enable STP on all VLANs, use the following command in Privileged mode:

```
set spantree enable all
```

Related solutions:	Found on page:
Configuring a Static VLAN on a Catalyst 5000 Series Switch	154
Configuring Multiple VLANs on a Catalyst 5000 Series Switch	154

Disabling STP on a Set/Clear Command-Based Switch

To disable STP on a Set/Clear command-based switch, use the following Privileged mode command:

```
catalyst5000> (enable) set spantree disable all
Spantree disabled.
```

Disabling STP on a Set/Clear Command-Based Switch by VLAN

To selectively disable specific ports on the switch by VLAN, use this Privileged mode command:

```
set spantree disable [VLAN]
set spantree disable all
```

For example, you could use disable STP on VLAN 2 with the following command:

```
set spantree disable 2
```

Viewing the STP Configuration on a Set/Clear Command-Based Switch

To view the current configuration of STP on your switch, use this Privileged mode command:

```
show spantree <VLAN number>
```

In the following example, the VLAN number is 5:

```
show spantree 5
```

The output should look similar to the following (Table 10.6 defines each of the fields in this output):

```
Spanning tree enabled
Spanning tree type            ieee
Designated Root               00--ac--15--22--a5--12
Designated Root Priority      8192
Designated Root Cost          0
Designated Root Port          1/0
Root Max Age 10 Sec           Hello Time 2 sec    Forward Delay 7 sec
Bridge ID MAC ADDR            00--ac--15--22--a5--12
Bridge ID Priority            8192
Bridge Max Age 20 Sec    Hello Time 2 sec     Forward Delay 15 sec

Port  vlan  Port-State  Cost  Priority  Fast-start  Group-Method
----  ----  ----------  ----  --------  ----------  ------------
5/1   2     forwarding  19    32        disabled
5/2   2     forwarding  19    32        disabled
5/3   2     blocking    19    32        disabled
5/4   2     blocking    19    32        disabled
```

The listing at the bottom of the output shows the ports in use in the spanning tree. It states the port, port-state, and priority, as well as whether Fast-Start (PortFast) is enabled.

Table 10.6   The show spantree command output fields.

Field	Description
Spanning tree enabled	Shows that STP is in use
Spanning tree type	Typically the IEEE standard
Designated Root	The 6-byte MAC address for the designated root bridge
Designated Root Priority	The 2-byte priority setting for the root bridge
Designated Root Cost	Total cost to get to the root bridge from this switch (0 indicates the root switch)
Designated Root Port	The port used to get to the root bridge
Root timers	Timer values of the root bridge or switch; these include the MaxAge, Hello Time, and Forward Delay timer values
Bridge ID MAC ADDR	The 6-byte address that the switch uses for its bridge ID
Bridge ID Priority	The 2-byte priority of this bridge
Bridge Max Age	The maximum values from the root bridge

Configuring STP on an IOS Command-Based Switch

Unlike the Set/Clear command-based switch, enabling the Spanning Tree Protocol on a Cisco IOS command-based switch is performed in Global Configuration mode. To enable STP, enter the following command:

```
spantree <VLAN list>
```

In the following example, 5 is the VLAN number and is considered a VLAN-list field; you can include up to 10 VLANs in the list:

```
spantree 5
```

Disabling STP on an IOS Command-Based Switch

To disable STP on a VLAN, in Global Configuration mode use this command:

```
no spantree <VLAN list>
```

In this example, 5 is the VLAN number and is considered a VLAN-list field:

```
no spantree 5
```

Viewing the STP Configuration on a Command Line Switch

To view the configuration, you use the same command you use for the Set/Clear command-based switches. However, you will receive much different output. Use this command:

```
show spantree
```

The output should look similar to this on your console:

```
VLAN1 is executing the IEEE compatible Spanning Tree Protocol
Bridge Identifier has priority 8192, address 002C.100A.AD51
Configured hello time 2, max age 20, forward delay 15
```

```
Current root has priority 8192, address 002C.100A.AD51
Root port is FastEthernet 1/1, cost of root path is 0
Topology change flag not set, detected flag not set
Topology changes 21, last topology change occurred 1d3h19m59s ago
Times: hold 1, topology change 9211
hello 2, max age 20, forward delay 15
Timers: hello 2, topology change 35, notification 2
Port Ethernet 0/5 of VLAN1 is Forwarding
Port path cost 0, Port priority 100
Designated root has priority 8192, address 002C.100A.AD51
Designated bridge has priority 8192, address 002C.100A.AD51
Designated port is Ethernet 0/5, path cost 10
Timers: message age 20, forward delay 15, hold 1
```

Configuring the STP Root Switch

To configure the switch to become the root bridge, enter the following command
in Privileged mode (Table 10.7 defines the syntax fields for this command):

```
set spantree root <vlan> dia <seconds> hello <seconds>
```

```
set spantree root 5 dia 3 hello 2
```

Configuring the STP Secondary Root Switch

To configure the switch to become the secondary root bridge, enter the following
Privileged mode command (Table 10.7 defines the syntax fields for this command):

```
set spantree root secondary <vlan> dia <seconds> hello <seconds>
```

```
catalyst5000> (enable) set spantree root secondary 1 dia 3 hello 2
VLAN 1 bridge priority set to 16384.
VLAN 1 bridge max aging time set to 12.
VLAN 1 bridge hello time set to 2.
VLAN 1 bridge forward delay set to 9.
catalyst5000> (enable)
```

Table 10.7   Root and secondary bridge configuration command parameters.

Command Parameter	Definition
root	Designates the root switch. The default priority of the root bridge is 8,192.
secondary (optional)	Used to designate the switch as a secondary root switch if the root bridge fails. The default priority of the secondary bridge is 16,384.
n (optional)	Specifies the VLAN. If you do not specify the VLAN, VLAN 1 is used. The valid value range is 1 through 1,005.
dia n (optional)	Specifies the diameter value discussed earlier in the chapter. It is essentially the number of bridges between any two points. The diameter should be measured starting from the root bridge. Valid values are 2 through 7.
hello n (optional)	Specifies in seconds how often configuration messages should be generated by the root switch. The valid values are 1 through 10.

Setting the Root Bridge for More than One VLAN on a Set/Clear Command-Based Switch

To set the primary root switch for more than one VLAN on a Set/Clear-based switch, use the Privileged mode command to change configuration to a root bridge. The default priority automatically changes to 8,192, which is the default when the command is used to configure the switch as the root bridge. Use the following command to specify the root bridge:

```
set spantree root <root|secondary> <VLAN list> dia <diameter>
```

The following command specifies the root bridge for VLANs 1 through 3:

```
set spantree root 1-3 dia 2
```

When the root bridge is configured correctly, the output on the console should be similar to this:

```
VLANs 1-3 bridge priority set to 8192
VLANs 1-3 bridge max aging time set to 10 seconds.
VLANS 1-3 bridge hello time set to 2 seconds.
VLANS 1-3 bridge forward delay set to 7 seconds.
Switch is now the root switch for active VLANs 1-3.
```

Assigning a Port Cost to a Port Using the Set/Clear Command-Based IOS

To manually change the port cost on a Set/Clear command-based switch, use the following Privileged mode command:

```
set spantree portcost <module/port> <port cost>
```

In the following example, 5 is the module number, 2 is the port number, and 100 is the configured port cost:

```
set spantree portcost 5/2 100
```

Assigning a Port Cost to a Port Using a CLI-Based Switch

To manually change the port cost on a Cisco IOS-based switch, use this Interface Configuration mode command:

```
spantree cost <port cost>
```

This example uses 100 as the port cost:

```
spantree cost 100
```

Verifying the Port Cost Configuration on Both a Set/Clear Command- and CLI-Based Interface

To verify the port cost on the port configured previously, use the following Privileged mode command:

```
show spantree <module/port>
```

The following command provides output on module 0, port 3:

```
show spantree 0/3
```

The output on the console should look similar to this:

```
Port      Vlan    Port-State    Cost    Priority Fast-StartGroup-method
--------  ------  ----------    ----    -------- ---------- ----------
    0/3     4     forwarding      10      32       disabled
```

Configuring the Port Priority on a Set/Clear Command-Based IOS

The port with the lowest priority value forwards frames for all VLANs. In the event that all ports have the same priority value, the port with the lowest port number will forward the frames. The possible port priority value range is from 0 to 63. The default port priority value is 32. To change a port's priority, enter the following Privileged mode command:

```
set spantree portpri <module/port> <port priority>
```

Here, 4 is the module number, 3 is the port number, and 10 is the port priority:

```
set spantree portpri 4/3 10
```

Configuring the Port Priority on a CLI-Based IOS

On a Cisco IOS command-based switch, the priority value is a numerical value from 0 to 255. To set the port priority on a Cisco IOS command-based switch, enter the following Interface Configuration mode command:

```
spantree priority <port priority>
```

In this example, 100 is the priority value:

```
spantree priority 100
```

Verifying the STP Port Priority on a Set/Clear Command-Based Switch

To verify the proper port priority setting, use this command (only the module and port numbers are required):

```
show spantree <module/port>
```

The following command provides output on module 2, port 3:

```
show spantree 2/3

Port          Vlan Port-State    Cost  Priority Portfast  Channel_id
------------  ---- ------------  ----  -------- --------- ----------
 2/3           1    not-connected  19        32 disabled  0
catalyst5000> (enable)
```

Verifying the VLAN Priority Settings

To verify the port's VLAN priority settings, enter the following command in Privileged mode (only the module and port number are required):

```
show spantree <module/port>
```

The following command provides output on module 3, port 5:

```
show spantree 3/5
```

Adjusting the FwdDelay Timer on a Set/Clear Command-Based IOS

To change the FwdDelay default setting, use the following Privileged mode command:

```
set spantree fwddelay <delay value> <VLAN>
```

In this example, 4 indicates a four-second delay and 3 indicates the VLAN:

```
set spantree fwddelay 4 3
```

Adjusting the Hello Timer on a Set/Clear Command-Based IOS

To change the default Hello Time on the bridge, use this Privileged mode command:

```
Set spantree hello <time value>
```

Use 4 to indicate a four-second interval:

```
set spantree hello 4
```

Adjusting the MaxAge Timer on a Set/Clear Command-Based IOS

To change the default MaxAge timer for a particular VLAN, use this Privileged mode command :

```
spantree maxage <time value> <VLAN>
```

In the following example, 5 refers to the MaxAge time and 1 refers to the VLAN:

```
spantree maxage 5 1
```

Preparing to Enable EtherChannel

When preparing to enable EtherChannel, you should check four items before configuring an EtherChannel bundle. They are as follows:

- If a bundle uses trunked ports, each port must be configured with the same allowed VLAN range. If the VLAN ranges are not configured identically for both ends of all the trunked links in the bundle, the data traffic for the particular missing VLAN traffic is not allowed and the frames for that VLAN are dropped.

- Trunked ports will not form a channel when set to the auto or desirable mode using the **set port channel** command. However, trunked ports on which VLANs are allowed will continue to transmit data traffic across their trunk links.

- You must verify that port security is disabled on all channeled ports. By enabling port security, the port shuts down when it receives packets containing a source address that doesn't match the secure address of the port.

- All ports in a channel must be enabled. Any disabled ports are considered link failures by the switch, and traffic for those ports is automatically transferred to any remaining ports in the bundle.

If these criteria are not met, then you will receive an error for each item that is not configured correctly when you try to configure EtherChannel.

Viewing the Port Setting for EtherChannel on a Set/Clear Command-Based Switch

To view the port settings on ports you are configuring for EtherChannel on a Set/Clear command-based switch, use the following command in Privileged mode. Use this command to compare the settings to make sure they match the other ports waiting to be configured as a bundle:

```
show port capabilities <module number/port number>
```

For this example, 2 is the module number and 1 is the port number. The output shows that the port is already configured to participate in a bundle:

```
catalyst5000> (enable) show port capabilities 2/1
Model                  WS-X5225R
Port                   2/1
Type                   10/100BaseTX
Speed                  auto,10,100
Duplex                 half,full
Trunk encap type       802.1Q,ISL
Trunk mode             on,off,desirable,auto,nonegotiate
Channel                2/1-2,2/1-4
Broadcast suppression  percentage(0-100)
Flow control           receive-(off,on),send-(off,on)
Security               yes
```

```
Membership              static,dynamic
Fast start              yes
QOS scheduling          rx-(none),tx-(none)
CoS rewrite             yes
ToS rewrite             IP-Precedence
Rewrite                 yes
UDLD                    yes
AuxiliaryVlan           1..1000,untagged,dot1p,none
SPAN                    source,destination
```

Creating an EtherChannel on a Set/Clear Command-Based Switch

To create an EtherChannel bundle, you must enable EtherChannel on two or more ports. On a Set/Clear command-based switch, use the following Privileged mode command to enable EtherChannel:

```
set port channel <port list> mode <on|off|desirable|auto>
```

The following output shows 2 as the module number and 1 through 4 as the port numbers:

```
catalyst5000> (enable) set port channel 2/1-4 ?
  <admin_group>           Admin group
  mode                    Channel mode

catalyst5000> (enable) set port channel 2/1-4 mode ?
  auto                    Channel auto mode
  desirable               Channel desirable mode
  off                     Turn off Channelling
  on                      Turn on Channelling
  <cr>

catalyst5000> (enable) set port channel 2/1-4 mode auto
Port(s) 2/1-4 channel mode set to auto.
catalyst5000> (enable)
```

Table 10.8 explains the syntaxes available for the **mode** option. The mode on each port can be set to **on**, **off**, **auto**, or **desirable**.

Table 10.8   The four mode options for configuring an EtherChannel bundle on a switch.

EtherChannel Mode Option	Description
on	Enables the port to channel or bundle without any negotiation.
off	Disables the port from channeling or creating a bundle.
auto	Enables a port to negotiate the state in which the port will respond to PAgP packets it receives. The syntax does not, however, initiate PAgP packet negotiation. This is the default setting.
desirable	Enables a port to actively negotiate creating a bundle with the port on the opposite side of the link by continuously sending PAgP packets.

NOTE: *Using the* **auto** *and* **desirable** *modes allows the configured ports to automatically negotiate whether to form a channel. The channel ports can be in different modes, as long as the modes are compatible. For example, if a port is in* **desirable** *mode, the port can form a bundle with another port that is in the* **desirable** *or* **auto** *mode.*

Verifying the EtherChannel Configuration

To verify the EtherChannel configuration on a Set/Clear command-based switch, use this command:

```
catalyst5000> (enable) show port channel ?
  info                    Show port channel information
  statistics              Show port channel statistics
  <mod>                   Module number
  <mod/port>              Module number and Port number(s)
  <cr>

catalyst5000> (enable) show port channel 2/1 ?
Usage: show port channel [mod[/port]] [statistics]
       show port channel [mod[/port]] info [type]
       (type = spantree|trunk|protocol|gmrp|gvrp|qos)
catalyst5000> (enable)

Port   Status      Channel              Admin Ch
                   Mode                 Group Id
----   ----------  -------------------- ---- ----
 2/1   notconnect  auto silent            16    0

Port   Device-ID                        Port-ID             Platform
----   -------------------------------  ------------------- ----------------
 2/1
```

Defining an EtherChannel Administrative Group

To define the administrative group, use the following Privileged mode command:

```
set port channel <module/port list> <administrative group number>
```

For example:

```
Catalyst5002> (enable) set port channel 2/1-4 10
Port(s) 2/1-4 are assigned to admin group 10.
```

Viewing an EtherChannel Administrative Group

To view an administrative group configuration, use the following command:

```
show channel group [administrative group number]
```

For example, to view group 10, use the following command:

```
Console> (enable) show channel group 10
Admin Port  Status      Channel              Channel
group                   Mode                 id
----  ----  ----------  -------------------- --------
  10  2/1   connected   auto silent                 0
  10  2/2   connected   auto silent                 0
  10  2/3   connected   auto silent                 0
  10  2/4   connected   auto silent                 0

Admin Port  Device-ID                        Port-ID          Platform
group
----  ----  -------------------------------- ---------------- ----------
  10  2/1
  10  2/2
  10  2/3
  10  2/4
```

Configuring EtherChannel on an IOS-Based Switch

To configure EtherChannel on an IOS command-based switch such as the 1900EN series and 2800 series switches, use the Global Configuration **port-channel** command followed by the mode (on, desirable, or auto):

```
port-channel mode <on|desirable|auto>
```

Here, the mode is auto:

```
port-channel auto
```

Identifying the Template Port

With the IOS-based switches, you must identify a template port for the **port-channel** parameters. To do so, use the following command in Global Configuration mode:

```
port-channel template-port <template port>
```

In this case, the FastEthernet 0/26 is port A on the 1900 series switch:

```
Catalyst1900(config)# port-channel template-port fastethernet 0/26
```

Verifying the EtherChannel Configuration on a Command Line Interface IOS

To verify the configuration on an IOS-based switch, use this Privileged mode command:

```
show interface
```

The output should look similar to the following on a CLI-based command switch:

```
PortChannel is Enabled
802.1d STP State: ForwardingForward Transitions: 1
Port-channel mode: auto, preserve-order: Disabled
Port parameters template port: A
Active port: A
PortMemberPriorityCap.PartnerPartnerPartnerPartner
Device-idPort-idPriorityCap.
-----------------------------
AYes128100-00-00-00-00-0000
BYes128100-00-00-00-00-0000
```

The output should look similar to the following on a Set/Clear command-based
IOS:

```
catalyst5000> (enable) show interface
sl0: flags=51<UP,POINTOPOINT,RUNNING>
     slip 0.0.0.0 dest 0.0.0.0
sc0: flags=63<UP,BROADCAST,RUNNING>
     vlan 1 inet 208.44.88.4 netmask 255.255.255.192 broadcast 208.44.88.63
catalyst5000> (enable)
```

Enabling PortFast on a Set/Clear Command-Based Switch

To enable PortFast on a Set/Clear command-based switch port, use the following
Privileged mode command:

```
set spantree portfast <module/port> enable
```

In this example, 2 is the module number and 1 is the port number:

```
catalyst5000> (enable) set spantree portfast ?
  <trcrf>                    Token Ring TRCRF vlan number
  <mod/port>                 Module number and Port number(s)
  bpdu-guard                 Portfast BPDU guard

catalyst5000> (enable) set spantree portfast 2/1 ?
  disable                    Disable port fast start
  enable                     Enable port fast start
catalyst5000> (enable) set spantree portfast 2/1 enable

Warning: Spantree port fast start should only be enabled on ports connected
to a single host.  Connecting hubs, concentrators, switches, bridges, etc.
to a fast start port can cause temporary spanning tree loops.  Use with
caution.

Spantree port  2/1 fast start enabled.
```

Disabling PortFast on a Set/Clear Command-Based Switch

To disable PortFast on a Set/Clear command-based switch port, use the following Privileged mode command:

```
set spantree portfast <module/port> disable
```

In this example, 3 is the module number and 8 is the port number:

```
set spantree portfast 3/8 disable
```

Enabling PortFast on a CLI-Based IOS Switch

To enable PortFast on a Cisco IOS command-based switch, use this Interface Configuration mode command:

```
spantree start-forwarding
```

Disabling PortFast on a CLI-Based IOS Switch

To disable PortFast on a Cisco IOS command-based switch, use this Interface Configuration mode command:

```
no spantree start-forwarding
```

Verifying the PortFast Configuration

To verify the PortFast configuration on a Set/Clear command-based switch, enter the following Privileged mode command:

```
show spantree <module/port>
```

To verify module 3 and port 8, do the following:

```
show spantree 3/8
```

Enabling UplinkFast on a Set/Clear Command-Based Switch

To enable UplinkFast on a Set/Clear command-based switch, use the following Privileged mode command:

```
catalyst5000> (enable) set spantree uplinkfast ?
  disable                    Disable spanning tree uplink fast
  enable                     Enable spanning tree uplink fast

catalyst5000> (enable) set spantree uplinkfast enable ?
  all-protocols              Enable uplink fast for all protocols
  rate                       Specify uplink fast rate
  <cr>

catalyst5000> (enable) set spantree uplinkfast enable all-protocols ?
  off                        All protocols off
  on                         All protocols on

catalyst5000> (enable) set spantree uplinkfast enable all-protocols on
VLANs 1-1005 bridge priority set to 49152.
The port cost and portvlancost of all ports set to above 3000.
Station update rate set to 15 packets/100ms.
uplinkfast update packets enabled for all protocols.
uplinkfast enabled for bridge.
```

TIP: *The* **set spantree uplinkfast** *command has other options, such as adding a station update rate or adding the on or off syntax for all protocols. The station update rate value is the number of multicast packets transmitted per 100 milliseconds (by default, it is set to 15 packets per millisecond). For more information on how to execute a change in the station update rate, use the Help command on the console.*

Disabling UplinkFast on a Set/Clear Command-Based Switch

To disable UplinkFast on a Set/Clear command-based switch, use the following Privileged mode command:

```
catalyst5000> (enable) set spantree uplinkfast disable
uplinkfast disabled for bridge.
Use clear spantree uplinkfast to return stp parameters to default.
```

You must clear the port and bridge costs modified by UplinkFast using the **clear spantree uplinkfast** command shown below:

```
catalyst5000> (enable) clear spantree uplinkfast
This command will cause all portcosts, portvlancosts, and the
bridge priority on all vlans to be set to default.
Do you want to continue (y/n) [n]? y
VLANs 1-1005 bridge priority set to 32768.
The port cost of all bridge ports set to default value.
The portvlancost of all bridge ports set to default value.
uplinkfast all-protocols field set to off.
uplinkfast disabled for bridge.
```

Verifying the UplinkFast Configuration

To verify the UplinkFast configuration on a Set/Clear command-based switch, you can use the following Privileged mode command:

```
show spantree uplinkfast
```

You should get output similar to the following—notice that the VLANs followed by a comma, module number, and port number are forwarding to 3/1:

```
station update rate set to 15 packets/100ms.
uplinkfast all-protocol field set to off.
VLAN        port list
------      ------------------------------------
1           3/1(fwd)
2           3/2(fwd),3/1
2           3/3(fwd),3/1
5           3/4(fwd),3/1
```

Enabling UplinkFast on a Cisco IOS Command-Based Switch

To enable UplinkFast on a Cisco IOS command-based switch, use this command in Global Configuration mode:

```
uplink-fast
```

Disabling UplinkFast on a Cisco IOS Command-Based Switch

To disable UplinkFast on a Cisco IOS command-based switch, use this command in Global Configuration mode:

```
no uplink-fast
```

Viewing the UplinkFast Configuration on an IOS-Based Switch

To view the UplinkFast configuration on an IOS command-based switch, enter the following Privileged mode command:

```
show uplink-fast
```

Viewing UplinkFast Statistics on an IOS-Based Switch

To view UplinkFast statistics, use this Privileged mode command:

```
show uplink-fast statistics
```

Enabling BackboneFast on a Set/Clear Command-Based Switch

To enable BackboneFast on a Set/Clear command-based switch, enter the following Privileged mode command:

```
set spantree backbonefast enable
```

Disabling BackboneFast on a Set/Clear Command-Based Switch

To disable BackboneFast on a Set/Clear command-based switch, enter the following Privileged mode command:

```
set spantree backbonefast disable
```

Viewing the BackboneFast Configuration

To view the BackboneFast configuration on a Set/Clear command-based switch, use the following Privileged mode command:

```
show spantree backbonefast
```

The output for this command is fairly simple:

```
Backbonefast is enabled.
Catalyst5002> (enable)
```

Chapter 11

Multilayer Switching

In Depth

Earlier in this book, I told you that switches were Layer 2 devices and routers were Layer 3 devices, which fit nicely into those well-known seven layers. You know the seven—the Open System Interconnection (OSI) Reference Model layers. Oh, did I forget to mention the Multilayer Switching Engine, multilayer switches, and Layer 3 switches?

Do you recall when it was easy to remember that Layer 2 devices use physical addresses and Layer 3 devices use logical addresses? These distinctions will seem much blurrier after you read this chapter.

For now, let's define what Multilayer Switching (MLS) does. MLS is a method for increasing the performance of IP routing. Whereas routers provide routing functionality with a central processing unit (CPU), MLS injects certain advanced modules—either available separately or built into switches—with Application-Specific Integrated Circuit (ASIC) silicon chips to handle Layers 3 and 4 routing. As a result, the switching hardware can handle the routing functions previously performed by routers at Layer 3. MLS combines the functions of switching and the functions of routing to increase the level of performance in the device.

Why Not Call Them Routers?

If MLS switches offer the same benefits as routers, why not just call them routers with a lot of interfaces? Although most multilayer switches are much faster and considerably less per port cost than routers, some MLS devices are simple, stackable workgroup switches that fall well short of the flexibility, protocol support, port density, and WAN features you find on most enterprise edition routers (with the exception of the Catalyst 6000, which now offers a FlexWAN Card).

Until the Cisco IOS version 12.1 was released, the only protocol supported by MLS was Internet Protocol (IP). Even now, MLS supports only IP and Internetwork Packet Exchange (IPX).

Let's examine how MLS works and the components used in MLS.

How MLS Works

Before we can analyze how MLS works, we need to understand how a network sends traffic from point A to point B. Cisco's implementation of MLS supports every Cisco routing protocol used in its product line, including the following:

- Border Gateway Protocol (BGP)
- Distance Vector Multicast Routing Protocol (DVMRP)
- Internet Group Multicast Protocol (IGMP)
- Open Shortest Path First (OSPF)
- Protocol-Independent Multicast (PIM)
- Routing Information Protocol (RIP)

However, Cisco's implementation of MLS supports only two Layer 3 routable protocols: IP and IPX.

IP and IPX are *connectionless* protocols. This means they attempt to deliver every packet in a best-effort manner. This method is similar to sending a piece of mail: You put it in the mailbox, but you have no guarantee that it will arrive—just the likelihood it will reach its destination.

Using other protocols, including those at Layer 2 and Layer 4, the network traffic is made up of a series of end-to-end conversations also known as *flows*. These flows are connection-oriented in nature. Connection-oriented data traffic is similar to a certified letter. You put the letter in the mailbox, and you receive a signed notice saying the letter reached its destination.

MLS identifies network flows from a network source to a network destination by using the Network and Transport layer information in the packet headers; it then forwards the packets. This sequence of packets is sent in one direction between a particular source and destination and uses the same protocol and Layer 4 header information.

Let's take a look at multiple flows. Suppose I am looking at Coriolis's Web site to determine when the last book I wrote will be released. At the same time, I am using FTP to send the latest chapter I have written for review. Both data flows are traversing back and forth from the same source to the same destination and vice versa—two flows of data are traveling at the same time between my PC and a server at Coriolis. How does my host, a router, or even the switch know which conversation I want on my screen? Why don't parts of the Coriolis Web site get mixed into the chapter I am uploading? The reason it works is that each flow is assigned an individual port number.

MLS should not be confused with NetFlow switching provided by the NetFlow Feature Card (NFFC) or the NFFC II, even though the NFFCs are used to provide MLS with the Catalyst 5000 and 6000 families of switches. MLS must use an external router or an internal route processor such as the Route Switch Module (RSM)

Prioritizing Traffic Flows

MLS identifies the unique flows between hosts by identifying the user application and classifying data traffic with the appropriate priority level. These flows can be either unicast or multicast traffic.

MLS identifies individual network traffic flows to provide predictable network services. It does this by supplying dedicated bandwidth to those applications that need it most. As an example, enterprise resource planning (ERP) application traffic (which can be mission-critical) can be identified as needing a higher priority and thus receive more network bandwidth than, say, Web or FTP traffic.

to provide the routing resolution for the initial packet that is routed in an MLS flow (the connection-oriented session). Each subsequent packet in the flow is processed by the switch, not the router.

Before we go into more detail on packet flows, let's take a more detailed look at the hardware and software used by MLS.

MLS Components

You should understand three components in the MLS process to resolve the destination path for the initial packet flow. These components are required in order to use MLS and send routing updates to Catalyst switches. The components are as follows:

- *MLS Switching Engine (MLS-SE)*—The switch supporting MLS
- *MLS Route Processor (MLS-RP)*—The internal route processor in the switch or external router that supports MLS
- *Multilayer Switch Protocol (MLSP)*—The protocol that runs between the MLS-SE and MLS-RP to enable MLS

Figure 11.1 shows the three MLS components contained in a single switch chassis, such as that of a Cisco Catalyst 5000 or 6000 family switch.

The Cisco 5000 and 6000 families of switches can use multiple internal route processors, such as the following:

- NetFlow Feature Card (NFFC)
- NetFlow Feature Card II (NFFC II)
- Route Switch Module (RSM)
- Route Switch Feature Card (RSFC)
- Multilayer Switch Feature Card (MSFC)
- Multilayer Switching Module (MSM)

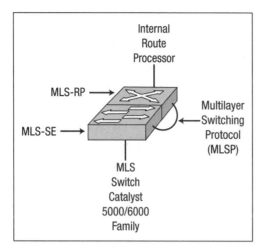

Figure 11.1   The MLS components using an internal route processor in an MLS switch.

NOTE: *The NFFC or NFFC II must be used as a daughtercard of the Supervisor Engine III. You can also use the Supervisor IIG or IIIG card with Supervisor Engine software release 4.1 or later, which provides the functionality of the NFFC without using an NFFC card. Newer Catalyst models have the MLS functionality built into the switch. These switches—known as Layer 3 (L3) switches—are the Cisco Catalyst 4908G-L3, the Cisco Catalyst 2926G-L3, and the Cisco Catalyst 2948G-L3. The RSM or RSFC can be used in the Catalyst 5000 family, and an MSM or MSFC can be used in the Catalyst 6000 family.*

You can use an external router instead of an internal route processor to resolve the initial packet routing information. You must use an external router that supports MLS. Figure 11.2 shows an external router providing MLS route resolution functionality for the MLS-SE (switch). MLS support is included in enterprise routers with the Cisco IOS version 11.3(2)WA4(4) or later. These routers include the following:

- Cisco 3600 series

- Cisco 4500 series

- Cisco 4700 series

- Cisco 7200 series

- Cisco 7500 series

- Cisco 8500 Gigabit Switch Router series

In order to understand the MLS process better, we need to examine how the data packets are forwarded in an MLS environment.

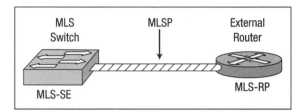

Figure 11.2   The MLS switch using an external router.

MLS Flows

When a flow process begins, the MLS-RP starts sending out multicast hello messages every 15 seconds to all switches in the network that accept MLS-RP messages. These messages inform each switch that the MLS-RP (router or internal route processor) is available to provide routing information to the MLS switches, allowing them to cache learned routes.

MLSP is the protocol used between the MLS-SE and the MLS-RP. It uses a Cisco Group Management Protocol (CGMP) multicast address, so each MLS-SE (switch) enabled for CGMP will hear the hello message. To distinguish between normal CGMP messages and the MLS messages, the MLS-RP uses a special protocol type in the hello message itself.

The MLSP hello message (which is also known as an MLS-RP *advertisement*) can contain the following information:

- The Media Access Control (MAC) addresses of the router interfaces participating in MLS

- The router's known virtual LAN (VLAN) information

- The MLS-RP's access lists

- Any known or updated routing information

A switch participating in MLS has an MLS-SE component. This component processes the hello message and records the MAC address of the MLS-RP interfaces into its Content Addressable Memory (CAM) table. If multiple MLS-RPs exist in the network, the MLS-SE assigns a unique 1-byte identifier called an *XTAG*, as shown in Figure 11.3. The XTAG is a number that distinguishes the network flows of each MLS-RP.

When a host from one VLAN on the network begins a network flow that is destined for a host on another VLAN, the MLS switch that received the first packet in the flow extracts the Layer 3 information for the flow. This information includes the destination address, source address, and protocol port numbers. The MLS-SE

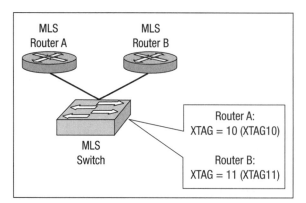

Figure 11.3   An individual XTAG number is assigned to each MLS router in the network.

then forwards the first packet to the MLS-RP for a routing resolution. MLSP is used to inform the MLS-SE of the path to the destination hosts communicating in the flow. Because this is the first packet, no cache entry exists; a partial MLS entry for this Layer 3 flow is created in the MLS cache.

When the MLS-RP receives the packet, it looks at its route table to determine the destination of the packet and applies any applicable policies, such as an inbound or outbound access list. The MLS-RP will then rewrite the MAC header, adding the MAC address of the destination host and using its own MAC address as the source address. The MLS-RP then sends the packet back to the MLS-SE.

At this point, an MLS router has resolved the first packet with either a VLAN or Layer 3 logical address to a Layer 2 MAC address. The MLS-SE can now use this address to make a forwarding decision and send the packet out the correct port connected to the destination node based on the entries the switch has in its CAM table. The MLS-SE also determines that the MAC address of the MLS router is the source address in the packet and that the packet's flow information matches a candidate entry in its MLS cache.

Now that the entry for the flow has been added to the MLS cache, any further packets that are identified as belonging to the same flow are handled by MLS-SE and switched based on the cached information. The MLS-SE rewrites the headers, reconditions the checksums, and forwards the packets without their having to go through the router. The MLS-SE rewrites the packets to look as if they had been forwarded by a router.

NOTE: *The MLS cache size can grow to a maximum of 128K. When the cache on the MLS-SE grows larger than 32K, it is likely that flows in the network will not be switched by the MLS-SE and forwarded to a router.*

When the conversation between the two nodes ends or discontinues for any reason, the MLS cache entry is aged out of the cache. For a new conversation to take place, the process must start again.

Access List Flow Masks

Flow masks are used by the MLS-SE to determine how the network flows are compared to the MLS cache entries. Which flow mask mode to use is determined by the types of access lists that are configured on the routers (MLS-RPs) participating in MLS. The MLS-SE is given this information via the MLSP messages from each MLS-RP for which the MLS-SE performs Layer 3 switching.

The three types of access list flow masks are as follows:

- Destination-IP
- Source-destination-IP
- IP-flow

Destination-IP Flow Mask

Only one flow mask is used at a time; the flow mask used is determined by the most stringent type of access list. The least stringent is a Destination-IP flow mask. It is used if no access lists are configured on any router participating in MLS, as shown in Figure 11.4. In this situation, the MLS-SE will maintain only one MLS entry for each destination IP address. Any flows that go to a given destination IP address will use this MLS entry.

WARNING! If a different flow mask is detected, the MLS-SE will automatically change the currently used flow mask to the most stringent flow mask detected on the network and purge its cached entries.

Source-Destination-IP Flow Mask

The Source-destination-IP is the next most stringent flow mask. This mask is used if any MLS-RP in the network is using a standard access list, as shown in Figure 11.5. Router B contains a standard access list. Even though router A has no access

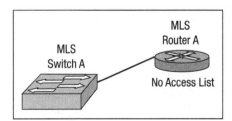

Figure 11.4   An MLS switch and one MLS router. The router has no access list configured, so the flow mask will be Destination-IP.

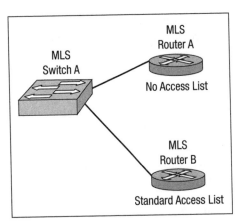

Figure 11.5   An MLS switch and two MLS routers.

lists configured, the flow mask is determined by the highest policies placed on a router. Therefore, the Source-destination-IP flow mask is used for all flows. The MLS-SE maintains one MLS entry for each source and destination IP address pair. Any flow between a given source and destination use this MLS entry, regardless of which IP protocol the interfaces use.

IP Access Lists and MLS Interaction

When any interface has an inbound access list applied, the interface where the access list is applied cannot be used for MLS. However, you can apply an output access list on an interface, and it will not affect MLS.

When MLS is enabled, standard and extended access lists are handled at the speed of the physical wire. Any modifications or changes to the access lists on any interface used for MLS take effect immediately after being applied to the interface on the MLS-SE, on any internal route processor, or on external routers.

If a flow has been established by the MLS-SE and a new access list is created on the MLS-RP, the MLS-SE learns of the change through MLSP. This immediately changes the flow mask and purges the cache entries from the MLS cache on all the MLS-SEs. Any new flows are created based on the new access list information.

IP-Flow Flow Mask

The IP-flow flow mask is the most stringent of all flow masks. This flow mask is used when any of the MLS-RPs has an extended access list configured on it, as shown in Figure 11.6. Router C contains an extended access list. This access list determines that the IP-flow flow mask is used for all flows. The MLS-SE creates a separate MLS cache entry for all IP flows. The IP-flow entry contains the source IP address, destination IP address, protocol, and protocol interfaces.

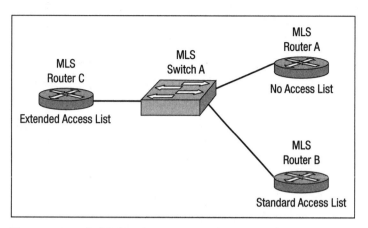

Figure 11.6　An MLS switch and three MLS routers.

MLS Troubleshooting Notes

There are a few pieces of information about MLS that will save you time when troubleshooting. Quite a few Cisco IOS commands can affect how MLS operates, and MLS doesn't work well with a few other data traffic features.

You may become confused when trying to troubleshoot MLS because the commands you need to watch out for are not directly related to MLS. Remember this basic rule: Any command that involves the router examining each packet to perform an action will disable MLS on an interface.

Let's take a look at some of these commands and the effect each command has on the interface:

- **clear ip route**—Clears all MLS cache entries for all the switches that are acting as MLS-SEs
- **ip security**—Disables MLS on the interface it is applied to
- **ip tcp header-compression**—Disables MLS on the interface it is applied to
- **ip tcp compression-connection**—Disables MLS on the interface it is applied to
- **no ip routing**—Purges all MLS caches and disables MLS on the interface it is applied to

The following IP features and protocols also have a negative impact on MLS:

- *Committed access rate (CAR)*—CAR will disable MLS on the interface.
- *Data encryption*—Any data encryption configured on the interface will cause MLS to fail.
- *IP accounting*—This feature will not work if MLS is enabled on an interface.

- *Network Address Translation (NAT)*—MLS is automatically disabled on an interface if NAT is enabled.

- *Policy route map*—MLS is disabled if policy route maps are used.

Now that we have discussed these issues, let's see how to configure MLS in your network. Even though this is a book on switching, in order for MLS to work properly in your network, you need to know how to configure both the MLS supporting switch and the MLS supporting router or internal route processor. In the next section, we will cover the configuration of both of these devices.

Configuring MLS

Configuring MLS involves tasks on both the MLS-RP and the MLS-SE. When using an internal route processor (such as an RSM) on the Catalyst 5000, the only tasks necessary are to verify that MLS is enabled on each interface and that all the interfaces are members of the same VLAN Trunking Protocol (VTP) domain. Because MLS is enabled by default, you need to re-enable MLS only on the interfaces that have been disabled. On a Catalyst 6000, no configuration is needed unless you have disabled MLS.

On the MLS-SE, you need to configure the switch to determine the IP destination of the MLS-RP, if it is an external router. If it is an internal MLS-RP, no configuration is necessary. The default behavior of IP is to maintain a cache entry for each destination IP address. This entry can be modified either to a source-destination pair or to a more specific IP flow.

On an external router being used as the MLS-RP, you need to configure the router to participate in MLS. If your switch has been configured to participate in a VTP domain, the MLS-RP must be in the same domain. You must configure each individual interface acting as an MLS-RP for MLS. Only one interface on the MLS-RP needs to be configured as the MLS management interface.

NOTE: *If the router is connected via non-trunk links to the switch, you need to configure a VLAN ID for each interface.*

When configuring MLS on both the switch and the router, you should pay attention to several items. This information can be helpful for troubleshooting and configuring MLS. Let's take a look at the following MLS features and components:

- MLS cache

- Aging timers

- VLAN IDs

- VTP domains

- Management interfaces

TIP: *On the Catalyst 2926G-L3, 4908G-L3, or 2948G-L3 switch, at least one MLS-RP must be configured. Multiple MLS-RPs can be configured in a single line; up to 16 MLS-RPs can participate in MLS.*

MLS Cache

The MLS cache is used to maintain the flow information for all active flows. The size of the MLS cache is limited to a maximum of 128K. This size limitation will occasionally cause MLS entries to be dropped from the MLS cache—usually if no traffic takes place in a network flow for 256 seconds. Certain routing changes and other network conditions can also force the MLS cache to purge its current entries.

Aging Timers

After the two hosts participating in a flow have completed their communication, you no longer need to maintain any entries regarding the flow. The quicker the end of the flow can be detected and the entries purged from the cache, the more effectively the switching process will function. Why? Because detecting and aging out these entries saves a lot of MLS cache space for real data traffic.

TIP: *Cisco recommends that the total MLS cache entries be kept below 32K. To implement this limit, set the initial aging time value to 128 seconds. If the cache entries continue to go over 32K, decrease the aging time setting and adjust it as necessary. If cache entries still continue to go over 32K, decrease the normal aging time in increments of 64 seconds from the 128-second default until the cache remains below 32K.*

You can adjust the amount of time the MLS cache keeps an entry in its table and set it to a value other than the default 128 seconds by using the **agingtime** command. This command is useful for eliminating short-lived entries in the cache, such as Domain Name Service (DNS).

The aging time can be configured from 8 to 2,032 seconds, in increments of 8 seconds. At the end of the aging time interval, if no further packets are seen in a network flow, the entries related to that flow will be purged from the MLS cache.

The **agingtime fast** command allows you to age out MLS cache entries quickly based on the number of packets received during a configured time period. The command has two parameters:

- **fastagingtime**—Identifies the amount of time an entry remains in the cache. The default for **fastagingtime** is 0, which means that the aging time is disabled and no fast aging occurs. This value can be configured for 32, 64, 96, or 128 seconds.

- **pkt_threshold**—Identifies the number of packets that must be detected during the configured **fastaging** time in order for the entry to remain in the MLS cache. The default parameter value is 0. You can configure this value to 0, 1, 3, 7, 15, 31, or 63 packets.

NOTE: If **fastagingtime** is not configured to one of the values indicated, it adjusts to the closest value.

On the Catalyst 6000, MLS aging is configured somewhat differently. You configure it on the switch using the **mls aging** command, which has three parameters:

- **normal**—Configures the waiting time before aging out and deleting shortcut entries in the Layer 3 table. This parameter can be set in the range of 32 to 4,092 seconds.

- **fast aging**—Used similarly to the Catalyst 5000 command for fast aging. Ages out entries created for flows that use a few packets and then are never used again. Both the fast aging threshold and time parameters are set with this command; they can be in the range of 1 to 128 seconds.

- **long**—Flushes entries that have been in use for the specified time value, even if the Layer 3 entry is still active. This parameter is used to prevent inaccurate statistics. The **long** parameter can be set in the range of 64 to 900 seconds.

MLS Cache Fast Aging Time

The processing of the MLS cache entries can cause performance problems on your switch. To keep this situation under control, it's good practice to monitor the IP cache and make sure it remains well under the maximum size of 128K. Doing so will prevent cache entries from being dropped continuously.

You can keep the size of the cache more manageable by having the MLS cache prune entries that are no longer needed. This type of pruning is known as *fast aging time*. This method configures a timer that checks for a certain number of packets to be sent for a flow during the configured amount of time. If the flow has not sent at least the configured number of packets during the configured time, the entries for the flow are dropped. Fast aging time is good for one-time-use entries, such as those used for DNS lookups and Trivial File Transfer Protocol (TFTP) transfers.

VLAN ID

MLS requires that inter-VLAN routing and packet-forwarding decisions be based on which VLANs have been configured on the ports. The internal route processors (such as the MSM, MSFC, RSM, and RSFC) use only VLAN IDs to identify their interfaces—it is not necessary to configure a VLAN ID for them.

An external route processor has no knowledge about VLANs, because these devices are configured using subnets. A VLAN ID must be assigned to them, if they are to participate in MLS. The interface on the external route processor must be an Ethernet or Fast Ethernet interface. You cannot configure the VLAN ID on a sub-interface.

VTP Domain

While configuring MLS, it is important to determine which of the MLS-RP interfaces will be MLS interfaces, and to add them to the VTP domain of which your other MLS switches are members. Remember, a switch can be a member of only one domain, and any interfaces participating in MLS on the switch or router must be configured members of that domain.

Management Interfaces

Only one interface on an MLS-RP needs to be configured to provide MLS management. The MLS management interface advertises MLSP hello messages, route changes, VLAN information, and MAC addresses. You must specify one of the MLS-RP's interfaces as a management interface, or MLSP packets will not be sent or received.

The management interface can be any MLS interface connected to the MLS switch. More than one management interface can be configured; however, doing so is unnecessary and only adds to the management overhead for the MLS-RP.

Immediate Solutions

Configuring an External MLS Route Processor

Configuring the MLS-RP for MLS involves the following tasks:

- Enabling MLSP on an MLS-RP
- Adding the VLAN ID to the router interface
- Adding the MLS interface to the VTP domain

Let's examine each of these tasks, as well as how to disable each of these features in case they are no longer needed on an interface.

Related Solutions:	Found on page:
Configuring a Hostname on an RSM	187

Enabling MLSP on an MLS-RP for IP

To enable the MLSP that runs between the MLS-SE and the MLS-RP, enter the following command in Global Configuration mode:

```
MLS-RP(config) mls rp ip
```

Disabling MLSP on an MLS-RP for IP

To disable MLSP on an interface, use the following command in Global Configuration mode:

```
MLS-RP(config) no mls rp ip
```

Enabling MLSP on an MLS-RP for IPX

If you are using version 12.0 or later of the Cisco IOS, you can also enable MLSP to multilayer-switch IPX packets. To do so, use the following command:

```
MLS-RP (config) mls rp ipx
```

Disabling MLSP on an MLS-RP for IPX

To disable MLSP for IPX, use the following command:

```
MLS-RP (config) no mls rp ipx
```

Assigning a VLAN ID

To configure a VLAN ID for an external router's interface, enter the following command:

```
mls rp vlan-id <vlan-id-num>
```

For example, here is how to assign VLAN 3 to an interface:

1. Enter the interface for which you want to assign the VLAN ID by using the following command:

   ```
   Router(config) interface fastethernet 1/1
   ```

2. To add the VLAN ID for VLAN 3, use the following command:

   ```
   Router(config-if) mls rp vlan-id 3
   ```

Adding an MLS Interface to a VTP Domain

Enter the following command to add an interface to a VTP domain:

```
mls rp vtp-domain <domain-name>
```

Here is an example of how to use this command:

1. Enter the interface for which you want to assign the VLAN ID:

   ```
   Router(config) interface fastethernet 1/1
   ```

2. To assign a VTP domain of *coriolis* to the interface, use the following command:

   ```
   Router(config) mls rp vtp-domain coriolis
   ```

WARNING! This step must be performed prior to using any of the other MLS interface commands on the MLS interface. If this command is not used first, the interface will be placed in a null domain and will be unable to perform MLS functions.

Enabling MLS on an Individual Interface

After MLS has been placed into a VTP domain, you must enable MLS on each interface that is to participate in MLS. To enable MLS on an interface, perform the following tasks:

1. Enter Interface Configuration mode on the interface for which you want to enable MLS using the following command:

```
Router(config)interface fastethernet 1/1
```

2. Use the following command to enable MLS on the interface:

```
Router(config-if)# mls rp ip
```

Disabling MLS on an External Router Interface

To disable MLS on an interface, perform these tasks:

1. Enter Interface Configuration mode on the interface for which you want to disable MLS using the following command:

```
Router(config)interface fastethernet 1/1
```

2. Use the following command to disable MLS on the interface:

```
Router(config-if)# no mls rp ip
```

Configuring the MLS Switch Engine

Configuring the MLS-SE (Catalyst 5000 and 6000) for MLS involves the following tasks:

- Re-enabling MLS
- Enabling aging timers
- Configuring the MLS Management Interface

Let's examine each of these tasks, as well as how to disable each of these features in case they are no longer needed on an interface.

Re-enabling MLS on a Catalyst 6000

By default, MLS is enabled on all Catalyst switches that support Layer 3 switching. To re-enable MLS on a Catalyst 6000, perform the following tasks:

1. Enter Interface Configuration mode for the VLAN interface. This example uses VLAN 11:

```
CAT6000(config)interface vlan 11
```

2. Enter the **mls ip** command to re-enable MLS on the VLAN interface:

```
CAT6000(config)mls ip
```

Re-enabling MLS on a Catalyst 5000

To re-enable MLS on a Catalyst 5000, use the following command:

```
CAT5000(enable) set mls enable
```

Disabling MLS on a Catalyst 6000

To disable MLS on a Catalyst 6000, use the following command:

```
CAT6000(config) no mls ip
```

Disabling MLS on a Catalyst 5000

To disable MLS on a Catalyst 5000, use the following command:

```
CAT5000(enable) set mls disable
```

Configuring the MLS Cache on the Catalyst 5000

To configure the MLS cache on a Catalyst 5000, use this command:

```
set mls agingtime <seconds>
```

An example is shown here:

```
Console>(enable) set mls agingtime 512
Multilayer switching aging time set to 512
```

Configuring Fast Aging on a Catalyst 5000

To configure the fast aging time on the Cisco Catalyst 5000, use the following command:

```
set mls agingtime fast <fastagingtime> <pkt_threshold>
```

An example of using this command looks like this:

```
CAT5000>(enable) set mls agingtime fast 32 7
Multilayer switching fast aging time set to 32 seconds for entries
with no more than 7 packets switched.
```

Configuring Fast Aging on a Catalyst 6000

To configure the fast aging time on the Cisco Catalyst 6000, use the following command:

```
mls aging fast threshold <packet_count> time <seconds>
```

An example of using the **mls aging fast** command is as follows:

```
CAT6000(config)# mls aging fast threshold 64 time 30
```

Disabling Fast Aging on a Catalyst 6000

To disable the fast aging time on the Cisco Catalyst 6000, use the following command:

```
no mls aging fast
```

Configuring Long Aging on the Catalyst 6000

To configure the long aging time on the Catalyst 6000, use the following command:

```
mls aging long <seconds>
```

An example of using the **mls aging long** command is as follows:

```
mls aging long 64
```

Disabling Long Aging on the Catalyst 6000

To disable the long aging time on the Catalyst 6000, use the following command:

```
no mls aging long
```

Configuring Normal Aging on the Catalyst 6000

To configure the normal aging time on the Catalyst 6000, use the following command:

```
mls aging normal <seconds>
```

An example is as follows:

```
mls aging normal 32
```

Disabling Normal Aging on the Catalyst 6000

To disable the normal aging time on the Catalyst 6000, use the following command:

```
no mls aging normal
```

Assigning MLS Management to an Interface on the Catalyst 5000

To enable an interface to be a management interface, follow these steps:

1. Enter Interface Configuration mode on the interface using the following command:

```
CAT5000(config)interface fastethernet 1/1
```

2. To enable the interface as the management interface, use the following command:

```
CAT5000(config)mls rp management-interface
```

Disabling MLS Management on an Interface on the Catalyst 5000

To disable a management interface, perform the following tasks:

1. Enter Interface Configuration mode on the interface using the following command:

```
CAT5000(config)interface fastethernet 1/1
```

2. To disable the interface as the management interface, use the following command:

```
CAT5000(config-if)no mls rp management-interface
```

Monitoring and Viewing the MLS Configuration

Commands on each MLS-SE and MLS-RP to monitor and view the configurations of each device are different. Let's take a look at the following commands:

- Viewing the MLS aging configuration on a Catalyst 6000
- Displaying the IP MLS configuration
- Viewing MLS-RPs
- Viewing MLS-RP specifics

- Displaying MLS VTP domain information
- Viewing the MLS VLAN interface information
- Viewing MLS statistics on the Catalyst 5000
- Viewing MLS statistics on the Catalyst 6000
- Viewing MLS entries

Viewing the MLS Aging Configuration on a Catalyst 6000

To see the MLS aging configuration on a Catalyst 6000, use the **show mls aging** command as shown here:

```
MLS-RP# show mls aging
             enable timeout  packet threshold
             ------ -------  ------ ---------
normal aging false     300      N/A
fast aging   false      32      100
long aging   false     900      N/A
```

Displaying the IP MLS Configuration

To display the MLS configuration for the MLS-RP, use the following command:

```
MLS-RP# show mls rp
```

The output should look similar to this:

```
ip multilayer switching is globally enabled
ipx multilayer switching is globally enabled
ipx mls inbound acl override is globally disabled
mls id is 0008.80e4.abd2
mls ip address 38.187.127.254
mls ip flow mask is destination
mls ipx flow mask is unknown
number of domains configured for mls 1
```

Viewing MLS-RPs

To see which MLS-RPs are configured on an MLS switch, use the following command:

```
MLS-RP> (enable) show mls include
Included MLS-RP
-------------------------------------
38.187.128.254
38.187.127.254
Console> (enable)
```

Viewing MLS-RP Specifics

To display MLS information for a specific MLS-RP on an MLS switch, enter the following:

```
MLS-RP> (enable) show mls rp 38.187.128.254
MLS-RP IP       MLS-RP ID       Xtag   MLS-RP MAC-Vlans
----------      ------------    ----   ----------------------
38.187.128.254  0000808dca20    2      00-00-80-08-dc-ca 1-20
```

Displaying MLS VTP Domain Information

To display the MLS VTP domain information, enter the following command:

```
MLS-RP# show mls rp vtp-domain coriolis
vlan domain name: coriolis
   current flow mask: ip-flow
   current sequence number: 88452194
   current/maximum retry count: 0/10
   current domain state: no-change
   current/next global purge: false/false
   current/next purge count: 0/0
   domain uptime: 13:07:36
   keepalive timer expires in 8 seconds
   retry timer not running
   change timer not running
   fcp subblock count = 7

   1 management interface(s) currently defined:
      fastethernet 1/1 on Vlan2

   1 mac-vlan(s) configured for multi-layer switching:

      mac 00e0.befc.4000
         vlan id(s)
         2

   router currently aware of following 1 switch(es):
      switch id 0080.abac.24ec
```

Related solutions:	Found on page:
Configuring VTP on a Set/Clear CLI Switch	164
Configuring VTP on a 1900 Cisco IOS CLI Switch	165

Viewing the MLS VLAN Interface Information

To view the MLS information about specific interfaces, use the **show mls rp interface vlan** command as shown here:

```
MLS-RP# show mls rp interface vlan 2
mls active on Vlan2, domain coriolis
```

Viewing MLS Statistics on the Catalyst 5000

This command illustrates how to display MLS information on the Catalyst 5000:

```
CAT5000> (enable) show mls
Multilayer switching enabled
Multilayer switching aging time = 256 seconds
Multilayer switching fast aging time = 0 seconds, packet threshold = 1
Destination-ip flow
Total packets switched = 105483
Active entries = 513
Netflow data export enabled
Netflow data export configured for port 8010 on host 10.1.1.25
Total packets exported = 20


MLS-RP IP    MLS-RP ID       Xtag   MLS-RP MAC-Vlans
----------  ------------     ----   ----------------------
38.187.128.254 0000808dade0    2      00-00-80-8c-dc-a2 1
38.187.127.254 0000808a22b2    3      00-00-80-8c-dc-a6 2
```

Viewing MLS Statistics on the Catalyst 6000

On the Catalyst 6000, you can get information similar to that provided by the previous command by entering the following:

```
CAT6000> (enable) show mls ip
Total Active MLS entries = 0
Total packets switched = 0
IP Multilayer switching enabled
IP Multilayer switching aging time = 256 seconds
IP Multilayer switching fast aging time = 0
seconds, packet threshold = 0
IP Flow mask: Full Flow
Configured flow mask is Destination flow
Active IP MLS entries = 0
Netflow Data Export version: 8
Netflow Data Export disabled
Netflow Data Export port/host is not configured
Total packets exported = 0
```

```
MSFC ID          Module XTAG MAC                Vlans
--------------   ------ ---- ---------------- ----------------
52.0.03          5      1    01-10-30-7b-0d-00 1,10,22
```

Viewing MLS Entries

To display all entries in the MLS cache, enter the following command:

```
CAT5000>(enable) show mls entry

Destination IP  Source IP       Port DstPrt SrcPrt Destination Mac
Vlan Port
--------------  --------------  ---- ------ ------ ----------------
MLS-RP 38.187.127.253:
38.187.123.5    38.187.127.254  UDP  6009   69     00-10-0b-16-98-00
1  1/1-2
38.187.123.9    38.187.127.254  UDP  6002   69     00-10-3a-00-a5-09
22   4/7
```

11. Multilayer Switching

Chapter 12

Hot Standby Routing Protocol

In Depth

Dynamic environments are constantly growing. I happen to work in one and I see the demand for 99.99 percent reliability increasing every day. However, even in a worldwide Enterprise network, high availability solutions are not prepared for various network failures. Here's an example: I manage a few hundred servers at a Fortune 100 company. I'm trying to get to a local intranet site and my browser just hangs. Then I try to ping the server that is across subnets and the request times out. I can ping everything and anything within my subnet, but then I try the default gateway. Does this sound all too familiar? Think of the customer impact, the data warehouses that are unreachable, or online training sessions where students cannot connect. I find it hard to believe sometimes that redundancy is not in place.

The point I'm trying to make is that department budgets or deep pockets do not always solve the problem. Network and systems administrators need help, especially when it is usually a team of about four to six engineers that manage a dynamic networked enterprise environment. If this was a Cisco switched campus model, which would overcome these IP-related issues and provide network redundancy, every device would have a backup device standing by in case of a failure. Route processor devices (such as internal cards in multilayer switches and routers) would have been among the hardest devices to configure for fast convergence redundancy.

The Cisco switched campus model builds redundancy into the Layer 2 switch block level devices. However, Hot Standby Routing Protocol (HSRP) is designed to build redundancy into the Layer 3 routing devices found in the Distribution layer of a network. It also provides convergence in seconds without manual intervention from a network administrator while remaining transparent between other interfaces on the network. HSRP can be applied to almost any LAN environment.

One primary feature of HSRP, which allows it to be so transparent to users, is its use of *priority schemes*. These priorities are used to determine which router is set as the default active router. When a router is manually assigned a priority, the standby interface that has a higher priority is selected as the active router.

HSRP is one of the best solutions when host interfaces on a local LAN segment require continuous access to network resources.

Routing Problems

Within a standard client/server network, the ability to exchange routing information between segments is allowed by Layer 3 address translation. However, although the clients may route the packet to its default gateway, they cannot route beyond their local LAN segment.

NOTE: *The default gateway is the protocol address for the route processor to which data packets containing a destination address outside the local segment are sent.*

In order for the client to route information out of its local LAN segment, it must use a manually configured IP stack; or, the client may be configured for Dynamic Host Configuration Protocol (DHCP) to determine a default gateway. In any event, if the Layer 3 routing device assigned as the default gateway fails or is offline, all devices located on that particular subnet or network will only be allowed to communicate with each other. The local collision or broadcast domain becomes the entire network in the eyes of each device. You can place another default gateway on the network, but there is no clear way to provide a secondary configuration to another default route without manually resetting the default gateway on either the client or server.

The next sections look at some ways that administrators and engineers have devised to overcome problems related to assigning default gateways, along with the benefits and difficulties in using each technique.

Routing Information Protocol

Once solution designed to inject Layer 3 routing redundancy allows nodes utilizing IP to use Routing Information Protocol (RIP) to discover secondary routers located on the network. This method allows the end-user node to maintain a routing table that determines the shortest path by calculating the number of hops and using the router with the fewest hops.

However, RIP has a very slow convergence time when a change in the network topology occurs. It may take up to three times the update interval setting before RIP chooses another default route from the table.

Proxy ARP

Another solution to creating redundancy for Layer 3 uses Proxy Address Resolution Protocol (Proxy ARP). The Proxy ARP broadcasts an IP ARP request for the Media Access Control (MAC) address of the router. The router replies with the MAC address of the requesting node.

If a failure occurs, however, the node configured for the default gateway has two options:

- Reboot the node.
- Wait for the ARP update and the flush period of the ARP entry to expire.

This delay creates a very high convergence period.

ICMP Router Discovery Protocol

ICMP Router Discovery Protocol (IRDP) is probably one of the longest protocol names to come along. IRDP is one of the most commonly used solutions for locating a redundant router in the event of a gateway failure. It is available only when HSRP is not configured.

IRDP is an extension of Internet Control Message Protocol (ICMP); it allows network administrators to use such commands as **ping** and **trace** between interfaces to diagnose network-related problems. ICMP provides mechanisms to allow routers to advertise default routes available for any network.

This protocol has many features—unlike RIP and Proxy ARP—for discovering the addresses of neighboring routers. ICMP requires no additional configuration by an administrator.

Hosts that use IRDP listen for IRDP advertisements from the default router. In the event a host interface does not receive IRDP advertisements during a predefined value (sometimes referred to as the *lifetime value*), the host interface considers the default route void and will begin to choose another route to a remote network.

IRDP has a high convergence time in the event of a failure. The default lifetime of the default route is 30 minutes, and advertisements are sent every 7 to 10 minutes. The router controls the interval at which the advertisement messages are sent. IRDP requires you to configure two separate intervals on the router: the minimum advertising interval and the maximum advertising interval. All advertisements are sent during that window of time. So, a change in the network topology can go unnoticed for almost 30 minutes.

Cisco developed HSRP to address and resolve these problems faced by network administrators.

The Solution

HSRP is a Cisco proprietary protocol developed for redundancy. It defines a group of routers working as one virtual router. It enables host interfaces to continue communicating outside the local segment even if a host interface's default route fails or the link is down. Basically, HSRP is a group of routers working together as a unit to provide fault tolerance.

HSRP works by assigning a group of routers a virtual IP address and a virtual MAC address. The routers in this group route packets to a virtual IP address so packets are still routed through the network even when their destination router is pushed off a shelf in the wiring closet. (Routers can fail for many reasons, most of which relate to electrical and component issues.)

HSRP also uses a priority scheme to determine which HSRP-configured router is the default active router. When you assign the standby interface a default priority that is higher than the priority of all other HSRP-configured route processor interfaces, that router is set as the active router. Once this active router is configured, multicast messages and advertising priorities are exchanged among HSRP-configured route processor interfaces. Now, if an active router fails to send a hello message (covered later in this chapter) within the configurable period of time, the standby router with the highest priority will be forced to become an active router.

HSRP is one of the best solutions when host interfaces on a local LAN segment require continuous access to the network resources. As shown in Figure 12.1, when a failure does occur, HSRP automatically lets the elected standby route processor assume the role and function of the offline router.

HSRP classifies the route processors on the network into standby groups. More than one standby group can be assigned to each route processor. The number of standby groups that can be assigned is limited by the physical topology being used. Table 12.1 shows the number of standby groups that can be configured on

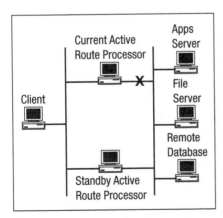

Figure 12.1   Two routers between various types of servers and clients. The standby route processor assumes the failed default route processor's position in the network.

Table 12.1   The maximum number of standby groups that can be assigned to a route processor based on the physical topology.

Topology	Standby Groups
Ethernet	255
FDDI	255
Token Ring	3

each type of physical LAN topology. Each group contains a route processor in each of the following roles:

- Active route processor
- Standby route processor
- Virtual route processor

All other route processors fall into the "other route processor" category.

WARNING! By increasing the number of standby groups on a route processor, you decrease the route processor's performance and increase latency. You'll increase the number of standby groups primarily to facilitate load sharing.

In the Immediate Solutions section, you will learn how to configure the standby priority. If it is not manually assigned, the priority is 100. But what if none of the route processors has been assigned a group priority? If multiple route processors in the group have equal priority, the route processor with the highest IP address for the respective group will be elected as the active route processor. The route processor with the second highest IP address will become the standby route processor. All the other route processors will be placed in a Listen state (see "The HSRP States").

The standby router will take over once the route processor that is currently active for the group does not receive three hello messages. The actual convergence time is contingent upon the HSRP timers for the group. The HSRP hellotime timer defaults to 3, and the holdtime timer defaults to 10. Interestingly, with HSRP, the standby route processor will take over even if the active router's LAN interface state is displaying the message *interface up line protocol down*.

Once the standby route processor becomes active, it will respond to any end station sending packets to the virtual MAC address. When an IP host interface sends an ARP request with the virtual route processor's address, HSRP will respond with the virtual route processor's MAC address—not its own. This virtual MAC address is the well-known MAC address of 0000.0c07.ac11, where 11 is the HSRP group identifier.

To find the current IP address of the virtual router, use the **show ip arp** command and look for the virtual route processor IP and hardware MAC address. You can also use the **show standby** command.

Route processors using HSRP can provide redundancy for a default gateway as well as load-balance traffic across VLANs and IP subnets (if multiple VLANs are being used, a separate HSRP standby group must be in place for each VLAN). Because route processors can be assigned as members of multiple HSRP standby groups, each standby group can have its own priority and its own active route processor. As shown in Figure 12.2, the active route processor for group 1 assigned to VLAN 1 uses route processor 2. VLAN 2 using standby group 2 will use route processor 2. In the event of a failure, the standby group will begin to use the other route processor. In this situation, load sharing will take place until a failure occurs.

Each standby group contains an IP address and a well-known MAC address assigned to the group. The IP address for the standby group is within the range of IP addresses belonging to the subnet or VLAN to which the route processor is providing services. The IP address cannot be assigned to any other device in the network except the standby group interfaces operating in the standby group.

Inter-Switch Link (ISL) links are used to transport VLAN information across the links to the different route processors used in each standby group. In order to pass HSRP standby group information between links for multiple VLANs, the interfaces in the group must be configured with ISL. The encapsulation format must be defined, and an IP address must be assigned to an interface.

NOTE: *Refer to Chapter 5 for information on configuring ISL encapsulation and assigning an IP address to an interface.*

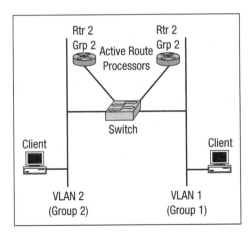

Figure 12.2   VLAN 1 and VLAN 2 utilize load balancing across the multiple route processors.

HSRP Message Format

All route processors in the HSRP standby group send and receive HSRP messages to one another. The messages are used to determine the roles of each route processor in the group. User Datagram Protocol (UDP) utilizing TCP port 17 encapsulates the data in the data portion of the UDP packet. The packet is then sent to an all-router multicast address with a time to live (TTL) of one hop.

The fields contained in an HSRP message are:

- *Version*—Indicates the HSRP version.

- *Op Code*—Describes the type of message contained in the packet. The three types of messages are as follows:
  - *Hello*—The first and most common message, which is sent to indicate that a route processor in the standby group is functioning in the group.
  - *Coup*—Indicates that a route processor wants to become the active route processor.
  - *Resign*—Notifies the other standby group members that a route processor no longer can or will participate as the active route processor.

- *State*—Indicates the current state of the route processor sending the message.

- *Hellotime*—Indicates the time period in seconds between hello messages that the sending route processor sends. The default is three seconds.

- *Holdtime*—Used when sending hello messages. This field indicates the length of time in seconds that the message should be considered valid. The holdtime should be at least three times the value assigned to hellotime. The default time is 10 seconds.

- *Priority*—Used to elect the active and standby route processors. The route processor with the highest priority in the HSRP group wins the election and becomes the active route processor.

- *Group*—Indicates the standby group number. The valid numbers are 0 to 255; 255 groups can be configured as valid HSRP groups.

- *Authentication data*—Contains an eight-character clear text password that is continuously reused.

- *Virtual address*—Contains the IP address of the router that is used by the HSRP group.

Just as in Spanning-Tree Protocol (STP), a route processor goes through different states before it becomes fully functional. In the next section, we'll look at these different states and how skipping one or more of the states affects HSRP.

The HSRP States

A route processor such as a router can transition through six HSRP states. The definitions of the states are included here:

- *Initial state*—All route processors begin in this state. In this starting state, HSRP is not running. The route processor can be found in this state after the power cycles or if a configuration change is applied to the route processor.

- *Learn state*—The route processor transitions to this state and remains in this state until it receives a hello message from the current active router. The hello message allows the route processor to learn the virtual IP address of the current virtual router.

- *Listen state*—In this state, the route processor has learned the IP address of the virtual router and is listening for more updated information through hello messages. In this state, the route processor is neither active nor standing by. Listen is basically a transitional state from the Learn state to the Speak state.

- *Speak state*—In this state, the route processor begins to forward its own periodic hello messages and to notify the other route processors that it is an active participant in the voting process to become an active or standby route processor. From here, it will forward to either the Active state or the Standby state.

- *Standby state*—In HSRP, there must be at least one standby route processor. If more than one exists, the route processors become what are known as *standby candidate route processors*. The route processor with the highest standby priority will enter the Active state in the event of a failure.

- *Active state*—The route processor in the Active state acts as the default gateway for the IP address assigned to the virtual router. It forwards any packets received for the virtual IP address or MAC address sent from any of the HSRP group's host interfaces. It also continues to send hello messages to the other route processors to verify that it holds this function.

HSRP Configuration

You can configure more than one HSRP group on a Route Switch Feature Card (RSFC) VLAN interface to provide a transparent route processor backup per network. Every VLAN interface within an HSRP group shares a virtual IP and MAC address. By configuring the end users' interfaces to use an HSRP virtual IP address as a default gateway, no interruption will occur in Layer 3 routing to the end users in the event of a failure of any route processor.

You can configure HSRP on a number of different types of Cisco route processors, including routers. You can configure multiple route processors on the same switch with interfaces for the same HSRP group. You can also configure multiple groups with multiple interfaces on the same route processor.

NOTE: *Route Switch Module (RSM), Multilayer Switch Feature Card (MSFC), and RSFC command sets are virtually identical.*

Disabling ICMP Redirects

It is important to disable all protocols that enable the host interfaces to discover the real MAC address of an HSRP standby group route processor interface. When enabling HSRP, ICMP redirects are automatically disabled. When you use the **show running-configuration** command under each VLAN interface configured for HSRP, a line will appear stating *no ip redirects*. This line indicates that ICMP redirects have been disabled. To re-enable an HSRP interface, enter Interface Configuration mode and use the command **no standby**, followed by the group number.

HSRP Interface Tracking

Interface tracking enables a standby group route processor to automatically adjust the priority levels based on the availability of the route processor. If a tracked interface becomes unavailable, the HSRP priority of the route processor is automatically decreased. When a route processor with HSRP tracking fails, it reduces the likelihood that a route processor with an unavailable interface will remain the active route processor for the standby group.

If a route processor fails, it automatically decrements its priority on that interface and stops transmitting hello messages out the interface. The standby route processor assumes the active router role when no hello messages are detected for the specified **holdtime** period.

Immediate Solutions

Opening a Session on an Internal Route Processor

To configure HSRP on an internal route processor such as an RSFC or RSM, you must start a session using the **session** command. To start a session on the RSM located in slot 3, use the following command from Privileged mode on the switch Internetwork Operating System (IOS):

```
HSN_5K>(enable) session 3
Trying Router-3...
Connected to Router-3
HSN_5KRSM>
```

Entering Configuration Mode on an RSM

Once you have started a configuration session, you need to enter Configuration mode for the VLAN interface that needs to be identified. To configure the interface for VLAN 3, use the following commands:

```
HSN_5KRSM>enable
HSN_5KRSM#configure terminal
Enter configuration commands, one per line. End with CNTL/Z.
HSN_5KRSM(config)#interface vlan 3
HSN_5KRSM(config-if)#
```

Enabling HSRP and Assigning an IP Address to a Standby Group

To enable HSRP and specify the virtual IP address, use the following command:

```
standby <group number> ip <virtual IP address>
```

For example, to make the group number 3 and the virtual IP address 63.78.39.254 you would enter the following:

```
standby 3 ip 63.78.39.254
```

TIP: *If you do not specify a group number, then group 0 is used by default. The IP address is the virtual IP address of the default gateway that you would assign manually or by DHCP to the end stations operating in this VLAN.*

Related solution:	Found on page:
Configuring Redundancy Using HSRP	203

Assigning an HSRP Interface Priority

You should increase the priority of the interface in the HSRP group that you would like to be active by default. Always remember that the interface with the highest priority becomes the active route processor for the HSRP group. To specify the priority for the HSRP interface, using the following command:

```
standby <standby group number> priority <priority>
```

In the following example, **3** refers to the HSRP standby group number corresponding to the VLAN interface number. The number **160** is the new priority for the HSRP group.

```
standby 3 priority 160
```

NOTE: *If no priority is configured, the interface priority defaults to 100.*

Assigning a Preempt Delay to a Standby Group

You can assign the standby group a preempt delay. Doing so allows the interface to preempt the current active HSRP interface and become active if the interface priority is higher than the priority of the current active interface. The syntax for this command is:

```
standby <standby group> preempt <preempt delay>
```

To set the standby group 3 to a preempt delay of 10, use the following command:

```
standby 3 preempt 10
```

Removing a Preempt Delay from a Standby Group

To remove the route processor from preempt status, use the following syntax:

```
no standby <group number> preempt
```

To remove the preempt status for group number 3, enter the following:

```
no standby 3 preempt
```

Setting the HSRP Hello and Hold Timers

The default values for the HSRP timers are 3 seconds for the hello timer and 10 seconds for the hold timer. All the interfaces in the HSRP group should use the same timer values on all member route processors in the group. To set the hello timer and hold timer, use the following:

```
standby <HSRP group> timers <hello timer> <hold timer>
```

To set the hello timer to 5 seconds and the hold timer to 15 seconds for HSRP group 3, use the following command:

```
standby 3 timers 5 15
```

Removing the HSRP Hello and Hold Timers

To remove the manual timer settings and return the settings to the default values for HSRP group 3, use the following command:

```
no standby 3 timers
```

Configuring a Clear-Text Password for HSRP Authentication

You can specify a clear-text password for the HSRP authentication string for the interface. All interfaces in the HSRP group use the same authentication string. The syntax is as follow:

```
standby <HSRP group> authentication <password>
```

To set the password book1 for HSRP group 3, use the following command:

```
standby 3 authentication book1
```

Configuring Two RSFC Interfaces as One HSRP Group

Now that you have learned the commands, let's look at an example. This project shows how to configure two RSFC interfaces as part of HSRP group 200 using all the required and optional commands I've discussed. Notice that on both route processors, the same virtual IP address is used for both groups.

Here is the configuration of the first RSFC for the HSRP standby group 200:

```
HSN_5KRSFC#configure terminal
Enter configuration commands, one per line. End with CNTL/Z.
HSN_5KRSFC(config)#interface vlan200
HSN_5KRSFC(config-if)#standby 200 ip 68.187.1.1
HSN_5KRSFC(config-if)#standby 200 priority 150
HSN_5KRSFC(config-if)#standby 200 preempt
HSN_5KRSFC(config-if)#standby 200 timers 5 15
HSN_5KRSFC(config-if)#standby 200 authentication password
HSN_5KRSFC(config-if)#^Z
HSN_5KRSFC#
```

The following is the configuration of the second RSFC. The priority setting here is lower than that of the first RSFC; thus the first RSFC is the active route processor (default gateway), and this RSFC is the standby route processor for the group:

```
HSN_KRSFC2#configure terminal
Enter configuration commands, one per line. End with CNTL/Z.
HSN_5KRSFC2(config)#interface vlan200
HSN_5KRSFC2(config-if)#standby 200 ip 68.187.1.1
HSN_5KRSFC2(config-if)#standby 200 priority 100
HSN_5KRSFC2(config-if)#standby 200 preempt
```

```
HSN_5KRSFC2(config-if)#standby 200 timers 5 15
HSN_5KRSFC2(config-if)#standby 200 authentication password
HSN_5KRSFC2(config-if)#^Z
HSN_5KRSFC#
```

Here's what happened:

1. You selected and entered the VLAN interface you want to have configured (vlan200).

2. You configured the HSRP group and entered the virtual default gateway IP address on that interface.

3. You set the priority accordingly, allowing one route processor to be active and the other to be standby.

4. You enabled **preempt** on both routers and you are not accepting the default timers. You have 5 seconds for the hello timer and 15 seconds for the hold timer (which specifies how long you want the hello timer to remain valid).

5. You have configured the clear-text authentication with the word "password".

The result will be that since HSN_5KRSFC has a higher priority than HSN_5KRSFC2, it will be the active standby route processor for HSRP group 200.

Enabling Interface Tracking

To configure tracking on the HSRP route processor interface, enter the following command in Interface Configuration mode:

```
standby <HSRP group> track <VLAN interface> <priority decrease>
```

For this example, we'll use HSRP standby group number 3, VLAN interface being tracked is 7, and 20 indicates the priority amount to decrease:

```
standby 3 track 7 20
```

Using the last setting, if the route processor's priority was 150 and the route processor were to fail, the tracking interface would decrease its priority by 20 to a value of 130.

TIP: *You can use the same command on an external route processor, as well. If you were in Interface Configuration mode for interface Ethernet1 and wanted to track the interface S1 for the same HSRP standby group, and with the same priority reduction setting, you would use the command* **standby 3 track s1 20**.

Using the **show standby** Command

To display the standby status of an HSRP interface, you must be in Exec mode and use the following command:

```
show standby vlan3 3
```

The **vlan3** command indicates the VLAN and **3** indicates the HSRP standby group. The output should look similar to this:

```
HSN_5KRSFC# show standby vlan3 3
Vlan3 - Group 3
   local state is Active, priority 160, may preempt
   Hellotime 5 holdtime 15
   Next hello sent in 00:00:02.922
   Hot standby IP address is 63.78.39.1 configured
   Active router is local
   Standby router is 63.78.39.2 expires in 00:00:05
   Standby virtual mac address is 0000.0c07.ac03
```

*TIP: To get a brief output of all the configured interfaces, you can use the **show standby brief** command.*

Using the **debug** Command

By enabling the **debug** command, it will list the changes in real-time for the HSRP group you specified. This includes the sending and receiving packets through the HSRP. To enable debugging of your HSRP group you need to use the following command at the Privileged Exec prompt:

```
debug standby
```

WARNING! The debugging feature is automatically assigned a high priority on the CPU, so this command can have a big impact on the internal route processor's performance.

To disable the debugging feature, enter either the **no debug standby** or the **no debug** command.

Chapter 13

Policy Networking

In Depth

Behind all switching implementations and configurations lies an area that, if left unattended, can render you and your network defenseless: access security policies. In this chapter, we will discuss the need for and creation of access security policies; we will also focus on how to implement these policies.

Security is one of the most important functions in today's networks. Without it, competitors would have access to various data warehouses, and hackers and common users would have an open invitation to your network. With e-commerce booming, the need to strengthen network security in order to reduce network intrusion and network vulnerabilities becomes increasingly important.

NOTE: *You can never count on network and data security even if it is in place, because it's only as secure as you make it. To implement strong security measures, you must begin at the physical device and extend them throughout your entire network.*

Once access policies have been created, it's a great advantage to you, as the network administrator, to know how to implement these policies and how to distribute them. The following sections will cover this material in depth and explain how it relates to Internet Protocol (IP) switching and routing.

Access Security Policies

An *access security policy* is designed to help define what your network needs in order to be secure from all possible intrusions. Creating this policy for your business or entity allows you, as the network administrator, to provide service-level agreements (SLAs) based on a set of defined traffic and security standards.

An access security policy should define the following:

- The physical security of all the devices in the network
- Control of user access to the network through the implementation of virtual LANs (VLANs) and port security
- What traffic should be allowed in and out of the network
- Route filters to determine the data that should be sent through the network and what route filters should be applied at the Distribution layer

- User groups that have access to each area of the network

- Types of access each user group should have to the network

Each layer of the network has a different function and applies policies differently. Figure 13.1 shows the policies and switches found at each layer of the network. Policies defined in the access security policy need to be applied to all the devices in your network. In the following sections, we will address how security should be applied at each individual layer of the network.

Core Layer Policies

By implementing security policies at the Core layer, also known as the backbone, you increase the elapsed amount of time between when a device requests access to a network and when it is allowed to transmit because of the amount of processing that is done on the switch. The job of the Core layer is to pass traffic as quickly as possible. Policies should be applied at the Access and Distribution layers before the data reaches this level. The Core layer should rely on the other two layers to provide filtering and security policies.

NOTE: *According to Cisco, the only policies at the Core layer should relate to Quality of Service (QoS)—features that allow for lower processing on the switch processor. This allows for a guarantee of a particular level of service for a given connection. Limiting policies this way will aid in congestion management and congestion avoidance.*

Switches	Policies	Device Types
CAT 1900 Series CAT 2900 Series CAT 3500 Series CAT 4000 Series CAT 5000 Series	Access Layer Policy	LAN Switches
CAT 4000 Series CAT 5500 Series CAT 6000 Series	Distribution Layer Policy	LAN Switches Multiplexed Switches
CAT 5500 Series CAT 6500 Series CAT 8500 Series	Core Layer Policy	Multilayer Switches

Figure 13.1   A short list of various switches overlapping into different areas of the policy layers.

Distribution Layer Policies

The Distribution layer is the primary layer for implementing security access policies. Implementation at this layer can be as simple as applying policy blocking to workgroups, or as complex as defining which paths different types of data should take through the network. The Distribution layer is also responsible for advertising correct routes, blocking identified traffic, and limiting the amount of data sent to the Core layer.

NOTE: *When you configure route summarization and distribution lists at the Distribution layer, they may have an adverse affect on the Core layer—mainly in the form of increased latency. Be sure you have a firm understanding of what you want to accomplish when configuring these policies.*

As the demarcation point between the Access and Core layers, the Distribution layer is the perfect location in the network to administer most of your policies. At this layer, you will define which resources and routes are to be sent to the Core layer, as well as what traffic should be allowed in or out of a switch block.

A good policy at this layer ensures that no unnecessary traffic or incorrect routes will be advertised to the Core layer. A good Distribution layer policy should define the following:

- *User traffic that can span different VLANs*—This policy can be defined by applying access lists to identified interfaces to permit or deny certain data traffic.

- *Routes that should be seen by the core switch block*—These can be defined by applying distribution lists, which are another form of access lists.

- *Services that will ultimately be advertised to the rest of the network*—These services include the Domain Name Service (DNS) and Dynamic Host Configuration Protocol (DHCP).

In this section, we will cover the following issues relating to the Distribution layer of the network:

- Access lists
- Managing virtual terminal access
- Managing Hypertext Transfer Protocol (HTTP) access

Access Lists

An *access list* is a list of conditions that control access to the switch, router, or route processor. IP, AppleTalk, and Internetwork Packet Exchange (IPX) access lists are like gatekeepers that control access from or to different segments of the network. After you build an access list, it can be applied to an inbound interface or an outbound interface. Once it has been applied to the interface, an implied "deny all" appears at the end of each access list.

The packets are filtered by comparing an identified value and acting upon a **permit** or **deny** statement. The list compares the packets receiving information (such as the source and destination addresses) to the values in your access list. If a match is made, the list follows the order to permit or deny the data. If a packet is denied, an Internet Control Message Protocol (ICMP) message is sent to the sending interface listed in the packet header, notifying the requester that the packet has been denied.

In Figure 13.2, the source address of 10.1.128.6 is trying to send a data packet to 10.1.128.10. Because the configured access list doesn't contain a **permit** statement for the source address, the access list automatically denies the packet.

Before you apply the access list to the currently used management station using a console port or virtual terminal port, always remember to check that you have a **permit** statement near the top of your access list for the management station you are using. You won't believe how many times we have had to deal with an administrator who is unfamiliar with access lists and who has locked himself out of his own internal or external route processor.

TIP: *It is important to remember that an access list is read in the order that it is configured. Here's an analogy: Suppose you're walking down a lane in a parking lot, looking for your car. Once you find your car, you don't continue looking. Access lists work the same way—if the access list makes a match, it does not continue looking for further instructions.*

Access List Types

There are two types of access lists: *standard* and *extended*. Both types permit or deny based on certain criteria. The standard access list allows a **permit** or **deny** statement based only on the source address. The extended access list is a bit more complex—it allows you to permit or deny based on the source address, destination address, protocol type, application type, or port number of the packet.

Standard IP and IPX addresses are the easiest to configure. The configuration statement requires an access list number, a **permit** or **deny** statement, and then the source address. This statement allows packets originating from the identified

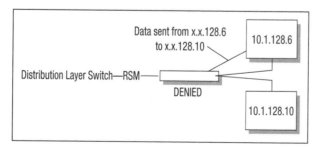

Figure 13.2   The request from x.x.128.6 to x.x.128.10 encounters an access list with no **permit** statement applied to the interface. As a result, the request is denied.

source address to be permitted or denied through the interface to which the access list is applied. Let's take a look at an example of permitting the source address from Figure 13.2 on access list 2:

```
CAT5KRSM (config)# access-list 2 permit 10.1.128.6
```

To identify a subnet in one statement, use a wildcard value after the IP address. If a wildcard value is not present, the source address must match completely. The wildcard value looks a lot like a subnet mask. A 0 in the wildcard string indicates that the value must match exactly in the same octet as the IP address; the value 255 allows any number in the corresponding octet of the IP address to be used. Let's look at the following access list string as an example:

```
access-list 2 permit 193.5.5.10 0.0.0.255 log
```

TIP: *An octet is the 8-bit value between each dotted decimal in an IP address. For the IP address of 193.5.5.10 the first octet is 193 and the fourth octet is 10. It is always important to remember which octet you want to mask.*

The 0.0.0 of the wildcard address means that the first three octets of the source interface's IP address must exactly match the first three octets of the network portion of the Class C IP address: 193.5.5. Because the last octet is 255, the last octet of the source interface of received data can be any value. This statement means that any host address with the network ID 193.5.5 will be permitted. Based on this IP scheme, you may be using variable-length subnet masks (VLSM).

To identify IP addresses that can be used within your chosen subnet mask, you must use the correct inverse address to identify those addresses. Table 13.1 shows the possible wildcard inverse addresses matched to the subnet mask.

Table 13.1 Possible wildcard inverse addresses.

Mask	Wildcard Inverse Address
255	0
254	1
252	3
248	7
240	15
224	31
192	63
128	127
0	255

There is an easy way to figure out the wildcard inverse mask for your access list or the first network available with any subnet mask. Always remember the magic number of 256, then subtract the network mask minus 1. For example, with 255.255.255.192, use the 192, subtract it from the magic number of 256, and you will get 64, which is your first network. Subtract one more and you will get the inverse wildcard mask for your access list identifying the network.

Here's another example. Say you have a class C subnet mask of 255.255.255.224. Subtract 224 from the magic number of 256 and you will get the first valid network of 32. Subtract 1 and you will get the network inverse mask of 31.

You can use the same magic number to subnet. Let's say you want to know the first and second networks of a 30-bit mask that is commonly used on point-to-point WAN links in order to conserve IP addresses. This would be a mask of 255.255.255.252. Taking the magic number of 256 and subtracting 252 we would get the number 4, which is our first valid network number. This time, instead of subtracting one, multiply by 2 and you get your second valid network, which is 8. This means that your valid hosts are 5 and 6 and your broadcast address is 7. This means we have just created a network with two hosts and wasted no IP addresses.

Let's look at another example using 255.255.255.240, which is a 28-bit mask. Table 13.2 shows the first three valid networks, the network numbers, the valid hosts for each network, and the broadcast address for each subnetted network.

Subnetting using variable length subnet masks (VLSM) seems pretty easy, doesn't it?

The type of access list defined is identified by the number you assign to the access list. Table 13.3 identifies the types of access lists that can be configured, along with the associated string of numbers that can be used with each type.

Extended access lists use many of the same configuration rules as standard access lists. An extended access list allows filtering based on source address, destination address, protocol type, application, or TCP port number.

NOTE: *Just as in standard access lists, an implied "deny all" exists at the end of each extended access list.*

The IP extended access list command is more complex than the standard access list command and offers many more options. The IP extended access list syntax is shown here:

```
access-list access-list-number {deny|permit} {protocol type}
source-address source-wildcard destination-address destination-wildcard
[protocol specific options|operator] [log]
```

Table 13.2   Example of subnetting 255.255.255.240.

Item	Network 1	Network 2	Network 3
Network	16	32	48
First Host	17	33	49
Last Host	30	46	62
Broadcast Address	31	47	63

Table 13.3   The available access list numbers and the associated access list types.

Available Numbers	Access List Type
1 through 99	IP standard
100 through 199	IP extended
200 through 299	Protocol-Type-Code
300 through 399	DECnet
600 through 699	AppleTalk
700 through 799	48-bit Media Access Control (MAC) address
800 through 899	IPX standard
900 through 999	IPX extended
1000 through 1099	IPX Service Advertising Protocol (SAP)
1100 through 1199	Extended 48-bit MAC address
1200 through 1299	IPX summary address

---

*TIP: You can use the syntax **any** as a parameter to replace the source or destination address; **any** implies all addresses. In IPX access lists, **A(n-1)** indicates an **any** syntax.*

Let's take a look at the syntax elements for the IP extended access list that are not included in the standard access list:

- *access-list-number*—For an IP extended access list, the range of possible numbers is 100 to 199.

- **deny|permit**—A **permit** indicates whether the source will be allowed in or out of an interface. A **deny** indicates that the data will be dropped and an ICMP message will be sent to the source address.

- *protocol type*—This syntax element indicates the protocol to match. Possible options include **eigrp**, **icmp**, **igrp**, **ip**, **nos**, **ospf**, **tcp**, **udp**, or any number from 0 to 255.

---

*TIP: The protocol syntax of **ip** indicates all protocol types.*

- *operator*—This syntax element compares source or destination ports. Possible syntaxes include **lt** (less than), **gt** (greater than), **eq** (equal), **neq** (not equal), and **range** (inclusive range).

- **log**—This syntax enables logging of information about packets that match access list entries.

WARNING! The log command is optional and logs information about all packets that match the access list entry. Enabling this feature uses considerable processing power. You should use it for trouble-shooting purposes only.

Let's take a look at the **any** parameter:

```
CAT5KRSM(config)# access-list 199 permit tcp 0.0.0.0 255.255.255.255
    0.0.0.0 255.255.255.255 gt 255
CAT5KRSM(config)# access-list 199 permit tcp any any gt 255
```

The first line permits any incoming IP address to any destination using any TCP port greater than port 255. The second line does the same thing, but replaces the source, destination, and wildcard addresses with the **any** command.

Now, let's examine how well-known TCP ports can work:

```
CAT5KRSM(config)# access-list 199 permit tcp any any eq 25
CAT5KRSM(config)# access-list 199 permit tcp any any eq smtp
```

The first line indicates that access list 199 permits any address to enter the interface for TCP port 25, which is the well-known TCP port for Simple Mail Transfer Protocol (SMTP). The second line does the same thing, but instead of using the TCP port number, it uses the acronym.

The **host** syntax indicates a single host, as shown in the source address in this example:

```
CAT5KRSM(config)# access-list 199 permit tcp host 38.187.128.6 any eq smtp
```

The following example permits User Datagram Protocol (UDP) packets with a DNS name as the destination:

```
CAT5KRSM(config)# access-list 199 permit udp any eq domain any
```

You can add a message in your access list by using the **remark** command. This command can help you identify lines in your access list. The following is an example of using the **remark** command:

```
CAT5KRSM(config)# access-list 1 remark Sabrina's IP Address
CAT5KRSM(config)# access-list 1 permit 18.1.12.25
CAT5KRSM(config)# access-list 1 remark Hanson's IP Address
CAT5KRSM(config)# access-list 1 deny 18.1.12.26
```

To remove a remark, use a command like the following:

```
CAT5KRSM(config)# no access-list 5 remark Sean's IP address
```

Applying Access Lists

Access lists are created in various ways. Once they're created, you can use different commands to apply an access list to various types of interfaces.

TIP: *To disallow the flow of data through any port or interface, use the **in** syntax. To allow data to flow through the switch but not exit out a certain interface or port, use the **out** syntax on the outbound interface.*

The following list shows the different commands and the types of interfaces associated with each command:

- **access-class**—Applies the access list to an interface for security purposes. This command identifies users of specified VTY lines. By default, five VTY lines come in to your Cisco Internetwork Operating System (IOS) or router. Because you do not know which one you will be using when you Telnet into your switch or router, you must apply the same access list to all the interfaces.

- **access-group**—Allows you to apply an access list configured in Global Configuration mode to an interface that can be used to filter data traffic based on source address, destination address, or many other protocol identifiers. For example, if a standard access list has been created and numbered access list 2 in Global Configuration mode and you want to deny traffic for the source address identified in the access list, use the command **ip access-group 2** followed by either **in** or **out**. The **in** or **out** syntax indicates whether data will be filtered based on traffic entering or exiting out of the interface.

- **distribute-list**—Identifies the routing update information that applies rules to allow the switch to learn new routes or advertise known routes to other routers or route processors. This is used on the (config-router) command mode when enabling a routing protocol.

- **ipx output-sap-filter**—Allows the applied access list to determine what IPX protocol services will be advertised in or out of an interface.

Applying Access Lists to Route Filtering

By controlling the routing tables at the Core layer, you can limit the size of the tables on your network devices. Doing so allows the switches to process data more quickly, prevents users from getting to networks that do not have a default or static route, and maintains routing information integrity.

To do this, apply an access list using the **distribute-list** command. After creating a standard access list, you can apply it to an inbound or outbound interface. The following is the **distribute-list** command and the syntax for an inbound interface:

```
distribute-list {access-list number|name} in [type number]
```

Here is the syntax when using the **distribute-list** command to apply an access list to an outbound interface:

```
distribute-list {access-list number|name} out
[interface name|routing process|autonomous system number]
```

Figure 13.3 shows a standard Class C network in which two subnets intersect at the Distribution layer switch. Subnet 128 belongs to a production network, and subnet 129 is used only for testing and development of new LAN topologies. We want subnet 128 to be permitted through to the Core layer on Gigabit Ethernet port g0/0, which connects to the Core layer switch. The second network is used for testing purposes only, so the access list should block any traffic from that subnet from reaching the Core layer switches. For this scenario, we will assume there are no other subnets in our switch block to contend with.

Let's create an access list that allows traffic from network 192.128.0.0 but denies traffic from interface192.129.0.0. Use the following command, keeping in mind that an implied "deny all" exists at the end of our access list:

```
access-list 2 permit 192.128.0.0 0.0.255.255
```

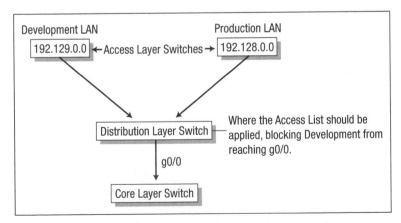

Figure 13.3   Two Class C IP subnets connected from the Access layer to the Distribution layer switch.

Next, you must specify a routing protocol: in this case, Enhanced Interior Gateway Routing Protocol (EIGRP). To do so, use the following command:

```
router eigrp 2
```

The last step is to apply the configured access list. Use the **distribute-list** command to interface g0/0 to filter outbound traffic from network 192.129.0.0:

```
distribute-list 2 out g0/0
```

Security at the Access Layer

The Access layer has very few policies to apply. The switches at this layer should rely on port-level security and passwords required on the network interfaces. The Access layer policy controls physical access to the components of the network. Physical access involves the following:

- Configuring users and passwords on the physical devices
- Limiting Telnet access
- Limiting access to network switches by implementing privilege levels
- Configuring banner messages
- Securing physical devices
- Implementing port security
- Managing VLANs

Configuring Passwords

Passwords can be configured on every access method to a Cisco Catalyst switch, by the VTY line, console, Web access, and auxiliary (AUX) ports.

Limiting Telnet Access

VTY access can be secured with a password—but when a careless administrator walks away from a logged-in Telnet session, the door is open with full access to the entire network. This situation allows anyone to access the open Telnet session and bring the network to its knees.

To lower the chances for this type of vulnerability, you may want to configure a time-out condition and apply it to unused VTY sessions. Cisco IOS calculates unused sessions in seconds or minutes, depending on the IOS version. Should the session not receive a character input from the administrator's session for the configured amount of time, the session is closed, and the administrator using the session is logged out.

Implementing Privilege Levels

Privilege levels can be assigned to limit switch users' abilities to perform certain commands or types of commands. You can configure two types of levels in the IOS: user levels and privilege levels. A *user level* allows a user to perform a subset of commands that does not allow for configuration changes or debug functions. A *privilege level*, on the other hand, allows the user to use all the available commands, including configuration change commands.

You can assign a user 16 different levels, from level 0 to level 15. Level 1 is set to User EXEC mode by default. This level gives the user very limited access, primarily to **show** commands. Level 15 defaults to the Privileged EXEC mode, which gives the user full access to all configuration commands in the IOS (including the **debug** command).

Privilege level 0 is a special level that allows the user to use a more specific defined set of commands. As an example, you could allow a certain user to use only the **show arp** command. This command is useful when a third party is using a sniffer on your network and needs to match a MAC address to an IP address and vice versa.

Configuring Banner Messages

You have probably messed around on a non-production router or switch and placed your own saying or name in a banner. In a production environment, your switch or router greets potential threats to your network with a banner message.

TIP: *Although this task seems miniscule, it is very important to your security. Many times, a hacker has gotten away with his crime and a district attorney has decided not to pursue hacking charges, because the greeting welcomed intruders into the network. Never use the word welcome in your banner messages!*

Physical Device Security

Physical access to all devices on your network should be included in your access policy. Because of all types of vulnerabilities and back doors that might be available, protecting the physical access of a machine on your network is extremely important. Any one person with physical access and the correct knowledge can easily apply known techniques on a given device and gain access. Therefore, it is important to have some physical barrier between your devices and the average user. In addition, passwords should be applied to all access points that are open via the network.

NOTE: *A proper physical environment allows for locking the room where devices are kept, locking device racks, and securing backup power sources and physical links. You should also verify that passwords are applied at all levels, and you should disable unused or unnecessary ports (including AUX ports) on your network.*

TIP: *Make sure that your room provides for proper ventilation and temperature controls while providing the listed security.*

Port Security

The Cisco IOS provides a feature called *port security* that lets you limit the MAC addresses that are allowed to use the ports on a switch. MAC addresses come pre-configured on a Network Interface Card (NIC), and because of applied industry-wide standards, no two NIC cards have the same MAC address. By configuring certain MAC addresses to use a switch port, you greatly increase control over which PCs can access the switch.

Here is how port security works: When a port on the switch receives data frames, it will compare the source MAC address to the secure source address learned by the switch. If a port receives data from a MAC address that has not yet been previously identified, the switch will lock that port and mark the port as disabled. A light on that port will then turn orange, indicating that the port has been disabled.

NOTE: *A trap link down message will automatically be sent to the SNMP manager if SNMP has been configured.*

You should know a few things before trying to apply port security:

- Do not apply port security to trunk links, because they carry data from multiple VLANs and MAC addresses.

- Port security cannot be enabled on a Switched Port Analyzer (SPAN) source or destination port.

- You cannot configure dynamic or static Content Addressable Memory (CAM) entries on a secure port.

- After you enable port security on any switch port, any static or dynamic CAM entries associated with the port are cleared, and any currently configured permanent CAM entries are treated as secure MAC addresses.

- Not all Cisco switches support port security. Check Cisco Connection Online (CCO) at **www.cisco.com** to see if your hardware and IOS version support port security.

The default settings of a switch allow all MAC addresses to access all ports on the switch. If you enable port security, immediately only those MAC addresses explicitly identified will be able to send data to the switch ports. You can configure ports with a static MAC address assignment or a dynamic MAC address assignment.

Static MAC Assignment vs. Dynamic MAC Assignment

Dynamic MAC address assignment allows the administrator to do basically nothing. Once port security is enabled, the first interface to broadcast its MAC address on the port becomes the port's secure MAC address. If another machine broadcasts a frame over the physical wire to the switch port with another MAC address, the port will automatically go into a locked-down, disabled mode.

Static MAC address assignment requires the network administrator to physically assign a MAC address to a port. This is the most secure way of creating the secure source address list, but it requires a lot of time and effort to manage. For smaller networks, this might be a good solution; but in bigger networks, it is not easily implemented.

VLAN Management

When you first provide the switch with an IOS, all the ports on the switch are assigned to VLAN1. In a typical environment, VLAN1 is also kept as the management VLAN. As a result, if the ports were not configured or were reset to their defaults, then anyone entering the network on VLAN1 would be in the management VLAN. Cisco recommends that the management VLAN be moved to a VLAN other than the default VLAN1 to prevent this type of problem.

13. Policy Networking

Immediate Solutions

Creating a Standard Access List

Here is the command used when creating an IP standard access list:

```
access-list access list number {permit|deny} source {source-mask}
```

As an example of creating an access list, let's say you want to allow an advertising company to FTP marketing material to your sales office. However, you do not want the whole world to have access to your FTP server.

To create the access list, perform the following steps:

1. Because the access list will be read in order, you first need to permit the addresses that can access the FTP server. FTP uses ports 20 and 21, so it should be configured like this:

```
HSNRSM(config)# access-list 100 permit tcp 192.5.5.0 0.0.0.255
    any eq 20
HSNRSM(config)# access-list 100 permit tcp 192.5.5.0 0.0.0.255
    any eq 21
```

2. The following commands will deny all the other traffic on ports 20 and 21:

```
HSNRSM(config)# access-list 100 deny tcp any any eq 20
HSNRSM(config)# access-list 100 deny tcp any any eq 21
```

3. Because the access list has an implied "deny all" at the end, you need to apply a rule that any other traffic can pass through. The **ip** indicates that all IP protocols are being identified:

```
HSNRSM(config)# access-list 100 permit ip any any
```

You do not want to apply the access list to an outbound interface, because then the FTP packets would span the switch fabric and use up bandwidth and processing power. You want to apply the access list immediately to the inbound interface to the company's Distribution layer switch.

To apply the access lists to an interface, follow these steps:

1. Access the interface to be configured. In this case, from Global Configuration mode, use the following command:

```
interface fastethernet0/0
```

2. Apply the access list to the interface to block access to inbound packets using the following command:

```
ip access-group 100 in
```

Unless the packets for FTP are coming from the advertising company, no one else will be able to access your FTP server.

Related solutions:	Found on page:
Opening a Session on an Internal Route Processor	381
Entering Configuration Mode on an RSM	381

Creating an Extended Access List

Creating an extended access list is very similar to creating a standard access list, but the options are more complex and can become quite lengthy. We suggest writing out your extended access list beforehand and then implementing it. Here's the syntax an Extended Access List can require for configuration:

```
access-list access-list-number {deny|permit} {protocol type}
source-address source-wildcard destination-address
destination-wildcard [protocol specific options|operator] [log]
```

Let's step through creating an extended access list that can be applied to an interface and deny any host on network 172.16.10.0 from going to any host on network 172.15.10.0. It will also deny ports 80, 23, 21, and 20. This will effectively disallow any access to World Wide Web services, Telnet, and FTP. Let's look at all the options:

1. For an extended access list we must identify an access list number between 100 and 199:

```
CoriolisRSM1(config)#access-list 199 ?
  deny      Specify packets to reject
  dynamic   Specify a DYNAMIC list of PERMITs or DENYs
  permit    Specify packets to forward
```

2. We must then choose who to deny. We are using TCP instead of IP so we can just identify the ports we want to deny. The first IP address identifies the network. The 0.0.0 identifies that the first three octets must be the same and the .255 identifies all the hosts in the last octet:

```
CoriolisRSM1(config)#access-list 199 deny tcp 172.16.10.0 0.0.0.255 ?
  A.B.C.D  Destination address
  any      Any destination host
  eq       Match only packets on a given port number
  gt       Match only packets with a greater port number
  host     A single destination host
  lt       Match only packets with a lower port number
  neq      Match only packets not on a given port number
  range    Match only packets in the range of port numbers
```

3. Now do the same for the destination address identifying the destination of 172.15.10.0:

```
CoriolisRSM1(config)# access-list 199 deny tcp 172.16.10.0 0.0.0.255
172.15.10.0 0.0.0.255 ?
  ack          Match on the ACK bit
  eq           Match only packets on a given port number
  established  Match established connections
  fin          Match on the FIN bit
  gt           Match only packets with a greater port number
  log          Log matches against this entry
  log-input    Log matches against this entry, including input interface
  lt           Match only packets with a lower port number
  neq          Match only packets not on a given port number
  precedence   Match packets with given precedence value
  psh          Match on the PSH bit
  range        Match only packets in the range of port numbers
  rst          Match on the RST bit
  syn          Match on the SYN bit
  tos          Match packets with given TOS value
  urg          Match on the URG bit
```

4. Now enter "eq" for equal to, and then identify the port numbers. Use a separate statement for each port number:

```
CoriolisRSM1(config)# access-list 199 deny tcp 172.16.10.0 0.0.0.255
    172.15.10.0 0.0.0.255 eq 80
CoriolisRSM1(config)# access-list 199 deny tcp 172.16.10.0 0.0.0.255
    172.15.10.0 0.0.0.255 eq 23
CoriolisRSM1(config)# access-list 199 deny tcp 172.16.10.0 0.0.0.255
    172.15.10.0 0.0.0.255 eq 21
CoriolisRSM1(config)# access-list 199 deny tcp 172.16.10.0 0.0.0.255
    172.15.10.0 0.0.0.255 eq 20
```

5. Now we have to identify addresses to permit or we will have effectively shut down the interface. Remember, there is an implicit "deny all" at the end of any access list:

```
CoriolisRSM1(config)#access-list 199 permit ?
  <0-255>  An IP protocol number
  ahp      Authentication Header Protocol
  eigrp    Cisco's EIGRP routing protocol
  esp      Encapsulation Security Payload
  gre      Cisco's GRE tunneling
  icmp     Internet Control Message Protocol
  igmp     Internet Gateway Message Protocol
  igrp     Cisco's IGRP routing protocol
  ip       Any Internet Protocol
  ipinip   IP in IP tunneling
  nos      KA9Q NOS compatible IP over IP tunneling
  ospf     OSPF routing protocol
  pcp      Payload Compression Protocol
  pim      Protocol Independent Multicast
  tcp      Transmission Control Protocol
  udp      User Datagram Protocol
```

6. We have to use the **ip** syntax, which means all IP protocols. If we only used the **tcp** syntax, we would only permit TCP ports:

```
CoriolisRSM1(config)#access-list 199 permit ip ?
  A.B.C.D  Source address
  any      Any source host
  host     A single source host
```

7. Since we want to identify everything else that can pass through the interface, we need to use the **any** syntax and identify the source address. You can identify a single host by using the **host** syntax followed by the IP address:

13. Policy Networking

```
CoriolisRSM1(config)#access-list 199 permit ip any ?
  A.B.C.D  Destination address
  any      Any destination host
  host     A single destination host
```

8. Just as in Step 7, we need to identify the destination addresses to permit:

```
CoriolisRSM1(config)#access-list 199 permit ip any any
CoriolisRSM1(config)#
```

You're not quite done yet. Even though you just created an access list, it still has to be applied to an interface before it will function.

Applying Access Lists Using **access-class**

Let's create an access list that allows Telnet access to the switch from the IP address 192.151.52.19 (this is the IP address of the only PC that will be used to Telnet into your switch). To do this, use the following command:

```
CAT5KRSM(config)# access-list 5 permit 192.151.52.19
```

Next, you need to enter Line Configuration mode for all five VTY lines with the following command:

```
CAT5KRSM (config)# line vty 0 4
CAT5KRSM (config-line)#
```

Finally, use the **access-class** command to apply the access list to an inbound interface with the following command:

```
CAT5KRSM(config-line)# access-class 5 in
```

Applying Access Lists Using **distribute-list**

To apply an access list using the **distribute-list** command, you need to have created a standard access list. Once your access list is configured, you can apply it to an inbound or outbound interface. Here is the syntax when using the **distribute-list** command to apply an access list to an outbound interface:

```
distribute-list {access-list number|name} out
[interface name|routing process|autonomous system number]
```

Let's say you have an access list that will allow network traffic from network 192.1.1.0 but denies traffic from interface 192.2.1.0. Do not forget that an implied "deny all" is attached to the access list:

```
access-list 1 permit 192.1.1.0 0.0.0.255
```

To use a distribution-list command you must also specify a routing protocol to use. In this case we will use OSPF:

```
router ospf 1
```

To apply the access list using the **distribute-list** command, you must attach the access list to the outbound interface you wish to filter. Let's say for this example it is Fast Ethernet port 0/0. Here is what you command might look like:

```
distribute-list 1 out fastethernet0/0
```

Configuring a Telnet Session Time-Out Value

To lower the chances for vulnerability when an administrator walks away from a logged-in Telnet session, you can configure and apply a time-out condition to unused VTY sessions. Here's how:

```
HSNRSM (config)# line vty 0 4
HSNRSM (config-line)# exec-timeout 5 0
```

We just set the timeout value to five minutes and zero seconds.

Related solution:	Found on page:
Configuring Telnet	67

Implementing Privilege Levels on a 1900EN

To assign a user a privilege level and a defined set of commands you first need to select a user and associate that user with a privilege level. To do this, use the following command in Global Configuration mode:

```
1900EN(config)# privilege configure level 3 password
```

You should assign a password for each configured privilege level. To assign the password brad1 to privilege level 3, use the following command:

```
1900EN (config)# enable secret level 3 brad1
```

When Brad wants to log in to the switch, he will use the following command:

```
1900EN (config)# username blarson password brad1
```

This setup allows the user blarson to use certain **show** commands by default, but gives him no access to the **debug** or configuration commands.

To allow the user to use all the **debug** commands in privilege level 3, use the following command:

```
1900EN (config)# privilege exec level 3 debug
```

To allow users with a privilege level 3 to use only a certain command syntax for **debug**, such as **debug ip**, use the following command:

```
1900EN (config)#  privilege exec level 3 debug ip
```

NOTE: *Privilege level 0 includes five commands associated with the privilege level:* ***disable, enable, exit, help,*** *and* ***logout***.

Configuring Line Console Time-Out Values

To configure a time-out value, use the following command. The time-out value is being set to five minutes, measured in seconds:

```
hsn(config)# line console
hsn(config)# time-out 300
```

TIP: *You can use the* ***lock*** *command to lock an unused Telnet session. After you issue the* ***lock*** *command, the system will ask you to enter and verify an unlocking password.*

To configure a Set/Clear command-based switch with a time-out value of five minutes, use the following command:

```
hsn# set logout 5
```

To configure the time-out value to five minutes on the console port of an IOS-based route processor or router, use the following command:

```
HSNRSM (config)# line console 0
HSNRSM (config-line)# exec-timeout 5
```

To configure the time-out value to five minutes on the VTY port of an IOS-based route processor or router, use the following command:

```
HSNRSM (config)# line vty 0 4
HSNRSM (config-line)# exec-timeout 5
```

TIP: *To configure seconds beyond a round number of minutes, you can add an additional value to the command. For example, if you want the **exec-timeout** to be 5 minutes and 10 seconds, the command is **exec-timeout 5 10**.*

Configuring Banner Messages

To configure a Message Of The Day (MOTD) banner on a Set/Clear command-based switch, use the following command from a Privileged mode prompt:

```
CAT5K(enable) set banner motd 'We Prosecute Unauthorized Access!'
```

To configure a MOTD banner on a Cisco IOS command-based switch or route processor, use the following command from a Global Configuration mode prompt:

```
1912EN(config)# banner login 'We Prosecute Unauthorized Access!'
```

Enabling HTTP Access

Starting with the release of version 11.0(6) of the Cisco IOS, Cisco included HTTP server software, which allows you manage the Cisco IOS from a Web browser. This software makes managing your switches easier—but opens one giant security hole.

By default, access through HTTP is disabled. To enable access through HTTP, use the following command:

```
CAT5KRSM(config)# ip http server
```

An access list can be configured to allow you to choose the IP address of the network device that can be used to access the switch. For example, use the following command to allow a PC with the IP address 15.47.112.10 for access list 2:

```
CAT5KRSM(config)# access-list 2 permit 15.47.112.10
```

Suppose this is the only statement in the access list. Because of the implied "deny all," once this access list is applied, only a PC with IP address 15.47.112.10 will be able to manage the switch. Before this filter will work, however, you must still apply the access list, state the authentication type, and configure the username and password. To apply the access list, use the following command:

```
CAT5KRSM(config)# ip http access-class 2
```

You can apply four types of authentication to HTTP access on a switch or router. Table 13.4 describes each of the four types of authentication.

To apply the authentication type, use the following command:

```
CAT5KRSM(config)# ip http authentication local
```

NOTE: To disable the configured authentication type, use the **no ip authentication** command.

To configure the username hsn with the password team, use the following command:

```
CAT5KRSM(config)# username hsn password team
```

You can provide an additional layer of protection when using Cisco's IOS ClickStart software or the Cisco Web browser interface. To do so, change the default TCP access port 80 to port 50, or any port you plan to use. To set the TCP port to 50, use the following command:

```
CAT5KRSM(config)# ip http port 50
```

Table 13.4   The four HTTP authentication types for a switch route processor or router.

Syntax	Description
aaa	Allows authentication, authorization, and accounting (AAA) to be used for authentication
enable	Allows the enable password method; the default method of HTTP server user authentication
local	Allows the local user database on the Cisco router, route processor, or access server to be used for authentication
tacacs	Allows the Terminal Area Security Access Control (TACACS) or Extended TACACS (XTACACS) server to be used for authentication

You can reset the HTTP TCP port to its default by using the following command:

```
CAT5KRSM(config)# no ip http 50
```

Enabling Port Security

To enable dynamic port security on a Set/Clear command-based switch for module 3 port 3, use the following command:

```
CAT5K>(enable) set port security 3/3 enable
Port 3/3 port security enabled with the learned mac address.
Trunking disabled for Port 3/3 due to Security Mode
```

To show a port configuration for port security, use the following **show** command:

```
CAT5K> (enable) show port 3/3
```

The output should look similar to this:

```
Port  Name              Status      Vlan  Level  Duplex Speed Type
----  ----------------  ----------  ----  ------ ------ ----  ----------
3/3                     connected   2     normal half   100   100BaseTX


Port Security Secure-Src-Addr   Last-Src-Addr     Shutdown Trap IfIndex
---- -------- ----------------  ----------------  -------- ---- ------
3/3  enabled  00-15-20-4c-78-a1 00-15-20-4c-78-a1


Port     Broadcast-Limit Broadcast-Drop
-------- --------------- --------------
3/3                    -              0


Port  Align-Err  FCS-Err    Xmit-Err   Rcv-Err    UnderSize
----  ---------- ---------- ---------- ---------- --------
3/3            0          0          0          0          0


Port Single-Col Multi-Coll Late-Coll Excess-Col Carri-Sen Runts Giants
---- ---------- ---------- -------- ---------- -------- ---- ------
3/3           0          0        0          0        0    0      0


Last-Time-Cleared
-------------------------
Fri Dec 22 2000, 19:53:38
```

To enable static port security for module 1 port 3, manually specify the secure MAC address of the attached interface 00-15-20-4c-78-a1 using the following command:

```
CAT5K> (enable) set port security 3/1 enable 00-15-20-4c-78-a1
Port 3/1 port security enabled with 00-15-20-4c-78-a1
  as the secure mac address
CAT5K> (enable)
```

On a Cisco IOS command-based switch, you can use the **port secure** interface configuration command to enable addressing security. In Interface Configuration mode, to assign a port to allow only one MAC address, use the following command:

```
2924XL(config-if)# port secure max-mac-count 1
```

TIP: You can assign **max-mac-count** a value between 1 and 132.

Displaying the MAC Address Table

Use the **show mac-address-table** command from Privileged EXEC Mode to display the MAC address table. Here is the command and syntax placement—Table 13.5 contains a description of each syntax element:

```
show mac-address-table [static|dynamic|secure|self|
   aging-time|count]
[address hw-addr] [interface interface] [atm slot/port][vlan vlan-id]
```

Table 13.5   The show mac-address-table command's optional syntax descriptions.

Syntax	Description
static	Displays the static addresses
dynamic	Displays the dynamic addresses
secure	Displays the secure addresses
self	Displays addresses added by the switch itself
aging-time	Displays aging-time for dynamic addresses for all VLANs
count	Displays a count for different kinds of MAC addresses
address	Displays information for a specific MAC address
hw-addr	Displays information for the given MAC address
interface	Displays addresses for the specific port
atm	Adds dynamic addresses to an ATM module slot/port

(continued)

Table 13.5 The show mac-address-table command's optional syntax descriptions (continued).

Syntax	Description
slot	Associates the dynamic address with a slot (1 or 2) port
port	Adds dynamic addresses to a port (the port number is always 0 for ATM interfaces)
vlan	Displays addresses for a specified VLAN
vlan-id	Displays addresses for the VLAN

The output from the **show mac-address-table** command should look like the following:

```
Dynamic Addresses Count:                5
Secure Addresses (User-defined) Count:  0
Static Addresses (User-defined) Count:  0
System Self Addresses Count:            12
Total MAC addresses:                    8

Non-static Address Table:

Destination Address   Address Type   VLAN   Destination Port
------------------    ------------   ----   -------------------
00-15-20-5c-80-a1     Dynamic          3    FastEthernet0/6
00-15-20-5c-80-a1     Dynamic          1    FastEthernet0/4
00-15-20-5c-80-b4     Dynamic          1    FastEthernet0/4
00-15-20-5c-80-12     Dynamic          3    FastEthernet0/6
00-15-20-5c-80-c5     Dynamic          3    FastEthernet0/6
```

TIP: You can use the **no port secure** command to disable addressing security or to set the maximum number of addresses allowed on the interface to the default value of 132.

13. Policy Networking

Chapter 14

Web Management

In Depth

Imagine having to manage all the com closets throughout your enterprise without the use of a remote management tool. It's a scary thought. What if you were in San Francisco and you needed to reconfigure a switch in Atlanta? Yes, Telnet would work, but Cisco also has a Web-based client management tool that is second to none: Cisco Visual Switch Manager (CVSM). The GUI interface helps make remote network management easier and less time consuming.

Standard and Enterprise Edition CVSM

Cisco Catalyst 1900 and 2820 series Ethernet switches both include the CVSM. However, if you are using the Standard Edition and you upgrade to the Enterprise Edition IOS, you will see a difference in the CVSM. The Standard Edition is designed to work out of the box; it simply connects desktops to its switch and then to high-speed network backbones. The Enterprise Edition, however, adds scalability. For example, when you're using the Standard Edition IOS, you can only join an existing switch cluster. If you're using an Enterprise Edition IOS, you can join and manage a clustered switch environment. This is just one example of the many differences between the two editions. The upgrade kits to the Enterprise Edition for the Catalyst 1900/2820 series switches are as follows:

- *Enterprise Edition Upgrade Kit*—WS-C19/28EEUG

- *Enterprise Edition Upgrade Kit, 10-pack*—WS-C19/28UG10

All Catalyst 1900 and 2820 series switches offer an intuitive and comprehensive Web-based management interface. The subtle differences between the two versions are that the Enterprise Edition software enables these switches to manage more complex networks when using the CVSM. It does this by integrating advanced features and more comprehensive switch management tools, such as options to manage Network Time Protocol, port spanning, and port grouping to ease enterprise switch management. The Enterprise Edition IOS is always preinstalled on Enterprise Edition switches, so no upgrade is needed.

CVSM Client Requirements

Let's look at the characteristics and functionality that are available using CVSM, how to perform these functions, what you need to get started, and various tips to better secure your CVSM environment.

The CVSM supports four OS platforms: Windows 95 (with Service Pack 1 update), Windows 98 (Second Edition), Windows NT 4 (with Service Pack 3 update), and Solaris 2.5.1 or higher (Cisco also recommends applying the Motif library patch 103461-24 found at **www.sun.com**). Cisco suggests the following hardware minimums for optimal system and Web site performance:

- *Windows-based system*—Pentium 166MHz, 64MB RAM, small fonts

- *SunOS 5.6 system*—SunUltra 1, 64MB RAM, small fonts

Cisco recommends using either Internet Explorer (IE) or Netscape Communicator as your browser. The following versions are supported:

- IE 4.01a, 5.0 (40- and 128-bit versions)

- Netscape Communicator 4.5, 4.51, and 4.611

IE is not supported on Solaris, and Netscape 4.6 is not supported at all. However, you can try to access the switch through your browser to determine whether your browser version is supported. If your browser is not supported, the switch will display an error message, and the session will not complete.

TIP: *IE 5.0 will automatically refresh with the latest real-time port configuration changes. For example, if you are logged on and you add an additional device to one of the switch's Ethernet ports, the CVSM will update your currently logged-on session with the port changes (this update takes 15 or 16 seconds). However, if you make a change from half duplex to full duplex in the Ports table, you must click on the browser's Refresh button to see the latest configuration changes. Finally, wait at least one minute before you turn off your switch, so the configuration changes will be saved to the switch's startup-config file (1900 and 2820 only).*

CVSM Access Levels

Once you are on your switch, you can configure privilege levels for users; you can grant up to 15 different user access levels. You can use these accounts and access levels for users to log on to the CVSM. The privilege access levels boil down to three types: User EXEC mode (level 1), Privileged EXEC mode (level 3), and Full Access (set by specifying 15). When configuring the accounts you can define passwords as well, as shown here:

```
enable password [level]{password}
enable secret [level]{password}
```

Level 1 specifies normal User EXEC mode privileges. When no level is specified, the privilege level defaults to Level 15.

NOTE: *It's important to remember that to access the CVSM for management from a Web browser, the switch will need to have a Full Access (level 15) password, an IP address, and the default gateway configured if the switch resides on another network segment.*

Once the accounts have been configured and you have logged on to the switch successfully, the default home page will be displayed.

CVSM Default Home Page

The CVSM uses standard Hypertext Transfer Protocol (HTTP) to access the switch's built-in Web server. After a connection is made through one of the switch's Ethernet ports, the embedded Web server (which resides in Flash memory) begins to initialize a session between it and the client. The CVSM home page will then be displayed, and a dialog box appears, requesting an account and password before you can log on. After you have successfully logged on, an image of your switch will appear; colored LEDs reflect your switch's current status by port. You can click on each port and configure it from there.

CVSM is a Web-based device-management tool for monitoring your switch, as well as managing its configuration. Because the switch is already configured, the CVSM allows you to view the current settings (the running-config file) the switch is using. You can change the configuration at will through its various settings, either by entering information in fields, adding and removing list items, or selecting checkboxes.

TIP: *The Cisco Catalyst 1900 Web Switch Manager uses JavaScript and frames. Be sure you have JavaScript enabled and that your browser fully supports the use of frames.*

When you are configuring your switch via the CVSM and entering information in the various fields, the changes become part of the running (current) configuration when you click on Apply. If you make a mistake and want to retype an entry, click on Cancel to undo your first entry.

NOTE: *Again, keep in mind that if you are using IE5, you must use the Refresh button in your browser after each configuration change to see the updates. Otherwise, you risk making a mistake down the line.*

The CVSM default home page also has a real-time display of your switch. As we mentioned earlier, each port has a colored LED display associated with it. Let's look at what these LEDs represent, because they correlate with the port's configuration.

The Switch Image

Each port on the switch image has an LED above it. The following LEDs, as a group or individually, display information about the switch and its individual ports:

- *Port Status (STAT)*—The default view of the switch image. It focuses on the actual status of the individual ports.

- *Bandwidth Utilization (UTL)*—The percentage of the switch's total bandwidth that is being used at any given time.

- *Full-Duplex Operation (FDUP)*—Which ports are operating in half- or full-duplex mode.

When you click on the Mode button on the switch image's home page, you will change the currently selected mode and the port LEDs. The LEDs change because they are related and work in conjunction with the mode that is selected. By default, when STAT is selected, it shows the current port status; using UTL displays the overall switch utilization; and FDUP displays which ports are configured and/or connected at full duplex. The LED is green for whatever mode has been selected and once the selected mode has been active for about 30 seconds, the switch will return to its default mode, illuminating the STAT LED. You can change the default mode by using the Console Settings menu on the management console.

On the top left side of the switch you will find another LED—System. The System LED's colors indicates the following:

- *Solid amber*—The switch is receiving power but is not functioning properly. One or more power on self tests (POSTs) have failed. The management console logon screen displays the failure.

- *Solid green*—The switch is operating as designed.

The Redundant Power Supply (RPS) LED's color means the following:

- *Solid green*—RPS is operational.

- *Blinking green*—AC power is on and RPS is up.

- *Black (off)*—RPS is off.

- *Solid amber*—RPS is connected but not working properly. A power supply in the RPS may have powered down, or the fan on the RPS is out.

The STAT LED's color indicates the following:

- *Solid amber*—The specified port is not forwarding packets. The port could be administratively disabled, disabled because of an address violation, or suspended by the Spanning-Tree Protocol (STP) because of network-related loops.

- *Alternating green and amber*—A problem exists, which may be due to any of the following: a link fault, error frames (which can cause connectivity issues), collisions, or cyclic redundancy checks (CRCs).

- *Black*—No link exists.

- *Solid green*—The link is operational.

In the Immediate Solutions section we'll walk through configuring the IP address and the Web CVSM configuration settings on the Standard Edition IOS. If you are using the command line interface, refer to Chapter 2, which explains how to configure the CLI for an IP address and a Level 15 password in order to use the CVSM. The last section of the Immediate Solutions section will walk you through the CVSM Web Management screens on the 1900 series switch, looking at each screen individually and identifying the configuration changes that can be made from each screen.

14. Web Management

Immediate Solutions

Configuring the Switch with an IP Address and Setting the Default Web Administration Port

When a switch is first plugged in and finishes initializing, no IP address is configured. You do not have to configure an IP address, but having one in place will help you manage your switch.

Follow these steps to set an IP address and identify the TCP port to be used. (These steps assume that a password has been configured on the switch.)

1. From the Main Menu on your Catalyst 1900, select [N] for Network Management.

2. At the Network Management Console, select [I] for IP Configuration.

3. Verify your address; or, if you do not have one, enter one at this point. Here's what you should see:

```
Catalyst 1900 - IP Configuration
Ethernet Address:  00-B0-64-75-65-40
--------------------- Settings -------------------------------------
[I] IP address                          192.1.2.1
[S] Subnet mask                         255.255.255.0
[G] Default gateway                     0.0.0.0
[V] Management VLAN                      1
[M] IP address of DNS server 1          0.0.0.0
[N] IP address of DNS server 2          0.0.0.0
[D] Domain name
[R] Use Routing Information Protocol     Enabled
--------------------- Actions --------------------------------------
[P] Ping
[C] Clear cached DNS entries
[X] Exit to previous menu
Enter Selection:
```

4. Once your IP configuration is set, back out to the Network Management menu.

5. Select [H] for HTTP Server Configuration. Notice that the default port is port 80. To reduce intrusion possibilities, we suggest using another port.

TIP: *Keep in mind that although port 443 is a very common port for HTTP-encrypted transmissions, in this case it is only a port—it is not secured at all.*

---

6. The HTTP server listens by default on TCP port 80 as seen here:

```
Catalyst 1900 - HTTP Server Configuration
---------- Settings ----------------
   [H] HTTP            Enabled
   [P] HTTP Port       80

   [X] Exit to previous menu

Enter Selection:  P
```

However, it can be configured to listen on any other user-defined port. Port 23 can't be used because it is reserved for Telnet. To change the default port, select [P] from the HTTP Server Configuration menu. Here is an example of changing the default HTTP port:

```
Enter HTTP port  (0 to 65535):
Current setting ===>   80
    New setting ===>   1024
```

We have now changed the HTTP port to 1024. You should use a numbering scheme that your department or organization believes to be the best.

Related solutions:	Found on page:
Configuring an IP Address and Netmask	57
Configuring Network Settings on the 1900 and 2820 Series	456

Connecting to the Web Management Console

Now that your port is configured and HTTP is enabled, you can connect to the Web Management Console. From any browser or address bar, type the address of your switch and the corresponding port number. For this example, the port number is 1024, and the URL should look something like **http://192.1.2.1:1024**.

NOTE: *You can connect by hostname and port (e.g. http://cat1900.xyz.com:1024) if DNS is configured on your network. However, keep in mind that in times of network troubleshooting, it's better to use native IP instead of DNS resolution.*

Once you enter your URL, you'll be prompted for an account and password. When you enter the password with no account specified, the switch will validate your password and redirect you to the Switch Manager Basic System Configuration Page shown in Figure 14.1.

Take some time to get to know what the Switch Manager has to offer. Beginning from the top, from left to right, you have the following options:

NOTE: *This list covers only the options located at the top of the frame. The left frame remains the same throughout the CVSM session.*

- *HOME*—The Basic System Configuration page and the page you are currently on.
- *PORT*—The Port Management page. This page allows you to configure every aspect of a switch port—the port's linkbeat, type of cast (uni- or multi-), congestion control, port name and/or description, and statistics. The page is shown in Figure 14.2.
- *ADDRESS*—The Address Table Management page. This page manages the Dynamic Address Table, the Permanent Unicast Address and Port Security Table, and the Multicast Address Table. Figure 14.3 shows an example.

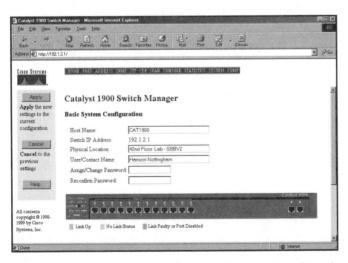

Figure 14.1   The home page of the Web Management Console.

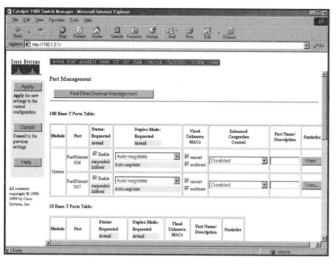

Figure 14.2   This page allows you the ability to configure port speeds, view statistics, name the ports, and manage various switch modules if they have been inserted into the switch.

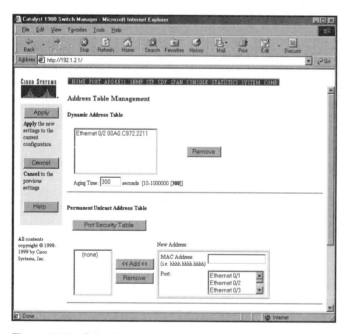

Figure 14.3   From here you can view and manage dynamic addresses and unicast and multicast tables.

- *SNMP*—The SNMP Management page. This page lets you manage and define where to send the SNMP information and who has read or write access to the SNMP information traps. Figure 14.4 shows this page.

- *STP*—The Spanning Tree Management page. This management page allows you to enable or disable STP on the specific switch ports, modify various Spanning Tree parameters, and configure STP. Among other things, you can set the path cost, priority, and port fast mode. For an example, see Figure 14.5.

- *CDP*—The CDP Management page. This page lists all the devices that have Cisco Discovery Protocol (CDP) enabled. You can browse them, access them by Telnet, and retrieve further details on the selected device. Figure 14.6 shows an example.

- *SPAN*—The SPAN Configuration and Port Monitoring page. Here you have the option of selecting the port to which you want to send the captured frames and the ports to be monitored. See Figure 14.7.

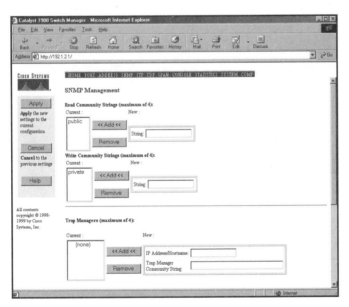

Figure 14.4   This page allows you to configure the SNMP properties, such as the community settings, and identify the IP address for the trap messages to be sent to.

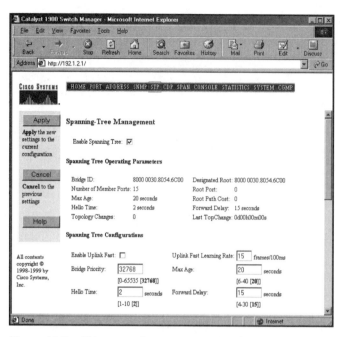

Figure 14.5   This page gives you more details and options for configuring STP.

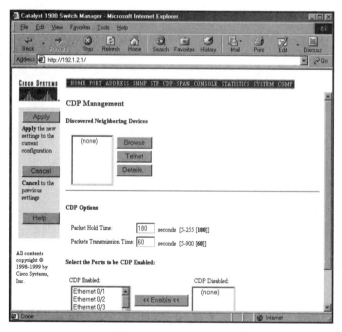

Figure 14.6   The CDP Management page allows you to choose which ports you want defined for CDP.

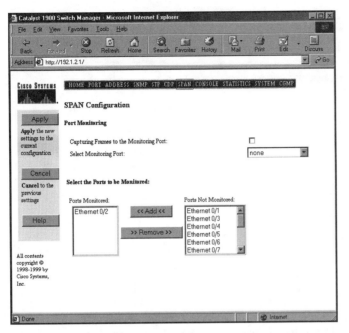

Figure 14.7   This page allows you to configure which ports to monitor and where they are monitored from.

- *CONSOLE*—The Console and Upgrade Configuration page. As you can see in Figure 14.8, this page is self explanatory. However, we wanted to bring to your attention the Accept Upgrade Transfer From Other Hosts option; it may be a vulnerability if you leave it selected.

NOTE: *Prior to a TFTP upgrade a dialog box will appear and say something like, "When you use this page to upgrade the switch, it may not respond for up to one minute. During this time do not unplug the switch. This behavior is normal." Once you click on OK, another dialog box will pop open and ask you, Do you wish to continue with the upgrade process?*

- *STATISTICS*—The Statistics Reports page. Here you can reset individual statistics or all statistics captured on each port. Figure 14.9 shows an example.
- *SYSTEM*—The System Management and Broadcast Storm Control page. This page is very much like the Main Menu accessed via the console port. Options include IP configuration, Mask, Domain Name, Gateway, DNS 1 and 2, RIP, Switching mode, and so on. See Figure 14.10.

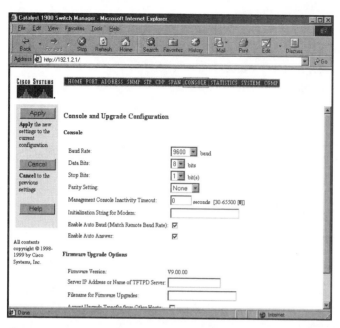

Figure 14.8   This page allows you to manage the console and firmware upgrades.

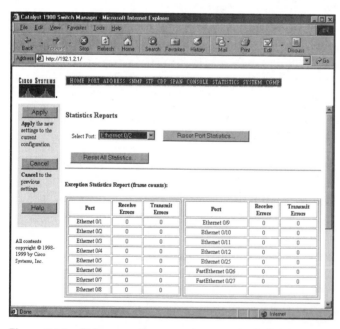

Figure 14.9   This page allows you to reset the individual ports or all ports on the switch. You can also view various receiving and forwarding information.

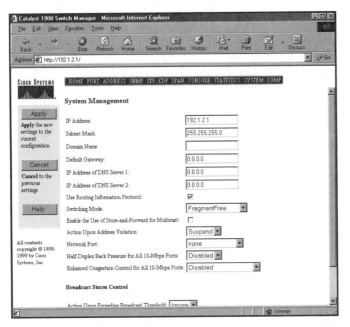

Figure 14.10   On this page you can control and manage broadcast storms and overall IP configuration of the switch.

14. Web Management

- *CGMP*—The CGMP Management page. By default, CGMP is enabled. This page allows you to configure the use of CGMP to dynamically discover end-user stations participating in multicast applications. In short, CGMP directs the packet to its destination rather than broadcasting the packet throughout the network. Figure 14.11 shows an example of the page.

Configuring the Switch Port Analyzer

You can configure the Switch Port Analyzer (SPAN) using the Web Management Console. When you implement switches, it is hard to see how the traffic flows in your network, because switches break up your broadcast and collision domains. This means that where you used to be able to connect a sniffer to a hub port to view the traffic and get statistics about the entire network segment, you no longer can with switches. SPAN allows you to connect a management device to a switch port and direct a replication of the traffic flowing in and out of the switch interfaces from either all the interfaces on the switch or those that you

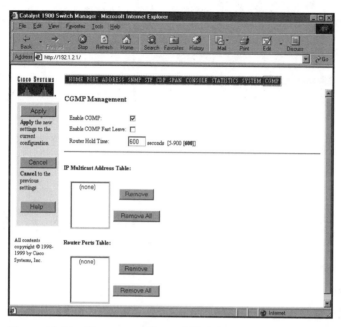

Figure 14.11   You can configure CGMP from this page.

identify to the interface connected to the management device. Follow these steps to configure SPAN:

1. To configure the SPAN via the Web Management Console, log on and go to the SPAN Configuration page (see Figure 14.7).

2. Click on the ports you want to monitor in the Ports Not Monitored window. Click on the Add button to move them to the Ports Monitored Window.

3. Select the port you wish to monitor from by choosing from the pull-down menu next to Select Monitoring Port. This port will usually be one of the trunk ports.

Related solution:	Found on page:
Enabling SNMP Contact	58

Chapter 15

The Standard Edition IOS

In Depth

The Cisco 1900 and 2820 switches come with two unique IOSs: Standard Edition and Enterprise Edition. The Standard Edition is a character-based IOS, and the Enterprise Edition is similar to the IOS on higher-end routers. The Cisco 3000 series is the only series of switches that comes with a unique IOS; this series offers a graphical user interface (GUI) to configure the switch. In this chapter, we will focus on the setup of the Standard Edition IOS in detail.

The 1900 and 2820 Series Switches

The Catalyst 1900 series switches are Cisco's entry point into Access layer managed switches. These switches are the only two that work at the Access layer; they can provide up to two 100BaseT or 100BaseFX uplink ports and up to twenty-four 10BaseT ports. The Catalyst 1900 is available in two models: the Standard Edition (SE) and the Enterprise Edition (EE).

The Standard Edition is a low-cost alternative for those migrating from a shared hub environment to a smaller workgroup environment. These switches were specifically designed to be plug-and-play right out of the box with no manual configuration. The Catalyst 1900 SE has 12 or 24 fixed 10BaseT ports with 2 high-speed 100BaseT, or one 100BaseT and one 100BaseFX ports. The Catalyst 1900 switch can be configured using the console port, its Web interface, or Cisco's Visual Switch Manager. Included in the Standard Edition is support for Domain Name Service (DNS) and Dynamic Host Control Protocol (DHCP) to help with ease of host management. The Standard Edition can be upgraded via the Flash to the Enterprise Edition.

The Enterprise Edition offers the features of the Standard Edition but also provides several high-end solutions. These include Fast EtherChannel, support for Dynamic Inter-Switch Link (DISL), an IOS Command Line Interface (CLI), and support for Cisco Group Management Protocol (CGMP).

The Catalyst 2820 series switch architecture is virtually identical to that of the Cisco Catalyst 1900 series switches. The switch is different because of its height and its uplink bays, which allow for high-speed uplink options such as Fiber Distributed Data Interface (FDDI), Copper Distributed Data Interface (CDDI), 100Mbps, and Asynchronous Transfer Mode (ATM) modules.

In this chapter, we will concentrate on the configuration of the Standard Edition IOS rather than the switch specifications for the 1900 and 2820 series switches.

NOTE: *The Catalyst 2820 series routers have been issued an End-of-Life (EOL) notice. This notice means the 2820 is no longer manufactured by Cisco. However, you still need to know how to configure these routers because they still exist in today's networks.*

Now, let's take a look at the menu-driven interface and how to configure the basics on a Standard Edition IOS on the Cisco Catalyst 1900 and 2820 series.

Main Menu Choices

When you log on to the 1900 switch you are presented with a Main Menu that looks similar to the following:

```
Catalyst 1900 - Main Menu

    [C] Console Settings
    [S] System
    [N] Network Management
    [P] Port Configuration
    [A] Port Addressing
    [D] Port Statistics Detail
    [M] Monitor
    [V] Virtual LAN
    [R] Multicast Registration
    [F] Firmware
    [I] RS-232 Interface
    [U] Usage Summaries
    [H] Help
    [K] Command Line

    [X] Exit Management Console

Enter Selection:
```

The following sections describe the Main Menu options. By typing the letter associated with each command on the Main Menu, you enter that configuration screen.

[C] Console Settings

The following shows the Console Settings menu on the Cisco Catalyst 1900 series:

```
Catalyst 1900 - Console Settings

          -------------------Settings-----------------
          [P] Password intrusion threshold         3 attempt(s)
          [S] Silent time upon intrusion detection None
          [T] Management Console inactivity timeout None
          [D] Default mode of status LED           Port Status


          ------------------Actions----------------
          [M] Modify password
          [E] Modify secret password

          [X] Exit to Main Menu

Enter Selection:
```

Here is what you'll see when you select the following settings:

- *[P] Password intrusion threshold*—This will limit the number of failed logon attempts and render the Management Console frozen for a predefined amount of time before allowing the next logon. This value may range from 0 to 65500 attempts. If you choose not to use a threshold, you should specify zero.

- *[S] Silent time upon intrusion detection*—This is the number of minutes the Management Console will be unavailable for use, due to an excessive number of failed attempts to log on. This value may range from 0 to 65500 minutes. Specify zero only for no silent time.

- *[T] Management Console inactivity timeout*—This can be configured to time out a session after a period of inactivity. Once a session has been timed out, the user must log on with a password to continue. The timeout can range from 30 to 65500 seconds. Setting the timeout to zero will indicate to use no timeout.

TIP: *A non-zero timeout should be set for security reasons.*

- *[D] Default mode of status LED*—This displays one of three status LEDs: port status, duplex status, and utilization of the switch. You can select the display mode by pressing the mode button on the front panel. Once a mode is selected and the mode button is released, the display automatically returns to the default status after 30 seconds.

- *[M] Modify password*—The Management Console password can help prevent unauthorized access. When specifying a password, use a minimum of four characters and a maximum of eight characters. The password is case-insensitive and can contain any character with a legal keyboard representation.

- *[E] Modify secret password*—The Management Console secret password can help prevent unauthorized access. This password is stored in encrypted form and thus provides enhanced security. When specifying a secret password, use a minimum of 1 character and maximum of 25 characters. The password is case-sensitive and can contain any character with a legal keyboard representation. This password will supersede the regular password.

- *[X] Exit to Main Menu*—This option returns you to the Main Menu.

[S] System Menu

You begin configuring the basic system settings by choosing S from the Main Menu. When you do, you'll see a menu similar to the following:

```
Catalyst 1900 - System Configuration
        System Revision: 5     Address Capacity: 2048
        System Last Reset:    Wed Sept 21 05:24:30 2000
        -----------------Settings--------------------
    [N] Name of system                      Coriolis Editings 2820
    [C] Contact Name                        Joe Snow (888)555-9700
    [L] Location                            Editor staff closet
    [S] Switching Mode                      FragmentFree
    [U] Use of store-and-forward for multicast Enabled
    [A] Action upon address violation       Disable
    [G] General alert on address violation  Disabled
    [I] Address aging time                  10 second(s)
    [P] Network Port                        None
        -----------------Actions----------------------
    [R] Reset system            [F] Reset to factory defaults
        -----------------Related Menus----------------
    [B] Broadcast storm control   [X] Exit to Main Menu
```

Let's look at each of the System Configuration commands. They are listed here with brief explanations:

- *[N] Name of system*—In multiple-switch environments, this option aids in determining which switch you are currently configuring. You can use up to 255 characters in the switch name, including spaces.

- *[C] Contact Name*—This option defines a contact name in case there are problems with the switch. This field can also contain up to 255 characters. Including a pager number or home contact information as part of the contact name can be helpful.

- *[L] Location*—This field can contain up to 255 characters. It provides additional information about where the switch physically resides.

- *[S] Switching Mode*—This option allows the switch to be configured for all three switching modes. The three configuration choices are: [1] Store-and-Forward, [2] FragmentFree, and [3] FastForward.

- *[U] Use of store-and-forward for multicast*—The switch will always use store-and-forward for broadcasts. This feature allows you to determine which method will be used for multicast frames. You can select from two options: [E] (enabled) allows the switch to use store-and forward for multicast frames, and [D] (disabled; the default) uses the method defined in the Switching Mode option from the System Configuration menu.

- *[A] Action upon address* violation—This option gives you three ways to inform the switch what to do when an address violation occurs. The option [S] (suspend) stops the port from forwarding frames of the violation. The option [D] (disable) turns off the port until an administrator disables it. The [I] (ignore) option indicates that no action will be taken.

- *[G] General alert on address violation*—This option indicates whether Simple Network Management Protocol (SNMP) trap messages are sent when an address violation occurs.

- *[I] Address aging time*—This option defines the number of seconds that dynamic entries will remain in the Media Access Control (MAC) address table. The valid settings are 10 to 1,000,000 seconds. The default is 300 seconds.

- *[P] Network Port*—This option specifies the port to which all unknown unicasts are forwarded. You can specify a port in the range of port numbers on the switch: A indicates port 25, B indicates port 26, AUI indicates the AUI port, and N indicates None.

- *[R] Reset system*—This option recycles the power on the switch.

- *[F] Reset to factory defaults*—This option clears all configuration settings back to the factory defaults.

WARNING! If you apply the [F] option, all manual configuration settings will be lost.

- *[B] Broadcast storm control*—This option launches the Broadcast Storm menu, which includes five options. (These options are discussed in "Configuring Broadcast Storm Control on Switch Ports" in the Immediate Solutions section.)

- *[X] Exit to Main Menu*—This option exits to the Main Menu.

[N] Network Management

By pressing N on the Main Menu, you reach the Network Management menu. This menu can be used to define an IP address for the system, Simple Network

Management Protocol (SNMP), Spanning-Tree Protocol (STP), Cisco Discovery Protocol (CDP), and Cisco Group Management Protocol (CGMP).

The following shows the Network Management menu:

```
Catalyst 1900 - Network Management

    [I] IP Configuration
    [S] SNMP Management
    [B] Bridge - Spanning Tree
    [C] Cisco Discovery Protocol
    [G] Cisco Group Management Protocol
    [H] HTTP Server Configuration
    [R] Cluster Management

    [X] Exit to Main Menu

Enter Selection:
```

Let's look at each option from this menu in more detail.

[I] IP Configuration

Choosing I from the Network Management menu brings up a menu that looks similar to the following:

```
Catalyst 1900 - IP Configuration

        Ethernet Address:    00-F3-1F-10-F1-06

    -------------------Settings--------------------
    [I] IP address                          10.17.18.254
    [S] Subnet mask                         255.255.0.0
    [G] Default gateway                     10.17.18.1
    [V] Management VLAN                      1

    [X] Exit to previous menu

Enter selection:
```

In order to use Telnet or SNMP to manage the switch, an IP address must be assigned to the switch. The following are the settings from the IP Configuration menu:

• *[I] IP address*—Configures the IP address on the switch.

• *[S] Subnet mask*—Configures the switch's subnet mask.

- *[G] Default gateway*—Configures the destination address for the route processor to which the switch will forward unknown or out-of-subnet addresses.

- *[V] Management VLAN*—Allows you to set the VLAN in which you will configure your switch. Cisco recommends that you choose a VLAN other than 1 because all ports are in VLAN1 by default. On the Standard Edition of the IOS software, the available VLANs are 1 through 4. The Enterprise Edition has 64 available VLANs.

- *[X] Exit to previous* menu—Exits back to the Network Management menu.

TIP: *When you change the IP address, the change takes effect immediately. However, all other options from the Network Management menu require a recycling of the power. Configuration changes on the 1900 and 2820 series are automatically saved, but the change can take up to 30 seconds to take effect.*

[S] SNMP Management

To make changes to SNMP, choose S from the Network Management menu. The following shows the Network Management (SNMP) Configuration menu options for a CAT 2820:

```
Catalyst 2820 - Network Management (SNMP) Configuration


                 -------------------Settings---------------------
        [R] READ   community string
        [W] WRITE community string
        [1] 1st WRITE manager IP address              0.0.0.0
        [2] 2nd WRITE manager IP address              0.0.0.0
        [3] 3rd WRITE manager IP address              0.0.0.0
        [4] 4th WRITE manager IP address              0.0.0.0

        [F] First TRAP community string               0.0.0.0
        [A] First TRAP manager IP address             0.0.0.0
        [S] Second TRAP community string              0.0.0.0
        [B] Second TRAP manager IP address            0.0.0.0
        [T] Third TRAP community string               0.0.0.0
        [C] Third TRAP manager IP address             0.0.0.0
        [U] Authentication Trap generation            Disabled
        [L] LinkUp/LinkDown trap generation           Disabled
                 -------------------Actions----------------------
        [X] Exit to previous Menu


Enter selection:
```

The options available from this menu are as follows:

- *[R] READ community string*—Identifies the community that is assigned to the management stations. Those management stations assigned to this community can read the trap messages sent from the switch. You can define a name up to 32 characters; the default is *public*.

NOTE: *When VLANs are implemented, the VLAN needs to be included in the string. For example, public in VLAN2 would be public2.*

- *[W] WRITE community string*—Identifies the community that is assigned to the management stations. Those management stations assigned to this community can read or set SNMP configurations on the switch. You can define a name up to 32 characters; the default is *private*.

- *WRITE manager IP address*—Allows you to define up to four SNMP management stations that can set SNMP configuration parameters on the switch.

- *TRAP*—Allows you to define which SNMP management stations can receive TRAP messages on the switch.

- *[U] Authentication Trap generation*—Allows you to enable or disable authentication trap message generation.

- *[L] LinkUp/LinkDown trap generation*—Informs the switch of the actions to take when the port changes its state from suspended, down, or up from STP. It also notifies the switch when an address violation has occurred, link errors are present, or a manual configuration error had been found.

- *[X] Exit to previous Menu*—Takes you back to the Network Management menu.

SNMP Default Trap Messages

By default, the Cisco Catalyst 1900 and Catalyst 2820 series switches send certain trap messages. Trap messages are sent by default in response to the following events:

- Port security violations
- Power recycling (powering on and off)
- Logon authentication failures
- STP port changes
- STP bridge assignments
- Broadcast threshold problems
- Power supply problems

15. The Standard Edition IOS

[B] Bridge - Spanning Tree

Selecting [B] Bridge - Spanning Tree from the Network Management menu will bring up the following menu. Here we use a 2820 for an example to show a more detailed list of available settings in an upgraded version of the IOS software:

```
Catalyst 2820 - VLAN 1 Spanning Tree Configuration
        Bridge ID:   0002 00-D3-1F-11-B1-05


      ------------------Information---------------------
      Designated root 0001 00-F3-1F-13-F3-11
      Number of member ports    27    Root port               3
      Max age (sec)             20    Root path cost       1000
      Forward Delay (sec)       15    Hello Time (sec)       10
      Topology changes           0    Last TopChange 245f08h12m22s


      ------------------Settings---------------------
      [S] Spanning Tree Algorithm & Protocol          Enabled
      [B] Bridge priority                             32,768
      [M] Max age when operating as root              20 second(s)
      [H] Hello time when operating as root           10 second(s)
      [F] Forward delay when operating as the root    15 second(s)


      ------------------Actions---------------------
      [N] Next VLAN bridge          [G] Goto VLAN bridge
      [P] Previous VLAN bridge      [X] Exit to previous menu

Enter Selection:
```

> **NOTE:** Spanning Tree Protocol and its defaults are covered in detail in Chapter 10.

[C] Cisco Discovery Protocol

Choosing C (Cisco Discovery Protocol) from the Network Management menu will bring up the following menu:

```
Catalyst 1900 - CDP Configuration/Status

    CDP enabled on: 1-24, AUI, A, B


      ------------------Settings---------------------
[V] Version                                    2
[H] Hold Time (secs)                         180
[T] Transmission Interval (secs)              60
```

```
------------------Actions----------------------
[E] Enable CDP on Port(s)
[D] Disable CDP on Port(s)
[S] Show Neighbor
[X] Exit to previous menu
```

```
Enter Selection:
```

The following list shows the commands from the CDP Configuration/Status menu:

- *[H] Hold Time (secs)*—Indicates how long a CDP multicast will remain in the CDP table. The valid entries are from 5 to 255 seconds, and the default is 180 seconds.

- *[T] Transmission Interval (secs)*—Defines the interval in which the switch will send CDP multicast messages.

- *[E] Enable CDP on Port(s)*—Identifies one or more ports on which to enable CDP. You can use the All setting to enable all ports, or you can identify blocks of ports by using a hyphen. For example, to identify ports 1 through 10, enter "1-10". You can use spaces to separate the variables; so, if you also want ports 12-15, enter "1-10 12-15".

- *[D] Disable CDP on Port(s)*—Identifies one or more ports on which to disable CDP.

- *[S] Show Neighbor*—Displays a list of neighboring Cisco devices together with their device ID, MAC address, port, capabilities, and device platform. The device's capabilities are indicated by letters: R indicates a router, T indicates a Trans Bridge, B indicates a Route Bridge, S indicates a switch, P indicates a repeater, H indicates a host, and I indicates IGMP.

- *[X] Exit to previous menu*—Returns you to the Network Management menu.

[G] Cisco Group Management Protocol

You configure Cisco Group Management protocol (CGMP) by selecting G (the last configuration option) on the Network Management menu. In order to function properly, CGMP needs all the ports on the switch to reside in the same VLAN. CGMP allows an intelligent means of limiting multicast flooding to specific ports.

The following shows the menu on a Catalyst 2820 when the G command is chosen from the Network Management menu:

```
Catalyst 2820 - Cisco Group Management Protocol (CGMP) Configuration

------------------Settings----------------------
[H] Router hold time (secs)              300
[C] CGMP                                 Enabled
```

15. The Standard
Edition IOS

```
-------------------Actions----------------------
[L] List IP multicast addresses

[X] Return to previous menu
```

The following list shows the commands and descriptions for the CGMP Configuration menu:

- *[H] Router hold time (secs)*—Indicates the amount of time the switch will keep CGMP multicast information. When the CGMP router fails or the power is recycled, the switch will flood multicast broadcasts out all the ports. The valid range is from 5 to 900 seconds; the default is 5 seconds.

- *[C] CGMP*—Enables or disables CGMP on the switch. There are two valid options: E (enabled) and D (disabled; the default).

- *[L] List IP multicast addresses*—Lists all multicast addresses learned by CGMP along with the VLAN, source MAC address, and port of the source address.

- *[X] Return to previous menu*—Returns you to the Network Management menu.

[P] Port Configuration

From the Main Menu, you can configure each port's settings from the Port Configuration menu. You must specify a port from Table 15.1.

The Port Configuration menu is as follows:

```
Catalyst 2820 - Port 24 Configuration

        -------------------Settings---------------------
        [D] Description/name of port        Port To Hanson's PC
        [S] Status of port                  Suspended-jabber

        -------------------Related Menus-----------------
        [A] Port addressing             [V] View port settings
        [N] Next port                   [G] Goto port
        [P] Previous port               [X] Exit to Main Menu

Enter Selection:
```

The following list shows the options and descriptions for the Port Configuration menu:

- *[D] Description/name of port*—This option allows the port name to be changed to a name with 60 characters or less, such as *Port to Hanson's PC*.

Table 15.1 The available configurable ports on a Catalyst 2820 from the Port Configuration menu.

Syntax	Port
A1	Port 25
B1	Port 26
AUI	The AUI port
1 through 24	An individual port on the switch

- *[S] Status of port*—This option has two configurable settings: E (enabled) and D (disabled). The default setting places all ports in the enabled mode.

Port Statuses

Although the administrator has only two configurable settings under the Status Of Port option, the port can be in any of the following statuses:

- *Enabled*—The port is available to send and receive data frames.
- *Disabled-mgmt*—The port has been manually disabled.
- *Suspended-linkbeat*—The port cannot detect a link at the other end of the cable. Possibly the cable has become unplugged, the device on the other end is turned off, or the port is not configured on the far-end device.
- *Suspended-jabber*—The port is temporarily disabled because of excessive jabber or indecipherable data frames.
- *Suspended-violation*—The port has been temporarily disabled because of an address violation. The port is automatically re-enabled once it discontinues receiving invalid source address information.
- *Suspended-ring down*—The port is using Fiber Distributed Data Interface (FDDI) links and cannot detect an attached FDDI ring.
- *Suspended-Spanning-Tree-Protocol*—The port is not participating in any STP forwarding state.
- *Suspended-not-present*—A module in an expansion slot (on the 2820 series only) cannot be detected.
- *Suspended-not-recognized*—The switch cannot detect the switch port or a module in the expansion slot (on the 2820 series only).
- *Disabled-self-test*—The port has been disabled due to a self-test failure.
- *Disabled-violation*—The port has been disabled due to an address violation. When a port is in this state it must manually be reset and enabled.
- *Reset*—The port has been manually reset and enabled.

- *[A] Port addressing*—This option is used to access the Port Addressing menu.

- *[V] View port settings*—This option is used to display individual port statistics.

- *[N] Next port*—This option is used to forward to the next configurable port.

- *[G] Goto port*—This option is used to configure any identified port.

- *[P] Previous port*—This option is used to configure the previous configurable port.

- *[X] Exit to Main Menu*—This option returns you to the Main Menu.

Let's take a look at the options available on the 2820 using an FDDI module on port A1:

```
Catalyst 2820 - Port A1 Configuration (Left Slot)

      Module Name: FDDI (Fiber SAS Model).  Version 00
      Description: Single Attached Station
      Ring Status: Not operational
      802.1d STP State: Blocking      Forwarding:  0
      -----------------Settings---------------------
      [D] Description/name of port
      ----------------Module Settings---------------
      [M] Module status                   Suspended-ring-down
      [I] Port priority (spanning tree)   128 (80 hex)
      [C] Path cost (spanning tree)       100
      [H] Port fast mode (spanning tree)  Disabled
      [L] Novell SNAP frame translation   Automatic
      [U] Unmatched SNAP frame destination  All
      -----------------Actions----------------------
      [R] Reset module              [F] Reset to factory defaults
      ----------------Related Menus-----------------
      [1] Basic FDDI settings       [2] Secondary FDDI settings
      [A] Port addressing           [V] View port settings
      [N] Next port                 [G] Goto port
      [P] Previous port             [X] Exit to Main Menu

Enter Selection:
```

The following list shows the menu options and an explanation of each:

- *[M] Module status*—This feature has three options. To see the status of the module, use the S option; the other two choices let you either enable or disable the module.

- *[I] Port priority (spanning tree)*—This option sets the port priority for the STP root port. The lower the number, the higher the priority. The valid range is from 0 to 255; the default is 128.

- *[C] Path cost (spanning tree)*—This option sets the path cost used to choose the STP root port.

- *[H] Port fast mode*—PortFast is an option that allows a port to immediately go into forwarding mode. This option offers two settings: E (enable) and D (disable). (The option is explained in detail in Chapter 10.)

- *[L] Novell SNAP frame translation*—This option determines whether manual or automatic frame-translation is used by IPX.

- *[U] Unmatched SNAP frame destination*—This option identifies the translation of frames for which the frame type cannot be determined. To use this option, option L should be set to automatic.

- *[R] Reset module*—This option resets the expansion modules.

- *[F] Reset to factory defaults*—This option resets the expansion modules' configuration to the factory defaults.

- *[1] Basic FDDI settings*—This option allows you to see the first expansion module's status and current configuration.

- *[2] Secondary FDDI settings*—This option displays the second screen of the expansion module's status and current configuration.

- *[A] Port addressing*—This option is used to access the Port Addressing menu.

- *[V] View port settings*—This option is used to display an individual port's statistics.

- *[N] Next port*—This option is used to forward to the next configurable port.

- *[G] Goto port*—This option is used to configure any identified port.

- *[P] Previous port*—This option is used to configure the previous configurable port.

- *[X] Exit to Main Menu*—This option returns you to the Main Menu.

[A] Port Addressing

The Port Addressing menu allows you to set up security and to add static MAC addresses to a port. When entering this option, you must first identify a port to configure, as listed in Table 15.2.

Table 15.2   The available configurable ports on a Catalyst 2820 from the Port Addressing menu.

Syntax	Port
A	Port 25
AUI	The AUI port
1 through 24	An individual port on the switch

Following is the Port Addressing configuration menu:

```
Catalyst 2820 - Port 2 Addressing


    Address:  Static    A0-00-F3-1F-11-34
    -------------------Settings---------------------
    [T] Address table size                     Unrestricted
    [S] Addressing security                    Disabled
    [U] Flood unknown unicast                  Enabled
    [M] Flood unregistered multicast           Enabled
    -------------------Actions----------------------
    [A] Add a static address
    [D] Define restricted static address
    [L] List addresses
    [E] Erase an address
    [R] Remove all addresses
    ----------------Related Menus----------------
    [C] Configure port          [V] View port statistics
    [N] Next port               [G] Goto port
    [P] Previous Port           [X] Return to Main Menu

Enter selection:
```

When the port is a secured port, its MAC address will be 00-00-00-00-00-00. The following is the list of options and parameters for the Port Addressing menu:

- *[T] Address table size*—Defines the number of allowable MAC addresses if the port is secure port enabled. The range can be any value from 1 to 132. The default is 132; it cannot be changed if the port is not secure port enabled.

- *[S] Addressing security*—Allows you to enable or disable secure port, which is also known as *addressing security*.

- *[U] Flood unknown unicast*—Allows you to enable or disable flooding of unknown unicasts out all the ports.

- *[M] Flood unregistered multicast*—Allows you to enable or disable flooding unregistered multicasts out all the ports.

- *[A] Add a static address*—Allows you to add a static unicast hexadecimal MAC address to the table, if the table is not full.
- *[D] Define restricted static address*—Allows a source MAC address to be identified, thereby allowing only the device using that MAC address to use the port.
- *[L] List addresses*—Displays all the static and dynamic MAC addresses that the switch has learned are attached to the port. The screen displays the first 15 entries beginning with those that have been statically configured.
- *[E] Erase an address*—Allows you to remove a statically or dynamically configured MAC address associated with the port.
- *[R] Remove all addresses*—Allows you to remove all statically or dynamically configured MAC address associated with the port.
- *[C] Configure port*—Provides a shortcut to the Port Configuration menu.
- *[V] View port statistics*—Displays individual port statistics.
- *[N] Next port*—Forwards to the next configurable port.
- *[G] Goto port*—Configures any identified port.
- *[P] Previous port*—Configures the previous configurable port.
- *[X] Exit to Main Menu*—Returns you to the main menu.

[D] Port Statistics Detail

The Port Statistics Detail displays the receive and transmit statistics for the port you select. This page can be used to help you identify performance or connectivity problems.

The options available from the Port Statistics Detail menu are as follows:

- *[A] Port Addressing*—Displays the Port Addressing menu.
- *[C] Configure Port*—Displays the Port Configuration menu.
- *[R] Reset Port Statistics*—Allows you to clear the port statistics. Enter [Y] (yes) to clear the port statistics.
- *[N] Next Port*—Displays the detailed port statistics for the next sequentially numbered Port on the switch.
- *[G] Go To Port*—Displays the detailed port statistics for a manually specified port.

[M] Monitor

Choosing M from the Main Menu will show you the following Monitoring Configuration menu:

```
Catalyst 1900 - Monitoring Configuration

          -------------------Settings-----------------
          [C] Capturing frames to the Monitor          Disabled
          [M] Monitor port assignment                  None
          Current capture list: 1-24, AUI

          -------------------Actions------------------
          [A] Add ports to capture list
          [D] Delete ports from capture list

          [X] Exit to Main Menu

Enter Selection:
```

The following list shows the Monitoring Configuration menu options and a description of each:

- *[C] Capturing frames to the Monitor*—Allows you to enable or disable port monitoring on the switch.

- *[M] Monitor port assignment*—Allows you to indicate the port to which captured frames are sent. The default is None.

- *[A] Add ports to capture list*—Allows the addition of ports you want to monitor. You can enter "all" to monitor all ports.

- *[D] Delete ports from capture list*—Allows the addition of ports you want to remove from monitoring. You can enter "all" to remove all ports.

- *[X] Exit to Main Menu*—Returns you to the Main Menu.

[V] Virtual LAN

To implement VLANs (covered in Chapter 5), use the V command from the Main Menu. Because the Standard Edition software does not support ISL and other high-end VLAN protocols, the VLAN menu is quite simple:

```
Catalyst 2820 - Virtual LAN Configuration

     VLAN   Name                          Member Ports
     ----   -------------------------     -----------
        1   VLAN 1                        1-24, AUI, A, B
     -------------Action---------------------------
     [C] Configure VLAN
     [X] Exit to Main Menu

Enter Selection:
```

This menu only gives two options. You can choose C to enter another menu that lets you configure a VLAN name and move member ports to another VLAN; or, you can exit to the Main Menu.

[R] Multicast Registration

By default, the switch forwards all multicast packets to all ports on the switch. To reduce the amount of multicast flooding on the switch, you can register multicast addresses and list the ports to which these packets are to be forwarded.

To display the Multicast Registration menu, enter the R option from the Main Menu. The following is a Multicast Registration menu from the Catalyst 2820:

```
Catalyst 2820 - Multicast Registration

    Registered multicast addresses: 1

    -------------------Actions-----------------
    [R] Register a multicast address
    [L] List all multicast addresses
    [U] Unregister a multicast address
    [E] Erase all multicast addresses

    [X] Exit to Main Menu

Enter Selection:
```

The first line of the menu displays the number of registered multicast addresses. The menu options are as follows:

- *[R] Register a multicast address*—Allows the addition of multicast addresses and ports to which multicasts can be forwarded. Invalid multicasts—such as unicasts, broadcasts, and reserved multicasts—are automatically rejected. The switch supports up to 64 IP multicast group registrations.

- *[L] List all multicast addresses*—Displays all registered multicast addresses that exist in the switch.

- *[U] Unregister a multicast address*—Removes registered multicast addresses.

- *[E] Erase all multicast addresses*—Removes all registered multicast addresses from the switch's address table.

- *[X] Exit to Main Menu*—Displays the management console Main Menu.

[F] Firmware

Loading an upgraded version of the system software is fairly simple. When you download the firmware to Flash memory, the switch does not respond to commands for approximately one minute. You should not turn off the switch until after the switch resets and begins using the new firmware.

NOTE: *Cisco periodically provides new firmware to implement enhancements and maintenance releases. New firmware releases can be downloaded from Cisco Connection Online (CCO), the Cisco Systems' customer Web site, at* **www.cisco.com**.

When you enter the Firmware Configuration menu, your display will look similar to this:

```
Catalyst 1900 - Firmware Configuration


        ---------------System Information------------
        FLASH: 1024K bytes
        V9.00.00 Standard Edition
        Upgrade status:
        No upgrade currently in progress.


        -------------------Settings-----------------
        [S] TFTP Server name or IP address
        [F] Filename for firmware upgrades
        [A] Accept upgrade transfer from other hosts    Disabled

        -------------------Actions------------------
        [U]System XMODEM upgrade      [D]Download test subsystem (XMODEM)
        [T]System TFTP upgrade        [X]Exit to Main Menu

Enter Selection:
```

The switch firmware version and the amount of Flash memory are displayed in the System Information area of the Firmware Configuration menu. The following list displays each option and its description:

- *[S] TFTP Server name or IP address*—Allows you to enter the server name or the IP address of the TFTP server where the upgrade file is located.

- *[F] Filename for firmware upgrades*—Lets you enter the name of the firmware upgrade file to be downloaded.

- *[A] Accept upgrade transfer from other hosts*—Allows you to enable or disable an upgrade from another host on the network. To prevent any unauthorized upgrades, disable this option after you upgrade your firmware.

- *[U] System XMODEM upgrade*—Allows you to begin the upgrade using the XMODEM protocol.

- *[T] System TFTP upgrade*—Allows you to begin the upgrade from a TFTP server. The address of the server and the name of the file must already be configured with options S and F.

- *[D] Download test subsystem (XMODEM)*—Available for Cisco personnel only. This option is not available during a Telnet session.

- *[X] Exit to Main Menu*—Returns you to the Main Menu.

[I] RS-232 Interface

The RS-232 Interface Configuration menu, which is available by choosing I from the Main Menu, configures the RS-232 interface on the switch:

```
Catalyst 1900 - RS-232 Interface Configuration


    ----------------Group Settings--------------
    [B] Baud rate                           9600 baud
    [D] Data bits                           8 bit(s)
    [S] Stop bits                           1 bit(s)
    [P] Parity setting                      None


    -------------------Settings-----------------
    [M] Match remote baud rate (auto baud)  Enabled
    [A] Auto answer                         Enabled
    [N] Number for dial-out connection
    [T] Time delay between dial attempts    300
    [I] Initialization string for modem


    -------------------Actions------------------
    [C] Cancel and restore previous group settings
    [G] Activate group settings

    [X] Exit to Main Menu

Enter Selection:
```

The following list explains the options available from the RS-232 Interface Configuration menu:

- *[B] Baud rate*—Lets you enter the baud rate. The possible settings are 2400, 9600, 19200, 38400, or 57600 for the console port. The default baud rate is 9600.

- *[D] Data bits*—Allows the configuration of data bits for the console port. The possible options are 7 and 8. The default is 8.

- *[S] Stop bits*—Allows the configuration of the stop bit value for the console port. The default is 1.

- *[P] Parity setting*—Changes the parity settings for the console port. The default is None.

- *[M] Match remote baud rate (auto baud)*—Allows you to enable or disable the console port from automatically matching the baud rate of an incoming call. The switch only matches a baud rate that is lower than its configured baud rate.

- *[A] Auto answer*—Allows you to enable the switch to automatically answer incoming calls or disable it from doing so.

- *[N] Number for dial-out connection*—Lets you enter the phone number the switch is configured to use when dialing out. This number is dialed when the switch is configured to communicate with a remote terminal upon power-up or power recycling.

- *[T] Time delay between dial attempts*—Configures the number of seconds between dial-out attempts. Zero (0) disables all retries. The default is 300 seconds.

- *[I] Initialization string for modem*—Allows you to change the initialization string to match your modem requirements.

- *[C] Cancel and restore previous group settings*—Allows you to undo any new values entered for the baud rate, data bits, stop bits, and parity settings.

- *[G] Activate group settings*—Allows you to activate the settings you have entered for baud rate, data bits, stops bits, and parity.

- *[X] Exit to Main Menu*—Returns you to the Main Menu.

[U] Usage Summaries

The Usage Summaries menu allows you to receive usage and summary reports. You can receive five types of reports based on the options shown here:

```
Catalyst 1900 - Usage Summaries


    [P] Port Status Report
    [A] Port Addressing Report
    [E] Exception Statistics Report
    [U] Utilization Statistics Report
    [B] Bandwidth Usage Report
```

```
    [X] Exit to Main Menu

Enter Selection:
```

The following list explains the options from the Usage Summaries menu:

- *[P] Port Status Report*—This option displays the Port Status Report, which displays the current connection status of ports. A sample of this report is as follows:

```
Catalyst 1900 - Port 3 Statistics Report
Receive Statistics                       Transmit Statistics
---------------------------------        ---------------------------------

Total good frames             9342   Total frames                  90269
Total octets                983976   Total octets                6147813
Broadcast/multicast frames     834   Broadcast/multicast frames    81389
Broadcast/multicast octets  133139   Broadcast/multicast octets  5492328
Good frames forwarded         9342   Deferrals                         1
Frames filtered                  0   Single collisions                 0
Runt frames                      0   Multiple collisions               0
No buffer discards               0   Excessive collisions              0
                                     Queue full discards               0
Errors:                              Errors:
  FCS errors                     0   Late collisions                   0
  Alignment errors               0   Excessive deferrals               0
  Giant frames                   0   Jabber errors                     0
  Address violations             0   Other transmit errors             0

Select [A] Port addressing, [C] Configure port,
       [N] Next port, [P] Previous port, [G] Goto port,
       [R] Reset port statistics, or [X] Exit to Main Menu:
```

- *[A] Port Addressing Report*—This option displays the Port Addressing report, which displays the number of MAC addresses and the MAC addresses assigned to a port:

```
Catalyst 1900 - Port 3 Addressing

     Address   :  Dynamic  00-60-8C-BA-52-14

------------------------- Settings -----------------------------------
   [T] Address table size                   Unrestricted
   [S] Addressing security                  Disabled
   [K] Clear addresses on link down         Disabled
   [U] Flood unknown unicasts               Enabled
   [M] Flood unregistered multicasts        Enabled
```

```
--------------------- Actions ------------------------------------
    [A] Add a static address
    [D] Define restricted static address
    [L] List addresses
    [E] Erase an address
    [R] Remove all addresses

    [C] Configure port          [V] View port statistics
    [N] Next port               [G] Goto port
    [P] Previous port           [X] Exit to Main Menu

Enter Selection:
```

- *[E] Exception Statistics Report*—This option display the Exception Statistics Report, which gives a summary of errors on a port:

```
Catalyst 1900 - Exception Statistics Report (Frame counts)


              Receive  Transmit Security
              Errors   Errors   Violations
             -------------------------------
      1  :       0        0         0
      2  :       0        0         0
      3  :       0        0         0
      4  :       0        0         0
      5  :       0        0         0
      6  :       1        0         0
      7  :       0        0         0
      8  :       0        0         0
      9  :       0        0         0
     10  :       0        0         0
     11  :       0        0         0
     12  :       0        0         0

    AUI:        0        0         0
    A  :        0        0         0
    B  :        0        0         0


Select [R] Reset all statistics, or [X] Exit to previous menu:
```

- *[U] Utilization Statistics Report*—This option displays the Utilization Statistics Report, which displays the utilization of each port:

```
Catalyst 1900 - Utilization Statistics Report (Frame counts)
```

```
         Receive    Forward   Transmit
        ------------------------------------
   1  :       0          0          0
   2  :       0          0          0
   3  :    9352       9352      90514
   4  :       0          0          0
   5  :       0          0          0
   6  :    3678       3677      81423
   7  :       0          0          0
   8  :       0          0          0
   9  :       0          0          0
  10  :       0          0          0
  11  :       0          0          0
  12  :       0          0          0

  AUI :       0          0      82461
   A  :       0          0          0
   B  :       0          0          0


Select [R] Reset all statistics, or [X] Exit to previous menu:
```

- *[B] Bandwidth Usage Report*—This option displays the Bandwidth Usage Report, which displays port-by-port bandwidth usage:

```
Catalyst 1900 - Bandwidth Usage Report

   --------------------- Information ----------------------------------
   Current Bandwidth Usage                     0 Mbps
   Peak Bandwidth Usage during this interval   0 Mbps
   Peak Time recorded since start up           1d 06h 58m 02s
   --------------------- Settings -------------------------------------
     [T] Capture time interval                 24 hour(s)
     [R] Reset capture
     [X] Exit to previous menu

Enter Selection:
```

- *[X] Exit*—This option returns you to the Main Menu.

Immediate Solutions

Configuring Network Settings on the 1900 and 2820 Series

To configure a 1900 or 2820 series switch, follow these steps:

1. Plug in your switch. You should see the following display:

```
Catalyst 1900 Management Console
Copyright (c) Cisco Systems, Inc.1993-1999
All rights reserved.

Standard Edition Software
Ethernet address:       00-F0-1D-30-BB-C2

     PCA Number: 25-41329-10
     PCA Serial Number: NBB02404421
     Model Number: WS-C1924-A
     System Serial Number: BBB02304561
     --------------------------------------
     User Interface Menu
     [M] Menus
     [I] IP Address
     [P] Console Password
Enter Selection:
```

The following list describes the three menu options:

- *[M] Menus*—Displays the switch's Main Menu.

- *[I] IP Address*—Available at log-on if the switch does not have a password configured.

- *[P] Console Password*—Allows you to enter an unencrypted privileged-level password to the switch management interface. This option is available at log-on only if the switch does not have a password. The password must be at least four characters and no more than eight characters long.

2. Choose selection [I] and enter an IP address that you have already pre-defined. Once you have completed the IP configuration, you need to select [S] from the following menu to enter the subnet mask for your segment:

```
Catalyst 1900 - IP Configuration


        Ethernet Address:   00-B0-64-75-65-40


        ------------------- Settings -----------------------------------
        [I] IP address                              192.1.2.1
        [S] Subnet mask                             255.255.255.0
        [G] Default gateway                         0.0.0.0
        [V] Management VLAN                          1
        [M] IP address of DNS server 1              0.0.0.0
        [N] IP address of DNS server 2              0.0.0.0
        [D] Domain name
        [R] Use Routing Information Protocol        Enabled


        ------------------- Actions ------------------------------------
        [P] Ping
        [C] Clear cached DNS entries
        [X] Exit to previous menu

Enter Selection:
```

3. Enter the Default Gateway by selecting [G]. This option will let you enter the DG information.

4. By default, the management VLAN is set to VLAN1. If you selected another VLAN prior to this configuration, you should verify that the correct management VLAN value is set.

5. Enter the DNS information by selecting [M] to enter the primary DNS server and then selecting [N] to enter the secondary DNS server.

6. Select [D]. You will be prompted to enter the name of the domain into which the switch falls.

7. Routing Information Protocol (RIP) is enabled by default. Because all changes are in real time, you can use one of the actions to verify connectivity. Select [P] (ping); then, if you have a client attached to your switch, try to ping a host on that particular subnet. If you can do so, your configuration was successful.

Related solutions:	Found on page:
Configuring an IP Address and Netmask	57
Configuring the Switch with an IP Address and Setting the Default Web Administration Port	421

Configuring Broadcast Storm Control on Switch Ports

The 1900 and 2820 series switches use one configuration for the entire switch; the configuration isn't port by port as with other Catalyst series switches. Therefore, all ports will use the same configuration. When you make a change to the Broadcast Storm Control menu it will affect all the ports on the switch. The following shows the Broadcast Storm Control menu:

```
Catalyst 2820 - Broadcast Storm Control


-------------------Settings-------------------
    [A] Action upon exceeding broadcast threshold    Block
    [G] Generate alert when threshold exceeded       Enabled
    [T] Broadcast Threshold (BC's received / sec)    1000
    [R] Broadcast re-enable threshold                300


    [X] Exit to previous menu

Enter Selection:
```

This menu allows you to control the propagation of broadcasts to each port. The following list gives a brief description of each setting:

- *[A] Action upon exceeding broadcast threshold*—Indicates what action will be taken in the event that the broadcast number threshold is exceeded. There are two settings: Option I ignores the excess broadcasts, and option B blocks them until the number of broadcasts becomes lower than the threshold setting.

- *[G] Generate alert when threshold exceeded*—Controls whether an SNMP trap is sent when the broadcast threshold has been exceeded. Two options are available: E (enabled) and D (disabled).

- *[T] Broadcast Threshold (BC's received / sec)*—Sets the broadcast threshold in broadcasts per second. The possible settings are 10 to 14,400; the default is 500 per second.

- *[R] Broadcast re-enable threshold*—Indicates the number of broadcasts per second at which the port will re-enable after an instance in which the threshold maximum disabled the port. The possible settings are 10 to 14,400; the default is 500 per second.

- *[X] Exit to previous menu*—Returns you to the System Configuration menu.

Configuring SNMP on the 1900 Series

To configure SNMP on the 1900 series switch, start from the Main Menu and do the following:

1. Select option [N] to go into the Network Management Menu. The following shows the Network Management menu:

```
Catalyst 1900 - Network Management

     [I] IP Configuration
     [S] SNMP Management
     [B] Bridge - Spanning Tree
     [C] Cisco Discovery Protocol
     [G] Cisco Group Management Protocol
     [H] HTTP Server Configuration
     [R] Cluster Management

     [X] Exit to Main Menu

Enter Selection:
```

2. Select [S] to enter the SNMP configuration menu, which looks like the following:

```
Catalyst 1900 - Network Management (SNMP) Configuration

     [R] READ configuration
     [W] WRITE configuration
     [T] TRAP configuration

     [X] Exit to previous menu

Enter Selection:
```

3. This menu has options to give a client read or write access to the local SNMP log files on the switch. Let's say we want to configure a read string for remote clients to access 1900 switch SNMP log files. And we want to

15. The Standard Edition IOS

change it from the default Public string to Techs. To do so, select [R], and then choose [1] to change the first string:

```
Catalyst 1900 - Network Management (SNMP) READ Configuration

--------------------- Settings -----------------------------------

    [1] First  READ community string
    [2] Second READ community string
    [3] Third  READ community string
    [4] Fourth READ community string

    [X] Exit to previous menu

Enter Selection:  1

This command configures the community string the switch will recognize
on all SNMP read (Get) requests. The string can be from 1 to 32
characters. Any character with a legal keyboard representation is
allowed.

Enter READ community string:

Current setting ===> public

    New setting ===> Techs
```

4. Remember that all SNMP traps are case sensitive, so you will want to have your SNMP configurations well documented to reduce human error. Once your community string has been set you will return to the previous menu.

5. Choose [X] to exit from the previous menu. We will now configure a Write Manager to allow write access to the SNMP log files and MIB objects. Select [W] from the Network Management SNMP configuration menu, and then [A] from the Network Management (SNMP) WRITE Configuration menu. Your screen should look like the following:

```
Catalyst 1900 - Network Management (SNMP) WRITE Configuration

--------------------- Settings -----------------------------------

    [1] First  WRITE community string
    [2] Second WRITE community string
    [3] Third  WRITE community string
    [4] Fourth WRITE community string
```

```
[A] First  WRITE manager name or IP address
[B] Second WRITE manager name or IP address
[C] Third  WRITE manager name or IP address
[D] Fourth WRITE manager name or IP address

[X] Exit to previous menu
```

```
Enter Selection:   A
```

```
SNMP Write Manager is the management station allowed to issue write
(Set) requests to the switch. Addresses or names for up to 4 such
stations can be defined. If no names or addresses are defined then any
management station can set the switch MIB objects.
```

```
Enter First  Write Manager name or IP address:
```

```
Current setting ===>
```

```
   New setting ===> 63.78.39.84
```

6. Notice that we have selected the Write Manager management station with
   the IP address 63.78.39.84. This will be the only client that has write access
   to the MIB objects and log files. After entering this information your screen
   will refresh and should look like this:

```
Catalyst 1900 - Network Management (SNMP) WRITE Configuration

--------------------- Settings ------------------------------------

[1] First  WRITE community string
[2] Second WRITE community string
[3] Third  WRITE community string
[4] Fourth WRITE community string

[A] First  WRITE manager name or IP address    63.78.39.84
[B] Second WRITE manager name or IP address
[C] Third  WRITE manager name or IP address
[D] Fourth WRITE manager name or IP address

[X] Exit to previous menu
```

7. At this point you can select option [1] and configure the WRITE community
   string and change the default community string from "private" to
   "techwrite," as we did in the following:

```
Catalyst 1900 - Network Management (SNMP) WRITE Configuration

--------------------- Settings ------------------------------------

   [1] First  WRITE community string
   [2] Second WRITE community string
   [3] Third  WRITE community string
   [4] Fourth WRITE community string

   [A] First  WRITE manager name or IP address    63.78.39.84
   [B] Second WRITE manager name or IP address
   [C] Third  WRITE manager name or IP address
   [D] Fourth WRITE manager name or IP address

   [X] Exit to previous menu

Enter Selection:  1

This command configures the community string the switch will recognize
on all SNMP read/write (Get/Set) requests. The string can be from 1 to
32 characters.  Any character with a legal keyboard representation is
allowed.

Enter WRITE community string:

Current setting ===> private

   New setting ===> techwrite
```

8. Again, once you have entered the new setting, your screen will automatically refresh. At this point, enter option [X] and return to the SNMP configuration menu.

9. At the Network Management (SNMP) Configuration Menu, select [T]. This will allow you to configure the trap message configuration settings:

```
Catalyst 1900 - Network Management (SNMP) Configuration

   [R] READ configuration
   [W] WRITE configuration
   [T] TRAP configuration

   [X] Exit to previous menu

Enter Selection:  T
```

```
Catalyst 1900 - Network Management (SNMP) TRAP Configuration

---------------------- Settings -------------------------------------

    [1] First  TRAP community string
    [A] First  TRAP manager name or IP address

    [2] Second TRAP community string
    [B] Second TRAP manager name or IP address

    [3] Third  TRAP community string
    [C] Third  TRAP manager name or IP address

    [4] Fourth TRAP community string
    [D] Fourth TRAP manager name or IP address

    [U] Authentication trap generation          Enabled
    [L] LinkUp/LinkDown trap generation          Enabled

    [X] Exit to previous menu

Enter Selection:
```

10. We now want to bind the IP address of our SNMP management station to the trap community string. To do this, enter the new community string, and select [1]. Then select [A] to enter the IP address. The following will appear on your screen:

```
Enter Trap Manager community string (32 characters max):

Current setting ===>

    New setting ===> Techtraps


    Catalyst 1900 - Network Management (SNMP) TRAP Configuration

    ---------------------- Settings -------------------------------------

        [1] First  TRAP community string              Techtraps
        [A] First  TRAP manager name or IP address

        [2] Second TRAP community string
        [B] Second TRAP manager name or IP address
```

```
[3] Third  TRAP community string
[C] Third  TRAP manager name or IP address

[4] Fourth TRAP community string
[D] Fourth TRAP manager name or IP address

[U] Authentication trap generation             Enabled
[L] LinkUp/LinkDown trap generation            Enabled

[X] Exit to previous menu

Enter Selection:  A

SNMP Trap Manager is the  management station to which the switch will
send any SNMP traps (alerts). The types of traps the switch can send
are authentication traps, linkUp/linkDown traps, among others. From the
Management Console, up to 4 Trap management stations can be defined.
If no trap managers are defined, the switch will not send any traps.

Enter First Trap Manager server name or IP address:

Current setting ===>

    New setting ===> 63.78.39.84
```

11. Notice that that IP address is the previously configured SNMP management station. Once this has been completed, you have successfully enabled SNMP on a Catalyst 1900 switch.

Related solution:	Found on page:
Enabling SNMP Contact	58

Configuring Port Monitoring on the Standard Edition IOS

To configure port monitoring, start from the Main Menu and do the following:

1. Select option [M] to begin to configure port monitoring.

2. To capture information you will need to add ports to monitor. In the following example, we will select all ports and enable capturing:

```
        Catalyst 1900 - Monitoring Configuration

    -------------------- Settings ----------------------------------
    [C] Capturing frames to the Monitor          Disabled
    [M] Monitor port assignment                  None
    Current capture list:  No ports in list


    -------------------- Actions -----------------------------------
    [A] Add ports to capture list
    [D] Delete ports from capture list

    [X] Exit to Main Menu

Enter Selection:  A


This command adds ports to the capture list. Actual monitoring takes
place only if all of the following information has been properly
configured:  1) the capturing status, 2) the identity of a port to which
monitored frames are sent, and 3) a non-empty capture list.

Port numbers should be separated by commas or spaces.  A port number
range  may also be specified. The word ALL indicates all ports. Example:
1, 7-11, AUI, 4, A

Enter port numbers:  ALL

This command enables or disables the monitoring (capturing) of frames
from ports that have been added to the capture list. Actual monitoring
takes  place only if all of the following information has been properly
configured:
1) the capturing status, 2) the identity of a port to which monitored
frames are sent, and 3) a non-empty capture list.

Capturing frames to the Monitor may be [E]nabled or [D]isabled:

Current setting ===> Disabled

   New setting ===> Enabled
```

3. At this point, we want to send the captured information to a specific port. To do so, select [A]. In this example, we have selected trunk port B:

```
Identify Port:  1 to 12[1-12], [AUI], [A], [B], or [N]one:
Select [1 - 12, AUI, A, B, N]: A
```

```
Current setting ===> None

    New setting ===> B
```

4. Now you want to select option [C] and enable "Capturing frames to monitor" to successfully complete the Port Monitoring configuration.

Configuring VLANs on the Standard Edition IOS

To configure VLANs on the Standard Edition IOS, do the following, starting at the Main Menu:

1. Select option [V] to open the Virtual LAN Configuration menu:

```
        Catalyst 1900 - Virtual LAN Configuration


----------------------- Information ------------------------------
VTP version: 1
Configuration revision: 0
Maximum VLANs supported locally: 1005
Number of existing VLANs: 5
Configuration last modified by: 63.78.39.164 at 00-00-0000 00:00:00


--------------------- Settings -----------------------------------
[N] Domain name                    VTPDomain1
[V] VTP mode control               Server
[F] VTP pruning mode               Enabled
[O] VTP traps                      Enabled


--------------------- Actions ------------------------------------
[L] List VLANs                     [A] Add VLAN
[M] Modify VLAN                    [D] Delete VLAN
[E] VLAN Membership                [S] VLAN Membership Servers
[T] Trunk Configuration            [W] VTP password
[P] VTP Statistics                 [X] Exit to Main Menu
```

2. Select [V], and accept the default setting of Server. Because the change we want to make is to add a server, we will take the defaults:

```
VTP mode may be set to [C]lient, [S]erver or [T]ransparent:

Current setting ===> Server

    New setting ===> Server
```

3. Select [A] to add an Ethernet VLAN to the switch. You'll see the following:

```
The following VLAN types can be added:
[1]Ethernet, [2]FDDI, [3]Token-Ring, [4]FDDI-Net, or [5]Token-Ring-Net

Select a VLAN type [1-5]: 1
```

4. Now we need to specify a name for the newly created VLAN. To change the name to "Techs" we need to select option [V], as shown in the following output:

```
Enter Selection:  V

This command selects the unique name of a VLAN.

Configuration change only takes effect when the VLAN SAVE command is
executed.

A string of up to 32 characters may be specified to name a VLAN.
Example: Engineering, Manufacturing, Blue

Enter VLAN name (32 characters max):

Current setting ===> VLAN0002

    New setting ===> Techs
```

5. Now you need to save the VLAN configuration. To do so, select option [S]. Save and exit.

6. To view information about your newly created VLAN, from the Virtual LAN Configuration menu, choose [M].

7. Next, select the VLAN you want information on. In this case, it's VLAN 2. Enter "2" and you should see the following:

```
    Catalyst 1900 - Modify Ethernet VLAN

-------------------- Information ------------------------------------
  Current member ports:
  Type: Ethernet
  VLAN Number: 2
-------------------- Settings ---------------------------------------
  [V] VLAN Name              Techs
  [I] 802.10 SAID            100002
  [M] MTU Size               1500
```

```
[L] Translational Bridge 1      0
[J] Translational Bridge 2      0
[T] VLAN State                  Enabled


-------------------- Related Menus ----------------------------------
[S] Save and Exit               [X] Cancel and Exit
[N] Cancel and goto Next VLAN   [G] Cancel and goto VLAN
[P] Cancel and goto Previous VLAN
```

8. To exit from this screen, select option [X].

9. To configure your trunk ports (Ax and/or Bx) to pass the VLAN information
    to neighboring switches, you must enable at least one of the trunk ports.
    From the Virtual LAN Configuration menu select option [T].

10. Now you need to enter a trunk port. We will be configuring port A:

```
Select a trunk port [A, B] : A
```

11. You should now see the Trunk A Configuration menu The next step is to
    enable trunking. To do so, select [T] from the menu, as shown here:

```
Catalyst 1900 - Trunk A Configuration Menu

Trunking status: Off        Encapsulation type: Unknown
-------------------- Information ------------------------------------
Transmit Flood traffic to VLANs         N/A
Receive Flood traffic from VLANs        N/A
Allowed VLANs                           1-1005
Pruning Eligible VLANs                  2-1001
-------------------- Settings --------------------------------------
[T] Trunking                            Off
-------------------- Actions ---------------------------------------
[S] List VLANs that Transmit Flood traffic
[R] List VLANs that Receive Flood traffic
[V] List Allowed VLANs
[F] List Pruning Eligible VLANs

[A] Add Allowed VLAN(s)      [E] Add Pruning Eligible VLAN(s)
[D] Delete Allowed VLAN(s)   [C] Delete Pruning Eligible VLAN(s)

[N] Next Trunk   [P] Previous Trunk   [X] Exit to Vlan Menu

Enter Selection:  T
```

This command configures the state of this trunk.
    [1] on - dictates that the port will always be a trunk.
    [2] off - allows an operator to specify that the specified port is never to be trunk, regardless of any dynamic mechanisms to the contrary.
    [3] desirable - is used to indicate that it is desirable for the port to become a trunk. The device will initiate any negotiation necessary to become a trunk but will not become a trunk unless it receives confirmation from other participants on the link.
    [4] auto - is used to indicate that the port is capable and willing to become a trunk but will not initiate trunking negotiations. Other participants on the link are required to either start negotiations or start sending encapsulated packets, on which event the specified port will become a trunk.
    [5] no-negotiate - dictates that the port will always be a trunk, like the on(1) state. However, The port will neither generate DISL frames nor process received DISL frames.
Trunking control state may be [1]On, [2]Off, [3] Desirable, [4]Auto, [5]No-negotiate:

Current setting ===> Off

    New setting ===> On

12. Now you want to pass the information through the specified trunk. You need to grant access to the VLANs so they know which trunk to send their information through. We are allowing the default VLAN (the management VLAN) and the newly created VLAN 2. To do so, select A from the Trunk A Configuration menu and enter "1-2":

This command adds one or more VLANs to the allowed VLAN list for this trunk.

VLAN numbers should be separated by commas or spaces. A VLAN number range may also be specified. The word ALL indicates all VLANs.
Example: 1, 2, 10-20

Enter VLAN numbers [1-1005] : 1-2

That's it. You completed the configuration.

Related solutions:	Found on page:
Configuring a Static VLAN on a Catalyst 5000 Series Switch	154
Configuring Multiple VLANs on a Catalyst 5000 Series Switch	154
Creating VLANs on a Catalyst 1900EN Series	155
Assigning a Static VLAN to an Interface on a 1900EN Series	156

Configuring Spanning Tree Protocol

To configure Spanning Tree Protocol, start from the Main Menu and do the following:

1. Select option [N], Network Management.

2. From the Network Management menu, select option [B]:

```
Catalyst 1900 - Network Management

[I] IP Configuration
[S] SNMP Management
[B] Bridge - Spanning Tree
[C] Cisco Discovery Protocol
[G] Cisco Group Management Protocol
[H] HTTP Server Configuration
[R] Cluster Management

[X] Exit to Main Menu

Enter Selection:  B
```

3. From this menu select option [U] for Uplink Fast. This allows for quick recovery should a root port fail:

```
Catalyst 1900 - Bridge - Spanning Tree Configuration

-------------------- Information --------------------------------------
   [S] VLAN spanning trees enabled        1-64

-------------------- Settings --------------------------------------
   [U] Uplink Fast                        Disabled
   [R] Uplink Fast Frame Generation rate  15
```

```
-------------------- Bridge Configuration ------------------------
  [1] Configuration option 1
  [2] Configuration option 2
  [3] Configuration option 3
  [4] Configuration option 4
  [0] VLAN bridge operating parameters
-------------------- Actions -------------------------------------
  [E] Enable spanning tree(s)    [D] Disable spanning tree(s)
  [C] Uplink Fast statistics     [X] Exit to previous menu

Enter Selection:  U
```

4. Select [E] to enable Uplink Fast:

```
Uplink fast may be [E]nabled or [D]isabled:

Current setting ===> Disabled

   New setting ===> Enabled
```

5. When you return to the Bridge Configuration menu, you can enable the Spanning Tree Protocol by selecting [E].

6. Select the VLAN you want to enable STP on. Notice we selected VLAN 2:

```
This command enables the Spanning Tree Protocol for a list of VLANs.
You may enable the Spanning Tree Protocol for a list of VLAN numbers.
VLAN numbers range from 1 to 1005.

VLAN numbers should be separated by commas or spaces. A VLAN number
range may also be specified. Example: 1, 2, 10-20

Enter VLAN numbers: 2
```

7. To disable STP on a particular VLAN, you need to select option [D] from the same menu:

```
This command disables the Spanning Tree Protocol for a list of VLANs.
You may disable the Spanning Tree Protocol for a list of VLAN numbers.
VLAN numbers range from 1 to 1005.

VLAN numbers should be separated by commas or spaces. A VLAN number
range may also be specified. Example: 1, 2, 10-20

Enter VLAN numbers: 1
```

Notice here we selected the management VLAN, VLAN 1.

Once you have configured STP and the Management VLAN you can see from the following output that only VLANs 2 through 64 are using the Spanning Tree Protocol:

```
    Catalyst 1900 - Bridge - Spanning Tree Configuration


-------------------- Information -------------------------------------
 [S] VLAN spanning trees enabled          2-64


-------------------- Settings ----------------------------------------
 [U] Uplink Fast                          Enabled
 [R] Uplink Fast Frame Generation rate    15


-------------------- Bridge Configuration ------------------------
 [1] Configuration option 1
 [2] Configuration option 2
 [3] Configuration option 3
 [4] Configuration option 4
 [O] VLAN bridge operating parameters
-------------------- Actions ------------------------------------------
 [E] Enable spanning tree(s)    [D] Disable spanning tree(s)
 [C] Uplink Fast statistics     [X] Exit to previous menu
```

Related solution:	Found on page:
Enabling STP on a Set/Clear Command-Based Switch	323

Chapter 16

Switch Troubleshooting

(continued)

In Depth

Switch troubleshooting includes both hardware and software. The switch hardware can be anything from a Supervisor Engine to a module, card, chassis, or even a power supply. The software can be the individual module software or the IOS.

In this chapter, we will focus on troubleshooting both the Command Line Interface (CLI) and the Set/Clear command-based IOS. First, I will concentrate on the physical hardware and then on the IOS troubleshooting commands. I will focus not only on the switch configuration but also on troubleshooting virtual LANs (VLANs) and the Spanning-Tree Protocol (STP).

Hardware Troubleshooting

The most common hardware problems are power supply problems, failed modules or interface problems, failed RAM, and cabling issues. Let's first take a look at what to do in the event of a power failure, the boot-up POST, and the different indicator lights that can be used for troubleshooting.

***WARNING!** The following steps are my recommendation, based on troubleshooting procedures I use every day. These steps do not come from Cisco documentation.*

No Power

The first indicator of a problem is the failure of a switch to power up. If there is no power to the switch, meaning the fan does not power up and no indicator lights appear lit on the front or back of the switch, follow these steps:

1. Check the physical cable for breaks or an unsecure connection.
2. Check the outlet with a multimeter for proper throughput.
3. Reseat the RAM in the chassis.
4. Check the connection and verify that all interfaces, cards, and modules are securely fastened in the chassis.

***WARNING!** Make sure you use proper grounding techniques before removing or touching any components, and that the switch is unplugged from all power sources.*

5. Make sure all gold-plated connections for the cards, modules, and RAM are not corroded and can make a good connection. To clean the gold-plated connections, I use an eraser from a pencil.

6. If necessary, contact Cisco Technical Assistance Center (TAC) or an authorized Cisco repair vendor for further troubleshooting steps and replacement parts.

TIP: *Heat from a failed fan followed by a cooling of components in the switch can cause a flexing of the connections. By reseating the connections, you can resolve the problem.*

POST

The power on self test (POST) can be a powerful tool in solving hardware issues. On the 1900 and 2820 series switches, the POST is not displayed on the screen. Instead, as the switch powers up, all the LEDs are lit except the LED that represents the test the switch is performing. The LEDs and their related tests are shown in Table 16.1.

TIP: *If the light turns green, the test has been passed. The switch will not boot if all the tests are not passed, with the exception of the realtime clock test. You can enter the Diagnostic Console on a 1900/2820 series switch to activate debugging or firmware upgrade options.*

Table 16.1   The LEDs and the POST tests they represent.

Port Number LED	Test
1	Ports (loopback)
2	Ethernet address PROM
3	CAM (MAC address) table
4	RS-232 console port
5	Realtime clock
6	CAM memory (SRAM)
7	Timer interrupt
8	Port control status
9	Flag memory (DRAM)
10	Buffer memory (DRAM)
11	Forwarding engine memory (SRAM)
12	Forwarding engine CPU
16/26	ECU memory (DRAM)

Indicator Lights

Indicator lights can be your biggest signal that a hardware, software, or configuration issue exists. In addition to the Catalyst 1900/2820 series switch LED tests, which were discussed in the last section, the Supervisor Engine on the Catalyst 5000 and 6000 family has five LEDs that can indicate a problem or tell you current utilization of the switch. The Supervisor Engine LEDs indicate the system, fan, power supplies, the load utilization, and whether the Supervisor Engine is active. Figure 16.1 shows the LEDs.

The switch load bar indicates the load on the switch. If the local device load is over 80 percent, then either there is a network problem such as a broadcast storm, or you need to upgrade the switching devices.

The system status lights indicate the following:

- *Red*—The diagnostics on the switch have failed.
- *Orange*—The PS2 power supply has failed.
- *Green*—All diagnostics have passed.

The fan LED indicates the following:

- *Red*—The fan has failed to power up.
- *Green*—The fan is operating correctly.

The PS1 and PS2 LEDs indicate the following:

- *Red*—The power supply has failed.
- *Green*—The power supply is operating normally.
- *Off*—The power supply bay is empty or off.

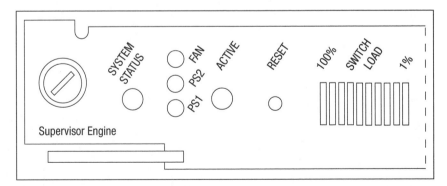

Figure 16.1   The Supervisor Engine LEDs.

The active LED indicates the following:

- *Orange*—The Supervisor Engine is in standby.
- *Green*—The Supervisor Engine is operating correctly.

Other LEDs are on the individual line modules, as shown in Figure 16.2. These LEDs indicate the status of each module. A green link light indicates a good established link. An orange or amber link light indicates a problem with the link. A red light indicates that a non-port test has failed.

NOTE: *A green switch port (SP) light indicates that the port is operating at 100BaseT. When the SP light is off, the port is operating in 10BaseT.*

Switch Cabling

The amount of data traffic that can float down a single pipe is almost unimaginable. With the introduction of 1- and 10Gbps links as well as Fast and Gigabit EtherChannel, data can move around today's networks at lightning speed. When gigabyte hard drives were first introduced for Intelligent Drive Electronics (IDE) drives, to copy one gigabyte to another drive took hours—even days. Now, you can send whole gigabytes over a network in mere seconds.

This higher speed adds complexity like never before. In early implementations, cable distances had greater flexibility. In today's high-speed networks, the distance limitations should be strictly adhered to. Many times, administrators will upgrade the network interface cards on both ends of a former 10Mbps link and find that the new 100Mbps link fails to work or has an excessive number of errors, forcing the link to become unusable. This happens because exceeding the 10BaseT cable limits didn't have the same detrimental effect as exceeding limits on 100BaseT.

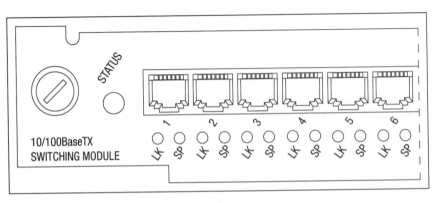

Figure 16.2   The 10/100 Ethernet module LEDs.

Table 16.2 Cable distance limitations.

Cable	Distance Limit	10/100Mbps Compatible
Category 3 cable	100 meters	10
Category 4 cable	100 meters	10
Category 5 copper	100 meters	10/100
Multimode fiber (half)	2,000 meters	10/100
Multimode fiber (full)	400 meters	10/100
Single-mode fiber	10,000 meters	10/100

You also may have a non-compatible cable type. For instance, 10BaseT will work over Category 3 twisted-pair, whereas 100BaseT requires Category 5. Table 16.2 shows the common cable limits for cabling in today's networks.

Switched Port Analyzers

It's hard to use a network sniffer on a switch the way you can in a flat topology network, because the switch isolates traffic, segments broadcast domains, and makes each port the collision domain. This isolation forces an administrator to manually connect a network sniffer to each port on a switch to monitor the traffic.

This problem is addressed by Cisco with the use of Switched Port Analyzer (SPAN). SPAN allows the switch to copy all the packets that are sent to nodes connected to the switch ports and direct them to another port. In essence, the designated switch port becomes a mirror of the monitored port or ports.

Cable Problems

When a cable problem surfaces, it usually appears as an intermittent problem; however, it can cause an immediate failure. Intermittent errors are hard to troubleshoot, and you must keep in mind that almost any connectivity issue can be cable related. You'll need to replace cables with a cable you know works in order to see if the change resolves your connectivity issue.

Multimeters, time domain reflectometers (TDRs), cable analyzers, and breakout boxes can be used to test for cable problems, but they may not always find the trouble. Just because cables were installed by a certified cable installer doesn't mean that they aren't improperly made, won't break, or don't have connector failures. Cables are moving parts, and any moving parts are subject to wear and tear as well as failures.

16. Switch Troubleshooting

Cross-Over Cables

When I am teaching classes, hardened Microsoft Certified Systems Engineers (MCSEs)s frequently have to ask me what a rollover or crossover cable is. This doesn't apply to all MCSE's of course, since I am one myself. I have always been on the networking side of technical support, so it is hard for me to believe that long-time network administrators don't know the differences between a straight-through and a cross-over cable or when to use them.

A connection to a network node from a switch or hub uses a straight-through cable. A crossover cable is used to connect two network devices: a hub to a hub, a switch to a switch, a switch to a router, and so on. Many times in my classroom or on the job, I have come across someone who couldn't get a connection between switches because they were using a straight-through cable and should have been using a crossover cable. See Chapter 2 for more information on cables and pinouts.

Switch Troubleshooting Tools

Catalyst switches provide quite a few diagnostic and administrative tools to assist administrators. These tools are located in the IOS command-line interface located on each Cisco device and in the CiscoWorks for Switched Internetworks (CWSI) external software for the end workstation.

Let's take a look at some of the components of CWSI. Then we'll examine the troubleshooting commands you can use on the Cisco IOS that are found on Cisco's line of enterprise switches.

CiscoWorks for Switched Internetworks

CWSI (also called Campus Manager) can run as a standalone application on Windows NT or Unix, including Solaris, HP-Unix, and AIX. This application includes a number of components that not only aid in troubleshooting but also help you during installation and monitoring. These components are as follows:

- *CiscoView*—A graphical user interface (GUI) application that provides a virtual look at the switch's chassis, configuration, and performance monitoring. This component provides very little in the way of troubleshooting functionality. A screen capture of CiscoView is shown in Figure 16.3.

- *User Tracking*—Used in the creation and management of dynamic VLANs. Cisco switches permit VLAN assignments based on dynamic VLAN assignments. This means the Media Access Control (MAC) address is used to assign the port to a specific VLAN. User Tracking defines these dynamic VLANs and maintains the whereabouts of workstations throughout the network.

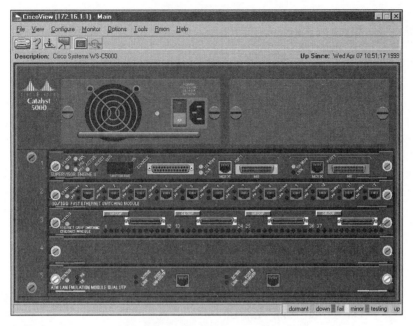

Figure 16.3   A screen capture from CiscoView.

- *VlanDirector*—Another GUI-based application. It is a very powerful tool to aid in the creation of multiple VLANs on a switch. This tool helps the administrator add users and assign ports, and it makes managing VLANs easy.

- *TrafficDirector*—A GUI component that is a great way to create usage baselines and to troubleshoot switched environments. This tool allows you to view the switched network as well as trunked and switched ports. A screen capture of TrafficDirector appears in Figure 16.4.

- *AtmDirector*—Used in Asynchronous Transfer Mode (ATM) networks. This tool can be used to configure, administer, and troubleshoot ATM switched networks.

IOS Software Troubleshooting Commands

Some command-line interface commands are available to aid you in troubleshooting a switch. You can also use a few GUI applications to simplify some of the functions involved in maintaining and configuring the Cisco IOS. These applications are helpful and will be discussed later in this chapter.

Let's look at some the commands that you can use to view the switch configuration and perform diagnostics in order to troubleshoot switch problems and configuration issues. We'll describe the following commands; then, in the Immediate Solutions section of this chapter, I'll give an example of the output you should see when using them:

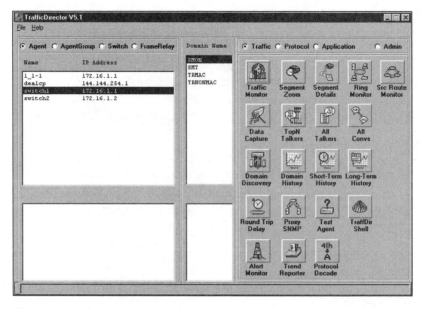

Figure 16.4 A screen capture from TrafficDirector.

- **show cam**
- **show cdp neighbors**
- **show config**
- **show flash**
- **show interface**
- **show log**
- **show mac**
- **show port**
- **show spantree**
- **show system**
- **show test**
- **show version**
- **show vtp domain controller**

show cam

The **show cam** command displays a switch's transparent bridging table (also known as the Content Addressable Memory [CAM] table). This is a table of the Layer 2 MAC addresses attached to each port that the switch has learned in order to make forwarding decisions.

Duplicate MAC Addresses

Occasionally, because of production mistakes, network devices are configured with identical MAC addresses on their interfaces. There are also some dual-homed Unix workstations that use manually assigned MAC addresses. This is a situation that leaves the door wide open for a duplicate MAC address in the network. This in turn can prevent communication in the local network. When the devices with the same MAC address are on the same broadcast domain, duplicate MAC addresses can become a substantial problem in your network.

By using the **show cam** command, you can view the list of known MAC addresses for interfaces attached to each switch port. If you are in a network where the administration of network devices is divided within the organization, I recommend that a central process be created to review and document assigned MAC addresses and thereby avoid this duplication problem.

NOTE: On the Cisco CLI-based IOS, use the **show mac** command.

---

show cdp neighbors

Cisco Discovery Protocol (CDP) is a Cisco proprietary protocol used to discover neighboring Cisco devices. The **show cdp neighbors** command displays the hardware, IOS version, and active interfaces. This information is passed between Cisco devices by CDP packets on physical media that support SNAP.

CDP packets are multicast packets that are advertised by the Cisco router or switches but not forwarded. This protocol is available on the Cisco IOS version 10.3 and later. You can use the **show cdp neighbors** command on both the CLI and Set/Clear command-based IOS.

show config

The **show config** command displays an incredible amount of troubleshooting information. With this command, you can obtain the entire configuration of switches and modules (except the Route Switch Module [RSM]) including passwords, system information, protocol settings, interface settings, and the system log settings.

NOTE: On the CLI-based IOS, use the **show running-config** command.

---

show flash

Cisco switches operate with software that is very similar to the Cisco IOS on routers. This software is stored and may be upgraded in flash stored on the Supervisor module. The **show flash** command reports the space required for the installed software and the version of the code, including the file names, software version numbers, and file sizes. Unfortunately, there is no comparable command on the 1900EN series switches.

16. Switch Troubleshooting

show interface

You can use the **show interface** command to get the IP configuration, interface flags, interface state, VLAN information from the Supervisor Console 0 (SCO) interface, and broadcast address. This command can be used on both the Set/Clear and CLI-based IOS.

show log

Using the **show log** command, you can look at significant events, including reboots of all the modules, traps, logged events, boot history, nonvolatile RAM (NVRAM) logs, module logs, and power supply failures. This command cannot be used on the 1900EN series switches.

show mac

The output from the **show mac** command is quite long. This command displays numerous counters that are maintained during normal operation. These counters include information on the traffic for each port, number of incoming frames, number of frame discards, total number of frames sent, and maximum transmission unit (MTU) violations.

NOTE: On the Cisco CLI-based IOS, use the **show usage** utilization command.

---

show port

Using the **show port** command, you can receive specific information about selected ports or all the ports on a specified module. This data includes the VLANs the port belongs to, port configuration information, port status, port speed, port duplex, port media type, security information, source MAC address of the last packet received, broadcast threshold, number of collisions, link error rate (LER), link error monitor (LEM), last report cleared time, and whether port trap is enabled.

Related solution:	Found on page:
Creating an EtherChannel on a Set/Clear Command-Based Switch	334

show spantree

The use of spanning trees is a necessity in today's networks in order to provide for redundant links and at the same time avoid a data looping problem. The **show spantree** command can be used to display the STP configuration crucial to the successful running of a switched network. The output from this command can tell you whether STP is enabled or disabled, the bridge or port priorities, the root bridge priorities, the path cost to the root, BPDU information, the bridge MAC address, timer information, the port states, and information on the fast-start configuration of each port. This command is similar on the Set/Clear IOS and the CLI-based IOS.

show system

Using the **show system** command, you can obtain a component status summary regarding the switch components. This information includes the system status, current traffic percentage, peak percentage, status of the fans, power supplies, and modem; uptime, and system identification configuration. There is no comparable command on the 1900EN series switches.

show test

The **show test** command can be used to obtain the status of the switch, interface cards, power supplies, Enhanced Address Recognition Logic (EARL) tests, or active loopback. It also displays the memory status of the read-only memory (ROM), flash electrically erasable programmable ROM (EEPROM), serial EEPROM, and non-volatile RAM. There is no comparable command on the 1900EN series switches.

show version

The **show version** command provides hardware and software version numbers, in addition to memory and the system uptime statistical information. This command can be used on both the Set/Clear IOS and the CLI-based IOS.

show vtp domain controller

The VLAN Trunking Protocol (VTP) maintains a consistent VLAN configuration throughout the network. In a VTP management domain, a configuration change is done only once on a VTP server-configured switch. The new configuration is propagated throughout the network. The **show vtp domain controller** command provides the status and configuration information for VTP.

16. Switch Troubleshooting

Immediate Solutions

Viewing the Set/Clear IOS Configuration

To view the Set/Clear IOS configuration, use the **show config** command. Let's take a look at an example of the output from this command:

```
Catalyst5002> (enable) show config

. . . . .

begin

!
set password $22$hgjhru^jf#sdc
set enablepass $22$hgjhru$fhkn
set prompt Catlayst5002
set length 24 default
set logout 0
set banner motd 'Unauthorized Use Prohibited!'


!
#system
set system baud  9600
set system modem disable
set system name  Catalyst5002
set system location Sacramento, CA
set system contact Sean Odom/Gina Galbraith
!
#snmp
set snmp community read-only      public
set snmp community read-write     private
set snmp community read-write-all all
set snmp rmon disable
set snmp trap enable  module
set snmp trap enable  chassis
set snmp trap enable  bridge
set snmp trap enable  repeater
set snmp trap enable  vtp
set snmp trap enable  auth
```

```
set snmp trap enable   ippermit
set snmp trap enable   vmps
!
#ip
set interface sc0 2 68.127.186.100 255.255.255.0 68.127.186.255
set interface sl0 0.0.0.0 0.0.0.0
set arp agingtime 1200
set ip redirect    enable
set ip unreachable    enable
set ip fragmentation enable
set ip route 0.0.0.0 68.127.186.254 0
set ip alias default 0.0.0.0

!
#Command alias

!
#vmps
set vmps server retry 3
set vmps server reconfirminterval 60
set vmps tftpserver 0.0.0.0 vmps-config-database.1
set vmps state disable

!
#dns
set ip dns disable
!
#tacacs+
set tacacs attempts 3
set tacacs directedrequest disable
set tacacs timeout 5
set authentication login tacacs disable
set authentication login local enable
set authentication enable tacacs disable
set authentication enable local enable
!
#bridge
set bridge ipx snaptoether 8023raw
set bridge ipx 8022toether 8023
set bridge ipx 8023rawtofddi snap
!
#vtp
set vtp domain Coriolis
set vtp mode server
set vtp v2 enable
set vtp pruneeligible 9-1005
```

```
clear vtp pruneeligible 1001-1005
set vlan 1 name default type ethernet mtu 1500 said 100001   state
 active
set vlan 1002 name fddi-default type fddi mtu 1500 said  101002 state
 active
set vlan 1004 name fddinet-default type fddinet mtu 1500  said 101004
 state active bridge 0x0 stp ieee
set vlan 1005 name trnet-default type trbrf mtu 1500 said  101005 state
 active bridge 0x0 stp ieee
set vlan 1003 name Token-Ring-default type trcrf mtu 1500  said 101003
 state active parent 0 ring 0x0 mode srb  aremaxhop 7 stemaxhop 7
!
#spantree

!
#uplinkfast groups
set spantree uplinkfast disable

!
#vlan 1
set spantree enable 1
set spantree fwddelay 15 1
set spantree hello 2 1
set spantree maxage 20 1
set spantree priority 32768 1

!
#vlan 2
set spantree enable 1
set spantree fwddelay 15 1
set spantree hello 2 1
set spantree maxage 20 1
set spantree priority 32768 1

!
#vlan 10
set spantree enable 1
set spantree fwddelay 15 1
set spantree hello 2 1
set spantree maxage 20 1
set spantree priority 32768 1

#vlan 1003
set spantree enable 1003
set spantree fwddelay 4 1003
```

```
set spantree hello 2 1003
set spantree maxage 10 1003
set spantree priority 32768 1003
set spantree portstate 1003 auto 0
set spantree portcost 1003 80
set spantree portpri 1003 4
set spantree portfast 1003 disable

#vlan 1005
set spantree enable 1005
set spantree fwddelay 15  1005
set spantree hello 2 1005
set spantree maxage 20 1005
set spantree priority 32768 1005
set spantree multicast-address 1005 ieee


!
#cgmp
set cgmp disable
set cgmp leave disable
!
#syslog
set logging console enable
set logging server disable
set logging level cdp 2 default
set logging level cgmp 2 default
set logging level disl 5 default
set logging level dvlan 2 default
set logging level earl 2 default
set logging level fddi 2 default
set logging level ip 2 default
set logging level pruning 2 default
set logging level snmp 2 default
set logging level spantree 2 default
set logging level sys 5 default
set logging level tac 2 default
set logging level tcp 2 default
set logging level telnet 2 default
set logging level tftp 2 default
set logging level vtp 2 default
set logging level vmps 2 default
set logging level kernel 2 default
set logging level filesys 2 default
set logging level drip 2 default
set logging level pagp 5 default
```

```
!
#ntp
set ntp broadcastclient disable
set ntp broadcastdelay 3000
set ntp client disable
set timezone PST 0 0
set summertime disable

!
#permit list
set ip permit disable
!
#drip
set tokenring reduction enable
set tokenring distrib-crf disable

!
#module 1 : 2-port 100BaseFX MM Supervisor
set module name 1
set vlan 1 1/1-2
set port channel 1/1-2 off
set port channel 1/1-2 auto
set port enable 1/1-2
set port level 1/1-2 normal
set port duplex 1/1-2 half
set port trap 1/1-2 enable
set port name 1/1-2
set port security 1/1-2 disable
set port broadcast 1/1-2 100%
set port membership 1/1-2 static
set cdp enable 1/1-2
set cdp interval 1/1-2 60
set trunk 1/1 auto 1-1005
set trunk 1/2 auto 1-1005
set spantree portfast 1/1-2 disable
set spantree portcost 1/1-2 19
set spantree portpri 1/1-2 32
set spantree portvlanpri 1/1 10
set spantree portvlanpri 1/2 10
set spantree portvlancost 1/1 cost 18
set spantree portvlancost 1/2 cost 18
!
#module 2 : 24-port 10/100BaseTX Ethernet
set module name    2
set module enable  2
set vlan 1 2/1-24
```

```
set port enable 2/1-24
set port level 2/1-24 normal
set port speed 2/11-24 auto
set port speed 2/19 10
set port duplex 2/1-2 full
set port trap 2/1-24  enable
set port name 2/1-24
set port security 2/1-24  disable
set port broadcast 2/1-24  0
set port membership 2/1-24  static
set cdp enable 2/1-24
set cdp interval 2/1-24 60
set spantree portfast    2/1-24 disable
set spantree portcost    2/11 10
set spantree portcost    2/12 10
set spantree portcost    2/17 10
set spantree portcost    2/18 10
set spantree portcost    2/19 100
set spantree portcost    2/21 10
set spantree portcost    2/1-10,2/13-16,2/20,2/22-24 19
set spantree portpri     2/1-24 32

!
#switch port analyzer
set span enable
!
#cam
set cam agingtime 1-2,10,1003,1005 300

end
```

Viewing the CLI-Based IOS Configuration

To view the CLI-based IOS configuration, use the **show running-config** command. Let's take a look at an example of the output from this command:

```
1912EN#show running-config
Building configuration...
Current configuration:
!
!
vtp domain "coriolis"
!
```

```
mac-address-table permanent 0030.194C.80A6 Ethernet 0/1
mac-address-table permanent 0000.0C00.4BD0 Ethernet 0/1
mac-address-table permanent 00A0.2457.2877 Ethernet 0/1
mac-address-table permanent 0000.0C33.4283 Ethernet 0/5
mac-address-table permanent 0000.0C33.4283 Ethernet 0/10
mac-address-table permanent 0000.0C33.4286 Ethernet 0/10
tftp server "68.127.186.39"
!
hostname "1912EN"
!
monitor-port monitored 0/1
monitor-port
!
network-port 0/8
!
address-violation ignore
!
multicast-store-and-forward
!
ip default-gateway 63.78.39.254
ip domain-name  "rcsis.com"
ip name-server 208.45.228.3
ip name-server 208.45.228.4
!
snmp-server location "Sean's Lab 1900EN"
snmp-server contact "Sean Odom"
!
enable password level 15 "book1"
!
interface Ethernet 0/1

1912EN#
```

Viewing the Software Version on a Set/Clear Command-Based IOS Module

To view the software version of a module on a Set/Clear command-based IOS, use the **show version** command. This command will not work on internal route processor modules, however. Let's look at the command and an example of its output:

```
show version <slot number>

Catalyst5002> (enable) show version 1
```

```
Mod Port Model       Serial #  Versions
-- ---- ----------   --------  ----------------------------------------
1   2   WS-X5530     006851332 Hw : 1.3
                               Fw : 3.1.2
                               Fw1: 4.2(1)
                               Sw : 4.2(1)
Console> (enable)
```

Viewing the IOS Version Information on a CLI-Based IOS

To view the IOS version information on a CLI-based IOS, use the **show version** command. Let's take a look at the command and its output:

```
1912EN#show version

Cisco Catalyst 1900/2820 Enterprise Edition Software
Version V8.01.02
Copyright (c) Cisco Systems, Inc.  1993-1998
1912EN uptime is 0day(s) 01hour(s) 33minute(s) 17second(s)
cisco Catalyst 1900 (486sxl) processor with 2048K/1024K bytes of memory
Hardware board revision is 5
Upgrade Status: No upgrade currently in progress.
Config File Status: No configuration upload/download is in progress
15 Fixed Ethernet/IEEE 802.3 interface(s)
Base Ethernet Address: 00-30-80-54-6C-00

1912EN#
```

Using the **show flash** Command on a Set/Clear Command-Based IOS

You can use the **show flash** command on a Set/Clear command-based IOS switch. You can view use optional syntaxes to view the individal chip or file system information. Let's take a look at the command and its output:

```
show flash [[m/]device:] [all|chips|filesys]

Catalyst5002> show flash
```

```
File            Version       Sector      Size    Built
-------------   -----------   ---------   ------  ----------------
c5000 nmp       3.1(213-Eng)  02-11       1316809 06/16/00 00:26:21
      epld      3.1           30            72920 06/14/99 19:33:06
      lcp atm   3.1           12-15         23747 06/14/99 11:16:06
      lcp tr    3.1           12-15         28737 06/14/99 11:17:19
      lcp c5ip  3.1           12-15         23723 06/14/99 11:26:40
      lcp 64k   3.1           12-15         57100 06/14/99 11:28:15
      atm/fddi  3.1           12-15         24502 06/14/99 11:47:07
      lcp 360   3.1(212)      12-15        120648 06/14/99 01:32:33
      mcp       3.1           12-15         26278 06/14/99 11:50:41

Catalyst5002>
```

NOTE: *There is no comparable command on the 1900EN series switches.*

Testing the Supervisor Engine Hardware on a Set/Clear Command-Based Switch

To test the Supervisor Engine module on a Set/Clear command-based switch, use the **show test** command. Let's take a look at the command, its optional syntax, and an example of its output:

```
show test [module number]

Catalyst5002> (enable) show test

Environmental Status (. = Pass, F = Fail, U = Unknown)
  PS (3.3V):   .  PS (12V): .  PS (24V):   .  PS1: .      PS2: .
  Temperature: .  Fan:      .  Clock(A/B): A   Chassis-Ser-  EEPROM: .

Module 1 : 2-port 100BaseFX MM Supervisor
Network Management Processor (NMP) Status:
(. = Pass, F =  Fail, U = Unknown)
  ROM:  .  Flash-EEPROM: .  Ser-EEPROM: .  NVRAM: .  MCP  Comm: .

  EARL Status :
      NewLearnTest:        .
      IndexLearnTest:      .
      DontForwardTest:     .
      MonitorTest          .
      DontLearn:           .
      FlushPacket:         .
```

```
        ConditionalLearn:       .
        EarlLearnDiscard:       .
        EarlTrapTest:           .

LCP Diag Status for Module 1  (. = Pass, F = Fail, N = N/A)
  CPU         : .   Sprom    : .   Bootcsum : .   Archsum  : N
  RAM         : .   LTL      : .   CBL      : .   DPRAM    : .   SAMBA : .
  Saints      : .   Pkt Bufs : .   Repeater : N   FLASH    : N

  MII Status:
  Ports 1  2
  ----------
        N  N

  SAINT/SAGE Status :
  Ports 1  2  3
  --------------
        .  .  .

  Packet Buffer Status :
  Ports 1  2  3
  --------------
        .  .  .

  Loopback Status [Reported by Module 1] :
  Ports  1  2  3
  --------------
         .  .  .

  Channel Status :
  Ports  1  2
  ----------
         .  .
```

NOTE: *There is no comparable command on the 1900EN series switches.*

16. Switch
Troubleshooting

Testing External Module Hardware on a Set/Clear Command-Based Switch

The Catalyst 5002 I am using has a Supervisor Engine in Slot 1. Slot 2 has a 10/100 Ethernet Interface Card with 24 ports. Let's look at the **show test** command, its optional syntax, and an example of a test on this module:

```
show test [module number]

Catalyst5002> (enable) show test 2

Module 2 : 24-port 10/100 Ethernet

LCP Diag Status for Module 2  (. = Pass, F = Fail, N = N/A)
  CPU        : .   Sprom    : .  Bootcsum : .   Archsum  : .
  RAM        : .   LTL      : .   CBL      : N   DPRAM    : N  SAMBA : .
  Saints     : .   Pkt Bufs : .  Repeater : N   FLASH    : .

  SAINT/SAGE Status :
  Ports 1 2 3 4 5 6 7 8 9 10 11 12 13 14 15 16 17 18 19 20 21 22 23 24
  -----------------------------------------------------------------


  Packet Buffer Status :
  Ports 1 2 3 4 5 6 7 8 9 10 11 12 13 14 15 16 17 18 19 20 21 22 23 24
  -----------------------------------------------------------------


  Loopback Status [Reported by Module 1] :
  Ports 1 2 3 4 5 6 7 8 9 10 11 12 13 14 15 16 17 18 19 20 21 22 23 24
  -----------------------------------------------------------------
```

NOTE: *There is no comparable command on the 1900EN series switches.*

Viewing the System Configuration on a Set/Clear Command-Based Switch

To view the system configuration on a Set/Clear command-based IOS switch, use the **show system** command. Let's take a look at the command and an example of its output:

```
Catalyst5002> (enable) show system

PS1Status PS2Status Fan-Status Temp-Alarm Sys-Status Uptime d,h:m:s Logout
--------- --------- ---------- ---------- ---------- -------------- ------
ok        off       ok         off        ok         93,3:21:60     none

PS1-Type   PS2-Type   Modem   Baud  Traffic Peak Peak-Time
---------- ---------- ------- ----- ------- ---- ----------------------
WS-C5008B  WS-C5008B  disable 9600 0%      0%   Sat Sep 09 2000, 8:16:58
```

```
System Name    System Location            System Contact
------------   ------------------------   --------------------
Catalyst5002   Sacramento, CA             Sean Odom
```

NOTE: *There is no comparable command on the 1900EN series switches.*

Viewing the VTP Domain Configuration on a Set/Clear IOS

The **show vtp domain** command can be used to obtain the VTP domain configuration on a Set/Clear command-based IOS switch. Let's take a look at the command and an example of the output associated with it:

```
Catalyst5002> (enable)  show vtp domain

Domain Name                      Domain Index VTP Version Local Mode Password
------------------------------   ------------ ----------- ---------- --------
Coriolis                              1            1       Server     -

Vlan-count Max-vlan-storage Config Revision Notifications
---------- ---------------- --------------- -------------
5          1023                   0          enabled

Last Updater     V2 Mode   Pruning  PruneEligible on Vlans
--------------   --------  -------- ------------------------
68.127.187.12    disabled disabled 2-1000
```

Viewing the VTP Domain Configuration on a CLI-Based IOS

The **show vtp** command displays the VTP domain configuration on an IOS-based switch. Let's look at the command, its available options, and an example of its output:

```
1912EN#show vtp ?
  statistics  Show VTP statistics
  <cr>
```

```
1912EN#show vtp
     VTP version: 1
     Configuration revision: 0
     Maximum VLANs supported locally: 1005
     Number of existing VLANs: 5
     VTP domain name      : coriolis
     VTP password         :
     VTP operating mode   : Server
     VTP pruning mode     : Disabled
     VTP traps generation : Enabled
     Configuration last modified by: 63.78.39.33 at 00-00-0000 00:00:00

1912EN#
```

Viewing the VLAN Configuration on a Set/Clear Command-Based Switch

To view the VLAN configuration on a Set/Clear command-based IOS switch, use the **show vlan** command. Several options are available for use with the command that allow you to see only trunked ports, only non-trunked ports, or an individual VLAN number. Let's look at the command, its optional syntaxes, and an example of its output:

```
show vlan [vlan] [trunk|no trunk]

Catalyst5002> show vlan

Virtual LAN ID:  1

   vLAN Trunk Interface:    FastEthernet1/0.1

   Protocols Configured:   Address:           Received:      Transmitted:
          IP               68.127.187.10      95563219847    81294682

Virtual LAN ID:  2 (Inter Switch Link Encapsulation)

   vLAN Trunk Interface:    FastEthernet1/0.2

   Protocols Configured:   Address:           Received:      Transmitted:
          IP               68.127.186.1       855147         854281

Catalyst5002>
```

Viewing the VLAN Configuration on a CLI-Based IOS

To view the VLAN configuration on a CLI-based IOS switch, use the **show vlan** command. Let's look at the command, its optional syntax, and an example of its output:

```
1912EN#show vlan ?
  <1-1005>  ISL VLAN index
  <cr>

1912EN#show vlan

VLAN Name                Status      Ports
-------------------------------------------
1    default             Enabled     6-12, AUI, A, B
2    Engineers           Enabled     1-3
3    Admins              Enabled     4-5
1002 fddi-default        Suspended
1003 token-ring-defau    Suspended
1004 fddinet-default     Suspended
1005 trnet-default       Suspended
-------------------------------------------


VLAN Type         SAID    MTU   Parent RingNo BridgeNo Stp  Trans1 Trans2
-------------------------------------------------------------------------
1    Ethernet     100001 1500   0      0      0        Unkn 1002   1003
2    Ethernet     100002 1500   0      0      0        Unkn 1002   1003
3    Ethernet     100003 1500   0      0      0        Unkn 1002   1003
10   Ethernet     100010 1500   0      0      0        Unkn 1002   1003
1002 FDDI         101002 1500   0      0      0        Unkn 1      1003
1003 Token-Ring   101003 1500   1005   1      0        Unkn 1      1002
1004 FDDI-Net     101004 1500   0      0      1        IEEE 0      0
1005 Token-Ring-Net 101005 1500 0      0      1        IEEE 0      0
-------------------------------------------------------------------------

1912EN#
```

Viewing the Spanning Tree Configuration on a Set/Clear Command-Based IOS

The **show spantree** command on the Set/Clear command-based IOS can be used to obtain configuration information and statistics on STP. You can use the command to view by VLAN number, module number, and module. You can also specify to see only active interfaces. Let's take a look at the command, its optional syntaxes, and an example of its output:

```
show spantree [VLAN|module number/port][active]

Catalyst5002> (enable) show spantree

VLAN 1
Spanning tree enabled
Spanning tree type         ieee

Designated Root            00-00-80-0c-a1-b3
Designated Root Priority   32768
Designated Root Cost       0
Designated Root Port       1/0
Root Max Age   20 sec    Hello Time 2  sec   Forward Delay  15 sec

Bridge ID MAC ADDR         00-00-80-0c-a1-b3
Bridge ID Priority         32768
Bridge Max Age 20 sec    Hello Time 2  sec   Forward Delay  15 sec

Port      Vlan  Port-State     Cost   Priority  Fast-Start  Group-method
--------  ----  ------------   ----   --------  ----------  ------------
 1/1       1    not-connected   19       32     disabled
 1/2       1    not-connected   19       32     disabled
 2/1       1    forwarding      10       32     disabled
 2/2       1    forwarding      10       32     disabled
 2/3       1    forwarding      10       32     disabled
 2/4       1    forwarding      10       32     disabled
 2/5       1    forwarding      10       32     disabled
 2/6       1    not-connected   19       32     disabled
 2/7       1    forwarding     100       32     disabled
 2/8       1    forwarding     100       32     disabled
 2/9       1    not-connected  100       32     disabled
 2/10      1    forwarding      10       32     disabled
 2/11      1    forwarding      10       20     disabled
 2/12      1    not-connected   19       32     disabled
 2/13      1    forwarding      10       32     disabled
 2/14      1    forwarding      10       32     disabled
 2/15      1    forwarding      10       32     disabled
 2/16      1    not-connected   19       32     disabled
 2/17      1    forwarding      10       10     disabled
 2/18      1    forwarding      10       32     disabled
 2/19      1    not-connected  100       10     disabled
 2/20      1    forwarding      10       32     disabled
```

```
2/21    1    forwarding        100    32    disabled
2/22    1    not-connected     100    32    disabled
2/23    1    forwarding         10    32    disabled
2/24    1    not-connected     100    32    disabled
```

Viewing the Spanning Tree Configuration on a CLI-Based IOS

The **show spantree** command can be used on a CLI-based IOS to obtain configuration information and statistics on STP. Let's take a look at the command, its optional syntaxes, and an example of its output:

```
show port <mod_num>
show port <mod_num/port_num>

1912EN#show spantree

VLAN1 is executing the IEEE compatible Spanning Tree Protocol
    Bridge Identifier has priority 32768, address 0030.8054.6C00
    Configured hello time 2, max age 20, forward delay 15
    Current root has priority 32768, address 0000.0C00.4BD0
    Root port is Ethernet 0/1, cost of root path is 100
    Topology change flag not set, detected flag not set
    Topology changes 0, last topology change occurred 0d00h00m00s ago
    Times:  hold 1, topology change 8960
            hello 2, max age 20, forward delay 15
    Timers: hello 2, topology change 35, notification 2
Port Ethernet 0/1 of VLAN2 is Forwarding
    Port path cost 100, Port priority 128
    Designated root has priority 32768, address 0000.0C00.4BD0
    Designated bridge has priority 32768, address 0000.0C00.4BD0
    Designated port is Ethernet 0/7, path cost 0
    Timers: message age 20, forward delay 15, hold 1
Port Ethernet 0/2 of VLAN2 is Forwarding
    Port path cost 100, Port priority 128
    Designated root has priority 32768, address 0000.0C00.4BD0
    Designated bridge has priority 32768, address 0030.8054.6C00
    Designated port is Ethernet 0/2, path cost 100
    Timers: message age 20, forward delay 15, hold 1
Port Ethernet 0/3 of VLAN2 is Forwarding
    Port path cost 100, Port priority 128
    Designated root has priority 32768, address 0000.0C00.4BD0
```

```
         Designated bridge has priority 32768, address 0030.8054.6C00
         Designated port is Ethernet 0/3, path cost 100
         Timers: message age 20, forward delay 15, hold 1
      Port Ethernet 0/4 of VLAN3 is Forwarding
         Port path cost 100, Port priority 128
         Designated root has priority 32768, address 0000.0C00.4BD0
         Designated bridge has priority 32768, address 0030.8054.6C00
         Designated port is Ethernet 0/4, path cost 100
         Timers: message age 20, forward delay 15, hold 1
      Port Ethernet 0/5 of VLAN3 is Forwarding
         Port path cost 100, Port priority 128
         Designated root has priority 32768, address 0000.0C00.4BD0
         Designated bridge has priority 32768, address 0030.8054.6C00
         Designated port is Ethernet 0/5, path cost 100
         Timers: message age 20, forward delay 15, hold 1
      Port Ethernet 0/6 of VLAN1 is Forwarding
         Port path cost 100, Port priority 128
         Designated root has priority 32768, address 0000.0C00.4BD0
         Designated bridge has priority 32768, address 0030.8054.6C00
         Designated port is Ethernet 0/6, path cost 100
         Timers: message age 20, forward delay 15, hold 1
      Port Ethernet 0/7 of VLAN1 is Forwarding
         Port path cost 100, Port priority 128
         Designated root has priority 32768, address 0000.0C00.4BD0
         Designated bridge has priority 32768, address 0030.8054.6C00
         Designated port is Ethernet 0/7, path cost 100
         Timers: message age 20, forward delay 15, hold 1
      Port Ethernet 0/8 of VLAN1 is Forwarding
         Port path cost 100, Port priority 128
         Designated root has priority 32768, address 0000.0C00.4BD0
         Designated bridge has priority 32768, address 0030.8054.6C00
         Designated port is Ethernet 0/8, path cost 100
         Timers: message age 20, forward delay 15, hold 1
      Port Ethernet 0/9 of VLAN1 is Forwarding
         Port path cost 100, Port priority 128
         Designated root has priority 32768, address 0000.0C00.4BD0
         Designated bridge has priority 32768, address 0030.8054.6C00
         Designated port is Ethernet 0/9, path cost 100
         Timers: message age 20, forward delay 15, hold 1
      Port Ethernet 0/10 of VLAN1 is Forwarding
         Port path cost 100, Port priority 128
         Designated root has priority 32768, address 0000.0C00.4BD0
         Designated bridge has priority 32768, address 0030.8054.6C00
         Designated port is Ethernet 0/10, path cost 100
         Timers: message age 20, forward delay 15, hold 1
```

```
Port Ethernet 0/11 of VLAN1 is Forwarding
    Port path cost 100, Port priority 128
    Designated root has priority 32768, address 0000.0C00.4BD0
    Designated bridge has priority 32768, address 0030.8054.6C00
    Designated port is Ethernet 0/11, path cost 100
    Timers: message age 20, forward delay 15, hold 1
Port Ethernet 0/12 of VLAN1 is Forwarding
    Port path cost 100, Port priority 128
    Designated root has priority 32768, address 0000.0C00.4BD0
    Designated bridge has priority 32768, address 0030.8054.6C00
    Designated port is Ethernet 0/12, path cost 100
    Timers: message age 20, forward delay 15, hold 1
Port Ethernet 0/25 of VLAN1 is Forwarding
    Port path cost 100, Port priority 128
    Designated root has priority 32768, address 0000.0C00.4BD0
    Designated bridge has priority 32768, address 0030.8054.6C00
    Designated port is Ethernet 0/25, path cost 100
    Timers: message age 20, forward delay 15, hold 1
Port FastEthernet 0/26 of VLAN1 is Blocking
    Port path cost 10, Port priority 128
    Designated root has priority 32768, address 0000.0C00.4BD0
    Designated bridge has priority 32768, address 0030.8054.6C00
    Designated port is FastEthernet 0/26, path cost 100
    Timers: message age 20, forward delay 15, hold 1
Port FastEthernet 0/27 of VLAN1 is Blocking
    Port path cost 10, Port priority 128
    Designated root has priority 32768, address 0000.0C00.4BD0
    Designated bridge has priority 32768, address 0030.8054.6C00
    Designated port is FastEthernet 0/27, path cost 100
    Timers: message age 20, forward delay 15, hold 1
```

Viewing the CAM (MAC Address) Table on a Set/Clear Command-Based IOS

A switch uses the CAM table to make forwarding decisions on the switch. Let's take a look at the available command options, syntaxes, and an example of the output using the **show cam** command:

```
Catalyst5002> (enable) show cam ?

Usage: show cam [count] <dynamic|static|permanent|system>     [vlan]
       show cam <dynamic|static|permanent> <mod_num/port_num>
```

```
        show cam <mac_addr> [vlan]
        show cam agingtime

Catalyst5002> (enable) show cam dynamic 2

VLAN  Dest MAC/Route Des  Destination Ports or VCs
2     00-30-19-4C-80-A6   2/4
2     00-30-19-4C-80-A8   2/18
2     00-30-19-4C-80-A6   2/15
2     00-30-19-4C-80-A6   2/12
2     00-30-19-4C-80-BC   2/9
2     00-30-19-4C-80-3F   2/10
2     00-30-19-4C-80-D4   2/6
2     00-30-19-4C-80-B3   2/7
2     00-30-19-4C-80-A2   2/2
2     00-80-00-00-12-D0   2/22
2     00-30-19-4C-80-C4   2/1
2     00-30-19-4C-80-3B   2/23
Total Matching CAM Entries Displayed = 12
```

Viewing the CAM (MAC Address) Table on a CLI-Based IOS

On a CLI-based IOS, the **show mac** command is used to view the CAM table that makes forwarding decisions for frames arriving on the switch. Let's take a look at the output using the **show mac** command:

```
1912EN#show mac

Number of permanent addresses : 5
Number of restricted static addresses : 0
Number of dynamic addresses : 1

Address          Dest Interface    Type       Source Interface List
-----------------------------------------------------------------------
0030.194C.80A6   Ethernet 0/1      Permanent  All
0000.0C00.4BD0   Ethernet 0/1      Permanent  All
00A0.2457.2877   Ethernet 0/1      Permanent  All
0000.0C33.4283   Ethernet 0/5      Permanent  All
0000.0C33.4283   Ethernet 0/10     Permanent  All
0000.0C33.4286   Ethernet 0/10     Permanent  All
0010.A4EF.92FB   Ethernet 0/6      Dynamic    All

1912EN#
```

Viewing the CDP Neighbors on a Set/Clear Command-Based IOS

The **show cdp neighbors** command is used to obtain details of the neighboring Cisco devices. Let's take a look at the optional syntaxes and an example of the output using the command:

```
show cdp neighbors [module number[/port number][detail]

Catalyst5002(enable) show cdp neighbor detail

Device-ID: Coriolis2514.coriolis.com
Device Addresses:
  IP Address: 68.27.187.254
Holdtime: 150 sec
Capabilities: ROUTER
Version:
Cisco Internetwork Operating System Software
IOS (tm) 2500 Software (C2500-IO-L), Version 12.0(5), RELEASE SOFTWARE (fc1)
Copyright (c) 1986-1999 by cisco Systems, Inc.
Platform: cisco 2500
Port-ID: FastEthernet0
Port: 2/1

Device-ID: 1900EN.coriolis.com
Device Addresses:
  IP Address: 68.27.187.253
Holdtime: 132 sec
Capabilities: SWITCH
Version:
Cisco Internetwork Operating System Software
Cisco Catalyst 1900/2820 Enterprise Edition Software
Version V8.01.02
Copyright (c) Cisco Systems, Inc.  1993-1998
Platform: cisco 1900/2820
Port-ID: FastEthernet0
Port: 2/2
```

Viewing the CDP Neighbors on a CLI-Based IOS

The **show cdp neighbors** command is used to obtain details of the neighboring Cisco devices on a CLI-based IOS. Let's take a look at the command and an example of its output:

```
1912EN#show cdp neighbors

Capability Codes: R - Router, T - Trans Bridge, B - Source Route Bridge
                  S - Switch, P - Repeater,   H - Host, I - IGMP
DeviceID      IP Addr         Local Port  Capability Platform     Remote Port
1005          68.127.187.254  Et0/1          R        cisco 1000   Ethernet0

1912EN#
```

Viewing Individual Port CAM Tables on a CLI-Based IOS

The **show mac interface** command allows you to view the MAC addresses associated with each individual port. Let's take a look at an example of the command:

```
show mac interface <Ethernet|fastethernet> <module/port>

1912EN#show mac interface ethernet 0/1

Address            Dest Interface    Type        Source Interface List
-------------------------------------------------------------------------
0030.194C.80A6     Ethernet 0/1      Permanent   All
0000.0C00.4BD0     Ethernet 0/1      Permanent   All
00A0.2457.2877     Ethernet 0/1      Permanent   All

1912EN#
```

Viewing Port Statistics on a Set/Clear IOS

To view the port statistics on a Set/Clear command-based IOS, use the **show mac** command. Let's look at the command and its quite lengthy output:

```
Catalyst5002> (enable) show mac

MAC Rcv-Frms Xmit-Frms Rcv-M Xmit-M Rcv-Broad Xmit-Broad
1/1        0         0     0      0         0          0
1/2        0         0     0      0         0          0
2/1    41840     23431    53    323      2342        887
2/2    23941     21026   132    432      1284         95
2/3     9892      6489   134    455      1345        178
2/4    23376     23179    34    124         1       2248
2/5   344951     16135   138    142     12412      13123
```

2/6	0	0	0	0	0	0
2/7	0	0	0	0	0	0
2/8	0	0	0	0	0	0
2/9	0	0	0	0	0	0
2/10	0	0	0	0	0	0
2/11	0	0	0	0	0	0
2/12	0	0	0	0	0	0
2/13	0	0	0	0	0	0
2/14	0	0	0	0	0	0
2/15	0	0	0	0	0	0
2/16	0	0	0	0	0	0
2/17	0	0	0	0	0	0
2/18	0	0	0	0	0	0
2/19	0	0	0	0	0	0
2/20	0	0	0	0	0	0
2/21	0	0	0	0	0	0
2/22	0	0	0	0	0	0
2/23	0	0	0	0	0	0
2/24	0	0	0	0	0	0

MAC	Dely-Exced	MTU-Exced	In-Dcrd	Lrn-Dcrd	In-Lost	Out-Lost
1/1	0	0	0	0	0	0
1/2	0	0	0	0	0	0
2/1	0	0	0	0	0	0
2/2	0	0	0	0	0	0
2/3	0	0	0	0	0	0
2/4	0	0	0	0	0	0
2/5	0	0	0	0	0	0
2/6	0	0	0	0	0	0
2/7	0	0	0	0	0	0
2/8	0	0	0	0	0	0
2/9	0	0	0	0	0	0
2/10	0	0	0	0	0	0
2/11	0	0	0	0	0	0
2/12	0	0	0	0	0	0

Port	Rcv-Unicast	Rcv-Multicast	Rcv-Broadcast
1/1	0	0	0
1/2	0	0	0
2/1	326653	3444	72348
2/2	2465834	1755	566432
2/3	99675	3467	66432
2/4	345562	453	77645
2/5	0	0	0
2/6	0	0	0

**16. Switch
Troubleshooting**

2/7	0	0	0
2/8	0	0	0
2/9	0	0	0
2/10	0	0	0
2/11	0	0	0
2/12	0	0	0

Port	Xmit-Unicast	Xmit-Multicast	Xmit-Broadcast
1/1	0	0	0
1/2	0	0	0
2/1	8809	431	227
2/2	5798	540	101
2/3	6260	895	83
2/4	7341	935	107
2/5	0	0	0
2/6	0	0	0
2/7	0	0	0
2/8	0	0	0
2/9	0	0	0
2/8	0	0	0
2/9	0	0	0
2/10	0	0	0
2/11	0	0	0
2/12	0	0	0

Port	Rcv-Octet	Xmit-Octet
1/1	0	0
1/2	0	0
2/1	3346321	437519
2/2	3442573	465421
2/3	6738753	6345326
2/4	234434	563002
2/5	3455	3225
2/6	0	0
2/7	0	0
2/8	0	0
2/9	0	0
2/10	0	0
2/11	0	0
2/12	0	0

```
Last-Time-Cleared
--------------------------
Sat Sep 23 2000, 11:29:11
```

Viewing Port Statistics on a CLI-Based IOS

To view the port statistics on a CLI-based IOS, use the **show usage** command. Let's take a look at the command, the options available, and an example of its output:

```
1912EN#show usage ?
  exception     Display exception statistics report
  utilization   Display utilization statistics report

1912EN#show usage utilization

          Receive    Forward    Transmit
          --------------------------------
  1  :      6301       5861        2252
  2  :         0          0           0
  3  :         1          0        4124
  4  :         0          0           0
  5  :       889        821        4124
  6  :      4217       4217        7857
  7  :         0          0           0
  8  :         0          0           6
  9  :         0          0           0
 10  :         0          0         693
 11  :         0          0           0
 12  :         0          0           0

 AUI :         0          0        4124
  A  :         0          0           0
  B  :         0          0           0
```

Here is the output using the **exception** syntax:

```
1912EN#show usage exception

          Receive    Transmit  Security
          Errors     Errors    Violations
          --------------------------------
  1  :       0          0           0
  2  :       0          0           0
  3  :       0          0           0
  4  :       0          0           0
  5  :       0          0           0
  6  :       0          0           0
  7  :       0          0           0
```

```
  8  :          0           0           0
  9  :          0           0           0
 10  :          0           0           0
 11  :          0           0           0
 12  :          0           0           0

 AUI:           0           0           0
 A   :          0           0           0
 B   :          0           0           0


 1912EN#
```

Using the Port Configuration on a Set/Clear Command-Based IOS

The **show port** command can be used on a Set/Clear command-based IOS switch to view the port configuration. Let's take a look at the command, its optional syntaxes, and an example of its output:

```
show port [module/port]
show port [module]


Catalyst5002> (enable) show port 2/1

Port  Name      Status    Vlan Level  Duplex Speed  Type
----  --------  --------  ---- ------  ------ ------ ------
2/1   Port1     normal     2           full    100 100BaseT

Port Security Secure-Src-Addr Last-Src-Addr  Shutdown Trap
---- -------- --------------- --------------- -------- --------
2/1  enabled  0090.80a3.32a0  0090.80a3.32a0 No        -

Port      Broadcast-Limit Broadcast-Drop
--------  --------------- ---------------
2/1                     -               0

Port   Status      Channel  Channel     Neighbor       Neighbor
                   Mode     status      device         port
----   ----------  -------  ----------  -------------- --------
2/1    connected   on       not channel
```

Port	Align-Err	FCS-Err	Xmit-Err	Rcv-Err	UnderSize
2/1	0	0	6	0	0

Port	Single-Col	Multi-Coll	Late-Coll	Excess-Col	Carri-Sen	Runts	Giants
2/1	3442	603	0	0	0	1	0

Using the **show port** Command on a CLI-Based IOS

The **show port** command can be used on a CLI-based IOS switch to view the port configuration. Let's take a look at the command, its syntaxes, and an example of its output:

```
1912EN#show port ?

   block     Forwarding of unknown unicast/multicast addresses
   monitor   Port monitoring
   system    System port configuration

1912EN#show port block ?
   multicast  Forwarding of unregisterd multicast addresses
   unicast    Forwarding of unknown unicast addresses

1912EN#show port block multicast
Ports receiving unregistered multicast addresses:
Ethernet 0/1, Ethernet 0/2, Ethernet 0/3, Ethernet 0/4
Ethernet 0/5, Ethernet 0/6, Ethernet 0/7, Ethernet 0/8
Ethernet 0/9, Ethernet 0/10, Ethernet 0/11, Ethernet 0/12
Ethernet 0/25, FastEthernet 0/26, FastEthernet 0/27

1912EN#show port block unicast
Ports receiving unmatched unicast addresses:
Ethernet 0/1, Ethernet 0/2, Ethernet 0/3, Ethernet 0/4
Ethernet 0/5, Ethernet 0/6, Ethernet 0/7, Ethernet 0/8
Ethernet 0/9, Ethernet 0/10, Ethernet 0/11, Ethernet 0/12
Ethernet 0/25, FastEthernet 0/26, FastEthernet 0/27

1912EN#show port monitor
Port monitoring state: Enabled
Monitor port: None
```

16. Switch Troubleshooting

```
Ports being monitored:
Ethernet 0/1

1912EN#show port system
Switching mode: FragmentFree
Use of store and forward for multicast: Enabled
Network port: Ethernet 0/8
Half duplex backpressure (10 Mbps ports): Disabled
Enhanced Congestion Control (10 Mbps ports): Disabled
Default port LED display mode: Port Status

1912EN#
```

Using the **show vlan** Command on a Set/Clear Command-Based IOS

You can use the **show vlan** command on a Set/Clear command-based IOS switch to obtain configuration information and protocol statistics for each VLAN. Let's look at the command, its optional syntaxes, and an example of its output:

```
show vlan [vlan] [trunk|notrunk]

Catalyst5002> show vlan

Virtual LAN ID:   1

    vLAN Trunk Interface:     FastEthernet1/0.1

    Protocols Configured:   Address:           Received:       Transmitted:
            IP              68.127.187.10      95563219847     81294682

Virtual LAN ID:   2 (Inter Switch Link Encapsulation)

    vLAN Trunk Interface:     FastEthernet1/0.2

    Protocols Configured:   Address:           Received:       Transmitted:
            IP              68.127.186.1       855147          854281

Catalyst5002>
```

Using the **show vlan** Command on a CLI-Based IOS

You can use the **show vlan** command on a CLI-based IOS switch to obtain configuration information for each VLAN. Let's look at the command, its optional syntaxes, and an example of its output:

```
show vlan <vlan>

1912EN#show vlan

VLAN Name              Status     Ports
----------------------------------------
1    default           Enabled    5-12, AUI, A, B
2    Engineering       Enabled    1-2
3    Admins            Enabled    3-4
1002 fddi-default      Suspended
1003 token-ring-defau  Suspended
1004 fddinet-default   Suspended
1005 trnet-default     Suspended
----------------------------------------


VLAN Type           SAID   MTU   Parent RingNo BridgeNo Stp  Trans1 Trans2
--------------------------------------------------------------------------
1    Ethernet       100001 1500  0      0      0        Unkn 1002   1003
2    Ethernet       100002 1500  0      0      0        Unkn 1002   1003
3    Ethernet       100003 1500  0      0      0        Unkn 1002   1003
1002 FDDI           101002 1500  0      0      0        Unkn 1      1003
1003 Token-Ring     101003 1500  1005   1      0        Unkn 1      1002
1004 FDDI-Net       101004 1500  0      0      1        IEEE 0      0
1005 Token-Ring-Net 101005 1500  0      0      1        IEEE 0      0
--------------------------------------------------------------------------

1912EN#
```

Using the **show interface** Command on a Set/Clear Command-Based IOS

You can view information about the switch network interfaces using the **show interface** command on a Set/Clear command-based IOS. Let's take a look at the command, its available option, and an example of its output:

```
show interface [trap]

Catalyst5002> (enable) show interface

sl0: flags=51<UP,POINTOPOINT,RUNNING>
    slip 0.0.0.0 dest 0.0.0.0
sc0: flags=63<UP,BROADCAST,RUNNING>
    vlan 1 inet 68.127.187.1 netmask 255.255.255.0 broadcast 68.127.187.255
```

Using the show interface Command on a CLI-Based IOS

You can view information about the switch network interfaces using the **show interface** command on a CLI-based IOS. Let's take a look at the command, its available options, and an example of its output:

```
show interface [module|port]

1912EN#show interface e0/5

Ethernet 0/5 is Enabled
Hardware is Built-in 10Base-T
Address is 0030.8054.6C05
MTU 1500 bytes, BW 10000 Kbits
802.1d STP State:  Forwarding    Forward Transitions:  1
Port monitoring: Disabled
Unknown unicast flooding: Enabled
Unregistered multicast flooding: Enabled
Description: port5
Duplex setting: Half duplex
Back pressure: Disabled
```

Receive Statistics		Transmit Statistics	
Total good frames	2504	Total frames	11745
Total octets	242467	Total octets	875657
Broadcast/multicast frames	359	Broadcast/multicast frames	11745
Broadcast/multicast octets	105187	Broadcast/multicast octets	875657
Good frames forwarded	360	Deferrals	0
Frames filtered	2144	Single collisions	0
Runt frames	0	Multiple collisions	0
No buffer discards	0	Excessive collisions	0
		Queue full discards	0

```
Errors:                              Errors:
  FCS errors                  0        Late collisions          0
  Alignment errors            0        Excessive deferrals      0
  Giant frames                0        Jabber errors            0
  Address violations          0        Other transmit errors    0

1912EN#
```

Using the **show log** Command on a Set/Clear Command-Based IOS

On the Set/Clear command-based IOS, you can view the stored logs by using the **show log** command. Let's look at the command, its optional syntax, and an example of its output:

```
show log [module number]

Catalyst5002> (enable) show log

Network Management Processor (ACTIVE NMP) Log:
  Reset count:    1
  Re-boot History:   Aug 04 2000 23:06:05 0

  Bootrom Checksum Failures:      0
  UART Failures:                  0
  Flash Checksum Failures:        0
  Flash Program Failures:         0
  Power Supply 1 Failures:        1
  Power Supply 2 Failures:        0
  Swapped to CLKA:                0
  Swapped to CLKB:                0
  Swapped to Processor 1:         0
  Swapped to Processor 2:         0
  DRAM Failures:                  0

  Exceptions:                     1
    Last Exception occurred on  ...
    Software version = 4.1
    Error Msg:
    PID = 0 Kernel
    PC: 10000D0C, Status: 2704, Vector: 007C
    sp+00: 14041000 0D0C007C 2604101F 0D3A00AC
    sp+10: 00000000 101785A2 00000030 102FB12C
```

```
sp+20:  10FFFF9C  10179C06  10357A90  102FB12C
sp+30:  10FFFFA8  101FB86E  00000000  10FFFFE8
sp+40:  101FC0D4  00000000  10278814  00002000
sp+50:  00000080  0000101F  B9862078  01000001
sp+60:  1CD80000  001E0000  00010000  00000000
sp+70:  00000000  00000000  00000007  68000000
sp+80:  00000000  00000000  00000000  00000000
sp+90:  00000000  103FFFEC  10000420  100009C2
sp+A0:  10000940  10000A4E  10001030  10001030
sp+B0:  10001030  10001030  10000BD0  10000AD0
sp+C0:  10000B28  10001030  10001030  10001030
sp+D0:  10001030  10001030  10001030  10001030
sp+E0:  10001030  10001030  10001030  10001030
sp+F0:  10001030  10001030  10001030  493798E4
D0: 00000000,  D1: 00000004,  D2: 00000030,  D3: 00005C05
D4: 11000000,  D5: 11000000,  D6: 10FF0008,  D7: 11000000
A0: 68000000,  A1: 00000000,  A2: 10357A90,  A3: 103C182C
A4: 103C182C,  A5: 64000000,  A6: 10FFFF8C,  sp: 10FFFF6C
```

```
NVRAM log:

Module 2 Log:
  Reset Count:   1
  Reset History: Fri Aug 04 2000, 8:07:12
```

NOTE: *There is no comparable command on the 1900EN series switches.*

Configuring SPAN for Port Monitoring on a Set/Clear Command-Based IOS

To configure the Set/Clear command-based IOS switch for SPAN, follow these steps:

1. To enable SPAN, use the **set span enable** command. The syntax for this command is as follows:

```
set span enable|disable
```

2. To enable SPAN for port monitoring, you must identify the source module, source port, destination module, destination port, and (optionally) whether

you want it to monitor received frames, transmitted frames, or both. The syntax for the command is as follows:

```
set span <source module/source port> <destination module/
    destination port>  [rx|tx|both]
```

NOTE: *RX stands for Receive, TX stands for Transmit.*

Configuring SPAN for VLAN Monitoring on a Set/Clear Command-Based IOS

To configure a Set/Clear command-based IOS switch for SPAN, follow these steps:

1. To enable SPAN, use the **set span enable** command. The syntax for this command is as follows:

```
set span enable|disable
```

2. To enable SPAN for VLAN monitoring, you must identify the source VLAN, destination module, destination port, and (optionally) whether you want it to monitor received frames, transmitted frames, or both. The syntax for the command is as follows:

```
set span <source VLAN> <destination module/
    destination port> [rx|tx|both]
```

Launching the Diagnostic Console on a Cisco 1900 or 2820 Series Switch

To launch the Diagnostic Console on the 1900 or 2820 series switch, follow these steps:

1. Attach a terminal or PC to the console port.

2. Press and hold down the Mode button, as shown in Figure 16.5, while cycling the power on the switch.

16. Switch Troubleshooting

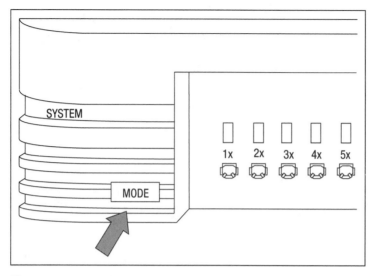

Figure 16.5   The Mode button on a 1900 Series switch.

3. Proceed through the following options:

```
--------------------------------------------------
Cisco Systems Diagnostic Console
Copyright(c) Cisco Systems, Inc. 1997
All rights reserved.
Ethernet Address: 00-30-80-54-6C-00
--------------------------------------------------
Press enter to continue.

    Diagnostic Console  - Systems Engineering

        Operation firmware version:  8.01.02    Status: valid
        Boot firmware version:  3.10

    [C] Continue with standard system start up
    [U] Upgrade operation firmware (XMODEM)
    [S] System debug interface

Enter Selection:
```

Using the Diagnostic Console to Upgrade the Firmware on a Cisco 1900 or 2820 Series Switch

Follow these steps to upgrade the firmware on a Cisco 1900 or 2820 series switch:

1. Press the Mode button on the front of the switch while booting, to enter the Diagnostic Console, as shown here:

```
------------------------------------------------
Cisco Systems Diagnostic Console
Copyright(c) Cisco Systems, Inc. 1997
All rights reserved.
Ethernet Address: 00-30-80-54-6C-00
------------------------------------------------
Press enter to continue.

    Diagnostic Console  - Systems Engineering

        Operation firmware version:  8.01.02   Status: valid
        Boot firmware version:  3.10

    [C] Continue with standard system start up
    [U] Upgrade operation firmware (XMODEM)
    [S] System debug interface

Enter Selection:
```

2. Use the [U] Upgrade Operation Firmware (XMODEM) option to upgrade the firmware (you must be using X-Modem compatible software on the network node attached to the switch):

```
Enter Selection:  U

The XMODEM protocol will be used to perform this firmware upgrade.
The user must initiate an XMODEM file transfer from the terminal
side using an appropriate terminal application specific command.

Do you wish to continue with the download process, [Y]es or [N]o?
```

3. By answering [Y]es here, the switch immediately deletes the IOS from the Flash. It doesn't give you any warning. The configuration is left to run on the new IOS that is installed:

```
Erasing invalid flash - may take up to 1 minute.
Erasure completed.
```

4. You now need to select the speed at which to upload the IOS. If you are using the console cable it should be 9600. If you are using a modem you can upload a new image at 57,600Kbps:

```
Do you wish to upgrade at [9]600 (console speed) or [5]7600? 9600

Waiting for image at the configured baud rate...
```

Using the Diagnostic Console for Debugging the Firmware and Hardware

Follow these steps to start debugging on the switch:

1. To enter the Diagnostic Console, press the Mode button on the front of the switch while booting.

2. Use the [S] System option to enter the debug interface, as follows:

```
Enter Selection:  S

    Diagnostic Console  - System debug interface


    [G] Generic I/O
    [M] Memory (CPU) I/O
    [F] Return system to factory defaults
    [R] Reset main console RS232 interface to 9600,8,1,N
    [V] View management console password

    [X] Exit to Previous Menu

Enter Selection:
```

Here is an example of the output from the [G] Generic I/O option:

```
Enter Selection:  G


    Diagnostic Console  - Generic I/O
```

```
----------------Settings------------------

[A] Autoincrement address        Yes
[F] From address location        0000H (0)
[L] Length in 16-bit words       0001H (1)
[T] Toggle byte/word display     Word
[V] Value for output             0000H (0)

----------------Actions------------------

[I] Input
[O] Output

[X] Exit to Previous Menu

Enter Selection:
```

Here is an example of the output from the [M] Memory (CPU) I/O option:

```
Enter Selection:  M


    Diagnostic Console  - Memory (CPU) I/O


    ----------------Settings------------------

    [F] From offset location        0000H (0)
    [L] Length in 16-bit words      0001H (1)
    [T] Toggle byte/word display    Word
    [V] Value for output            0000H (0)

    ----------------Actions------------------

    [I] Input
    [O] Output

    [X] Exit to Previous Menu

Enter Selection:
```

Here is an example of the output from the [F] Return System To Factory Defaults option:

```
Enter Selection:  F

Reset system with factory defaults, [Y]es or [N]o? Yes
```

Here is an example of the output from the [R] Reset Main Console RS232 Interface To 9600,8,1,N option:

```
Enter Selection:  R

Reset main console RS232 interface to 9600,8,1,N, [Y]es or [N]o? Yes
```

Here is an example of the output from the [V] View management console password option:

```
Enter Selection:  V

The current management console password is: 62592

Press any key to continue.
```

Appendix A
Study Resources

Books

McDysan, David E. and Darren L. Spohn, *ATM Theory and Application*, McGraw-Hill: New York, 1998. ISBN: 0-07045-346-2. This book is a great resource on Asynchronous Transfer Mode (ATM) and LAN Emulation (LANE).

Odom, Sean and Douglas Hammond, *CCNP Switching Exam Prep*, The Coriolis Group: Scottsdale, AZ, 2000. ISBN: 1-57610-689-6. This book covers the curriculum for the Cisco Switching Exam number 640-504.

Cisco Group Study and Users Groups

Some of the best resources for Cisco information are Cisco users groups and group study Web sites. Most major cities have one or both. Joining a group is a great way to keep up on technical information and gain a network of friends off of whom you can bounce troubleshooting questions. The following are some of the best Cisco user groups we've found:

- *Atlanta Cisco Certification Study Group (ACCSG), Georgia*— **www.brainslap.com**
- *Capital District Cisco Users Group, Albany, New York*—**www.cdcug.org**
- *Cisco Users Group for Central Iowa*—**http://cisco.knis.com**
- *Dallas/Ft.Worth Cisco Users Group, Texas*—**http://dfw.cisco-users.org**
- *Denver Cisco Users Group, Colorado*—**www.twpm.com/dcug/**
- *Groupstudy.Com*—**www.groupstudy.com**
- *Kansas City Cisco Users Group, Kansas*—**www.cugkansas.com/home.cfm**
- *New England Cisco Systems Users Group*—**www.ciscousers.com**
- *Northern California Cisco Users Group, Sacramento, California*— **www.csecnet.com/cisco/index.htm**

- *Omaha Cisco User Group, Nebraska*—**www.teklnk.com**

- *Sacramento Placer County Cisco Users Group, California*—**www.cisco-cert.org**

- *Southern California Cisco Users Group*—**www.sccug.org**

Live Cisco Training/Internet-Based Labs/Study Resources

- *The Quest for Certification*—Author Sean Odom's Web site—Meet Joe Snow and get valuable updates to this book—**www.thequestforcertification.com**

- *ExamCram.com*—The latest certification information and study questions—**www.examcram.com**

- *e-Business Process Solutions*—Cisco Internet Training/VAR—**www.e-bps.com**

- *VLABS-MentorLabs.Com*—Online Cisco labs and equipment—**www.mentorlabs.com**

- *CCNP Study*—CCNP information, interviews, and book reviews—**www.ccnp-study.com**

Online Resources

Multiple documents are available on the Web, but the best place for information is the Cisco Web site. Cisco is one of the best companies at providing documentation on its products. You can find the Cisco Web site at **www.cisco.com**.

Asynchronous Transfer Mode

- *ATM fundamentals information on an 8500 Series switch*—**www.cisco.com/univercd/cc/td/doc/product/atm/c8540/wa5/12_0/3a_11/atm_tech/basics.htm**

- *Configuring ATM accounting and ATM RMON*—**www.cisco.com/univercd/cc/td/doc/product/atm/c8540/wa5/12_0/12_3/sw_conf/act_rmon.htm**

- *ATM Features For LightStream Switches*—**www.cisco.com/univercd/cc/td/doc/product/dsl_prod/ios_dsl/rel121/rel_3/ol068201.htm**

- *Configuring ATM signaling and ATM Internetworking*—**www.cisco.com/warp/public/614/12.html**

Cisco IOS

- *The Cisco IOS Easy IP*—**www.cisco.com/warp/public/cc/pd/iosw/ioft/ ionetn/tech/ezip1_wp.htm**
- *IOS troubleshooting commands*—**www.cisco.com/univercd/cc/td/doc/ product/software/ios113ed/113ed_cr/fun_r/frprt4/frtroubl.htm**
- *Configuring User Interface*—**www.cisco.com/univercd/cc/td/doc/product/ atm/c8540/wa5/12_0/12_3/sw_conf/admin.htm**

Hot Standby Router Protocol

- *HSRP frequently asked questions*—**www.cisco.com/warp/public/619/ 3.html**
- *Frequently asked questions and solutions*—**www.cisco.com/warp/public/ 619/3.html**
- *Sample configuration of HSRP*—**www.cisco.com/univercd/cc/td/doc/ cisintwk/ics/cs009.htm**

Inter-Switch Link

- *ISL Functional Specification*—**www.cisco.com/warp/public/741/4.html**
- *ISL Trunking on the Catalyst 5000 and 6000 Family Switches*—**www.cisco. com/warp/public/793/lan_switching/2.html**

IP Multicast

- *Higher-level Protocols Used with Multicast*—**www.ipmulticast.com/ community/whitepapers/highprot.html**
- *IP Multicast Routing Commands*—**www.cisco.com/univercd/cc/td/doc/ product/software/ios121/121cgcr/ip_r/iprprt3/1rdmulti.htm**
- *Simple Multicast Routing Protocol*—**www.cisco.com/univercd/cc/td/doc/ cisintwk/ito_doc/smrp.htm**

Multilayer Switching

- *Configuring IP Multicast Multilayer Multicast Switching*—**www.cisco.com/ univercd/cc/td/doc/product/software/ios121/121cgcr/switch_c/xcprt5/ xcdmmsc.htm**
- *Configuring IP Multilayer Switching for IOS 12.1*—**www.cisco.com/ univercd/cc/td/doc/product/software/ios121/121cgcr/switch_c/xcprt5/ xcdmsc.htm**

- *Configuring IPX Multilayer Switching*—**www.cisco.com/univercd/cc/td/
doc/product/software/ios121/121cgcr/switch_c/xcprt5/xcdmsipx.htm**

Quality of Service

- *Quality of Service Overview*—**www.cisco.com/univercd/cc/td/doc/
product/software/ios121/121cgcr/qos_c/qcdintro.htm**

- *Configuring Quality of Service on a Cisco Catalyst 6000*—**www.cisco.com/
univercd/cc/td/doc/product/lan/cat6000/sw_5_4/config/qos.htm**

- *Configuring IOS Quality of Service on the Catalyst 6000 Family*—
**www.cisco.com/univercd/cc/td/doc/product/lan/cat6000/ios127xe/
qos.htm**

Spanning Tree Protocol

- *Configuring STP on a Cisco Catalyst 2900*—**www.cisco.com/univercd/cc/
td/doc/product/lan/c2900xl/29_35sa6/olhelp/stphelp.htm**

- *Configuring STP on a Cisco Catalyst 6000*—**www.cisco.com/univercd/cc/
td/doc/product/lan/cat6000/sw_5_3/cofigide/spantree.htm**

TACACS+

- *Configuring TACACS+ and RADIUS on the Catalyst 5000, 5500, 4000, and
2900 Series*—**www.cisco.com/warp/public/473/cat_tacacs_plus.html**

- *Configuration examples using TACACS+*—**www.cisco.com/univercd/cc/td/
doc/product/software/ios121/121cgcr/secur_c/scprt1/scdathor.htm**

VLANs

- *VLAN and router technical tips*—**www.cisco.com/warp/public/741/10.html**

- *IEEE 802.10 VLAN encapsulation information*—**www.cisco.com/warp/
public/741/3.html**

- *VLAN configuration issues on the Catalyst 5000*—**www.cisco.com/warp/
public/741/9.html**

Standards Organizations

- *American National Standards Institute (ANSI)*—This organization coordi-
nates many specialized standards organizations and technical committees.
ANSI's Web site can be found at **www.ansi.org**.

- *Electronic Industries Alliance (EIA)*—This is the parent organization for a
number of standards groups, including the Telecommunications Industry

Association (TIA). TIA/EIA standards relate mostly to cabling. The TIA members are providers of communications and information technology products and services. The TIA/EIA Web site can be found at **www.tiaonline.org**.

- *Gigabit Ethernet Alliance*—This group was formed to promote industry cooperation in developing Gigabit Ethernet. You can find this group's Web site at **www.gigabit-ethernet.org**.

- *High Speed Token Ring Alliance*—This group was formed by Token Ring vendors to establish high-speed solutions for Token Ring. Their Web site can be found at **www.hstra.com**.

- *Institute for Electrical and Electronics Engineers (IEEE)*—This standards organization creates and publishes standards related to electronic technologies. It is best known for its 802 committee, which has produced a series of standards documents that describe LAN protocols and physical transmission topology standards. The IEEE's Web site can be found at **www.ieee.org**.

- *International Organization for Standardization (ISO)*—This organization is best known for the Open System Interconnection (OSI) Model. It creates and publishes standards that cover a wide range of topics. The ISO Web site can be found at **www.iso.ch**.

- *International Telecommunications Union Telecommunication Standardization Sector (ITU-T)*—This organization is responsible for the networking standards relating to Asynchronous Transfer Mode (ATM). The ITU-T Web site can be found at **www.itu.int**.

- *Internet Engineering Task Force (IETF)*—This organization is responsible for the TCP/IP, Simple Network Management Protocol (SNMP), and Internet standards. A lot of its work relates to upgrading and enlarging the TCP/IP protocol suite and networks utilizing that protocol. The IETF Web site can be found at **www.ietf.org**.

- *National Committee for Information Technology Standards (NCITS)*—This organization was formed to produce market condition standards for storage devices, multimedia, programming languages, and security. The T11 committee is responsible for fiber channel standards. You can find the NCITS T11 Web site at **www.t11.org**.

Cisco Job Search Sites

- **www.americanjobs.com**
- **www.cisco.com/pcgi-bin/jobs.pl**
- **www.computerjobs.com**

Appendix A
Study Resources

- www.computerjobsbank.com
- www.computerpeople.com
- www.computerwork.com
- www.dice.com
- www.hotjobs.com
- www.ishunter.com
- it.careershop.com
- www.jobbankusa.com
- www.jobserve.com
- www.monster.com
- www.preferredjobs.com
- www.selectjobs.com
- www.winjobs.com

Appendix B

Basic IOS CLI-to-Set/Clear Commands

Many features are supported by the Set/Clear-based switches, which include the Catalyst 5000 and 6000 families of switches. Most basic commands on a Command Line Interface (CLI)-based IOS can be mapped to commands that provide similar functionality on the Set/Clear-based CLI.

Table B.1 maps the 1900EN commands with those of the 5000 family of switches.

Table B.1   1900EN commands mapped to 5000 commands.

1900EN IOS-Based Switch	Description	Set/Clear-Based Switch
description *<description_string>*	Configures the port name	set port name *<modnumber>* *<description>*
duplex <auto|full|full-flow-control|half> *<mod|number>*	Sets the port duplex	set port duplex <half|full>
enable password level 1 *<password>*	Sets the switch password	set password
enable password level 15 *<password>*	Sets the enable password	set enablepass
hostname *<name>*	Sets the prompt/hostname	set prompt *<name>*
ip address *<ip_address> <netmask>*	Sets the IP address	set interface sc0 *<ip_address><netmask>*
N/A	Sets the port speed	set port speed *<mod/number>* <10|100|auto>
N/A	Sets the system name	set system name *<name>*
no trunk-vlan *<vlan_range>*	Clears a trunk port	clear trunk *<mod/num>* *<vlan_range>*
no spantree *<vlan-list>*	Disables Spanning-Tree Protocol (STP)	set spantree disable *<modnumber>*
port-channel mode *<on|off|auto|desirable>*	Sets the port channel mode	set port channel *<modnumber>* <on|off|auto|desirable>
show interface*<type><mod|port>*	Shows the port configuration	show port *<mod/number>*
show ip	Shows the configured IP address	show interface

(continued)

Table B.1   1900EN commands mapped to 5000 commands *(continued).*

1900EN IOS-Based Switch	Description	Set/Clear-Based Switch
show running-config	Shows the running configuration	**show config**
show spantree *<vlan>*	Shows the spanning-tree configuration	**show spantree** *<vlan>*
show uplink-fast	Shows the UplinkFast configuration	**show spantree uplinkfast**
show vlan	Shows the VLAN configuration	**show vlan**
show vtp	Shows the VLAN Trunking Protocol (VTP) configuration	**show vtp domain**
spantree *<vlan-list>*	Configures STP	**set spantree enable** *<mod/number>* **hello** *<hellotime>*
spantree cost *<cost-value>*	Configures the port cost	**set spantree portcost** *<mod/number cost>*
spantree priority *<priority-value>*	Configures the port priority	**set spantree portpri** *<mod/number><priority>*
spantree start-forwarding	Enables PortFast	**set spantree portfast** *<mod/number>* **enable**
spantree-template	Sets the FwdDelay timer	**set spantree fwddelay** *[vlan] delay-value*
spantree-template	Sets the STP HelloTime	**timer set spantree hello** *<interval>*
spantree-template	Sets the MaxAge timer	**set spantree maxage agingtime** *[vlan]* **time**
uplink-fast	Enables UplinkFast	**set spantree uplinkfast enable**
trunk <on|off|desirable|auto|nonegotiate>	Configures the trunk port	**set trunk** *<mod/num>* <on|off|desirable|auto|no-negotiate>
vlan *<vlan_number>* **name** *<vlan_name>*	Configures the VLAN name	**set vlan** *<vlan_num>* **name** *<vlan_name>*
vlan-membership static *<vlan>*	Assigns a port to a VLAN	**set vlan** *<vlan_num>* *<mod/number>*
vtp *<mode>*	Configures the VTP mode: Transparent, Server, or Client	**set vtp mode** *<mode>*
vtp *<name>*	Configures the VTP domain	**set vtp domain** *<name>*
vtp password *<password>*	Configures the VTP domain password	**set vtp passwd** *<password>*

Appendix C
The Cisco Consultant

On the side, I run a small consulting company. When I tell people that I am a Cisco consultant, they usually reply, "Oh"; or, they ask how well Cisco's stock is currently doing. Consulting means that you work from one project to another on a freelance basis. Usually, if you're the consultant for a Cisco partner, the customer has found you—so the first part of your job is rather easy.

The following is a list of steps to help ensure that you meet your customer's expectations:

1. Establish your credibility.
2. Assess the customer's current needs.
3. Assess the customer's future needs.
4. Research solutions.
5. Propose several solutions and provide a cost estimate for each.
6. Explain to the customer the expectations of each solution.
7. Under-promise and over-deliver.

Not all your work requires technical knowledge. You should have the following business skills:

- Good speaking skills
- Good estimating skills
- Access to parts and device costs
- Good sales ability

Because you are selling Cisco gear, if you follow these rules, the only way you can fail at your job is if you stink at configuring and troubleshooting networks or if you have a difficult personality. I am going to assume that you possess neither of those two characteristics. Of course, you probably won't last long if you give away the house, either.

The first thing to do is to establish credibility with the customer. How do you do this? Let's take a look.

Establishing Credibility

There are many ways you can project a good degree of credibility with your customer. Here are a few suggestions:

- Wear the proper attire.
- Come prepared.
- Make the customer feel like they're important to you.
- Show your certifications.

When you first meet the prospective customer, it's a good idea to wear your company attire (a logo shirt and slacks). If the company doesn't have a standard outfit, make sure you make your first impression (depending on your gender) in a white shirt, tie, and slacks or a blouse, slacks or a dress. (Wearing tennis shoes is not a good complement to this attire.)

Take a current price list, including all the latest Cisco devices, their basic abilities, available modules, and prices. (Knowing the products will help you price things correctly, as well.) Almost every Cisco device has modules, cards, power supplies, and other accessories you can purchase separately, By the way—this Black Book is a great item to carry in your bag!

Make sure you are on time for your first appointment with the customer. Turn off your cellular phone (let voice mail be useful for once) and put your pager on vibrate. You want to project to the customer that he or she is the most important person in the world at that moment. No one wants to buy something from someone who frustrates them by answering a cellular phone or pager every five minutes.

Put your certifications on your business card. You need to show the customer that you are a skilled network consultant, and nothing does that better than industry-recognized certifications such as those Cisco has to offer. Displaying at least a CCNA or CCDA on your card projects to the customer that you are a proven professional in the industry. Although your peers may know that a CCNA is entry level, to the customer (who has no technical ability) you have a networking black belt. (Of course, I have found that writing a book on the subject never hurt, either!)

You need to keep your certifications current—and never lie about them. It is too easy for any business entity to do a quick check and see if you are who you say you are. If you don't have any certifications, you should hit the books, take a class, and get certified. One of the students in my class a few weeks ago put it this way: "I am taking your class because getting a Cisco certification is just like printing truckloads of money!" And in many ways, he is right.

Come Off As an Expert

When I am not consulting or writing books, I am teaching Cisco-related courses. One of the main characteristics I like to project to my students is not only looking smart, but sounding smart. The best way to sound smart is to know the equipment you are trying to sell to the customer, to have an extensive knowledge of the way devices and protocols work in the network, and to know the layers in which the devices and protocols can be found. Always stay tuned to what is new on Cisco's Web site—particularly its press releases and End-of-Life (EOL) notices. Nothing is worse than having the customer tell you about new Cisco products that are available.

Bringing a list of your previous clientele can't hurt. You may want to have letters from previous clients included in the packet of materials you give to the client with your estimate or with your brochure. If you are just starting out, you may not have such a list or letters available to show the client. If you have previous work experience, use clientele from that job. However, you shouldn't spend too much time gloating—remember, your goal is to sell the client, not talk his ear off. You can sometimes lose a job just because the client felt you talked too much or overstated your abilities.

Designing a Solution

When you finally get the chance to make a proposal, you need to design a solution. Many pieces of software are available from Cisco to help you in the design process. If you don't have access to this software or you need to make the proposal at the customer's site, a Web page is dedicated to this task on the Cisco Connection Online (CCO) site.

You need to imagine and draw every piece of the network you are designing. If you forget to include every cable you'll need, you will be in trouble. As you know, Cisco devices and cabling are quite expensive.

I like to draw a diagram of the building, placing a picture of every piece of equipment and every cable I will need. Doing so will help you decide on the modules you will need in the switches as well as the number of specific ports. Don't forget to look at the aggregate bandwidth of all the ports on the switches. Remember, the amount of bandwidth that can be sent on all these ports may be more than the trunk links can handle, if the correct network design is not implemented.

When submitting a proposal, keep in mind that you should actually make two proposals: one that includes the equipment needed to handle the immediate and short-term solutions and another that covers both the immediate and long-term solutions. In the proposal, you might want to explain the term "forklift upgrades" (briefly, this term refers to the fact that buying equipment correctly up front will be significantly cheaper than upgrading individual components later when it becomes necessary). Customers may not want to invest more money than they have to in the short term, but sometimes they will—and you wind up making a much bigger sale. Occasionally, your customers will find wisdom in investing in the future.

Estimating the Cost

When estimating the cost of a proposal, I add all the equipment costs and then add an additional 10 percent to the total, just in case I forgot something such as cables, tape, or tools. (I always have to go to the store for something I had no way of knowing I'd need.)

Make sure you factor in small things, such as tape, cables, cable straps, bundle holders, connectors, cable converters, extra RAM, cable testers, and the like. Don't forget to include parking costs—especially in San Francisco at $17 to $30 per day.

TIP: *If you are really trying to bid competitively, you may want to make the equipment costs appear lower and increase the labor cost by just a few dollars or increase the labor time estimate.*

Presenting the Final Proposal and Creating Expectations

The process of creating a proposal may seem difficult; but once you make a successful proposal, you can use the same one over and over, with modifications. The final proposal should break down the costs of the equipment, software, your labor, and licensing (software and hardware), and it should include network diagrams if possible. The proposal should look professional, including diagrams created using software such as Visio, to show how the equipment will be placed, and spreadsheets listing the equipment costs and the amount of realistic labor for installing each item.

At the very least, the proposal cover should be full color. A picture of the customer's building is great to include. I once had a manager who had a sign that

read, "THE PROPOSAL: Dumb people like pictures." Of course, you don't want to call your customers dumb—but they lack your knowledge. If they didn't, you wouldn't be there.

Don't get too in-depth, such as estimating the number of feet of cable needed for each room. That's a little too much. Just include a single "cabling" item on the proposal.

However, you should go into great detail as to the steps you will take to complete the job. Be sure that these steps are outlined in a language that the customer can understand. Assume that the customer does not know such terms as CPU, RAM, and CSU/DSU. Explain what each device does and why it is needed. A proposal that the customer can't understand won't help you get the job. I have seen some proposals that included a list of acronyms or a glossary.

Along with the proposal the customer is expecting, I include a higher-end proposal outlining what the customer could purchase for future needs, as well as a separate proposal to help negotiate the cost of continued support after the installation. Someone has to support the equipment after it is installed—might as well be you or someone who works with you.

WARNING! *Unless the customer asks, avoid contracts and proposals that keep the total amount open. A contract or proposal that states you'll work for $75 per hour until the job is done will most likely be unfavorable—unless you're contracting with the government, and then I highly recommend it (that was a joke). Customers want to know the final total up front.*

The last thing you should do is place an expiration date on the proposal. Equipment costs change, and so do your time constraints. Usually I make mine good for 90 days. This limit gives the customer plenty of time review the proposal and come to a decision.

Contracting

When you first go into business as a consultant, you should have a contract that is created by an attorney and authorized by your insurance carrier. Once you have the contract in a word-processing document form that outlines your liabilities and those of the customer, you can modify the contract to suit each individual customer. The investment is worth it—not just in case you are ever in a legal bind, but because good contracts help keep you *out* of a legal bind.

Make sure that the contract restates your deadlines, because the period between the time the proposal was made and approved may have been quite lengthy. During that period, your time constraints or the availability of the equipment may have changed.

Other than making sure that the person who signs your contract is authorized to do so, you're ready. After the contracts are signed, sealed, and delivered, go to work!

Document, Document, Document

Because you are the one who installed the components, the customer will most likely come back to you for support. When a doctor works on a patient, he documents everything so he knows what worked, what didn't work, and what has been tried before, for many reasons (including legal). You should treat each network just like your own patient.

Occasionally, you will be called back only to find that a less-than-knowledgeable person did some work on the network. Having the working configuration in hand makes for a quick resolution. If there is a problem with a component or if a component needs an upgrade, your documentation should show you exactly what you need to order to remain compatible with the current equipment.

Even though you're a high-paid Cisco consultant, you should get a few weeks of vacation a year, too. If you're the only one who knows the network, you'll be working on your vacation days.

The Way to Fail

Throughout history, great achievers have learned to manage themselves and their time. If you don't learn to manage yourself, you may encounter many points of failure.

Lots of things can ruin your reputation and can actually get you replaced on a job. Let's look at a few:

- Failing to be there when promised or rushing through the job
- Failing to manage your time
- Assuming you understand the customer's needs
- Failing to take responsibility

Failing to Be There When Promised, or Rushing through the Job

Let me tell you a story of an experience I had with a bad contractor, who always promised and never delivered. I had some remodeling done on my bathroom. The contractor and I spent a whole night working through every detail of how I wanted the bathroom to look, from the flooring all the way to the paint and lighting. The job was going to be very expensive, and I hired a person who worked for himself. Because the materials were charged separately and reimbursed to the contractor, he purchased all the materials and then left them in our living room. This was his first mistake, because I had to convince my wife that the materials would only be there a week or so.

The first day the contractor showed up, we gave him the initial payment for his work. He did a great day of work, removing the old flooring, vents, cabinets, toilet, and other fixtures. He said he would be back the next day to work some more—but the next day came and went, and he failed to show up. I called him, and he said a personal situation had come up and he was unable to make it. He assured me he would be there the next day to get most of the work done. The next day he showed up, worked about an hour, and then left, saying nothing. I could tell by the quality of his work that he was rushed and in a hurry to be somewhere else instead of where he was paid to be.

This went on for days—the contractor either didn't show up on time, didn't come at all, or worked a short period and disappeared. My wife finally told me that we needed to find someone else. Because I was the one who had been calling and getting a different excuse every time, I called the contractor and warned him that we were getting upset. He returned the next day, worked for quite some time, and then again returned to his habit of not showing up.

After three weeks, my wife demanded that we get someone else to finish the job. She was tired of having mirrors and cabinets sitting in the hallway. The following day, I called the contractor, informed him that he would no longer be allowed in our home, and told him we would hire someone else to complete the job he had started.

Failing to Manage Your Time

One of the biggest issues I have noticed about other consultants is their time management. When consultants contract a job, they get much of the money up front. To make matters worse, they have to do this to survive, because they always try to undercut their competitors' prices so much that they don't make enough money to live their desired lifestyle as a self-employed consultant. Therefore, they like to contract as much as they possibly can—only to wind up getting too much work.

You should make sure that you can complete each job and that you allow extra time in case configuration problems or hardware problems pop up when you least expect them. Booking your time both day and night does not allow for overtime to complete a job that has gotten behind. Be sure you have enough time to get the job done.

I had a great mentor who always said, "Over-promise and under-deliver". This means you should over-estimate your time and get the job done more quickly than you promised. By telling the customer you will finish the job in a week when you know it will only take two days, you leave time for emergencies. And when you get it done in three days, the customer is tickled pink and recommends you to his friends, neighbors, and grandmother.

Assuming You Know What the Customer Needs

An easy way to fail at a job is to assume what the customer needs. As a consultant, you need to verify with the customer exactly what he or she needs. You should also explain what each component you're installing does and describe its features. Don't assume because you have used it before that the hardware or software you have chosen to install is the same thing the customer has dreamed of having.

If you can't find the contracted item for one reason or another, don't get a substitute without first consulting with the customer. If you fail to get a solution that addresses the needs of your customer (or the needs the customer has forgotten to pass on to you), the experience can be a terrible ordeal. For this reason, you need to picture the environment you are designing and make sure the customer has been properly queried on his or her needs.

Don't forget to include something a client asked for. Always log conversations with the customer and note what is still needed and the action items you need to perform. Keeping a note pad and a checklist handy can be helpful. In the event of an unforeseen legal issue, it also helps to have a paper trail of all conversations.

Failing to Take Responsibility

If you realize that you failed to contract an item, you should absorb the cost if it is small. No one feels more nickeled and dimed than a person who has hired a consultant, when the consultant says he forgot to add a cable and will be charging another $10 five times. You can absorb small costs into the 10 percent padding I discussed earlier. If it is a large charge, debate notifying the customer. If it is too large to absorb, explain to the customer that you are at fault for not realizing you needed the part, and that you need to add an additional charge. Doing this more than once can be hazardous to your client/consultant relationship— just a helpful hint.

You will leave resentment in the customer's mind if you try to blame him by telling him he did not tell you he needed a particular component. The customer is not the professional who needed to realize he needed something—you are.

Conclusion

As a consultant, you must remember to manage your time and yourself. You are your own project manager. In fact, not only are you the project manager, you are the employee who is going to do the work. You'll probably make many mistakes in the beginning—but, I hope, none that can't be overcome. I'll leave you with one last quote that I like: "Experience is a tough teacher. You get the test first; then you're going to learn the lesson." I am not sure who wrote it, but it sure does make a good point.

Appendix D

Cisco 1912EN and Catalyst 5000 Configuration Practice Lab

Today Joe Snow, our imaginary consultant, has received a Catalyst 1912EN switch, a Catalyst 5000 with a Supervisor Engine III, and a 24-port 10/100 Ethernet module.

Joe has taken both the switches out of the box and has assembled all the devices into a rack. At present, neither switch is configured; Joe will be configuring both switches for a lab.

Required Equipment

To complete this lab, you will need:

- One Cisco Catalyst 5000 (Cisco 2926G, 2948G, 2980G, 5002, 5500, 5505, 5509, 6006, 6009, 6506, or 6509 are great Set/Clear command-based IOS substitutes).

- One Supervisor Engine III Module for the Cisco Catalyst 5000 running IOS version 5.5(2), as shown here in my **show version** output:

```
Catalyst5000> (enable) show version

WS-C5000 Software, Version McpSW: 5.5(2) NmpSW: 5.5(2)
Copyright (c) 1995-2000 by Cisco Systems
NMP S/W compiled on Jul 28 2000, 16:43:52
MCP S/W compiled on Jul 28 2000, 16:38:40

System Bootstrap Version: 3.1.2

Hardware Version: 2.0  Model: WS-C5000  Serial #: 011454261

Mod Port Model      Serial # Versions
--- ---- ---------- -------- ----------------------------------------
1   0    WS-X5530   011454261 Hw : 2.0
                              Fw : 3.1.2
                              Fw1: 4.2(1)
                              Sw : 5.5(2)
```

```
                WS-F5521    011455134 Hw : 1.1
     2    24     WS-X5225R   013405523 Hw : 3.1
                                       Fw : 4.3(1)
                                       Sw : 5.5(2)
             DRAM                    FLASH                   NVRAM
     Module Total    Used    Free    Total   Used    Free    Total Used  Free
     ------ ------   ------   -----   ------  ------  ------  ----  ----  ----

     1      32640K   20331K  12309K   8192K   5548K   2644K   512K  185K  327K


     Uptime is 2 days, 19 hours, 3 minutes

     Catalyst5000> (enable)
```

- One 24-port 10/100BaseTX module, as shown in the following **show module**
  output (you can substitute any 10/00 Ethernet module):

```
     Catalyst5000> (enable) show module

     Mod Slot Ports Module-Type                Model               Sub Status
     --- ---- ----  -------------------------  ------------------  --  --------
     1   1    0     Supervisor III             WS-X5530            yes ok
     2   2    24    10/100BaseTX Ethernet       WS-X5225R           no  ok


     Mod Module-Name         Serial-Num
     -- -----------------    --------------------
     1                       00011454261
     2                       00013405523



     Mod MAC-Address(es)                         Hw     Fw          Sw
     -- --------------------------------------  ------  ----------  ----------
     1   00-50-bd-a0-b0-00 to 00-50-bd-a0-b3-ff 2.0     3.1.2       5.5(2)
     2   00-50-0f-b7-ff-50 to 00-50-0f-b7-ff-67 3.1     4.3(1)      5.5(2)


     Mod Sub-Type Sub-Model Sub-Serial Sub-Hw
     -- -------- --------- ---------- ------
     1   NFFC     WS-F5521  0011455134 1.1

     Catalyst5000> (enable)
```

- One Cisco 1912EN using version 9 of the Catalyst IOS, as shown here
  (1924EN, 2822, or 2828 are great Access layer substitutes with Enterprise
  Network Edition of the CLI-based IOS):

```
1912EN#show version

Cisco Catalyst 1900/2820 Enterprise Edition Software
Version V9.00.00
Copyright (c) Cisco Systems, Inc.  1993-1999
1912EN uptime is 9day(s) 10hour(s) 26minute(s) 36second(s)
Cisco Catalyst 1900 (486sxl) processor with 2048K/1024K bytes of memory
Hardware board revision is 5
Upgrade Status: No upgrade currently in progress.
Config File Status: No configuration upload/download is in progress
15 Fixed Ethernet/IEEE 802.3 interface(s)
Base Ethernet Address: 00-30-80-54-6C-00
```

- One Cisco 2600 router. (Any Cisco router from the 2600 series through the 7000 series will work fine as a substitute as long as it has at least two 10/100 Ethernet ports. A 10Mbps attachment unit interface [AUI] port will not work, because Inter-Switch Link [ISL] needs to use a 100BaseTX port for optimum trunking support.)

NOTE: *For this lab, the Cisco 2620 series router has been previously configured with its basic configuration.*

- Two Ethernet crossover cables to run between devices.
- One console cable and connector.

Lab Objectives

During this lab, you will complete the following tasks:

- Configure the basic switch configuration on the Cisco 1912EN. Configure the basic passwords, the hostname, and IP information. Set up three VLANs: VLAN 2, named CAD; VLAN 3, named Graphics; and VLAN 4, named DocProduction.

- Configure the basic switch configuration on the Cisco Catalyst 5000. Configure the basic passwords, the hostname, and IP information.

- Enable trunking on port f0/27 on the 1912EN to trunk to port 2/2 on the Cisco Catalyst 5000 using Dynamic ISL (DISL) on the 1912EN side and ISL on the Catalyst 5000 side.

- Create a trunk port on the Catalyst 5000 port 2/24 to the Fast Ethernet 0/2 interface on the 2600 router using ISL.

- Enable a VLAN Trunking Protocol (VTP) domain named *Coriolis*. Make the 1912EN a VTP server and the Catalyst 5000 a client in order to propagate the 1912EN's VLAN configuration.

The diagram shown in Figure D.1 illustrates the configuration.

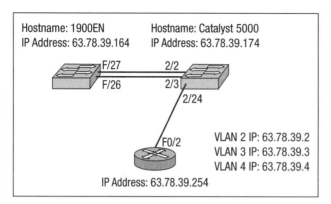

Figure D.1   The sample configuration.

Possible Solution

More than one solution exists to any problem; however, here is the suggested solution to configuring the Cisco Catalyst 1912EN, the Cisco Catalyst 5000, and the Cisco 2620 trunked interface.

The 1912 Basic Configuration

To configure the Cisco Catalyst 1912EN, follow these steps:

1. Access the Cisco Catalyst through the Console port and configure the switch. Choose K to access the command-line interface. The initial password is to just press Enter, as shown here:

```
Catalyst 1900 Management Console

Copyright (c) Cisco Systems, Inc.  1993-1999
All rights reserved.
Enterprise Edition Software
Ethernet Address:        00-30-80-54-6C-00

PCA Number:              73-3122-04
PCA Serial Number:       FAB03263DNB
Model Number:            WS-C1912-EN
System Serial Number:    FAB0335V70D
Power Supply S/N:        APQ0325005M
PCB Serial Number:       FAB03263DNB,73-3122-04
------------------------------------------------

1 user(s) now active on Management Console.

          User Interface Menu
```

```
    [M] Menus
    [K] Command Line

Enter Selection: K

    CLI session with the switch is open.
    To end the CLI session, enter [Exit].


>enable
Enter password:

#
```

2. Just like on a router, enter the **conf terminal** command to configure an interface:

```
#conf terminal
```

3. Configure the hostname:

```
(config)#hostname 1912EN
1912EN(config)#
```

4. Configure a password for the switch:

```
1912EN(config)# enable password ?
  level   Set exec level password

1912EN(config)# enable password level ?
  <1-15>  Level number

1912EN(config)# enable password level 1 coriolis1
1912EN(config)# enable password level 15 coriolis2
1912EN (config)# enable secret coriolispass
```

5. Enter Interface Configuration mode to configure the Fast Ethernet 0/27 port on the 1912EN. Enter the switch's IP address and the default gateway (router):

```
(config)# interface f0/27

(config-if)#ip address 63.78.39.164 255.255.255.0
(config)#
```

```
1912EN(config)#ip default-gateway 63.78.39.254
1912EN(config)#
```

6. Enable trunking on this port to always be on:

```
1912EN(config-if)#trunk ?
  auto        Set DISL state to AUTO
  desirable   Set DISL state to DESIRABLE
  nonegotiate Set DISL state to NONEGOTIATE
  off         Set DISL state to OFF
  on          Set DISL state to ON

1912EN(config-if)#trunk on

1912EN(config-if)# exit
1912EN (config)#
```

7. Assign VLAN names:

```
1912EN(config)#vlan 2 name CAD
1912EN(config)#vlan 3 name Graphics
1912EN(config)#vlan 4 name DocProduction
```

8. Assign the VLAN number that matches the Ethernet port number on the front of the switch:

```
1912EN#config terminal
Enter configuration commands, one per line.  End with CNTL/Z.

1912EN(config)#interface e0/2
1912EN(config-if)#vlan-membership static ?
  <1-1005>  ISL VLAN index

1912EN(config-if)#vlan-membership static 2
1912EN(confi-if)# exit

1912EN(config)#interface e0/3
1912EN(config-if)#vlan-membership static 3
1912EN(confi-if)# exit

1912EN(config)#interface e0/4
1912EN(config-if)#vlan-membership static 4
1912EN(config-if)#exit
```

9. Enable this device to be a VTP server for the Coriolis VTP domain:

```
1912EN(config)#vtp ?
  client       VTP client
  domain       Set VTP domain name
  password     Set VTP password
  pruning      VTP pruning
  server       VTP server
  transparent  VTP transparent
  trap         VTP trap

1912EN(config)#vtp domain ?
  WORD  Name of the VTP management domain

1912EN(config)#vtp domain Coriolis

1912EN(config)#vtp domain server
1912EN(config)# exit
```

NOTE: *The configuration on the 1912EN is saved automatically, so you do not need to save the configuration.*

The Catalyst 5000 Basic Configuration

To configure the Cisco Catalyst 5000 10/100 Ethernet module and Supervisor Engine, follow these steps:

1. Access the Cisco Catalyst 5000 through the Console port located on the Supervisor Engine III. The initial password is to press Enter, as shown here:

```
Cisco Systems Console

Enter password:

Console> enable

Enter password:
Console>(enable)
```

2. Configure the hostname:

```
Console>(enable) set prompt Catalyst5000>
Catalyst5000> (enable)
```

3. Configure a password for the switch. Press Enter for the old password if none has ever been configured:

```
Catalyst5000> (enable) set password
Enter old password:

Enter new password: coriolis1
Retype new password: coriolis1
Password changed.
```

4. Configure the password for Enable mode. Press Enter for the old password if none has ever been configured:

```
Catalyst5000> (enable) set enablepass
Enter old password:
Enter new password: coriolis2
Retype new password: coriolis2
Password changed.
Catalyst5000(enable)
```

5. Enter the IP address and the default gateway (router) for the switch. The switch must be configured on the SC0 interface:

```
Catalyst5000> (enable) set interface sc0 63.78.39.174 255.255.255.0
Interface sc0 IP address and netmask set.
Catalyst5000> (enable) set ip route default 38.68.127.254
Route added.
```

6. Enable trunking on interface 2/2 to complete your trunk link to the 1912EN switch and on interface 2/24 to the router for interVLAN routing:

```
Catalyst5000> (enable) set trunk 2/2 mode on isl
Port(s) 2/2 trunk mode set to on.
Port(s) 2/2 trunk type set to isl.
2000 Oct 19 12:31:54 %DTP-5-TRUNKPORTON:Port 2/2

Catalyst5000> (enable) set trunk 2/24 mode on isl
Port(s) 2/24 trunk mode set to on.
Port(s) 2/24 trunk type set to isl.
2000 Oct 19 12:32:46 %DTP-5-TRUNKPORTON:Port 2/24
```

7. Enable this switch to be a VTP client for the Coriolis VTP domain. By doing
    this step you will propagate VLAN information to and from the 1912EN
    switch:

```
Catalyst5000> (enable) set vtp domain ?
Usage: set vtp [domain <name>] [mode <mode>] [passwd <passwd>]
               [pruning <enable|disable>] [v2 <enable|disable>
(mode = client|server|transparent Use passwd '0' to clear vtp password)
Usage: set vtp pruneeligible <vlans>
(vlans = 2..1000 An example of vlans is 2-10,1000)

Catalyst5000> (enable) set vtp domain Coriolis mode client
VTP domain Coriolis modified
```

Configuring the Cisco 2621 Interface for ISL Trunking

To configure the Cisco 2621 interface, follow these steps:

1. Enter Interface Configuration mode for the Fast Ethernet 0/2 interface and
    force the port to use full duplex. Disable any IPs and use the **no shutdown**
    command:

```
Cisco2621(conf)# interface fastethernet 0/2
Cisco2621(conf-if)# no ip address
Cisco2621(conf-if)# no shutdown
Cisco2621(conf-if)# full-duplex
```

2. Create a subinterface for each VLAN. Assign a description (optional), an IP
    address for the VLAN, and an encapsulation type, as well as the VLAN
    number:

```
Cisco2621(conf-if)# interface fastethernet 0/2.2
Cisco2621(conf-if)# description vlan2
Cisco2621(conf-if)# ip address 63.78.39.2 255.255.255.0
Cisco2621(conf-if)# encapsulation isl 2
Cisco2621(conf-if)# interface fastethernet 0/2.3
Cisco2621(conf-if)# description vlan3
Cisco2621(conf-if)# ip address 63.78.39.3 255.255.255.0
Cisco2621(conf-if)# encapsulation isl 3
Cisco2621(conf-ip)# interface fastethernet 0/2.4
Cisco2621(conf-if)# description vlan4
Cisco2621(conf-if)# ip address 63.78.39.4 255.255.255.0
Cisco2621(conf-if)# encapsulation isl 4
```

NOTE: *Don't forget to save your configurations. Use the* **show config** *command on each device to verify the configurations.*

Appendix E

Switch Features

This appendix is dedicated to helping you determine which switch needs to be placed in your network. If the wrong switch is placed in each point in your network the load can cause severe problems, including bottlenecks or load failures. We will break down the switches into the layers in which Cisco feels they should reside, based on their latest certification curriculum.

Access Layer Switches

The Access layer is the access point where the workgroup layer or end-user interface enters the network. This layer provides the means to connect to the devices located in the Distribution layer and provide connections to both local and remote devices. The goals of this layer are to pass traffic to the network for valid network users and to filter traffic that is passed along. Because the Access layer is the entry point to the network, only port security-based decisions, such as those based on the Layer 2 hardware addresses, can be made here.

Devices found at this layer and covered in this chapter are as follows:

- Cisco Catalyst 1900 series
- Cisco Catalyst 2820 series
- Cisco Catalyst 2900G series, including the new 2980G series
- Cisco Catalyst 2900 XL series
- Cisco Catalyst 3000 series
- Cisco Catalyst 3500 XL series
- Cisco Catalyst 3900 series

Cisco Catalyst 1900

The Catalyst 1900 is the entry point for Cisco's switch line. There are two types of Catalyst 1900 switches: the Standard Edition (SE) and the Enterprise Edition (EN).

The Standard Edition, as explained in Chapter 15, is a low-cost alternative for administrators migrating from a shared hub environment or smaller scale installations. The SE uses a menu-driven IOS and cannot handle some of the more advanced features available in the Enterprise Edition of the IOS.

The Enterprise Edition contains all the features of the Standard Edition but provides several high-end solutions, including Fast EtherChannel, support for Inter-Switch Link (ISL), an IOS Command Line Interface (CLI), and support for Cisco Group Management Protocol (CGMP).

The 1900 series offers two different models: the Cisco Catalyst 1912 and the Cisco Catalyst 1924. They are identified by the number of standard ports. Table E.1 shows the features of each switch.

Cisco Catalyst 2820

For an environment that needs high-speed links to the wiring closet for 20 or so users, the Catalyst 2820 is an ideal solution. This switch is perfect for smaller wiring closets where it is not economical to purchase a high-end solution such as a Cisco Catalyst 5000 series switch.

The Catalyst 2820 series switch architecture is virtually identical to that of the Cisco Catalyst 1900 series switches, differing mainly in its height and uplink bays. The switch has two uplink bays that allow for high-speed uplink options such as Fiber Distributed Data Interface (FDDI), Copper Distributed Data Interface (CDDI), 100Mbps, and Asynchronous Transfer Mode (ATM) modules.

The 2820 series comes in two models: the Cisco Catalyst 2822 and the Cisco Catalyst 2828. On both switches, you will find twenty-four 10BaseT Ethernet ports and one 10Mbps attachment unit interface (AUI) port. All the features listed earlier for the Catalyst 1924 apply to the Catalyst 2822 and the Catalyst 2828, as shown in Table E.2, with the exception of the number of allowable MAC addresses.

Table E.1   Features available for the Cisco Catalyst 1912 and Catalyst 1924.

Feature	1912	1924
Ports	12	24
Backplane	1Gbps	1Gbps
Processor	80486 CPU	80486 CPU
Flash	1MB	1MB
DRAM	2MB	2MB
Forwarding rate	370 pps	370 pps
Max MAC addresses	1,024	2,048

Table E.2   Features available for the Cisco Catalyst 2822 and Catalyst 2828.

Feature	2822	2828
Ports	24	24
Backplane	1Gbps	1Gbps
Processor	80486 CPU	80486 CPU
Flash	1MB	1MB
DRAM	2MB	2MB
Forwarding rate	370 pps	370 pps

Cisco Catalyst 2900

Two quite significantly different architectures are found in the 2900 series of switches: the 2900 series switches and the XL version of the 2900 series switches. About the only similarity between these series is their low cost; if you compare the Catalyst 2900 family of switches' performance and features to other Cisco Catalyst switches, this series is one of the best values for your money.

The 2900 series includes the 2901, 2902, 2926, and 2948G. These switches use an architecture similar to that of the Cisco Catalyst 5000 series of switches. This series uses the Set/Clear command-based CLI, allowing the switch to support advanced features such as ISL.

The XL series was introduced long after Cisco released its prized Catalyst 5000 series of switches, and it causes great confusion to customers of Cisco resellers because the 2900 XL series has a lower model number. In most cases, vendors assign higher model numbers to newer, better, and faster models. One of the most noticeable differences between the 2900 XL series and the 5000 series, which uses a Set/Clear CLI, is that the XL series uses the true Cisco IOS, which is almost identical to that of Cisco routers. The 2900 XL series is the wiring closet workhorse for 10/100 auto-negotiation. Auto-negotiation allows the switch to negotiate the switch port speed and duplex based on the type of traffic being sent to the switch by the sending interface. The models available in this series are the 2908 XL, 2912 XL, 2916 XL, and the 2924 XL.

The 2900 XL series supports some comprehensive management features including a built-in Hypertext Transfer Protocol (HTTP) server for the Web-based Cisco Visual Switch Manager, Simple Network Management Protocol (SNMP), Cisco Discovery Protocol (CDP), CiscoWorks for Switched Internetworks (CWSI), and embedded agent support for four groups of Remote Monitoring (RMON).

Its security and redundancy features support user-selectable port security, multilevel console security, Cisco IOS IP access lists, Terminal Access Controller

Table E.3   The models and features available for the standard version of each Cisco Catalyst 2900 XL series switch.

Feature	2908 XL	2912 MFXL	2916 XL	2924 MXL	2924 CXL
10/100 ports	8	0	16	24	22
100BaseFX ports	0	12	0	0	2
Expansion slots	0	2	0	2	0
Enterprise Edition	Yes	Yes	Yes	Yes	Yes
Standard Edition	Yes	No	Yes	Yes	Yes
Backplane	3.2Gbps	3.2Gbps	3.2Gbps	3.2Gbps	3.2Gbps
Flash	4MB	4MB	4MB	4MB	4MB
DRAM	8MB	8MB	8MB	8MB	8MB
Modularity	No	Yes	Yes	Yes	No
Forwarding rate	3 million pps	3 million pps	3 million pps	3 million pps	3 million pps
Max VLANs	64	64	64	64	64

Access Control System Plus (TACACS+) authentication, and IEEE 802.1D spanning-tree support. Take a look at Table E.3 to see the hardware features of each switch.

The Cisco Catalyst 2926 and the 2948G are both similar to the architecture of the Cisco Catalyst 5000 series. These switches are store-and-forward mode switches with many high-end features:

- A high-performance 24Gbps non-blocking architecture switching fabric capable of delivering over 1 million packets per second (pps).

- The capability for users to configure each port with priority levels to accommodate time-sensitive applications such as voice and video.

- Support of Fast EtherChannel (FEC) uplink bundles for up to 400Mbps on the Catalyst 2926T and 2926F. The Catalyst 2926GS and 2926GL each support uplinks of up to 800Mbps. These FEC ports can be configured between two switches, two routers, or a switch and a router. Special configurations and Network Interface Cards (NICs) also allow a server to be configured with FEC uplinks to a router or switch. This ability results in a very efficient high-speed backbone and data center uplinks with automatic load balancing and failover for port failures.

- Support for RMON statistics, which give a good picture of network activity in the form of statistics, history, events, and alarms groups.

- Support for VLAN load-balancing and Spanning-Tree on multiple parallel Fast Ethernet ISL trunks to increase capacity and fault tolerance between switches.

- Support for ISL, Dynamic Inter-Switch Link (DISL), CDP, VLAN Trunk Protocol (VTP), VLAN Membership Policy Server (VMPS), Dynamic VLANs, and port security based on the MAC address.

- Support for complete SNMP management for Ethernet Management Information Base (MIB), bridge MIB, MIB II, and VTP.

- Support for management with CWSI, CiscoView, TrafficDirector, and VlanDirector.

- The 2948G supports advanced scalability for Fast EtherChannel, Dynamic VLANs, and 802.1Q trunking and bandwidth control using Quality of Service (QoS) features such as protocol filtering, link load balancing, per-port security, TACACS+ authentication, and IP permit lists.

The hardware features available for the Cisco Catalyst 2900 series switches are listed in Table E.4.

Cisco Catalyst 3000

The Cisco Catalyst 3000 has a completely different architecture than any other Cisco switch. However, this series of switches received an End-of-Life (EOL) notice from Cisco, so we will include only a basic overview in this chapter.

Table E.4 The models and features available for the standard version of the Cisco Catalyst 2926, 2948G, and 2980G switches.

Feature	2926T/F	2926GS/GL	2948G	2980G
10/100 ports	24	24	48	80
100MB FE	2	0	0	0
Gb ports	0	2	2	2
Expansion slots	0	0	2	0
Enterprise Edition	Yes	Yes	Yes	Yes
Standard Edition	No	No	No	No
Backplane	1.2Gbps	1.2Gbps	1.2Gbps	24Gbps
Flash	4MB	8MB	12MB	0
RAM	20MB	32MB	64MB	NA
Modularity	No	No	Yes	NA
Forwarding rate	1 million pps	1 million pps	1 million pps	18 million pps
Max VLANs	1,024	1,024	1,024	N/A

Appendix E
Switch Features

The Catalyst 3000 series provides the following features:

- Stacked switch platforms that are manageable as if they were a single logical entity. These switches automatically configure themselves as new switches are added or removed.

- Cut-through switching technology delivering wire-speed, low-latency switching. The Catalyst 3000 also has the ability to use FragmentFree or Runtless switching, which automatically changes to store-and-forward when an error rate has been exceeded.

- Optional modules to provide additional interfaces for more Ethernet ports, Fast Ethernet ports, ATM ports, and WAN connectivity.

- User definable per-port and secure-mode filtering that provides access control for sensitive information resources.

- Support for up to 64 VLANs using Cisco's LAN Emulation (LANE)-based ATM, and ISL-based Fast Ethernet VLANs to extend switched VLANs throughout the enterprise.

- Spanning-Tree Protocol (STP) implemented by VLAN for loop detection.

- An optional stack port interface module that connects one 3000 series switch to another. This Catalyst Matrix delivers 280Mbps per switch of bandwidth for unrestricted traffic flow.

Some of the basic hardware features of the Cisco Catalyst 3000 series of switches are listed in Table E.5.

Cisco Catalyst 3500 Series XL

The Cisco Systems Catalyst 3500 series XL is a scalable line of stackable 10/100 and Gigabit Ethernet switches. These switches provide high performance and investment protection for companies that are expanding their switched networks. The three major applications for the 3500 series XL are as follows:

- In the enterprise wiring closet at the enterprise edge, aggregated to a larger Catalyst switch

Table E.5   The key features of the Cisco Catalyst 3000 series switches.

Feature	3000	3100	3200
10BaseT ports	16	24	0
Flex slots	0	1	1
Expansion slots	0	1	7
Max VLANs	1,700	1,700	1,700

- In a branch office where it can provide a LAN backbone and desktop connectivity

- In a multilayer network where it can be deployed with a Layer 3 switch for a low cost solution

Each Catalyst 3500 XL comes with 2 Gigabit Ethernet interfaces that come with 12, 24, or 48 Gigabit Interface Converter (GBIC) ports and auto-sensing 10BaseT/100BaseTX ports. The 3508G XL provides eight Gigabit Ethernet ports for GBIC Ethernet aggregation. It also has built-in support for Voice Over IP telephony, in addition to built-in support for up to 250 port-based VLANs and ISL VTP.

In addition, the 3500 series supports many of the features of the 1900 and 2900 series, such as DNS and DHCP. The series is offered in both Standard and Enterprise Editions. Table E.6 shows the features of the Catalyst 3500 series.

Cisco Catalyst 3900 Series

The Catalyst 3900 and 3920 are low-cost solutions for Token Ring users to migrate from a shared-media hub to a switched environment. Like the 3500 series, the 3900 is a stackable switch with the ability to provide a variety of high-speed uplinks, network management, and support for multiple VLANs.

The Catalyst 3900 provides an ISL module for connections between wiring closets. This module consists of two ports, which can be either fiber or copper. Two feature cards can be used in the 3900. This link can provide up to 100Mbps uplink connectivity. Also supported is an ATM module that provides Token Ring users with ATM access to campus backbones. The module provides a single 155Mbps connection with a multimode fiber interface. In addition, optional four-port Token Ring modules can be added to the expansion ports in the Catalyst 3900. These

Table E.6   The Cisco Catalyst 3500 series key switching features.

Feature	3512	3524	3548	3508
10/100 ports	12	24	48	0
GBIC ports	2	2	2	8
Enterprise Edition	Yes	Yes	Yes	Yes
Standard Edition	Yes	Yes	Yes	Yes
Backplane	10.8Gbps	10.8Gbps	10.8Gbps	10Gbps
Flash	4MB	4MB	4MB	4MB
DRAM	8MB	8MB	16MB	8MB
Stackable	Yes	Yes	Yes	Yes
Forwarding Rate	4.8 million pps	6.5 million pps	8.8 million pps	7.5 million pps

cards allow for expansion of up to 28 Token Ring ports. Up to eight units can be stacked using the optional stack port module and the Catalyst Matrix, for a total of 224 Token Ring ports. The four-port fiber module supports IEEE 802.5J standard for ring-in/ring-out (RI/RO) and the fiber lobe attachment of end stations.

The Catalyst Switch Matrix is an eight-port interface that connects up to eight Catalyst 3900 series switches. A Cisco Catalyst 3900 has the ability to detect if it is connected to another Catalyst 3900 switch that is connected to a Catalyst Matrix. The connected Catalyst 3900 series switches then connect in the switch block to make a stack that logically appears to be one switch.

One of the great features of the Catalyst Matrix in the 3900 series is the switch's ability to connect any combination of up to eight Catalyst 3900 switches or to remove any one switch without needing to have the power cycled or turned off. A Cisco Systems proprietary shielded cable (1 meter long, with a 50-pin connector at each end) is used to connect the switches participating in the switch stack. The cable uses cross-over wiring so either end can be used for either side of the connection. The cable plugs into a stack port I/O connector on the back of each Catalyst Matrix. The other end of the cable is plugged into a Catalyst stack port module interface card that is installed in an expansion slot on another Catalyst 3900 series switch.

The 3900 series supports three types of bridging:

- Source Route Bridging (SRB)
- Source Route Transparent Bridging (SRT)
- Source Route Switched Bridging

Key Features and Benefits

The Catalyst 3900 has the following features:

- Twenty shielded Token Ring ports for 150-ohm shielded twisted pair (STP) or 100-ohm unshielded twisted pair (UTP) connectivity
- FlexSlot accommodating two expansion modules or one double-wide module for future expansion
- Nine-pin EIA/TIA-232 interface for local console or modem connectivity
- Automatic 4-, 16-, and 32Mbps speed adaptation
- TokenChannel switch interconnect
- MAC address and protocol (DSAP/SNAP) filters
- IEEE and IBM Spanning-Tree Protocol

The Catalyst 3920 provides the following features:

- Twenty-four shielded Token Ring ports for 150-ohm STP or 100-ohm UTP connectivity
- Nine-pin EIA/TIA-232 interface for local console or modem connectivity
- Automatic 4-, 16- and 32Mbps speed adaptation
- TokenChannel switch interconnect
- MAC address and protocol (DSAP/SNAP) filters
- Spanning-Tree Protocol

When you need to upgrade the Catalyst 3900 or 3920 IOS, you can do so by using the same serial port that is used for configuration. You can upgrade code by using Trivial File Transfer Protocol (TFTP) from a TFTP server or uploaded through the workstation using HyperTerminal. Table E.7 shows key features of the Catalyst 3900 series.

Distribution Layer Switches

The Distribution layer is the demarcation point between the Access and Core layers. This level terminates the traffic that originates in the Access layer connections and summarizes the traffic before passing it along to the Core layer. It can best be described as the layer that provides policy-based connectivity.

The main focus of the Distribution layer is to define the boundaries for the network and to provide packet manipulation of the network traffic. It provides isolation from topology changes, manages the size of the routing table, and aggregates network traffic.

In addition, interdomain traffic is redistributed at the Distribution layer, and static and dynamic route redistribution occurs at this point. This layer is also commonly

Table E.7   The key features of the Cisco Catalyst 3900 series.

Feature	3900	3920
Ports	20/24/28	24
Stack slot	1	1
Expansion slots	1 FlexSlot	None
Backplane	520Mbps	520Mbps
Processor	Intel 960SA	Intel 960SA
DRAM	Up to 8MB	Up to 8MB
Stackable	Yes	Yes

used as the point at which remote sites connect to the network. Let's take a look at the different switches typically found at this layer.

In this section we'll be looking at the following switches:

- Catalyst 4000 series
- Catalyst 5000 series
- Catalyst 6000 series

Cisco Catalyst 4000 Series

The Catalyst 4000 series provides very fast and intelligent Layer 2 switching services using a 24Gbps switching fabric. It is used in Ethernet networks utilizing 10-, 100-, and 100Mbps switching. Let's take a look at the features of each of the Catalyst 4000 series switches in Table E.8.

Catalyst 5000 Series

With the introduction of applications such as video, audio, and interactive programs, a new set of challenges were introduced in the intranet world. They can be summarized as follows:

- *Scalability*—The new intranet client/server model inverses the old 80/20 rule because most intranet traffic crosses workgroup boundaries to reach servers located all across the campus. This traffic flow requires network scalability and performance for both Layer 2 and Layer 3 switching.

- *Performance*—Usage of the network through network-enabled applications is causing an increase in network traffic, requiring faster devices and media in the network.

- *Critical application integrity*—With the convergence of mission-critical business and multimedia applications on the common intranet, there is an increasing need for QoS and support for multicast-intensive applications.

Table E.8   Catalyst 4000 series key features.

Feature	4003	4006	4908G	4912G
Slots	3	6	Fixed	Fixed
Max ports	96	240	8	12
Max MAC addresses	16,000	16,000	16,000	16,000
Max VLANs	1,024	1,024	1,024	1,024
Backplane	24Gbps	60Gpbs	22Gbps	24Gbps

The Catalyst 5002 delivers features in a small package for the needs of smaller wiring closets, but still switches 1 million pps. The 5000 continues to address the needs of switched wiring closets with 1 to 3 million pps performance. The 5505 has a five-slot chassis like the Catalyst 5000, and is made for the high-end wiring closet with performance from 1 to 25 million pps. The 5509 supports 10/100 Ethernet, or Gigabit Ethernet for backbone applications, with over 25 million pps switching performance. The 5500 is the most versatile switch in the Catalyst series, with the ability to support LightStream 1010 ATM switching or Catalyst 8500 Layer 3 switching line cards as well as all the Catalyst 5000 series line cards. The Catalyst 5500 is positioned as a high-capacity wiring closet or data center switch, with over 25 million pps of switching performance.

Key Features

Key features of the Catalyst 5000 series of switches are as follows:

- High-speed connectivity using standard Fast Ethernet, FDDI, or ATM interfaces

- Fast EtherChannel supported on Supervisor Engine II ports and Fast Ethernet line cards, providing up to 800Mbps of load sharing, redundant point-to-point connections

- Support for all Supervisor Engines, including the NetFlow Switching feature card option on Supervisor Engine II, which scales to multimillion pps forwarding across campus

- Dual redundant switching engines, power supplies, and a passive backplane design that ensures full system redundancy for mission-critical environments

- Cisco's Virtual Trunking Protocol (VTP), which supports dynamic VLANs and dynamic trunk configuration across all switches

- Support for all advanced switching features of the Cisco IOS software

- Support for advanced multicasting with CGMP

The Catalyst 5000 series of switches uses an architecture based on Supervisor Engines I, II, and III. The Supervisor Engine provides network management and uplink ports. The Supervisor Engine II uses a fixed configuration, but it supports Fast EtherChannel technology on all uplink ports. The Supervisor Engine III module can be deployed in any Catalyst chassis. In a Catalyst 5500, 5505, or 5509, the Supervisor Engine III enables the 3.6Gbps crossbar fabric. The Supervisor Engine III also has modular uplinks, with Fast EtherChannel and Gigabit Ethernet support.

NetFlow LAN Switching provides multilayer switching for the Catalyst 5000 series. It is supported through the NetFlow feature card, an upgrade that is available for Supervisor Engine III. Table E.9 shows the key features of the Catalyst 5000 family of switches.

Table E.9   The key features of the Catalyst 5000 family of switches.

Feature	5000	5002	5500	5505	5509
Modular slots	5	2	13	5	9
Backplane	1.2Gbps	1.2Gbps	3.6Gbps	3.6Gbps	3.6Gbps
Forwarding rate	1 million pps	3 million pps	25 million pps	25 million pps	25 million pps
Max VLANs	1,000	1,000	1,000	1,000	1,000

Table E.10 shows the switching modules, the ports available for each module, and the maximum allowable ports on each switch chassis.

The Catalyst 5000 series has many switching modules that have made it popular for high-density wiring closets and data center connectivity. These switching modules provide the ability to have a high port density for connectivity to the desktop, in addition to a high-speed uplink.

Catalyst 6000 Series

The Catalyst 6000 series has become the popular choice for those upgrading from the Catalyst 5000 series. These switches are designed to address the needs for gigabit scalability, high availability, and multilayer switching in distribution and server-aggregation environments. The Catalyst 6000 family complements the Catalyst 5000 series and 8500 series switches.

Table E.10   Catalyst 5000 family port densities for each switch chassis.

Switching Module	Ports Supported per Module	Max Ports per Chassis				
		5002	5000	5505	5509	5500
Gigabit Ethernet	2, 3, 9	3	20	20	38	32
Group-Switched	48	48	192	192	384	528
10BaseT Ethernet	24/48	48	192	192	384	528
Switched 10BaseT	24/48	24	96	96	192	264
Switched 10BaseFL	12	12	48	48	96	132
Group-Switched	24	24	96	96	192	264
Switched 10/100BaseTX	12/24	26	98	98	194	266
Switched 10/100BaseTX	24	26	98	98	194	266
Switched 100BaseFX	12	12	50	50	98	134
ATM Uplink	1 (dual-PHY)	1	4	4	7	7
CDDI/FDDI	1	1	4	4	8	11

The Catalyst 6000 family is capable of scaling bandwidth from T1 to OC-192 in the WAN/MAN, and from Ethernet to 10 Gigabit Ethernet in the LAN. The Catalyst 6000 series uses a Cisco IOS software base with ASICs to deliver wire-speed traffic management services end-to-end. The Catalyst 6000 series also offers a range of WAN/MAN protocols and media, as well as future scalability for direct analog and digital connectivity to existing voice infrastructures, to allow easy migration from existing networks to high-speed converged LAN/WAN/MAN networks and Voice Over IP architectures.

The Catalyst 6000 and 6500 series switches offer multilayer services using interchangeable line cards. The first of these cards is the PFC, which is an integral part of the CiscoAssure end-to-end QoS and policy-based security solution. The PFC can identify user applications and classify traffic with the appropriate priority level. For example, a video conferencing packet can be given higher priority than, say, a Web page request.

The second of these services is the MSFC, which, in combination with the PFC, provides 15 million pps of forwarding performance for IP, IPX, and IP Multicast traffic. The MSFC also supports Hot Standby Routing Protocol (HSRP) for routing redundancy between MSFCs in the same chassis, across Catalyst 6000 family switches, or between a Catalyst 6000 series switch and a standalone Cisco router.

The MSFC also supports traffic-statistics collection and accounting with no impact on switching performance.

In addition, Cisco offers the FlexWAN module, which accepts up to two Cisco 7200/7500 series WAN port adapters, supporting asynchronous and synchronous serial interfaces at speeds from 56Kbps to 155Mbps. The FlexWAN module provides native support of the Frame Relay, ATM, Packet over SONET (PoS), Point-to-Point Protocol (PPP), and High-Level Data Link Control (HDLC) protocols along with a range of interfaces, including T1/E1, T3/E3, High-Speed Serial Interface (HSSI), and OC-3. Up to eight FlexWAN modules are supported in a Catalyst 6000 family switch. However, this module does not support modules for Ethernet, Token Ring, FDDI, channel port adapters, encryption service modules, compression service modules, and doublewide port adapters.

Table E.11 shows the key features of the Catalyst 6000 series.

Table E.11   The key features of the Cisco Catalyst 6000 family.

Feature	6006	6009	6506	6509
Backplane	32Gbps	32Gbps	256Gbps	256Gbps
Forwarding rate	15 million pps	15 million pps	150 million pps	150 million pps

(continued)

Table E.11   The key features of the Cisco Catalyst 6000 family *(continued)*.

Feature	6006	6009	6506	6509
Modular slots	6	9	6	9
Max Gigabit ports	130	130	130	130
Max 100FX ports	192	192	130	130
Max 10/100 ports	240	384	240	384
Max 10BaseFL	192	192	192	192
Max ATM	8	8	8	8
Max VLANs	1,000	1,000	1,000	1,000

Core Layer/WAN Switches

The Core layer and WAN switches are used for high-speed switching backbones and WAN implementations to switch packets as quickly as possible. The Core layer is usually designed with optimal redundancy, because it must be highly reliable. Fast convergence is also a requirement of the Core layer.

In this section we'll be discussing the following switches:

- Catalyst 8400 series
- Catalyst 8500 series
- BPX 8600 series
- MGX 8800 series
- Catalyst 12000 series

NOTE: *Cisco considers the Catalyst 5500 and the Catalyst 6500 series switches as versatile Distribution and Core layer switches.*

Cisco Catalyst 8400 Series

The Catalyst 8400 series wide-area switches provide the backbone services to deliver data, voice, fax, and video applications. The IGX 8400 series integrates with other Cisco WAN products to offer end-to-end solutions. The Catalyst 8400 series integrates several QoS features, including:

- *Automatic routing management*—The switches perform a connection admission control (CAC) function on all types of connections in the network. Distributed network intelligence enables the CAC function to automatically route connections over optimal paths while guaranteeing QoS.

- *Dynamic buffer management*—The switch dynamically assigns buffers to individual virtual circuits based on the amount of traffic and service-level agreements.

- *Optimized bandwidth management*—The 8400 switch guarantees fair and cost-efficient bandwidth utilization using various techniques such as voice compression and Voice Activity Detection (VAD) for voice, and Repetitive Pattern Suppression (RPS) for circuit-switching data traffic.

Catalyst 8400 Modules

The Catalyst 8400 series is available with 8 slots on the 8410, 16 slots on the 8420, and 32 slots on the 8430. These switches use a 1.2Gbps redundant cell bus. They support a wide array of modules for OC-3/STM-1 ATM interfaces, T3/E3 ATM interfaces, T1/E1 Frame Relay interfaces, V.35 Frame Relay interfaces, X.21 Frame Relay interfaces, HSSI Frame Relay interfaces, EIA/TIA-232 circuit data interfaces, and one- or two-port voice modules using either T1, E1, or J1.

Catalyst 8400 Services

The Catalyst 8400 series offers standards-compliant ATM user-to-network interface/network-to-network interface on a variety of interfaces. All ATM interfaces support per-VC queuing, rate scheduling, and multiple classes of service including those defined by the ATM forum, such as constant bit rate (CBR), variable bit rate real time (VBR-RT), variable bit rate non real time (VBR-NRT), available bit rate (ABR), and unspecified bit rate (UBR). It also offers ATM interfaces that can be customized to meet performance requirements.

The advanced traffic management features of the Catalyst 8400 series enable built-in congestion avoidance mechanisms for Frame Relay traffic. Standards-based messaging on the user-network interface (UNI) enables the Catalyst switch to extend traffic management features to Cisco routers, delivering high QoS across the entire Frame Relay network. Enhanced Local Management Interface (ELMI) also enables automatic Frame Relay traffic-shaping parameter configuration on Cisco routers.

Cisco's Tag Switching technology provides you with a highly scalable, reliable means of integrating IP traffic with ATM traffic.

The Catalyst 8400 switch offers efficient, high-quality voice connectivity across the wide-area backbone. All voice interfaces can be directly attached to voice switches for voice or fax/data connectivity via a T1/E1 interface. The Catalyst 8400 series voice interfaces support standards-based voice compression schemes and onboard echo cancellation. Voice compression reduces the amount of bandwidth required for voice connections across the WAN. The Catalyst switch supports the following voice compression techniques:

- Adaptive Differential Pulse Code Modulation (ADPCM) at 16Kbps, 24Kbps, and 32Kbps

- Low-Delay, Code-Excited Linear Prediction (LD-CELP) at 16Kbps
- Conjugate-Structured, Algebraic Code-Excited Linear Prediction (CS-ACELP) at 8Kbps

The IGX voice interfaces also support the VAD silence suppression technique, which sends cells on the trunk only when there is something to send. With most voice connections consisting of up to 60 percent silence, VAD technology enables the IGX 8400 series to achieve an average two-to-one compression ratio, thus saving additional bandwidth. When combined with ADPCM, LD-CELP, or CS-ACELP compression schemes, VAD enables you to achieve compression ratios beyond eight to one.

In addition, the voice interfaces support fax and modem data transport. For Group 3 fax, the Universal Voice Module supports Fax Relay, whereby it demodulates and remodulates the signal and transports a fax across the network using only 9.6Kbps of network capacity.

The Catalyst 8400 series also supports voice switching capabilities using the Voice Network Switching (VNS) system. VNS enables a Catalyst 8400 network to function as a tandem voice network that receives signaling, interprets it, and dynamically establishes voice connections between the source and destination ports. The network routes each voice channel on a per-call basis and extends advanced voice features (such as transfer, caller ID, and camp-on) across the wide-area network. With VNS, available trunk capacity can be dynamically used by bandwidth-hungry data applications, thus maximizing the efficiency of available network resources. The network ensures an optimal connection for each call, reducing delay and improving voice quality by minimizing compression cycles.

IGX 8400 series circuit data capabilities enable synchronous or asynchronous legacy data or video to be transported across the WAN through a fixed-delay, fixed-throughput, zero discard, or point-to-point data connection. Available speeds range from 1.2Kbps to T1/E1 for synchronous data and from 1.2Kbps to 19.2Kbps for asynchronous data using standard serial interfaces such as V.28/RS-232, V.11/X.21, V.35, EIA/TIA-449, and T1/E1.

A network of Catalyst multiservice ATM switches can be deployed with a variety of trunk interfaces and speeds ranging from 64Kbps to OC-3/STM-1.

Network Management

The Catalyst 8400 can be managed using the CiscoView GUI management tool or Cisco Strata View Plus for integration with NetView or HP OpenView. The Strata View Plus software also provides management applications using SNMP, application programming interfaces (APIs), and SQL-based API for database inquiries.

Cisco Catalyst 8500 Series

The Catalyst 8500 series multiservice switch routers integrate multiservice ATM switching with wire-speed multiprotocol routing and Layer 3 switching into a single platform that supports Cisco IOS services for QoS and security. The Catalyst 8500 family delivers campus and metropolitan network solutions with scalable performance and lower cost of ownership.

Large-scale deployment of server farms and the continued growth of intranet applications are driving the substantial increase of traffic volumes in enterprise networks. The traffic volumes are coupled with shifts in traffic patterns that do not conform to traditional network design principles such as the 80/20 rule. Common applications for the Catalyst 8500 series switches include centralized server farms, transport of mission-critical applications, and intranets.

The Catalyst 8500 series consists of the Catalyst 8510 and 8540, which are 5- and 13-slot modular chassis-based implementations of the Catalyst 8500 technology. Table E.12 lists key features of the Catalyst 8500 series switches.

BPX 8600 Series

The BPX 8600 series provides a scalable set of solutions delivering ATM, Frame Relay, SNA, voice, and circuit emulation services, plus Voice Over IP, IP-based Virtual Private Networks (VPNs), managed intranets, and Internet services.

The BPX 8650 IP+ATM switch provides ATM-based broadband services, and supports MPLS to deliver IP services. The BPX 8680 Universal Service Node offers broadband, narrowband, and MPLS, and can be upgraded to OC-48c speeds.

The BPX 8600 series can be configured to support broadband, narrowband, and IP services, depending on specific needs. The switch supports the following interfaces: T3/E3 ATM, OC-3/STM-1, ATMOC-12/STM-4 ATM, T1/E1 ATM, n x T1/E1 IMA, Frame Relay, high-speed Frame Relay, SNA, circuit emulation, ATM UNI 3.0/3.1, and SMDS.

The switches also supports IP VPNs, Voice Over IP, managed intranets, premium Internet services, and IP Fax Relay.

Table E.12 The key features of the Cisco Catalyst 8510 and 8540.

Feature	8510	8540
Modular slots	5	13
Forwarding rate	6 million pps	24 million pps
Backplane	10Gbps	40Gbps

The BPX 8600 series switch includes a 20Gbps crosspoint switching fabric in a 15-slot chassis. Three slots are reserved for common control modules, and 12 slots are provided for interface modules.

The broadband control card (BCC) is usually configured redundantly; it supports ATM cell switching, internal and remote-node communication, node synchronization, network-management communication, and shelf-management communication. The alarm status monitor card (ASM) monitors the power supply voltage and shelf temperature of the BPX 8600. The ASM card also includes telco-standard relays, which can activate switch alarm indicators. The switch also supports BXM cards that enable you to configure both PVCs and SVCs for ATM services.

The Cisco BPX 8600 series switch enables video on demand, IP Multicasting, distance learning, and videoconferencing. Multicast functionality ensures that latency-sensitive video traffic is delivered with the required bandwidth.

BPX 8680 Universal Service Node

The BPX 8680 Universal Service Node is a scalable IP+ATM WAN edge switch that combines the benefits of Cisco IOS IP with the extensive queuing, buffering, scalability, and QoS capabilities provided by the BPX 8600 series.

The BPX 8680 consists of one or more MGX 8850s connected as feeders to a BPX 8620. Designed for very large installations, the BPX 8680 can scale to 16,000 DS1s by adding up to 16 MGX 8850 concentrator shelves while still being managed as a single node.

This switch supports a Crosspoint Switch Fabric with a peak switching capacity of 19.2Gbps. It does this with twelve 800 or 1600Mbps switch ports that support up to OC-12/STM-4 cell rates. The arbiter establishes up to 20 million cell connections per second, making this a very fast WAN solution. This switch supports many WAN speeds including OC-12c/STM-4, OC-3c/STM-1, T3, E3, Channelized T3 (down to DS0), n x T1/E1, T1/E1, Channelized T1 (DS0 and DS0A), Channelized E1, HSSI, X.21, V.35, and LAN solutions including Ethernet, Fast Ethernet, and FDDI.

MGX 8800 Series

The Cisco MGX 8800 series wide-area edge switches integrate Cisco IOS software IP capabilities and carrier-class ATM in a single platform. The MGX 8850 switch enables delivery of differentiated services while scaling from DS0 to OC-48c/STM-16 speeds. The MGX platform provides a cost-effective edge infrastructure for volume services, such as Frame Relay.

Key Features

Key features of the Catalyst 8800 series are as follows:

- Flexible IP+ATM multiservice platform
- Scalable from 1.2- to 45Gbps of non-blocking throughput with a single chassis
- Managed by Cisco's IP+ATM service management tools

Services

Services provided by the Catalyst 8800 series include the following:

- IP VPNs using Cisco IOS software-based multiprotocol label switching (MPLS)/tag switching
- Full suite of Voice Over IP, Voice Over ATM, and Voice Over Frame Relay capabilities with full interworking
- High-density Point-to-Point protocol (PPP) for Internet access and aggregation
- SNA outsourcing
- Full-featured narrowband ATM for managed data, voice, and video services
- High-density broadband ATM for wholesale ATM services
- Circuit emulation for private line replacement

The MGX 8850 wide-area edge switch is designed for carrier-class reliability. Every system component can be configured for 100-percent redundancy, and all MGX 8850 switch modules can be removed and reinserted without impacting service delivery or affecting the performance of other modules. Background diagnostics continually monitor switch functions on active as well as standby modules, ensuring fault-tolerant operation. As a result, Cisco wide-area switches routinely deliver high service availability.

The Cisco MGX 8850 switch supports industry-standard, automatic protection switching (APS) for all Synchronous Optical Network (SONET) and Synchronous Digital Hierarchy (SDH) interfaces. If a fiber is cut or a card fails, APS performs switching to the backup fiber within milliseconds.

The Cisco MGX 8850 switch provides cost-effective 1:n redundancy of service interfaces to enhance overall reliability and service availability. With support of 1:n redundancy, a single standby service module will automatically take over the traffic functions of any failed service module of the same type within seconds.

The MGX 8800 RPM supports all major routing protocols, including Internet Gateway Routing Protocol (IGRP), Enhanced IGRP (EIGRP), Open Shortest Path First (OSPF), Intermediate System-to-Intermediate System (IS-IS), Border Gateway

Protocol 4 (BGP4), Routing Information Protocol (RIP) versions 1 and 2, static routes, and route redistribution. It also supports many QoS features including Policy Based Routing, QoS Policy Propagation via BGP, and Committed Access Rate.

Congestion management is provided with the following methods:

- First in, first out queuing (FIFO)
- Priority queuing
- Custom queuing
- Weighted fair queuing (WFQ)

The MGX 8800 RPM also supports MPLS. It can act as a label edge router or label switch router. It also supports MPLS-VPNs via mulitprotocol BGP extentions, VPN route-target extended BGP community attributes, MPLS forwarding across backbone, and multiple routing/forwarding instances on the provider edge router.

As mentioned earlier, the Route Processor Module has an ATM deluxe port adaptor interface to the chassis backplane.

Advanced traffic management features are as follows:

- ATM service classes: nrt-VBR, ABR, and UBR
- Traffic shaping (per VC)
- High-performance architecture
- Extended VC capabilities
- Up to 4,096 VCs
- Up to 200 concurrent segmentation and reassemblies (SARs)
- ATM adaptation layer 5 (AAL5) for data traffic

Advanced traffic management mechanisms in the ATM port adaptor (PA) architecture allow for the support of bursty, client/server traffic, while supporting applications that require guaranteed or best-effort service. The ATM PA traffic management capabilities—based on ATM Forum specifications—surpass those of any existing ATM interface in high-end routers.

12000 Series Gigabit Switch Routers

The 12000 series Gigabit Switch Router (GSR) is designed and developed for the core of service provider and enterprise IP backbones. The Cisco 12000 GSR family includes three models:

- *12008*—An eight-slot chassis switch that can be used to support up to 84 DS3, 28 OC-3c/STM-1c, and 28 OC-12c/STM-4c or 7 OC-48c/STM-16c interfaces

- *12012*—Has 12 slots that can be used to support up to 132 DS3, 44 OC-3c/STM-1c, 44 OC-12c/STM-4c, or 11 OC-48c/STM-16c interfaces

- *12016*—The new 5Tbps GSR terabit system, which has 16 slots that can be used to support up to 180 DS3, 60 OC-3c/STM-1c, and 60 OC-12c/STM-4c or 15 OC-48c/STM16c interfaces, with support for 15 OC-192c/STM-64c interfaces in the future

You may wonder why a router is being featured in a book about switches. The 12000 series belongs in this book because of its integrated switching fabric. At the heart of the Cisco 12000 GSR is a multigigabit crossbar switch fabric that is optimized to provide high-capacity switching at gigabit rates.

The crossbar switch enables high performance for two reasons: Connections from the LCs to a centralized fabric are point-to-point links that can operate at very high speeds; and, multiple bus transactions can be supported simultaneously, increasing the aggregate bandwidth of the system. A GSR system can be configured as 40Gbps for the 12008, 60Gbps for the 12012, and 80Gbps for the 12016, scalable to 5 terabits.

The switch fabric includes two card types: switch-fabric cards (SFCs) and clock and scheduler cards (CSC). Each GSR must have at least one CSC in the chassis. The SFCs receive the scheduling information and clocking reference from the CSC cards and perform the switching functions.

The Gigabit Route Processor (GRP) is a high-performance engine that provides the routing intelligence for the 12000 GSR family. It is dedicated to determining the network topology and calculating the best path across the network. The GRP has the following hardware characteristics:

- 200MHz R5000 CPU

- Optionally, up to 256MB CPU DRAM (default 128MB)

- 512K Layer 2 cache

- 512K configuration nonvolitile RAM (NVRAM)

- 8MB boot flash

- Two PC Card Type II software upgrades

- Ethernet (RJ-45 and MII connectors) for network management access

- Local console and modem ports (DB-25/EIA/TIA-232c)

The GRP provides the following key functions:

- Processes interior gateway protocols (IGPs) such as Intermediate System-to-Intermediate System (IS-IS), Interior Gateway Routing Protocol (IGRP), Open

Shortest Path First (OSPF), and Enhanced IGRP (EIGRP) to determine the network topology

- Processes external gateway protocols (EGPs) such as Border Gateway Protocol (BGP)

- Creates and maintains the routing table (up to 1 million route entries)

- Distributes and updates Express Forwarding (EF) tables on the LCs and maintains copies of the tables of each LC for card initialization

- Handles general maintenance functions such as diagnostics, console support, and LC monitoring

- Processes in-band management through Simple Network Management Protocol (SNMP), Management Information Base (MIB), Telnet, Bootstrap Protocol (BOOTP), and Trivial File Transfer Protocol (TFTP)

Glossary

10Base2—The IEEE 802.3 standard for running Ethernet at 10Mbps over a thinnet coaxial cable. The maximum length for a 10Base2 segment is 185 meters (607 feet).

10Base5—The IEEE 802.3 standard for running Ethernet at 10Mbps over a thicknet coaxial cable. The maximum length for a 10Base5 segment is 500 meters (1,640 feet).

10BaseT—The IEEE 802.3 standard for running Ethernet at 10Mbps over shielded or unshielded twisted-pair wiring. The maximum length for a 10BaseT segment is 100 meters (328) feet.

100BaseFX—An IEEE standard for running Fast Ethernet over fiber-optic cable.

100BaseT—The IEEE 802.3U standard for running Ethernet at 100Mbps over a shielded or unshielded twisted-pair cable. Also known as *Fast Ethernet*.

100BaseT4—A technology that allows the use of Fast Ethernet technology over existing Category 3 and Category 4 wiring, utilizing all four pairs of wires.

100BaseVG (Voice Grade) AnyLAN—The IEEE 802.12 standard that allows data transmissions of 100Mbps over Category 3 or data-grade wiring, utilizing all sets of wires.

802.10—Used within FDDI backbones. This Cisco mechanism is used to implement VLANs. It was originally developed by the IEEE as a standard to implement FDDI into metropolitan area networks (MANs).

1000BaseX—This IEEE 802.3Z standard that defines standards for data transmissions of 1,000Mbps. Also known as *Gigabit Ethernet*.

Access layer—In the campus hierarchical model, the layer where the workstation connects to the network. Hubs or switches reside at this layer, and workgroups access the network here.

access link—The user's entry point into the switched network. This link connects the NIC in the user's local resource to a switch or other device such as a bridge or hub that in turn connects to the network backbone or higher-layer switches and routers.

access list—A security feature used with the Cisco IOS to filter traffic types as part of data routing. Access lists are also used to filter traffic between different VLAN numbers.

active route processor (active-RP)—The active router or route process in HSRP that is currently handling routing decisions and discovering routes for the attached segments.

address—A set of numbers, usually expressed in binary format, used to identify and locate a resource or device on a network.

address filter—A feature of the Cisco Catalyst 3000 series. It is a way of using Layer 2 MAC addresses or switching ports to filter traffic. This process allows you to filter traffic and restrict access without the use of VLANs. It uses a process similar to access lists on the Cisco IOS. However, you can apply multiple address filters to the same interface.

Address Resolution Protocol (ARP)—The protocol used to map the IP address to the MAC address.

adjacency table—Works with the FIB and the CEF ASIC to keep a table of nodes that are adjacent to or within a single hop of the switch. CEF uses the adjacency table to prepend Layer 2 address table information.

administrator—A person responsible for the control and security of the user accounts, resources, and data flow on the network.

All Routes Explorer (ARE)—On a Token Ring network, if the node of destination is not found on the local network segment, an ARE frame is sent to all the bridges. Each bridge receiving an ARE updates the frame with a RIF and then forwards the frame out all the ports.

American National Standards Institute (ANSI)—The organization that publishes standards for communications, programming languages, and networking.

ANDing—The process of comparing the bits of an IP address with the bits in a subnet mask to determine how a packet will be handled.

anycast address—An address used in ATM for shared multiple-end systems. An anycast address allows a frame to be sent to specific groups of hosts.

Application layer—The layer of the OSI model that provides support for end users and for application programs using network resources.

Application-Specific Integrated Circuit (ASIC)—A feature of many LAN controllers. ASICs are internal to the switch. They work in conjunction with the internal processor to make Layer 2 forwarding decisions. However, they lack the ability to make flexible software-implemented forwarding decisions. Their ability to perform small tasks quickly and inexpensively makes them a key in the switching process. ASICs used in Cisco switches and routers are the Phoenix, FE, LMA, PFPA, SAMBA, SAGE, SAINT, and CEF.

Asymmetric Digital Subscriber Line (ADSL)—A service that transmits digital voice and data over existing (analog) phone lines.

Asynchronous Transfer Mode (ATM)—An international standard originally developed by the International Telecommunications Union Telecommunication Standardization Sector (ITU-T), used in high-speed transmission media such as E3, Synchronous Optical Network (SONET), and T3 for cell relay. It can be used in multiple service types such as voice, video, or data, and it's sent in fixed-length, 53-byte cells. ATM has become common on today's corporate networks. It guarantees throughput and minimizes delay. It can provide scalable speeds up to multiple gigabits per second.

Asynchronous Transmission Synchronization (ATS)—A process used in serial data transfer in which a start bit and a stop bit are added so the receiving station knows when a particular bit has been transferred. Also known as *bit synchronization.*

ATM Adaptation layer (AAL)—The ATM layer that adapts data to the ATM 48-byte payload. There are a number of adaptations to this layer, such as AAL1, AAL2, AAL3/4, and AAL5. AAL5 is by far the most common in today's networks. AAL5 defines how data from a node on the network such as a PC or server handles ATM cells. It is also used by Cisco Catalyst switches with LANE to perform segmentation and reassembly of ATM frames into cells and cells into frames.

ATM System Processor (ASP)—A Cisco ATM cell-switching processing card, located on the Cisco Catalyst 5500 chassis or slot 2 on the LS1010 chassis.

attachment unit interface (AUI)—IEEE 802.3 specification used between a Multistation Access Unit (MAU) and a NIC.

attachment unit interface (AUI) connector—A 15-pin D-type connector sometimes used with Ethernet connections.

attenuation—The loss of signal that is experienced as data is transmitted across network media.

Glossary

Automated Packet Recognition and Translation (APaRT)—A FDDI line module feature found on Cisco Catalyst 2820 and 5000 series switches that allows for the automatic detection of frame types with translational bridging. It uses the CAM table to get the frame-type information for all end nodes.

backbone—A high-capacity infrastructure system that provides optimal transport on a LAN. Typically in a LAN, the data running from router to router, switch to switch, or switch to router is transported through a faster physical topology than the rest of the local area or virtual LAN devices. The physical cable is called the backbone.

BackboneFast—Initiated when a root port or blocked port receives an inferior BPDU from its designated bridge. It allows the secondary or backup port to immediately begin forwarding after a link fault with the root link. BackboneFast bypasses the MaxAge timer.

backplane—Similar to the motherboard in a PC. The backplane is the primary data/control bus located on a Cisco Catalyst switch. It interconnects all the modules inside the switch chassis.

bandwidth—The rated throughput capacity of a given network protocol or medium.

base bandwidth—The difference between the lowest and highest frequencies available for network signals. The term is also used to describe the rated throughput capacity of a given network protocol or medium.

Basic Rate Interface (BRI)—An ISDN digital communications line that consists of three independent channels: two Bearer (or B) channels, each at 64Kbps, and one Data (or D) channel at 16Kbps. ISDN BRI is often referred to as *2B+D*.

baud rate—The speed or rate of signal transfer. This term is named after French telegraphy expert J. M. Baudot.

binary—A Base 2 numbering system, characterized by 1s and 0s, used in digital signaling.

binding—The process of associating a protocol and a NIC.

bit—An electronic digit used in the binary numbering system.

blackout—A total loss of electrical power.

blocking architecture—A condition in which the total bandwidth of the ports is greater than the capacity of the switching fabric.

bridge—A device that connects and passes packets between two network segments that use the same communications protocol. Bridges operate at the Data

Link layer of the OSI Reference Model. A bridge filters, forwards, or floods an incoming frame based on the MAC address of that frame.

Bridge Protocol Data Unit (BPDU)—A multicast frame generated by the switch that carries information about itself and changes in the network topology.

bridging address table—A list of MAC addresses kept by bridges and used when packets are received to determine which segment the destination address is on before sending the packet to the next interface or dropping the packet if it is on the same segment as the sending node.

broadband—A communications strategy that uses analog signaling over multiple communications channels.

Broadband Interexchange Carrier Interconnect (B-ICI)—An interface that connects two ATM carriers.

broadcast—A packet delivery system in which a copy of a packet is given to all hosts attached to the network.

broadcast domain—In a none-switched network, all the devices that can receive a broadcast from one machine in the network sent on the physical wire. The broadcast domain is a segment not separated by a Layer 3 device or Layer 2 device that can filter broadcasts. On a switched network using VLANs, the broadcast domain is all the ports or collision domains that belong to the same VLAN.

broadcast storm—Occurs when broadcasts throughout the LAN become so numerous that they use up all the available bandwidth, thus grinding the network to a halt.

brouter—A device that can be used to combine the benefits of both routers and bridges. It's commonly used to route routable protocols at the Network layer and to bridge nonroutable protocols at the Data Link layer.

brownout—A short-term decrease in the voltage level, usually caused by the startup demands of other electrical devices.

bus—A path used by electrical signals to travel between the CPU and the attached hardware.

bus mastering—A bus accessing method in which the NIC takes control of the bus in order to send data through the bus directly to the system memory, bypassing the CPU.

bus topology—A linear LAN architecture that uses a common cable with multipoint connections for the flow of data in a serial progression to all nodes on that network segment.

Glossary

byte—A set of bits (usually eight) operating as a unit to signify a character.

cable modem—A modem that provides Internet access over cable television lines.

campus—A group of buildings in a fixed geographical location, owned and controlled by the organization.

Carrier Access Module (CAM)—A module attached to the ATM cell-switching bus. A CAM can support two port-adapter modules to provide physical ATM line-ports used by end nodes. A CAM can be placed in the Cisco Catalyst 5500 in slot 9, 10, 11, or 12. It can also be placed in the LS1010 in slot 0, 1, 3, or 4.

Carrier Sense Multiple Access with Collision Avoidance (CSMA/CA)—A media-access method that uses collision avoidance techniques.

Carrier Sense Multiple Access with Collision Detection (CSMA/CD)—A media-access method that uses collision detection and that listens to the network to see if it is in use. If the network is clear, data is transmitted. If a collision occurs, both stations will retransmit their data.

change control—A process in which a detailed record of every change made to the network is documented.

channel—A communications path used for data transmission.

Channel Service Unit (CSU)—A network communications device used to connect to the digital equipment lines of the common carrier, usually over a dedicated line or Frame Relay. CSU is used in conjunction with a Data Service Unit (DSU).

Circuit Emulation Services (CES)—A Port to Application Mapping (PAM) module that allows no ATM devices utilizing either T1 or E1 interfaces to attach to an ATM switch backplane. This module can be used to connect private branch exchange (PBX), video conferencing, and non-ATM routers to the network backbone.

Cisco Discovery Protocol (CDP)—A Cisco protocol that gathers and stores information about neighboring devices on the network. It can be used in Ethernet, Token Ring, Serial, and FDDI media types. All Cisco devices including hubs support CDP.

Cisco Express Forwarding (CEF)—Used in the CEF ASIC (CEFA) and Distributed Cisco Express Forwarding (dCEF) ASIC, Cisco's newest ASICs. These ASICs, which are used in Cisco's high-end devices, are the most functional and efficient ASICs in the Cisco product line. They use a CEF search engine, which makes IP prefix-based switching decisions using an adjacency table. The CEFA operates at both Layer 2 and Layer 3, using ARP to resolve next-hop adjacencies at Layer 2. A network interface is said to be *adjacent* if it can be reached in a single hop. This component looks at the first 64 bytes of an incoming frame, obtains as much information as possible, and then uses the switch's CAM table to rewrite the relevant source MAC address, destination MAC address, or destination network address to the frame or packet header.

Cisco Group Management Protocol (CGMP)—A Cisco protocol used by the Catalyst switch to forward multicast frames intelligently. CGMP dynamically discovers end-user stations participating in multicast applications. When receiving a multicast, it forwards the multicast directly to the end users instead of broadcasting the multicast throughout the network.

Class A network—A TCP/IP network that uses addresses starting between 1 and 126 and supports up to 126 networks with up to 16,777,214 unique hosts each. 127 is a Class A address but is used for loopback testing on Ethernet interfaces.

Class B network—A TCP/IP network that uses addresses starting between 128 and 191 and supports up to 16,384 networks with 65,534 unique hosts each.

Class C network—A TCP/IP network that uses addresses starting between 192 and 254 and supports up to 2,097,152 networks with 254 unique hosts each.

Classless Inter-Domain Routing (CIDR)—A technique that allows multiple addresses to be consolidated into a single entry.

Clear Header—A field (part of the 802.10 header) that copies the encrypted Protected Header for security purposes to help guarantee against tampering with the frame. Also known as the *Secure Data Exchange (SDE) Protocol Data Unit*.

ClearChannel Architecture—The switching architecture found in the Cisco Catalyst series 1900 and 2820 switches. The architecture is made up of the 1Gbps Packet Exchange Bus, Forwarding Engine, Embedded Control Unit, a management interface, and a 3MB shared memory buffer.

client—A node that requests a service from another node on a network.

client/server networking—A networking architecture utilizing front-end demand nodes that request and process data stored by the back end or resource node.

coaxial cable—Data cable, commonly referred to as *coax*, made of a solid copper core, which is insulated and surrounded by braided metal and covered with a thick plastic or rubber covering. This is the standard cable used in cable TV and in older bus topology networks.

collapsed core—A design in which both the Core and Distribution layers' functions are combined into one layer.

collision—The result of two frames transmitting simultaneously in an Ethernet network and colliding, thereby destroying both frames.

Glossary

collision domain—All the interfaces on a single segment that can send data on the same physical wire. In the case of a switch, all the nodes connected to each individual port are in their own collision domain. In a hub, all the interfaces connected to the hub ports are in their own collision domain.

Color Blocking Logic (CBL)—A feature of the SAMBA ASIC used to cause the EARL to make forwarding decisions. It also ensures that a tagged frame that comes from a particular VLAN does not exit through a port belonging to another VLAN. CBL also assists in placing ports in one of four different modes for Spanning-Tree Protocol: blocking, learning, listening, or forwarding.

common carrier—A supplier of communications utilities, such as phone lines, to the general public.

communication—The transfer of information between nodes on a network.

connection-oriented communication—Packet transfer in which the delivery is guaranteed.

connectionless communication—Packet transfer in which the delivery is not guaranteed.

connectivity—The linking of nodes on a network in order for communication to take place.

Content Addressable Memory (CAM)—A table used by a bridge to make forwarding and filtering decisions. The CAM table contains MAC addresses with port addresses leading to the physical interfaces. The CAM table uses a specialized interface that is faster than RAM to make forwarding and filtering decisions. It examines frames it receives from a segment and then updates the table with the source MAC address from the frame.

control plane—Functions that dictate how data actually flows through the switching fabric.

Copper Distributed Data Interface (CDDI)—The implementation of the FDDI standard using electrical cable rather than optical cable.

Core block—The end point for networks. It requires fast access and no policy implementation.

Core layer—In the Cisco Hierarchical Model, the backbone of the network, designed for high-speed data transmission.

crosstalk—Electronic interference caused when two wires get too close to each other.

cut-through packet switching—A switching method that does not copy the entire packet into the switch buffers. Instead, the destination address is placed in buffers, the route to the destination node is determined, and the packet is quickly sent out the corresponding port. The switch begins forwarding the frame as soon as the first 13 bytes and MAC address are received. It relies on the receiving device to discard the frame if there is corruption. Cut-through packet switching maintains a low latency.

cyclical redundancy check (CRC)—A method used to check for errors in packets that have been transferred across a network. A computation bit is added to the packet and recalculated at the destination to determine if the entire packet contents have been transferred correctly.

D connectors—Connectors shaped like the letter *D* that use pins and sockets to establish connections between peripheral devices using serial or parallel ports. The number that follows is the number of pins the connector uses for connectivity. For example, a DB-9 connector has 9 pins, and a DB-25 has 25 pins.

data field—In a frame, the field or section that contains the data.

Data Link layer—Layer 2 of the OSI Reference Model. The Data Link layer is above the Physical layer. Data comes off the cable, through the Physical layer, and into the Data Link layer.

data plane—Functions applied directly against the actual data being directed in and out of the switching fabric.

Data Service Unit (DSU)—A component that formats and controls data for transmission over digital lines. It is used in conjunction with a Channel Service Unit (CSU).

Data Terminal Equipment (DTE)—A device—at the user end of a user-network interface—that serves as a data source, a destination, or both. These devices include computers, protocol translators, and multiplexers.

datagram—Information groupings that are transmitted as a unit at the Network layer.

DB-9—A connector that has nine pins and is used for a serial-port or parallel-port connection between PCs and peripheral devices.

DB-25—A connector that has 25 pins and is used for a serial-port or parallel-port connection between PCs and peripheral devices.

dedicated line—Generally used in WANs to provide a constant connection between two points.

Glossary

default gateway—Normally a router or a multihomed computer to which packets are sent when they are destined for a host that's not on their segment of the network.

demand node—Any end user or interface that requests and accesses network resources such as servers or printers.

destination address—The network address to which the frame is being sent. In a packet, this address is encapsulated in a field of the packet so all nodes know where the frame is being sent.

Destination Service Access Point (DSAP)—A one-byte field in the frame that combines with the service access point (SAP) to inform the receiving host of the identity of the destination host.

dialed number identification service—The method for delivery of automatic number identification using out-of-band signaling.

dial-up networking—The connection of a remote node to a network using POTS or PSTN.

diameter—A unit of measurement between the root switch and child switches, calculated from the root bridge with the root bridge counting as the first switch. Each subsequent child switch out from the root bridge is added to come up with the diameter number.

Digital Subscriber Line (DSL)—A public network technology that delivers high bandwidth over conventional copper wiring at limited distances.

distributed switching—An implementation in which switching decisions are made at the local port or the line module.

Distribution layer—Functions as the separation point between the Core and Access layers of the network OSI Reference Model. The devices in the Distribution layer implement the policies that define how packets are to be distributed to the groups within the network.

domain—A logical grouping of interfaces in a network or intranet to identify a controlled network of nodes that are grouped as an administrative unit.

Dual Attached Stations (DAS)—A connection that allows a device to connect to both FDDI counter-rotating rings.

dual-attachment concentrator (DAC)—A device connected to the FDDI counter-rotating rings. The DAC serves as a hub to provide passive connections to the rings for peripheral devices.

Glossary

dual-homed—A FDDI end station attached to two DACs for redundancy.

dumb terminal—An end-user station that can access another computer or switch but cannot provide any processing at the local level.

Dynamic Host Configuration Protocol (DHCP)—A protocol that provides an IP address to requesting nodes on the network.

Dynamic ISL—A protocol that performs trunking negotiation. It also verifies that two connected ports can become trunk links. A Dynamic ISL port can be configured in one of four modes: On, Off, Desirable, or Auto.

Dynamic VLAN port—A VLAN number assigned to a certain MAC address. The node attaching to any dynamic port on the switch is a member of the VLAN assigned to the MAC address. Dynamically assigned VLANs are configured using CiscoWorks 2000 or CiscoWorks for Switched Internetworks software.

dynamic window—A mechanism that prevents the sender of data from overwhelming the receiver. The amount of data that can be buffered in a dynamic window can vary.

electromagnetic interference (EMI)—External interference from electromagnetic signals that causes reduction of data integrity and increased error rates in a transmission medium.

Electronic Industries Association (EIA)—A group that specifies electrical transmission standards.

Embedded Control Unit (ECU)—A component of the ClearChannel Architecture that handles frame switching on the Cisco Catalyst series 1900 and 2820 switches in software. The ECU is an Intel 486 processor, Flash memory module, and 512K DRAM. It is also used in initializing the switch, using STP on a per-VLAN basis, controlling the LEDs on the chassis, maintaining RMON statistics, and handling in-band and out-of-band management of the switch.

emulated LAN (ELAN)—A feature used by ATM LANE to perform the basic functionality of a VLAN in Token Ring or Ethernet environments. ELANs, like VLANs, require a route processor such as a router to route frames between ELANs.

encapsulation—The technique used by layered protocols in which a layer adds header information to the Protocol Data Unit (PDU) from the layer above.

Encoded Address Recognition Logic (EARL) ASIC—An ASIC located on the Catalyst 5000 family of switches that sees all the frames that cross the bus. It performs a task similar to that of the CAM. The ASIC is responsible for making switching decisions based on the MAC address and the source VLAN. It is also responsible for updating the address table.

Glossary

encryption—The modification of data for security purposes prior to transmission so that it is not comprehensible without the decoding method.

enterprise services—Services that involve crossing the backbone to achieve access. These services are typically located on a separate subnet from the rest of the network devices.

EtherChannel—A connection used on the Catalyst 3000 family or Kalpana switches. It allows as many as seven Ethernet links to be bundled and load-balanced frame by frame to provide up to 140Mbps of bandwidth. It can utilize half-duplex or full-duplex links.

Extended Industry Standard Architecture (EISA)—The successor to the ISA standard. It provides a 32-bit bus interface used in PCs.

Fast EtherChannel (FEC)—A connection used on the Catalyst 5000 family of switches. It allows as many as seven Ethernet links to be bundled and load-balanced frame by frame to provide up to 800Mbps of bandwidth. It can utilize half-duplex or full-duplex links.

Fast Ethernet—IEEE 802.3 specification for data transfers of up to 100Mbps.

fault tolerance—A theoretical concept defined as a resistance to failure. It is not an absolute and can be defined only in degrees.

fiber channel or fibre channel—A technology that defines full gigabit-per-second data transfer over fiber-optic cable.

Fiber Distributed Data Interface (FDDI)—A high-speed data-transfer technology designed to extend the capabilities of existing LANs using a dual rotating-ring technology similar to Token Ring.

fiber-optic cable—A physical medium capable of conducting modulated light transmissions. Compared with other transmission media, fiber-optic cable is more expensive; but it is not susceptible to electromagnetic interference and is capable of higher data rates. Also known as *fiber optics* or *optical fiber*.

File Transfer Protocol (FTP)—The set of standards or protocols that allows you to transfer complete files between different computer hosts.

Flash memory—A type of memory that keeps its contents (usually the operating system) when the power is cycled.

flow control—A method used to control the amount of data transmitted within a given period of time. There are different types of flow control. See also *dynamic window* and *static window*.

forward delay—The length of time a port will remain in one of four protocol states in Spanning Tree Protocol.

Forwarding Engine (FE)—A major component of ASIC; part of the ClearChannel Architecture on the Cisco Catalyst series 1900 and 2820 switches. It is responsible for learning addresses, allocating buffer space in the shared memory space, frame queuing, forwarding decisions, and maintaining statistics.

Forwarding Information Base (FIB)—A mirror image of the IP routing table's routing information, similar to a routing table or information base. It updates routing information when routing or topology changes occur in the network and recalculates the next-hop information. The FIB maintains a list of all known routes and eliminates the need for route cache maintenance associated with fast switching or optimum switching. FIB is used with the CEF ASIC.

FragmentFree switching—A fast packet-switching method that reads the first 64 bytes of the frame to determine if the frame is corrupted. If this first part is intact, the frame is forwarded. Also known as *Runtless switching*.

frame—Grouping of information transmitted as a unit across the network at the Data Link layer.

Frame Check Sequence field—A field that performs a cyclic redundancy check (CRC) to ensure that all the frame's data arrives intact.

frame filtering—A process useful for VLANs, which utilizes a filtering table to drop frames based on a certain value contained in any one of the many fields in the data frame, such as the source or destination address. As part of normal operations, switches share filter tables. The frame's contents are compared to the filter table in the switch, thereby increasing the latency of the switch. Frame filtering is not used to implement VLANs in the Cisco Catalyst 5000 or 6000 family of switches.

Frame Length field—In a data frame, the field that specifies the length of a frame. The maximum length for an 802.3 frame is 1,518 bytes.

Frame Relay—A Data Link layer switching protocol used across multiple virtual circuits of a common carrier, giving the end user the appearance of a dedicated line.

frame tagging—A VLAN implementation method used to add VLAN information to data frames. As a frame enters the switch, it is tagged with VLAN information. It retains this information through the switching fabric; the tagging is removed before the frame exits the switch port with the attached destination interface. The process is transparent to the sending and receiving interfaces.

Frame Type field—In a data frame, the field that names the protocol being sent in the frame.

Frequency Division Multiplexing (FDM)—A technology that divides the output channel into multiple, smaller-bandwidth channels, each using a different frequency range.

full backup—A backup method in which every file on the hard drive is copied.

full duplex—A transmission method in which the sending and receiving (Rx and Tx) channels are separate; therefore, collisions cannot occur. Data is transmitted in two directions simultaneously on separate physical wires.

gateway—A hardware and software solution that enables communication between two dissimilar networking systems or protocols. Gateways usually operate at the upper layers of the OSI protocol stack, above the Transport layer.

gigabit (Gb)—One billion bits or one thousand megabits.

Gigabit Ethernet—IEEE specification for transfer rates up to one gigabit per second.

guaranteed flow control—A method of flow control in which the sending and receiving hosts agree upon a rate of data transmission. After they agree on a rate, the communication will take place at the guaranteed rate until the sender is finished. No buffering takes place at the receiver.

half duplex—A circuit designed for data transmission in both directions, but not simultaneously.

head-of-line blocking—A situation in which congestion on an outbound port limits throughput to uncongested ports. It is completely different from oversubscription. Physical data from another source device blocks the data of the sending device.

High-Speed Serial Interface (HSSI)—The network standard for high-speed serial communications over WAN links. It includes Frame Relay, T1, T3, E1, and ISDN.

host—Any system on a network. In the Unix world, any device that is assigned an IP address is a host.

host ID—A unique identifier for a client or resource on a network.

hostname—The NetBIOS name of the computer or node, given to the first element of the Internet fully qualified domain name (FQDN). It must be unique on your network.

Hot Standby Routing Protocol (HSRP)—A Cisco protocol that provides a redundant route processor on a segment. Should a route processor or link to a route processor fail, another configured router in a Standby Group can take over the routing responsibilities. The routers participating in an HSRP Standby Group are configured with a virtual MAC address and a virtual IP address. A separate instance of HSRP can exist for each VLAN.

hub—A hardware device that connects multiple independent nodes. Also known as a *concentrator* or *multiport repeater.*

Hypertext Transfer Protocol (HTTP)—A protocol used by Web browsers to transfer pages and files from a remote node to your computer.

IEEE—See *Institute of Electrical and Electronics Engineers.*

IEEE 802.1—Standard that defines the OSI model's Physical and Data Link layers. This standard allows two IEEE LAN stations to communicate over a LAN or WAN and is often referred to as the *internetworking standard.* It also includes the Spanning-Tree Algorithm specifications.

IEEE 802.2—Standard that defines the Logical Link Control (LLC) sublayer for the entire series of protocols covered by the 802.x standards. This standard specifies the adding of header fields, which tell the receiving host which upper layer sent the information. It also defines specifications for the implementation of the LLC sublayer of the Data Link layer.

IEEE 802.3—Standard that specifies Physical-layer attributes—such as signaling types, data rates, and topologies—and the media-access method used. It also defines specifications for the implementation of the Physical layer and the MAC sublayer of the Data Link layer, using CSMA/CD. This standard also includes the original specifications for Fast Ethernet.

IEEE 802.4—Standard that defines how production machines should communicate and establishes a common protocol for use in connecting these machines. It also defines specifications for the implementation of the Physical layer and the MAC sublayer of the Data Link layer using Token Ring access over a bus topology.

IEEE 802.5—Standard often used to define Token Ring. However, it does not specify a particular topology or transmission medium. It provides specifications for the implementation of the Physical layer and the MAC sublayer of the Data Link layer using a token-passing media-access method over a ring topology.

IEEE 802.6—Standard that defines the Distributed Queue Dual Bus (DQDB) technology to transfer high-speed data between nodes. It provides specifications for the implementation of metropolitan area networks (MANs).

IEEE 802.7—Standard that defines the design, installation, and testing of broadband-based communications and related physical media connectivity.

Glossary

IEEE 802.8—Standard that defines a group of people who advise the other 802-standard committees on various fiber-optic technologies and standards. This advisory group is called the Fiber Optic Technical Advisory Group.

IEEE 802.9—Standard that defines the integration of voice and data transmissions using isochronous Ethernet (IsoEnet).

IEEE 802.10—Another Cisco proprietary protocol, used primarily to transport VLAN information over FDDI. You will find this protocol primarily used in FDDI backbones to transport VLAN information and data.

IEEE 802.11—Standard that defines the implementation of wireless technologies, such as infrared and spread-spectrum radio.

IEEE 802.12—Standard that defines 100BaseVG/AnyLAN, which uses a 1000Mbps signaling rate and a special media-access method allowing 100Mbps data traffic over voice-grade cable.

IEEE 802.1Q—Standard for inserting a frame tag VLAN identifier in the frame header. As a frame enters the switching fabric, it is tagged with additional information regarding the VLAN properties. The tag remains in the frame as it is forwarded between switches and is removed prior to exiting the access link to the destination interface. This process is completely transparent to the end user.

Industry Standards Architecture (ISA)—The standard of the older, more common 8-bit and 16-bit bus and card architectures.

input/output (I/O)—Any operation in which data either enters a node or is sent out of a node.

Institute of Electrical and Electronics Engineers (IEEE)—A professional organization that develops standards for networking and communications.

Integrated Local Management Interface (ILMI)—A protocol created by the ATM forum to allow any ATM switch and ATM device to communicate using SNMP.

Integrated Services Digital Network (ISDN)—An internationally adopted standard for end-to-end digital communications over PSTN that permits telephone networks to carry data, voice, and other source traffic.

intelligent hub—A hub that contains some management or monitoring capability.

interface—A device, such as a card or a plug, that connects pieces of hardware with the computer so that information can be moved from place to place (for example, between computers and printers, hard disks, and other devices, or between two or more nodes on a network).

Glossary

internal IPX address—A unique eight-digit number that is used to identify a server. It is usually generated at random when the server is installed.

internal loopback address—Used for testing with TCP/IP. This address—127.0.0.1—allows a test packet to reflect back into the sending adapter to determine if it is functioning properly.

International Standards Organization (ISO)—A voluntary organization, founded in 1946, that is responsible for creating international standards in many areas, including communications and computers.

Internet Assigned Numbers Authority (IANA)—The organization responsible for Internet protocol addresses, domain names, and protocol parameters.

Internet Control Message Protocol (ICMP)—Network-layer Internet protocol, documented in RFC 792, that reports errors and provides other information relevant to IP packet processing.

Internet Engineering Task Force (IETF)—A group of research volunteers responsible for specifying the protocols used on the Internet and for specifying the architecture of the Internet.

Internet Group Management Protocol (IGMP)—Protocol responsible for managing and reporting IP multicast group memberships.

Internet layer—In the TCP/IP architectural model, the layer responsible for the addressing, packaging, and routing functions. Protocols operating at this layer of the model are responsible for encapsulating packets into Internet datagrams. All necessary routing algorithms are run here.

Internet Network Information Center (InterNIC)—The group that provides Internet services, such as domain registration and information and directory and database services.

Internet Protocol (IP)—Network-layer protocol, documented in RFC 791, that offers a connectionless internetwork service. IP provides features for addressing, packet fragmentation and reassembly, type-of-service specification, and security.

Internet Research Task Force (IRTF)—The research arm of the Internet Architecture Board. This group performs research in areas of Internet protocols, applications, architecture, and technology.

internetwork—A group of networks that are connected by routers or other connectivity devices so that the networks function as one network.

Internetwork Operating System (IOS)—Cisco's proprietary operating system, used in its routers and switches.

Internetwork Packet Exchange (IPX)—The Network-layer protocol generally used by Novell's NetWare network operating system. IPX provides connectionless communication, supporting packet sizes up to 64K.

Internetwork Packet Exchange/Sequenced Packet Exchange (IPX/SPX)—Default protocol used in NetWare networks. It is a combination of the IPX protocol to provide addressing and SPX to provide guaranteed delivery. IPX/SPX is similar to its counterpart, TCP/IP.

Inter-Switch Link (ISL)—A special Cisco proprietary Ethernet protocol that assigns a 26-byte header to an encapsulated frame and a 4-byte checksum, sometimes referred to as the FCS or the CRC. This protocol is used to send more than one VLAN between Cisco network devices configured for trunk links.

IPSec—A protocol designed for virtual private networks (VPNs). It's used to provide strong security standards for encryption and authentication.

IPX address—The unique address used to identify a node in the network.

kilobit (Kb)—One thousand bits.

kilobyte (K)—One thousand bytes (transmission rate).

LAN Emulation (LANE)—A standard created by the ATM forum to govern the connections of ATM end stations to either Ethernet or Token Ring devices. LANE provides a bridge from devices using ATM to Layer 2 devices using Ethernet and Token Ring.

LAN Module ASIC (LMA)—An ASIC in the Cisco Catalyst 3000 series switch that provides frame buffering, address learning, bus arbitration, and switching decisions for Ethernet ports.

latency—The time used to forward a packet in and out of a device. This term is commonly used in reference to routing and switching.

Layer 2 Forwarding Protocol (L2F)—A dial-up VPN protocol designed to work in conjunction with PPP to support authentication standards, such as TACACS+ and RADIUS, for secure transmissions over the Internet.

Layer 2 Tunneling Protocol (L2TP)—A dial-up VPN protocol that defines its own tunneling protocol and works with the advanced security methods of IPSec. L2TP allows PPP sessions to be tunneled across an arbitrary medium to a *home gateway* at an ISP or corporation.

learning bridge—A bridge that builds its own bridging address table, rather than requiring you to enter information manually.

Line Module Communication Processor (LCP)—Provides communications for the MCP located on the Supervisor Engine. The LCP is located on each line module.

local area network (LAN)—A group of connected computers that are located in a geographic area, usually a building or campus, and that share data and services.

local broadcast—A broadcast on the local network, looking for the IP address of the destination host.

local service—Service where the device supplying the service resides on the same subnet as the device requesting the service.

Local Target Logic (LTL)—A feature of some line modules that assists the EARL in making forwarding decisions.

local VLAN—Beneficial for networks whose resources are centralized and in one geographical location. The VLAN can span one switch or many switches within the same floor or building.

logical addressing scheme—The addressing method used in providing manually assigned node addressing.

Logical Link Control (LLC)—A sublayer of the Data Link layer of the OSI Reference Model. It provides an interface for the Network-layer protocols and the MAC sublayer; it's also part of the Data Link layer.

loop—A continuous circle that a packet takes through a series of nodes in a network until it eventually times out. Without a protocol such as STP to detect loops, if no life cycle is assigned to the packet, the data could continuously encircle the network.

loopback plug—A device used for loopback testing.

loopback testing—A troubleshooting method used to verify the usability of interfaces. The output and input wires are crossed or shorted in a manner that allows all outgoing data to be routed back into the card.

management—Fault, capacity, accounting, performance, and security control for a network.

Master Communication Processor (MCP)—A feature of the Supervisor Engine that takes commands from the Network Management Processor (NMP) and forwards them to the correct LCP. The MCP is also responsible for testing and configuring the local ports and controlling the ports using LTL and CBL. It also performs diagnostics on the memory, SAINT ASICs, LTL, and CBL. In addition, the MCP is responsible for downloading software to the line modules.

Media Access Control (MAC) address—A six-octet number that uniquely identifies a host on a network. It is a unique number that is burned into the NIC, so it cannot be changed.

Media Access Control (MAC) layer—In the OSI model, the lower of the two sublayers of the Data Link layer. It's defined by the IEEE as responsible for interaction with the Physical layer.

Media Access Unit (MAU)—IEEE 802.3 specification referring to a transceiver. Not to be confused with a Token Ring MAU (Multistation Access Unit), which is sometimes abbreviated MSAU.

megabit (Mb or Mbit)—One million bits. This term is used to rate transmission transfer speeds (not to be confused with *megabyte*).

megabyte (MB)—One million transmission bytes. This term usually refers to file size, in which case it would be 1,048,576 bytes.

message—A portion of information that is sent from one node to another. Messages are created at the upper layers of the OSI Reference Model.

microsegmentation—The process of using switches to divide a network into smaller segments.

microwaves—Very short radio waves used to transmit data over 890MHz.

modem—A device used to modulate and demodulate the signals that pass through it. It converts the direct current pulses of the serial digital code from the controller into the analog signal that is compatible with the telephone network.

multicast—A single packet transmission from one sender to a specific group of destination nodes.

multilayer switches—A combination of Layer 2, 3, and 4 switches that use the concept of route once, switch many.

multiprocessor—Support for multiple processors in a single machine.

Multiprotocol Over ATM (MPOA)—An ATM forum standard that includes enhancements to LANE and adds Layer 3 switching capabilities to ATM switches.

Multistation Access Unit (MAU or MSAU)—A concentrator or hub used in a Token Ring network. It organizes the connected nodes into an internal ring and uses the RI (ring in) and RO (ring out) connectors to expand to other MAUs on the network.

NetFlow Switching—A feature incorporated into the Multilayer Switching Module (MSM), NetFlow Feature Card (NFFC), and NFFC II that was originally instituted and developed for Cisco's enterprise routers. NetFlow allows for transparent switching in hardware while incorporating QoS features including security, multicast forwarding, multilayer switching, NetFlow data exporting, and packet filtering at Layer 3 and Layer 4 application ports.

NetWare Core Protocol (NCP)—NetWare protocol that provides a method for hosts to make calls to a NetWare server for services and network resources.

network down—Situation in which the clients are unable to utilize the services of the network. This can be administrative, scheduled downtime for upgrades or maintenance, or it can be the result of a serious error.

Network Driver Interface Specification (NDIS)—Microsoft proprietary specification or standard for a protocol-independent device driver. These drivers allow multiple protocols to be bound to the same NIC, allowing the card to be used by multiple operating systems. NDIS is similar to Open Data-Link Interface (ODI).

network ID—The part of the TCP/IP address that specifies the network portion of the IP address. It is determined by the class of the address, which is determined by the subnet mask used.

Network Interface Card (NIC)—The hardware component that serves as the interface, or connecting component, between your network and the node. It has a transceiver, a MAC address, and a physical connector for the network cable. Also known as a *network adapter*.

Network Interface layer—The bottom layer of the TCP/IP architectural model, which maps to the bottom two layers of the OSI Reference Model. It's responsible for sending, receiving, and interacting with bits at the Physical layer.

Network layer—The third layer of the OSI Reference Model, where routing based on node addresses (IP or IPX addresses) occurs.

Network Management Processor (NMP)—A feature of the Catalyst Supervisor Engine that is responsible for general control and some management functions of the switch. It is responsible for executing the system's configuration changes, the Command Line Interface (CLI), and running diagnostics on boot components as well as new components.

Network Time Protocol (NTP)—A protocol that allows all network equipment to synchronize the date and time on the private or internetwork environment.

Glossary

network-to-network interface (NNI)—An interface that provides connectivity between two ATM switches.

non-blocking—A condition in which the fabric contains more bandwidth than the sum total of all the ports' bandwidth combined.

nonvolatile RAM (NVRAM)—Static memory similar to that of the Flash. Information stored in the NVRAM does not get lost when the power is cycled on the device. On a switch, the NVRAM stores the VLAN configuration, system configuration, SNMP parameters, STP configuration, and configuration of each port.

Novell Directory Services (NDS)—The user, group, and security information database of network resources utilized in a NetWare 4.x and/or NetWare 5.x internetwork.

Open System Interconnection (OSI) model—A seven-layer model created by the ISO to standardize and explain the interactions of networking protocols.

oversubscription—A condition in which the total bandwidth of the ports is greater than the capacity of the switching fabric. Also referred to as a *blocking architecture*.

Packet Internet Groper (PING)—A TCP/IP protocol-stack utility that works with Internet Control Message Protocol (ICMP) and uses an echo request and reply to test connectivity to other systems.

password—A set of characters used with a username to authenticate a user on the network and to provide the user with rights and permissions to files and resources.

patch panel—A device where the wiring used in coaxial or twisted-pair networks converges in a central location and is then connected to the back of the panel.

peer-to-peer networking—A network environment without dedicated servers, where communication occurs between similarly capable network nodes that act as both client and server.

permanent virtual circuit (PVC)—A logical path established in packet-switching networks between two locations. It's similar to a dedicated leased line. Also known as a *permanent virtual connection* in ATM terminology (not to be confused with Private Virtual Circuit, also known as a PVC).

permission—Authorization provided to users, allowing them to access objects on the network. Network administrators generally assign permissions. Slightly different from but often used with *rights*.

physical addressing scheme—The MAC address on every network card manufactured. It cannot be changed.

Physical layer—The bottom layer (Layer 1) of the OSI Reference Model, where all physical connectivity is defined.

plain old telephone service (POTS)—The current analog public telephone system. Also known as the PSTN.

Plug and Play—Architecture designed to allow hardware devices to be detected by the operating system and for the driver to be automatically loaded.

Point-to-Point Protocol (PPP)—A common dial-up networking protocol that includes provisions for security and protocol negotiation and provides host-to-network and switch-to-switch connections for one or more user sessions. PPP is the common modem connection used for Internet dial-up.

Point-To-Point Tunneling Protocol (PPTP)—A protocol that encapsulates private network data in IP packets. These packets are transmitted over synchronous and asynchronous circuits to hide the underlying routing and switching infrastructure of the Internet from both senders and receivers.

polling—The media-access method for transmitting data, in which a controlling device is used to contact each node to determine if it has data to send.

Port Adapter Modules—Modules attached to the Carrier Access Modules on the LS1010 ATM and Catalyst 5500 series ATM bus that provide physical ATM line ports for the end-user stations.

Port Aggregation Protocol (PAgP)—Manages the Fast EtherChannel bundles and aids in the automatic creation of Fast EtherChannel links.

PortFast—A protocol that forces an STP port to enter the forwarding state immediately after startup for a single workstation or server connected to a switch port.

power on self test (POST)—A series of tests run on a Cisco Catalyst switch when the power is turned on. POST tests the hardware, memory, processors, ports, and ASICs to verify they are functioning properly.

Presentation layer—Layer 6 of the OSI Reference Model. This layer prepares information to be used by the Application layer.

Primary Rate Interface (PRI)—A higher-level network interface standard for use with ISDN. Defined at the rate of 1.544Mbps, it consists of a single 64Kbps D channel plus 23 (T1) or 30 (E1) B channels for voice or data.

Private Virtual Circuit (PVC)—A logical connection between locations through a Frame Relay and ATM cloud. When a company has three branch offices, and each location physically connects to the Frame Relay provider's network cloud through a series of switches, it appears to the end users as if the three branch

Glossary

offices are directly connected to the local network. (Not to be confused with a Permanent Virtual Circuit, also known as a PVC.)

proprietary—A standard or specification that is created by a manufacturer, vendor, or other private enterprise and is not always a recognized standard.

Proprietary Fat Pipe ASIC (PFPA)—An ASIC utilized on the Catalyst 3000 series switches that use no 10BaseT ports such as Fast Ethernet, 100VG/AnyLAN, ATM, or the Stackport of the Stack Port Matrix. Functionally, the PFPA is the same as the LMA.

protocol—*A* set of rules that govern network communications between networks, computers, peripherals, and operating systems.

Protocol Identification field—In a frame, a five-byte field used to identify to the destination node the protocol that is being used in the data transmission.

protocol stack—Two or more protocols that work together, such as TCP and IP or IPX and SPX. Also known as a *protocol suite.*

Proxy ARP—Used by end-stations to discover the IP address of the default gateway. The end-stations dynamically acquire the IP and MAC address of the default gateway. The IP address of the default gateway is manually configured on the node running Proxy ARP.

Public Switched Telephone Network (PSTN)—All the telephone networks and services in the world. The same as POTS, PSTN refers to the world's collection of interconnected public telephone networks that are both commercial and government owned. PSTN is a digital network, with the exception of the connection between local exchanges and customers, which remains analog.

Quality of Service (QoS)—A guarantee of a particular level of service for a connection. QoS uses queuing and other methods to guarantee that bandwidth is available for a certain protocol, application, or address. QoS is important for implementing applications such as voice and video.

queuing—Uses buffering and priority control mechanisms to control data congestion on the network. Another term for *QoS*.

read/writes—The counting of packets on the ingress (read) as well as the egress (write) from the switching fabric.

Remote Monitoring (RMON)—An IETF standard that defines how devices gather and share network monitoring information. This information can be used to send information gathered to an SNMP management station. RMON gathers Layer 2 information concerning bandwidth use, collisions, and errors. Catalyst switches can gather four of the nine different information types: Statistics, History, Alarm, and Event. The other five groups can be monitored using a SPAN port and an attached protocol analyzer or probe.

remote node—A node or computer that is connected to the network through a dial-up connection. Dialing in to the Internet from home is a perfect example of the remote node concept.

remote services—Services where the device supplying the services resides on a separate subnet from the device requesting the services.

repeater—A device that regenerates and retransmits the signal on a network. A repeater is generally used to strengthen signals going long distances.

Request For Comments (RFC)—Method used to post documents regarding networking or Internet-related standards or ideas. Some have been adopted and accepted by the Internet Architecture Board as standards.

resource node—An interface on the network that provides a service for a demand node. Resource nodes can be such items as servers, printers, and other devices available to connect to a network to provide services.

rights—Authorization provided to users, allowing them to perform certain tasks. Network administrators generally assign rights. Slightly different from but often used with *permissions*.

ring in (RI)—A connector used in an IBM Token-Ring network on a Multistation Access Unit (MAU) to expand to other MAUs on the network. Counterpart to the ring out (RO), the RI connector on the MAU connects to the media to accept the token from the ring.

ring out (RO)—A connector used in an IBM Token-Ring network on a Multistation Access Unit (MAU) to expand to other MAUs on the network. Counterpart to the ring in (RI), the RO connector on the MAU connects to the media to send the token out to the ring.

RJ-11 connector—Used with telephone systems; can have either four or six conductors. A red/green pair of wires is used for voice and data; a black/white pair is used for low-voltage signals.

RJ-45 connector—An Ethernet cable connector used with twisted-pair cable, which can support eight conductors for four pairs of wires.

Route Switch Feature Card (RSFC)—A Cisco router on a card running the Cisco IOS. This card allows the switch to disregard installing an RSM or daughter cards, because they are built into the modules.

Glossary

Route Switch Module (RSM)—Cisco's first multiprotocol multilayer switch module, which utilizes the full support of the Cisco IOS for performing Layer 3 routing from a slot internally on a Layer 2 switch. This module provides for interVLAN connectivity.

Routing Information Field (RIF)—A field on Source Route Bridge Token Ring frames that contains information about the rings and bridges that the frame must travel to the destination interface.

Routing Information Protocol (RIP)—Protocol that uses hop counts as a routing metric to control the direction and flow of packets between routers and switches on an internetwork.

Runtless switching—A switching method in which the switch reads the first 64 bytes to verify that there is no corruption of the packet. If there is corruption, a preset maximum of errors changes the switching type from cut-through switching to store-and-forward switching. Also known as *FragmentFree switching*.

Secure Data Exchange (SDE) Protocol Data Unit—A field (part of the 802.10 header) that copies the encrypted Protected Header for security purposes to help guarantee against tampering with the frame. Also known as the *Clear Header*.

Security Association Identifier (SAID)—One of the three values that make up a Clear Header on the FDDI frame type. It is used for security for the Clear Header. The Clear Header contains a SAID, Link Service Access Point (LSAP), and Management Defined field (MDF).

Sequenced Packet Exchange (SPX)—Protocol used in conjunction with IPX when connection-oriented delivery is required. It is used mainly in NetWare network environments.

server—A resource node that fulfills service requests for demand nodes. Usually referred to by the type of service it performs, such as file server, email server, or print server.

service access point (SAP)—A field in a frame that tells the receiving host which protocol the frame is intended for.

Service Advertising Protocol (SAP)—NetWare protocol used on an IPX network. SAP maintains server information tables, listing each service that has been advertised to it, and provides this information to any nodes attempting to locate a service.

Service Advertising Protocol agent (SAP agent)—Router or other node on an IPX network that maintains a server information table. This table lists each service that has been advertised to it and provides this information to any nodes attempting to locate a service.

session—The dialog that exists between two computers.

Session layer—The fifth layer of the OSI Reference Model, which establishes, manages, and terminates sessions between applications on different nodes.

shared system—The infrastructure component routed directly into the backbone of an internetwork for optimal systems access. It provides connectivity to servers and other shared systems.

shielded twisted-pair (STP)—Twisted-pair network cable that has shielding to insulate the cable from electromagnetic interference.

Simple Network Management Protocol (SNMP)—A protocol used with TCP/IP networks to provide network devices with a method to monitor and control network devices. It is used to manage configurations, statistics collection, performance, and security, and to report network management information to a management console that is a member of the same community.

Simple Network Management Protocol (SNMP) trap—An SNMP protocol utility that sends out an alarm in an identified community notifying members of the community that some network activity differs from the established threshold, as defined by the administrator.

Simple Server Redundancy Protocol (SSRP)—A Cisco protocol that provides redundancy for all LANE server components.

Single Attached Station (SAS)—A FDDI device that has only a single connection to a single DAC.

smart bridge—A bridge that builds its own bridging address table. No manual configuration or intervention is required. Also known as a *learning bridge*.

socket—A logical interprocess communications mechanism through which a program communicates with another program or with a network.

socket identifier—An eight-bit number used to identify the socket. Developers and designers of services and protocols usually assign socket identifiers. Also known as a *socket number*.

source address—The address of the host who sent the frame. It is contained in the frame so the destination node knows who sent the data.

Source Route Bridging (SRB)—A type of bridging used to segment Token Ring networks. It requires all rings and bridges to have a unique number.

Source Route Switching (SRS)—A type of bridging that combines SRB and SRT, developed to allow more physical rings on the network. It allows for growing bandwidth needs while preserving the benefits of SRB.

Glossary

Source Route Translational Bridging (SR/TRB)—A type of bridging that bridges a Token Ring segment to another physical media type such as Ethernet or FDDI. It is transparent to the source and destination interfaces.

Source Route Transparent Bridging (SRT)—A type of bridging that combines SRB and TB. Using SRT, the bridge places a RIF into a frame traveling from the TB to the SRB side. It then strips out the RIF when the frame travels from the SRB port to the TB port.

Source Service Access Point (SSAP)—A one-byte field in the frame that combines with the SAP to tell the receiving host the identity of the source or sending host.

Spanning-Tree Algorithm (STA)—Defined by IEEE 802.1 as part of the Spanning-Tree Protocol (STP) to eliminate loops in an internetwork with multiple paths. The STA is responsible for performing STP topology recalculations when a switch is powered up and when a topology change occurs.

Spanning-Tree Protocol (STP)—Protocol developed to eliminate the loops caused by the multiple paths in an internetwork. It's defined by IEEE 802.1. STP communicates topology changes from switch to switch with the use of BPDUs.

Standby Route Processor—The router standing by in an HSRP Standby Group, waiting to take over in the event the active route processor fails.

static IP addresses—IP addresses that are assigned to each network device individually; often referred to as *hard-coded*.

static VLAN port—A port on a switch manually assigned a VLAN number. Any node or interface connected to the port automatically becomes a member of the assigned VLAN.

static window—A mechanism used in flow control that prevents the sender of data from overwhelming the receiver. Only a set amount of data can be buffered in a static window.

station IPX address—A 12-digit number that is used to uniquely identify each device on an IPX network.

storage area network—A subnetwork of storage devices, usually found on high-speed networks and shared by all servers on the network.

store-and-forward—A fast packet-switching method that produces a higher latency than other switching methods. The switch waits for the entire packet to arrive before checking the CRC. It then forwards or discards the packet.

StreetTalk—A global naming service created by Banyan and included with the Banyan Vines network operating system.

subnet mask—A 32-bit address that is used to mask or screen a portion of the IP address to differentiate the part of the address that designates the network and the part that designates the host.

subnetting—The process of dividing your assigned IP address range into smaller clusters of hosts.

Subnetwork Access Protocol (SNAP)—An Internet protocol that specifies a standard method of encapsulating IP datagrams and ARP messages on a network.

supernetting—Aggregating IP network addresses and advertising them as a single classless network address.

switch—A Layer 2 networking device that forwards frames based on destination addresses.

switch block—Switching devices located in wiring closets, requiring high-speed uplinks and redundancy. The switch block connects end-user stations to the switches that connect to the Distribution layer.

Switched Multimegabit Data Service (SMDS)—Defined by IEEE 802.6; the Physical-layer implementation for data transmission over public lines at speeds between 1.544Mbps (T1) and 44.736Mbps using cell relay and fixed-length cells.

Switched Port Analyzer (SPAN)—A port at which traffic from another port or group of ports is attached to a protocol analyzer or probe device. The SPAN aids in the diagnoses of problems related to traffic patterns on the network.

switched virtual circuit—A virtual circuit that is established dynamically on demand to form a dedicated link and is then broken when transmission is complete. Also known as a *switched virtual connection* in ATM terminology.

switching fabric—The "highway" the data takes to get from the input port on a switch to the output port.

synchronous transmission—Digital signal transmission method using a precise clocking method and a predefined number of bits sent at a constant rate.

syslog—Messages sent to a remote machine regarding the switch system configuration, such as software and configuration changes.

T1—Digital WAN carrier facility that transmits DS-1-formatted data at 1.544Mbps through the telephone switching network, using AMI or B8ZS coding.

Glossary

TCP/IP—See *Transmission Control Protocol/Internet Protocol.*

Telecommunications Industry Association (TIA)—An organization that develops standards—with the EIA (Electronics Industries Association)—for telecommunications technologies.

Telnet—Standard terminal-emulation protocol in the TCP/IP protocol stack. It is used to perform terminal emulation over TCP/IP via remote terminal connections, enabling users to log in to remote systems and use resources as if they were connected to a local system.

Terminal Access Controller Access Control System Plus (TACACS+)—A security feature that uses an MD5 encrypted algorithm to enforce strict authentication controls. It requires both a user name and password, allowing administrators to better track network usage and changes based on user accounts.

thicknet coax—Thick cable (usually about .375 inch in diameter) most commonly found in the backbone of a coaxial network.

thinnet coax—Cable that is thinner than thicknet (about .25 inch in diameter). It is commonly used in older bus topologies to connect the nodes to the network.

token—A frame that provides controlling information. In a Token Ring network, the node that possesses the token is allowed to transmit next.

Token Ring—An IBM proprietary token-passing LAN topology defined by the IEEE 802.5 standard. It operates at either 4- or 16Mbps in a star topology.

Token Ring adapters—Traditional ISA or Microchannel devices with 4- or 16Mbps transfer capability, used to connect nodes to a Token Ring network.

topology—The shape or layout of a physical network and the flow of data through the network.

Transmission Control Protocol (TCP)—Part of the TCP/IP protocol stack. TCP is a connection-oriented, reliable data-transmission communication service that operates at the OSI Transport layer.

Transmission Control Protocol/Internet Protocol (TCP/IP)—The suite of protocols combining TCP and IP, developed to support the construction of worldwide internetworks. See *Transmission Control Protocol* and *Internet Protocol.*

Transmission Control Protocol/Internet Protocol (TCP/IP) socket—A socket, or connection to an endpoint, used in TCP/IP communication transmissions.

transmit—The process of sending data using light, electronic, or electric signals. In networking, this is usually done in the form of digital signals composed of bits.

Transparent Bridging (TB)—A bridging type that uses the MAC address to make forwarding and filtering decisions transparent to the sender and receiver interfaces. TB is used in Ethernet.

Transport layer—Layer 4 of the OSI Reference Model. It controls the flow of information.

Trivial File Transfer Protocol (TFTP)—A simplified version of FTP, allowing files to be transferred over a network from one computer to another. It's also used to install the Cisco IOS on an IOS-based switch, router, or Gigabit Switch Router (GSR).

trunk link—A special type of VLAN connection. Unlike a user port, trunk links expect the device at the other end of the connection to understand the inserted frame tags. Standard Ethernet and Token Ring cards do not understand frame tags. Trunk links use an encapsulation method that allows them to carry the data of more than one VLAN through the switched internetwork. Devices that support trunk links are switches, routers, and some specialized NICs meant for servers.

twisted-pair—A type of cable that uses multiple twisted pairs of copper wire.

unicast—A frame in which the destination MAC address specifies the single destination computer. Unicast can be summarized as direct network traffic between two individual nodes.

unshielded twisted-pair (UTP)—A type of cable that uses multiple twisted pairs of copper wire in a casing that does not provide much protection from EMI. The most common network cable in Ethernet networks, it is rated in five categories.

UplinkFast—Provides fast convergence after an STP topology change and achieves load balancing between redundant links.

User Datagram Protocol (UDP)—A communications protocol that provides connectionless, unreliable communications services and operates at the Transport layer of the OSI model. It requires a transmission protocol such as IP to guide it to the destination host.

user-network interface (UNI)—An interface that provides a connection between an ATM end-station interface and an ATM switch interface.

virtual LAN (VLAN)—Allows a network administrator to divide a bridged network into several broadcast domains. Each VLAN is considered its own separate subnet, and Layer 3 routing is still required to route between VLANs. VLANs can be based on the port identifier of the switch, the MAC address, Layer 3 address, directory information, or application information. VLANs can be implemented on different media types such as Ethernet, FDDI, Token Ring, or ATM. The benefits of VLANs are limited broadcast domains, added security, and redundancy.

Glossary

virtual private network (VPN)—A network that uses a public network such as the Internet as a backbone to connect two or more private networks. A VPN provides users with the equivalent of a private network in terms of security.

VLAN Trunking Protocol (VTP)—A protocol used to enhance and configure the extension of broadcast domains across multiple switches. VTP dynamically reports the addition of VLANs throughout the switched network, in turn creating a consistent switched network.

VLAN Trunking Protocol (VTP) pruning—A protocol used to reduce the number of switches participating in VTP by removing switches from the database that do not have certain VLANs' numbered ports. For example, if switch 1 and switch 2 have ports belonging to VLAN 6 and switch 3 does not, it will not forward VLAN 6 traffic on the trunk link to switch 3 unless switch 3 is a gateway to another switch that has VLAN 6 member ports. If VTP pruning were not enabled on a trunk port, all VLAN traffic would travel through the trunk links to all the switches whether they had destination ports or not.

wide area network (WAN)—Data communications network that serves users across a broad geographical area. A WAN often uses transmission devices such as modems and Channel Service Units/Data Service Units (CSU/DSU) to carry signals over leased lines or common carrier lines.

window flow control—A flow-control method in which the receiving host buffers the data it receives and holds it in the buffer until it can be processed. After it is processed, an acknowledgment is sent to the sender.

X-TAG—A one-byte value used as an identifier Multilayer Switch Route Processor (MLS-RP).

Glossary

Index

Windows® 2000 Titles from Coriolis

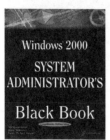